# Trapped in the Cold War

# Trapped in the Cold War

*The Ordeal of an American Family*

Hermann Field and Kate Field

*Afterword by Norman M. Naimark*

Stanford University Press

Stanford, California

1999

Stanford University Press
Stanford, California
© 1999 by the Board of Trustees of the
Leland Stanford Junior University
Printed in the United States of America
CIP data appear at the end of the book

*For our children, Hugh, Alan, and Alison,*
*and to the memory of*
*Elsie Field and Stanislaw Mierzenski*

# Acknowledgments

We wish to express our appreciation to the many people who have made publication of an American edition possible. Peter Shepherd of Harold Ober Associates has been supportive from the beginning. Along the journey we have received invaluable assistance from many friends and particularly our three children, who made editorial suggestions and helped us handle the complexities of the computer. Jobst-Christian Rojahn did an excellent job of translating our original English manuscript for the German edition, which appeared in 1996, and we incorporated many of his editorial suggestions in the present volume. Anne Canright has fine-tuned the prose with skill and sensitivity. We are also indebted to Professor Igor Lukes for introducing us to Professor Norman Naimark and Stanford University Press, where Muriel Bell and John Feneron have been most supportive in the final stretch.

# Contents

*14 pages of illustrations follow page 418*

A cow was enjoying her afternoon siesta in a Polish meadow when suddenly she saw a hare loping toward her at breakneck speed from across the Russian border.

"Hey, what's the hurry?"

The hare came to a breathless halt. "What's the hurry? Didn't you know they're rounding up camels over there?"

"Did you say camels? What's that got to do with you?"

The hare shook his ears pityingly at the cow's sluggishness of mind. "But my friend, that's just it. How can I prove I'm not a camel?"

And he dashed on, obsessed by that awful thought.

*—version of an after-dinner joke of the 1930s*

# Prologue

T oday, at the end of the twentieth century, it is perhaps hard for Americans to recapture the international atmosphere of the late 1940s and early 1950s, when the Cold War was at its height. But the switch from wartime collaboration between the United States and the Soviet Union was rapid and ruthless. Ours is the story of an American family caught up in that change and catapulted into an international intrigue of historic proportions. Our account is based on detailed recollections that we wrote down independently of each other in 1955, at the end of our ordeal. They were filed away when we resumed our normal lives.

In 1949, when our story begins, Hermann, at age thirty-nine, was building a career as an architect and had been selected to become head of the architecture school of Western Reserve University in Cleveland, Ohio. Kate was beginning a new career as a lecturer in economics at Cleveland College, after having had two children. Two years earlier, in 1947, both had gone with a dozen architects and planners on a tour of Europe, led by Hermann, studying the reconstruction of cities after the devastation of World War II. The group had visited countries in both Western and Eastern Europe. Particularly memorable was the sight of Warsaw, still digging itself out of the rubble.

Hermann intended to repeat this venture in 1949, but owing to the increased tensions of the Cold War there were few applicants and the tour was canceled. He was also planning to attend a conference in Italy of the International Congresses of Modern Architecture, which would include such luminaries as the architects Le Corbusier, Walter Gropius, and Jose Luis Sert, as well as delegates from the communist countries. Through this organization and his previous tour Hermann had met the Polish architect couple Szymon and Helena Syrkus, who were involved in planning the reconstruction of Warsaw and who invited him to make another visit.

In the United States, Senator Joseph McCarthy and the House Un-American Activities Committee were actively pursuing both real and supposed Communists in any influential position. One outgrowth of this effort was the trial in New York of Alger Hiss, a former member of the State Department and, in 1945, secretary to the United Nations Founding Conference in San Francisco. Hiss had been accused of perjury for denying that he had passed documents to the Russians back in the 1930s. In the course of this trial, the name of Hermann's elder brother, Noel, had come up, he having been a State Department colleague of Hiss in the same period.

We were part of the generation that reached maturity in the aftermath of the First World War. Hermann was born in 1910 in Switzerland, the son of Herbert Haviland Field, an American Quaker, pacifist, and dedicated internationalist, who headed a zoological institute in Zurich. His mother was English, and after her husband's premature death in 1921, in order to carry out his wish that his children should grow up as Americans, she transplanted her family of four to Cambridge, Massachusetts. So Hermann always felt he had one foot on each continent, a feeling that followed him throughout his life. After graduating from Harvard, he returned to Europe in 1934 and completed his architectural studies in Zurich. His first professional assignment was in England, where he met Kate in 1938.

Kate was born in 1912 in London. Her father was Oliver Thornycroft, an internal combustion engineer and son of the sculptor Hamo Thornycroft; her mother was Dorothy Rose, daughter of Edward Rose, theater critic and playwright and an early member of the Fabian Society. Kate's parents were both graduates of Cambridge University, where Kate also earned an honors degree in economics. She then spent a year at Smith College in Massachusetts before returning to England in 1935.

After World War I, the Russian revolution of 1917 had radically changed the international landscape. Much of Western diplomacy from then on was focused on parrying this new social order seen as a threat to our own. Meanwhile, the ravages of inflation and unemployment in Germany undermined both internal and international stability, and the Great Depression in the United States and Britain demonstrated to us young people the shortcomings of our own economic system. Losing confidence in the ability of our societies to solve the problem of misery in the midst of plenty, we were searching for solutions.

Our parents' faith in the League of Nations as guardian of collective security was proving to be unjustified. The United States dissociated itself from it at its birth. Japanese aggression in Manchuria was followed by Mussolini's assault on Abyssinia, then by Franco's attack on the Spanish Republic with the help of Hitler and Mussolini. Hitler successively moved into the Saar, the Rhineland, and Austria without any effective opposition from the Western democracies. Finally in 1938, in a deal made with Hitler behind the back of an isolated Czechoslovakia, England and France agreed at Munich to hand over the Sudetenland to Germany, leaving Czechoslovakia without defensible borders. While this betrayal was rationalized as necessary to maintain "peace in our time," it was followed inevitably half a year later by Hitler's seizure of the truncated remains of Czechoslovakia, Central Europe's last remaining democracy. Stalin's Soviet Union, supposedly Czechoslovakia's committed ally, was determined not to be caught alone in a military confrontation with Nazi Germany. Stalin finally cut his own fatal deal with Hitler over the body of Poland. On September 1, 1939, Hitler's invasion of that country plunged us into the Second World War.

In the 1930s it seemed to many of us young people that the USSR had a clearer grasp of the steady drift toward war resulting from aggressive fascism than did the West. For geopolitical as well as ideological reasons the Russians promoted the so-called Popular Front to bring together all groups opposed to fascism, for whom the negative aspects of Stalinism were relegated to the back burner, if perceived at all. It was rather easy to dismiss as capitalist propaganda stories of human rights violations, or to justify the Moscow treason trials of high Communist officials as being a necessary defense of an embattled Soviet Union. Nearer to home, the evident failure of our own capitalist societies to maintain an equitable social order made the Marxist socialist alternative seem a viable vision for a better future. Thus the Soviet Union was looked up to as its first tentative embodiment, despite all the flaws of trying to apply it to a signally unsuitable agricultural society.

As a young graduate student, dunked into the maelstrom of a Europe girding for war, Hermann saw in the communist left the most tenacious and effective ally for peace and social justice. Though distancing himself from the strictures of party membership and its unquestioning discipline, he became part of the heady activism of the Marxist student exiles in Zurich.

Kate, a member of the British Labour Party, also held strongly antifascist opinions and actively worked to uphold them. She had organized a home for sixty refugee Basque children from bombed Bilbao in Spain and worked for the British Committee for Refugees from Czechoslovakia from its inception.

When World War II finally came, we were both working for the British-sponsored Czech Refugee Trust Fund, Hermann in Krakow and Kate in London. After Hermann's escape from Poland we continued this work in England for another year; we then married and took the last American liner from Ireland back to New York. There Hermann resumed his architectural career, and Kate worked first for the British Press Service, then for Time, Inc.

During the war Hermann worked on the design of U.S. army embarkation camps, and in 1944, when the United States and the Soviet Union were still allies, he helped organize the Architects' Committee for Soviet-American Friendship, formed under the auspices of the New York chapter of the American Institute of Architects.

After the wartime alliance with the USSR, the switch to the Cold War came as a shock. Hermann, still with ties to communist friends in Europe dating from his graduate student days in Switzerland and his work for refugees, was easily persuaded by his sister-in-law to set out in search of his brother, Noel, who had mysteriously disappeared in May on a visit to Prague. Hermann underestimated the finality of Churchill's "Iron Curtain."

Now, some fifty years later, both the faded dream of a more equitable society and the actuality of its betrayal in the Soviet Union place a responsibility on those of us who experienced that telling moment of our time, to add our piece to historical memory.

*Valley Farm, Shirley, Massachusetts, April 1999*

# 1

## August Afternoon in 1949

A drowsy August afternoon like any other, the anticipation of evening coolness in the air. Behind me the loudspeaker was droning the names of passengers, flight departures, arrivals. Occasionally a familiar word: Krakow, Poznan, Gdynia . . . Through the open window of the ticketing hall I waved a last farewell to my Polish hosts, the architect couple Szymon and Helena Syrkus, and Mela Granowska of the Polish Energy Ministry. Slowly their car swung on the gravel and headed back onto the Warsaw road. Szymon had an urgent appointment in town at 5:30.

And I? I had almost a quarter of the earth to traverse to my university project in Cleveland. I was returning home to America, but also returning with redoubled urgency to the question that could not be evaded: What about my brother Noel? The past seven days here had merely been a futile respite. Day and night since Noel's wife, Herta, had told me in Geneva of his disappearance I had been racking my brain for some explanation, some clue. Last May his letters to her from Prague had stopped. Since then, no trace, only a growing sense of something preposterous, unreal, that injected itself unspoken into everything.

And so it was, too, that I felt a foreboding, not yet identified, in my goodbye to my friends here. Hadn't some wedge been driven between our worlds, theirs and mine? Was it still possible to stand with one foot in each? To find a meeting ground between East and West where none existed any longer? The incident that morning as I was waiting for the bus flashed across my mind. We had all laughed afterward, but it had left a distinct uneasiness. And what about Lolek and Anka's strange silence? No response to my phone call from Prague; their locked apartment door. What a contrast to my reunion with them on my visit to Warsaw in 1947. And just now, Mela's parting remark: "Promise to write a card tonight from Prague that you are all right." There seemed indeed a finality in the dusty wake of the departing car.

"Pan Field, *prosze*"—Mr. Field, please. The loudspeaker cut across my thoughts; the drone surrounding me took sudden form. I turned from the window. At the counter only my processed ticket was handed back to me. "Your passport you will get on the plane." A porter picked up my checked-in baggage and beckoned me to follow. We cut across the gravel drive to the arrivals and departures shed. Customs, each passenger called one at a time. Some desultory poking around among my things, an objection to some Polish currency I had failed to spend, a mute signal from another official on the sidelines to forget it, a nod to the porter to pick up my suitcase again, and I was on my way once more, pleased at not having been asked about my undeveloped color films. Carrying them inconspicuously in my pocket had been a good idea.

I followed the porter into the little adjoining departure room facing the flight apron. Apparently I was the first passenger processed. But no, a man was standing inconspicuously over by the far wall. Funny how I hadn't noticed him at first. He was staring intently at me. Without taking his eyes off me, he shifted toward the point where I had entered. Involuntarily, I glanced back too. My suitcase had been set down just inside the room, and already the door was closing behind the porter's back. I turned toward the glazed door facing the airfield. Maybe I could see the plane.

"*Dokumente.*" The man suddenly came to life. "Passport."

I was surprised. "Haven't . . . *Niema* . . . On plane," and groping for an adequate Polish word, I pointed toward the field. He had moved over to that door himself and beckoned me to follow. I started to, but then he pointed back to my suitcase. Why, of course, take it along: an official ushering me to the plane. But there was something strange and imperative about this man. And why no porter? He opened the door and beckoned me to go ahead, suitcase in hand. How odd; no plane anywhere in sight.

"*Prosze,*" and he pointed to an open door on my right just beyond the one we had emerged from. I entered with the stranger close on my heels. Maybe it was just a matter of having to change that Polish money into Czech currency before leaving. I recalled the nod of the customs official a few moments earlier. Of course.

The triple shift from customs through one door, then another, and now through a third had the predetermined air of sleep walking. As the door closed behind me I found myself in a small corner room and, facing me, two men standing behind a large table. One was in uniform, apparently an officer; the second was a rather heavyset civilian with a cigarette drooping from the corner of his mouth.

"Empty your pockets," the latter ordered in German, as if this were perfectly routine. He even looked surprised when I said, "I don't understand." The demand was repeated, now with unmistakable firmness.

I experienced a moment of hesitation, a "why?" and a feeling of amazement, followed by an awareness of not being surprised at all. And then the flash of recognition, even relief. Obviously: it was those color films in my pocket! How stupid to have created suspicion by not declaring them myself, especially after the incident that morning.

"Please, if that's what you want," and with a forced smile I deposited the two film cartridges on the table. "Since you have no facilities for color developing in Warsaw, I was advised to . . ."

"Quickly, quickly," the man with the drooping cigarette broke in. "Empty all your pockets."

I shrugged and did as I was told. He pointed to a chair. I sat down. Silence settled over the room, the three men casually observing me from their various positions. The man with the cigarette picked up one of the film cartridges and inspected it. This was my cue. "They require special developing since they're color."

He looked up, amused. "We'll take care of them for you, all right."

I gave up. A pity if my efforts to make a record of Warsaw's reconstruction progress were spoiled.

Outside I heard airplane motors not far away. Through the upper part of the curtained side window I could see the top of the control tower. Occasionally the man in it glanced down this way as if aware that something unusual was going on in here.

Five minutes went by in silence, ten. Why this absurd inactivity? I looked ostentatiously at my watch. It was almost departure time. "Excuse me, but I think I should be going to the plane." The man with the cigarette nodded indulgently.

Again a stretch of silence. Maybe, I thought, the plane is late on the run here from Prague, and on account of this film business they want me to wait here instead of with the other passengers and they'll put me on at the last moment. Yet I knew better. That wasn't it. Well then, what? Instinctively I shied away from further speculation. I should have desisted from taking any color pictures in the absence of proper processing facilities here. Obviously the incident that morning had caused suspicion and the confiscation now.

That morning I had been waiting for the bus at the intersection of the Alea Niepodlegloszci and the Sierpnia and decided to photograph a rather promising apartment block with balconies under construction across the road. As I was getting my exposure reading, I felt a tap on my shoulder. I looked around. A youth in his teens seemed to be asking what I was doing. I pointed to my camera and then to the construction site. The youth shook his head. "*Nie wolno*"—Not allowed. I shrugged and answered in English, "Okay, I won't in that case," put my light meter away, and turned back to the bus stop. But the youth stuck to me, tugging at my jacket and beckoning me to follow him into the high, modernistic office building just behind us. To a uniformed official at a reception window I again tried to explain, but evidently his German was not up to it, and English was even more futile. He told me to take a seat while he got busy volubly on a telephone.

I waited fifteen minutes and was getting impatient, as I had been on my way to a lunch date in the center of town with a leading Polish city planner. The man behind the window merely shrugged. Judging from the flow of officers checking in and out, I concluded that this was some military establishment. Another fifteen minutes. I became more insistent and showed my passport. Again some telephoning. After another half hour a militia officer appeared and, addressing me in German, asked to see my passport, listened to my explanation, and then apologized at my having been detained, pointing out that the error had arisen due to my intending to photograph a defense building. Advising me to be more careful henceforth, he left as abruptly as he had appeared. I asked the man at the window whether I could now go on my way. He nodded, all smiles and apologies.

Before I got through the door, I bumped into a second officer coming in all out of breath. He stopped me and asked me to follow him upstairs into a small office. "It will be necessary to take down a protocol about this before you leave," he explained in good German. On a blank white sheet he put down my personal data, and then he asked: "What were you doing in front of the Ministry of National Defense?" So that's where I was. Laboriously he noted down that my interest had been not in it but in the apartment building going up across the street, and that anyway I had not actually taken a picture but only a meter reading. I signed the sheet, and as I left at last the officer admonished me that as an architect I should recognize the nature of a building! Getting into a taxi, I had glanced almost in fear of new trouble toward the fateful, scaffold-surrounded construction. It looked just as innocent as before—obviously an apartment house in the making. Nevertheless, clearly suspicions had been aroused by all my photographing this past week, and this airport scene was the payoff.

In the little room, the silent passage of time was unnerving. A growing dread forced my mind into ever smaller circles, shutting out all but the little pile of things from my pockets on the table, the three uncommunicative faces, the telephone on the wall in the corner, the top of the control tower through the window, until all finally dissolved into one urgent reality: the plane. The plane—would it go without me?

Another half hour must have passed by in silence. The sun's rays had crept from the floor to the wall. At one point there was a flurry of airplane motors, but then quiet again settled in outside. The plane. I did not even dare look at my watch lest it confirm my growing dread. Make a scene? But I felt silly, guilty somehow. The fact was that I had evaded declaring those films. There they lay right before me, the cause of all this trouble. But was that all there was to it? If only someone would say something.

The man at the door pulled its window curtain a little to one side and peered out. He nodded to the man with the cigarette, who went over to the telephone. Some arrangements were made in a muted tone. He hung up. Again the room settled into a long silence. After a while a motor was audible close by outside. It stopped. The man at the door slipped out, then returned. The man with the cigarette said in German, "Please, take your suitcase and follow this gentleman."

I went through the door—and stopped abruptly. I found myself looking directly into the open rear-end of a small delivery van. I set my suitcase down and turned inquiringly to the men.

"*Predzej*"—Quickly, get on in. They lined up solidly between me and the building. The half-perceived flash of an idea passed through my mind: Demand contact with my embassy. Still better, just make a dash for it across the field and shout for help. But I knew: that sort of thing only happens in the movies. And so, as if in a dream, I found myself clambering onto the floor of the van, the original stranger close behind me with my suitcase.

The door swung shut. I was in semidarkness, the only light coming in through a little oval pane in the rear door. Through it I could see the other two men get into a second vehicle, which rapidly receded as we got under way, swaying and bumping over the grass. I tried to think, but it was all too preposterous to find a starting point. Obviously there was no question of the plane anymore, but that was not yet a disaster. I could take the night train instead. Of course, Herta and Karel would get a fright at the airport in Prague when they found I was not on the plane as arranged. At once Noel's disappearance would come to their minds. If only I could phone through before they drove out there, to let them know I would be delayed until tomorrow. I would try. I felt better.

I concentrated on the little cut-out with its images racing into the distance behind us. I tried to establish where we were going. We were speeding along a highway in wide open country, the car by now close behind us. Several times I caught a glimpse of the receding airport tower. Some modern apartment buildings were on the right. Why yes: the Rakowiec housing project, designed by the Syrkuses, which I had inspected with them only a few hours earlier on the way to the airport. So I was heading back to the city along the same road on which I had just left it. But where to? I strained to identify buildings, road signs,

streetcars as they flashed by. The Filtrova, for sure, and then I spotted the col-
onnade of the Polytechnic Institute and, shortly after, the familiar balconies behind their scaffolding—the unfortunate starting point of this crazy day. A short
distance farther along the Sierpnia we cut across the Marszalkowska, Warsaw's
Fifth Avenue, full of rush hour traffic in spite of the ruins. We slowed down.
Our horn tooted as we swung across an unidentifiable street and passed
through an iron gate guarded by uniformed security militia. After some maneuvering in the shadowed courtyard of a tall building we came to a stop. The
motor was turned off, and in rapid sequence the door swung open, my traveling
companion crawled out with my suitcase, and the heavyset man with the cigarette appeared and beckoned me to climb down and follow him through a door
within a step or two of the back of the van.

Proceeding down a long carpeted corridor with doors on either side, I was
ushered into a small room with heavy drawn curtains, even though it was still
daylight outside. The sole furniture: a writing table and three chairs. The uncommunicative man entered behind me, carrying my suitcase. Once more we
were alone together. He came over and tapped me on the arm and indicated
that I should raise my hands over my head. To my surprise he promptly started
frisking me from my shoulders to the bottom of my trousers. This was too
much. I should demand contact with the embassy and put an end to this! But
then I was struck by the humor and incongruity of finding myself so suddenly
in such ignoble circumstances. "Our guest from America . . ."; "Our architect
friend . . ."; "Our honored colleague from Cleveland and friend of the new Poland." These words still rang in my ears. And now? If my erstwhile hosts could
only see me.

He pointed to a chair in the corner, which I took. He then tackled my suitcase with concentration, dumping its contents onto the table, fingering each
item in turn as if expecting at any moment to make some momentous discovery.

His search was interrupted by the entrance of a severe-looking woman in
her thirties, who sat down at the table and started all over again with my things,
listing them on a sheet of paper: pajamas, toothpaste, letters, architectural
drawings, socks—every smallest thing, occasionally asking me in excellent
German to identify a doubtful item.

If they go on this way, I thought, I'll miss the night train too. But she speaks
German. I can make myself understood, at least. I began: "Where am I?"

She looked up sarcastically. "You know very well where you are."

I tried again: "What's the meaning of all this?"

All I got was an enigmatic "You know very well."

"I asked a reasonable question and expect a reasonable answer. I had a plane to catch and you made me miss it."

She kept on writing. "That's up to you and not our problem."

I tried a new line: "But I was to be met at Prague airport, and . . ." She looked up. For the first time she seemed really to notice me. She turned to the uncommunicative man and consulted with him in a low tone. He went out. I felt triumphant. At least they know now that they can't drag this on and on without anyone noticing. Probably now they'll agree to put me on the night train if I telegraph to Prague and allay fears by stating that I had simply missed the plane.

The heavyset man appeared in the door. My earlier passivity was now gone. I turned on him angrily. "What does all this mean? I'm an American architect and was here by invitation. You have no right to interfere with my departure. You are violating my rights."

In a calculatedly deliberate manner, he pulled a chair over and straddled it, leaning on the back rail, the cigarette drooping from his lips. He stared at me for a moment and then with pointed emphasis said: "Long before Hermann Field chose to come to Warsaw we were well aware of whom we were dealing with."

I was dumbfounded. But I ignored the ominousness in his voice and merely said, "If you know who I am, then why all this now? You must be aware that I came here because of my friendly interest in your reconstruction and to visit colleagues."

"And perhaps see other friends too?"

"Yes, to see Dr. Gecow and his wife, old prewar friends from student days."

"And did you see them? No?"

"I tried to, but they were away on vacation."

"On vacation?" He nodded with exaggerated seriousness and whispered something to the woman; they both smiled. I felt more and more agitated. I raised the matter of the Prague airport again: "I was to be met at the plane in Prague. I must let them know that I am delayed."

An indulgent nod, and then, as if in afterthought: "And who are 'they'?"

"My sister-in-law and a Czech friend."

He got out a notebook. "And their names?" I gave them.

"Noel Field's wife perhaps?" So he knew my brother's name. "And where is he?"

What should I say? If they learned about his disappearance, wouldn't that at once redouble their suspicions about me? "I don't know at the moment."

He repeated with feigned surprise: "So you don't *know* . . ." Then, after a pause: "And how can your friends be reached in Prague?" I pointed, feeling more hopeful, to my address book on the table. He reached over and took it and found the information. Then he whispered something to the woman and got up and went out, whereupon the uncommunicative man reappeared, like an alter ego.

The woman laid her list to one side while the man scooped my things haphazardly back into the suitcase. She pulled a number of sheets of lined paper out of the table drawer and wrote some sort of long heading. I felt still more hopeful. Was there time to make the night train? The woman looked at her watch as if she had read my thoughts.

"Your full name, please, and your date of birth."

So it wasn't over yet. I told her.

"Your father?"

I told her: Herbert Haviland Field. Yes, American, born in Brooklyn Heights in 1868, zoologist, dead. Mother, Nina. Died two years ago; born in London in 1874. Me? Born 1910 in Zurich. I explained that I had grown up in Switzerland because my father was director of an international zoological institute there until his death in 1921, when the family returned to America. Our home there? In Cambridge, Massachusetts (how she struggled with that word!). Went to school there, two years of grammar school and four of high school. Then? Harvard University. Yes, also in Cambridge. Graduate studies in Zurich. Profession? Architect in Cleveland, Ohio.

She looked annoyed. "You are not answering properly. That is too sketchy. We will start again with when you finished the university."

"But how much longer will this take? Since you made me miss my plane, I must catch the train tonight for Prague. Surely you don't want to create an international incident with this?"

I was getting worried again. Would this stupidity jeopardize any last chance of prying Noel quietly out of whatever trouble had hit him? The whole point of my going earlier that month to Prague, where he apparently had disappeared, had been to approach the Czech authorities privately through friends in the hope of locating him without fanfare. Although I was skeptical that this plan would work, Herta had pleaded for it in view of the controversy around Noel at home in connection with the trial of Alger Hiss, which would make his disappearance a front-page sensation. Until I learned from Herta whether our efforts had succeeded or failed, it was essential that nothing catapult Noel's disappearance into the press. If the news was negative, there would be no recourse other than to put the whole thing in Washington's lap, where I was convinced it belonged in any case. The urgent matter now, though, was for me to have the final picture from Herta. I would then be leaving for home from London with Kate and the boys ten days hence.

In response to my protest the woman simply said, "It's all up to you. The more detailed you are, the quicker we'll be finished." She came back to the matter of my return to Europe in 1934. Had I been married?

"Yes, my first wife, Jean, and I came on separate graduate fellowships for study in Switzerland, I in architecture and she in German literature." On our way there, I pointed out, I had attended a summer seminar on city planning at Moscow University. I also mentioned our month's adventure as farm laborers on a state farm between the Volga and the Urals. Surely that would work in my favor, indicating at least a sympathetic interest toward the Soviet Union. We proceeded to Jean's and my two years as students in Zurich and then my three years in England on my first architectural assignment, and Jean's and my eventual separation and divorce in 1939. Then that strange, unplanned interlude of activity on behalf of refugees from Czechoslovakia following Hitler's takeover of the rump of that country that same year, which took me to Prague and Krakow and pitched me into the center of the German invasion of Poland in September. I pointed out that among the many I was instrumental in saving at that time were a number of Czech communists who were playing a prominent role in the current regime. Then the first winter of war in England with Kate; the next summer, newly married and taking the last American evacuation ship from Ireland; and the remaining war years in New York, working for the U.S. Army Corps of Engineers and developing an interest in the problem of rebuilding war-devastated cities. I emphasized the help given to visiting Russian architects and building engineers through my efforts in New York, and also my interest in Czech and Polish reconstruction, as evidenced by my including both countries in my architectural study tour of Europe in 1947 and my visit again this year.

Impatiently she interrupted me: "Go back to your work in Krakow in 1939."

What was there to say? It was ten years ago and I had given it little thought since then.

By now exhausted, I had stopped thinking about the night train. That too was behind me, and the hours were going by with no more meaning than in a dream. And as in a dream, it began to seem as if the monotonous drone of my voice came from someone outside myself. The only other sound in the room was the incessant scratching of the pen, on which I tried to fix my eyes in the idle hope that the faster it moved the nearer we would be to the end. At some point I ate a sandwich and drank some beer.

On and on the questioning went. New York again. Midnight passed. The shift in 1947 to my downtown center planning project in Cleveland. My impending architectural deanship at Western Reserve University. How unreal and far away it all sounded! The present: 1949. We had to have reached the end at last.

"And your brother?"

Yes, here it was, the question I had been hoping in vain would be forgotten.

"Your brother, when did you last see him?"

"Two years ago. In 1947."

"Where?"

"In Paris."

"And where is he now?" For the first time she looked up to watch my response.

It was no use. To hedge would only look as if I had something to conceal and make things worse. "He disappeared from his hotel in Prague in May, a few days after arriving via Paris from Geneva, where he and his wife live. The Czech authorities are investigating the matter for me, and that is why it is so urgent I get back to Prague without delay." I went on to describe Herta's call for help from Geneva just after I had arrived in London to join Kate and the boys; my response of flying on to see her and her subsequent plea that after my conference in Italy I go to Prague, where I had loyal friends from the refugee relief days before the war; and my decision while they were looking into the matter to come briefly to Warsaw, where I had already been invited by my colleagues Szymon and Helena Syrkus.

She looked up. "And why didn't you go at once to the U.S. authorities? After all, isn't that the usual thing when one of your kind gets into trouble?" I couldn't fail to sense the sarcasm in her voice. I was furious. Was that the thanks I got for trying to protect Poland's neighbors, the Czechs, from inevitable embarrassment about this inexplicable incident within their own borders?

"I shouldn't have to explain that to you," I blurted out bitterly.

This time she didn't even bother to look up, didn't show the slightest reaction. Her pen was moving steadily across the sheet, on and on. But now with every new word I felt I was being sucked willy-nilly into something beyond my control or comprehension. Somehow, imperceptibly, the whole affair had taken a new turn.

But what in fact had I done? Nothing whatsoever. All they had to do was develop my films to establish that. At most I'd exercised bad judgment, but without hostile intent. And yet, was the intrusion of Noel's disappearance merely a coincidence? Could there be any connection between this craziness and my search for him? "One of your kind"—the words rang ominously in my ears. I had the sickening sensation of treading in a morass and sinking ever deeper.

"Tell me what you know about your brother."

Wasn't this my chance to make them understand that they should be concerned about Noel? Hadn't he proved his friendship for the new Poland immediately after the war, when as European director of the Boston-based Unitarian

Service Committee he had taken the difficult initiative of establishing an American-sponsored hospital in the devastated mining region of Silesia? The effort had received wide international recognition and had the full support of the Polish health authorities. I emphasized that more recently, in the emerging Cold War climate, Noel had come under attack at home, accused of bias toward communists in his relief work, even of being a communist himself. That should impress them!

"But go back earlier."

I told her that in 1936 he left the State Department, where he had been its specialist on the successive naval disarmament conferences, and shifted to the disarmament section of the League of Nations in Geneva. Then in 1938, with the republican defeat in the Spanish civil war, he was appointed a member of the League commission for the evacuation of the international volunteers caught in the final retreat. His dedication then and later, during the war, when many of these people were lingering in French internment camps, had saved many lives—including the lives of many Poles. Surely now the authorities should be concerned with what had happened to him rather than complicating everything by delaying my departure.

Another hour passed. When the door finally opened and the man with the cigarette stood before me and nodded for me to follow him out into the corridor, I saw him as if through a haze. I rose automatically. I had no will left to challenge him, wanted just to put an end to tonight. All I was aware of in the room I entered was the sofa in front of me, on which I dropped and immediately escaped into overwhelming sleep.

# 2

## Warsaw Courtyard

The youth set down a glass of hot milk and a plate with two rolls, a slice of ham, and a large chunk of butter. "*Gut appetit*," he said in broken German and smiled, then retired courteously to the sofa on which I had just had a few hours of exhausted sleep.

The table I sat at looked out a window onto a courtyard. With daylight and fresh air pouring in and my breakfast delivered right to me, I felt a rather light-headed optimism crowd away the nightmarish recollections with which I had awoken. True, I was cut off from the outside world for the moment, under detention without a word of explanation. True, too, there was a wire mesh across my window, and while I slept a light bulb had shone down on me and two silent figures had kept watch from their chairs in the half dark by the door. Nonetheless, now there was a casualness about everything, as if I were merely a houseguest here. Even the neatly designed monogram on the plate and cutlery had a touch of genteel elegance—though as I stared at the three letters, MBP, I suddenly realized what they stood for: Ministry of Public Security, Poland's secret police. No ordinary restaurant this.

Two new young men came in. While my guards of the night packed up their things, the four of them engaged in a lively chatter. For them, it was just the beginning of another day. My new guards smiled at me and settled down on the sofa. Mere youths in their teens, they soon opened up their briefcases, got out textbooks, and began to study as if everything was just as it was supposed to be.

I got up from the table and started to walk back and forth. Actually, had anything unsalvageable happened? Surely this mix-up would be clarified in the course of the day, now that they had my whole story. No doubt Herta and Karel Markus, my loyal friend from Krakow days, had had a fright yesterday evening when I didn't arrive; but they would assume I had merely missed my plane and would turn up on the same flight today. And why not? It was another ten hours until departure time, which should be plenty. I had allowed a four-day stopover in Prague before flying on to London the afternoon of the twenty-sixth. Although I had the clear impression that the Czechs were giving us the runaround about Noel's disappearance and knew more than they chose to say, I had no choice but to play along. Once I got a final answer from them, as well as Herta's views on the state of things, I would be in a better position to plan the next steps as soon as I reached London. We would have to manage on three days now, but it would be enough.

"*Hallo! Hallo! Nie wolno*"—Not allowed! I turned. Both youths were beckoning me excitedly to come away from the window. I shrugged and resumed my pacing. The youths laughed at my evident perplexity. To impress me with the serious consequences of my dereliction, the younger one made a cutting sweep across his throat. Amused, I pointed questioningly to myself. No, no; he shook his head and pointed to himself and his colleague. All three of us laughed.

Naturally, this prohibition only heightened my interest in the courtyard. What else had I to occupy myself with? Each time I turned in my pacing I gave a quick glance. I noticed some young men doing filing in a room across from mine. Every now and then a shiny black chauffeur-driven car would pull up outside and disgorge some serious-looking civilian with his briefcase. A platoon of uniformed security militia lined up at attention, responded to various commands, and then marched off around the corner of the building opposite. Presumably that was where the entrance to the courtyard was. Every time a car passed in or out I could hear the clanking of a metal gate, probably the one I had passed through the previous evening.

This doing nothing began to be wearing. Had they forgotten me? I indicated to the youths that I wanted to speak to someone. They nodded reassuringly: soon, soon. Noon passed. My earlier tranquillity had left me. One of the youths went out and a few minutes later returned with some soup, and on a second trip with a plate of meat and vegetables and a glass of watery stewed apples. I ate with relish; at least it was something to do. Then I returned to my pacing with renewed impatience. I complained again, but it was obvious I would get the same friendly answer: Soon, soon, with a smile that suggested, What's the hurry? My mood swung from anger to a feeling of helpless resignation and back again. These people seemed to have no sense of time. Or maybe it's just that we Americans have an exaggerated compulsion in that direction.

The door opened silently, and someone whispered to one of the youths. He beckoned to me. We went out into the corridor and stopped three doors down to the left. He knocked. A man's voice inside said "*Prosze.*" It was the room of the previous evening, the heavy curtains drawn though it was early afternoon. At the side of the table sat the hard-faced woman just as before, but the empty chair behind it was now occupied by a young man in civilian clothes, attempting to look twice his years as he tried in silence to stare me down. He started to write laboriously. He spoke in Polish to the woman, and she in turn to me in German: "The officer asks you to give your name and where and when you were born."

I was amazed. "But we went over all that last night, and today it was just a matter of finishing about my present trip here."

She looked at me as if I were awfully dumb. "Last night has no bearing. From now on I'm merely here as interpreter. The officer wishes to start over."

I gasped. "But that's impossible. You can't go on and on this way."

"Why not? We have time. The clearer and franker you are with us, the quicker it will go."

"But this won't get us anywhere. I have been delayed almost twenty-four hours without any explanation."

"You know very well why you are here. What is your full name?"

And so we were off on a new round that seemed designed to defy time and patience. First the young man thought, then he formulated a question, then he put it to the woman in Polish; she repeated it to me in German; I answered; she translated it back into Polish, sentence by sentence; after another spell of thinking, he wrote something down. There was a pause for supper at seven, and then another long stretch in the evening. Before stopping on both occasions everything that had been written down was translated for me, confirmed by my signature at the bottom of each page and at the end the statement "The foregoing answers have been reread to me in German and represent a true statement of my testimony."

Afternoon had passed into evening, evening into night, and as I once more dropped on the sofa with the broken springs I realized I was much further from the end than twenty-four hours earlier. Again and again I had protested, asked for an explanation, pointed out the urgency of my being in Prague, warned about the adverse effects for all concerned of a scandal, even threatened that Poland would be held responsible in view of my being a foreign national. It was like talking to a wall. The stock reply: You have only yourself to blame for the slow progress, and you had better stop with your interruptions.

Back in my room with the couch, I tried to reassure myself that I would still have two days in Prague. However, a new fear began to intrude on the problem of my stopover there. What if day after tomorrow comes and I'm still here? I had written Kate what plane I would be arriving on in London the evening of the twenty-sixth. What if there were no sign of me? What would she think? Although Herta had insisted that I should avoid any concrete reference to Noel's disappearance in correspondence, Kate was aware that something serious had happened to him. In my last letter two days ago, I had hinted as much as I dared. And for there suddenly to be no news from me too? I tried to push the thought aside, but it recurred ever more pressingly as my watch ticked on toward that moment in London.

And Noel . . . How could anyone disappear without a trace? My mind rushed through the by now familiar sequence: The mysterious letter and telegram from Herta. Then in Geneva, Herta pulling me into her apartment without a word and quickly closing the door behind me. In a hushed voice: "Hermann, he's disappeared. In Prague. Not a word since May. No telephone response. No letters. And now it's July. Hermann, for the sake of your love for your brother . . ." She broke down as she released this secret she had apparently told no one.

But why such secretiveness? Why hadn't she alerted the U.S. embassy? "It's not that simple, Hermann . . ." Gradually an incredible picture of paralysis and inaction had emerged, based on complexities in my brother's political life of which I had been only vaguely aware, but which left his wife in a sea of uncertainty as to what to do. On top of accusations of communist leanings in his wartime and postwar relief work, his name had now come up in the Hiss trial in New York—at which moment precisely he turns up in communist Czechoslovakia and promptly disappears. Was it to avoid facing the music at home in the changed climate of the Cold War? Or was he a victim of somebody's scheming in the twilight zone of international intrigue? But what someone? If indeed he was a Communist, why would he disappear in Prague, of all places? With the Communists now in control, wouldn't they have received him with open arms?

Herta was beset by fear of an international scandal, which would freeze all positions in the new Cold War atmosphere, whoever was to blame. She pleaded with me to try a quiet approach and go to the Czech authorities unofficially, before being forced to go public. It all seemed crazy to me. But of course Herta knew more about Noel than I; I had to trust her judgment. It would not be an irremediable step anyway, and if nothing came of it Herta agreed to ask for the help of our government, at last. So immediately after the architectural congress in Italy I had flown to Prague, with Herta following me a few days later.

The Czech communist authorities had claimed to be as mystified as we were. They said it would take them a week to report back. Rather than sitting around, I had decided to accept my Polish colleagues' invitation to see the progress of reconstruction here in Warsaw since my visit two years earlier.

Instinctively my mind shifted to my photographing—how irresponsible that had been in view of the business about Noel. I fell into a delirious sleep.

My third day of living between these two rooms, either pacing back and forth in the twelve-foot length between window and door or sitting hour after hour in the corner facing the drawn curtains and the eternal questions and sound of scribbling, I began to live entirely with that coming moment when the plane's wheels would touch ground in England without me on board. Already I was sure I would not be there. It was only a vain hope that I might still be able to alert Kate that I was even delayed. If I could do just that, everything else would be all right. The *Batory*, on which we were planning to return, would not reach Southampton until the twenty-ninth. Three days' grace. Wasn't that all that mattered? That I could no longer do anything about Noel was evident.

August 25 came without the slightest change in routine. All morning long I was ignored, with nothing to do except watch the hours go by and pace back and forth in the room. If only there was something I could occupy my mind with. I had repeatedly asked for a book from my suitcase but was ignored. I had then asked for any book, even one in Polish. To my surprise, I was told that books were forbidden. I found part of an East Berlin newspaper in my coat pocket and started reading and rereading that. It was taken away: "You are not allowed to read." I looked at my watch. "You are not allowed to have a watch." I had to hand it over. The guards had made a checkerboard, with checkers and chess figures fashioned from bread, with which they helped to while away their boredom. They were not averse to an occasional game with me. That, too, turned out to be forbidden. I tried to make conversation with my companions in a mixture of German, French, and Polish. The next day I was reprimanded: "Please refrain from talking with your guards." What could I do? In desperation I tried to sing as I walked back and forth. It did not work: my mind swung inexorably to that London-bound plane that would soon be leaving Prague.

At last I was called into the room with the drawn curtains. "Tell us about each of your friends during your studies in Zurich from 1934 to 1936."

I flared up and point blank refused to continue, demanding to speak at once to a responsible official. The two consulted. The man got up and went out. A little later there was a knock on the door. I was told to return to my room. I noticed the time on the watch of one of the guards. The plane had left by now; Kate and the boys would be full of anticipation. I tried to pace. I lay down and drew my raincoat over me and tried to drowse as a kind of thought anesthesia. I searched desperately for something to deaden my awareness of the time. I got up and watched the guards playing their chess. How I envied them! I followed every move with utmost concentration. If only I could play too, just this once. In spite of the experience a few days back, I asked. They looked up, surprised: "*Nie wolno*"—not allowed—but something about my expression made them soften. They looked at each other, then toward the door. Then one batted his hand dismissively and indicated I should play standing where I was; if the door opened we would pretend I was just watching. We started. I was soundly beaten. I pleaded for just one more try. They seemed to understand. This time I held my ground better.

It was getting dark outside. I was fighting, fighting with all my will to concentrate. It seeped through nonetheless, the dazing realization: She knows now. Kate knows by now that I did not arrive. It was the boys' bedtime. There had already been supper, quite different from anticipated. "Mummy, why didn't Daddy come?" What could she say? Would the boys sense the dread behind her reassurances as she kissed them good night? "Tomorrow." I grappled on with the chess. Night came. Why wasn't there the usual evening session in the other room?

The guards changed. The new ones came in full of the world outside that had moved along as usual while here everything stood still. Tanned by the August sun, they recounted their exploits with Halka and Jadwiga and were full of scorn for a certain Kowalski. And there were the snapshots taken at the beach, a sizing up of the object revealed, grudging approval, a pointed comment, and laughter all around. Life. I could fight no longer. I threw myself down on the sofa and turned my back to the room, my raincoat over my head.

Darkness. Quiet. Now at last I let it surge through me, my whole consciousness focusing on the house this same night off in London, which had suddenly been sucked into the orbit of this awfulness. And exactly like me in the days just past, Kate would be holding off the reality, telling herself against her deeper awareness that the morrow would bring an explanation, that everything would turn out all right. I fell into a feverish sleep, which released me for the moment from my preoccupation.

August 27 came and went. The sessions in the curtained room resumed. The only reference to the previous day's demand was, "You have only yourself to blame for any delay." I wanted to retort that I was available every morning at nine o'clock. This workday that for some reason began in the afternoon and ended deep in the night was enough in itself to drive one mad. There had been a definite stiffening in attitude toward me. I desisted, seeing no point in making things worse. There was a new formality. "The officer requests you follow instructions more promptly," or "The officer instructs you to sit politely. It is not allowed to cross your knees that way."

I could not shake off the pervasive sense of unreality. It destroyed any capacity for a genuine outburst. There was nothing to do except keep going. I formulated each new point as simply as possible, trying imperceptibly to mark time—focusing on details and avoiding any suggestion of hurry. I refrained from wrangling about the weird way my answers were summarized when they were finally read back to me to sign. It wasn't so much intentional distortion, I thought, as the limitation of the mind of the man before me, who could not re-state a sequence of events from an environment completely strange to him. What did it matter? There was nothing there that anyone could take exception to, even though the end product would be a biographical grotesque. My one job was to concentrate on my recounting, which would end with my seizure at the airport. At that point there was bound to be a change of routine, a reappraisal, a decision. Perhaps release with some face-saving device? So long as it came be-fore the next deadline, the *Batory*'s sailing for America two days hence. I tried not to think about Kate's mounting anxiety, about her uncertainty as the sailing hour approached. Would she get all packed and set, hoping I would turn up at the last moment?

And then came August 29: the *Batory* had come to Southampton and gone. Was the distance between Kate and me and the boys increasing every minute, or had they stayed behind at the last moment? How awful for them to be faced with such paralyzing uncertainty. Kate knew that I would never of my own free will miss our trip home. Somehow, with the decisive sailing hour behind me, my tension dropped. I had lost another round. In normal life I would have thrown up my hands in despair. Now, though, I cut my losses and simply felt consoled by the possible reprieve of a last-minute direct flight home.

Up to now I had refrained from demanding contact with our embassy in Warsaw. At first I had thought it would only worsen the situation by forcing the authorities to justify an apparently minor infraction. Later it became evident that no matter how much I demanded this right, no one would pay any atten-tion. The only effect would be to heighten their suspicions that I had been up to something with my photographing. Clearly, there was more to lose than to gain. Instead I would continue to emphasize every detail in my life that could be construed as sympathetic to the communists. I would draw attention to friend-ships and acquaintanceships with persons in positions of responsibility in pres-ent-day Poland and Czechoslovakia, most of them growing out of my efforts ten years earlier to save their lives from the Nazis. What better references could I have? Through them, too, the authorities could check the accuracy of my ac-count. Gradually I would be able to persuade my interrogators that they had made an unfortunate mistake. They would be keen to avoid a disagreeable scandal, and I could even assure them that I would make no issue of what had happened provided they released me in time to get back to Cleveland for my work.

September 1 came, the tenth anniversary of Hitler's 1939 assault on Poland, which I had witnessed at such close range. How ironic that this day should find me in these circumstances here, after all I had given of myself ten years earlier! The sky was clear and blue, just like that dawn when I had watched incredulously from my window as the first bombs fell on the outskirts of Krakow, not knowing it was the start of World War II.

Today was a holiday. The courtyard was still and deserted. Above, a formation of planes passed across the small cutout of sky as if to mock me. My companions brought in big headlined anniversary issues of the newspapers filled with reminiscences of those first awful weeks of war and dissolution. I never guessed then that this tenth anniversary would find me a prisoner here, the very course of my life and my career in the far-off heartland of America threatened.

Two days later, I recalled Mela's regret as we had driven out to the airport ten days earlier. "What a shame you won't be here on the third. There are a number of survivors of our Krakow evacuation here in Warsaw. We could organize a little celebration. Imagine their excitement with you among us. What a pity!"

Well, I was here. And while I was not part of their celebration, my mind drifted back to that long line of ill-fed, ill-clad stragglers tramping with their pitiful bundles of worldly goods through thick, choking dust, on a trek eastward that in fact had led nowhere. Mela Granowska had been one of the Polish Jewish locals in Krakow who during the preceding months had given much of her youthful energy as a grassroots ombudsman for our refugees. On the third day of the war, September 3, 1939, when in the face of the advancing Germans evacuation on foot had become the only recourse left to our refugee community, Mela had agreed to throw in her lot with us as one of our guides, an invaluable help in an alien country in the process of dissolution.

And now? Here, right outside my window and in the rooms all around me, people were going about their daily tasks just as in thousands of office buildings everywhere. Yet here too, unknown to most of the others around me, was I, for whom all time had stopped in a captivity that defied sanity. I could call out and draw attention to my plight, but I would simply be ignored like an inmate of a mental institution. How close I still was to life, and at the same time how far away! All I had to do was put on my coat and open the door, walk down the corridor, and join the others on their way home. But just try! I did not want to think of the consequences if, even for one moment, I attempted to do what everyone else took for granted.

As one September day followed another, the numb dread that filled me was only heightened by the endless stretches with nothing to occupy my mind. It pursued a continuous circuit of worry about the meaning of my detention, about Kate and the boys, about Noel, and about the profound setback my professional career was likely suffering. My tension mounted as I realized that at any moment the news of my disappearance, and of Noel's, would take over the headlines. Once that happened the issue would be beyond redemption. A situation was taking shape in which I was a heretic in both camps, as the meeting ground I had sought receded in the distance. Whatever the outcome now, the world around me had been profoundly shaken, of that I had no doubt.

Initially, I was convinced that I was the only person in this weird detention. Obviously it was not a prison, which was a hopeful sign. Everything underlined this: the coming and going outside of ordinary people occupied with everyday routines and the sight of office work going on across the courtyard; the absence of any grilles or bars in any of the windows opposite; the improvised setup in the room—not even a locked door! My youthful guards were rank amateurs and found it quite beyond their capacity to assume the bearing befitting their role. Despite several reprimands, our room became a friendly fraternity based on a fellowship of boredom and confinement. During hours when superiors were likely to be around, a strict aloofness was maintained. At other times, and especially during the weekends, we slipped into an easy informality, with conversations pieced together laboriously from three different tongues. Their favorite subject: women; second, America.

And yet I began to sense that something else was going on close by, something I could not put my finger on. For example: next to my room on the left was a stairwell that led up through the building and down to a basement, with an entry from the courtyard. From what I could hear through the wall, the staircase was little used, but once a day at one o'clock, Sundays included, a covered jeep swung in through the courtyard and backed up to the basement entry. Almost at once the aroma of soup drifted in through the window, and sure enough a moment later two men in faded uniforms lifted a huge metal tureen out from the back of the jeep and carried it into the building and down the stairs. Some fifteen minutes later they emerged with the same tureen, now obviously empty.

Sometimes in the quiet of the night I felt sure I heard grating noises coming from somewhere beneath the floor. On one such occasion I glanced up at the guard sitting at the table. He responded with a somewhat sheepish grin. There was something mysterious about the corridor, too. In the after-work hours, especially at night, I became aware of footsteps passing along it. I noticed also that at such times my guards wouldn't enter the corridor themselves. And whenever I was to be accompanied along the corridor, either to the curtained room or in the opposite direction to the WC and washroom, or from there back to my room, the guard would first slip out for a moment to survey the scene and only then nod to me to follow.

This was always the case—with a single exception, which at once brought everything into focus. That night I was about to return from the washroom, and my youthful companion's mind was evidently so filled with his latest amorous conquests that he quite forgot to take the customary peek first. So it happened that as we were advancing from our end, two figures rapidly approached us from the other. I almost stopped; I knew in a flash. I stared. He stared. And we passed each other. For hours afterward I could not shake off the memory of that frightened unshaven face that seemed all eyes and yet looked at me without human recognition, as if from another world. Never had I seen skin so strangely taut and white, and hair so black. Accompanied by a uniformed nonentity who set a brisk pace, he had shuffled by, incredibly emaciated, his shoes without laces, in a bedraggled, too big suit without belt and a collarless shirt.

What life of crime, what kind of neglect could have produced such a wretch? I recalled the face again—and the eyes, the eyes—and I felt ashamed. Of course I knew better, but the truth was too fearful to admit: not long ago he had looked just like me. This frightening grotesque of a man had been fashioned in the cellar beneath my feet. I shivered, trying to shake off the feeling of proximity. I wished I had not seen, not observed so conscientiously. Each day at one o'clock the jeep with the soup forced me to remember. Was it really possible, after all the horrible lessons of the Nazis and the war, that a society that had been so victimized now saw fit to keep people, whatever their guilt, in a cellar in circumstances that drove all human likeness out of them? Desperately I tried to persuade myself that I had made some false deduction.

In this situation, even the hated sessions in the curtained room became the release for which I waited each day. Not only was it an activity, but it was the sole element of progression. In the end they would tire. As September 8 neared I pointed out that on this day I would be expected back at my university. I referred to a presentation to the board of directors on my project and to the opening session of my course and expressed the opinion that all hell would break loose if there were no sign of me. Did Poland really want that? I explained as calmly as I knew how that an international scandal at Poland's expense could still be averted if I were permitted to fly back at once.

When the eighth arrived my tension became almost unbearable. I argued ever more sharply and again demanded to speak to a person of authority. I did this at intervals throughout the day, even getting the guards to pass my request on to their superiors. At night I tossed and turned, nightmare-filled sleep alternating with anxiety-plagued wakefulness. For the first time I allowed myself to entertain visions of escape. If only I knew just what street I was on. It could not be more than a few blocks from the American embassy, on the Alea Stalina. That I could give my guards the slip I was sure. I looked at them. One was sound asleep, curled up on top of the table—his usual spot when he had night duty—and snoring loudly. The only older man among my six rotating roommates, he was, in spite of his nighttime siestas, the only one who performed his role with a degree of professionalism. It was he who was in charge of the others and was rarely willing to make any concession in my favor. Unlike the youths, who were immaculately dressed, however, he usually looked grubby and uncouth.

His companion that night was sitting on a chair, having fallen asleep reading a book, which lay open on his lap. He had placed himself in what he presumed was a position that blocked the door, so that he would be awakened by anyone trying to get by. In fact, however, he had slumped so far sideways that with great care one might be able to sneak by unnoticed. Certainly before these two knew anything about it, I could escape into the courtyard. There was no locked door to that point, I was sure. But what then? The only exit from there was past the iron gate, which was guarded day and night, and I had already noticed that people leaving invariably took out their identity cards as they turned the corner of the building. No, that way of escape was hopeless. I thought of another: through one of the office doors on the opposite side of the corridor and out the window there. Chances were it might be on a back street. But then, how would I know which direction to run? Not to mention all the other incalculables I couldn't anticipate. No, that too was a delusion, I decided.

The eighth had come and gone. I felt a new numbness, though I had not really expected anything to be different. Noticing my agitation, the interpreter surprised me by commenting, "Tomorrow we'll work longer and try to finish up, just as you wish." Could it really be? I swung now from despair to cautious waiting. Sure enough, the next day I was brought into the other room in the middle of the morning, unusually early. "Can I speak to someone at last?" For the first time, I got an answer: "Yes, when we are finished."

In fact, we did wind up in the middle of the afternoon. Even more surprising, the last part was handled very sketchily, as if there were a definite deadline to meet. As I got up to return to my room the interpreter smiled and said, "You see, I told you we'd hurry up and finish."

Back in my room I found the guards tidying up, the friendly youth who had been in charge of the petty cash for food busily doing last-minute accounts. I told him he showed all the aptitude of a Swiss hotelier. After they had packed up their belongings, everyone sat down, expectantly waiting for something. Once again the vision came to me of the 5:30 plane. These preparations seemed to fit the time. I would be taken straight to the plane, probably without any official explanation. How else could they save face? The guards by now knew all about my work in Cleveland and my anxiety to get there on time. I joked about my regrets at having to say good-bye, told them they should come visit me in America. They laughed and said they would. We got onto the subject of the transatlantic flight, the stops en route, the weather, the plane types. The atmosphere in the room got ever jollier. One of the youths pointed to the jam jar on the table. "Better finish it. A pity to waste it." The excitement and anticipation had made me hungry. I took the spoon and slowly ate the sweet preserves. To me, the jam jar seemed conclusive evidence of impending departure.

Time passed. It was late afternoon already. What was holding us up? Departure time for the connecting flight to London via Prague had passed. Perhaps another route had been decided on, for more direct connection with a transatlantic flight. Stockholm, perhaps, or Berlin? I felt some uncertainty but tried to drive it back.

As dusk settled, we were all still waiting for something to happen. The night guards appeared at their appointed time, though without their usual packs, and they were not the guards I expected. One of them was the old grubby fellow who slept on the table. With him was another older man who had stood watch several times before. I had felt ill at ease in his presence; unlike the youths, he seemed always to be observing me out of the corner of his eye. The four talked briefly in an undertone, and as the day shift left I shook hands with them and thanked them for their friendliness. The room settled into silence. The two men looked at me unsmilingly; both smoked nervously, as if anticipating some impending unpleasant responsibility.

It was getting dark, and I was feeling more and more alarmed. There was a whispered conversation at the door. One of the men began collecting my things. He asked whether my shaving kit was all together. I opened the zipper of the leather case and checked, entertaining a momentary impulse to slip a razor blade into my pocket. The second fellow's eyes were on me; it was impossible. Then I noticed that there was no lid on a bottle of sleeping pills I always had along when traveling. I could tip them unnoticed into the palm of my hand as I closed the case. Somehow I felt they might come in handy, though I had no idea just how. Successful, I handed the case back with a nod. A moment later, however, I tried to shake them unnoticed into my outside jacket pocket and one slipped through my fingers and fell to the floor. At once the second man with the penetrating eyes jumped toward me in alarm and demanded to see what I was hiding. I had no choice. I emptied my pocket. Each pill was carefully collected, laid in some folded paper, and deposited in the guard's pocket.

This mishap and the sullen watchfulness of the guards thereafter filled me with new foreboding. If I weren't going to a plane or train, what was going on? What was the alternative at so late an hour? A hotel for the night, perhaps? I didn't even pretend to believe that. But hadn't I heard a car's horn and the sound of a motor?

The door opened and for the first time since that first evening after my arrest the heavyset man with the cigarette stood before me.

"Put on your coat and come with me."

Silently I followed him out into the corridor, the two guards close behind me. But I had to get a clear answer right now. "Mister, please, I must have a word with you."

The man with the cigarette shook his head. "No, not now. This is not the place for that. Later."

Later. So there was to be a later.

# 3

## Journey to Nowhere

A gain I and my suitcase were jouncing along inside a paneled delivery van, the small oval window in the rear door covered now by a flap of canvas. Opposite me were the two guards. The rumpled one was smoking and staring at the floor; the other had his eyes fixed disconcertingly on me. Overhead a weak electric bulb illuminated the silent scene.

It had all happened so smoothly. I had emerged from my corridor into the dark courtyard only to find myself once more staring into the open rear of this vehicle. A moment later the door had shut behind the three of us. It was strange, moving along inside this completely enclosed space, isolated from visual contact with the changing environment outside. The sounds that penetrated, though, seemed to bring it doubly close somehow—the sudden clanking of a streetcar right beside me, the tinny rattle of an old car on the cobblestone pavement, horns, the swish-swish of cars going the other way, the squeak of tires, someone shouting. At first we moved haltingly, slowing down, stopping—traffic lights—starting up after a minute, accompanied by the general rumble of other cars accelerating in low gear. Warsaw in the evening, part of an unseen stream.

But which way were we heading? Toward the station? We should have reached it by now, if so. Then again, hadn't he said he would speak with me "later"? Maybe he had meant some last-minute statement in the train, an official expulsion order with a face-saving justification. And yet why go on fooling myself? The whole atmosphere of the past hours pointed unmistakably to something very different.

I listened intently, alert to the feel of the road under us. We seemed to be in much lighter traffic. We had turned to the right onto a very smooth boulevard. Suddenly there were no intersections; the varied resonances that seemed to suggest the proximity of buildings had vanished. Why were we without transition in the countryside? Could it be the highway to the airport after all? My hopes rose. There was a slight swish at regular intervals, and each time a little crack of light showed around the edges of the canvas flap. Then it came to me: we had been crossing a long bridge. And now we were on the other side. Again there was twisting and weaving and stops. Again a streetcar clanked nearby. Then the sounds of cars became rarer again. Our speed picked up. We had left the city behind us.

We must have been going half an hour, and the air filtering through was different, colder. Open country. By now we would have reached the airport. Perhaps I'm to be taken all the way to the frontier in this vehicle, I thought. My heart almost stopped. What frontier? Hadn't we crossed a long bridge earlier? It could only be the Vistula. That meant we were heading east. And what frontier was that? It was the nearest one to Warsaw—much, much nearer than before the war. Maybe an hour of fast driving, though I could not tell how long we had actually been under way. The roads were getting worse and worse; we seemed to have left the highway and were bouncing along country lanes. We seemed to have turned so many times that I had not the faintest idea anymore of direction, but weren't the worsening roads the surest sign we were going east, approaching the Soviet border? My dread mounted. For the first time a new concept, with all its implications, pushed through my consciousness—Siberia.

We drove on and on into the night. The two men seemed oblivious and merely sat hunched up smoking, as if this were a routine journey made for the hundredth time. Then, after several sharp turns that sent us tipping into one another, the van slowed down, came to a stop, and sounded its horn. How loud it sounded, the only thing in this absolute stillness! Something like a metal gate clattered and creaked. We moved ahead slowly on very rough ground, then again came to a stop. Muffled voices, approaching footsteps, whispered remarks to the driver, someone getting out up front, footsteps along my side. The door opened a crack and the old guard crept over, then nodded. The little light overhead went out. Pitch darkness. The door swung open with a burst of chilly, aromatic country air, recalling at once September nights on the terrace of our summer home, Valley Farm, in Massachusetts. Gradually I could distinguish the silhouettes of people outside in the moonless night. There was not one light anywhere in sight, only the periodic glow of a cigarette. Someone approached and leaned in.

"We will now bind your eyes and then you will be led from the van."

I recognized "Cigarette's" voice. I felt a little reassured. Perhaps this was the "later" he had promised. Anyway, at least there was some continuity. I wasn't among strangers. Still on Polish soil.

The old guard was untangling a shiny black object with ribbons hanging from it. He squatted in front of me. Soft pads were fitted compactly into my eye sockets while two ribbons were tied tight about my head. I was blindfolded. A comical flash from childhood hit me: playing blind man's buff.

Someone took hold of each arm and steadied me as I crawled out of the vehicle onto the ground. Grass. I waited. Hands closed in on my arms and guided me straight ahead. I groped my way along. My mind was a blank. I seemed to have receded far into myself, and my body appeared to be carrying on automatically, independent of me. My feet bumped against a hard curb. I stopped. A hand tapped my knee. I raised it. A step. Some more. A concrete exterior staircase. I could feel warmth radiating toward me. An open house door; a threshold. Musty air with a smell of old wood and plaster. Now I was walking on a creaky wooden floor. I had the distinct impression of being in an old farmhouse. Could there be anything more unlikely?

Judging from the resonance, we were proceeding down a corridor, a narrow one, since there was not room to go three abreast. Then a turn to the right across another threshold. The resonance had changed, and the air too: muffled now and stale, with the smell of new furniture. I felt a rug under my feet. I was eased backward a few steps and discovered myself against a chair. I sat down. The hands left my arms. I waited, sightless, and in the prevailing silence felt eyes fixed on me. There were hurried steps on the wood floor of the corridor. A door to my left opened and was closed, cautiously. A slight movement of air as someone tiptoed past me on the rug. Whispering, almost inaudible. It must be a big room. To my right, close by, a match was struck—someone lighting a cigarette.

If only I could have one. The need became overwhelming: I must have one. I would ask. It would be a first test of their attitude, of what to expect—were they hostile or friendly? Instinctively I fell into pantomime: instead of asking, I raised my hand in the direction of the sound and then put my fingers to my mouth and inhaled. There was a slight chuckling, and then I felt a tap on my hand. Someone was putting a lighted cigarette between my fingers and pushing my hand toward my face. I drew strongly on it. Strange, I was basically a nonsmoker. It was wonderful, though; not just the taste, but the warmth of an unspoken gesture of civility.

I smoked on in silence, and as I did my mood shifted from numb resignation to ebullient optimism. If I wasn't on my way to Siberia, then what was the purpose of the mysterious rendezvous?

Suddenly it came to me: yes, of course, a rendezvous! I grasped at the idea eagerly. I was to meet someone, but I was not to know where. Everything was clear at last. I understood the weeks of questioning and now this mysterious trip. Tomorrow I would be free and on my way, but before that, tonight, I was to come face to face with the one I had sought in vain—my brother. I would hear from Noel's own mouth why he had been detained. Or perhaps he had even disappeared voluntarily, to avoid being drawn into the trial of Alger Hiss. Although Hiss and he had apparently known each other only slightly, their terms at the State Department had overlapped briefly and they seemed to have moved in the same circle of left-wing friends. Herta had dismissed the idea when I had suggested it in Geneva, and yet Noel's gentleness coupled with his ill health during the past year might have convinced him that he would not endure the strain of being called as a witness. Removing himself from the scene might have seemed the only option.

Noel's life had been in a turmoil the last few years. Herta told me he had gone to Prague in April to apply for a teaching post at Prague's Charles University. That should have been sufficient to put him on the sidelines. So why, in addition, disappear without trace? There were doubtless a lot of factors I did not know that Herta had chosen not to tell me. Our lives had diverged greatly during our adult years. Even this summer when I had responded to Herta's SOS from Geneva and had agreed to help her look for him, it had been on condition that I keep out of his problems and merely act as an intermediary through my contacts in Prague and Warsaw.

Although deep inside I knew better, with every moment the idea of a rendezvous took a stronger hold on me. The door opened again, and once more I sensed tiptoed movements on the rug. It was probably Noel being brought in, blindfolded too. Whatever the meaning of all this, the thought of seeing my brother's familiar face was quite overwhelming. I would rush over and throw my arms around him and forgive him, no matter how much I and Kate and the boys had suffered because of him in the past days. Maybe the situation had been unforeseen and beyond his control. Hadn't I apparently disappeared without trace too? I sat tensely staring with sightless eyes across the room to where I sensed he was sitting.

A hand reached to the back of my head and untied the blindfold. The mask slipped from my face; the sudden light dazzled me. I was at one end of a fairly big room. At the other end, behind a big desk, sat a stranger staring at me in silence. I sank back in my chair, dazed. So I had been wrong. At once the mirage was dispelled and I saw my wishful fantasy for what it had been. Was my grip on reality slipping? I pulled myself up and looked slowly around. To the right, on a chair almost facing me, sat the disheveled old guard. He gave a nod of recognition. Although he did not smile, there was a distinctly friendly something in his eyes. The serious-faced guard stood close by to my left. Behind him was the door through which I apparently had come. It was a corner room with heavy drawn curtains; a resplendent Turkish rug covered almost the entire floor and a modern globe lamp on a rod hung from the center of the ceiling. Over in the right-hand corner there was a couch. The newly painted walls and the contemporary light-colored desk gave a rather superior impression, in strange contrast to the farmhouse environment I had sensed on entering.

Maybe they are planning to keep me in this room temporarily. It was so much nicer than the one in Warsaw—a promising sign, perhaps after all a transition to being freed.

The stranger behind the desk got up, sauntered in front of it, and sat down on its edge, his legs dangling. He seemed amused. Hardly more than a youth, he had an unpleasant, cocky manner.

"*Auskleid*," he said in faulty German, indicating with his hands that I should undress, then pointed to the couch: "*Lieg.*"

I was puzzled. What business did he have to talk that way? I took off my trench coat. That did not satisfy him. I took off my jacket. He pointed to my pants. I took them off too, then stopped as if I didn't understand. I looked down at myself and felt a momentary urge to grin. He got cross and waved his arms: "*Alles! Alles!*"

When I was finally stark naked, he pointed once again to the couch. As I lay there he began examining my clothes, piece by piece. He tugged so roughly at the lining of my suit jacket that I was sure he would wreck it. I exclaimed with a forced laugh: "*Nicht kaput machen*"—Don't destroy.

He looked up at me and guffawed, then with a nod of mocking solicitude and reassurance said, "*Nein, nein, nicht kaput,*" and again laughed and winked at the others.

Finally he came over to me. He made me turn over on my stomach and then crouch for rectal inspection. On my back again I had to raise my arms and open my mouth and raise my tongue. Then he returned my clothes, minus raincoat, belt, necktie, and shoelaces.

I had barely finished dressing when Cigarette appeared in the door and beckoned: "Come with me for some supper downstairs."

I got up. I decided I was not going to let this opportunity go by, and as I passed him into the corridor I said, "I want to speak with you. What is the meaning of all this? I was told it was all finished. You know how urgent it is that I return to Cleveland."

He was cross. "Ssh. Not so loud. Not now. How quickly it goes is entirely up to you. Now, go on, go on."

How often had I heard that before? The corridor along which I had come earlier was indeed narrow. Everything about the place had a definitely rural feel, small and old and unpretentious. Once more I wondered: Could it be a frontier transfer point?

A man ahead beckoned to me to turn left just before the door at the end, onto a small landing with a narrow wooden staircase twisting down between two walls. "Supper downstairs," Cigarette had said. I went down the worn steps, the man at my back. "Quicker." I reached a dimly lit brick floor at the bottom and stepped through the narrow opening in a thick whitewashed wall with a heavy metal door. It was rather like going through an emergency bulkhead on shipboard. I hesitated. In the half-dark it indeed seemed as if I was looking down the underdeck gallery of an old ship. As far as I could see door followed door along a damp, low corridor—heavy, narrow doors with big, wide bolts. All were closed except one not far down on the left, from the opening of which bright light poured into the cellar.

"Quicker, quicker." Mechanically I proceeded. "Here. Here." Someone pushed me toward the opening and gave me a heave so that I tripped over the high sill and almost landed on my hands. The first thing I noticed was a small closed barred window up near the ceiling. My second sensation was of bareness and damp cold. I stopped and instinctively stepped back: a tomb. I turned inquiringly to the man standing in the low door opening. He was a frightening spectacle, with a big shock of hair on his head, which shook as he gesticulated emphatically, one eye wandering out of line with the other in his excitement: "Hands up, hands up! Shoo, shoo! To the wall. Shoo!"

My head reeled. Was I awake? What Dantesque inferno had I descended into? My hands went up instinctively, as much out of a strange hypnosis as real fear.

"To the wall! Shoo! Shoo!"

I backed toward it. No, not good enough; he kept on yelling at me and swinging his arms and rolling his eyes until I had turned around and faced the wall with my hands straight over my head. The door banged behind me with a hollow echo. A key turned, followed by the crash of a heavy bolt. What now? Gradually I lowered my hands. Somehow I felt ridiculous standing that way, like a bad kid in school.

I turned, half expecting a new commotion. I was in an almost square cellar room with rough whitewashed cement walls and a damp-looking brick floor. The furnishings consisted of a bucket with a wooden lid in the corner near me and two rectangular metal pipe frames resting on sawed-off pipe legs cemented into the floor, each about nine inches high. The one was adorned merely with planks; the second had in addition a dilapidated oblong canvas sack from which straw was spilling onto the floor. From a beam across the middle of the room hung a small padlocked wire basket with an exposed electric light bulb glaring from it. Uncertain what to do next, I instinctively looked toward the door, which was narrow and barely high enough to pass through. It consisted of two square panels in a heavy frame without any handle or lock on this side. The strange thing, however, which distinguished it from any other door I had ever come across, was an oblong splayed slit at about eye level with what looked like a still narrower strip of glass on the corridor side. At once I was sure that unseen eyes were staring at me through it.

There was a crashing noise at the door. I stood transfixed. What now? Once more the wandering eyes, the gesticulating, the very epitome of fury: "Shoo, shoo! Hands up! To the wall!"

I was so spellbound by this insane behavior that it took me a moment to comprehend that I was the object of it. He started making sallies across the threshold as if he were shooing geese. I turned and faced the wall and again held my hands above my head. If I were the victim of a revolt in an insane asylum, wouldn't I likewise simply do as I was told? It was all so extreme that it was not quite convincing. For something to be really horrible and terrifying, one must have something to relate it to out of one's experience, and I could find nothing in mine that gave me purchase. I was more like an observer from outside accommodating myself to an unintelligible rite.

A second man came in and walked over beside me. He was tall and athletic looking, wearing a pullover, with a rather handsome face and small cold eyes. Instinctively I turned and dropped my hands, but once again came Shoo's voice: "Wall, wall! Hands up!" The second fellow came right up to me, his face a few inches from mine. Laughing, he gave my hair a little pull: "Afraid, aren't you?" He spoke good German, in contrast to Shoo's almost unintelligible hodgepodge. "There are your things. Make your bed and let's have your shirt and underwear. And whenever the door opens, go at once to the wall with your back to the door and hands over your head. Understand?" A moment later the cell echoed with the slamming of the door and the crash of the bolt.

All was silence, hollow, tomblike silence. I waited a bit, then I dropped my hands and looked toward the straw sack. Still nothing happened. I saw two folded blankets and some white things. I went over: a sheet, a pillowcase, some long-legged underpants with ribbons at the bottom, a collarless shirt with three buttons down the middle. Where had I seen that recently? Immediately I knew: in the corridor in Warsaw that night. I glanced toward the cutout in the door, half expecting a new commotion any minute.

On the floor by the door I noticed a brown enamel mug with a slice of black bread lying on top of it. When had that gotten there? I went over and inspected it. Hot tea, bread with lard, and pieces of smoked sausage. So that was the "supper downstairs." I went back to the straw sack and inspected it. In addition to being torn, it was stained and mildewed. I felt the straw that oozed out of it. It was damp and dirty. The small square pillow was also filled with straw. I shifted the blankets and linen to the bare plank frame opposite and tried to bundle the loose sack into some sort of usable mattress. Then I spread the freshly ironed sheet over it. An agreeable and comforting cleanness now hid the unappetizing sack. Next the pillowcase. No covering sheet, just the blankets. The bed was made, a human touch at least. Next my clothes. I cast off my incredibly dirty shirt and underwear, which I had lived in day and night for almost three weeks. The new underwear felt reassuringly clean, in spite of its strange appearance.

I continued my exploration, doing the stocktaking one sees zoo animals do when they are first put into a new cage. I inspected the pail, half full of water—presumably in lieu of a toilet. The window. Tightly closed, it had two small, hinged wings about a foot square each, the glass obscured by paint. I could not hear any sounds through it. In fact, it seemed rather like a fake window of a stage set. Raising myself on tiptoe, I looked through the rusted metal screen on the inside face of the wall into the deep window recess and saw a lot of dried leaves lying on the bottom, as well as bits of dried bread and mouse leavings. So the window had been open and someone had amused himself feeding mice that had come in from outside. I looked closer at the bars halfway between the window and the screen in front, one horizontal with four verticals welded to it, the ends firmly embedded in the concrete of the opening. The whitewash was still fairly new looking, as it was throughout the cell. While this building was certainly old, its conversion to its present use, whatever that was, could hardly be more than a year or so back.

In the angle between ceiling and exterior wall there was a boxed-in beam. I reached up and tapped it: hollow, not a beam at all, probably a pipe enclosure. I looked at the floor more carefully. The joints between the bricks had either decayed or never been mortared. I stooped and scraped—damp, soft. Everywhere ground moisture was seeping through. Judging from the height of the windowsill, the ground outside must be about at eye level.

I looked more closely at the two "bedsteads." Wasn't that what they were? In that case, this cell was sometimes used for two persons. Or maybe the one without the mattress was meant for sitting on as a kind of bench. There were spiral wire markings all along the pipe frame, and the planks looked very new and unsoiled, as did the cement closure of the pipe stumps that served as diminutive legs. Some changes had been made recently. Maybe these beds had been some sort of first aid litter for carrying wounded. But of course, it was absurd to make them of metal pipe. And why had the wire springs been removed? Surely they would make more sense than these hard planks.

I went over to the door and picked up the mug and slice of bread, and took a close look at the opening in the door. It was cut through wood two inches thick—a solid door all right, considering it was under two feet wide and only about six feet high. Could one see through the slot? Was the corridor dark? I brought my face right up against it. Behind the narrow strip of glass there seemed to be a closure with two pinholes punctured in it, one of them revealing a little light. In the left-hand corner of the slot there was a small cutout behind the glass. Why couldn't I see any sign of light here? I looked still closer, and almost dropped my mug. I had the distinct feeling I had been staring at the pupil of a human eye.

Trying to look matter-of-fact, I sauntered over to the plank frame. I would sit on it even though it was uncomfortably low, and give myself a much needed moment of quiet to reflect while I ate. No doubt it was late, and I felt distinctly hungry. I set down my mug and laid the slice beside it. I had barely sat down when the door went through convulsions and Shoo stood in it, outraged and furious. "*Nie wolno!*" Not allowed.

I got up and started toward the wall, but already the door had slammed shut. What wasn't allowed? Eating? Or was there something sacred about this plank frame? Well, I could sit on my bed, but that would be rather unsteady, and what if it was a still more sacred taboo? To play it safe I stayed where I was, on my feet, and munched my bread and drank my tea standing in the middle of the cell. I was already feeling triumphant at having gotten through my meal without being disturbed when the key turned again and the sliding bolt echoed through the void. I hurried over to the window wall and faced it, hands over head. A voice behind me shouted, "*Appell*"—Taps. The door slammed shut. I turned to look for something new at the door. Maybe he wanted the mug. I picked it up and stood irresolutely waiting. Once more the key and the bolt. As the door flew open I held out my mug. This time it was the man with the small, hard eyes. He came in with a swagger, hands in pockets, and looked me fixedly in the face as if waiting for something: "*Nu*, what? Forgotten so soon? *Cholera*—Damn. Hands up and to the wall. And just mind in the future."

There I stood, motionless, the enamel mug high over my head.

"*Appell. Appell.* Didn't you hear? Off with your suit and shoes and into bed." He watched me a moment longer, then turned and swaggered out. I waited until I was sure the door was locked and bolted. I quickly slipped out of my suit—but where should I put it? After all, I couldn't hold my shoes and socks and suit and mug all above my head! No matter what I did, I was sure I was in for further trouble, so I laid the things neatly at the foot of my bed and crawled in under the blankets. What a relief to be able to stretch out at last.

Again the crashing of the door. I tried to look matter-of-fact, lying on my back, my eyes on the ceiling.

"*Cholera*, what's the matter with you? No ears, what? To the wall. Didn't I just tell you?"

I scrambled out and hurried barefoot to the spot in front of the window bars, which by now was becoming quite familiar. I raised my hands.

"Hands higher! Stand straighter! All right. You'd better mind down here, or else. What do you think this is, a sanatorium? And your clothes, next time, there on the floor in front of the door." He went over to the bed and picked up my things. The door crashed. Absolute silence.

I crawled back into bed. The electric light bulb glared in my eyes. I couldn't shake off the penetrating chill of this cellar. I turned toward the wall and pulled the blankets way up over my ears. I would be dead to the world for a few hours, and in the morning I would have a better head to figure all this out. Almost at once there was the key again and the bolt.

I scrambled to my feet. What had I done wrong now? Deliberate steps behind me and again those small eyes looking mockingly at me.

"You're not allowed to lie that way. No putting your hands under the covers. On your back with your arms outside. Do you understand?" He looked me up and down as if I were the dumbest creature he had ever come across, then sauntered back to the door.

For the third time I crawled under the blankets. I lay as directed. All I wanted was to be left alone. To rid myself of the eye glare, I turned my head and surveyed every item in this subterranean world into which I had fallen: four silent, bare walls, a ceiling and a floor, an electric light beating down on me mercilessly. Strange to think there were other human beings on both sides of me, across the corridor too, locked up in similar walls of silence. Were they German war criminals? Or might they also be victims of a chase after nonexistent crimes?

Once more I reviewed all the explanations I could think of. Clearly, this was no short and passing event. I was in for it now, whatever it was. More and more I was haunted by the notion of a frontier post. Disappearance, cellars, Siberia—how often in recent years had there been hints of this pattern, on a mass scale? Why hadn't I paid more attention? Could this now be the first lap? But this was Poland, not Stalin's Russia! And even though the personnel here were still Polish, couldn't it be a secret transit spot? Tomorrow might find me handed over to some Russian escorts, once more on my way, this time to certain oblivion in the vast reaches of the steppes. But why me? Why me, of all people?

I tried to sift in my mind everything I had ever heard or read about disappearances in Stalin's hinterland. In the prewar days I had regarded much of it with a degree of skepticism; it seemed too much part of the Nazi propaganda mill, and the communist left had kept up a barrage of denial. Although the reports in recent years had a much more reliable ring, I had written them off, thinking that this was but an unfortunate Russian heritage from tsarism that would not repeat itself in countries with Western traditions such as Czechoslovakia and Poland. And now in all likelihood I would be paying for my wishful thinking.

I shivered. Was this to be the end of my life as I had known it? Were Kate and the boys and Cleveland, and America itself, gradually to become distant memories, part of a wonder that once was called life, with everything henceforth being just a long wait for death? And no one would ever know what had happened. Theories would be put out that would remain unanswered forever. Noel? How blind of me not to have seen the writing on the wall. First him, and now me, and doubtless Herta too, to obliterate the last possible leak. I recalled Karel's ill-concealed worry in Prague: "Don't stay alone after dark. Let me know when you want to return to the house and I will fetch you in the car." I had laughed. "Don't worry. What could anyone have against me?"

Unable to get to sleep, I tossed and turned. The naked light bulb shone straight down on my face. My hands and arms were cold. The hollow silence of the cell was becoming ever more oppressive. Occasionally there was a flurry of noise in the corridor, a swish of movement past my door, the floor runner deadening the sound; a telephone ringing nearby, a muffled answer; bolts clanging somewhere; something like feet running upstairs. Then complete silence. I was too absorbed by my own problems to listen carefully. When would they turn off this glaring light and blot out the sight of these walls and the door with the omnipresent eye, this oppressive space in which I found myself without knowing what structure it was a part of or where it was?

Images of my brother enveloped me as I searched, searched for a clue. Noel in Paris the last time I had seen him, in 1947, a brief encounter at the air terminal during a stopover. He was depressed. I gathered that the controversy about his political bias in directing the European office of the Unitarian Service Committee was likely to cause his forced departure from the work he had given so much of himself to during the war years. I went farther back, into my childhood. Zurich. The moment in 1921, when I was eleven, when everything had changed with my father's premature death. Noel, six years my senior, becoming my mentor, determined that my father's Quaker humanism should continue to guide us as a family. My mother's decision that she and her four children should return to America so we could grow up in our father's culture, rather than in the only one we knew in the isolation of war-surrounded Switzerland. The image of Noel, before we left in 1922, addressing a student No More War rally in the big hall of our villa overlooking the lake and the Alps.

Our new home in Cambridge, with Noel at Harvard and weekend outings that provided continuity with Switzerland in their focus on peace and social equity. Me, the kid brother sitting on the fringes, but listening, absorbing; Noel, emerging from his Harvard studies as an authority on world disarmament. The sudden wrench when he went off to Washington with Herta, his grade-school love from Zurich who had followed him here to become his wife. Our relationship now was conducted mainly through correspondence. Noel at the State Department, in charge of a series of naval disarmament conferences. My return to Switzerland in 1934, then in 1936 his switch to Geneva and the disarmament section of the League of Nations. Both of us back in the land of our childhood. Noel . . .

# 4

## Vacation's End

My summer vacation in England visiting my parents with my two boys, Hugh, aged six, and Alan, four, was coming to an end. It was August 25, and Hermann had written that he would arrive by air from Prague that evening. I was in Sussex, visiting my grandmother for a last time, so I had written Hermann to take the train straight down there.

Everyone else had gone to bed. I was sitting in front of the dying fire, waiting. Hermann would take a taxi from the station, and any minute the doorbell would ring. I waited, but it didn't ring. He must have missed the train. Perhaps the plane had been late? In that case, he would take the next train. I continued to wait, but the time for that train passed too. Could he have changed his plans? But in that case I knew he would have let me know. Even though there was no telephone here at my grandmother's, he could have wired. If only I were in London, I could have checked with the airport. Perhaps there was a message there for me. Or perhaps he had stayed the night in London with my parents and didn't want to wake me with a wire. Anyway, there was no point sitting up any longer. All would doubtless become clear in the morning. Feeling uneasy, I went to bed.

The next morning a neighbor came over to say that my mother was on their telephone and wanted to speak to me. I ran over there. This would be the explanation. My mother sounded excited. A letter had come for me from Herta in Prague, as well as a telegram, which read: "Hermann delayed Warsaw. Helena informed. Letters en route." Helena Syrkus was a Polish architect whom Hermann knew through the international architectural congress they had both just attended in Italy.

All my apprehension returned. Something was seriously wrong: Hermann had not even got back to Prague. I packed up the children and brought them to London. My mother met us at Victoria Station. She had brought Herta's letter, which read:

Dear Kate:

I am very much disturbed about Hermann. As you know, he flew to Warsaw on August 15th, intending to come back on August 22nd. On Monday evening I went with his friends to the airport to meet him but he was not on the plane, although the passenger list carried his name and the flight personnel confirmed that they had expected a fifth passenger, who failed to show up . . .

Herta said she had then phoned Helena Syrkus but that she was away. She would try again the next day and send me a wire. But, she wrote, "unless Helena can tell me something tomorrow I am really at my wit's end . . . I doubt if anything more can be done from here . . ." She went on to tell me not to be too alarmed but that there might have been an accident, or Hermann might have gotten into trouble taking photographs. "I think we can trust Hermann to kick up no end of a row in such a situation, but that may not be enough to get him out of trouble, particularly since he can't swear in Polish . . ."

The letter was signed with a small capital H, scratched lightly with the pen, and headed only "August 24th," with no address. But it was postmarked Prague, and I did not doubt it was from Herta.

I felt sick. Something had happened to Hermann four days ago already, and no one knew what. "That camera of his may be to blame," Herta had written. "Of course, that will be cleared up eventually." I clung to the hope that she was right and checked our luggage in at the station, ready for the boat train in three days' time.

What on earth should I do? I had never thought of how to handle such a situation, in spite of the anxieties that had plagued my vacation ever since Herta's letter and telegram had arrived back in July begging Hermann to go and see her at once. It was in response to her SOS that I had booked a flight for Hermann to go on to Geneva the very next day after his arrival in England from Ohio, and I had since had no opportunity to learn from him what the trouble was. All I had was his note written after he had seen Herta in which he said that something had happened to Noel—but that information was for me alone; for everyone else, Noel was simply ill. Had this same "something" now happened to Hermann? Herta seemed to be banking on the Polish architects, whose guest Hermann had been, to get him out of any trouble.

The Cold War was on, and he was an American caught in a communist country. Our government was hostile to the Polish government, and vice versa. Would an inquiry from the State Department merely annoy the Poles—especially if, perhaps at this very moment, they were on the verge of letting him go? I knew so little about this sort of situation that I even thought an inquiry by the American government might confirm the Poles' suspicion that Hermann was involved in some activity against them—if that's what was going on. Later I learned that it works exactly the opposite way: a protest from one's government is expected, and its absence may be taken as evidence that the suspect is a spy. But what wife of an ordinary citizen knows the correct procedure if her husband is mistaken for a spy? The very word *spy* was terrifying. I thought of spying as a purely wartime activity. People were shot for it. But this was peace, wasn't it?

My father said that in case Hermann was going to be accused of spying, the State Department ought to know about it right away. I took his advice and rang the American embassy.

"I want to report the disappearance of my husband." It sounded somehow ridiculous.

The voice said she would put me through. I started again, this time with a man: "My husband has disappeared in Poland." "Oh!" He sounded startled. He would put me through to someone else. Once more I started: "Yes, disappeared . . ." But again I was stopped. I would be put through to a first secretary.

At last I was able to explain: "He was visiting Warsaw. He's an architect, and he met some Polish architects at a conference in Italy, and then he went to Warsaw for a week as their guest. I can give you their address . . . He was due in Prague last Monday, and in London last night." He asked me a question. "Oh yes, he'd have written or wired. Very reliable, he'd always let me know if he'd changed his plans. Couldn't the American embassy in Warsaw find out something?"

He promised to make inquiries right away. I felt better. Now it was in the hands of the experts. But Herta had given me Helena Syrkus's telephone number. That was practically an invitation to ring her, and she might be able to tell me something. It's uncanny how easy it was to put through a call to Warsaw; one wouldn't know there was an Iron Curtain. But the voice on the other end replied: "Mrs. Syrkus is not in her office. Ring tomorrow morning." So I sent a wire to her home asking her to phone me. She didn't. Next morning I rang her office again. This time the voice replied with a different message: "Mrs. Syrkus is away but may be back next week." The curtain had rung down on Hermann.

A second letter arrived from Herta, again from Prague, dated August 25th. She had talked to Helena Syrkus, who was surprised that Hermann had not arrived in Prague, since she herself had taken him to the airport, though she had left before he had passed through customs. She thought his undeveloped films might have gotten him into trouble and promised to do all she could to get the matter straightened out. She had gotten Hermann his Polish visa, so felt doubly responsible for him. Herta felt his case was in good hands, "although it's horribly awkward all around." She thought it unnecessary to take official steps at this point:

Kate dear, don't be too upset. One doesn't get lost between the customs and the plane. I am much relieved, because yesterday I really thought there might have been an accident. And Helena is the best person to handle such a situation. . . . And in the future Hermann better specialize in taking nice portraits of his family, and could I have some samples of his work?

This time the letter was properly signed, in what I presumed was her normal handwriting. She had even added, "In case you don't have it, my address is Hotel Paris, tel. 602-21." Obviously she felt much better, in spite of seeming to think that Hermann had been arrested—though it was strange to regard that as such a minor thing. She was quite confident that Helena Syrkus could clear things up quickly. Since Herta had given me her address, I thought I ought to let her know what I'd done, so on the twenty-ninth I wired her: "Your letters received . . . Have asked American Embassy to make inquiries. Sailing Monday, selling extra ticket"—for clearly Hermann would never arrive in time to use his. I searched about frantically for a purchaser.

All weekend I waited for the telephone to ring with some news from the embassy. Although Herta would have disapproved of my bringing them in on the case, I feared she might be being completely unrealistic. While I had no reason to trust her judgment, I nevertheless clung to her optimism.

"Why hasn't Daddy come?" asked Hugh, the six-year-old.

"He couldn't. He will as soon as he can."

"But why couldn't he?"

Why indeed! What explanation could I give that would satisfy yet not frighten him?

"He just couldn't make it, that's all. He'll come soon." Perhaps just the saying of it would make it come true.

Saturday night, and still no news. I grabbed at sleep for escape. But in sleep the carefully constructed bulwarks of optimism began to give way; my subconscious knowledge of the truth flooded through and shocked me wide awake.

In front of me was my half-curtained window in the moonlight. Just four panes of glass showing—a cross of iron it looked, a prison window. Hermann was in prison. That was the reality. He was facing a little barred window like that. I could see him lying awake in a bare cell. Awake now, as I was, but so far away. I imagined him lying there unable to grasp that such a thing could happen—had happened—to him. And then I could see his startled, incredulous eyes as he tried to protest his innocence to unbelieving Polish police. I could see him explaining that he had led a tour of architects there just two years before because he believed that, regardless of differences in our social systems, people should be willing to see what was being done in each other's countries. And that this time he was the guest of the well-known Polish architects the Syrkuses, who had been anxious that he should see the reconstruction of Warsaw.

But would those hardheaded Polish police be convinced? He was not a communist. Were not all noncommunists their enemy? Did they make allowances for people, like Hermann, who never seemed suspicious or to sense danger? What irony I now found in Helena Syrkus's postscript to Hermann's last letter to me: "It is a shame that you never come with Hermann to Warsaw. Next year we don't let him enter our house without you!" Would she be able to get him out of trouble now?

Suppose she did not. How would I manage alone with the children in Cleveland? Miles from everyone—my parents in England, and Hermann's only other living relative, his sister Elsie, far away in Illinois. If it went on long I should run short of money, but worse still, who would comfort and advise me? Above all, how could I face being alone in that big house, which we had only just finished furnishing together as our first real home? The picture of our home came so vividly before my eyes that I felt that, once there, I would surely just walk about all day in tears.

Yet according to plan, in two days the children and I would be aboard the *Batory* bound for New York. A Polish ship. But if Hermann were a Polish prisoner, could something happen to us on that voyage? I knew Hermann was innocent. Perhaps they might want to get rid of me; it was easy to push people into the sea. I felt ashamed of these fears—but why take the chance? In general, I found it paid to obey my intuitions. In any case, by staying here I would be nearer to Hermann. I decided not to take the *Batory* and to try to sell those tickets in the morning.

Alan was sleeping peacefully in his cot at the foot of my bed. Poor little boy, he didn't know what a cruel world he'd come into. I picked him up and put him in my bed and lay beside him. It was comforting to feel his small, warm body. Thank God I still had my little boys with me. I slept.

Monday came, the day we should have sailed. I rang the embassy, but they still had nothing to report from Warsaw. Then I wrote to Elsie, for as Hermann's sister I felt she should know. She had a new baby and I hated to worry her, so I phrased the news as calmly as I could: "The Embassy assures me that this sort of thing is by no means uncommon, that we have no need to worry about his personal safety because he was seen to the airport; it is clear he could not have been unlawfully waylaid. However, they say that even when it's a matter of trivial technicality it sometimes takes a few weeks (!!) to clear up, as the red tape unravels very slowly."

The next day I wrote to Herbert Hunsaker, dean of Cleveland College, Hermann's employers, in the same vein: "As soon as he can he will want to fly back to the U.S.A. . . . . I will probably not be able to teach my course in Economics this semester."

That same day, Tuesday the thirtieth, the embassy telephoned me at last. They had a message from Warsaw that Mr. Syrkus said Hermann had left for Prague on the twenty-second as planned. I wondered if that were true. Syrkus ought to know; after all, it was his wife who Herta said was making inquiries. Could this information be the result of the inquiries? And yet, there was Herta's original letter: "He was not on the plane, although the passenger list carried his name . . ."

I scanned the newspaper for clues and saw the headline "Revolt Crushed Says Prague." The Czechs said they had forestalled a revolt during this last weekend. I rang the embassy again. Was it possible, I asked, that Hermann had been taken off the plane at the Prague end of the journey—before Herta could see him? Obviously the Czechs were in a state of jitters and might have suspected him, being an American. The embassy promised to persevere.

In those days I learned that suspense could really be sickening. I felt a continuous ache inside. I could not bear to leave the house for fear of missing a telephone call from the embassy or Herta. But from her there was no sound. Four days later, on September 3, the embassy had another message from Warsaw. The original flight manifest of Czechoslovak Airlines flight 563 of August 22, they said, listed Hermann and four others as departing from Warsaw at 6:20 P.M. The manifest was signed by Czech Flight Captain Schorr. Our embassy in Warsaw had been informed by a Polish Security Police official that Hermann's name would not have been on the signed manifest had he not been on the aircraft. This official also stated that he had no recollection of any "incidents" involving Czechoslovak Airlines for several months, and there was no evidence in Warsaw that an incident did occur.

Given this news our embassy in Prague was brought in on the job, and on September 6 they reported that they had seen the flight manifest of Hermann's plane too, but although his name was listed, it had been crossed off. The Czechs said it was crossed off by the stewardess when she found Hermann was not on the plane.

Who was to be believed—the Czechs or the Poles?

This vacation had gone terribly wrong. I went over in my mind how it had all started. On June 6, under the great elms of our home in Cleveland, we had a birthday party for Alan, who would be four the next day. By then, though, he, Hugh, and I would be steaming across the Atlantic for England; Hermann, who could not get so long a vacation, would join us in six weeks.

That evening Hermann drove us to the station. The great train steamed in, its bell clanging. I still found American trains romantic. To me they suggested vast distances, with their cowcatchers and their great wheels, as different from the domestic-sized English trains as a tiger is from a cat.

We were in New York before breakfast the next day. Hugh had brought his bicycle and Alan his tricycle, and they pedaled delightedly down Grand Central Station. We were sailing on the Polish liner *Batory*, the only ship the travel agency had been able to find space on. On her last trip the *Batory* had attracted some rather sensational attention when Gerhart Eisler, a German communist refugee wanted by the FBI on suspicion of espionage, had stowed away on her, and now her crew were not allowed to go ashore in New York. So I had the strange feeling of being involved in an international incident at one remove.

The voyage was pleasant enough, with nothing to remind one that the ship was sailing under a communist flag. Every morning Captain Jan Cwilinski, looking very businesslike, marched around the decks inspecting, his officers neatly lined up behind him. As we passed up and down the main staircase, a large painting of Stefan Batory, the heroic king of Poland who fought Ivan the Terrible in the sixteenth century, looked down upon us in his red robe.

Eight days, and we were reaching Southampton. One of the ship's officers said politely that it was a pity I was leaving the ship there. Conditions were so bad in England, whereas in Poland I would get some really good food. The gangplank went down, and there was my mother's familiar figure on the dock.

Time passed, and Hermann would soon be with us. But before he arrived the letter from Herta had come. So I booked passage for Hermann to fly to Geneva on July 20. It would give us only a few days together, but what else could I do?

Then came a wire from Hermann saying his plane was delayed by two days. That was really annoying. But finally he phoned from the air terminal in London, and my first glimpse of him was as he walked up our street, Corringham Road, a suitcase in each hand and the boys running to meet him.

It was good to be together again after six weeks. We had plenty to talk about, but scarcely time. His plane left the next morning. Everything was overshadowed by Herta's mysterious cry for help. What did it mean? Had something happened to Noel? We so seldom heard from the two of them now that they lived in Switzerland. The only time I had actually spent with them was when they came to New York in 1946 and stayed with us in Brooklyn. Noel seemed to worry about his health, and Herta I remembered as a comfortable, homey person. But since then, in the new atmosphere of the Cold War, an unsympathetic spotlight had been turned on Noel. He had been asked to resign from his position as European director of the Unitarian Service Committee be-cause of his "friendliness" toward communists. He had also been named as an associate of Alger Hiss, now on trial in New York for perjury.

Hermann agreed that the only thing was for him to go to Geneva and find out what was the matter. So the next morning he was off again. I was really un-happy about it. I had not said half the things I wanted to, and I felt vaguely ap-prehensive. Would he really take care? I knew from the war that Hermann was fearless when other people's lives were at stake. He had nearly lost his life in Po-land in 1939 trying to help refugees from Hitler, and I had been a month without news of him. I did not want to live through anything like that again.

For the next few weeks I waited for Herta's mystery to be cleared up. Her-mann sent letters and postcards from Bergamo, Italy, where he was having a lovely time at the international congress of modern architecture. What had happened to Noel, however, remained unexplained. I deduced that Hermann had not seen him. Finally he wrote that on August 1 he would be going to Prague with Herta, as "there was no point in her staying in Geneva"—though, he commented, she was "wonderfully optimistic, in spite of present troubles." Our suspicion that something had happened to Noel was correct, but this was for me alone, for everyone else "illness."

I felt completely sick. Noel must have disappeared. Now Herta's mysteri-ousness had entered Hermann's letters. I was left with this horrible uncertain-ty, and not allowed to discuss it with anyone, not even my parents. But if something had happened to Noel, why was Hermann going on to Prague? I felt he was being influenced by Herta, that she was exploiting his affection for his brother to induce him to take risks. By the time I knew it, he was already in Prague. How could I write him on such a subject? The iron curtain stood be-tween us.

At intervals postcards arrived to reassure me. One was of the many bridges of Prague, looking as stable as when I had been there myself in 1947, before the communists came to power. And then a letter, saying he was off to Warsaw for a week. It seemed he was simply doing a repeat of the architectural tour he had led in 1947. Perhaps everything would turn out all right after all.

But now my fears had come true and he was gone.

# 5

## But Muffin Could Hear

"Muffin couldn't see outside the box. But Muffin could hear . . ." During the days and weeks that followed I often recalled a favorite record of my boys about a little black-haired dog called Muffin. He was a city dog who, when vacation time came, was dispatched in a traveling box to the country, to an entirely new world that at first he could not see, a world entirely of sounds. Temporarily deprived of sight, Muffin was all ears, and as each successive noise filtered through to him he asked himself: "What was that?" There were the daytime noises and there were the nighttime ones. He heard the noises of the train. A call: "What was that?" A crow. "And that?" Gradually, in spite of his basket prison or the darkness of night, he became familiar with his new country world even though he had never seen it. For Muffin could hear. And I, too, I could hear.

That first morning I had awoken with a start. What was that? Where was I? I had the sensation that I was hearing this noise a second time, it was something familiar, like the calling of one's name. I opened my eyes and found myself blinking in the glare of the electric light. Quickly the events of the previous evening came back to me, and at once I recognized the sound, now louder and nearer than before. It was the successive opening and closing of cell doors along the corridor. I jumped onto the damp brick floor. Already it was my door's turn, and the cell echoed convulsively. When the flurry had passed I dropped my hands and turned from the wall to find my jacket and trousers and shoes scattered across the floor as if blown in by a gust that had swept on as suddenly as it had arrived.

I collected the things one by one, dusted them off, and slipped them on quickly as protection from the cold. The little barred window near the ceiling looked as impenetrable as ever. Still night in the world outside. The noise of keys and bolts and slamming doors had meanwhile receded down the corridor, only to switch again and proceed back to the starting point up a little way to the right. The procedure now, however, was in slow motion, with a lot of new sound elements. After a door had been opened, there was a clicking sound out in the corridor like a loud switch being turned, and then in place of the closing sound there were quick muffled steps and a swish of movement past my door. A bit later there followed the clatter of a pail way off on the left, and after a long pause more hurried footsteps and at last the door-closing noise. Almost at once the same sequence repeated itself from a point a little closer. Then it was right next door already, and this time I could distinguish a pail being picked up off the floor just on the other side of my wall. I had sized up the meaning: the first round had been the clothes; this one was to empty the buckets. As the key turned I picked it up from the corner and stood ready in front of the door as it swung open.

A startled figure drew back into the darkness of the corridor. The flawless mime spell was broken: "*Cholera!*" The stranger gesticulated frantically for me to get away from the door as a second man rushed up and joined the excited exhortations. So I was in trouble again. Better start over. I set my pail down and hastened to the far wall with my hands above my head. But the exhortations in Polish behind me continued. The pail? Surely they didn't expect me to hold it above my head too!

A wave of obstinacy came over me. I was following protocol; the next move was up to them. There was a clicking from the door similar to what I had heard earlier. Not a switch at all, but the snapping of fingers. Now, what on earth could that mean? More *Cholera*'s, then some whispering, then several *Sssh*'s. A *Hallo*. I held my ground and kept staring at the bars of the little window. My first gesture of retaliation. I couldn't be expected to see through the back of my head. Some steps approaching gingerly, an emissary. A tap on my shoulder. I turned my face without shifting my raised hands and found myself looking at a shortish, perplexed man in a brown smock who started pointing alternately to my jacket, to the pail, and to the door.

I went over and once more picked up the pail, but again was rewarded with a flood of protests. The man tugged at my jacket and shirt, all the time keeping a furtive eye on the door as if expecting to be eaten alive at any moment. I shrugged. They shrugged. Deadlock. Maybe I shouldn't have dressed yet. I took off my jacket. The two guards nodded eagerly. I started to take off my pants. New consternation. I put them on again. The man pointed once more to my shirt. I pulled it off over my head and stood stripped to the waist. The response from the door was gratifying: renewed nodding and even an incipient smile of amusement. As I squeezed at last with my pail through the narrow door opening, the two faces radiated a mixture of triumph and relief that reason had won in the end.

I wandered uncertainly in the below-decks darkness of the corridor. To my left just beyond my cell the passage bulged into a windowless space about the size of a small room; a brick pier took the place of the missing corridor wall, and against it stood a table with a shielded lamp and what looked like an army field telephone. The farther wall was lined with curtained-off wooden shelves.

"*Predzej*"—Quickly.

Apparently they didn't like my turning my head to look. I slopped along as fast as my laceless shoes permitted, trying to keep the pail from sloshing over. Beyond the guard's space the corridor floor dropped two steps, a succession of low bolted doors on either side. As I went along I counted a total of eight on this end. In the half dark I could distinguish the little metal slides about half an inch wide and four inches long, at eye level, with pinpoints of light in each. The silent witness of unknown occupants. The far end of the corridor had been raised three steps and made into a sort of doorless alcove with toilet and washbasin. This was the only source of light in the whole length of corridor. In spite of an icy blast of predawn air that poured in through a slightly opened window with painted-out glass, an unpleasant odor pervaded the place.

I emptied the bucket, balancing with spread feet on the slightly higher floor along the walls to keep my shoes from submerging in the murky puddle that lay over the rest of the space. The guard had followed close behind me, hissing, "*Predzej, predzej,*" each time I seemed to show interest in my surroundings. He now pointed to a long-handled brush, and step by step I learned the whole procedure: empty the pail, don't pull the chain, rinse and scrub the pail, empty it again, fill it half full, set it down on the floor; do teeth with the toothbrush handed to you; before the draft freezes you stiff, wash head and arms and hands under the icy water from the faucet; finally, dry with the individual towel provided, fold the towel, stick the end of the toothbrush into it, pick up the pail with the other hand, and hurry back—"*Predzej, predzej*"—along the corridor without glancing right or left (though you do anyhow). Dropping the towel on a chair as you pass the open space at the middle of the cellar, you go on into your cell and set the pail back in the corner as the bolt crashes shut behind you.

I slipped my shirt and jacket on again and started pacing back and forth to get warm. I noted the slow succession of door openings receding down toward the washroom, fourteen times in all. So I had at least thirteen unknown companions down here. What a strange setup. Who had ever heard of a prison so small? And yet what other function could this handful of cellar cells have?

My window was acquiring a pinkish hue; an ever growing sense of light penetrated the thick layer of white paint. Dawn. It must have been about six and I had probably been up an hour. So my day had started at five.

Gradually as the day advanced the initial nothingness took shape in terms of successive routines of which I was a part, and these in turn became my clock, the signposts of time passed and of endurance. The bucket cycle was followed after a short period of silence by the serving of breakfast, a mug of watery grain coffee with two slices of black bread with lard and cheese, set on the floor inside the door just as supper had been. After another flurry during which the empty mugs were collected, the cellar settled into what seemed an endless somnolence. Inside my cell daylight showed itself merely in the lifeless translucency of the patch of painted glass, the only reminder of a world that continued outside these walls.

There was something submerged, anesthetized, about this hollow silence, broken only by the occasional ringing of the telephone, a muffled conversation, a flurry of whispering in the corridor. With nothing to occupy my mind or hands in this suspension of time, there were just two things to do as my mind raced around in a circle of ifs and whys: pace back and forth the twelve feet between door and window until my legs began to sag; then sit down on the plank frame (for some reason no one seemed to mind today) and stare at the floor until the damp chill became unbearable; then return to the pacing—searching, searching all the while for an answer to the riddle.

It wasn't until the next cycle at lunchtime that the spell was broken. I was the fourth identity in a sequence of fourteen, starting off to my right and ending down by the washroom. Two enameled eating bowls, a wooden ladle, and an enameled mug appeared on the floor at the door. I retreated with my find to the planked frame like a caged animal that hauls its bone off to a secluded corner. My greed was partly genuine hunger brought on by the endless pacing and the cold, but more than that it was simply an activity on which I could concentrate.

As I wolfed down the pea soup, the pork and cabbage and potatoes, and finally the watery stewed apples, I felt I had weathered the day's low point. As if in justification for my improved spirits, a pleasant surprise occurred when the dishes were picked up. Steps approached and, when I looked up, there stood the old guard from Warsaw who had slept on the table and who had given me the cigarette the previous evening. It was like meeting an old friend. He smiled in an amicable way and, with the help of another guard at the door, explained that I no longer needed to stand facing the wall with raised hands when the door opened. He added that I could sit down on the plank frame whenever I wanted to and that I was allowed to take an afternoon nap if I wished, and I could even have my window slightly open. I felt quite overwhelmed with all this sudden consideration, though I did wonder at the weird unpredictability of everything here.

And so that first day shrank enormously. Sleep was partly responsible. Not that I was consciously tired, but like eating it was a method of killing time and my thoughts. The fresh country air now pouring in over the top of my window also helped, washing away the most acute sensations of claustrophobia.

Just as with Muffin, in the weeks and months and years that followed there were two distinct worlds of sounds, those of the night and those of the day, which constantly pieced themselves together into larger concepts that became as concrete as if I had actually seen them. That second night as I lay on my straw sack I could hear the putter of a solitary motorcycle on some country road; the purr of a truck traveling fast along a highway; the rumble of a train far off. Then these more distant sounds were drowned out by the barking of a dog nearby and the answer of another farther off, and still another, each presumably the guardian of some lonely farmyard. Then there was the barking of a pack of dogs, first far off, then swinging this way, dogs on a scent in a growing frenzy of excitement. Police hounds perhaps? A supplement to the bars and bolts and masonry down here? I shivered at a sudden upsurge in the chorus, very near at hand. Closing in on their prey. Was this what would meet me if somehow I contrived to break out of this cellar? No doubt the inhabitants of the other thirteen cells were lying listening just as I was, feeling the same horror at the vivid image evoked by this continuous barking in the night.

In time I came also to recognize the sounds of approaching day. The first was a steadily increasing rumble of trains with laboring engines. Often they came to a stop, whistled impatiently, then started again with a clatter that passed from car to car. Freight trains. From where? To where? Freight trains converging on a sleeping metropolis with the goods for the coming day. But what metropolis?

Another signal of the awakening day was the clop-clop of horses' hoofs on a macadam road, pulling rubber-tired peasant carts to market. It recalled the stretch of highway between Krakow and Katowice, which I had often driven after dark during my work in 1939; such carts, laden with produce for the Krakow market, would abruptly loom up out of the night, lightless, with the driver fast asleep.

Finally there was the first crowing of a cock, and another, and another, and I knew that any moment the cellar would go through its first convulsion of the new day and suit after suit would be catapulted through fourteen doors.

Then there were the sounds of the day. The distant chugging of a tractor, which brought to my mind the image of the New England fall with all its resplendent beauty, the red-leafed maples in our valley and the roadside stands piled high with squashes and pumpkins and apples and rows of cider bottles. Or a car horn tooting not far away, feet running on the gravel past my window, the clanking of an iron gate; an automobile shifting gears, accelerating, nearer then farther, then suddenly whooshing past close by and coming to a stop. Car doors slamming, voices, laughter.

There were less familiar sounds as well. A periodic clatter on gravel, accompanied by a voice shouting, "Whoa . . . whoa"—evidently a horse plowing a field, turning at each pass on a strip of gravel. Or that distant whining, rising and falling, sometimes angry, sputtering—what could that be? A threshing machine, I finally decided. I also heard the mooing of cows, and the high voices of children calling in the middle of some game—how infinitely sweet, bringing to mind so many memories. These were all country sounds. This hideous cellar seemed to be in the middle of a peaceful rural landscape.

Then there was the steady drone, soft, then louder, and finally receding into nothingness, exactly the same each day. A passenger plane on its scheduled flight. I even spotted it once almost overhead in the small patch of sky I could see above my window, getting ready for landing with the undercarriage down. I could not be far from a major airport. I counted ten or more flights somewhere within earshot every day.

Or the sudden sputtering of a two-cycle motor without any gears, which buzzed away, then returned closer and closer, and finally came to a stop with a couple of gasps as suddenly as it had started. What could that be? A motorcycle? No. A farm machine? No. I had it at last: an outboard motorboat. I must be near a lake.

Or even more significantly, once there was a loud blast from a whistle close by, high and shrill. I listened for the rumbling of wheels. Instead I heard something else, a strange swish accompanied by a chopping noise, almost like an old mill wheel at home. What could that be? Why of course, a riverboat, a sidewheeler, and I recalled the crowded day boats going up the Hudson on a Sunday. So it wasn't a lake but a river. I began to explore my geographic memory. What river in Poland within an hour's drive from Warsaw was navigable? The Bug, the Narew? Possibly. But what about the many trains, the distant factory whistles shortly after dawn, the airplanes coming in for a landing?

As the days went by, I felt ever surer that in spite of my long trip in the delivery van I was in fact quite close to Warsaw, and that it was Poland's mighty Vistula that flowed within earshot of this cellar. This was a big discovery indeed, for in that case it could not be the Russian border after all; whatever the meaning of all this madness, I was still firmly on Polish soil. This seemed confirmed, too, by the bits of conversation I heard spoken by occasional passersby outside. To date I hadn't heard one word of Russian in here or through the window gap. What an achievement, to banish the vision of oblivion in the Arctic bleakness of Siberia, that point of no return! As long as I was still in Poland, something had to happen. No matter how unpleasant the next turn might be, at least it held the chance inherent in every change.

I kept on recalling the map of this part of Poland, trying to define all characteristics that might tie in with the sounds outside. From the dawn red I established that my window faced northeast. I was acquainted with the reconstruction plan for the Warsaw region, the lay of the main railway lines and highways, the location of the Vistula bridges, the main flight directions out of Okecie Airport. All evidence seemed to suggest that I was somewhere on the east bank to the south of the city—all except the distance I had traveled that night, which placed me much farther away. How could I account for this discrepancy?

In this cellar, however, there was another area for Muffin's ears, namely, the sounds that penetrated into my cell through the cracks around the door and even through the massive walls of the cell and the ceiling above. Unlike the outdoor sounds of the country, which had by and large become a source of reassurance and strength, these inside sounds increasingly took on the character of a nightmare, the more defined they became. Of course, there were those most common ones, like the opening and closing of cell doors. These were not too disturbing, especially if they occurred as part of the daily cycles that traveled the length of corridor as regularly as a clock. There were usually nine such cycles, beginning with the return of the clothes at getting-up time to the calling of "*Appell*" at seven in the evening when the clothes were collected once more.

These routines were the station stops along the hard fourteen-hour route from waking to sleep. They had lost the unpredictability of the first night and day and soon seemed eminently regular and reasonable. Like most animals, man is a creature of habit. The shouting, the hands over head against the wall, had passed like a storm and given way to a casualness and correctness, though always circumscribed by an immutable law by which it was my lot to receive my food on the floor like a zoo animal and the human language was replaced by a snap of the fingers. Even my suit's status had improved. It now landed gently in the morning, not all scattered across the floor.

Saturday had its special merits, with an extra routine that came only once a week: a shave and body wash, inserted between the getting-up routine and that of breakfast. The most important aspect of this event was that it allowed a broader occasion for contact than any of the other daily activities. This is how it went: First a guard proceeded from cell to cell with an old pickle can half full of hot water, a stick of shaving soap, a brush in a little metal bowl, and a safety razor. While a second guard kept watch at the door, he dipped the brush in the stubbly water of the can, worked up a lather on the face of the prisoner standing in the middle of the cell before him, and then hacked away with the razor. The resistance of a week's stubble combined with a dull blade and the heavyhandedness of a lumberjack ensured that my face became a crisscross of bleeding cuts. At least the sight of it, which I was spared, produced a human reaction, in the form of a lot of shrugging and the grinning explanation that the blade was genuine *Amerikanski*, so how could he be blamed? This guilty collaboration between my face and the razor established, the hacking continued without the slightest effort toward a gentler touch. I couldn't help feeling grateful that my cell was No. 4 and not 14, with regard to both the feel of the blade and the contents of the pickle can. With the last stroke of the razor, the guard marched out of the cell and on to No. 5, leaving me ready for the next stage of this streamlined process. This followed anywhere from five to fifteen minutes later when my door opened and a bucket of hot water was set on the floor with a square of laundry soap, my towel, and a fresh sheet, shirt, and ribboned long johns. It is amazing how much a sense of cleanliness and a change of body linen can do to boost one's spirits in circumstances like these.

One inside noise puzzled me a long time, and it was actually only weeks later that I spotted its source visually. Almost every morning there was a fifteen- or twenty-minute stretch during which there was a steady click-clack over in the direction of the stairs at my end of the corridor, rather like a very laboriously moving pendulum. Often it paused for a moment, only to pick up again. What could it be? It usually happened again before lunch and in the evening as well. In spite of its regularity, I was sure it represented a manmade rhythm. Although its source eluded me for the time being, it became one of the best-remembered indoor sounds. I did not yet know that all the water for this building had to be pumped by hand.

Sometimes the outside and inside worlds suddenly intersected. One night an unusually strong draft poured in through my window and howled under my door, as the big leaves of a creeper outside tapped impatiently against the glass. A deep booming came from outside and immediately was blotted up by the silent walls of my cell. Again a second time, even louder. It was thunder, a worm's-ear impression of it. Almost at once the light bulb flickered, glowed weakly, and then went out. How delicious this complete darkness was! Throughout life we seem in search of light, but the unbroken glare of these weeks had already made the blackness of night a thing sweet beyond comparison.

At once there was running hither and thither in the corridor, the telephone started ringing, for a moment a flashlight beam shone in through the door slit, and then there was a noise like someone cranking an old car—and sure enough a motor sputtered, going into a roar and then back into a steady hum as the light came on again weakly with a flickering reddish color. An emergency generator saw to it that under every circumstance these cages of human misery should be observable to the unseen eye beyond the slit in the door. Why such concern about darkness for even a moment? Only gradually did I come to understand the specter of suicide that hung over this cellar, the key to which lay in the other indoor sounds.

The first night I had vaguely noticed them but without any attempt at identification. With each succeeding night, however, I concentrated increasingly on them until they became the most compelling reality of all in this new subterranean world. They started mainly after I had crawled into bed and often did not subside until the early hours of the morning. First there was the ringing of the telephone in the guard space next to me. Then a coming to life in the far reaches of the cellar that seemed to spread past me and up the stairs. Hardly had this wave subsided than a new ringing started off a second wave. Some nights there were as many as six or seven in succession. Then there was a quiet period again down below and I would finally fall asleep, only to be awakened sometime during the night by a sudden bedlam of what seemed like stamping and running, starting upstairs and ending each time with the crashing of a cell bolt somewhere along the corridor.

By the third night I had a sick feeling. The sounds had begun to take form. There were two phases: With the ringing of the telephone the guards proceeded to a specified cell. After a pause, presumably for dressing, a prisoner was hurried past my door and up the narrow wooden stairs with a guard close on his heels. Then I could hear them both on the wooden corridor floor above. They stopped. There was a knock on some door. The prisoner entered and the door closed behind him. The guard returned downstairs. A few minutes later the phone rang again, and the same performance happened with a second prisoner, a third, a fourth. Then silence.

I lay tense. Any moment, I knew, the second phase would begin, the real pandemonium. An hour might have gone by, or a second. I fell off to sleep, but awoke instantly as the phone rang. I heard a guard go upstairs by himself and along the corridor. I held my breath. Now. Yes—there they go: a sudden confusion of feet, racing along almost overhead, then crashing and banging on the wooden stairs like a whole lot of crates had broken loose, then a less defined commotion. They had reached the carpet runner down here. The skirmish rolled along ever closer to my door, two people running, panting to the sound of incessant flogging, until it all abruptly stopped as a door closed somewhere down the corridor and a bolt slammed into place.

Hardly had the cellar settled back into silence than the phone rang again, and once more a prisoner went upstairs, followed later by the mad chase. Sometimes there was a gasp or a groan, a "*predzej, zcurvisyn, predzej*"—quicker, you son of a bitch, quicker—but usually the whole thing transpired in eerie silence. This nightmare sequence I came to call the rabbit hunt. It was too unreal to give it any other name. I did not want to hear it; I knew it would only continue to upset me. But how to escape the sounds? I pulled the covers over my head, but the moment the telephone rang I was wide awake, waiting, waiting. In desperation I stuffed balls of bread in my ears when I went to bed. It didn't help. No matter how deeply I had fallen asleep, I was fully aware in an instant.

The picture became fuller. Not everyone in this cellar seemed to be treated the same. There were those who went in the morning, for example, and those who went in the afternoon. Some walked quietly to their interrogations upstairs and came down undisturbed, while others went in a half trot but still without audible signs of prodding. The "rabbits" were at the bottom of the hierarchy. But even among them I soon discovered gradations and variations in procedure. There was a rabbit in a cell a little farther down, it seemed like No. 6, who went up one night on the run, only to be on his way back in a mad scramble a few minutes later. After a momentary lull the bolt of his door crashed again, and once more he was scurrying, panting, toward the stairs with a guard behind him, but again he came tumbling back down after having hardly reached the interrogation room, the slap of blows accompanying him all the way to his cell. The ensuing silence was short-lived, however. It was the same door again. I put my head under my pillow and held my hands over my ears. It didn't help. This particular rabbit made another five trips up and down before real silence settled upon the cellar and I felt able to let go of my ears.

It wasn't just the night sounds from the corridor that I found so distressing. The room above my cell was one of those used for interrogations. The insulation of the ceiling was insufficient to dampen the noise during the stretches of complete silence in the cellar when there was no activity in the corridor. While I usually couldn't catch individual words, the general atmosphere that prevailed was often all too clear. Sometimes it was so quiet above that I couldn't even hear the voices; the only sign of someone being there was the occasional shifting of a chair or footsteps going back and forth. At other times there would be constant tirades, broken by hardly audible replies. Then there were moments when again, feeling sick, I held my breath, moments when the shouting and cursing suddenly changed into an undefined confusion of movement and thuds, followed by a sudden rush of words in a high unnatural voice, some more tirades, renewed confusion, and finally the telephone outside, then labored footsteps coming down the stairs, passing by outside, faltering heavy breathing, a groan, whispers, and, after considerable delay, the closing of a cell door. More often than not, these episodes involved the prisoner in the cell exactly opposite mine.

Already on my second day below I had noticed that the corridor opposite me was different. Instead of a cell door there was a narrow opening leading to a small space about five feet deep and nine feet wide, the same width as my cell. In the far wall were two regular cell doors, bolts and peek slots and all. Every time my door opened I could steal a quick glimpse in that direction. Usually the space was dark. There was no doubt that one of the two doors led to a cell with someone in it all the time. The other was in use intermittently, often for only short periods and at night, in conjunction with the rabbit hunts.

Once the door of this cell stood open and I could see that it was pitch dark inside, a mere windowless hole about four feet by six feet without even a place to lie down. The one next to it could be no bigger. How could a person be kept in a space that small? What did it mean? I was alert for every sound that would provide an answer, and the more I listened the weirder it all seemed. Sometimes a guard posted himself in front of one of the doors for hours, turning a light switch on and off almost continuously or, in alternation, sliding the bolt back and forth in a rapid staccato. Once in a while the door really flew open, followed by a scuffle and by slapping sounds from inside the cell as if on a bare body. Occasionally the opening of the door was followed by a big splash of water and a gasp, the bucket then being set on the brick floor as the door slammed shut.

In time I realized that the alternating switching on and off of the light and banging with the bolt were inducements to keep the inmate awake and on his feet when he could no longer resist sleep, and that dousing with cold water or flogging was the next stage if the milder version lost its effect. From what I could make out, inmates of these two holes seemed to be put in there stark naked, probably both as further incentive to become compliant and as a precautionary measure against any attempt to use the darkness to end their miseries.

It was the second of these cubicle cells opposite me that housed the unfortunate rabbit whose tribulations upstairs I unwillingly followed through my ceiling. He also seemed to have a strange way of falling off his chair, or whatever he was sitting on upstairs, and landing on the floor again and again with a thud as two different voices shouted at him at the same time. On certain occasions, a third person would knock on the door and join the other two; a series of regularly spaced, hardly audible thuds close to the floor ensued, interrupted periodically by the loud repetition of a question. On the mornings following such events I could distinguish a guard sitting in the vestibule opposite with this particular rabbit, working with scissors and tearing something. The impression was of someone being given a surgical dressing. It was a further characteristic of these two cells that their inmates often missed part or all of the normal routines of the day.

Slowly and painfully the picture filled itself out. I was opposite two "special treatment" cells used when all other methods of persuasion had failed. The meaning of the sounds emanating from there turned all hearing at such moments into hell. Had I been placed within earshot by design or by chance? I became preoccupied with wondering whether the rabbit hunts and their extreme form opposite were all part of a standard processing to which every inmate of the cellar was sooner or later subjected. Inevitably, despite the dread and loathing that filled me, I became obsessed with observing and interpreting every indoor sound, wondering each night I heard the telephone ring and the bunch of keys being picked up from the table whether the steps outside would stop in front of cell No. 4 and I, too, would become a rabbit.

This dread produced a state of paralysis, such that I couldn't even demand to speak to someone of authority. Wasn't authority responsible for what I heard each night? Shouldn't I consider myself lucky to be forgotten for the moment in the security of my four walls, my mouse hole? Time had already lost all meaning. Everything that could have happened in the world outside already had. There were no more date lines of last defense; they had all gone by. Kate knew now beyond the slightest doubt that something of incalculable seriousness had happened which no hopeful thinking could explain away. By now the newspapers knew it, and Cleveland. My university development project, my home, my career, the impending deanship at Western Reserve University—how far away they all were, in another world.

For the hundredth time I went through all the what-if scenarios. If I had stayed in the United States this summer, as originally planned after an architectural reconstruction tour fell through, I would have had a quiet month at Valley Farm. But Kate and the boys had already gone to England for the summer and there had been the International Congress of Modern Architecture at Bergamo, to which I was a delegate, so it made sense to go to Europe.

Or the second if: if I had refused to go to Prague and had insisted instead on taking the matter up at once through U.S. consular channels, or even after deciding to go, if I had insisted on Herta's staying behind in Geneva where she would be at hand to explain what had happened, things would surely be different. No doubt in Prague she, too, had been picked up before she could give any warning. And what would prevent the Poles from putting out false scents to shift scrutiny away from their doorstep? They might, say, have sent Kate a fake telegram placing me far from the scene of the crime, in Berlin or Copenhagen, for example, which I might reasonably have visited on my way back to London. For that matter, what would prevent the Poles from claiming that I had been the victim of some criminal act or a car accident in which identification was no longer possible? If they really wanted me to disappear without trace, there were hundreds of ways. But again, why me of all people? Why?

If only I had stayed right in Prague with Herta under Karel Markus's protective eye and not been tempted to take a second look at Warsaw's reconstruction while the Czech government supposedly investigated Noel's disappearance. Or, if only I had registered at our embassy here on arrival, or gone back that last day to report the incident with my photographing. Even during those weeks in the Security Police headquarters, couldn't I still have retrieved the situation by refusing to respond, by fighting back? Instead I had fooled myself into simply believing that everything was bound to clear up. I had assumed that all I could do was try to be as cooperative as possible. And what good had that done? But could I have achieved anything by any other course? At police headquarters, after all, there had been a cellar as well, and the noises here always recalled the apparition I had encountered in the corridor there, an apparition that became the embodiment of the rabbit image of this cellar now.

If, if, if, if . . . Far from providing any useful answers, against my will this second-guessing seemed only to suck me deeper into the horrible world of sounds from which there was no escape. No one could help me anymore, because no one, not even Kate, would know where to start. Disappeared without trace. All cards, every last one, had slipped from my hands . . . Rabbit . . . Oblivion.

# 6

---

## Shock

I had been part of this cellar inferno of sounds a little over a week when what night after night I had been anticipating with dread finally happened. For what seemed like an hour I had been lying on my straw pallet. Several cells had already disgorged their rabbits for their first lap upstairs. Once again the telephone tinkled on the other side of the wall. "*Slucham*"—I'm listening . . . It seemed to me the muffled interchange was longer than usual. Finally: "*Dobra*"—All right.

Someone picked up the bunch of keys, unmistakable signal that a prisoner would soon be on his way. Probably the one down in No. 8; they didn't miss him a single night. I heard the keys again, this time close, the sound of looking for the right one in the bunch. Opposite? No, here. So this was it at last. The key turned, the bolt slid; without comment or sign the guard deposited my suit and shoes on the floor. The door slammed shut again with a doomlike echo.

I jumped out of bed and quickly slipped into my suit and laceless shoes. Through the window crack I could hear the nightly barking of the dog pack, now nearby, now farther away. When the door opened again I waited for the finger snapping that would start my journey upstairs. Instead the guard entered carrying my raincoat and two short pieces of string. I put the string through the top eyelets of my shoes and tied them firmly, remembering the hectic descent usual on the return downstairs. But why my raincoat—in this collarless shirt, without any socks, unshaved, at night? What could this mean? My misgivings mounted.

An officer with shining jackboots appeared in the door. Without a word he gave something to the guard, who came over to where I stood in my raincoat. It was the familiar blindfold of black satin, and before I grasped what was happening the ribbons were pulled tight about my head and I found myself in sudden darkness. My heart was pounding; I was breathing heavily. Again the unknown—Siberia. The beginning of a journey. Where would it end? The rabbit hunt, with all its horror, had at least the advantage of being somewhat known, a cycle that would bring me back finally to the shelter of my mouse hole here. But this? Barely perceived images, ever more ominous, flashed through my mind.

There was a pause. I could hear steps around me but not one spoken word. A hand took hold of my arm and guided me ahead. I stumbled over the threshold of my cell door as I was steered to the right into the corridor. In a moment we would start up the wooden stairs. But the hand held me back. We came to a stop. A key turned in a metal door straight ahead. Suddenly the cold night air was blowing on me. Different from last time, certainly different from what the rabbits experienced. We moved forward again, slowly up some stone steps out of doors. How loud the dog pack now sounded.

Gravel underfoot. Again a pause. The hand left my arm. I drew in the night air, trying to steady my breathing. There was a hurrying of footsteps and a dull flapping noise behind me. In the next moment something heavy came down from above and enveloped me, almost knocking me to the ground. I felt entangled. Groping, I found myself inside a semirigid covering that hung down on all sides from my head right down to my knees. The night air was gone and instead everything reeked of a suffocating mixture of oil and canvas, reminding me of a garage. Then I realized what it was: a heavy tarpaulin, tied at the waist, through which strong hands now gripped each arm and, without letting go, gave me a shove ahead. I staggered forward, then caught myself. Fear and the weight of the tarpaulin almost made my knees give way.

An elemental instinct of self-preservation made everything in me focus on a search for meaning. We were on grass, heading onto some pathless field. Not even a truck to crawl into this time. A human form with a cover thrown over it; the silent walk into the night; the sound of feet beside and behind me; the officer in parade uniform for some special occasion—but what occasion? Suddenly I knew. With me, they had just dispensed with the interrogation upstairs, with the rabbit hunt. They were in a hurry to get rid of all traces. Siberia was too far. Oblivion right here, right now. Long-forgotten images of executions flashed across my mind. Always a little party going out into a field or to a wall, in their midst the ungainly form of the hooded victim, sightless and led by the arms, then a moving apart and in the flash of a second a signal and the shots from behind. Could I be mistaken? No. It all added up to this. At last the anonymity of this forgotten cellar made sense.

I was wet from head to foot with fear. I found it hard to breathe against the wall of canvas pressing against my face. On and on I went in this death walk to some unseen wall. My legs moved mechanically, as if they weren't mine. It was too late now. There was nothing I could do, with that grip on my arms and those steps I could hear all around me. It would happen in sixty seconds, or forty, or right now even as I walked. If it would only happen quickly, before the waiting went beyond endurance. How frightfully lonesome this last moment was. How much comfort Kate and the boys could give me now with their warmth and love, obliterating the distance to the final second. How much they would want to help me; how much they would want to know they really had done so.

Here Kate, here, take my hand hard. And you, Hughie, and you, Alan, both of you hold on this side. Just this one last time, all united together and strong, the way we once were before all this happened. That's it. I am counting now, Hughie. Remember how I taught you numbers? So let's count together. It won't be long now. And you too, Kate. We're marching side by side, helping each other. We're almost there. Keep counting. And Katie, if Alan should forget, you always tell him how he held my hand and helped even though it wouldn't go properly with the counting. How is it, Hughie—it's so hard to keep my mind on it, have we reached a hundred? Isn't it strange, us four walking, walking this way together? Hold my hand tighter now. The counting will be over any moment.

Kate and Hughie and Alan and I, we stopped, held back by a pulling on my arms. Gravel again. The barking of dogs very close, echoing as from a wall just ahead. A pulling close of the tarpaulin around my waist. In front of me, some metal squeaking with a tinny sound. A slight push on my back, the hands guiding me forward again as if to get me into exact position for something, as if wanting me to bend. I stooped. My legs struck against a sharp edge about a foot from the ground. I felt strong pressure from behind, and, unable to extricate my hands from under the tarpaulin, I lost my balance and pitched headlong into a narrow metallic space.

Had I been shot? I had no clear conception of just what had happened. All I knew was that I seemed pinned between two walls made of metal. Why had I fallen? Was I dying?

No, it hadn't ended yet. I wasn't shot. At once, however, I sensed a new danger, a new horror. Not only was I half smothered under this tarpaulin, but I had been shoved into some sort of chamber, shallow and long and narrow, just the size of my body. I recalled the creaking of a metal door. I was gasping for breath. Could it be? Abruptly the vision of the Nazi gas chambers came to me. Could it be? Quieter than shooting.

I lay stiff, unable to move, overwhelmed by a sense of suffocation. I was prone on my face with my hands under me and my feet hanging out of the mouth of the contraption. I heard some cursing: "*Cholera.*" How strange, after all this silence. Then, "Shoo . . . shoo." Someone was tugging at my feet, and now straight in front of my head something was happening too. It seemed as if a metal door had been opened just a few inches from my head. Someone grabbed me under my shoulders through the tarpaulin and tried to raise me. Limp and will-less, I was dragged up on my knees, then tipped sideways, where I landed on something soft and springy. Apparently the wall on that side had been barely a foot high ... All at once everything took form: a car—I was half lying, half sitting, on the back seat of a car. I steadied myself. Someone sat down to the left of me, someone else to the right. A voice said in German, "Hands over here, on the rail, and mind you keep them there at all times." The tarpaulin was raised sufficiently to allow me to reach out and grasp a long thin bar—the rug rail along the back of the front seat.

A tinny door slammed in front; a starter whined; the motor coughed, and almost at once we began to move. Under the tarpaulin I sat bolt upright on the edge of the seat, the only way I could hold the rug bar. The sounds and a cold wind swirling about me and even penetrating my canvas covering made it clear that I was in the backseat of an open car, old and with a four-cylinder engine. The succession of dreads, certainties, and reprieves had brought me to a state of numb shock in which I kept waiting for the worst to happen. I was by now quite incapable of visualizing ever coming out of this alive. It had merely been a matter of overhasty interpretation of how the end would come.

Through the tarpaulin barrier I sensed we were weaving and bumping along a country lane. Then there seemed a change of resonance, and I was quite sure I had caught the smell of pines. So we had entered a forest.

But why a forest? At once a new dread gripped me. Hadn't forests been one of the favorite spots for Nazi execution squads? Weren't there tens of thousands of Poles and Jews and Russians in unknown forest graves stretching from the Baltic to the Black Sea? It was the most convenient way of obliterating all traces, and besides, the victim can be made to do the work of digging the trench himself. All that remained afterward was to fill it in again.

That had been the Nazis, however. Well, what about Katyn Forest, the site of the mass grave of thousands of Polish officers discovered toward the end of the war in Nazi-occupied Poland, in an area earlier occupied by the Russians? I had never been sure as to the identity of the perpetrators in that atrocity, after all. It had been wartime, and Russia had been our ally.

We were going deeper and deeper along a twisting trail into some woods. We slowed down, turned left, then right. I was perspiring from head to foot, waiting, waiting for the moment when we would stop.

But we didn't stop. The car gradually picked up speed, the road became smoother and straighter, the smell of pines gave way to cold country air; a motor growled by, followed a while later by a motorcycle. For some time we moved along at an uninterrupted pace on what seemed like a highway. For the first time I began to feel chilled by the clammy wetness of my clothes as the night air worked its way through the tarpaulin and rushed about my legs. Another car and another, then tooting, slowing down, the sound of brakes. An intersection. A little while later I was completely alert. What was that? A clattering noise, now just beside us. A streetcar—people. A kind of delirium swept over me: we must be in a town! Small? Big? Polish? Russian? I was all ears. After some twisting and stops we hit a straight smooth stretch with short swishing sounds—hadn't that happened on the trip out that night too? Again city traffic. I wondered if anyone had bothered to look our way in the light of a street lamp. What a queer sight I must be, rather like a draped clay sculpture on an armature in an art school. We were slowing down again, tooting, turning sharply to the right, and coming to a stop. Some calls were exchanged. Already I was sure, though I didn't dare risk disappointment: Warsaw, life. I held myself in check and listened. The grating sound of a gate. We drove in slowly. We stopped, the motor was turned off. Someone began pulling off the tarpaulin, then undid the eye blind. I stared in confusion. I was sitting in the back of a small, open canvas-topped car, on the one side of me "Shoo" and on the other my old friend who slept on the table. As I climbed unsteadily out I looked toward the door of the building in front of me. It was the same courtyard door I had passed through on two previous occasions.

So I wasn't dead. So I was back in the world among people. Even this courtyard, even the familiar corridor through which I passed, seemed like a long-lost paradise. I felt drunk. The nightmare was almost over. I wanted to shake the hands of the two guards at my side, to clap them on the back in celebration. I needed an outlet for the overwhelming joy that swept through me: alive, alive, did you hear, Kate and Hughie and Alan, we made it, we got through and will soon be reunited in life, not death! The dam of tension in me had broken. I felt washed along helplessly by tears that wouldn't come and laughter that wouldn't either. How crazy all my fears had been! And yet, what a weird prelude to my return here. And why?

We entered a brightly lit anteroom with desk and telephone, probably occupied in daytime by a secretary. The inevitable picture of President Bierut was on the wall; a door on either side led to adjoining rooms. I was shown to a chair in the corner. I sat down, aching and bruised and my shirt sticking to my back. My guards settled down silently on a bench against one of the side walls. I wanted to smile at them, but they looked stolidly at the floor and puffed at their cigarettes. The door on the left opened, and to my surprise one of the friendly youths who had shared my courtyard room in August went past me to the corridor door. I gave a big grin of recognition, but he acted as if he had never seen me, in fact as if this encounter were embarrassing. Why this atmosphere of gloom? Maybe it was my incredibly bedraggled appearance.

I felt my hair. It was sticky and disheveled. My face had several days' worth of stubble on it, not to speak of old cuts and new bruises. My raincoat was crumpled, my suit in worse shape than ever after this journey, my shirt stained and wet, my legs sockless, and my shoes tied merely with bits of string. No belt, no collar, no necktie. Through the door on the right I could vaguely hear voices. Probably I was waiting to be ushered in there to come face to face at last with a responsible official who would explain all this madness.

The door opened and the same immaculately groomed officer whom I had seen for a moment in the door of my cell before I was blindfolded stood severely before me. The two guards jumped up and tried to look formal. The officer pointed to a coat rack beside me. I took off my coat, amazed at the way my hands were still trembling. The officer beckoned me to proceed ahead of him through the door.

I found myself in a rather impressive room with a large Persian rug, heavy curtains, and a big map of Poland on the opposite wall. The room was dominated by two shiny mahogany desks, one parallel to the window wall at about the center of the room, the other at right angles to it like the top of a capital T. Behind the first sat a black-haired, lean-faced man about my age, staring at me poker-faced out of self-assured, cunning eyes. At the end a delicate-looking youth was busy with a pencil and pad, and facing him across the two desktops at the second desk sat two more civilians, a man with a rather monumental face and a big shock of graying hair and, set back a bit, the familiar heavyset figure of Cigarette. These two men, too, were staring at me intently. At the angle of the T was an empty chair to which the first man pointed without a word. The officer in uniform sat down unobtrusively on a chair beside the door. Not far from him a big, old-fashioned wall clock was ticking away as its pendulum swung. It was 9:40. I had not seen accurate time for almost a month.

The silence and staring continued as if I were some strange laboratory subject. The black-haired man reached over to a big candy tin standing on the desk, then pushed it in the direction of his colleagues. My eyes followed the tin, my mouth and throat completely parched. I felt an irresistible urge to suck a candy too. Behind this need lay also an almost hysterical impulse to prove the casualness of this occasion to myself and the others in this room, to prove that none of what had happened just now had seemed the least bit strange to me, that my nerves were in excellent condition. I pointed to the tin and smiled weakly: "May I?"

I had broken the spell of staring. The black-haired man nodded, a sarcastic expression perceptible around his mouth. The tin was pushed in my direction. I reached in, took one, two, three hard candies into my hand, and put them all in my mouth. They tasted wonderful. Meanwhile, we had settled right back into the silent staring. I already sensed that the dark-haired man was in charge, with the others merely in attendance; and in fact it was he who at last spoke up, in perfect German: "How are you?"

What an absurd question! He said it the same way you say hello of a morning in the elevator on your way to your office. Instinctively I answered in kind with the same casualness: "*Es geht, danke*"—All right, thank you—and at once I felt frightfully silly. What could be more beyond dispute than my battered and bedraggled self? And sure enough, an indulgent smile of amusement spread slowly over the black-haired man's face. It was catching somehow, and against my will I found myself doing the same. The ridiculousness was too apparent. My behavior reminded me of childhood and getting an irrepressible urge to giggle in the presence of adults for no reason except that it was exactly the thing not to do. I felt embarrassed. I must get a grip on myself. What if this man is the MBP minister himself? Involuntarily I glanced up at a black-and-white framed portrait on the wall above the desk: a rather youngish official face of nondescript character, probably the boss. I looked at the man before me again. No, there was no similarity.

"Tell me, what are you actually?"

"What do you mean, my profession?"

"Yes—sure, sure, your profession." He cast a quick amused glance at his colleagues. Again I couldn't resist smiling too, rather like a dog that wags its tail every time you look at him.

"Well, surely you know that I am an architect."

"Oh, I see, so you're an architect." There was a pause, and again he glanced with amusement at the other men, who were silently watching me from the sidelines. "An architect. Now, that's really interesting. You're quite sure? Not perhaps an archaeologist instead, how about that?" He gave a chuckle and, stretching out in the chair, looked at me as if we had a good mutual joke.

"Archaeologist? Why archaeologist?" I had hardly asked the question before his amusement had again spread to me as surely as a dog's tail starts wagging. What in heaven's name was the matter with me?

He nodded encouragingly as if to say, See how we understand each other? Then he remarked, "Noah's ark too perhaps? Come, come now. Nice archaeology, nice architecture." He was in high humor, and his eyes suggested a good-natured tolerance in the face of attempted naiveté.

"But, I don't understand you." At once I felt I sounded feeble and insincere. The fact was, I had suddenly identified just what he was driving at. Quite by chance several months earlier I had noticed an item in the newspapers that had worked the Russians into a lather of suspicion. An American archaeological expedition proposed to look for traces of Noah's ark on the slopes of Mount

Ararat, and the Russian retort was that the American interest was not old Noah at all but the much more tangible and visible Soviet-Turkish border close by. But for me to admit recognition of the reference would lend color to the implied aptness of the parallel. I decided to ignore the dig. Somehow, however, the whole thing struck me as so ludicrous that I couldn't keep a straight face.

The black-haired man looked triumphant. "Well, well, so you're an architect, an American architect. Well, we'll have plenty of time to go into that." And then, as if an afterthought: "But, Mr. Architect, you were in Krakow in 1939, weren't you? And what were you doing? Building skyscrapers?"

Again I felt silly and defensive, as if I had been caught out. He had singled out the one period in my life in which I had certainly not been engaged in architectural activity. "Well, I was administrator for the Czech Refugee Trust Fund to help rescue anti-Nazi refugees following the occupation of Czechoslovakia..."

He interrupted. "We know all that. But who sent you? For whom were you working?"

Obviously for the British refugee committee in London, but at once I felt embarrassed. That wasn't the whole story by any means. After I got to Krakow, yes, but while the funds had been provided by the committee, my original covert expedition to Prague in April of 1939 had had its origins rather in that twilight world of political struggle against Hitler. I had actually been approached directly by some of the refugee leaders in London who had already been given asylum in England and, with the unofficial blessing of the committee, were seeking a way of rescuing some of their most jeopardized colleagues still in Prague.

"I went to Prague originally to help rescue some highly endangered German and Austrian Communists caught there by the German occupation. They included a number who were to receive British visas..."

Again he interrupted. "Communists?" He smiled indulgently. "I know very well what your rescue work looked like. Only too well. But you still haven't told me whom you did it for. Who was it who sent you?"

From the way he stared at me I got the feeling I had done something wrong back then. How strange, since in that Prague venture the Communists had been among the main beneficiaries. I explained how it came about that I had agreed to try to help these people between architectural jobs, and how circumstances changed the initial clandestine Prague venture of a week into the longer unintended interlude in Krakow on behalf of the refugee committee itself. It seemed incongruous for me to be explaining to a Communist official that a rescue of this sort in the atmosphere of the late thirties was not bound by legal niceties. Since when had communists become sticklers on such matters? Surely it was obvious that without the alibi provided by the mission, that I was retrieving a Czech film for International Pictures, and without the resultant entry permit that I wangled out of the Gestapo, I would never have gotten to Prague, nor would any relief body have committed itself officially on anything so risky. I had been utterly on my own.

"Yes, yes we know all this, but for whom did you actually go?"

I tried to recall the names of the refugee leaders I had spoken with on that occasion in London. It was ten years back. In the last analysis it had been Kate who had first approached me. "Well, I guess it was at my wife's suggestion."

"And your brother? It wasn't he who sent you perhaps?"

But what did Noel have to do with this? Yes, years later during the war, after his permanent position at the League of Nations had folded under him, he had turned to the relief field and served with the American Unitarian Service Committee, first at its Marseilles center and then in Geneva and Paris as European director. But in 1939 he was still at the league, and by the time he entered the relief field I had long since been back in architecture in New York, far from the European scene. My interrogator was putting the cart before the horse.

"Didn't you see your brother in Geneva in 1939 just before you left for Prague?"

"Yes, I saw him some weeks earlier on my way back from a brief visit in Switzerland in connection with winding down my building job in England. It was a purely personal visit, and I had no idea at that point that I might be going to Prague. It was only later, after my return to London, that my wife mentioned the plight of these people."

"All right then, let's hear right from the beginning the whole story of what you claim you did in 1939, from the moment you left London in April until your return during the war six months later."

Hadn't he even bothered to read those reports written with such labor during my initial weeks here? Well, perhaps it would be all to the good to state the story in my own words without the distorting element of an interpreter. Although it had been ten years, I had come to regard my rescue work in 1939 as a highwater mark in my life in which I had given my all, at the risk of death, to protect human rights that were being violated. Given the failures of the spineless governments of that period, it had been a positive achievement whose reward I had found again in recent years in a community of friendship scattered over half a dozen countries. I felt reassured. I had felt nearer to the communists then than at any time before or after in my life. What had impressed me most was their unremitting and courageous resistance against the Nazis when acquiescence was the easy way out. While numerically they represented only a small part of those we had managed to save, they were, I thought, my trump card at this moment. I could point to a number of Czech, German, and Austrian communists who could substantiate that I had contributed to their being alive today.

Quietly and with increasing confidence I began my account. The three men listened intently without once interrupting me. The youth at the side of the desk jotted down the names of every place and person I mentioned. I made a point of singling out every communist I could remember from those days—the ones who had gone to England, to Australia; the ones who had been among my helpers in the work in Krakow when no outside administrative assistance was available; the ones who had been caught by the war on Polish soil and had participated in our forlorn trek by foot on the first days of the invasion. I described the final debacle when Vilem Novy and I decided in Luck in the Polish Ukraine that it was all over and, using the protection afforded by the Bank of Poland's gold convoy, which was heading for the Rumanian border under cover of night, fled south to escape seizure by the Germans.

The black-haired man broke in for the first time. "But why did Mr. Novy and you flee south some hundred kilometers to Rumania when you could much more easily have fled to the Russian border only fifty kilometers to the east?"

"I can't answer for Mr. Novy, but obviously my desire was to get back to England to report to the committee, to whom I was responsible. I don't see how fleeing east would have helped that."

"And you had no other reason?" Again that sarcastic tone. Maybe this was because I had mentioned Kate.

"Yes, I was naturally eager to get back to the woman I wanted to marry."

"But isn't it a little strange that Novy, an important Czech communist, chose this route too? After all, Gottwald was in Moscow, not London. Was it perhaps that you persuaded Novy? Did you perhaps have some special plans for him?"

"I can't recall what was on his mind. That was ten years ago. Certainly he was not a man to be persuaded by me. Under the bombing and general disintegration in Poland and the scattering of our refugees, there was nothing more we could do and the logical course was to take the first escape possibility that offered itself."

"And that was with the fascists who dragged Poland to defeat and plundered her gold?"

"Well, I don't know about that. It was as part of the gold transport of the Bank of Poland, which wanted to avoid the country's gold reserves falling into the hands of the Germans. When the news of the Soviet advance reached us at the Rumanian border, Novy in fact did decide to turn back, but it was too late. I remember his also going to the Russian legation in Bucharest and asking for contact with Mr. Gottwald in Moscow, but he got no answer; I couldn't keep on postponing my departure for London on his account, so suggested that Novy come along with me in view of the risks he faced staying on alone in Rumania."

The man with the black hair continued to probe this point until finally I could not take it any longer. "If you want to know why Mr. Novy went with me to London instead of to Gottwald in Moscow, why don't you go and ask him yourself? I'm not his keeper, am I? How can I tell what was in his mind on a certain afternoon ten years ago? As for my work in Krakow, I think it was as fair as the insuperable difficulties I faced allowed. Hundreds of people came through the Krakow office. Jews and a great many opponents of Hitler, among them communists, owe the fact that they are alive today to my perseverance then."

"Yes, yes I know only too well what it looked like and who benefited from it." Again the sarcastic smile. He pointed to the big map of Poland on the far wall. "Will you please trace with your finger the route of your September refugee evacuation."

I got up and walked over. I showed the route of the train that took the Katowice group on September 1 as far as Kielce, which they reached two days later—a journey of little more than an hour normally. I indicated the section we did on foot, many hundreds strong on the route out of Krakow; the point where we were cut through by a German tank column; and then the spot where, in ever dwindling numbers, we crossed the river Dniester at Zaleszczyki some ten days later. As I returned to my chair I glanced at the wall clock. It was past midnight. But what did all this mean? Why this sudden interest in 1939 to the exclusion of everything else?

As if he had read my thoughts, the man with the large face looked up and asked in German with a heavy Slavic accent: "Where is your brother?"

I was taken aback by the sudden shift in subject. I shrugged. "That's just what I'd like to know." To say outright that I suspected he had been kidnapped by the Russians might only get me into worse trouble. How could I know whether this man wasn't Russian, perhaps an official from the NKVD, the Commissariat of Internal Affairs? "The Czech authorities are trying to find out for me."

"But you're an American. Another American disappears in a foreign country; wouldn't the normal thing be for you to go to your embassy and make a big fuss? Who ever heard of going to the country where it happened, especially if it's a communist one? A little queer, isn't it?" He looked across to the black-haired man and winked.

I could hardly believe my ears. My willingness to try for a solution that would help the Czechs avoid a scandal was simply a matter of amusement to these men! I wanted to yell out how completely I agreed with him and what a fool I had been. Didn't this man realize how much easier it would have been for me to have gone to the U.S. authorities at once? I began to tremble all over with conflicting emotions as I tried to find words, tried to explain.

"We didn't want to embarrass the Czech government on something that might not be their doing at all," I finally said. "You know how easily such a thing can become an international scandal in the present atmosphere of tension. My wish has always been to increase cultural understanding and interchange between East and West, and I was willing to try a direct approach to the Czechs on those grounds."

"What do you mean by saying it might not be the responsibility of the Czechs?"

Again I was face to face with this dangerous question. I tried to evade it. "In Prague there were two telegrams from my brother after his disappearance. The first was from Bratislava, the second from Vienna. The Czech authorities suggested to my sister-in-law that perhaps he had been lured away by American undercover agents to ensure his being at hand as a witness in a trial at home." Although this was patent nonsense and I had never believed this theory concocted from the telegrams, I recalled how strongly the Czechs had tried to impress that possibility on Herta, which only added to her sense of helplessness and disorientation. I was determined not to be the first to mention the word "Russian" in this room.

"Oh, the Americans. And you never thought of any other possibility?"

There was smiling all round the room, and once again I found myself sucked in against my will. It was all so obvious, but I was determined to play dumb. "Who else could be interested in such a thing? Or maybe he was the victim of a robbery or accident or of amnesia. That can happen too." I could see from their faces that they knew very well I wasn't that naive. However, they chose to let it go.

The questions shifted to identifying everyone I had seen in Europe since my departure from Cleveland in July. Throughout the evening Cigarette had remained silent, rather like a proud circus trainer. One o'clock struck. By now I had become increasingly aware that this session was not about to lead to my release either. Quite the contrary, I had a growing sense of getting tangled up in an ever more ominous misunderstanding. This feeling had become so strong that I couldn't even bring myself to ask point blank for an explanation and for an end to my detention. I was afraid to force the issue, afraid of what I would find if I did. Not once had there been a question about my photography, only the constant hinting at some awful, concealed guilt, of my being the archvillain in some unknown drama. All my efforts to play up my past sympathies had the effect merely of heightening the sarcasm from across the desk.

The black-haired man looked at the clock. It was almost two. "Well, it's been long enough. We'll stop for tonight." And he got up. The officer in the corner came to life and went over to open the door. I stood beside my chair a moment trying to decide what to say. Surely I had to protest and insist on my rights. Before I could say a word, though, the black-haired man intervened, speaking with a studied seriousness: "Good night, Mr. Architect. We will be meeting each other again, and then we will see whether there still is any way out for you."

I was not surprised to find myself clambering into the small delivery van, the two guards at my heels. For the first time I knew where I was going. What a contrast to the horror that had marked the beginning of this evening. For once there was no mystery, merely a return to that cellar.

As we jounced along in silence, dimly lit by the little bulb in the ceiling, Shoo and his colleague looked so familiar, so normal. Had they any idea what I had thought and felt on our last trip together? How much of it had been a calculated softening-up for my evening session here? How well did the organizers of this expedition understand the workings of the mind after ten days of solitude in that cellar-nowhere with its sounds? I suspected that they knew very well and found this knowledge useful.

As we drove through the night I kept on hearing the parting words in that room: "We will see whether there is still any way out for you." What did that mean? The more I reflected over the remark, the more ominous it appeared. "Way out?" And if we did not find a way out, what then? But what had I done to be faced with such an alternative? What did they want of me? How was I to cope with something so unknown? Gradually the word took form that I had even been afraid to whisper to myself: *Spy . . . spy . . .* That was what I had become from one day to the next. For that I had disappeared into the cellar, and for that, oblivion now hung over my head. Siberia after all? No, more likely the noose. But if only I knew how I had become a spy. Was it possible to be one without knowing it? The incredible had become so normal that I was not sure of anything anymore. Without knowing it, without knowing it—a spy? To my confused mind came the recollection of that unhappy hare dumbfounded with the problem of proving he wasn't a camel. But really, how did he know he was not?

# 7

## Days and Nights

Right after breakfast the next morning I was visited by the previous night's officer in jackboots. He had paper and pencil in hand and a stiff piece of cardboard as a writing surface. Then and there he wanted me to write the complete story of the 1939 refugee interlude just as I had told it a few hours before in Warsaw. "And be sure to mention the reasons you and Mr. Novy went to England instead of Russia."

While I was amazed at being asked to go over all this ground again, the fourth time by now, it seemed an auspicious sign that they wanted it in writing directly from me, to supersede the garbled version made originally through the interpreter. I sat completely absorbed all day on the plank frame, the board on my knees, filling page after page. Whenever I ran out of paper or my pencil required sharpening, I knocked and my needs were attended to at once. I was an entity again, something human. At last the initiative lay in my hands. I was doing something, applying my mind. Even Muffin's world of sounds temporarily ceased to exist.

My optimism seemed justified when the next day in the middle of the morning I was ushered politely upstairs into a sun-bathed corner office across from the one I had seen the first night, large and light and comfortable with muslin curtains obscuring the lower half of the windows.

"How are you?"

Again this confusing casualness, as if we had gathered for an afternoon cup of coffee at the Hotel Polonia. Behind a large desk at the far end of the room sat a new interrogator, a young officer in a captain's uniform, blond and handsome with an uncomplicated face rather like that of a college track star. The interpreter beside him was the woman I knew already from Warsaw. Beside them on the desk lay the product of my days of intensive writing.

"The officer wishes to ask you about your work in 1939 with the Czech refugees."

So we were off on the same tack once more—the fifth time! I didn't care. This sunny room was a lot better than the cellar. Let them ask a hundred times. During the initial weeks in Warsaw every additional sentence they demanded had almost driven me crazy with impatience. Now, in contrast, I delighted in every time-consuming translation or digression. It took us all of five days to complete our journey, once more across that bridge over the Dniester into Rumania, secure from German bombing.

Then the cellar closed in upon me again, with all the weight of isolation and unbroken pacing from morning to night, a return too to Muffin's world of sounds and to the dead ends of speculation and uncertainty. "We will see whether there is still any way out for you." A hundred times each day I came back to these words. Every evening I hoped that the guard would appear again with my raincoat to take me to the city. Hadn't he said, "We will be seeing each other again"? What was he waiting for? I no longer expected sudden freedom, but I was still waiting to be told at last of what I was accused. That was all I asked for. I was sure that once I knew the accusation I would be able to fight back and eventually clear myself.

Meanwhile, from all sorts of scraps of observation I tried to piece together a clearer picture of my immediate environment. Each expedition beyond my cell, whether with my pail along the cellar corridor or upstairs to the sunny corner room, revealed something new: the extent of piping and electric wiring; the location, construction, and thickness of walls, piers, floors, and ceilings. Or I might catch accidental glimpses through a hastily closed door upstairs. Once I had an unintended encounter at the foot of the cellar stairs with a youth shoving a lever back and forth. So, the familiar clicking sound I had so often heard was a hand-operated water pump.

The building was of very simple masonry construction, the interior walls running through from cellar to roof so that cell sizes coincided generally with the sizes of the rooms above. The image that gradually took shape in my mind was that of a converted single-story residence, perhaps of a country squire—not more than 120 feet long and 30 wide—overgrown with big-leafed vines. With its single row of eight windows interrupted by a disused entrance portico of some sort at the center, I could even imagine two whitewashed doric columns—as much a touch of status in the Polish countryside as in our own American South—with a covered terrace opposite on the back for shelter from the heat of an August afternoon. The existence of this terrace was confirmed by a bit of wall I could see jutting out just beside my cell window, which in the morning cut off the rays of the rising sun. By smell and sound I also discovered that the kitchen was upstairs, and beneath it in the cellar was a laundry and boiler room, and nearby the emergency generator, all reached by doors from the hallway of the cellar stairs. Much, much later, when for the first time I actually set my eyes on the building, I was able to establish that the image I had created in these first weeks was essentially correct.

But who had ever heard of keeping prisoners in such an incongruous setting, so out of the way that its water had to be pumped by hand? Outside the walls, rural innocence; inside, behind obscured cellar windows overhung with leaves, the inmates of fourteen cells; and behind thick drawn curtains above, the nighttime rabbit hunts and agony that turned human beings into pitiful, degraded animals. No wonder that at times the bracing air that poured in through the triangle above my window and the hauntingly beautiful sounds of the countryside created a horrible sense of split reality that seemed almost more than sanity could bear. Only as the years went by did I come to understand fully that the incongruity of my immediate environment reflected a split which dominated every aspect of the communist "paradise."

For a week nothing happened. Then one morning I was again taken to the sun-bathed corner office. It is difficult to describe how magical the world that burst in on me there seemed: daylight, blue sky with scudding clouds, the swaying tops of big trees, the muted warmth of a furnished room, casual conversation. "How are you?" I was asked with a polite smile. At once all the pent-up rebellion seemed to wash away, replaced by an irresistible optimism, almost gratitude.

"Last time you complained that you had nothing to do down below. I have some work for you." The young officer was walking back and forth slowly in front of the desk as if reflecting.

Work. I was excited. I had had enough of the appalling vacuum that descends on a human being in solitary confinement with none of the normal activities of life to occupy him. Most of us have not had the occasion to acquire the philosopher's reflective capacity that feeds on itself; contemporary life impels us to a mental pattern in which our mind becomes essentially an adjunct to activity, and without this catalyst it is lost. Take away all normal life, take away every external thing on which the mind can fix, and the result is a floundering in a void that, with every hour, day, and week, becomes more suffocating and unbearable. The communist interrogation system exploits this vulnerability in modern man to the full, knowing well that it is an ally in breaking victims' morale. Through careful manipulation, a whole series of psychological and physical "pressures" work finally to transgress human endurance, leaving only a pliant animal without will.

The officer went on to explain that he had some more writing for me to do. What he wanted were detailed biographical sketches of all the persons relating to my activities over the years.

At first I felt worried. What right had I to report on other people's lives? Couldn't I do them harm? But in fact, what was there to hide? The people I knew were either not politically minded at all, benevolently neutral, or else outright partisans of the communist cause. By describing a large number of people of my acquaintance, I should be able to make clear the repercussions my disappearance was bound to have. The Polish authorities would be forced to realize that they could not count on my being forgotten. If I stuck to the truth I had nothing to fear, either for myself or my friends. Let them check and recheck every detail, even if it took weeks and months. In the absence of any means of producing evidence myself, this was my only recourse. In the end my innocence was bound to prevail.

So I agreed to start all over again.

I was hardly back down in the cellar than a small square table with a shiny plywood top was maneuvered into my cell together with a bentwood chair to match. I felt like a king. I walked around and around the table with tears in my eyes, touching it, stroking it, this symbol of everything I had missed in the past weeks. The cell at once looked different, infused with a bit of humanity. And so began a series of days I was hardly aware of in my fever of work. The morning and evening trip with the bucket, mealtimes—the treasured "station stops" that had given sole definition to the hours between getting up and going to bed— went almost unnoticed now. There was a new freedom. I could knock on the door whenever I needed paper or my pencil sharpened. I could ignore *appell* and work late into the night. I could set my food bowls on the table before me. I even was allowed to make a magazine-page shield around the lamp cage to cut down the glare.

Again it was my refugee work of 1939 that provided most of my ammunition. I started with the communists I could recall. After all, they were my best defense. Then the sympathizers. Then on to the broad category of sundry opponents of Hitler. I tried to say something about everyone whom I could recall having had the slightest contact with. Then personal friends over the years—in America, in Europe. Architects and other professionals. It was a really rich lode to draw upon. I smiled to myself as the heap of written pages grew and grew. What a bureaucratic paradise I was creating! Almost every evening the guard collecting the day's pile asked whether I was finished, to which I shook my head: "Oh no, not for a long time yet."

After five days of this writing spree, I was called upstairs. On the desk lay a truly formidable stack of paper. At once, however, I sensed a chilly atmosphere. The officer got up, picked up the pile before him, and started pacing back and forth, glancing severely at me several times. He shook the papers in his hand. "Pan Field, this is altogether unsatisfactory. We have looked through what you have written here. There is a lot about people whom we are obviously not interested in, and much too little about those whom you don't want to tell us about. What do we care about some reactionary architect in America or some Corbusier? Why are you so afraid to tell us about the activities of your communist friends?"

Why this emphasis on their own people? As for left-wing political activity, I had certainly reported everything I knew. Admittedly, in most cases it was very little. Except with regard to something I was directly connected with myself, such as the refugee work in 1939, I had had no reason to follow these matters. Not ever having been part in that exclusive inner circle of communists, I had always thought it was none of my business what form their activity took.

I tried to explain that I had in fact reported everything I knew. "By now you should have been able to establish that while I have never felt that I could isolate myself from the world around me and I have been willing to do my share when called upon to do so by circumstances, my life interest has never been politics but the profession for which I trained."

"Pan Field, Pan Field. We are not children. It would be much better if you talked less about architecture and more about that which is the cause of your sitting here in this room."

"But what do you want of me? Look, it's not my fault if you are going after something that doesn't exist. I never did the smallest thing against your country." Somehow I was afraid to use the word "spy," and yet I knew that was what we were talking about.

"Pan Field, you are obstinate. We will give you another chance. We are patient. Go down now to your cell and think it over and then start once more to write down for us what you really know about the activities of those friends that interest us."

I shrugged. "I'll try, but I don't think there's anything that I can add." I wanted to gain time, and above all, I didn't want to lose the possibilities provided by having pencil and paper in my possession. As I prepared to return to my cell, I expected to have the papers I had written up to then given back to me as reference for what I had left out.

"No, it's not a matter of adding, Pan Field. You don't need this. It's junk from beginning to end. You understand me very well. I want you to start all over again, and this time tell the truth."

Back in my cell I was at a loss for what to do. The productive fever of the previous days was gone. This writing was getting me nowhere. In fact, the only result was an ominous coolness upstairs. Clearly I would have to redo the biographies of my left-wing acquaintances at the very least. While there was essentially nothing new I could say about them, I would change the emphasis and focus on whatever scraps I knew of their political activities and associations, letting everything else recede into the background. I would try to get this all done by the next evening and then use the full day thereafter for a detailed statement of my case, refuting any possible grounds for suspicion. By the time they discovered what I was doing it would be down in black and white.

Gradually, the statement took form. "You are holding me here," I wrote, "because for some reason you believe that I am a spy masquerading as an architect and friend. If I were a free man with access to all sources of evidence, I could prove very easily that your suspicions are ill-founded. In my present circumstances, deprived of all normal means of defense, all I can do to clear up this horrible mistake is to give you a frank picture of myself, of how I think about things, of the attitudes that have grown in me over the years toward the world in which I live, of the heritage of humanism handed down to me by my father and mother."

I wrote that while I never was a communist myself, it was at the same time impossible by my deepest nature to have engaged in espionage against them or, for that matter, against anyone. I described the basis of the friendships that had endured between me and some active communists in their countries and why these could not possibly have had any other purpose than simple mutual goodwill. Through knowing me as I am, the authorities would see that suspicions that had arisen from my photographing, or from my search for my brother, or from whatever else, were unfounded.

"I appeal to you to read this with an honesty equal to the sincerity with which I am reporting to you about myself. Perhaps in this way the completely senseless and wasteful harm that this awful misunderstanding is bringing not only on me but on your cause as well, can still be ended."

I wrote about my Quaker father with his dual dedication to science and to peace; the ethical concepts that gradually took form in me and the generally socialist inclination to which these had led me; my sympathetic interest in the huge social and economic changes in Russia since the October revolution of 1917; my despair with the international amorality of the thirties, which had increasingly drawn me into political action on the same side as the communists.

I explained some of my reasons for not becoming a communist nonetheless, especially my belief that my life lay in helping to provide human shelter through my chosen field of architecture and that it was here that I felt I had a contribution to make, not in politics.

I shifted to my brother to point up the differences in our approach to the world. Six years older than me, he had spent his adolescent years within hearing of the thunder of war on the other side of the Swiss border and had been taken to visit the French battlefields by my father soon after cessation of hostilities.

These experiences had left an indelible mark. From then onward his interest focused, like my father's before him, on a search for the social and political preconditions for peace.

While I had seen little of him during my adult life, I was of course aware of his steady gravitation toward the left. It had become especially evident in the mid-1930s with his shift from the U.S. State Department to the disarmament desk at the League of Nations in Geneva, and especially once he joined the League of Nations commission for the evacuation of the international brigades from Spain in 1938. This work had exposed him to the final stages of the defeat of Republican Spain by General Franco with massive support from Hitler and Mussolini. The Spanish debacle made a profound impression on him, as reflected in his intense concern after the outbreak of war in 1939 over the fate of the "brigaders" of many nationalities now stranded and facing increasing danger and deprivation in internment camps in southern France. It was as European director of the Boston-based Unitarian Service Committee that he threw himself into an intense refugee rescue mission in both Marseilles and Geneva during the early 1940s and continuing into the first postwar years.

Precisely what form his political thinking had taken by then I could only surmise. He had never chosen to say. I did recall that he and Herta had finally visited the Soviet Union in the winter of 1937–1938. Theirs coincided with a similar visit by Paul and Hede Massing, close friends of theirs in Geneva whom I knew as well. The Massings in those years had an aura of mystery for me as persons deeply involved in the anti-Hitler communist underground in Germany. After the Hitler-Stalin pact they became outspoken critics of Stalinist Russia, though Mrs. Massing revealed that through most of the 1930s she had in fact been an undercover recruiting agent for the Soviets.

While it was likely that Noel's convictions had by the late 1930s drawn him into the communist camp, I was skeptical of the accusations in the American press of activities during his tenure in the State Department—or later, for that matter—directed against his own country. Such disloyalty would have denied the profound ethical principles he had inherited from our father. That did not preclude, however, the possibility of involvement during his years in Geneva with various facets of the international communist movement abroad. From my own interlude with refugee aid I was well aware how difficult the tightrope walk of independence was, even given the advancing threat of fascism and war. How much more difficult it must have been in Noel's case with the end of hostilities, caught off guard as he no doubt was by the sudden dissolution of wartime alliance with the coming of the Cold War.

My reason for turning to the subject of my brother as I wrote that day down in the cellar was to make clear that his mysterious disappearance could not possibly have arisen out of hostile activities on his part, and that my search for him in turn had been completely innocent of any hidden motives. While I still tried to blame my photography, I increasingly suspected that my troubles derived from my having come too close to the truth in my brother's disappearance and that I was being held to prevent my raising the issue in the world outside.

It grew late. The guard with the unpleasant small eyes came in, ostensibly to collect the sheets I had written that day, though I was sure he had come more out of curiosity. He knew some German and no doubt intended to take a quick look at the pages of writing in his hands while he waited for me to undress and hand him my suit and shoes. It wasn't every day they landed a foreigner down here, and he could not have failed to notice the label on the inside of my jacket: BOND'S, Made in Rochester, N.Y.

As he leafed through the penciled pages, his eyes caught something that at once drew his attention. He couldn't resist. "Are you related to Noel Field?"

I was amazed. How could a guard down here, carefully isolated even from the identity of the handful of prisoners in his care, know something about my brother who had disappeared in Prague? When I nodded, he looked at me with pitying amusement, clucking his tongue in mock disapproval. As he closed the door he added further emphasis by shaking his head, as if to indicate he was glad not to be in my shoes.

The next morning I again asked for pencil and paper. The guard on duty shrugged and said there wasn't any: "*Niema.*" I paced nervously. Toward the middle of the morning I knocked. This time the head guard appeared. Pointedly he said there would be no more paper for me henceforth; then he slammed the door shut. By now I knew that shifts in attitude down below were not accidental. I sat there, waiting for some response. It didn't come. Instead there was a gradual stepping up of the burden of my isolation with well-aimed thrusts. The occasional friendly smile or word disappeared. I was abruptly deprived of the right to sleep for a few hours in the afternoon. I was shouted at at every opportunity—"Faster! *Predzej!*"—and in the morning there seemed a new delight in catapulting my clothes in a big arc across the room.

A few days later there was another incident that could have provided a critical clue if only I had known to look for it. By a strange fluke, a vital bit of news lay before my eyes without my being aware of it. During my writing stretch I had been given an innocuous page of a sports magazine to wrap around the bulb cage to reduce the glare, a small but significant gesture of improvement. To keep grease from food bowls off the tabletop and off my writing paper, I used this same page as a mat at mealtimes. After a few days it was so soiled that the old guard, whom I had had in Warsaw and who often went out of his way to be helpful, replaced it with the first thing he found to hand outside, a page from a discarded Polish newspaper. Normally this would never have happened, given the systematic secrecy and isolation that prevailed in that cellar. In my case, however, the guard had observed that I didn't know a word of Polish.

With nothing to occupy me, I began a game at meal times of trying to decipher bits of the newspaper to see how much I could piece together. There were some reports on the results of the harvesting just completed, something about trade negotiations with Hungary, a vituperative article about the new federal German regime just formed under Adenauer. The main abuse, however, seemed reserved for the defendants in some big political trial in Hungary. It was all about a "Banda Rajk." Judging from the fat black captions it was something pretty important, but all I could make out was a lot of froth about conspiracies involving Titoist gangsters and agents of American imperialism. No doubt it was just a new beating of the drums on the familiar old theme that had started with the Tito-Cominform split the year before. I passed on to the next caption, which looked more interesting, something about the new six-year plan for Warsaw's reconstruction. I became so absorbed, I slowed down with my eating and wasn't finished when the door opened for my bowls and wooden ladle to be collected. This breach of routine was just the sort of thing the small-eyed guard liked, and sure enough it was he who sauntered in and stopped in front of the table, contemplating the most effective point of attack. His eyes fell on the soiled bit of newspaper and suddenly took focus. He pulled it impetuously from the table, sending one of the bowls clattering to the floor. Shaking the paper in front of my nose, he shouted at me: "What were you reading? Tell me what you were reading!"

Surprised at this outburst, I answered: "About Warsaw reconstruction."

He turned to his colleague at the door and exploded in Polish: "Did you hear what that son of a bitch said?" and he mimicked: "Warsaw reconstruction, just Warsaw reconstruction." Then turning on me again and shaking his finger an inch from my eyes, he warned: "You just wait and see," and as he turned to leave he swept his hand around his neck in the gesture of a noose being tightened. At the time I sensed there was more to this incident than mere nastiness, that I had inadvertently trodden on some forbidden territory. It took a further two months for me to realize its full import.

My main enemy, however, was the indiscipline of my mind in the face of total inactivity. With each passing day I found it more difficult to focus for any length of time on anything but the endless spiral of speculation about my circumstances, the undermining sallies into hindsight, the ever more absurd "ifs" and "if nots," the visualization of Kate and the children's plight, the damage in Cleveland to the project that had become so much a part of me, my sister Elsie's shock in far-off Illinois at the vanishing of both her brothers. Had Kate delayed her departure home? What if she had been incautious enough to have returned on the *Batory*? The arm of the MBP could reach her there. Might they find it convenient to have her disappear? An accident, a person overboard? All day long, day after day, I hopped from one dread to another with no way to stop myself, and each round left its corrosive mark.

Soon I began to realize, though, that in a situation like mine the first job was to conserve every bit of my strength. If I didn't help myself, no one would. Sickness was unthinkable, as was losing my mental grip. Already my nervous condition was causing stomach cramps, and the penetrating cold of the cellar kept me awake at night. I started with countermeasures on the physical side, doing basic sit-ups at first to get some appetite for breakfast. It became a game, as I devised ever new movements based on the normal-life activities that were missing. I introduced a second round of basic exercises before lunch, another before supper, and a final one to warm up before bed. In doing so, I added several new "station stops" to the routine of my days, and to that extent they shrank a bit. The exertion and discipline in turn were reflected in a stronger will to cope with my mental disarray.

In the first weeks in Warsaw I had sometimes filled in the time by softly singing folk songs. Down here I quickly discovered that singing out loud led to sharp rebuke as a dangerous form of demonstration. But I found I could sing without making an audible sound. This provided a whole new series of "stations": a selection of traditional English songs right after breakfast; in mid-morning, after the changing of the guards, the tenor parts from choral music learned in the Harvard Glee Club in college days; after lunch, some German lieder and songs from childhood in Switzerland; and before *appell* in the evening, a piecing together of bits of symphonic music. I reveled in Bach's B Minor Mass and Brahms's Requiem and the life-affirming final chorus of Beethoven's Ninth Symphony, which came back to me with all the imagery of those glorious moments of immersion onstage in Symphony Hall with Koussevitzky sweeping us off our feet. As never before, this music became a great support in threatening moments of despair.

I discovered another area of interest as well. Like every cellar, this one had spiders, and I began a minute observation of their habits. Still more satisfaction came from some field mice, which often clambered into the window recess in search of food. I had always been very fond of animals, and ever since having some mice as childhood pets I had regretted the unfortunate clash of interests that made them the object of merciless treatment on the part of humans. Thus as the days went by, my window visitors and I became friends, and while I helped them out with tidbits of sausage and cheese and bread—which they finally came to eat from my outstretched hand—they helped me as the one tender link between me and all of life outside. They cheered me up with their irrepressible vitality and playfulness. How fortunate they were to lack the perception that could tell them of the virtual certainty of sudden, painful death long before the natural term of their lives was done!

One day, unwittingly, I rewarded their trust in human friendliness with sudden disaster. Apparently eyes on the other side of my door had observed my pastime. While I was delighting in the touch of a little tongue licking the lard off my finger and the feel of a warm body and rapidly beating heart, a shadow suddenly passed across the dull glass of the window and it banged shut. The mouse had fled up the wire screen into a corner of the window recess, where it clung in panic as the cell door opened. I returned to my lunch bowls on the table as two guards walked over to the window. I felt tense from the imminent tragedy but was determined not to give the men the satisfaction of seeing how upset I was. They were looking along the bottom and did not see the mouse. I felt somewhat hopeful. If only they didn't look up. There in the corner, though, a tail looped through the wire mesh.

A third guard appeared in the door, probably the one who had closed the window. The other two were just about to give up and leave the cell when their colleague called out and pointed. He had spotted the mouse's tail; he excitedly left the door and headed toward the window. From their usual extreme caution regarding prison security, these men had lapsed into almost comical carelessness in their preoccupation with my mouse. I was sitting between them and the wide-open cell door with the keys hanging in the lock. In one quick swoop I could have reversed our situation, locking the full complement of guards into my cell and gaining the freedom of the corridor and the means of unlocking all the cell doors. For a moment the idea of doing just that flashed through my mind. Not that I had any illusion of a successful break, but as an act of defiance and revenge—and then I heard the plaintive squealing of the mouse being pulled through the grille and flung to the floor, where it was crushed by a boot to the accompaniment of curses. As the men walked laughing out of the cell, swinging the crushed little body for my special benefit, I was trembling with anger and bitterness. For days thereafter this incident haunted me. Already I had learned to treasure life with the intensity that comes of deprivation, and I could not help feeling deeply aware of a close parallel in the ruthlessness with which both I and the mouse that had befriended me had fallen victim.

The little crack at the top of my window often provided a glimpse of a cloud moving against the blue of the sky. At night it revealed the bulb of a lamp post outside, which sometimes acted as a backdrop to streaks of rain—a visual confirmation of the clatter I heard in a nearby downspout. And one night—truly a

wonder—I saw the bright, clear disk of a full moon with fluffs of cloud scudding across it. A special visitation for me in my tomb, by the world that I had
once known and been a part of. Somewhere far off, this same moon hung over
the night in which Kate and the boys slept. Perhaps she had noticed it too and
had the same thought that it could be seen by both of us, a bond beyond the
reach of man's inhumanity. It happened just that one night. It was over a year
before I caught a glimpse of the moon again.

As my mind rotated continuously through every detail of the weeks before
my disappearance sifting for further clues, it focused increasingly on a third-
floor apartment in a modern block on Warsaw's Szostego Sierpnia, where I had
spent several nights on a spare couch during my visit two years before. It was
there that Lolek—Dr. Leon Gecow—and his pediatrician wife, Anka, lived, old
friends of mine from student days in Zurich. In the first moment of meeting at
the airport in 1947 I had hardly recognized Lolek, for before me stood a colonel
in the Polish army. I could not help laughing at the change: how comically incongruous, nonconformist Lolek in uniform, and with medals at that! As we
embraced, the hilarity spread to them too. It was all part of this unbelievably
changing world, and the most unbelievable thing of all was the unlikely chance
that had, against all logic, brought us together again in the postwar ruins of
Warsaw.

My mind went back ten years to that weekend in August 1939 when the
refugees in Krakow, many hundreds strong, were assisting the civilian population dig zigzag shelter trenches in the parks. Out of the blue I had received a call
from Lodz, the center of Poland's textile industry, lying roughly halfway to
Warsaw.

"Hermann, it's Lolek. We've still got to see each other." There had been an
urgency in his voice. The word "still."

With the clear threat of war in the air, I yearned for his counsel and
strength. I had responded without hesitation: "I'll take the afternoon train tomorrow and then the three of us can be together all of Saturday and most of
Sunday."

I had first met Lolek in the fall of 1934, shortly after I had started my architectural studies in Zurich. Jean and I had just spent the summer in Russia at an
Anglo-American summer school at Moscow University, under the auspices of
the Institute of International Education in New York, which had also negotiated our fellowships in Switzerland. The Russian segment of our journey was a
heady one in that exciting summer following the Roosevelt-Litvinov rap-
prochement and our belated recognition of the Soviet Union. Not only did the
summer school provide a breadth of contact with ordinary Soviet citizens unknown before or later, but some like myself used it also as a jumping-off point

for still broader exploration. After completing six weeks on a city planning seminar with visits to state planning offices, architects, and housing projects, followed by the usual circuit tour of a half dozen show cities, I had felt an overwhelming urge to get a glimpse of the real Russia—rural Russia. Thanks to our own youthful persistence and the imaginative enterprise of a woman official of the Commissariat of State Farms, Jean and I got a good deal more than we had bargained for, spending six weeks as farm laborers on the steppes between the Volga and the Ural Mountains. At last, in an ethnic enclave there of German settlers created by Catherine the Great, language was no barrier to firsthand contact. During those weeks we found ourselves in the conclusive reality of the primitive, suffering Soviet countryside in the aftermath of Stalin's collectivization. While it shocked us, in our ignorance we responded to it as something inevitable, an epochal change long overdue, an agony of birth justified by the promise of a future of abundance. If it seemed violent and ruthless, we explained it away as a uniquely Russian phenomenon!

This baptism in the Soviet experience across the Polish border was our badge of admission to the circle of foreign students to which Lolek and Anka belonged in Zurich. Both were studying medicine at the university, exiles from their own country because of political activity and the fact that as Jews they were discriminated against in admission quotas. Marxist in their general outlook but passionately independent in their thinking, they had shunned the party-line blinkers of some of their fellow antifascist students in Zurich.

Unlike most radicals of the time, Lolek somehow had managed to combine tolerance and an exploring mind with his Marxism, never for a moment losing his awareness of the individual. During my two years in Zurich it was he who provided me with the closest intellectual contact with radical thought. It was he, too, who alerted me to many aspects of the left that I could never accept. While basically regarding himself as a communist, he was merciless in his attacks when he regarded their tactics wrong or when he sensed distortion of theory to suit expediency. It was from him during the first Stalinist purges of the mid-1930s that I had heard the tale of the encounter between the Russian hare and the Polish cow.

Through Lolek I had come in touch for the first time with that atmosphere of intense theoretical preoccupation that I associated with the early flowering of socialist thought in Germany at the turn of the century and also with the long winter darkness around the samovar of czarist Russia. Whenever my eyes became tired at the drafting board of an evening, I would head down the four flights from our mansard room and along the Stapferstrasse to the smoke-filled basement rooms that Lolek and Anka shared, a feverish Central European microcosm in the midst of the clean Swiss mountain air where the ills of the world were invariably being dissected. And whenever a special delicacy in the form of goose fat or Polish sausage had arrived from home, the two of them would climb up to Jean's and my place and we would organize a little feast, adding yogurt and cucumbers and black bread and the cheapest local wine to round out the meal.

Their medical degrees in 1936 brought Lolek and Anka to a dead end. Their Swiss student visas had run out, and Lolek had no choice but to return to Poland for military service. Anka, like so many other antifascist exiles in Zurich, took off for Spain. The Spanish civil war was at its height then, and so Anka went underground to Barcelona, volunteering her medical services to one of the various groups supporting the Republican cause. The particular group she linked up with, composed mainly of the Catalonian anarcho-syndicalist unions, soon ran afoul of the Russians, who increasingly called the shots as the West sold the republic down the river to Franco. Anka finally left, discouraged both by the West's betrayal of the republic and by the internecine struggles among its defenders. Switzerland refused to readmit her. She had no choice but to return home to Lodz as well—and to permanent unemployment in Poland.

And then in August 1939, with Poland on the brink of war, came that phone call in Krakow and the weekend that followed. In Lodz, Lolek's father made available his car and chauffeur to take us deep into the Polish countryside, to a little guest house in a village where, undisturbed by the gathering storm, we could stay until it was time to catch the late-afternoon train back to Krakow on Sunday. The sudden quiet and simplicity of that rural scene was overwhelming. It was as if we had slipped back fifty years into Tolstoy's world with its diminutive wooden farmhouses. I felt intoxicated by the sudden opportunity to unburden myself and to respond to Lolek's questions. He was his old self, never quite satisfied with appearances, examining every alternative interpretation. He was still not fully convinced that war was imminent. The Polish colonels, he said, were too much like Hitler himself in their general ideology. If it came down to it, they might well prefer going with the Nazis against the Russians rather than turning to the Soviet Union as a partner against German aggression.

But hadn't that option been brutally wiped out by the Molotov-Ribbentrop nonaggression pact, signed just a few days before in Moscow? Although nothing had seemed impossible in the aftermath of Munich, didn't this newest twist stand everything on its head? What would be the ultimate impact of the current move on Poland, on war and on peace? At what point in the diplomatic web that had been spun these past months had war become inevitable? Wasn't it in fact Stalin's misguided riposte to the Munich Pact, which essentially invited Hitler to turn east rather than west, that was to blame? And how did we fit into all of this, I from far-off America and they who were destined to share Poland's fate, whatever that was to be?

Imperceptibly, the human jungle of Krakow had melted into just the three of us hunting desperately for answers to these questions. That this was but a last precious moment before the storm's full fury was unleashed seemed sadly inescapable as, from the rear platform of my train back to Krakow, I watched the two figures of Lolek and Anka recede in the distance. When would we see each other again, if ever?

During the war I often thought about that last encounter and wondered about the fate of my two friends. I knew they had inevitably been exposed to the double menace of racial extermination and successive military campaigns that rolled back and forth across their country. Survival would be a miracle indeed. And yet it had happened, and there they had stood, representatives of an unknown Poland barely risen from its ruins, to welcome me and my colleagues two years ago at the airport.

Lolek now held the important position of the army's representative to the Polish Red Cross, while Anka was practicing in a Warsaw children's clinic. Somehow, despite his critical temperament, Lolek had managed to get along with the new regime. He admitted to the deep hostility and distrust faced by the communists, not just on ideological grounds but above all as part of a deeply anti-Russian tradition, the long lesson of Poland's history. As he said with his ironic smile, "Here it's an affliction even among comrades." And unfortunately, the recent experiences during the war had only served to reinforce all the misgivings about their neighbor to the east. Lolek acknowledged that the communists had a frightful lot to live down, but there was nothing to turn back to. Time and the manifest benefits he saw in the course they had set would in the end heal the wounds and bring the population to their support—"provided we meet the size of the responsibility with an equal amount of intelligence," he couldn't help adding. Knowing Lolek and Anka as I did, however, I did not doubt their basic loyalty to the Polish communist regime.

In the perplexing problem of Noel's disappearance, it had been natural that I had thought to turn to Lolek for advice. I wrote from Prague but had received no answer. My first evening in Warsaw I had gone to his and Anka's apartment, only to be told through the closed door that neither of them was at home. To my further question of how I could reach them, the voice claimed not to know their address or when they would be back.

I had gone again several days later, but this time no one even answered the door. Finally I rang up Lolek's office at the Ministry of Defense. His secretary was evasive and refused to give me his vacation address or any indication of when he would be back. Only a few hours before my own disappearance I had made a final visit to their apartment hoping he might have returned that weekend. My concern grew when a phone call to Anka's clinic elicited the reply that she had ceased working there some months before and that her present workplace was unknown. Now, as I paced back and forth in my cell, I recalled that when I had mentioned Lolek as a character reference the night I was picked up, it evoked an exchange of amused glances between Cigarette and the woman who was taking notes, as if to say, "Didn't I tell you so?" And since then I had been asked more than once to describe the whole history of my contacts with him.

Gradually the uneasiness of August had shifted to suspicion, and by now I was convinced that Lolek and Anka had disappeared just like my brother Noel and me. But why? Had Lolek expressed himself too freely? I could imagine that he would have been troubled by the increasing subservience to Soviet dictates. I recalled the reports of the previous spring of the trouncing the party had given Poland's only really popular communist leader, Wladyslaw Gomulka, for resisting the Russianizing trend. My conviction that the Gecows had disappeared became so strong that I listened to coughs and footsteps in the corridor with redoubled attention to see if they were familiar.

The mystery of Lolek and Anka's disappearance heightened my dread that I had fallen into something much bigger and more menacing than could be explained by my photography or even by my search for Noel. But what possible connection could I, coming from far-off America and a professional life long since removed from any political activity, have with all this except that I was aware of the others' disappearance? Was it simply that I had stuck my nose into something that was considered none of my business and so had to be gotten out of the way? Every time my cycle of thought reached this point, I felt a new wave of horror: oblivion.

One Saturday while shaving me, one of the guards who knew a little French asked me about prisons in America. I told him that with us, prisoners could always have books and something to keep them busy. He said it was the same in Poland too. Seeing my surprise, he laughed and said: "No, of course not out here, but in prison, yes—after trial and sentencing." This was indeed a significant scrap of information. So he assumed I would be brought to trial and this cellar was only transitional. Henceforth, whenever the round-and-round journey of my mind brought me to my worst fear, oblivion, I countered it with this clear prospect of a trial, and soon these two concepts became the extreme poles of my continual pendulum swing between hope and despair.

My improvised calendar showed me that it was already October. So did the increasingly frigid air that howled through the gap in my window and under the door. I kept track of the days by means of a hooked piece of straw, which every morning I moved one slot farther along the bottom of the expanded metal grille of the window opening. A few days ago it had reached the thirtieth slot almost at the opposite corner: the end of September. Now it was creeping along once more from the first slot on the left.

Soon it would be the twelfth—Columbus Day. The Macy's parade in New York. I mentally called up all the Columbus Days I could remember—1946, 1945, Hughie on my shoulders, beside me hand in hand, Kate and me by ourselves. Or another image: the final blaze of color of the New England fall. How bittersweet the memory of the sky at Valley Farm, of the stream winding its way through the tufts of uncut brown grass! And soon it would be Thanksgiving. Would it find me still in this distant tomb? Or would all my past gradually become only a hazy memory? I looked at the second straw, which I moved once a week; it recorded the passage of weeks since that August afternoon when life as I knew it had abruptly ended. Tomorrow it would be seven slots up: forty-nine days. There was still a long way till it reached the top, the twenty-second slot. What would I do then? I shivered and turned away.

The only result from my written appeal seemed to be that my existence was forgotten altogether. By now all my hopes focused on the mere chance to speak up, to be heard. For hours each day I went over what I would say when that great moment came. Gradually I memorized it, and it got to be a game to see how many rounds of the room it would take to say it, and then how many times I could say it between breakfast and the changing of the guards at ten o'clock. "Pan Kapiten . . ." it always began. "Pan Kapiten . . . Pan Kapiten . . ." He wouldn't be able to ignore me. I had to speak to him. It became an obsession: I would speak to him and everything would be all right.

Each morning on returning from the washroom I told the guard that I wanted to speak to someone. At first the reply was "Dobra"—All right. Then they didn't bother to say anything anymore. I began to make the same request at mealtimes. Finally I even began to knock on the door in the middle of the morning, after the bell had rung several times and other cells had been opened and the inmates gone upstairs. A few times the guards responded, but then batted their hand in disgust as soon as I started, slamming the door shut again in my face. I began even to envy the rabbits of the night. Wasn't it worth a flogging to get upstairs face to face just for the one time that would clear it all up?

At last one morning the telephone rang and it was in my door that the key turned. After the constant artificial light, my knees almost buckled under me as I entered the corner room upstairs and saw real daylight pouring in through the windows. I dropped to the stool in the corner and in a haze stared at the officer and interpreter waiting silently across the long room.

"Pan Kapiten . . ." My mind went blank. I faltered, tried again. He sat there with a blank sheet in front of him. Then he spoke through the interpreter, interrupting me: "Pan Field, all this doesn't interest us. You don't look well. You are slipping. Why are you so stubborn?"

"But Pan Kapiten, listen to me . . ."

He got up and, a flush of anger spreading across his face, sauntered over toward me. He pointed to my jacket. I followed his look to the ear of rye I had stuck into the lapel. I had plucked it, a delicate frond with a lovely sweep, out of the straw spilling from the torn mattress and adopted it as a kind of talisman to represent nostalgia for the world I could only hear through the crack of my window but no longer see. What was wrong in that?

"Take that off at once and give it to me. Such demonstrations won't get you anywhere here." He returned to the desk.

"Pan Kapiten, for the hundredth time, what is it you want of me?"

"Pan Field, you are doing yourself no good by not talking about what you must. We will not be patient with you forever. In the end you will talk anyway, and meanwhile you have only yourself to thank."

I stared at him in despair. "But Pan Kapiten, let me tell you . . . if it is that you are expecting me to talk about some espionage I committed, then let me tell you it will never, never happen because there is nothing to say. There is nothing to say because I never was a spy for one moment in my life, and you know that as well as I do. I demand an end to this insanity. I demand . . ."

The door opened, and the guard beckoned for me to come. I wanted to ignore him, but the officer got up and snarled, "Stop that, and leave the room at once, do you hear? Go down and think some more about it. I'm not your lawyer."

As I turned I flung back: "That's just it. If there were a lawyer here, as there is everywhere else in the world . . ." I was trembling with anger.

"*Predzej.*" The guard hustled me through the door.

Back in the cellar depression swept over me. More and more I was haunted by a nagging question: what would happen if they didn't believe that I had nothing to hide? They had closed all avenues to any defense, to any means of uncovering their mistake. They were interested in one thing only, and that thing happened not to exist. The more I thought about my plight, the more unbearable it became. Was I doomed to waste the remaining years of my life in this cellar just because I was innocent? How lucky were those of my unknown fellow prisoners who actually had something to confess and be brought to trial for. Down here I would end up going insane, and then what?

A trial—that was it, that was what I needed. If I were tried, my disappearance could no longer be kept a secret. Kate would know what had happened. I would receive a sentence, so many years, but what was that compared with this unendurable void? Still, a trial—in the end that wouldn't help me at all, since they would only try me on the basis of espionage, which didn't exist.

All the cellar sounds came alive again, and they now acquired a new meaning, a new urgency. It was essential to know them well, to be prepared. Wouldn't that be the next stage? If I didn't confess voluntarily, then other means would be used to make me do so. A new horror stood before me. What if they simply kept on and on? If I had held something back, of course, I could always end the agony by confessing. But that relief was not available to me. So they would continue, extending indefinitely this ghastly deadlock that could find no solution. Convinced that the breaking point would be reached at last and that I would confess, they did not know that I did not have that escape in my grasp at all.

But—perhaps I did. I still had time. I could create something for such an emergency. Thinking only of that day which would inevitably come, I feverishly began to recast myself in a role that would bring relief when I could no longer endure. It was not an easy task, and I concocted one conspiracy after another, only to find each inadequate. My story had to be completely credible. Otherwise, if they suspected a fabrication, things would be worse than ever and there would be nothing left to me when I reached the breaking point upstairs. It could also not involve any persons who might as a result fall into the hands of the secret police. From the other side, I wanted to make sure that those who knew me in the West, and above all Kate, could at once spot what I had done if the trial became known, as there was a good chance it would. I was sure the communists would not be able to resist the opportunity of a propaganda turn that would provide an excuse for what they had done. Perhaps I could even go back on my confession once my case reached the courts, provided newspaper correspondents from the West were present. I felt fairly skeptical about this possibility, however; the MBP, the Polish security police, undoubtedly would protect itself against any such contingency. Whatever happened, confession and trial at least meant that the shadow of oblivion would be removed once and for all. I would be out of this cellar. No matter what the verdict, there would be a sentence, a prison term, and I could not be forgotten. Kate would know where I was and what had happened and would be able to fight back.

During the next days a plot took form; inconsistencies were overcome. My fantasy flowed ever more freely. I almost felt proud of the smooth intelligence agent whose careful operations I could recount in such detail. I was excited and almost happy with the release that came from having something to occupy my mind, something constructive at last in place of passive drift. I had decided to set my nefarious activities in the recent postwar period only. My prewar refugee interlude was quite unusable for such distortion. Not only would a story from those times involve some people in the East who might be hurt, but my interrogators would never believe me in any case, no matter what hidden trickery I now revealed—there were simply too many people with whom they could check who would ridicule the whole idea. The benefits the communists had shared in the refugee rescue mission were too evident, as was the record of the lives saved and the affection for me of those who had been a part of those experiences.

Instead, my "spying" had to center on my photography. It was a natural. Both my temporary arrest that Monday morning in front of the Ministry of National Defense and the discovery of my undeveloped film could be made to work in my favor. Hadn't I in effect been caught red-handed attempting to smuggle material out of the country? Hadn't I photographed various government buildings? After all, in this nationalized economy every administrative or industrial building could be placed under this heading. Then there were my many photographs of the new east-west arterial bridge across the Vistula with its tunnel extension right under the heart of Warsaw—a strategic communication line, a natural bombing target in case of hostilities. The fact that I had not photographed anything that could not be found also in hundreds of pictures in newspaper and magazine illustrations could be conveniently ignored. For even the most innocent picture of reconstruction, some subtle hidden intention could no doubt be claimed.

But the most helpful angle was my 1947 study tour, when I and my colleagues—Americans all—had photographed like mad. At that time we had avoided the color film problem by having a small amount of black-and-white film developed and simply saying nothing about the color rolls for which no processing facilities existed. Responsible Poles themselves had recommended this course to me, and more than likely the customs officials had quite consciously closed their eyes. Now, as a consequence, the MBP had no way of knowing what was in those pictures. I was free to "reveal" this information and fit it to my group's espionage "assignment." We had traveled very widely through the country from north to south, had visited important factories such as the railway car plant in Wroclaw, and had made an extensive inspection tour by boat through the harbor installations in war-devastated Szczecyn. What a paradise of possibilities! According to this scenario, my spying activities could have been done completely unbeknownst to the Czechs and Poles we had met, who were merely innocent dupes, fooled by the respect in which I was held for my 1939 relief work. My sole handler, from whom I received my secret instructions, was safely far beyond the border.

The person I chose for this role was real. This was important to enable me to describe all details of circumstances and environment without any slips or inconsistencies, and also to prevent premature discovery of the fiction in any checking the Polish authorities might be able to do in the West. He was in fact a neighbor to whom I had shown my slides in 1948 and who since that time had taken a position in Europe on an educational project. In my story this "educational" work, like my reconstruction study tour, had only been a cover for actual intelligence activity, my friend's assignment being connected with a secret strategic photo file on numerous aspects of the communist countries. I would claim that I had been one of his operatives on my trip in 1947 and again during my visit this summer.

The thing that gave me the most trouble was motivation. Hadn't I just written an impassioned plea stating the impossibility of my ever having engaged in spying? Money as motivation was out; it fit neither my circumstances nor my character. Professional agent in a double life was equally questionable. The record of 1939 and my recent analysis of my beliefs made it just as difficult to dress myself in the garb of anticommunist crusader.

Finally I had it: I had slid into this spying against my will as a result of political blackmail at home. I would paint a lurid picture of the political climate in America after the war. There had been plenty in the press about hounding not only communists but also liberals and people with occasional left-wing associations like myself. In the planning of an important university development project I concocted some trouble with the FBI because of my participation in efforts on behalf of Soviet reconstruction and the controversy in which my brother was alleged to be a Soviet agent. My story went that I was told that I would not be molested, but only if I used my contacts in the communist satellite countries and went there under the guise of friendly architect to fulfill specific U.S. intelligence assignments. To save my career, I agreed. That cover, corroborated by my photographing, would, I felt sure, fit the psychology of my interrogators like a glove. Wasn't it exactly in line with that opening remark the night I was taken to Warsaw? "Architect? You're sure you're not an archaeologist instead?" I could see Blackie's sarcastic smile.

I was well satisfied with my construction. The nighttime sounds through my door and ceiling no longer frightened me so much. I was ready.

After two months of uncertainty and isolation in the cellar world, my mind had begun to follow a pattern it took me years to overcome. As a result of the mouse-cage wheel of thought that takes possession of a human being in such circumstances, the slightest crack, appearing at first only on the periphery of the mind's activities, at once sucks in all of consciousness. From that point on the person builds and builds upon a weak foundation, believing that the one answer has at last been found. The pent-up inactivity releases a sort of chain reaction that is impossible to hold back, in which everything that went before is recast to fit the picture and all "ifs" are brought in as ammunition. In a frenzy of unrealistic planning everything is set on that ultimate goal, and no warning doubts are tolerated, as they would mean a return to the void and the mouse wheel. During the past months I had already attempted several such mental flights, only to crash miserably back to reality in the end. I was still smarting from the experience of writing my appeal some weeks before. How many times in the years ahead was I to repeat this sort of zigzag performance, with its demoralizing aftereffects on discovering how completely my judgment had failed me.

The night following my final decision to take the initiative I lay awake until the early hours of the morning perfecting every smallest detail. I would be sitting again in the sun-bathed room, the endless waiting broken, the preparation for my trial having taken its place. I would no longer be a forgotten nobody. The moment would soon come when Kate would know I was alive.

I had spent the last hours in such intense absorption with my new identity that I was hardly aware it had nothing whatsoever to do with reality. At breakfast time, therefore, I told the head guard to report to the *kapiten* that I had thought things over as he had suggested and that I now had something specific to say to him.

It was Saturday. At lunchtime I was told the officer would see me on Monday. I was disappointed; I wanted to get it over with, now that I had burned my bridges behind me. I paced back and forth hour after hour. That night I again went over it all for the hundredth time. Sunday came. My enthusiasm began to wear off and the first doubts appeared. What if my story were so plausible that even Kate was persuaded? And all my friends, what would they think? Would the final record charge me with duplicity, a double life? What effect would it have on Hugh and Alan? And wouldn't the publicity wreck the career of my friend? Even if the U.S. authorities knew it was a fabrication, it would still have an element of plausibility. Some doubt would remain. And could I count on my status as a foreigner to be a mitigating factor in the sentencing? If I took this step, there would be no way back. If I were sentenced to life imprisonment or even given death, I would have only myself to blame.

All Sunday night I wavered. Finally the overwhelming polarity of my story pushed me in the opposite direction with equal conviction. I gasped at the danger I had almost brought down on my head. It had been sheer insanity. By the morning I had decided I would not go through with the confession under any circumstance, not even with the severest torture. But now I was in panic. What would I say? I thought feverishly. The morning advanced. All I could finally think of was the names of some people I had forgotten at the time of writing my account. I would tell him about them as the reason for wanting to speak to him, and then once again I would assert the impossibility of my being a spy.

The key turned. I went upstairs. I said good morning. The two faces across the room looked at me with keen expectation. She said, "You have thought things over. You have asked to speak to the captain. Well then, please proceed."

For a moment I had the wild idea of making the confession after all. How easy it would be. I was keenly aware of the mysterious grille in the ceiling exactly over my head. I had noticed it uneasily each time I had been up here. Was it meant to intimidate any prisoner who found himself sitting here? Or was there something more ominous to it?

No, I couldn't. I wouldn't, not under any circumstance. I began uncertainly. "Yes, I thought you might like to know . . . it is that I recalled several important names that I neglected to include in my biographies . . ."

She was already translating what I was saying. I saw his face harden. "Pan Field." She repeated his words as he rose behind the desk. "Pan Field, is that all you have to say?" He seemed to hiss the question at me.

I nodded. "But Pan Kapiten . . . ," and I started on the plea I had half prepared. The door opened before I had said half a sentence and I was hustled from the room without a word.

Day followed day again in monotonous sequence. Now it seemed as if my cell had sunk into the timelessness of a tomb. Even the life of the cellar, restricted as it was, seemed to bypass door No. 4. The cold down here had become ever more unbearable. My clothes were less than I normally wore in midsummer. In spite of the blankets wrapped around me and over my head, I felt continuously chilled through. At night, as a result, I struggled, turning and curling up between wakefulness and sleep, never able to get warm. What would happen when December came, or January? How would I survive?

Again the maddening what-ifs. What if I hadn't received the architectural fellowship in Zurich in 1934. What if my father hadn't died in 1921. What if I hadn't gotten to know Kate in 1938.

I played a game with myself each day: What chance was there still of a trial? How great was the likelihood of the alternative, that I was on my way to disappearing for good? In October I had thought 50-50. Then it had gone down to forty percent in favor of a trial. By now, I thought, the odds had sunk to ten percent—as had my morale, to the same degree. So, with life it was all over. Hughie and Alan would grow up, marry, but for me they would never be more than two little boys aged six and four. When a person dies, he is spared the pain of seeing the world go on without him. It soon forgets even that he ever existed. I, however, was dead and alive at the same time; yes—buried alive in a tomb. Ten years from now it would be just the same in here, but outside ten full years of happenings would have left their mark on everything. Blessed be the dead.

To break the morbidity of my thoughts I tried to occupy my fingers by breaking straw into small slivers and then making abstract designs on the table top, as I sat on my chair with my back to the door and the Judas eye. Imperceptibly the patterns began to take concrete form. Letters emerged: my name in golden capitals across the middle of the table. I became fascinated; how defiant it looked in this anonymity! I went on, did a second line: AMERICAN ARCHITECT. Like an echo—my nationality, the career that had been mine in life; like looking at something back in time. I made a frame of straw lines around it. There was something missing: dates. Laboriously I did a third line: "1910," and then "–1949." My hand was trembling. My epitaph. It looked bleak. I thought of my talisman: the ear of rye. I went over to my straw sack and picked out two especially delicate ones and arranged them with their stems crossing in the blank space just below the dates. I got up and surveyed my handiwork from all sides, quite forgetting about the Judas eye in the door. Well, at least my existence in here had been recorded once. There, shining golden under the glare of the electric bulb, was testimony to the fact that I had existed, had been a part of this world for all of thirty-nine years. Nothing my tormentors did could undo this fact.

The key turned, the bolts rattled, breaking the spell. The head guard walked over to the table. He stared silently at the epitaph, then at me. What storm had I precipitated now? He shook his head slowly and stood undecided for a moment. Then he reached out and swept the pieces off the table and into his hand. As he left the cell he said in German, "Very bad. Forbidden. This time I didn't see." The door closed. I stared forlornly at the blank tabletop, but at the same time I appreciated the touch of human decency and felt grateful for it.

Usually the cellar was relatively peaceful during the day. The quiet was accentuated by the felt slippers worn by the guards as they moved from Judas eye to Judas eye. It was typical of the perversity of everything here that it was only when the prisoners, after fourteen hours of being on their feet, at last could retire exhausted to their beds that their presence became noticed, as both floors of the building exploded into the cycle of nocturnal activity. Sometimes, however, certain cells—especially the "special" miniature ones opposite me—were kept in commotion twenty-four hours a day.

One afternoon a sudden crescendo of activity focused on three cells. On two, the bolts were slammed back and forth at intervals like the firing of guns. Opposite, a light was continually switched on and off. I sat at the table with my back to the door, listening and getting more and more worked up. I could imagine the hapless individual approaching the point of collapse. Suddenly the door opposite flew open. A commotion. The splash of water. I winced as if the target had been me. How could a human being survive such an ordeal? A quiet settled across the corridor. I felt instinctively that someone was outside looking through the Judas eye at my back. I was still boiling inside and pretended not to notice, but just sat unmoving at the table.

Suddenly the key was inserted and the bolt flew back as the door opened. I looked around and got up. A young fair-haired man stood in the door staring angrily at me. I stood immobile and stared back, trembling. So this was the beast who had been amusing himself across the corridor. He took a few steps toward me and glanced around the cell as if looking for something wrong. His eyes fixed on the straw spilling out at the foot end of my bed from the disintegrating sack. He pointed to it and hissed in German, "What's that? Prefers to live like a pig in here, eh?"

I shrugged. What did he want of me? I held myself back, sensing that trouble was brewing. "There's nothing I can do about it. The sack is torn."

He strode over and in one swoop grabbed one end of my mattress and swung it with its covers and pillow in a big arc across the cell, scattering its contents of crumbled straw from one end to the other. "Now get going, you." (He was using the familiar *du* as an added insult.) "Mind that you make order here and that you pick up every single piece of straw—every single piece, do you hear? You'll learn it doesn't pay to live like a pig. Do you understand?" And he shook his finger close to my face.

I didn't move. I didn't know whether I was more afraid of him or of myself and what I might do. I had a momentary impulse to spit in his face. If he dared to touch me, I would strike back with everything in me. I was trembling with anger and humiliation.

"Well, how about it?"

I was silent. He stared at me dubiously. The expression in his eyes and play about his mouth suggested the worst. Abruptly, however, he turned toward the door, saying: "I'll give you fifteen minutes to tidy up here—and mind you, not one piece of straw on the floor."

The door slammed shut. I stood alone in the chaos around me. I stared at the door. Let him come back in fifteen minutes; I would leave everything just as it was. But did that make sense? Shouldn't all my efforts go in just the one direction of making survival possible at whatever cost, even if it meant cringing like a whipped dog? Yes, even at that cost. What was pride in circumstances such as mine?

I picked up the blanket and sheet. I gathered together the main scatterings of straw, then I tried to brush together the thinner bits, using a bundle of straw as a broom. It didn't work, so I started on hands and knees at one corner of the cell, picking up pieces individually with my fingers. I didn't finish until supper, by which time I was in an almost contented frame of mind. No matter what it might be, at least it was something to do and had made the hours go by faster than they would have otherwise. I almost smiled to myself. I'd foxed him after all!

After the sad incident weeks before with my little friend the mouse I had stopped putting food in the window opening to discourage others from coming in. As my solitude and despair increased, though, so did my yearning for contact with these small visitors. I waited each day for a head to pop up over the window sill, and if none appeared I felt deprived. I lay awake at night waiting for the rustling sound among the dried leaves behind the bars. I missed their presence, the living warmth of their little bodies. I recalled a wearisome childhood sickness that was transformed into happy play by some tame white mice that I was allowed to put into my bed for a while each day. I remembered how they scurried around between the sheets, making little tunnels as they went, in perpetual movement. If only I could have one of my little visitors in the cell with me now, something alive to share my loneliness; then I could turn my back on all of man's evil work. That was out of the question, though; it would be noticed running around and quickly dispatched. But what if I did the same as when I was a child? What if I kept it hidden away in my bed? It would be as safe there as outside. Hadn't I noticed the silhouette of a prowling cat, to which several mice had already fallen victim? The need became irresistible.

And so it came about that one morning a Polish field mouse descended quite against its will into my cell and found itself deposited on my pillow, whence it took prompt refuge under the covers just as I had anticipated. I had a cell mate, a fellow prisoner. That night I lay immobile, keyed for the slightest movement. I was rewarded when finally I felt something hot and soft brush against my leg, circle my foot, come up the other side, then hustle back along the same route. It was the happiest moment since my descent into this cellar. I was no longer alone. I lay still all night, hardly daring to move lest I accidentally crush my little ally against solitude. Often when I woke up for a moment I could feel it here or there, up near my pillow or down at the other end. Every now and then I could sense the lightning movements of its paws in that face-cleaning ritual that was a sure sign of contentment.

The next afternoon the door suddenly opened and Shoo dragged in a new straw mattress packed tight as a sausage. He pointed to my bed and indicated that he wanted to have the old one. But my mouse? When I took off the covers it would jump on the floor and be discovered. I gathered everything in one bundle, hoping the mouse would be picked up together with the covers, and laid

the heap carefully on the table. Out it all went with Shoo. Alone again, I placed
the mountainous sack on the frame. A wonderful smell of fresh straw pervaded
the cell, evoking a chain of nostalgic remembrances of harvesting in the fall, of
nights spent in Swiss mountain barns on school expeditions.

As I laid out the covers one by one over the mattress I felt desolate, feeling
the keen loss of my little friend. How delighted I was, then, when, having returned from the evening bucket cycle, the door closed again behind me, I saw a
mouse scampering along the wall! It must have slipped back in from the corridor unnoticed while I was in the wash cubicle. Soon it had taken refuge somewhere in my bed. *Appell* came and I clambered up onto the straw mountain,
finding myself eighteen inches higher from the floor than before. It was difficult
getting under the covers, they were pulled so tight. Again I waited for the feel of
the warm vibrant body hurrying along my side. Several times I imagined it, but
always it turned out to be nothing. Several times during the night I woke up and
looked around the floor to see if it had perhaps left the bed. No sign anywhere.
By the morning I was alarmed. I took the covers off, one by one. No mouse.
Then I rolled the mattress over on the plank frame. There it was—dead,
crushed. It had apparently crawled under the sack when I got into bed and had
been pinned there by the weight of my body. So I had been the cause of destroying this mouse's life, too.

A person living a normal life simply cannot comprehend how sharply such
apparently trivial happenings affect a human being deprived of all living contact and driven to the very edge of loneliness. I had suffered already so much
from human ruthlessness that I felt disgust with myself at the egotism that had
wantonly increased the world's load of suffering, even if it was only the agony of
a small mouse. Life had become infinitely precious to me, and yet I had
thoughtlessly deprived this little animal of something it had as much right to as
I. Even with a mouse, could the need to make my own lot more bearable justify
sacrificing its one life? Surely one ruthlessness doesn't justify another in a sort of
chain of evil.

My despair grew. I tried to shake it off by creating elaborate escape fantasies.
Sometimes my escape focused on one of those freight trains I could hear before
dawn. I would work out detailed plans for every contingency—except, of
course, the initial problem of how to get out of the cellar, for which I had no
solution. Sometimes the escape would be on foot. Once in town, I would hide
in the dark near the entrance to the Hotel Bristol until a car bearing the official
American emblem would stop outside. I would slip in unnoticed, revealing
myself only once it was under way, and we would make a dash for the embassy
compound, American soil. This was but one of a hundred different variants.

At other times I countered self-pity by reminding myself that I was not by any means alone in my misery. For the first time in my life, wasn't I in fact in the mainstream of humanity? Wasn't I exaggerating my misfortune as something that should shock the world? Although I kept asking, How could such a thing happen? wasn't it more apt to ask, How could such a thing happen to *me*, Hermann Field, American, Harvard Class of '32? Such things and much, much worse were commonplace. They were happening all the time, all over the face of the earth, and always had. Not just in the form I was experiencing, but injustice, brutality, death, famine, maiming disease, war. The score went into the millions. Heretofore I had been among the small fortunate minority. Now I was getting a taste of that other side, the vast well of human suffering. I began to think about people I had known who had gone through searing experiences in the course of their lives. I thought about those who had lost out.

I tried to put myself in the situation faced by people in the Nazi extermination camps, during the Warsaw uprising, in Hiroshima, or the people dragged from their homes for no reason whatsoever to waste away as a new type of slave in Siberia. It was a never-ending stream, just that of our own time alone, of the last decade, so pervasive that it lost dimension altogether as I looked back through the history of man. Here I was no longer alone. Here there was much to learn from. Why in normal life does it mean so little to us? Can we begin to see only when we are struck down ourselves?

Increasingly there were times, too, when I could not focus my mind at all anymore, when the void opened wide before me. As I walked around and around the table in the small floor space, a hundred circles clockwise and then a hundred the other way, and then back again, all I could do was concentrate on the patterns of the bricks, the irregularities created by patches of moisture, the shadows of the table and chair and plank frames. Gradually they became animated; as my attention fixed on them, I recognized the contours of familiar faces. A bearded professor I had known; a friend from my youth; the sculpturesque features of the Italian prime minister DeGasperi—a gallery of changing portraits.

Then I saw a lovely boy's head, face averted, sad, ever so familiar. I felt panic, a crowding sense of guilt. It was Hughie, troubled and hurt, unable to comprehend the sudden dissolution of his family security. On the next pass, I tried not to look at that spot but searched among the bricks for something else—I knew I shouldn't, but I couldn't resist. I found it: Kate—there over near the door where the moisture had come through. I didn't dare stop, but waited with suspense until the next round would bring me to the same point again. There was no mistaking it: she was looking up with her slightly upturned nose.

I was breathless. I kept going, faster, faster. Again I saw her. It got to be the focal point of each pass around the cell. Hughie, Kate. Hughie, Kate, faster, faster, one hundred rounds, two hundred, three, four, pacing ever faster, my eyes focused on the bricks rushing by beneath me. Why didn't I get dizzy? Why didn't I lose consciousness and fall and break this inescapable circle of images and bricks and hectic chasing after nothing? But I knew I wouldn't. I knew I could go on till the clatter of bolts announced a temporary halt for food, and then again on along my circular course until the next station stop—night, and the goal at last: dazed exhaustion and heavy sleep.

Was I going crazy? Once the thought rose in my mind it brought a new terror to my existence. If I even once lost a grip on myself, everything would be lost. I recalled the accounts I had read of the hell of mental institutions, even in our supposedly enlightened age. I had a vivid memory of one I had visited as part of a course in college. In the inferno in which I found myself now, it was not difficult to imagine how such a thing would be dealt with. Perhaps the two inmates of the cells across from me had gone crazy and that was the reason for the special load of misery that had descended on them. I knew I must forestall any such possibility.

My mind shifted to another emerging preoccupation: simply putting an end to it all. Better now, when I still had the will for it and the strength to carry it through. I had been searching for some way. There was the sheet, of course, but nothing high enough in the cell to tie it to. And anyway, such an attempt would be noticed long before I could achieve my goal. I had thoughts of diving off the table onto the brick floor. But wouldn't a reflex prevent full impact? It would probably just lead to permanent crippling, nothing more.

Finally I began to explore another approach. The buttons of my prison shirt and underpants were made of cloth-covered thin metal disks on a cardboard backing. On Saturday I handed back my shirt with a button missing. No one noticed. I took it apart at night under my covers and on successive nights sharpened it surreptitiously on the metal frame. It turned out to be too small and weak to pierce the skin. The next Saturday I removed a larger one, which again went unnoticed. This time I tried to sharpen it on the wood plank frame, a little every night, to try to avoid breaking the edges in the process. Again I failed. I started a third button. If only I could succeed. This way everything could happen in bed, with no one noticing until it was too late. But it was no use.

A new blow fell. My table was the one thing that gave my cell a faintly human character. I had feared it would be taken away when my writing stopped, but it had survived successive worsenings of my circumstances. Suddenly one afternoon, though, the door opened and Shoo and a new, unpleasant-looking guard with a diminutive mustache marched in and without a word lugged it out, together with the chair. I stood desolate in the barren cell. When so little is left, each thing acquires an importance out of all proportion. It seemed to me I had lost another round.

By the next day I had gotten over the first shock of my loss. I suspected, though, that this setback in my cellar existence was merely a portent of something more. Without knowing why, I waited with increasing dread of further change. It was not long in coming.

# 8

## London 1949

How I longed for the nights, and sleep. "Sleep that knots up the ravelled sleeve of care . . ." How true it was. In sleep one's spirit is mended a little, enough to face another day, which again will unravel it. Without sleep one breaks. Often the night was not long enough and I fought to stay asleep, to postpone coming back to the thought that always jolted me awake: This thing has happened to us. He is suffering, and I cannot help him.

Odd scraps of poetry, or of the Bible, would come back to me and run endlessly in my head, their profound human understanding revealed to me often for the first time.

I was generally the first one downstairs in the mornings, where I anxiously pulled the newspapers from the letterbox to scan them for clues. And here one came: the *Times,* September 10, 1949—"The Hungarian government indicts Laszlo Rajk for treason . . . Noel Field denounced as American agent." Rajk had been Hungary's foreign minister and a high-ranking communist. I read on in amazement and horror. Here in black and white was Noel's name—our family's name. He was being accused by the communists, when Hermann was in their hands, and Herta in their territory. And where was he?

I leaned against the stair rail feeling utterly ill. The words of Hermann's letter came back to me: that something had happened to Noel was for me alone; for everyone else, illness. To keep that up was no longer possible. Herta's optimism was wrong, completely.

My father came down and I showed him the paper.

"Where is Noel, anyway?"

"I don't know. And I don't think Herta and Hermann do either. We'll have to talk to the embassy."

I hardly knew Noel. I knew that he had worked during the war helping refugees from Hitler's Germany and the various countries that Germany had over-run. I believed he was a Good Samaritan who had sacrificed his health and risked his safety doing this. I had also heard that he was at least somewhat sym-pathetic to communism, which made it seem absurd to suggest that he had spied for America against the communist states. At home in the Hiss trial it had even been suggested that he was a Russian agent. What a fantastic situation, to be accused by both sides at the same time!

The House Committee on Un-American Activities was trying to show that under Roosevelt communists had gotten footholds in the administration that could be dangerous now that the wartime alliance with the USSR was over. In the summer of 1948 they found an ex-communist, Whittaker Chambers, who stated that Alger Hiss of the State Department, who had been the United States delegate to the founding conference of the United Nations in San Francisco, had been in a communist group in the State Department way back in the 1930s. Chambers said that Hiss had passed official papers to him. Hiss denied the charge and sued Chambers for slander. Although so much time had passed since these events that Hiss could no longer be accused of espionage, he was charged with perjury for his denial.

The first Hiss trial started on May 31, 1949. Evidence revealed that Hiss knew Noel Field, who in the 1930s was also a young man working in the State Depart-ment. Noel left the department in 1936, after participating in the London Naval Conference of 1934. He had become increasingly unhappy with U.S. foreign pol-icy, particularly its failure to take a stand against the threat of fascism in Europe. I thought that probably he no longer wanted to be in a position of promoting a policy he had ceased to believe in. He had always been a person of strong opinions, and by 1949 he was suspected of being a communist sympathizer.

I could see how in the current climate of American public opinion, if Noel had been subpoenaed as a witness, he might well have done harm to Hiss.

We waited expectantly to see if Noel would be produced as a witness in the Rajk trial—perhaps even Hermann as well—though it was hard to see why ei-ther of them should be in Hungary. But the trial ended without giving us any real evidence as to where they were. Allen Dulles, head of the Central Intelli-gence Agency and formerly with the wartime Office of Strategic Services, had also been accused in the trial, but no one suggested that the Hungarians were holding him. No more did they need to have Noel. Nevertheless, the State De-partment now started to make inquiries for Noel and Herta. Neither I nor her friends in Switzerland had heard from Herta since August 26, and the theory that she was still waiting quietly in Prague for Hermann to turn up had to be abandoned. Perhaps it was no mere accident that Rajk had not been tried until two weeks after Noel's closest relatives had also disappeared.

The proceedings of the Rajk trial, published in Budapest by the Hungarian government and printed in English under the title *Laszlo Rajk and His Accomplices before the People's Court*, were on sale in England at a low price. Presumably they thought it was good propaganda, but at 315 pages it was hardly attractive to the general reader. Yet perhaps even its stodginess could be an asset, making it appear a painstaking document, while few people would bother to read it to the end to grasp its full absurdity. For me it had a real interest: to discover how Noel's name had become involved, as well as any clues that might help get our family out of its present mess.

It was also an interesting political document, because around Rajk and his "accomplices" a whole communist thesis was developed that I could see would set a pattern for similar show trials to come. The indictment accused Laszlo Rajk and others of "attempts to overthrow the democratic order of Hungary and other crimes." In twenty pages the prosecution's case was outlined, ending with this political conclusion:

Laszlo Rajk and his companions set up an organization which had for its aim the overthrow of Hungarian democracy which is secured by constitutional law, the destruction of the independence of Hungary, and Hungary's enslavement to a foreign power. Rajk and his band set themselves the aim of tearing Hungary out of the camp of the defenders of peace, which is the only guarantee of the freedom and happiness of our people, of chaining our country to the imperialist war front and thus lowering it to be a satellite and toy of the imperialists. They hoped to realize this aim with the armed help of the present leaders of the Yugoslav state, Tito, Rankovich, Kardelj and Djilas.

Rajk and his band wanted to annihilate all the great achievements of the Hungarian people's democracy, to give the land distributed to the peasants back to the great landowners, the mines and factories to the big capitalists, again to shackle the hands of the working people and again to put the enemies of the Hungarian people who had fled to the west into power.

The conspirators wanted to lower Hungary to be a Yugoslav colony, a colony of Tito, who together with his band deserted from the camp of Socialism and of the democracies, who deserted into the camp of foreign capital and reaction, and thus made Yugoslavia a satellite of the imperialists.

Behind the plan of Rajk and his companions, too, there stood American imperialism which, in the German and Austrian zones of occupation, has already assembled its bloodhounds, those arrow-cross, fascist, Horthyist ex-officers and ex-gendarmes who are calculating that, as in 1944, they can again wade knee-deep in the blood of the Hungarian working people, and again—this time in the interests not of German fascism but of American imperialism—can sell Hungary and thus ruin and annihilate all the results of our Liberation and reconstruction.

Laszlo Rajk and his companions, in order to attain these criminal and base aims, did not stop at any banditry. . .

Rajk was one of the top men of the Hungarian Communist Party. He had been minister of internal affairs but after Tito's split with the Russian-sponsored Communist Information Bureau (Cominform) was given the less crucial, but still important, position of foreign minister. His codefendants also had long records of Communist Party service. With such backgrounds, I could not conceive of any motive that would be sufficient to induce these men to embark on a hazardous attempt to "restore capitalism" in Hungary.

Naturally, I approached the trial from a lay Westerner's viewpoint. The extraordinary fact was that all the defendants pleaded guilty, then proceeded in enormous detail to recount their crimes. In fact, they produced all the evidence against themselves. As if to prove its genuineness, the trial was open to the press, and reporters from fourteen countries were present—including the United States and Britain. Some reported that the accused seemed to be stating their confessions as if they were learned by heart. The more I read of the actual proceedings, the clearer I could see the "lessons" to be drawn from the confessions—confessions the political content of which seemed more appropriate to a Marxist treatise than to a speech by a man on trial for his life. It seemed that, far from defending themselves, the accused were merely helping the prosecutor develop his thesis. Andras Szalai's hearing ended this way:

Szalai: It was hypocrisy...
Prosecutor: Deceit.
Szalai: It was deceit.
Prosecutor: Treason.
Szalai: It was treason.
Prosecutor: So this was your activity. I have no more questions.
President of the Court: Does the Defense have any questions?
(None). Return to your seat, Andras Szalai.

The defense never did have any questions. Every statement of the accused was accepted. And when it came to the formal speeches for the defense at the end, the counsel were careful to assume the guilt of their clients on all major charges, thus making it impossible for anyone to take seriously any appeals for a "lenient sentence," as was made for Rajk himself.

The confession of the accused in a capital case should not be sufficient in itself to convict. In this case there were also the statements of the various accused incriminating each other, and there were some witnesses. There was no indication in the printed report of the trial that the witnesses were also under arrest, but considerably later I discovered that this was so in the case of at least one witness, Sandor Cseresnyes. An American businessman who was arrested in Hungary not long after the Rajk trial, Robert Vogeler, shared a cell with Cseresnyes, whose story he tells in his book *I Was Stalin's Prisoner*, incidentally revealing that Cseresnyes had been imprisoned since May 25—after Noel disappeared, and just before Rajk was arrested. Vogeler also describes the methods used to force Cseresnyes to incriminate Rajk.

In the trial neither the accused nor the witnesses were sworn to tell the truth, though the president of the court had evidently heard of such a procedure, since, after hearing one witness, he quaintly asked: "Is there a proposal to put the witness under oath? (None. The Court waived its right to make the witness take the oath.)"

Noel's name appeared frequently in the trial. In the indictment he was referred to as "One of the chiefs in Switzerland of the American espionage organization known as the 'Office of Strategic Services' (O.S.S.)." Dr. Tibor Szonyi in particular was accused of being connected with Noel in Switzerland, as well as with Allen Dulles, for "Field specialized in recruiting spies from among so-called 'left-wing' elements, and the various émigré espionage groups of different nationalities in Switzerland were subordinate to him." Nowhere in the trial was there any attempt to prove these assertions. Yet such proof was crucial, for unless Noel truly was acting as an American spy, the elaborate structure built on this assumption would fall to the ground.

Even supposing Noel had indeed met some of these Hungarians when they were in exile, there could be alternative explanations. He had met hundreds of refugees, including communists, in the course of his work for the Unitarian Service Committee, and had helped them in various ways. That he had any connection with the OSS, or with any intelligence agency, was news to both me and his sister, Elsie. We did not know whether to believe it, and thought it unlikely to be true. But even if it were true, there was still a perfectly reasonable explanation: during the Second World War we and the Russians were allies against Germany. Underground movements in the territories occupied by or allied with Hitler were considered a legitimate part of our war effort. Any of these refugees cooperating in such efforts would have done so as a part of their personal fight against Hitlerism. If any of the Hungarian communists in question had helped the OSS, it would have been against Hitler's ally, Admiral Horthy of Hungary, not against a nonexistent postwar regime, destined to be communist.

The trial revealed an interesting sequence of dates. We found later that Noel had disappeared from Prague on May 12. Dr. Tibor Szonyi, whose confession suggested that he had in fact met Noel, was arrested on May 18, on the same day as Andras Szalai, whose testimony also contained many references to Noel. Rajk was arrested on May 30. It could be that in questioning Noel they had come upon Szonyi and Szalai, who in turn had given them a lead to Rajk. But if the

Hungarians had been picking Noel's brain, why had they not produced him as a witness? If he had really been an American agent against them, his testimony would have been invaluable to the prosecution. The natural inference was that Noel had been no such thing and that the Hungarians had failed to get a false confession from him or felt that he could not be relied on to give one in court.

Yet another alternative existed: that the Hungarians did not themselves hold Noel but had only been given information obtained from him. After all, so far as we knew Noel had not intended to go to Hungary. Hermann had disappeared in Poland, and possibly now Herta in Prague. This had become an international mystery of a sinister sort. People drew parallels between the Rajk trial and trials that had gone on in Russia from time to time, ever since the revolution. Was Russia behind the scenes, stage-managing it all?

With the passage of death sentences on Rajk, Szonyi, and Szalai and the imprisonment of the others, the macabre affair was over. The evidence was unconvincing, but the fact that they were communists prevented any great sympathy for them abroad, and possibly even at home. But the personal tragedies remained, one more monument to man's inhumanity to man. Their comrades in the communist movement all over the world would, of course, believe them guilty. I had no doubt they were men who had devoted their lives to the cause of communism, believing it to be good. But the philosophy that the end justifies the means had borne bitter fruit, demanding the sacrifice even of these faithful servants. Didn't one see how impossible it was for them to defend themselves? What, in the end, had they to live for?

What were the real reasons for this trial? It was unlikely that the Hungarian Communist Party could afford to decimate its leadership without some compelling reason. Yet the trial showed that in fact little, if anything, had actually happened. These men were supposed to be involved in a conspiracy, but as counsel for Rajk admitted, "He shrank from taking the final steps. It is a fact that before anything could have happened, the conspiracy was discovered." They were sentenced, then, for acts they *might* commit in the future.

Perhaps Rajk was a man who thought too much, or knew too much, or was simply too Hungarian. Although the trial was reminiscent of those in the Soviet Union in the 1930s, the basic reason for it lay in the special circumstances of the world after World War II, the competition between the communist and noncommunist states.

Moscow had fathered the Cominform, which was ostensibly a clearing house for information to be shared by those Communist Parties in control of national governments. That it was in fact more than this had been clearly shown in 1948, when Marshal Tito declined to take Russian advice on how the revolution should proceed in Yugoslavia and brought down on his head a shower of abuse. The Cominform supported Moscow, and Tito was expelled from it.

This meant that Moscow could no longer control Yugoslavia. Its Communist Party had become a renegade group, no longer willing to be influenced by the paternalistic party of the Soviet Union. Particularly in the Cold War, this was a serious defeat for Stalin, and he set about seeing that it would not be repeated in other countries.

But how could he make sure of this? Once the rift had occurred, he would have lost the upper hand. How could he openly intervene to make a Communist Party desert its leadership and follow the Moscow line? The surest thing was to prevent the situation from ever arising, and this could be done only by removing from positions of leadership in the satellite parties any men who might show the independence of Tito.

At the same time, this had to be done without revealing that Moscow had played a role in it. The U.S. State Department believed there were Soviet advisers attached to the security police of the satellite states, as well as Soviet agents working among them. Through such channels it would be possible to achieve Rajk's downfall, bypassing the Hungarian Communist Party as such.

The trial was also a convenient occasion to read a lecture to all the satellite peoples, propounding the Soviet thesis on the machinations of the United States and Yugoslavia. The people should be made to feel that everything the West did, even the charitable work of religious organizations, was only a "cloak for espionage activities." We were not to be trusted—and even the leaders of their own Communist Party were not to be trusted too much. Russia was their real friend.

The trial also indicated that Hungary would not be alone in undergoing a cleansing. The Yugoslav defendant, Brankov, said that Tito had plans to subvert Rumania and Poland as well, and had hopes of doing this through Wladyslaw Gomulka, secretary of the Polish Communist Party, "But he did not carry it out and admitted this was a wrong line." In 1949 Gomulka duly went into obscurity. Czechoslovakia was not forgotten either, and Szonyi asserted that through Noel the OSS "had established a similar contact with the Czechoslovak group, notably with Pavlik [a Czech] . . . and further with a German Trotskyist group whose leader was Politzer, and with other countries, notably with the Polish political émigré groups."

All this I studied with a sinking heart. It showed only too clearly that the matter was one of high communist policy, and Hermann was not involved through a minor error by an overzealous border official.

THE PAPER BATTLE BEGINS

The first formal approach by the State Department on behalf of Hermann was made on September 13, 1949—exactly three weeks after his arrest. Before that date the inquiries had been informal, with the object of obtaining maximum evidence on which to base a note. The State Department, after all, only had my word for it—and indirectly Herta's—that Hermann had been in Poland in the first place. And until they had checked the airline passenger lists they had no corroborating evidence of when or where he had disappeared.

On September 13, three days after the bombshell of the Rajk trial report, the American embassy in Warsaw presented a formal note to the Polish Foreign Office inquiring about Hermann's whereabouts and asking whether he had actually departed from Poland. It also asked about the existence of official records other than flight manifests, such as customs and immigration records.

The Polish Foreign Office replied that the case would be investigated immediately and a report made.

The next day the U.S. embassy in Warsaw made an oral inquiry and was told that, although the investigation was not yet complete, Hermann had not been arrested or taken into custody by Polish authorities.

Since there was no written reply by the following day, the embassy asked whether Hermann had been "detained, or otherwise prevented from boarding the plane by Polish customs authorities, security police or other agents of the Polish Government, or agents of any other government." It also expressed the "American Government's concern at Field's disappearance and requested a prompt report." The Poles said no information was yet available but that the embassy would be informed immediately when something was learned.

I did not know of these negotiations when I decided to go to my grandmother's in the country for a few days. The embassy had no objection. I had been in a state of nervous suspense for three weeks, and everyone thought a change would do me good. But the enforced quiet of country life only heightened my tension. What if something happened while I was away? I was incapable of relaxing or even of sitting still.

One wet evening a newspaperman appeared on the doorstep, having been sent over from Brighton, fourteen miles away, to get my story. I was terrified. I did not know whether it had been decided to make the matter public or the story had leaked to the press. All I remember saying was "Can't you leave unhappy people in peace?" as I sent the poor young man away empty-handed.

Next morning I phoned the embassy. They told me of their note to Poland regarding Hermann and that it had been decided to make the matter public in the hope of "winkling him out." But I still did not issue any statement myself, for I was fearful of saying the wrong thing.

Nine days after the note to Poland was delivered, it still had no written reply. Our ambassador in Warsaw was away, so the chargé d'affaires called at the Foreign Office and was told that "as far as the Polish authorities have been able to ascertain" Hermann was not in Poland. He had apparently passed through airport customs; he was in no jail in Poland; he had not been taken into custody by the security police, the military police, or other agents of the Polish government, or agents of any other government. They said the investigation was continuing.

Next day the chargé d'affaires telephoned for "definite information on Field for transmittal to the press." He was told that no further information was available. Two days later he called at the Foreign Office again, where an official said he was "really mystified." And three days after that he requested an appointment with the acting foreign minister, who, on September 28, told him that he had no information but that an answer would be forthcoming "as soon as the investigating authorities provided it."

Altogether some fourteen approaches were made to the Poles in this period, yet the American note remained without a written answer. Orally, however, they asserted that Hermann was not held in Poland.

As to Noel and Herta, the State Department certainly wanted more information before making diplomatic approaches on their behalf. With the doubts regarding Noel's political sympathies, the question of voluntary disappearance arose. Yet the Rajk trial suggested that his position might be anything but comfortable, and whatever his politics he was still an American citizen.

By unofficial inquiries the State Department found that Noel had gone to Prague from Switzerland in early May, staying at the Palace Hotel. He had walked out of the hotel on May 12, accompanied by two men whom nobody seemed to know. It appeared that he had intended to be back, for he left his luggage in his room, and even a quantity of personal papers. But he never returned. Later, the hotel got a telegram from Bratislava, close to the Hungarian border, apparently from Noel, saying he was making a short trip to Budapest and asking them to keep the room for him. In June they got another one, this time from Vienna, saying that he would not be needing the room any longer. This wire asked that his belongings be given to a Mr. Kimel of Bratislava, who would be calling for them. In due course Mr. Kimel had appeared and was given Noel's things.

When the embassy checked on this story several strange things came to light. Noel had had an important appointment in Prague on May 12, and he had not kept it. The originals of the telegrams were neither written nor signed in

Noel's writing. "Mr. Kimel" could not be found, and his address in Bratislava was nonexistent.

Upon learning all this I felt quite sure that Noel had not been free after leaving the hotel with those two strange men. If one started believing telegrams, which could be sent by anyone, one might follow false trails all over the world. I decided the only thing was to stress that the last time Noel had been free was on May 12, in Prague. This is the position his sister, Elsie, and I always stuck to.

As to Herta, our only evidence was negative. She was staying at the Hotel Paris in Prague on August 26, the date of her last known letter, and waiting for Hermann. Obviously she would not voluntarily leave Prague without informing any of her family or friends. Letters and telegrams had apparently not reached her, but neither were they returned to the senders. Certainly an inquiry was in order for her too.

Since the oral replies of the Poles regarding Hermann had been negative, it was decided to approach the Czechs officially in his case as well. On October 7, 1949, the U.S. government sent its first note to the Czechs, "requesting information on the whereabouts of the American citizens Noel, Herta and Hermann Field."

But the Hungarians were also involved. They had made many references to Noel in the Rajk trial, and it was possible that the second telegram, even if not sent by Noel himself, did reflect the truth in saying that he had gone to Hungary. But by now that was four months ago, and as evidence it was not solid enough to support a really strong note. Again the State Department had to ask for information rather than demand it. On October 10 they asked if Noel were currently in Hungary, or had recently been there. Two weeks later the Hungarian Foreign Office replied informally that none of the Fields had been in their country within the past three months. Two months later they confirmed this in an official note, stating categorically that none of the Fields had been there since May 1. That was two weeks before Noel had disappeared.

Despite all this, the Hungarian police were keenly interested in Noel. As part of their campaign against Western contacts they arrested another relief worker that same October, Israel Jacobson, who had worked for the American Jewish Joint Distribution Committee, the agency for Jewish relief. The Americans protested, and after ten days he was released. Elsie, Hermann's sister, managed to see him after his return home and he told her that the Hungarians had asked him what he knew of Noel. In reply he had asked whether they had held Noel and was told no, but that they "wished they had."

During that fall of 1949 there was a wave of arrests of Western nationals. Soon after Hermann disappeared, a Frenchman, Robineau, also disappeared at Warsaw airport. In this case, his father had come to see him off and carefully waited to see that he boarded the plane. When he did not, the father got the plane searched at its next stop, and the French threatened to hold it until Robineau was produced. At first the Poles said he had taken the plane, but when the French stood firm they found they had him after all. True, he was sentenced to three years, but he was never lost.

A contrary case was that of Edith Bone, a British subject but Hungarian born, who visited Hungary and was coming home alone by air, via Prague. She never reached England. The Hungarians said she had left, the Czechs that she had not arrived, and there were no witnesses.

The most publicized case was that of the American businessman Robert Vogeler and his English colleague Edgar Sanders, both working in Budapest for the International Telephone and Telegraph Company. Vogeler was returning to Vienna alone, by car, and failed to arrive. His wife promptly made inquiries and found that he had not crossed the border into Austria. Shortly after, she made all her information public. The Americans promptly sent a note "requesting an investigation into the disappearance" and followed this up with daily requests at a high level in Budapest. After at first insisting, in the usual way, that they had "no knowledge of the whereabouts" of Vogeler, the Hungarians finally admitted that they held him.

If these cases had occurred before Hermann's, I think I would have known better how to act. One thing they showed clearly: the communists would admit holding foreigners only when faced with incontrovertible evidence that they did.

## DESPERATE RELATIVES

I found the accusations against Noel in the Rajk trial totally bizarre. Terrified that equivalent charges would be made against Hermann because of his work for the Czechoslovak refugees, I felt I must somehow try to convince whoever was holding him that he was no spy.

Many people in England knew the work we had both done for the refugees. In the hope of getting some publicity explaining Hermann's wartime activities that might be read by his captors, I went to see Kingsley Martin, editor of the *New Statesman*, an independent weekly with generally liberal tendencies. Martin was an energetic middle-aged man with a shock of unruly graying hair and penetrating eyes. He received me in his unpretentious newspaper office and listened to my story. He understood my dilemma and promised to do whatever he could that would be helpful.

When I left, Kingsley Martin rose and gave me a friendly peck on the cheek, telling me to have courage. I could not help thinking that when a newspaper editor you have just met for the first time gives you a parting kiss, things must be pretty bad. Later on his paper did publish a lengthy and accurate account of Hermann's work and disappearance.

I also visited a former colleague, a woman who had worked with us for the Czech Refugee Trust Fund during the war. I knew she was a communist, but I thought she knew that Hermann was no spy and that she might get that word across somehow. But, she asked, how would she know if he were a spy or not? After all, if he were, he would not even tell his wife. Then she added, "The only person I'd be sure was not a spy is you, Kate. You're too muddleheaded!"

The shock of Hermann's disappearance thrust all minor complications from my mind. Yet eventually they claimed my attention. There was our home in Cleveland. Who would keep an eye on the empty house, the Plymouth standing deserted in the garage? And money, it would soon run out, though luckily there was still some in the bank I could send for. And clothes: the children and I had only summer things with us, and it was already chilly. But to find someone to go to our home and send off the right clothes was far too difficult; our friends in the States were busy doing more important things for us. I would simply have to buy a few warm things in England.

In the summer I had bought a new winter coat and had it shipped directly to the *Batory*. It had its own adventures. No one could prevent its going off to New York. There, of course, no one claimed it; so back it came to Southampton, up to Gdynia in Poland, and again to Southampton—and still I could not arrange to retrieve it. So it crossed the Atlantic a third time—but on this trip I had arranged with one of the passengers to claim it for me in New York. She succeeded, and sent it back to me by mail.

I still clung to the idea that there must be news of Hermann soon. Embassy officials had at first said he might turn up in West Berlin at any time. Then they warned it might take "several weeks" to clear things up. I had booked on the Cunard line for the middle of November, thinking there would surely be news by then. But the diplomatic front was unyielding. The note to Poland failed to "winkle him out," and on October 24 the Czech Foreign Office sent a formal note saying that they had "no knowledge of the Fields having made a stay in Czechoslovakia, but the appropriate authorities have undertaken to trace them."

As our sailing date again drew near, I visualized what it would be like spending the winter alone with the children in Cleveland. I felt I could not face it and canceled the passage. Instead, my mother found places for the children in King Alfred School, the old progressive day school just up the road alongside Hampstead Heath, and from then on they marched off together every morning, the six-year-old in charge of the four-year-old, two little American boys in their long corduroy pants, starting their first winter in England.

Having put Hermann's case in the hands of our government, at first I felt confident. But soon I began to feel I must do more. Everything was going so slowly. Was everything possible being done? People began to suggest that it was not, that the only way to get more action out of a government is constantly to pester them, to organize pressure, so that your particular problem, instead of being a small one among many weightier ones, becomes a real headache that insists on being cured.

Only one member of Hermann's immediate family was still alive and free: his sister Elsie. Elsie was a physician, married to Joseph Doob, a professor of mathematics at the University of Illinois. Their sons, Stephen and Peter, were only a year older than my two. They also had a daughter, Deborah, who had been born in July, only a month before her uncle Hermann disappeared.

It was a terrible shock to Elsie to hear from me that her brothers were missing. She had never been much interested in politics, nor had she done any refugee work. Instead she had worked hard on her medical career, at a time when it was not easy for a woman to become a doctor. But Elsie and her two brothers shared a very deep affection, perhaps especially deep because they had all been born abroad and come to the United States as teenagers with their mother, after their father's death in Switzerland.

When Elsie heard of the disappearances she immediately plunged into action, and we were in constant touch. Since I was in England, she went to Washington in November to see what could be done. Joe was left in charge of the boys, but Deborah, only four months old, had to go with her. Despite this burden she managed to see various high officials in the State Department. She came away with the impression that they were really working for us, but only in the form of repeated diplomatic requests for information.

I had previously raised the question of sanctions to back up the diplomatic requests and been told that trade with Poland and Czechoslovakia was negligible, that there were very few private loans, that the government could not stop them even if it wanted to, that a ban on travel by American citizens would only please the other side because they wanted to reduce contacts with the West to a minimum and in any event few people went now except on official business. In short, these sanctions would be ineffective. The ultimate sanction of breaking off diplomatic relations the State Department was frankly not prepared to take. It was too important to have representation in Poland and Czechoslovakia.

Certainly one could not be sure that a mild sanction would be effective, and the State Department was unwilling to try such an approach, for then they would be stuck with it. In Hermann's case, however, I began to see that any sanction would have helped, even if it did not produce his immediate release. It would at least have been an incentive to answer notes unequivocally, or if not that, then to keep Hermann alive so he could be produced as a bargaining chip at some future date when the trade, loans, or travel of Americans might be of greater interest to Russia or the country concerned.

But alongside the belief that a mild sanction would be ineffective, I began to see another factor in the State Department's reluctance to act, which arose out of the prevailing Cold War situation. Indeed, it seemed that the communists were trying to provoke us to break off contact with them altogether. Perhaps the Russians were the ringleaders, afraid we were still exerting an influence in those satellite countries. Yet we seemed simply to shrug off those attacks, refusing to be provoked. It was clear that we were as keen to stay in that part of the world as the Russians were to get us out. And if this were our general policy, clearly it conflicted with taking any strong action in support of an individual national who got into trouble.

If this was the situation, the need for us as a family to exert pressure was critical. Western Reserve University and Hermann's architectural colleagues were prepared to press the State Department in his support. We also received help from some members of Congress, but we needed much more—a resolution of Congress, say, to overcome the State Department's reluctance to use sanctions.

Pressure on the State Department was one strategy, perhaps the only one that could have produced any result. And yet at the time there was also the unanswered question of whether we, the family, could get anything out of the communists ourselves. If I, as Hermann's wife, an ordinary citizen committed to no official policy, went and appealed to them to look at the case more carefully, swore that Hermann had been involved in no subversive activity, and begged them to help me find him—might not my very sincerity impress them and make them think again? I had seen from the Rajk trial how Noel, whom I believed innocent, had been used to convict local nationals. I was afraid that the same thing might be done with Hermann. Perhaps I could convince the communists that by accusing Hermann wrongly they would also be hurting themselves. This line of thought rested on the possibility that the wave of arrests and accusations was not part of a well-laid plan of purging but was the product of Cold War paranoia, a fear of "Western agents" so all-embracing that the security police could no longer distinguish between those who were spies and those who were not.

If only this analysis proved to be true, and the communists were willing to listen to me, I might after all convince them that Hermann should be released. Reason said, why should they listen to me, a mere wife? Yet the faint hope remained, and I knew I would not be able to rid my mind of it until I had put it to the test by going to the communist embassies. This was not easy for me because

I was so afraid. I knew that embassies were technically foreign soil, and I had seen what happened to our family when they entered communist territory. I thought it was probably the height of foolishness to go and put myself also in their hands. Supposing they wanted to hold me in their embassy; could anyone ever prove that I had gone in and not come out again? Would they say, "Yes, we were expecting Mrs. Field but she never arrived" and meanwhile I would be sitting in a back room as they waited to whisk me away under cover of darkness? It sounds fantastic, and yet I remembered the case of the Russian governess, Mrs. Kosenkina, who was held in the Russian consulate in New York shortly before we left Cleveland. The Russians had said she had chosen to go there, but she gave them the lie by leaping out a back window when they weren't looking. True, I was not a Russian, but with Noel, Herta, and Hermann prisoners I felt I was next on the list. I still had the feeling that because I knew they were innocent the communists would like to be rid of me as an inconvenient witness. Then there would be no one on the outside who could answer any accusations against Hermann.

However, I realized that I might be exaggerating both my own importance and the lengths to which communists would go in their embassies abroad, and I decided to go ahead, taking the precaution of not going alone but with my mother, a British subject, as witness.

Already in September I had tried to meet with the Polish ambassador, but he would not see me. With the Czechs I tried a different method and without seeking an appointment simply walked into their embassy one day in November and asked to see the ambassador on "personal business."

The waiting room was deserted, the whole building quite silent. I remembered the only other occasion I had been there, two years earlier, when I had applied for a visitor's visa so that I could join Hermann's architects' tour of the region that summer. That was in the days of the Benes coalition government, before the communists took over, and the embassy had been buzzing with life and animated conversation, crowded with people wanting documents and visas. Now there were only a few Czech officials, with little to do, it seemed, and no one to talk to.

The message came back: the ambassador would see me. I went up with a silent girl in the elevator and was shown into a large room. The ambassador sat at his desk. He was a pleasant, unpretentious-looking man who would have looked more comfortable in a less showy office. His English was imperfect, but he understood me, and as I related how my husband had failed to return I felt his surprise to be genuine. I asked simply for his help, reiterating that I knew my husband had never intended any crime and that the Czech government would be making a terrible mistake if they thought otherwise. I also said that unless the matter were cleared up quickly it would become a first-class international scandal. While I spoke he seemed to become increasingly uncomfortable, but he listened, and when I had finished he said quite kindly that, although it was not properly the concern of his embassy, since Hermann was not British, he would make a personal inquiry in Prague and let me know.

I thanked him and left. Downstairs my mother was waiting, and we left that quiet building together. For a while I thought I might hear something and telephoned a few times for an answer, but none came and finally I gave up.

As for the Russians, I made no attempt to approach them at this time. They could not have admitted being involved, since it would have been a case of gross interference in the affairs of Poland and Czechoslovakia, two supposedly sovereign states. Procommunists, of course, held that such interference did not exist. The State Department naturally disagreed, but thought it useless or even harmful to approach Russia in our case.

Communist embassies in London could always say our case was not their concern, since we were American citizens, but in Washington they had no such easy way out. Elsie managed to get an interview at the Polish embassy when she went to Washington in December. They told her that a serious investigation had been made in September and from it the Polish government could say that Hermann was not detained in Poland. She even raised the question of whether any other power or secret police could be operating on their territory and received an indignant no. Some days later she went back to see the Polish ambassador himself; he disclaimed the previous statement and said that an investigation was still going on. This was the same story the Poles had told the State Department.

Also in December, Elsie got an interview with the Czech ambassador. He said that in October a search had been made and the Czechs knew nothing about the Fields' whereabouts. He also emphatically denied that any other country could be operating in Czech territory. His explanation was that all three people had wanted to disappear; he also suggested that the State Department was "not telling us everything" and that it in fact was not doing its best for us. Although we were both firmly convinced that Hermann and the others were being held against their will in miserable conditions, we could not prove it to a skeptic. And the rumor that kept cropping up, particularly with regard to Noel and Herta, that they had disappeared voluntarily, was dangerous: it provided all authorities with such a convenient excuse to simply drop the case. The ambassador's second suggestion—that our government was not doing its best for us—was also one that we heard on many occasions. It was easy for things to look that way, since the State Department seldom made public its approaches and did not invoke sanctions.

The Czech ambassadors whom Elsie and I saw were recalled to Prague in February 1951 "for consultations" after the disappearance of their foreign minister, Clementis. They never returned to their posts in Washington and London.

Neither Elsie nor I called on the Hungarians. I had no cause to, since Hermann had never been to Hungary nor had he been mentioned in the Rajk trial. As to Noel and Herta, we believed that there was insufficient evidence, especially since they had both apparently lost their freedom in Prague. Although we gained very little from our personal approaches to the communists, at least I felt we had tried everything.

The months went by, and still no formal charges were made by our family members' captors. The State Department had not gotten to first base; they were still sending notes trying to "ascertain the whereabouts" of the missing people.

I felt an urge to answer the accusation against Noel in the Rajk trial that he was an American agent. Yet the charges were really nothing more than a smear; no formal charges were made.

From studying the Rajk trial I could see one possible explanation: that it was a frame-up by the Russians to eliminate any chance of defection by the Hungarian Communist Party from the Cominform. On the other hand, if the trial had been initiated by the Hungarians themselves, it was hard to see how it could strengthen their communist leadership. In either case, even if Noel were innocent of espionage, as I believed, they were hanging other innocents. Clearly, though, no loyal communist could take that view once Noel's guilt had been assumed in the Rajk trial. One communist rumor was that eventually, when all his accomplices were rounded up, Noel would be tried and convicted. Another was that American officials had indicated by odd remarks that Noel was indeed one of their agents. Such rumors I regarded with skepticism.

Although in the beginning it seemed obvious to me that Hermann could not be a spy, being far too transparent a character as well as too talkative, after a while I realized this would mean nothing to someone who did not know him. A complete underworld existed to which I had never given a thought: the world of intelligence and counterintelligence. And when I said, "But he's completely the wrong sort of person to be a spy: he's artistic, and would always be giving himself away," I was met with, "Ah, but those are the people who make the best spies, because no one suspects them." Dealing with such an Alice-in-Wonderland world seemed hopeless. I had always thought of espionage as a wartime occupation between belligerents, but now it seemed it was carried on in peacetime too. With this underworld living side by side with us ordinary people, there seemed no reason why any traveler should not be taken for a spy, using his tourism as a "cover" for his other activities. And if he appeared friendly, naturally he was more effective—and therefore more dangerous! I found myself apologizing for Hermann's naiveté in traveling alone through the Iron Curtain.

The point that depressed me most of all was that if Hermann *was* a spy, I would not know it. I had complete faith in him, but that faith, I realized, was worthless. In my impotence I thought back on Hermann's life and how it might look to the suspicious eyes of security police, or to what use it could be put by Machiavellians interested only in political expediency. Hermann, after all, had had more contact with Europe than the average American. His early years in Switzerland had given him an affinity for European ways, and a second mother tongue, German. Not only that, but his father had been intensely interested in international affairs, particularly in the cause of peace.

When I met Hermann in the summer of 1938, although I was English and he American, we found we shared much the same views: against the rise of dictatorships, against the brutality of anti-Semitism, and against the aggressive nationalism of Mussolini and Hitler.

In September 1938 Neville Chamberlain, the British prime minister, signed the Munich Agreement with Hitler, which handed over the Sudetenland of Czechoslovakia to Germany. The whole region was to be transferred from democratic Czechoslovakia to dictatorial Germany; those who did not think they could survive under the Nazis had to leave their homes behind them and flee. At the same time, an even graver danger now befell the antifascist refugees from Germany and Austria whose asylum in what remained of Czechoslovakia was no longer assured.

The *News Chronicle*, a Liberal newspaper under the chairmanship of Walter Layton, an old family friend, launched an appeal for funds to help the refugees, as did the lord mayor of London. The public's response was immediate, and a committee was formed to administer the money. Layton's daughter Margaret, who had been at Cambridge University with me, was made the committee's chief executive officer and secretary. I, with others, was in charge of finding accommodations for the refugees, either in private homes or in hostels that we set up for the purpose. I remember the first discussion as being in the home of Maynard Keynes, the economist, in Bloomsbury, but once we were fully operational we had to take over a whole house. Thus was born the British Committee for Refugees from Czechoslovakia, later to become the Czech Refugee Trust Fund.

When the Munich Agreement was signed I had only recently met Hermann, and a few months later his architectural job was completed and he was preparing to go home to America. As many of us had foreseen, though, Munich was not the end but the beginning. With Czechoslovakia's natural defense lines gone, in March 1939 Hitler marched into Prague. Our work for refugees became enormously enlarged. More funds were made available; we were overwhelmed with work and short of people qualified to carry it out. Moreover, under the German occupation British relief workers could not get into Prague to help those caught there escape to Katowice in Poland, where the British vice consulate was issuing visas for England that had already been authorized in London.

I thought of Hermann. His American passport might make it easier for him to get into the occupied territory, and he was certainly well qualified with his fluent German. Although I would miss him, it was only to be for a week or two and he would be back. I suggested it to him and he accepted without hesitation.

After successfully completing his mission in Prague, he continued on to Poland. There he found that large numbers of refugees were fleeing over the Tatra mountains, and even as the British vice consulate in Katowice tried to help the original group it was overwhelmed by the new arrivals. These were heading mainly toward Krakow, farther from the frontier but without anyone to help. So instead of returning to England, Hermann organized a second reception center in Krakow, and was still there when war broke out in September. He tried to organize an evacuation of the refugees stuck in Poland, but the German advance, the first blitzkrieg, was too swift and swept over them. Some managed to get out later through the Baltic states, and Hermann himself, despite being bombed, was lucky enough to get out through Rumania and so back to England.

For me September was an awful month, when I knew that Germany had attacked Poland and was advancing over her and there was no news of Hermann. England was at war for the second time in my life, and London was hastily being sandbagged, while we all walked around carrying gas masks. By now I was head of the department dealing with the housing of the refugees and had to try to transfer as many as possible from London. By the end of the month our whole office had been moved out too, and still there was no word of Hermann. I was terribly worried and unhappy. With the whole of Poland overrun, his chances of getting out alive did not look good. And then, at the beginning of October, a telephone call from the *News Chronicle*: their correspondent had found Hermann in Rumania—and he was safe!

I have no doubt that many people—men, women, and children—owe their lives to the work Hermann managed to do in Krakow. They were of all sorts, for the policy of the committee was to be politically evenhanded. The purpose was to save those who were in the direst need, those who would be most endangered if not given haven in England. This policy was agreed to by the British Home Office, which decided to whom visas should be given. Some sought refuge on religious and racial grounds—they were Jewish. Most sought refuge on political grounds: they had in some way opposed Hitler, either in their writings—many

were members of the "PEN" club, an international writers organization—or by
their political or trade-unionist activities. There were Democrats, Liberals, Social Democrats, and Communists. Some had originally fled from Germany itself, or from Austria or the Sudetenland, and had already been refugees in
Czechoslovakia. It was a great snowball of humanity—all people uprooted by
intolerance. And although there were rivalries among the different groups and
even quarrels, I do not think that any denied the right of survival to the others.

In those days, back in 1938 and 1939, we did not think of communists as being a threat. Not only was the Communist Party in England tiny, but it was also
the time of the Popular Front, a European effort to combine the forces of Liberals, Social Democrats, and Communists to oppose first fascism under Mussolini, with his war on Abyssinia, then Franco in Spain and Hitler with his expansion of Nazi Germany. The Communists were among the most dedicated in this
struggle, and consequently among the first to be persecuted by the Nazis.

After March 1939, when Hitler occupied the rest of Czechoslovakia, a loan
was made by the British government to the Czechoslovak government and
earmarked for refugees, and our relief committee was turned into the more
formal Czech Refugee Trust Fund, with Sir Henry Bunbury, a retired civil servant, as director and some well-known public men as trustees to represent the
British Home Office, the trade unions, and the Jewish community. In all, some
seven thousand people were rescued.

After the outbreak of war with Germany the refugees had to appear before
Aliens Tribunals, which decided whether it was safe to leave them at large or
whether they should be interned. Many Germans and Austrians were interned
as "enemy aliens" on the Isle of Man. So were some of the Sudeten German
communists. Others were sent to camps in Australia and Canada.

Some of the refugees we got to know personally, especially if they were
prominent in their particular political or other "group." Many more we just
knew by name. Some of them finally settled abroad, in groups or singly, but
many spent the war in England and then returned to their homeland hoping to
rebuild their lives there. No doubt among all these people there remained a
residue of goodwill toward the British public, for it was probably the most
comprehensive rescue effort prior to the actual outbreak of war.

As I went over all this in my mind, it seemed ironic that people who had
given so much of themselves for the refugees should now come under suspicion
from the communists. No one in 1939 could have foreseen what the world
would be like ten years later, or that Eastern Europe would have communist
governments. This was trial by hindsight. The world had changed out of all recognition: the war against the Nazis was over; the Cold War against the commu-

nists was on. Then, the acid test had been: Are you pro-Nazi? Now it was: Are you a communist?

Now it was the fall of 1949. I saw in the papers that Evzen Loebl, the Czech deputy minister for foreign trade, had disappeared from his Prague office a short while before; so had Vilem Novy, editor of the communist daily *Rude Pravo*. Both men had been refugees in England during the war, and Hermann and I knew them both. I jumped to the conclusion that their downfall was due to Hermann's arrest and that endless interrogations had dragged the whole story of his refugee work out of him. I suspected, by analogy with Noel's case, that they were going to call Hermann an American, or perhaps British, agent too. And once that was done and a lot of Czechs wrongly hanged for knowing him, could they ever let him out? It seemed a race against time. I pestered the American Embassy mercilessly, insisting that something be done.

Then one day they gave me the State Department's current view: all three had been kidnapped by Russian agents. I was stunned. If this were true, how could one ever reach them? They could have been taken anywhere—shot perhaps—and no one could ever be held responsible. Would I ever see Hermann again? Yet despite this depressing theory, the State Department was still willing to go on trying. They said there was a possibility that continued pestering of the satellite countries might finally induce Russia to release them—that this was the only hope. A direct approach to Russia would not only be useless, they said, but it might be disastrous.

I told one or two English people of the State Department's kidnap theory, and they were shocked. Somehow they did not quite believe things were done that way, even by the Russians. They thought that Poles and Czechs might arrest people, but they would hold on to their prisoners.

After four months of thinking of nothing else, my nerves began to go. Bicycling in Golders Green one day I saw Hermann blindfolded and tied to a post for execution—but it was only the power standard with a white band of paint on it. I did not dare walk across Hampstead Heath alone at night, for fear of being liquidated by some unknown assailant, and one day I arrived home breathless from cycling away from a car that I believed was following me. Believing that I knew too much, I began to feel that my papers were not safe in our house.

I was becoming paranoid. I did not know whose judgment to trust, and so trusted no one. I tried to figure things out for myself, but it was all beyond me; I needed expert advice. Desperately I developed the hope that if only I could get a lawyer, he would be able to achieve what I could not. But when I found one he said that the whole matter was outside the law and lawyers could not help.

However, he offered me the use of a small room in his offices, where I could work on the case. From that time on I frequently went down there, where I was undisturbed.

One night in late December, unable to sleep, I laid out all my correspondence and news clippings on the dining room table to see what I could make of them. Then suddenly I saw it: the State Department had put the entire onus of producing Hermann on Poland. There was not one clipping that suggested Czechoslovakia might be responsible. Always Hermann had disappeared "at Warsaw airport" or "in Poland"; never was there any suggestion that the abduction might have occurred at the Prague end of the flight! Yet to me, Poland had far less reason to be interested in him than Czechoslovakia. It was Czech refugees he had helped before the war, and the Czechs had produced no proof that Hermann had not traveled to Prague and been arrested immediately on arrival at the airport. Moreover, Herta and Noel had disappeared in Prague.

I felt I had made a great discovery, and once more went to the embassy to try and convince the U.S. officials. They agreed it was conceivable, but I think Washington still thought the whole thing was engineered by the Russians, and since the Russians would never admit to such interference, the only thing was to continue pressing the Poles.

How much better it would have been for me, and for those around me, if I simply left it to the State Department to do the thinking and worrying, and myself gone on with my life confident that everything possible was being done. Several of my friends advised me to do just that, but I still felt that since I was on the outside, it was up to me to get Hermann out by pressing constantly. I noticed that most people arrested by the communists were put on trial within two or three months. They had had Hermann for four, and every day I feared the surprise announcement of a trial. I was still sleeping badly, and my father insisted I go to the doctor. When I told him my story he gave me sleeping pills and something to increase my blood pressure, which was very low.

Christmas was coming. I had never felt less like celebrating, but somehow I knew I had to appear to enjoy it for the sake of Hugh and Alan. They must be given a good time and not share the adults' depression. Last Christmas we had all been together with Elsie and her family in America. Hermann had played Santa Claus and distributed the presents—but Alan had recognized him by his shoes. How far away all that was now: another world.

I walked through my part in a daze, imagining how Hermann might be spending his Christmas, alone.

# 9

---

## London 1950

Here was I, waiting for news of Hermann, back in the Hampstead Garden Suburb I could just remember from my infancy.

I was two when the First World War began, and even through the security of my nursery world, with its patterned wallpaper and Nanny spreading bread-and-butter for tea, the knowledge of a dangerous outside world had penetrated, one that even my mother could not control—a world that sent her hurrying home from the stores with me because an air raid alarm had sounded, that sometimes made her get us out of bed at night and sit huddled in the telephone cupboard under the stairs.

And then suddenly the whole thing was over. The war, which seemed to have gone on all my life, was finished. Everyone said there would never be another war. My parents said there was going to be a League of Nations that would settle disputes, and the countries would not need to fight each other again. I was very reassured, and visualized the world getting nicer and nicer to be in. As I grew up, this belief in the possibility of replacing force by reason endured, combined with the feeling of individual responsibility: that I ought to do my bit to make the world a better, kinder, saner place.

My father, Oliver Thornycroft, the son of a sculptor who had been knighted for his work, was himself an enthusiastic internal combustion engineer and a graduate of Cambridge University. In the First World War he worked on the development of tanks, and I remember his taking me inside one, and being properly frightened because I had not grasped that only the caterpillar track turned over and over, not the whole lozenge-shaped vehicle.

Between the wars my father worked with his friend Harry Ricardo designing internal combustion engines. He was also a keen mountaineer, climbing in North Wales and the Alps, and we children took part in some of these expeditions. Politically he generally supported the Liberal Party. During the Second World War he worked for the Admiralty and was involved in the design of "underwater weapons," for which he was awarded the order of Commander of the Bath. At the time of Hermann's disappearance he was still doing research for the Admiralty in London.

My mother, Dorothy, was the daughter of Edward Rose, theater critic and dramatist and an early member of the Fabian Society, that group of English socialists who believed in the necessity of gradualism. She graduated from Cambridge in 1911 with an honors degree in economics, married shortly thereafter, and had five children, of whom I was the eldest. She always had interests outside the family, was a nonconformist by temperament, and joined the Labour Party. Both my parents helped refugees from Hitler before the war.

When my parents returned to live in Hampstead after the Second World War, my mother was again active in the Labour Party and was elected to Hendon Borough Council, and later to Middlesex County Council.

My mother had a strong influence on us children. So did Bedales, the coeducational boarding school to which we were sent, run by the pioneer educator J. H. Badley, a Unitarian. Because of the all-inclusive nature of Badley's religious instruction and the progressive educational methods, many nonconforming intellectuals and foreigners sent their children to the school, where the atmosphere was freer than in a typical English boarding school.

This background had something to do with my decision to study economics and politics at Cambridge University with professors such as Joan Robinson and John Maynard Keynes. I took part in demonstrations for the League of Nations and peace, and when the unemployed Hunger Marchers came through Cambridge we gave them meals.

The Great Depression was still on when I graduated in 1934 with an honors degree in economics. The only job I was offered was as a teller in a bank. Instead I accepted a one-year fellowship at Smith College in Massachusetts and set sail for the United States.

My year at Smith was an eye-opener in many ways, with wonderful, friendly people, interesting professors, fabulously good food, and good friends. But the contrasts were not lost on me. In the depth of the depression one of the girls arrived on a private plane from California. Meanwhile I took part in a study of the conditions of the unemployed in nearby Easthampton, where the mill had shut down and all the workers were living on nothing but minimal food packages provided by welfare.

Supporting trade unions was the issue of the day for students. I made a trip to Hartford, Connecticut, to picket the Colt firearms factory in support of striking workers, and in the spring I drove with friends down to Chattanooga,

Tennessee, where I stayed at the Highlander Folk School, run by Myles Horton and his father, which was actively supporting the attempt to organize unions in the South. Floodlights shone into my bedroom to prevent nighttime sniping, and one of the staff limped around with a bullet wound in her leg.

From there I went on to stay with the Arthur Morgan family in Norris. Morgan was in charge of the dam then being constructed there by the TVA to generate electricity for the whole Tennessee Valley. This impressed me greatly. That year, too, President Roosevelt introduced the first Social Security legislation, a truly radical innovation.

Although I was appalled by the social inequality I saw, which somehow was more obvious here than in England, I still held on to the optimism of my onetime college lecturer, Maynard Keynes, and hoped that "priming the pump" through federal spending would get the United States out of the depression. While my stay in America made my thinking more radical than before, and I made some attempts at reading Marx, by temperament I was not a revolutionary.

I returned to England, became a schoolteacher, and joined the Labour Party. The political scene was going from bad to worse. Hitler achieved his *Anschluss* with Austria, and in 1936 the newly formed Republican government of Spain was being attacked by his and Mussolini's air forces. Many educated British were convinced that if the fascists took control of Spain, the rest of Western Europe would be seriously weakened. When the Nazis bombed Bilbao, capital of the Basque country, the first wave of Spanish refugees arrived in England.

In affiliation with the newly formed Basque Children's Committee, my mother and I undertook to care for sixty young refugees. We got our town of Worthing, in Sussex, to loan us a large, empty house and we received these children, accompanied by a couple of Spanish señoritas. They stayed several years as the Spanish war continued to drag on. When Franco finally won, some were asked for by surviving parents and they were repatriated.

I accompanied a trainload of these children across France to Hendaye, on the Spanish frontier. They had been in England several years, and their last memories of their homeland had been of brutal bombings from which they had taken shelter in the sewers of Bilbao. Anticipation of seeing their parents again was mixed with fear.

We took them to the long international bridge at Hendaye. At the far end we could see a small contingent of the fascist police, their black helmets looking like coal scuttles. Then they advanced to the center of the bridge. The señoritas leading the children advanced to meet them, and we watched the guards march them all off into the distance.

Meanwhile refugees were arriving from Germany and Austria, either political opponents of Hitler or Jews. My parents gave a home to several of them, and I became involved in the rescue of refugees from Czechoslovakia.

After the war, by a strange gravitation my parents came back to the same Hampstead Garden Suburb of my childhood. The cook, the maid, and the nanny were gone. My mother cooked and my father washed the dishes. When I came back in 1949 they had a lodger, and Hugh, Alan, and I shared the remaining two bedrooms. We visited all my relatives, and I felt proud of my two little American boys.

The problem of Hermann's disappearance was not the only one my parents had to contend with. My younger sister, Priscilla, had married Hans Siebert, a German refugee, and was now living with him and their two daughters in East Berlin. We had given a home to Hans in 1936 when he had managed to escape from Germany after having been incarcerated as a Communist. He was released through the intervention of Adam von Trott zu Solz, an aristocratic German who was later hanged for his part in the 1944 plot by General von Stauffenberg to assassinate Hitler. Hans lived with us and helped with our home for Basque refugee children. During the war he was interned for a while on the Isle of Man as an "enemy alien." In 1947 he returned to Germany, followed the next year by my sister and their children. He remained a Communist and held a good position in the ministry of education in East Berlin.

With the allegations against Noel, followed by his and Hermann's disappearance, we were fearful for Priscilla and her family. Hans lost his job in Berlin in the summer of 1950, but soon thereafter was given the title of professor and was later transferred to Dresden to set up a teachers' training college. Priscilla, an artist, was able to continue her work of writing and illustrating children's books, and as far as we knew they did not suffer further due to the allegations against Hermann. But their safety remained a nagging anxiety to my parents.

## SOMETHING FOR THE PRESS

As 1950 approached I began working on a statement for the press. Up to now I had not made one, fearing to say the wrong thing.

I outlined Hermann's work for refugees in 1939 and how he had been caught in Poland for the first month of the war while trying to evacuate people from Krakow, out of the path of the German invasion. And how, in 1947, he had led a group of architects studying reconstruction in both Western and Eastern Europe and "been particularly impressed by the work done in Poland, especially the rebuilding of Warsaw." I said that he was a "genuine believer in democracy and a staunch antifascist" as well as a keen photographer.

I took my draft to the first secretary at the American embassy and asked his opinion. I watched his face as he read. There was a silence, and then: "Mrs. Field, if the American people read this they would say your husband was a Communist, or at least a fellow traveler, and had gotten his just deserts."

I was stunned. As I walked down the stairs I realized I had been completely on the wrong track. I did not have to convince the communists that Hermann was not a spy; I had to convince his own country that he was worth saving.

That might not be easy, with Senator Joseph McCarthy busy rooting out real or supposed Communists in the United States. Hermann's willingness to visit communist countries after the war could certainly be interpreted as "fellow-traveling." So I went home and worked on a new statement that I hoped would satisfy the Americans without necessarily aiding the communists.

There had been some talk about the State Department considering further action, but nothing had happened and I was becoming desperate. Finally, four days after Christmas 1949, I dictated my statement over the telephone to the major press agencies, which said it would be sent to all the big English newspapers.

First thing in the morning I bicycled to the stores and bought the papers. I opened the London *Times.* There was nothing. I searched through the *Daily Telegraph.* Again nothing. I quickly went through them all, and only in one was there a short paragraph. This staggering, shocking story—how could it not be of general interest? However, the picture looked a little different when I got the American papers. The *New York Times* had printed quite a full report and I felt somewhat better, though I was cured of thinking that anything I said would, as the English say, "set the Thames on fire."

The same day in the papers there was a news item from Washington that America was pressing the Czechs and Poles again regarding our family. It seemed possible that some sanction, such as a travel ban, might be taken to bolster the demand for information. One thing was clear: for Hermann, the pressure was being put on the Poles.

A new year, 1950, had begun, and my father had the idea of calling on his old friend Walter, now Lord Layton, for help. Walter was a prominent member of the Liberal Party and still chairman of the *News Chronicle*, the newspaper that in 1938 had sponsored the fund for refugees from Czechoslovakia. In addition, one of his daughters had married a Czech and now lived in Prague. So Walter had a keen interest in our case. Through him I could get good advice and access to the press, and he had useful connections in both London and Washington.

I went to Walter's apartment in Westminster, near the Houses of Parliament, and laid my problem before him. He was completely sympathetic and willing to do anything in his power to help. With a lifetime of diplomatic experience behind him and numerous contacts in high places, his concern heartened me tremendously. From then on I kept him informed of developments and consulted him before making any statement to the press.

On January 25, 1950, the second trial of Alger Hiss ended; he was found guilty of perjury and sentenced to five years in prison. At the time I think I read everything published on the trial, yet could not shake the feeling that there were possible alternative explanations of how certain unclassified papers had gotten out of a government department in the 1930s. In my view, Hiss could well have been speaking the truth.

But the climate of opinion in the United States continued to become more fervently anticommunist, and this made it hard to fight for Noel, whose pro-communist leaning was well known. I was in fact warned at the embassy that there was a difference between Noel's case and Hermann's—to which my father had responded, in his dogged British way, "Well, Noel is still an American citizen." It was in practice difficult to separate the two cases, particularly for us: the two brothers were, after all, both family.

## MORE CLUES

Evidence of the Soviet Union's intervention in Eastern Europe was not lacking. During the winter of 1949, its hand took an increasingly firm grasp. In Poland, Marshal Rokossovsky, whose Russian troops had encircled the Nazis under General von Paulus at Stalingrad, was appointed minister of national defense and so became head of the Polish army. It was announced that the Russians had placed him "at the disposal of the Polish army" at the request of President Bierut, who had chosen him on grounds of his Polish origin and popularity among the people of Poland. That he was really popular is most doubtful, since he had been in command of the Russians on the east bank of the river Vistula at the time of the ill-fated Warsaw uprising against the Nazis and had failed to come to the Poles' aid, and even refused the Allies the right to use Russian airfields in support of the Poles.

A few days after Rokossovsky's appointment his second in command, General Ochab, attacked Wladyslaw Gomulka, the former vice premier and secretary-general of the communist Polish Workers Party and one of the few people who had opposed the excommunication of Marshal Tito, head of the Yugoslav communist party, from the Cominform. Gomulka's eclipse had been hinted at in the Rajk trial. Within a week, he and two others were expelled from the central committee of the Polish Workers Party, and Rokossovsky was co-opted onto it. It was a nice example of how the Russians perfected their control.

One of the two men expelled with Gomulka was General Marjan Spychalski, described as minister for reconstruction, formerly a vice minister of national defense. I had never heard of him before, but when I read that he was an architect and had been appointed mayor of Warsaw after the war, I began to wonder whether Hermann's name might be dragged into an attack on Spychalski. Yet I knew it was the Syrkuses who had shown Hermann around, and I believed they were still free; it seemed that if the Poles held Hermann, the Syrkuses should also have been arrested.

On the diplomatic front, the year 1950 opened with a definite reply from the Czech government, delivered to the American embassy on January 6. It confirmed that Noel had arrived by air on May 5, 1949, and was granted a residence permit valid until May 15. He made no application for its prolongation and "it is to be presumed that Noel Field left Czechoslovakia most probably still at the time when he had a valid residence permit." There was no record in the passport or other control files of his departure, which must therefore have occurred "at a time when the present control had not yet been introduced."

Herta had arrived in Prague from Zurich by air on August 3, stayed at the Hotel Paris until August 27, then registered at the Hotel Carlton-Savoy in Bratislava and stayed there until September 6, when she left Czechoslovakia. The note failed to state her point of departure or her destination.

Hermann had arrived by air from Zurich on August 1 and left on August 15. His destination was also not stated. The note concluded that these investigations "were carried out with the greatest possible care and conscientiousness" and the "results can be considered as definite."

It was hard to know how much importance to attach to the Czech report. The arrival dates in each case agreed with our own belief and were clearly taken from immigration records. But Noel's departure was distinctly vague; it was "presumed" he had left. An equally plausible explanation was that he had been arrested prior to May 15—perhaps on the twelfth, as we believed. The story on Herta was more complete, and if one believed it, might indicate that she had been abducted from Prague, then kept quietly in Bratislava until the coast was clear and she could be gotten out of the country. But where to?

On Hermann the note added nothing to what we already knew, which meant that here was I, five months after the event, still with no news. What to do next I really did not know, but I did think that Elsie and I should discuss a plan of action. I was still in a very nervous state, and it was agreed that it would not be good, either for the children or for me, to try to get along alone at home in Cleveland. Moreover, Elsie felt that she might be able to learn something by coming to Europe, so she came over in February, bringing her baby daughter, Deborah.

The failure of diplomatic methods made me decide once again to try the direct approach. On February 15 I sent identical telegrams appealing for help to the Polish minister of public security, Radkiewicz, and to the Czech minister of the interior, Vaclav Nosek, who had been in Krakow in 1939 and then in England. One of these two men should know where Hermann was, I felt, even if their foreign offices did not.

My telegrams were quoted in British and American papers. I sent copies to the Polish and Czech embassies in London, with a request to see someone in charge. Eventually I was granted an interview with a second secretary at the Polish embassy who promised to make an inquiry, but no answer ever arrived.

Ten days later I received a telegram direct from Prague signed "Secretariat of the Minister of Interior." It said the same as the Foreign Office, but it was strange to be holding in my hand a telegram dispatched from the other side of the Great Divide. At least it meant my telegram had reached the Czech police, perhaps Nosek himself.

Only one week later, on the evening of March 3, I was sitting with Elsie in front of the fire listening to the BBC's news bulletin. The announcer was saying, "At the recent meeting of the Central Committee of the Czechoslovak Communist Party, Mr. Ladislav Kopriva called for increased vigilance against Titoite plots and underground activity . . ." I listened intently. According to Kopriva, agents of the Tito clique, on lines similar to Rajk's, were trying to get the country subordinated to Yugoslav agents who served the Anglo-American imperialists. Vilem Novy, the editor in chief of *Rude Pravo,* the Czech Communist Party daily newspaper, had been deprived of his function and recalled as a member of the National Assembly.

Vilem Novy! This was the man who had escaped the German invasion of Poland and turned up in Rumania with Hermann. My heart was thumping, and every second I expected to hear Hermann's name.

The statement went on. According to Kopriva, in 1939 Novy had been entrusted by the Communist Party with the welfare of Czechoslovak émigrés in Poland but had abandoned them and left for France. He was "helped by a national of a Western state," with whom, though he learned that this man was suspected of espionage, Novy maintained contact during his later stay in Britain.

After his return home Novy had misled the Party by asserting that the foreigner in question had rendered important services to Czechoslovak exiles. He also failed to inform the Party that "that agent of a foreign intelligence service" had twice visited Czechoslovakia, at which time Novy had introduced him to leading political and economic functionaries to enable him to acquire the information he wanted. Novy, Kopriva reported, "worked as an agent of Western imperialists in that he betrayed state secrets to their intelligence service and gave them information." He did it, according to Novy's own admission, because he wanted to prevent the "foreign espionage center" from compromising him before the Communist Party for his cowardly and treacherous behavior toward the Czech exiles in Poland and "because his relations toward the bourgeoisie and the West were closer than his relations to the working class and the USSR..."

I grasped Elsie's hand and whispered, "This is it." For I recognized at once this travesty of history. This "national of a Western state" could be none other than Hermann, though what he had done, and what Novy had done, had been quite different from what Kopriva described.

As soon as the broadcast was over I phoned Walter Layton and asked his advice. Perhaps if I identified Hermann they would be afraid to attack him further, seeing that someone on the outside knew as much as they did. My father drove me to Fleet Street at once. I was almost beside myself with excitement and fury, feeling that strange exhilaration that makes one imagine one can take on the whole world.

We discussed with Walter whether to identify Hermann as the individual Kopriva had referred to, and finally decided to do it. By being frank, we thought, we might make it clear that Hermann had nothing to be ashamed of and no secret dealings.

Late that night my reply was released to the press: "My husband is the man who helped Vilem Novy escape from the Nazis through Poland in the early days of the war..." He had, I further stated, helped hundreds of Czech refugees of all opinions, for no other reason than to save human lives. Vilem Novy had come to England because it was the policy of the Czech communist leaders of the time to accept British asylum. Hermann's experience of being bombed in Poland had given him a deep interest in postwar reconstruction, and that was why he had returned in 1947 and 1949. "He has never been an agent of any kind."

My statement was printed in full the next day by the *News Chronicle,* Walter's paper. Other newspapers reported briefly that the mysterious "Western national" was Hermann, though some correspondents thought it was Noel.

One wondered why Kopriva did not mention the name Field. Perhaps it was to keep not outsiders but the Czechs in the dark. After all, they had recently denied that any of the Fields could be in Czechoslovakia. Kopriva himself hinted that this was the case, for at the end of his accusations he thanked the Cominform for having exposed the Anglo-American conspiracy and declared that all Czech Communist Party members should pay heed to "the experience of the All-Union Communist Party of Bolsheviks," that is, the Russian party.

Kopriva, who was one of the Czech delegates to the Cominform, thanked that body for telling him which of his own party were spies—people, in other words, who knew things that Minister Nosek did not. Shortly afterward, police authority in Czechoslovakia was reorganized as in Poland: the secret police were put under a new Ministry of Public Security, its first minister being none other than Ladislav Kopriva.

I shall never forget the night of Kopriva's attack. When I got back from Fleet Street it was midnight. I was dead tired, no longer buoyed up by adrenalin. I lay in bed shivering and wept. Man's inhumanity to man was never-ending. What I had feared for six months had begun to happen, and its advance seemed inexorable. How soon would I hear that Hermann was on trial for his life, as I sat hundreds of miles away with no way of helping him?

That all who had disappeared were under arrest was obvious. Novy, they said, had done these things "according to his own admission." In other words, that burly, tough man had been broken into making a false confession. Then there was Kopriva's reference to the Ministry of Foreign Trade—Evzen Loebl's ministry. Wasn't this a veiled reference to this other "Londoner"? I remembered that he had a wife and little boy. What would happen to them, and to the families of all the other people being summarily locked up all over Czechoslovakia? What a terrible end to the hopes of all those who had returned home there after the war. I remembered a shocking account I had read of the death of Colonel Lukas by beating. He had been with the Czech forces in England during the war, and I had met him then. My prayer for Hermann, which so far had been "Keep him safe and bring him home," now came to be "Let him not suffer."

I was terrified that if we did not put pressure on the Czechs they would decide Hermann was a spy and therefore "expendable." Eventually I got an interview with American Ambassador Douglas and put my questions to him: What was U.S. policy? How should I act? He felt that public statements by me made no difference; "But," he said, "I may be wrong . . . there is no general line of policy one can follow in these cases . . . "

So there I was again: still needing to do my own thinking.

Elsie and I went on trying to gather up any loose threads of evidence. We learned that two English people had been on Hermann's plane out of Warsaw, and when I appealed in the press for them to come forward they wrote to me. They could not remember the details of a journey that had taken place so long ago, but, they said, they had not noticed any other English-speaking person on board. I felt it was a serious oversight that no one had contacted them earlier.

We decided to find out for ourselves how a man could be snatched from an international airline without anyone knowing. Elsie got the help of a lawyer who specialized in airline work. He told us of the International Air Code, to which all the main airlines subscribed, including the nationalized Czech airlines. This code had quite elaborate provisions designed to protect passengers against just what had apparently happened to Hermann. Before a plane takes off, the flight captain has to sign the passenger manifest. A copy of this remains at the airport of departure, while the original is taken on the plane. In signing the manifest, the captain, on behalf of his company, accepts responsibility for all the passengers listed. If one of them fails to board the plane, the captain should be given a new list without the name of the missing person and sign that.

In Hermann's case the captain signed the list with his name on it, and no new list was made. If, as the Czechs later contended, the stewardess had struck his name when she found he was not on the plane, it was in contravention of the international code and resulted in responsibility for Hermann being unfixed. It was even quite possible that he had been arrested at Prague airport without Herta's seeing it.

Whatever had happened, we had a case against Czech Airlines. But when we came to consider how to proceed, everyone shrugged. The State Department did not think they could get anywhere with it, and the only way I could sue the Czechs was in a Czech court, since Hermann had bought his round-trip ticket to Warsaw in Prague.

The search for clues went on, and one day I heard of a Czech woman who had recently left Prague and was in London. I went to see her, and she was able to confirm that Novy and Loebl had disappeared. In her circles in Prague, moreover, people believed their disappearance had some connection with the Field brothers. Karel Markus, with whom Hermann had stayed on his last visit, had disappeared quite soon after Hermann, she said. She knew the Markuses and described the awful suffering of his wife, Sonia, who was left alone with her old mother and two very small children. People had tried to persuade Sonia to take a job "to take her mind off it," but she said she had to stay at home. I knew so well how Sonia must have felt. And then I asked how she was now.

"Sonia is dead," the woman said. "After the denunciation of Novy, she and her children were found dead in their flat. They say that she killed herself and the children."

## TIGHTENING OF THE SCREWS IN CZECHOSLOVAKIA

It was impossible to convince me, knowing that Hermann must be a prisoner, that the great United States could do nothing to get either Poland or Czechoslovakia to admit holding him captive. I always had the gnawing feeling that I must somehow be more effective.

I had already become convinced in the winter of 1949 that Czechoslovakia, not Poland, was more likely to be responsible. For one thing, Szymon Syrkus had told American intelligence that Hermann had left for Prague by air as planned. Syrkus would not deliberately mislead the search. Moreover, his wife, Helena, attended an architectural conference in Paris in the spring of 1950. It seemed unlikely that she would be free to travel to the West if the Poles were holding Hermann. And although the Polish ambassador in London refused to see me, I heard from him indirectly that Hermann was not in Poland.

But perhaps the strongest factors in my believing the Czechs guilty were that Hermann and I had so much more connection with Czechoslovakia, that Noel and Herta had disappeared there, and that Czechs who had spent the war years in London were disappearing.

Already in November 1949 we had seen the dramatic recall of Foreign Minister Vladimir Clementis from Lake Success, where he was leading the Czech delegation to the United Nations. Clementis had worked with the Czech government in exile in London. People warned him not to go home, but his conscience was clear and he thought he had nothing to fear. To my horror, his wife came from Prague to join him, and they both went back, Clementis stoutly denying that he could be in any danger.

In January 1950 *Rude Pravo* published sharp attacks on the wartime government in exile in London, of which Clementis and Vaclav Nosek were the only two former members still in office in Prague. That March Prague announced that Clementis had been replaced as foreign minister; he was given an insignificant job in a bank.

All that year the Czech communists scrutinized each other. At the Slovak Communist Party congress in May Clementis was accused of "bourgeois nationalism." Dr. Gustav Husak and Laco Novomesky, cabinet members representing Slovak interests in the Czech government and friends of Clementis, were also castigated. All three were called upon to confess their errors, but only the "self-criticism" of Husak and Novomesky was accepted.

In July the Central Committee of the Czech Communist Party put all its members on probation. A further purge of ex-Londoners started with the arrest of Otto Sling, general secretary for the Brno district. Sling had married an Englishwoman, spent time in Moscow, and knew Rudolf Slansky, general secretary of the Czech Communist Party, and his assistant, Maria Svermova. Svermova was later arrested and accused of plotting with Sling.

In November, Antonin Gregor, minister of foreign trade, returned from Moscow where he had signed a five-year trade agreement with Russia. Clearly the trade policy of the satellite countries was now being directed from Moscow, and trade with the West carefully controlled.

Contacts with the West were also being reduced as Czechs of various backgrounds were tried for being "traitors and spies" following contact with Western nationals. In January 1950 the government had issued a decree forbidding non-Communists to practice law, so there was no danger of a defense lawyer putting the interests of his client before those of the Party.

The offices of Western charity organizations in Prague were shut down and a number of diplomats expelled. The American and British Information Services and the offices of the British Council were closed on the grounds that they were slandering the regime.

I was frantic, and while everyone agreed that diplomatic approaches had to be left in the hands of the State Department, it was also thought that personal appeals on humanitarian grounds could do no harm. Despite the Cold War, some individuals in the West still had contact with the Russians, and I determined to seek a few out.

There was Dr. Hewlett Johnson, for example, dean of Canterbury Cathedral, a patrician figure who, because of his willingness to cooperate with the communists against fascism before the war and subsequent efforts in favor of peaceful coexistence with the USSR, was known as the Red Dean.

On Saturday, April 1, Elsie, six-month-old Deborah, and I took the train to Canterbury. The deanery was an ancient stone building close to the cathedral. The dean received us in his study, where a nice open fire burned. He had heard of our case, and I explained my fear that Hermann would be put on trial as a spy while we had no way of defending him. He listened sympathetically and said a trial might never come. He urged us not to give up hope, he would soon be going to a peace conference in Australia, he said, that he hoped would abate the Cold War, and then perhaps Hermann and Noel would be released. He did not see what more he could do.

Elsie was very disappointed and rather angry, and tired little Deborah's screams were echoing down the stone corridor. The dean offered to show us around the cathedral and, whisking Deborah in her carrier up onto his shoulders, strode out into the dusk. It was an unforgettable sight, this tall man in gaiters, white hair flowing, a small howling baby on his back.

Hermann did have supporters at home. Herbert Hunsaker, the dean of Cleveland College and our employer, enlisted the help of Dr. John Millis, president of Western Reserve University. Ralph Walker, president of the American Institute of Architects, of which Hermann was a member, also took up his case with the State Department. Elsie and I even turned to Congress, especially to our representatives from Ohio, Senator Robert Taft and Representative Frances Bolton.

Mrs. Bolton went to the State Department on our behalf in April, whereupon I received a four-page report explaining the department's policy. Among other things, this report responded to my complaint that the government seemed not to be pressing the Czechs as hard as the Poles, despite Hermann's connections with Czech nationals, saying in part:

> The Polish government has never made a reply to the American Notes. . . . In the absence of any written reply . . . the United States Government has continued to press the Poles. . . . The representatives of the Czechoslovak Government have been more definite than the Polish Government in their informal statements disclaiming that your husband was in their country. A Deputy Vice Minister (Hajdu) stated to Ambassador Briggs on November 30 in the presence of Acting Foreign Minister Siroky that it was certain that none of the Fields were in Czechoslovakia.

The report clarified, however, that in view of Kopriva's apparent reference to Hermann in the case of Vilem Novy, the department had, on April 13, sent a further note to the Czechoslovak government asking the following questions:

> 1. Was Hermann Field arrested at the Prague airport on August 22 before passing through customs?
> 2. Will the Czechoslovak authorities after further search state definitely whether or not Hermann Field is in Czechoslovakia?
> 3. If Hermann Field is now being detained in Czechoslovakia, would the Czechoslovak authorities inform the Embassy of any charges against him and permit him to be visited by an American consular official?

To my request that the State Department issue a public denial if Hermann were charged with espionage on behalf of the American government, they replied that they could not do this without knowing the exact charges, but "would make clear that he was never employed by the United States Government."

At the same time, the American ambassador to Poland, Joseph Flack, was instructed to take up the case again with the Polish acting foreign minister. Flack reminded him that for eight months the United States had been trying to obtain a report from the Poles on Hermann's disappearance. Was it really possible that an investigation was still being pursued? The minister replied that it was indeed continuing, and as soon as he had some information he would transmit it to the ambassador.

As for the Czechs, in a curt note of April 27 they said that they had nothing to add to their previous statements and would not indulge in "clairvoyance" as to what Ladislav Kopriva might have meant—something it accused the State Department of doing. Not only was this note lacking in the usual diplomatic courtesies, but it also made clear that the Czech Foreign Office was not going to risk asking its own security police to whom their allegations referred. A month later the State Department replied, stating that in view of the "paucity of positive information" provided by the Czechs regarding the whereabouts of Noel, Herta, and Hermann, it must "hold the Czechoslovak Government responsible for the welfare of these three American citizens in the event that they should have been in Czechoslovakia since their respective disappearances last year."

From Poland no information was forthcoming, and so on June 22 the American embassy in Warsaw sent the Poles a fresh note, stating that in default of further information from them the U.S. government must hold the Polish government responsible for Hermann's welfare in the event that he had been in Poland after his disappearance.

Elsie and I considered these notes terribly weak; they seemed to suggest that we had no evidence at all. We would have greatly preferred some form of sanction that would operate until Poland or Czechoslovakia cleared itself by providing evidence against another country.

One member of Congress suggested to the State Department that Americans be banned from traveling to Poland and Czechoslovakia. Not only did that not happen, but economic ties remained in place as well. The *New York Times* of June 9, 1950, for example, reported that a three-way trade agreement involving Austria, Poland, and the American Economic Cooperation Administration (ECA) had been arranged with Washington's consent.

I was furious and wrote to the State Department that the consent should have been conditional on the Poles immediately answering their note regarding Hermann. I further asked yet again that, as a minimum sanction, all travel by Americans to Poland be banned until a reply was received.

No such action was forthcoming, and my irritation with the Poles was not reduced when I read that, shortly after concluding their agreement with the ECA, they signed a new one with the USSR "to reduce their dependence on the capitalist countries." It seemed they were getting the best of both worlds.

I concluded that our policy was to maintain as many contacts as possible, through trade, travel, and diplomatic representation. The initiative in trying to cut these ties came repeatedly from the communist side, in the form of attacks on Western organizations of all sorts, whether they were charities, the British and American Information Centers, journalists, or even diplomats. We turned the other cheek whenever possible, though in the grosser cases we had to give tit for tat. Whenever a mere private individual got arrested strong public protest was needed to induce the State Department to decide, regretfully, that reprisal was necessary.

The days of "gunboat diplomacy" to defend U.S. nationals caught in enemy territory were over. It finally hit home that the interests of a person so detained were in direct opposition to the interests of his country. He was a hostage, and something would have to be given up to achieve his release.

It looked to me as if the underlying reason for the communist provocations in Eastern European countries, coming so frequently in 1949 and 1950, was the desire of Russia to dissipate what little goodwill remained toward the Western democracies that had been their former allies in the war. And behind this was, I believe, the Russian fear that one of her other satellites might break away, as had Tito's Yugoslavia. These were in essence preemptive strikes against any potentially dissident communist party. Naturally, the policy of Washington was to oppose this, to maintain American influence and contacts in the satellite countries. This doomed many of our efforts to failure.

The only sanction ever taken in support of Hermann was by the American Institute of Architects. Their president, Ralph Walker, discussed the case with the State Department, and, having found that they would not apply any sanction, the AIA passed a resolution, addressed to the Union Internationale des Architectes, with which it was affiliated, stating that the Americans would send "no delegate to Poland or anywhere within that area" until something was heard regarding Hermann.

Ralph Walker reported to Elsie that this was followed up at the next meeting of the UIA that spring in Paris, where the discussion revolved a great deal around Hermann. The Polish delegation included Helena Syrkus. Mrs. Syrkus—who of course had invited Hermann to come to Poland and had accompanied him to the airport on that last day—argued that his situation was unusual in that he had come on his own, whereas members of the AIA would be invited by the Polish government, which would guarantee their safety.

This was a bit much, and the next scheduled meeting of the UIA, scheduled to be held in Warsaw, was canceled. Although this action by his colleagues was valuable in showing that Hermann was somebody who was known and cared about, it could not produce his release.

The State Department had, of course, weightier matters to deal with. Americans were losing their lives in Korea, and relations between East and West were at a new low. The communists themselves, however, sometimes provided us with a news item that enabled us to keep the Field case alive. As a friendly newsman from the Associated Press reminded me, "The squeaky wheel gets the grease." And so I continued to make myself heard.

## ANOTHER DISAPPEARANCE

On September 2, 1950, the press reported that six high officials of the East German communist party, the Socialist Unity Party, had been expelled for associating with Noel, "the American spy." A secret meeting of the Central Committee had been held on August 24, at which Secretary-General Walter Ulbricht had accused many of his colleagues of forming "a nest of class enemies" within the party. Significantly, they were also charged with "lacking trust in the Soviet Union as the leading progressive force."

Dr. Fritz Kaul, an East German lawyer, said that Noel could be produced as a prosecution witness if needed. This prompted the U.S. High Commissioner in Germany to ask the Soviet authorities in Berlin for help in locating "this American citizen." But there was no response.

Thus the repercussions of the Field case were publicly extended to a third country, Germany. The international connection was clear, though in each case the accusations were carefully made by a national of the country concerned. And in each case the same type of person was hit: a communist who had been a refugee in the West during or before the war and who later held a position of importance in his native country.

Hot on the heels of this new evidence that the Field case was a matter of high policy and that Noel, at least, was under arrest came a letter from Elsie saying she had heard that Erica Wallach was intending to go to Germany in the hope of finding Noel.

Erica had lived with Noel and Herta in Switzerland during the war years as their foster daughter. She and her parents, Dr. and Mrs. Glaser, were opponents of Hitler who had left their country estate in Germany and found refuge in Majorca. When the Franco rebellion overtook Spain, Dr. Glaser volunteered his medical services on the Republican side. After Franco's victory the Glasers eventually came to England and worked for the Czech Refugee Trust Fund, where I met them.

Erica, still only a teenager, had been suffering from typhoid and was evacuated from Spain by Noel and Herta, then on the League of Nations Evacuation Commission. They took her with them to their home in Geneva, where she remained during the war. In 1945 she returned to Germany in uniform with the U.S. military government, and eventually married an American GI, Robert Wallach. They had two small children and were living in Paris.

I had never met Erica, and did not even know her married name. But Elsie's news alarmed me. How on earth could she help Noel by going to Germany? If she went to East Germany, I felt sure, she would not return.

I sat down and wrote her a letter explaining why I thought she should not go: "We have to face the hard and bitter fact that the Fields are pawns in a vast political scene . . . It is a matter of top Cominform policy . . ."

It was now a year since Hermann had been taken. My parents made valiant efforts to give Hugh and Alan a good summer in spite of the ever-present shadow over our lives. One Sunday we all drove to St. Albans, wandered around the abbey and across the meadows to the river. Suddenly Alan was gone. I became frantic and dashed about asking people to help. Then we found him, sitting calmly in the car. I hugged him with tears running down my cheeks, and he wondered what was wrong with me.

We drove home, full of thankfulness that this time the nightmare had been a false alarm. As I opened the door the phone rang: "This is the Associated Press. Mrs. Field, what do you know about Erica Wallach? She disappeared in Berlin on August 26." That was two weeks ago already. My warning letter had been too late.

Apparently Erica had gone to Berlin two days after the East German communist purge. One of those ousted was Leo Bauer, chief editor of the radio station Deutschlandsender. She had gotten to know him during the war, and later, when she was stationed in Germany with the U.S. occupation administration, she had renewed her contact with him. It was said that Erica had been planning to see him, in the hope that he could help find Noel. She had promised her husband she would not be away more than two days and that she would phone him after arriving at Tempelhof Airport in West Berlin, but he heard nothing.

A few days later, on August 31, the official East German newspaper, *Neues Deutschland,* published a detailed account of the supposed activities of Noel and his connection with the purged Germans, and Erica's name was also mentioned. Clearly she would be arrested, if possible. Perhaps she had been invited to Berlin for that purpose.

Just as the Czech Kopriva had modeled his statement on the thesis of the Rajk trial in Hungary, so this purge of Germans elaborated the same theme, and the proceedings of the earlier trials were used as evidence against the present victims: "The trials against the bands of spies, saboteurs, and murderers of the traitor Rajk in Hungary (September 1949) and Kostov in Bulgaria (December 1949) produced ample proof that the Anglo-American Secret Services began their preparations for a Third World War against the Soviet Union and its Allied countries already long before the end of the Second World War." In the East German case, moreover, the entire argument depended on Noel's guilt: "With all ten persons involved, the starting point is the same: long-standing connections maintained until recently with representatives of the Anglo-American Secret Services, especially with the American spy Noel H. Field, who camouflaged himself as a 'Good Samaritan.'"

Noel was supposedly not in Germany, yet the prosecution lawyer Kaul had rashly told newsmen that he could be produced if necessary. We tried, unsuccessfully, to follow up this thread. The communists, however, were too wary to have Noel appear, and I rather doubted that the East Germans even had a chance to cross-examine him. In any case, all the people named in the purges disappeared completely from the scene. The expected public trial never came, but a year later it was reported that one of the accused men, Willi Kreikemeyer, had been sentenced by a Russian military court for espionage. Once again the international connection was underlined.

On October 27, the Cominform's journal, published in Bucharest, carried an article entitled "Agents of American Imperialism Exposed" that recapitulated the German purge, including the allegations against Noel. In all this it was conveniently forgotten that Noel had left the Department of State in 1936. His later work was thus referred to as if he were still a State Department official, with events long past being reinterpreted to fit the communists' present theory. He had been pronounced a spy by the highest authorities, to whom there was simply no effective reply.

# 10

## Face to Face

The white translucency of the two small panes of glass had changed to an impenetrable gray. Once more darkness had descended on the unseen world outside and I began counting to see how many hundred circuits from door to window and back would bring me to supper and the conquest of another day.

It was mid-November, and a steadily more penetrating cold crept through our cellar. I fought it by using both blankets as part of my daytime apparel, one wrapped cumbersomely like a tube around me from below my arms almost to my ankles, the other pulled tightly over my shoulders. In this new strategy of survival every action was directed against the strength-sapping onslaught of cold, and every added hour of warmth was a victory, in which the mug of tea at supper became an ally not only for the liquid heat it diffused through the body but for the warmth transferred through the metal to my hands until the last drop was gone.

I stopped a moment to listen. Hadn't I heard the rattle of the keys just now close by? The bolt of my door slammed back with an echo. At once I was tense, my keyed-up perception telling me that an important moment had arrived. Too early for supper. The wrong time for interrogation. My table and chair gone, the cell contained nothing but the straw sack, the pail, and myself—nothing more to remove.

As the door flew open I could hardly believe my eyes. In his hands the guard was holding not just my battered pants and jacket but objects I hadn't seen since that moment over two months before when I had first sleepwalked into this haunted building: my shirt and necktie, my underwear, even my belt. He beckoned for me to take them. Seeing my continued perplexity in the face of the obvious, he pointed to the blankets draped around me and mimed an unwrapping movement. The door closed again. With a mixture of dread and anticipation I shed my covers, my battered suit, my prison shirt and long-johns, and started from scratch with the once-familiar routine of dressing. As I finished, the door opened. The guard smiled apologetically as he held up the ragged remnant that had once been my socks. I adjusted them as best I could around my feet and slipped back into my laceless moccasins. A thought seemed to come to him and he disappeared, returning triumphantly with two shoelaces and a shoe brush.

In my mind just one question kept revolving: For what am I being dressed up this way? The guard was fumbling in his breast pocket and pulled out a comb and handed it to me, pointing to my hair. My heart pounded harder still. How I wanted to recognize the incipient surge of hope inside me, but instinctively I fought it back, retreating into an emotionless passivity.

He left, and I was alone. Suddenly I remembered: the metal button I had been sharpening tediously every night, which was hidden between the planks and the frame of the cot. Given the unknown turns that lay ahead I didn't want to be separated from it. I sat down on the straw sack and tried inconspicuously to pry it out, but already the door was opening again. This time it was the head guard and he was carrying my raincoat. So it was definite: I was leaving. I felt a rush of wild yet suppressed hope. The guard handed me a hat, which turned out not to be mine at all, much to his embarrassment. No wonder! Before he took it back from me I noticed something most interesting: the maker's name and address. Its rightful owner, presumably like me an inhabitant of this cellar, had apparently bought it on Regent Street in London. But before I had time to reflect on this, the familiar black-velvet eye pads were produced from the head guard's pocket and I was pitched into darkness.

This time there was no tarpaulin, no expedition across unseen fields. Immediately on leaving the building I bumped into what turned out to be the rear end of my old friend, the delivery van. As I crawled in, guided by two sturdy hands, I stumbled against a hard object, which I identified as my suitcase. So it was accompanying me on my unknown journey. I could have hugged it. Wasn't the fact that we had been reunited the surest sign that I had left this cellar for good?

I waited for someone to remove the eye pads. After all, the interior of this truck was no secret to me, nor was the courtyard of the MBP headquarters in Warsaw, presumably our destination. But nothing happened.

We drove along bumpy and winding roads, on and on. I listened closely for signs that we were approaching the city: other cars; smoother, straighter roads; streetcars; stops at intersections. They failed to materialize, even after what must have been half an hour. A new dull realization sunk in: not Warsaw this time; and at once the question: What then? And the inevitable sickening answer: east, east at last. It had come. My suitcase and I were to be delivered at the frontier. And then? On and on, east, east—Siberia and oblivion. Yes, I am leaving Poland today, but not in the direction I had hoped.

I retreated far into myself and passively waited for whatever might come. We were twisting and winding more than ever. We stopped abruptly and the horn sounded. After a moment of complete country stillness a metal gate began creaking—a familiar sound by now, and not at all promising. We had reached our destination and it appeared to be no more urban than the place we had left. After a short uphill we maneuvered and again came to a stop. The motor was turned off. Someone opened the door.

It was like a repeat performance of that first journey into the night in September. The cold country air rushed in as my invisible companions tugged at my sleeves and helped me to the ground. Somewhere close by from inside a building I could hear a motor humming. It seemed we were going straight toward the sound. I stumbled up two stone steps and found myself inside an echoing hallway. A new set of stone steps, this time down. I counted eight of them, as the din of the motor rose to a crescendo, drowning out all other sounds and echoing weirdly as if in an endless vaulted space. There was a peculiar smell of newness about the place, of fresh plaster and lumber. We turned to the left on a cement floor and then again left as I stumbled over a low threshold onto a resounding wooden floor. I sensed we had entered a much smaller space.

Someone undid my blindfold and I found myself looking straight into Shoo's perspiring face. Apparently he noticed my surprise, and a sheepish grin played around his mouth. "Nu, nu," he muttered almost good-naturedly, as if gently scolding a trained seal that had forgotten to take its turn; then suddenly he shook his shock of unkempt hair, his face full of frenzy, as he pointed toward the far wall. Without even bothering to see whether I was obeying he turned abruptly and shuffled out into the dark corridor as the wide door closed noisily behind him, leaving me standing there wondering how he had reentered my life. Here at the edge of nowhere it almost seemed like meeting an old friend.

With intense curiosity I looked around at my new surroundings. Though reminiscent of my previous quarters, the room also had significant differences, which impressed me the more I explored. The basic elements were the same: again a cellar cell of some sort; an obscured, barred and grilled window; whitewashed masonry walls; a bolted door with a peephole; a pail with wooden lid in the corner; and a bulging straw mattress on a cot. The difference was that between an obsolete model, battered from use, and the latest design. While this space was much more confined than the cell I had lived in, hardly more than half its width, about six feet across and eleven long with a ceiling so low I could almost touch it, that didn't worry me. The first thing I noticed was that it was warm and cozy. Sure enough, there under the window was a thick loop of welded pipe. I went over and felt it: it was hot, and I almost cried with relief.

I observed the other improvements, one after another. The horizontal two-wing window was more than double the previous window in size and would be sufficient to provide daylight in spite of the thick coat of white paint that obscured the glass. Instead of damp bricks there was a planed plank floor, so new that each footstep left a mark on it. The whitewashed walls were spotlessly clean, as if they had been done that very day. The light bulb, instead of glaring inescapably from the middle of the ceiling, was in a caged reflecting box recessed into the side wall. The door was metal clad and strangely wide, rather like a hospital door, just as the previous one had been extreme in its narrowness; and in place of the variable oblong observation slot it had a circular, splayed Judas eye.

What attracted my attention most, however, was the sleeping arrangement—not so much the fact that the blanket, sheet, and pillowcase lying folded on the straw sack were obviously completely new, as was the sack itself, but that it all rested unmistakably on an American army cot with diagonal strut legs, looking as if it had just been brought down from the attic of Valley Farm. At that moment it seemed the most precious thing on earth, a bit of my homeland to keep me company here, to give me strength and solace. At odd moments that evening, while making the bed and afterward lying on it, I kept making surreptitious inspections of each part of it, and sure enough I soon came upon an army Q.M. number on the underside of the canvas with a date early in 1945. How in heaven's name had it ended up in a Polish secret police cellar? Yes, if only it could speak.

Looking around my tiny world as I lay awake long into the night, I felt almost happy. I had the eerie feeling of being the only inmate of this cellar. It was not exactly a reassuring thought. Even the awareness of unknown companions in misery in the other place had lent a kind of solidarity to the suffering. And why had I alone been singled out for this weird one-man operation? By the next morning I felt a little reassured: I discovered we were two. I had a neighbor somewhere to the right of me who also received his clothes, went with his pail to the washroom, and had food shoved in through his door. His presence became unmistakable a little later that morning. Someone was crying far away in the hollow of the cellar. It was a sort of crying I had never heard before, on and on as if to himself, in complete desolation and abandonment. How strange to imagine a man doing this. I could not conceive of crying myself; it went against a basic instinct for survival that froze all normal emotion. Perhaps my neighbor was a mere youth in his first hours of solitude and self-pity. His crying was strangely high pitched and resonant, almost mechanical, like a child weeping itself to sleep.

My cell was apparently right beside the main entrance to the building, and with every arrival or departure the scrape of shoes on the stone steps reverberated through the thick wall. It was evidently half a flight up to the floor above, the other half being the one that had brought me blindfolded down into the cellar. The entrance hall was bounded by an inner and outer door, and everyone going in or out was guided by a second individual, a doorman with keys who kept both doors carefully locked. There was also a great deal of lugging in of heavy objects. In fact, during the day I heard a continual racket of hammering and sawing inside and out, typical of the last stages of a building operation. In the cellar, pipes were being cut and joined, wooden floors similar to mine, presumably, being laid. Outside I could hear bricklayers at work on a scaffolding that in the early morning hours threw its silhouette across my window. More than that, it revealed a projecting wall right beside me, and from the shape of its shadow I decided that the entrance hall protruded from the rest of the building in a semicircle. From this silhouette, and also from the stair sounds, I established that I found myself in a single-story building.

On my trips twice a day to the washroom with my pail I visually supplemented the sounds of my new environment. This confirmed my first impression that I was in a superior version of the facility I had been in before, about the same length and width, with cells ranged on both sides of a central corridor, the building probably made from the shell of some existing farm structure if not entirely new. The cellar was higher out of the ground, more like a basement with wide, obscured windows at each end of the corridor like the one in my cell. This meant that during the day sufficient light came in from outside to eliminate the need for continuous artificial light, this being maintained only during the hours of darkness. On my side of the corridor there were seven doors, the one in the middle leading to the stair hall, the other six opening into cells, of which mine was the fourth as indicated by a number on the jamb.

The north side of the corridor was subdivided similarly, but only two of the spaces turned out to be cells, bringing the total to not more than eight for the entire basement. The rest of the north side consisted of a number of service rooms, which I gradually came to identify. In one of these, at the center opposite the stair hall, was the erratic motor that made such an infernal noise for unpredictable spells throughout the day. I soon established that it was an automatic water pump. The interesting thing was that it was called on to produce a volume of water quite out of line with the little dribble consumed in this basement, a sure sign that it serviced other buildings in the vicinity. Opposite me was an open curtained space of the same size as my cell. It was the guard's enclave, with a telephone. Beyond it in turn, entered through a narrow side door, was the boiler room, which was serviced by the guards themselves. Along the boiler room's doorless corridor wall, narrow wooden carpeted stairs led to the floor above without any sort of barrier, as innocently as in a private residence.

The most surprising thing in the basement, however, was at the opposite end of the north side, across from cell No. 1: the washroom—and what a washroom it was! About twelve feet by twelve, it had a big obscured horizontal window in each outside wall and was equipped with a bathing area with four showerheads with elaborate individual controls and thermometers, two large washbasins on the opposite wall, two WCs separated by projecting wing walls, a urinal, and in the inside corner by the door, a built-in coal range with a cylindrical water tank on brackets above it—all evidently just installed and on a scale fit for an army company. With all this, I waited in vain for the big influx of bathers, but the washroom was never to be used by more than the handful of prisoners who happened to be kept in the building and by the guards who tended us.

In the days that followed I examined every little clue to explain my shift from cell No. 4 in location x to cell No. 4 in location y, with a twenty- or twenty-five-mile trip in between. Whatever the reasons, I sensed a strange continuity. While everything here had the mark of newness and a relaxation relative to the inhuman conditions of the other cellar, my new abode was nonetheless in all essentials merely a kid-glove variant. It was as if I had simply shifted from third to second class on the same unfortunate ghost ship. I experienced the same succession of routines—on a relaxed level—from morning to night. And most marked of all, there was the same blustering buffooning Shoo, even though subdued to a degree in keeping with his changed surroundings. And to bear out the analogy further, each night after I was under my blanket, my neighbor, whose unrestrained crying had startled me so that first morning, was quietly guided upstairs for interrogation, but without the slightest indication of a rabbit hunt.

The interrogation room was almost above me, and at times the sound of excited voices came through from above, especially the prisoner's. He had an amazingly high, hysterical voice and often launched into long, impetuous tirades, not letting the interrogator get a word in. As a result of these nightly outbursts I came to characterize my neighbor in No. 3 as "the man with the high voice."

I noticed something else about him. Saturdays now provided the great treat of a real wash under a hot shower, a tremendous improvement over trying to get clean with a bucket of water in an icy cell. After some careful listening I discovered that my neighbor was not given his turn under the shower; rather, hot water was carried in to him in a big enamel basin (which I had spotted in the washroom), to be collected from his cell when he signaled with a knock on the door that he was finished. Perhaps he was an invalid or had some sickness, which also could account for his crying and excitability upstairs.

The most difficult things to identify were the outside sounds, since my window was kept tightly sealed despite repeated requests for even a crack of fresh air. Even so, I heard the cocks crowing in the dawn and later the twitter of birds outside my window, the distant chugging of a tractor—the same country sounds that Muffin had heard before. And then once unmistakably, too, the rising and falling purr of an outboard motor boat. What a strange coincidence! And on several occasions, just before lunch, didn't I also catch the sound of an airplane passing close overhead at the usual time?

Once when I left my cell, bucket in hand, I found that someone had forgotten to pull the curtain that concealed the guards' space opposite. My eyes immediately fell on the guard's table. Why of course, it was the very one removed from my cell in the other cellar only a few days ahead of me. Even the same chair. I had an urge to stop and stroke them. Why would anyone take the trouble to ship them miles across the countryside to this far-off spot? Yet here they were.

The same thing happened in another area as well. While, like everything else here, the bowl and mug and wooden ladle that appeared on my floor at mealtimes were all brand new, the prison fare itself had not undergone the slightest change. In fact, it seemed as if the cook had made the trip along with me, so unmistakably was the food prepared by the same hands. The sausage sections were laid on the bread just the same way and the hamburger patty had the identical shape. But that was crazy. Why would they have shifted the cook along with me?

Soon I made another discovery. There was no cook hidden in this building, nor even a kitchen. Thus I noticed a sequence of footsteps along the path outside, up through the entry, and down the corridor stairs as the signal that heralded a meal, and quickly established that our food was brought on a tray from a building somewhere to the east of the one I was in. The same kitchen as before? Surely that was impossible. Yet didn't everything here defy logic?

And so I began to suspect every more strongly that, far from being within a stone's throw of the Russian border, I hadn't even left the general locality in which I had spent the previous months. Could it be that this driving on twisty country roads had no more significance than to turn me round and round in a mad game of blind man's buff? Filling in the picture became a favorite pastime in the months ahead, but only much, much later did I realize how very near, in fact, the new cell No. 4 was to the old one.

Here there was only one guard at a time except when the cell door was opened; at those times whoever happened to be doorman upstairs or the guard previously on duty would act as reinforcement. The three who spelled each other in the cellar were Shoo, who seemed to be in charge; a little fellow with a diminutive stub mustache whom I had seen once before in the other cellar; and an older man who initially had the worried and somewhat embarrassed expression of a beginner.

Of this trio, who for long stretches were to provide my sole contact with the human species, the little fellow proved the most unattractive. He was like Shoo's shadow and did his best to emulate all of his worst traits. What in Shoo was a kind of unpredictable madness, which could come on without thought or premeditation yet often contained an element of good-natured buffoonery, in his understudy took the form of calculated sallies of the cat-and-mouse variety. Not that he ever did physical violence to me or was guilty of direct sadism. It was merely that the "Mean One," as I came to call him, had an irrepressible urge, sparked no doubt by his diminutive size and colorless personality, to be a somebody. His mustache helped, but still he was simply the type one could easily ignore and push around. Here in the basement, however, he was suddenly transformed into the man of authority, and every time he opened the cell door he acted his part to the hilt, always on the lookout to humiliate. Long after Shoo had given up the face-the-wall-and-hands-above-the head procedure with me, the Mean One continued to take delight in using this and many other modes of calculated degradation. My defiance, however, only grew as the weeks went by. It was the first sign of a toughening that eventually locked me into an almost continuous fight with my captors, even to the very edge of death.

The third guard—I named him "Fatty"—was quite different from the other two. He took his job seriously, as, I suspected, he would have any job. He had a German air about him, and I wouldn't have been surprised if he came from one of the western sections of Poland with strong Germanic influences. All that Fatty cared about was orderliness and routine. Within that framework he had an almost paternalistic concern for the welfare of his charge, treating me much as he would his master's stable horse. He demanded obedience, not to assert himself but because that was in the order of things. Cleanliness was also important to him. While Shoo and the Mean One thought nothing of hacking my chin into a bloody pulp on a Saturday shave as something that I deserved, Fatty sweated and blushed every time he made the smallest cut, shaking his head apologetically. Unlike the other two he knew isolated German words, usually expressed in imperatives in the familiar *du* form: Go . . . Stop . . . Eat . . . Hurry . . . Forbidden. These were his favorites. Perhaps he had been a prisoner himself during the war and had had to learn to obey these words. In any case they were said without insult or malice.

Though I had reason to appreciate the great improvement in my physical circumstances, the essential problem remained unchanged. I was still swallowed up by an inexplicable nothingness with no idea of what might lie ahead; still deprived of any sort of activity, with no external focus for my thoughts, no outside inputs I could seize upon to fill the vacuum from sleep to sleep.

After having suffered from persistent cold before, I now found myself facing the opposite extreme: excessive heat. Shivering was replaced by perspiring; instead of wrapping myself in a mountain of blankets, I paced the cell in just shirt and long johns. Still I felt no relief. In large part my growing discomfort stemmed from inadequate air. Twenty-four hours a day I was consuming the limited oxygen provided by less than six hundred cubic feet of almost hermetically sealed space. The double-pane window was firmly closed. The only changes of air came during the short interval my door stood open while I went to the washroom each morning and evening. Meanwhile all my pleas to have the window opened, even briefly, were ignored.

This lack of air had a strong depressive effect. Physically it heightened a tendency toward abdominal pains in the afternoon, a symptom that had already begun in the tension of the other cellar. Now, too, my mouth became inflamed. Although I always received enough food, and the midday meal was in fact incongruously good for prison fare, without doubt it was deficient in vitamins.

It was no wonder that my health began to suffer. Yet at the same time, I saw the situation as an opportunity to test the attitude of my captors. If faced with my becoming critically ill, what would they do? If the intention was to have me disappear for good, a fatal sickness might be rather convenient for them, or at least a matter of indifference. If, however, they wanted to keep me in cold storage for some future eventuality, they would be forced to take action.

I began by explaining my complaint as best I could to Shoo. He scratched his head and nodded. Nothing happened. Perhaps he hadn't understood. I tried Fatty next, tapping into his limited German vocabulary. He listened seriously and said he would report the matter. Again I waited. The next day I even had a go at the Mean One. When after another day still nothing happened I began to fear the worst. I decided to make one more attempt, this time saying nothing but dramatizing my complaint to make certain it was understood. At the onset of pain in the afternoon I grabbed my pillow and started pacing back and forth holding it pressed against my abdomen, screwing up my face periodically. I must have been an alarming spectacle, and I didn't fail to notice that the little cover on the Judas eye often shifted and the telephone rang several times during the next hour in the guards' space opposite.

I had barely lain down that evening when I heard someone unlocking the door of the room above my cell. There was some moving about of chairs. The phone rang opposite and a moment later my suit was dropped into my cell and I was told to get dressed. I was led up the corridor stairs to a curtained door, beside which I had to stand facing the wall while the guard knocked. I was ushered into a brightly lit office with the usual heavily curtained window, a modern desk, and a big Persian rug rolled up on the floor. A solidly built man with a hairless cannonball head and thick horn-rimmed glasses sat on a chair staring mutely at me. But what drew my attention was the second man standing behind him. It was the noncommunicative individual who had been waiting for me in that room at the airport and whom I hadn't seen since that unfortunate afternoon.

I was so taken aback that I looked blankly at the seated man as he said in perfect German: "I understand you have some complaint with your health."

It dawned on me that this was a doctor and that I was up here no doubt in direct consequence of my pillow performance. I was so excited by the implication I almost forgot what the problem was. I tried to explain but got all tangled up. It was so long since I had spoken with anyone who could understand me that I felt quite drunk and my words came out in a torrent. Even more than explaining my ailment, I wanted to use the occasion to draw this man's attention to my plight in general. However, as soon as he caught my drift the uncommunicative individual opened his mouth for the first time and in Polish told me sharply to stop. The doctor then examined me without comment, and as soon as I was back in my clothes I was hustled on the run back down to my cell. I did not care, though; I was happy and felt triumphant. My strategy had brought results, and the test was positive beyond any doubt: they did not want me to die, at least not at this point. And what heartened me especially was that I had, for the first time since I left the world, been treated as a human being.

All my feelings of that evening were reinforced the next morning at breakfast when to my surprise a mug of hot milk and white French bread with butter replaced the usual watery grain coffee and black bread and cheese. Lunch, too, was completely changed, now consisting of a bowl of barley broth; a plate of grated raw carrots flavored with lemon, topped with two soft-boiled eggs; and some dried white bread. For supper again a mug of milk, this time soured and set, and once more white bread and butter. I felt delight. Not because I really liked the food better—in fact, loss of the midday meal was to prove quite a deprivation. Not even because I knew this diet would help me avoid serious illness. But because I now had evidence that I was not expendable, that maintenance of my life was a matter of close concern to my captors.

A few days after the incident with the doctor I was called upstairs in the late afternoon. The doctor again? When I entered I found a shortish, fair-haired man with a bushy mustache and probing eyes sitting behind the desk, his gaze fixed on me rigidly. I sat down on a stool in the corner beside the door and stared back. The staring session continued silently. In spite of his strange behavior I had the impression of a more mature and sympathetic individual than any I had met so far. He was about my own age and somewhat of an intellectual, judging from his informally tasteful clothes, a tweed suit and hand-woven wool necktie.

At last he broke the silence: "How long have you been under detention?" His voice was quiet and unaggressive, and he spoke excellent German.

"About twelve weeks."

He reflected on this a while, his eyes all the time on me. Then, quite casually, he asked how my health was bearing up. I mentioned my ailment and the doctor's visit, to which he replied: "Yes, I have heard from other prisoners too that he is a conscientious and competent man." And after a pause: "You see, we can help you if we want to."

· Another short silence, then in a measured voice he continued: "You know, your circumstances can change a lot. They can become better, as you have seen. Also a lot worse. That lies entirely in our power. I think you understand me. It seems to me we have reached a stage when we can sit down together and not beat about the bush. We can approach our subject together as two thoroughly familiar with it, and with an objectivity like that of colleagues in a laboratory."

I could not quite make out what he was driving at, but I was tremendously relieved by his quiet reasonableness. And most important, we could talk directly to each other in a common language. I nodded eagerly: "Why yes, that is just what I would like to do. As you can imagine, I certainly want to get to the bottom of this whole awful mistake. I can't believe its perpetuation can be of any value to you either."

Again there was silence. He leaned back in his chair as if turning my remark over carefully in his mind. Now as he spoke he looked at me still more probingly.

"Mistake, Mr. Field? That you are at last forced to lay your cards on the table? Or do you mean the game itself? For years you have been playing against us with particular cunning. The truth was bound to come out eventually. The game is up and you are in our power. Surely it must be evident to you by now that the only intelligent course for you is to assist us in undoing your handiwork of the past. I am hoping that it is in this spirit that we will be working together in this room."

Unable to contain myself, I blurted out: "But for heaven's sake, *what* game? What have I been playing against you?"

Ignoring my question, he went on, emphasizing every word: "Yes, you were like all the rest. You felt secure, and as a result you overplayed your hand. You reckoned on the lack of vigilance of the people's power, on our inexperience. But you and your backers miscalculated, Mr. Field, and your presence here represents a great defeat for the class enemy. Yours was not the last conspiracy against us, but we have struck at the core and paralyzed the biggest threat since we won our freedom. Damage already done has been great. We were slow, but our strength lies in our determination to extirpate every last vestige."

Again I broke in, dumbfounded by the certainty of his tone: "But you're not talking sense. What conspiracy? Tell me what have I done to you. Give me just one example!"

He got up and started walking slowly back and forth between window and door. Then he stopped abruptly in front of me.

"And who is Allen Dulles?"

"Allen Dulles? I don't know. Why?" I tried to recall. Hadn't the name come up sometime before the war in Switzerland in connection with the Bank of International Settlements? I hazarded: "There's a John Foster Dulles. That's the only one I'm sure of. He's some sort of adviser on foreign affairs to the Republican Party and has been at many international conferences. Probably this one is some relative of his, a son or brother. It's quite a well-known family."

He had resumed his pacing: "Mr. Field, tell me precisely, what were your contacts with Allen Dulles, and what was the nature of your assignments from him?"

"Assignments? But I just told you, I know nothing about the man. I never met him."

"Yes, perhaps you haven't actually seen him. That wasn't necessary for your work, for your directives." He fell into silence again and then abruptly changed the subject.

"When did you last see your brother?"

"In the summer of 1947 in Paris."

"And where did you go after seeing him?"

"To Switzerland."

"Yes, for two days. And then?"

"To Czechoslovakia."

"And tell me, did you briefly see your brother in the spring of 1939?"

"Yes. I stopped in Geneva for two days on my way back to England."

"And where did you go from England?"

"Well, I planned to return home to America, since I had finished my architectural work abroad, and . . ."

"Exactly, the normal thing would have been to return home. But what did you do instead, a few days after arriving in London from seeing your brother in Geneva? Where in fact did you go?"

"I went to Prague at the suggestion of my future wife, who was working for the British refugee committee, to help anti-Nazi refugees in imminent danger of their lives following Hitler's seizure of Czechoslovakia."

"Yes, so you went to Czechoslovakia after seeing him, as you did later in 1947." He walked back and forth in silence and then sat down behind the desk. "And tell me, this past summer, you planned to see your brother? Where?"

"Why yes, I had hoped to see him in Geneva. Then I thought he was in Prague, but . . ."

"But that plan went wrong somehow, didn't it?" He smiled. "And you didn't see him."

"No, unfortunately I could not find him." I was feeling increasingly uneasy. Where were these probes leading?

"Unfortunately, you could not find him," he repeated with emphasis. "You said in your written depositions that he disappeared at the beginning of May. But you waited until August to do something about it. In other words, until you had your directives."

"I didn't know about it until I saw my brother's wife in Geneva in July."

"And it was she who gave you your directives?"

"I offered to help her, in whatever way she deemed most useful, to try to locate her husband."

"And the directive was again Prague, as it had been in 1939 and 1947?"

"You know very well that if I imagined I might come under suspicion of some activity against one of your countries, I would hardly have proceeded to Prague after the warning of my brother's disappearance there. The fact of my flying to Czechoslovakia and appealing to the authorities there, followed by my brother's wife two days later, proves our innocence."

"Oh no doubt you would have preferred to stay away. But you were under orders. You had no choice. You had to warn your coworkers here in Prague and Warsaw. And perhaps Berlin too?" He opened the drawer and pulled out my brown appointments diary. "You had some Berlin addresses in here, didn't you?" he said as he turned to the last page. "Yes, Berlin. Is that your writing?" He handed it over to me.

"No, my sister-in-law's. She thought perhaps these people might be willing to help, as acquaintances of my brother's here in the East."

"Your sister-in-law's writing . . ." He put the little book back in the drawer and looked sharply at me. "It was a desperate gamble, Mr. Field—this innocence—but it failed, as is evidenced by your sitting here today."

I felt like I was in an insane asylum. Why was I being crowded step by step into a defensive posture? Up to now I was sure my misfortune, if not triggered by my misguided photographing venture, was the result of my looking into my brother's disappearance and coming too close on his trail, so that in turn my disappearance became a necessity. The mere fact of my searching for him behind Communist lines could be twisted into an act of espionage. What else could it be?

"I don't understand what you're driving at with these directives and conspiracies." Once more I went over the reasons for my three visits to Czechoslovakia and Poland in 1939, 1947, and that summer. Once more I admitted the one irregularity in regard to my photography and the reasons for it. Yes, it had been irresponsible in view of the tense atmosphere that now prevailed. Though I had done nothing with any hostile intent, I was perfectly willing to stand trial for this act and be convicted to the degree that I had trespassed against their laws.

My interrogator listened with increasing impatience. "Why bring up this photographing all the time? Have we insisted on inquiring about it? We are well aware of the liberties you took in this respect. You were temporarily under arrest on the morning of the twenty-second on that score, but we released you, didn't we? We had good cause to hold you then, but we chose not to, as it wasn't your camera that interested us. It was in fact merely one of your props of innocence, just as was your interest in our reconstruction. We are not children, Mr. Field."

So they were not concerned about my photographing. At least that was established. In a way I was relieved, since I had been hampered by a guilty conscience about this. In all other respects, though, my record was clean and my actions friendly beyond doubt. So far as culpability was concerned, then, there remained only my fruitless efforts to find Noel, coupled perhaps with complicating angles in his life about which I knew nothing.

After a pause I spoke up again: "All right, if it wasn't my photography that got me into this scrape, I am being penalized simply because of my wish to help my brother and his wife in a very compelling and human situation. Wouldn't you have done the same thing if you had been in my place?"

"Mr. Field, why always bring up your brother? Let us be clear: You are sitting here because of yourself, not because of him. Do you understand? It is you and your actions that are the subject of our joint study now, as I believe we agreed at the outset. Yes, perhaps your brother has a lot to answer for in his own right. We may even come to agree that his work was even more effective than yours, more at the nerve center than you may have realized yourself. Not that I belittle the damage you pulled off in your own capacity before we put a stop to it."

He looked at his watch. "But I am disappointed. We aren't making a very good start, are we? I suggest we break off now for supper and then continue later this evening, when we will have all the time we need."

He pressed a button under the edge of the desk. A moment later the Mean One entered and, snapping his fingers, made a sweeping movement with his arm. I got up and passed into the semidarkness of the corridor. When I entered my warm cell down below the mug of sour milk and bread were already sitting on the threshold.

I was glad to be back in my quiet retreat, where I could try to collect my thoughts in the face of this staggering new turn. So it was neither Noel nor the photographing they were after. It was me, myself. The clue lay in my own life, somewhere in the very texture of my own activities. I gulped down the milk, wolfed the bread, and then started pacing back and forth, racking my brain for an answer. Was it perhaps that I had been too close to the communists and at the same time too far? Wasn't the ultimate scorn reserved for the incorrigible independent who could not be corralled into the ranks of the faithful? Would they now try to apply Communist Party vengeance on me, even though I had never been one of them? It seemed possible, like the recent sentencing of men for views and actions of an earlier decade before the communist state in question even existed.

The more I thought about this, the more troubled I became. How unenviable in times like these to be neither fish nor fowl. How easy my father's generation had it in comparison, able to live simply by ethical standards and principles of human dignity. I had no constituency, neither the satisfaction of the reactionary who could find justification in hate and feel at the center of a cause, nor the balm of the dedicated communist who could subordinate his plight to a historical vision in which everything would come out right in the end.

Bedtime came. I lay a long time thinking. On the other side of the wall was the usual coming and going of heavier and lighter boots, the succession of lockings and unlockings of the inner and outer entry doors. And then I heard something that brought me immediately alert. Wasn't that the key of the room above me being turned? A light switch clicked on; a chair was shifted. Someone had sat down. The telephone rang in the guard's space across the corridor: "*Slucham, slucham. Dobra.*" Activity, the key in my door, and my clothes on the floor.

Then there I was again, sitting in the corner facing the desk. Again we were sparring, relentlessly circling around something that didn't exist.

". . . And tell me, the refugees in Krakow in 1939 were evacuated to England on the basis of British visas you obtained for them?"

"No, not directly. On the basis of visas the refugee committee in London negotiated with the British Home Office."

"But on the basis of lists and recommendations supplied from Poland."

"Yes, mainly, although my office was subordinate at first to the one at the

British vice consulate in Katowice, and this in turn to London, which made the actual selection. Except on one occasion when a Home Office team came out here to speed up the process and made its choice on the spot direct from interviews and our lists."

"And you say communists were included in these grants of visas, is that correct?"

"Yes, quite a few. That is correct." I was glad we had turned back to 1939. Here the benefits the communists had shared were beyond dispute. This would surely stand me in good stead.

"Now Mr. Field, let's for a moment pretend we are statesmen, specifically British statesmen of 1939. What interest would you suggest we, the government of Neville Chamberlain who negotiated the Munich agreement with Hitler, would have in being so suddenly magnanimous toward communists? Wouldn't it have been more in line with our objectives, as guardians of capitalism and the British Empire, to have these communists disappear for good in Hitler's concentration camps?"

I reflected a moment. "Probably the explanation lies mainly in the bad conscience the British public felt in the aftermath of Munich. They felt the least they could do was to help those who were likely to suffer at the hands of the Gestapo for their anti-Nazi activities. Especially endangered were the left wing refugees from Germany and Austria who had up to then been given shelter in Czechoslovakia. Also the social democrats, communists, and trade unionists who opposed the pro-Nazi irredentist movement in the Sudetenland. With the Sudeten area now incorporated into Germany, these people needed immediate escape irrespective of party label. There was pressure from all political quarters, which the British government could not ignore."

He smiled from across the desk. "So in your opinion the British Home Office gave all those visas to communists just out of a bad conscience. Really, doesn't that sound a bit naive?"

I said that without public pressure it was doubtful whether the British government would have given a second thought to the plight of anti-Nazis stranded in occupied Czechoslovakia.

His skepticism was evident. "Helplessly acting against its own interests just because some people are making a fuss? Saddled with a whole lot of foreign communists for no reason just as war is about to break out? Even paying their passage to England? The left hand of British diplomacy unaware of what the right is doing? Come, come, Mr. Field. How old are you—thirty-nine? And able to sit here with a straight face and tell me such a tale? Where have you been all these years?"

I did feel a little silly under his hammering. Somehow he had a point, for which the answer eluded me. "Well, maybe they also had some concrete national considerations not apparent on the surface. I certainly don't deny that these may have played a role too."

"Go on, go on . . . yes. Like what, for example?"

"Like the fact that the international situation in 1938 and 1939 was very fluid. Anything could happen, and alternatives had to be prepared for. That Germany still might strike west could not be excluded—even despite all the efforts to induce it to go east, at Munich and afterward. The communists could be an asset in that case, with their experience in underground struggle against the Nazis at home and in Czechoslovakia. In the event of war it could be put to good use, as in fact it eventually was."

"How about other reasons for trying to get the cadres of the Czech and German communist movements conveniently onto British soil?" He paused. "To help organize future communist parties perhaps?"

"Well no, obviously not, but what I just said . . . And what about the other alternative—England joining Hitler in a war against Russia? It would be convenient to have these leaders safely interned on the British Isles and be able to keep tabs on them."

My interrogator looked pleased. "So you admit that the visa granting may not have been quite as altruistic as you first made out. And yet, why do you skirt the most obvious reason for this strange hospitality?"

"I don't understand."

"To become *partners,* Mr. Field, partners after victory. Trusted outposts of IS at the very heart of any new people's democracies."

I was more and more puzzled. "What is IS?"

A flash of anger passed over his face but he controlled himself. What had I done wrong? Why did he look at me so incredulously when I asked that? I racked my brain as to what these mysterious initials I was supposed to know could mean. Probably some well-known industrial conglomerate like Britain's ICI, Imperial Chemical Industries. But how was that related?

He got up without answering. He paced back and forth in silence, then reached down and pressed the invisible button. "Mr. Field, I am patient, but this won't do. You will return downstairs."

And so, abruptly, I found myself slopping down the steps to my cell again in my laceless moccasins. In a way I was glad. I felt exhausted and I wanted to piece together the new elements of this craziness. However, I had hardly handed in my suit and slipped under the blanket before I heard the telephone ring again. The door opened and my suit was back on the floor. A few moments later I was ushered once more into the curtained room upstairs.

I was worried. Would we again tangle over these mysterious initials? Somehow I felt on the defensive for not knowing them. To my relief, though, he seemed to have shifted his interest. He was once more sitting behind the desk, his eyes focused steadily on me.

He said in a quiet voice, "Mr. Field, let us start over a different way. Tell me, who sent you to Prague in 1939? Whose directives were you following?"

So we were back in that old groove. "As I have already stated on several occasions, it was Kate who suggested I go. We weren't married yet then. After Hitler's takeover in March of what was left of Czechoslovakia she had been asked if she knew someone who might succeed in breaking through to Prague and making contact primarily with the communist refugees in hiding there who had failed to be rescued before the invasion. Although they already had been authorized to receive British visas, their processing had lagged behind the other categories of political refugees, and now it was too late. The only way out was across the border into Poland, and to head for the British vice consulate in Katowice." And yet again I went over the details of my covert expedition to Prague.

He made no attempt to challenge my account, but confined himself to getting me to repeat this or that aspect in greater detail, especially of my Krakow operation. Whenever I stopped he would simply say, "And then?" At least this time I didn't have to go through the mincing machine of translation but could give a coherent account at last.

Hours seemed to go by as my voice droned on. Increasingly, as I began to fight hunger and sleep, I felt as if I were hearing a record being played outside myself. Several times the voice opposite me broke in to say that although the sequence of my account was generally true, I was describing that part of the iceberg visible to the eye, whereas our joint endeavor concerned that bigger part below the surface. And then abruptly at some point he pushed the button and a moment later I was weaving my way, stiff and in a sort of stupor, along the corridor down to my cell.

A new routine had begun that was to continue for a month. In spite of the growing exhaustion in which the endless night hours upstairs left me, I felt a renewed vigor and optimism. For one thing, something was finally happening. The endless days and nights with no purpose, no form, nothing to occupy my mind, no sign of change, had come to an end. Time had ceased to be oppressive. My mind had something to focus on, and each day brought its new quota to mull over from the session the night before.

For another, I had found an escape from loneliness and the establishment of a specific human relationship. I had an identity again. I was Mr. Field. The atmosphere in the curtained room upstairs was strangely reminiscent of the intimacy of the psychoanalyst's consulting room; the only thing missing was the couch. There was no hint of the bludgeoning and violence and humiliation I had come to associate with such nightly sessions from my sojourn in the other cellar. The illusion was maintained with consummate artistry, and I took great care never to violate it, hoping to avoid a change of mood.

My interrogator had a matter-of-fact manner, as if our sessions together were the most natural thing in the world. There was nothing hurried or imperative about them. It was a sort of seminar of madness in which we could afford to give humor and human frailty its due place. Sometimes we would digress into hours-long philosophical discussions. I found him quite knowledgeable in literature and on occasion we drifted off into this as well, like the afternoon we spent on Goethe and an interpretation of *Faust*. Another time we might explore architecture in depth.

I responded to these opportunities with an almost childish compulsion. Never was it suggested that there was anything strange or irregular in the fact that I was here at all, that I, an American architect responsible for a university development project in far-off Cleveland, married with wife and children and a home, was filed away in a cellar somewhere in Poland unbeknownst to the outside world, on tap to be hauled up at any moment of the day or night, set on a stool in a corner for hour after hour of some fantastic quiz game, only to be filed away once more at the press of a button. The whole assumption was so unreal that it hypnotized me into acquiescence. Whereas in August and September I had made demands and protests, now I was careful to do nothing that might jar the delicate balance. Already the past seemed so far away, so fantastic. All concepts of the world I had been a part of had gradually washed away, and meanwhile I was resigned to sitting night after night in this room, convinced that it was the one route that someday, given enough patience, might bring me out of this nightmare.

On the evidence of these sessions it seemed to me that my biggest dread, that of permanent disappearance, was unfounded. Everything pointed toward a plan to involve me in some trial; and a trial, whatever its outcome, was an encouraging prospect. One night following a digression into the complexity of human personality, my interrogator said that I'd be pleased to know that the judge being considered for my trial was a complicated fellow like myself who would be able to understand me. I was surprised: "But really, are you planning to try me? When?"

"Probably, yes. That depends on you."

Despite my general acceptance of the situation, the unreality of these sessions became more and more staggering. Increasingly I began to ask myself if I wasn't suffering some strange form of insanity, a split personality where a macabre fantasy had pushed out reality. I recalled a famous German motion picture of the 1920s, *The Cabinet of Dr. Caligari*. In it we see an eerie twilight world of fear and persecution by a Mephistophelian character, and at the end it turns out the whole story was nothing more than the distorted visions of an insane asylum inmate. I had the sense of being in a mental institution, but one in which the insane were in control and persecuting me, who was normal.

But how did I know it wasn't the other way around? That all this wasn't my own hallucination, one I could not break out of? As the days of hammering away, of accusation and sparring, continued and turned into weeks, I became obsessed with a vague sense of guilt in spite of reason, a defensiveness, such that sometimes I hardly dared look my accuser in the face. It had to mean something. If not consciously, then without knowing, had I somehow done things that were quite different from what I had supposed or intended? That was irrelevant, said my interrogator. My reality was a subjective one. In this room we were dealing with objective reality—and we promptly launched into an hour's discussion about subjective and objective reality. That I had been part of a major intelligence operation in Krakow, as he claimed, may have been true for all I knew. He conceded that I may not have been aware that my superior in Katowice was a British agent, but it didn't change the objective situation that in my activity I had, through her, become an agent myself.

But if I had, even if unknowingly, become a collaborator in a covert strategy that turned the moments I prized most in my life into something to be ashamed of, how could I claim innocence? Imperceptibly, my sense of guilt mounted. In quiet moments, this frightened me more than anything else. Was I losing my grip on reality? Was the persistence of the man across the desk driving me to assume the role for which he sought to condemn me? Often upstairs in the early morning hours, exhausted, I caught myself saying that he might be right somehow. And yet the link that would bring us to agreement at last never materialized.

A long discussion on character traits, for example, ended with him remarking, "One can't go just by appearances. Look at you, for example. Certainly one gets the impression of a very decent, idealistic, and attractive type. And yet look what you've been up to all these years behind your mask of culture. It served you in your double life and fooled everyone—maybe even yourself?"

Myself? That became our stumbling block. "You have told me all about your life quite truthfully," he commented. "We have ninety percent of your story, but how much longer are we going to beat about the bush with the remaining bit, the ten percent, the other side? You have described the horrible sequence of events of 1939 in Krakow factually but ignored the specific role you played in them, as if you were merely a cog unaware of the purpose of your actions. If we will finally agree as to the real nature of your role there, we will have completed most of our task up here; the rest of your activities are of minor importance beside this. I have never met anyone so hardheaded and obstinate as you. And to what end?"

Yes indeed, to what end?

And so, day after day the sheets of testimony piled higher. We had advanced a long, long way since that first evening, and the atmosphere had become increasingly strained. Successively the picture of my guilt became more specific, better defined: I had gone to Prague in 1939 as part of an English (or American, or Anglo-American—this detail seemed to vary) intelligence scheme directed against the Czech and German communist movements. Why, asked my interrogator, was a leading German communist to whom I had given funds in Prague for escape to Poland caught by the Gestapo at the frontier when I was supposedly waiting for him in Katowice at the British vice consulate, "a notorious center of British intelligence activity"? Was it coincidence that a "Nazi agent" worked on the staff there, specifically dealing with refugee records? Wasn't my direct superior for a time in Poland known as a British agent? Wasn't I thus in effect passing all refugee records to the IS—the British Intelligence Service? Furthermore, weren't all requests for visas reviewed by the British Home Office? Wasn't it in turn an arm of British intelligence? Hence, since all my directives come via the aforementioned agent or the British vice consulate, and through them from the Home Office, didn't that mean I was in fact working for British intelligence itself? It was a clear logical progression, so how could I turn around and say it was false?

After nights of hammering and threats, I finally yielded. Yes, if all the above was true, then I seemed to have worked in Krakow on behalf of British intelligence. That refugee work should be associated with a vipers' nest of intrigue did not surprise me. As far as I was concerned, anything was possible. Even at the time, in 1939, I had had strong suspicions of activities going on, on both the left and the right, that did not coincide with the refugees' best interests.

My initial optimism had evaporated. Although I increasingly asked myself how this would all end, at the same time I developed a sort of passivity, as if I were two people at once. Somehow it didn't really seem to be *my* fate that was hanging in the balance. Often I felt as though I were dictating my reminiscences to a biographer. But while the facts were never challenged, in the end the motivation for everything I did was always stood on its head. So consistent was this that again and again I wondered whether it was I who was insane. Things I had done without a thought now seemed laden with calculation.

Only when he pressed too hard and lost his patience did I fight back. I accused the communist countries of a cannibalism in which they gleefully devoured each other and their friends rather than concerning themselves about their real enemies. I likened the communist security authority to a fire department running after false alarms while the fire burned elsewhere. The tension would mount almost to the breaking point, with my interrogator pacing back and forth in front of me, until I could hardly keep from smiling at the fierceness of his face. And then as suddenly he would sit down and quietly start on a new tack.

Somehow, the more I emphasized the help I had given to endangered communist refugees in Krakow in 1939, the more triumphant my interrogator seemed.

"Yes, yes, our records bear out all you say . . ." He reflected a moment and then held up a folder.

"And what about your relations with the Krakow police, with Starosta Woynarowski? Fortunately we have the police records of that period right here, and they are most revealing."

He continued: How was it that I, who was helping victims of fascism, was also cooperating with a Polish fascist police department that worked hand-in-glove with the Nazis across the border?

I didn't want to get involved in an argument over Poland's prewar government. Certainly there was much it could be blamed for, and its right-wing bias and anti-Semitism had been notorious. As a result of those traits, protecting the antifascist refugees in their makeshift domiciles had often seemed like a precarious tightrope walk. I pointed out that in my position the goodwill of the local authorities had been essential; without it, the whole effort would have collapsed.

"And the police raids and roundups in the summer, leading to the mass delivery of refugees across the border directly into the hands of the Gestapo—was that part of your cooperation?"

He had hit upon the most trying, most heartbreaking misfortune I had had to endure in all those heartbreaking months of 1939. In fact, I had never been able to come to terms with it quite and I suspected it would haunt me the rest of my life. In the face of rapidly mounting refugee arrivals, with a corresponding reduction of visas to a trickle, I had found myself with close to five hundred refugees on my hands, most of whom had not the slightest chance of emigration. Originally, after the March invasion of Czechoslovakia, Warsaw had grudgingly acceded to a British diplomatic request to facilitate transit of refugees with British visas through Poland to Sweden and then to England. As the weeks went by, the Polish authorities became alarmed at the evident pileup in Krakow and Katowice, seeing it as an abuse of a circumscribed concession.

In a manner typical of those times, they decided to deal with the situation by instructing local police departments to undertake a gradual clearance by shipping the refugees back across the border—right into the hands of the waiting Gestapo. Thus the Krakow police department seemed to have no choice but to do as it was told, and there was nothing I could do to stop it, since I had no way of pulling five hundred visas out of my hat.

I had gone to great pains to maintain a friendly official contact with Starosta Woynarowski, who held the dual role of mayor and police commissioner. Such diplomacy seemed a prerequisite for our relief work, which also had considerable support from the local Krakow communities in terms of shelter and provisioning. In response to my complaint that he was disrupting the process of moving the refugees to England as rapidly as possible, he agreed to help neutralize the effects of his raids while still following the letter of his instructions from Warsaw.

This is what he did. He insisted on a weekly roundup before dawn somewhere in town; although this landed some fifty random refugees in the lockup, he promised the release of any who I could vouch were being processed for a visa. Both of us knew we were stretching a point, and by this method I could at least salvage the most endangered and compelling cases, regardless of the reality of an impending visa. Yet it put me in the ghastly role of arbiter in a macabre game of wits, one that determined the life or death of those concerned. Together with my assistants I tried to set up very exact priorities to guide me when I sat later before the *starosta* with the list of his human catch, there to bargain with him for the maximum percentage he would be willing to release against those to be trucked back to the German border.

The identities of the lucky few checked off, the *starosta* had left it to me to hurry to the lockup courtyard to ensure their release. On each occasion I had to stand by as the prisoners were separated into two groups. I remembered how I had waited with dread each week for the predawn phone call announcing a raid and the beginning of another heartbreaking ordeal. How could any person with an elementary sense of human decency be expected to make such decisions, even though we managed in a rough way to save the most endangered people and avoid the total collapse of our effort? Even the plainclothes police inspector who conducted the raids, Wyszniewski, came to my aid for some strange reason, tipping me off as to their time and place, thereby enabling me to get some of those I could not otherwise protect out of harm's way. His motivation, he claimed, was concern over the fate of prominent Czechs who might be swept into his net, and of the women and children. "I am a family man, Pan Field," he explained, "and I was given refuge in Prague in the Great War."

Clearly, my interrogator was now focusing all his attention on this aspect of my Krakow work. He began by venturing that the person behind these raids had been none other than myself, that I had put the Polish Ministry of the Interior up to it in order to sweep out the communists.

I was dumbfounded. My instructions from London had been to save the most endangered people. This group certainly included the communists, not one of whom had been shipped back to the border. I cited some Czechs who could substantiate this fact.

He looked triumphant and laughed: "You are perfectly right: not one. Not so astounding, was it, considering your game? First, get them into your power . . ." He reflected a moment.

"And why did you supervise the freeing yourself? Wouldn't the logical thing have been for the *starosta* to pick up the phone and read the names to his inspector down in the lockup? Why did you come into this purely internal police procedure? Because you were necessary! Because you took your chosen prisoners to the little room in the back. And for what purpose? Not just women, as Inspector Wyszniewski did in his own game. No, your intentions were less frivolous—to tell each, 'I can save you, release you right this moment. But first we have a little business to do. In return for your release and the British visa you will in due course receive, you will sign this statement that you will in future place yourself at the disposal of the British Intelligence Service for any task they may assign you. If not, I regret, I cannot prevent your falling into the hands of the Gestapo at the frontier.'"

The face across the desk broke into a triumphant smile: "And 1945 came and your Krakow friends returned to their Czech homeland and rose to positions of high responsibility in the new life of their country. And in whose service? In the service of the masters to whom you delivered them in the back room of the Krakow lockup."

I was dazed. So even my best efforts in this case had taken a macabre twist. A similar distortion was made of my refusal to abandon the refugees in the last days before the German invasion of Poland, despite the urgings of Noel in Geneva and the American embassy in Warsaw; my work in England with the Czech Refugee Trust Fund during the first months of the war; and later occasions in America when I helped one or another refugee achieve asylum there.

As if these cruel fabrications were not enough, I was told that there was no doubt my brother was himself an unmasked American agent. Yes, my interrogator announced, by now the whole world knew it. In fact, he had used the same system of recruitment in the internment camps in France, coupling freedom with future undercover work for American intelligence. The alternative: the extermination trains to Auschwitz. He, even more than I, had been highly successful getting his agents into the very heart of the postwar people's democracies.

The madness I felt engulfing me left me with nothing to hold on to, nothing more I could say. I waited dully for the push of the button, the knock on the door. Release.

One evening I was confronted with a statement to sign that went something like this: Question: "In what ways did I work for the intelligence service of the United States?" Answer: "In that I helped my brother, an agent of American intelligence, in his work with refugees during the war, I admit that I worked on behalf of American intelligence."

I read it amazed and point blank refused.

"Mr. Field, what is the point of continuing to deny what everyone already knows. You are a stubborn man. Your brother was much more realistic. He cooperated with us as soon as he realized the game was up."

My heart almost stopped. This was the first frank admission I had heard that my brother was in fact in the hands of one of the communist countries and that the Polish security police was familiar with his interrogation. But I was determined not to be bludgeoned into further foolishness. I was sure Noel's wartime efforts had been no more connected with undermining communist countries that didn't yet exist than had mine.

He continued: "I grant that perhaps you weren't aware of the actual nature of your brother's work, just as he may not have fully known about yours. Secrecy is key in work like yours that it is sharply compartmentalized. Let us assume for the moment that in spite of the similarity of your work, you may have had some illusions as to your brother's life and ideals, perhaps as a matter of policy. But will you agree with the statement I read to you if we can prove your brother's role?"

"But that's out of the question."

He persisted: "But if we could *prove* it in black and white?"

I shrugged. "Yes, maybe."

He opened the drawer and pulled out a reddish paperbound book with lots of marker slips in it. He handed it to me. "Does that ring a bell? Did he ever mention these names to you?"

I looked at the cover. It was in Polish. Apparently the report of a trial in Hungary, of a Rajk, a Szonyi, and others some months earlier in Budapest. I recalled that I had come across these names not long before, but surely not from Noel. Suddenly I remembered: the page of newspaper I had used as a lamp shade, only to have it snatched away when I tried to read it.

"Yes, I read something about this trial down in my cell."

He stiffened. "How so?" I described the incident last September. "And about your brother?"

"What about my brother?"

He pointed to the markers. I opened the book at the first one. My eyes at once spotted the underlined passage, somebody's testimony, and sure enough there was my brother's name in black and white: ". . . the chief agent of OSS in Europe." I was dumbfounded. By all appearances, this trial had been held only three months ago in public and was important enough for the transcript to be printed in languages other than Hungarian. I turned to the next marker, and the next. A silence descended over the room as I studied page after page. Even though I had to struggle with the Polish, the gist was unmistakable. Witness after witness seemed to be saying the same thing: that Noel was a central link between Allen Dulles and the defendants in a vast conspiratorial network masterminded by the American Office of Strategic Services in the last years of the war and during the Cold War period since. Again and again, former Hungarian, Yugoslav, and Czech exiles had returned home from the West, then set about using the trust of their high positions to overthrow the new communist states, with Noel as the expediter. I felt dazed and numb with horror.

"But did my brother testify himself at the trial?"

"No. It wasn't necessary and not practicable. This was not his trial. However, testimony taken from him was read out at the trial."

"I would like to see it, and in a language I can fully understand."

"I will try to get it for you."

At last, was this the missing piece? If Noel had in fact led a double life, obviously the communists would assume by analogy that I had done the same. Noel had on several occasions mentioned some sort of wartime association with OSS. And the end of the war had found him in American uniform in Germany for a period. For all I knew, his life these past years at the heart of the international scene in Geneva had been an indirect continuation of those wartime efforts. I pulled myself up. How could I think such a thing? Noel had been the embodiment of my father's humanity and idealism! It was all utterly out of character. I felt ashamed.

"But sir, what about the Hiss trial and the attack on my brother's loyalty at home?"

"A smoke screen. The best disguise when all else begins to fail." And he cited a number of cases of men who had spent years in prison just to make themselves convincing to the other side. He came back to the written question and answer he had confronted me with at the beginning of the evening. Was I convinced now? Surely on this point it was no longer possible to plead innocence.

I remained silent. Once more he went over the various pieces of evidence from my brother's life, culminating in the book in my hands. Once more I paged through it. My interrogator's tone sharpened: "We have been exceedingly patient with you, but you are obviously not responding."

At once everything that had happened to me became clear. It all came down to guilt by association. I reread the question and my proposed answer. Actually, it said nothing. I wrote in the word "occasionally." Now it read, "In that I occasionally helped . . ." I then added "in effect," so that it read, "I admit that in effect I worked . . ." I felt a bit better. This way, wasn't I simply confirming that I knew nothing about Noel's activities? If he actually was an anticommunist agent, then it was a logical conclusion that any intervention on my part, even if only on rare occasions, to help some hapless individual escape the Germans might be construed as an indirect contribution to his intelligence work. If it somehow turned out that the statements of witnesses at the trial were false and Noel's activity had the humanitarian basis I had always assumed, or even the communist slant of which he was accused at home, then this whole statement would automatically go by the board and become meaningless.

I capitulated and signed.

I had almost forgotten the passing of time these last weeks, but that night as I staggered downstairs I noticed snowy boot prints on the rug of the corridor. So winter had come, a winter that in the hermetically sealed isolation of my cell I came to know only from the banging of boots in the entryway, the quiet muffling of footsteps outside, and the occasional ice formation made by condensation on my obscured window.

All the next day—I worked out that it was the second Sunday in December and we had been at it for three weeks, night after night—I paced back and forth going over every detail of my brother's life, weighing every contact I had had with him since my childhood in Zurich, when in a way he had taken my father's place in my upbringing. Every Sunday after the family had gathered around my father's grave in the small private cemetery overlooking the lake, Noel, six years my senior, took my arm for the walk home and we indulged in serious conversation about the ethics of human relations, about moderating our own ego drives and learning to see things through the eyes of others, about the greater joy of giving than of receiving. Throughout these talks, the image of my father always hovered in the background. I listened and invariably found myself resolving to do a better job the following week.

During my teen years in Cambridge, Massachusetts, Noel continued to act as a father substitute to us three younger children. At the same time he accomplished the feat of graduating from Harvard College in two years, going on to graduate studies there in international law. All the while he was involved in peace activism, and I recall large summer weekend outings and more intimate lectures by various leaders of the peace movement. Excitement was in the air, a sense of braving the conservative complacency of the pre-depression twenties, which was only reinforced by our attendance as a family each Sunday at the Cambridge Friends' meeting.

It was not surprising, therefore, that already in high school I felt called upon to do my bit. As editor of our school magazine, the *Review,* I wrote an editorial that raised a few eyebrows, to the effect that November 11th, Armistice Day, was a day that above all others should be dedicated to peace, not to memorializing past feats of war. When we were called in to school assembly to celebrate the occasion I immediately felt betrayed. I could stomach having bemedaled veterans on stage, but then the guest speaker, a legionnaire, launched into the glories of battles won and the need to maintain a strong military. It was little more than incitement for us to become soldiers all over again, and this on Armistice Day! When his harangue ended and we were asked to stand to salute the flag, I felt it would be a confirmation of all that had been wrong about the day. Impetuously I remained in my seat in the front row, much to the shock of all those gathered on the platform.

Retribution was prompt. I was called out of my class to the principal's office and subjected to a long sermon. How could I in my public position as editor of the school's monthly bring such insult on my institution. The only option was to suspend me forthwith. Then, as tempers eased, the principal decided that would only create more adverse public notice. The best thing would be to place me on probation and close the incident. And the editorship? That went unchanged. I felt triumphant—a first lesson in politics: act from a position of strength. I had no regrets.

In those years, under Noel's tutelage, I developed a belief in the League of Nations, in the social pact in our everyday lives, and a sense that a commitment to peace also meant a commitment to social change. But once Noel began his career and married, we saw each other but rarely. In fact, I knew very little of Noel's inner life then. He had taken a position in Washington with Frederick Libby's National Council for the Prevention of War as that centrist group's specialist on disarmament. While there he published a study on that topic that drew the interest of the State Department, where in due course he became the assistant on disarmament matters, attending successive international conferences. Like my mother, in his private life he was an early advocate of racial equality, and with his black Washington friends he tried to break the color barrier in the capital's theaters and movie houses. He was outraged by the execution of Sacco and Vanzetti, and openly supported the 1932 bonus march on Washington, which President Hoover suppressed with the violent intervention of the National Guard, let by General MacArthur. Clearly he had come to identify with the underprivileged in our society.

And now? All this was supposed to have been a cover for something else? It seemed incredible. Yet during these past months everything had come to seem all too credible, and I was incapable of feeling surprise. Even if someone sought to prove that my two boys, hardly able to read yet, were cogs in a conspiracy, I would shrug—maybe. Or if Truman turned out to be an undercover member of Russia's Politburo.

This day, being Sunday, there was no interrogation. Normal people were enjoying their weekend. Soon they would be doing their Christmas shopping. I imagined Euclid Avenue in Cleveland in the swirling snow, everyone crowding along past the gaily lit store windows, the Salvation Army troop singing carols at the corner of the Public Square.

By the evening I began to feel bitterness. What Noel did with his own life was his concern. But what right did he have to use us as pawns in matters we had no chance of knowing about. If he wanted to lead a double existence, he should have taken every precaution to ensure that none of those close to him were affected. Surely within a family like ours such double play and pretense had no place. Subversion and secrecy were a form of violence and lawlessness. And look at the innocent people who had been drawn into the debacle. Herta, his wife—perhaps she had known, but if so it was inconceivable that she would knowingly have sent me off to almost certain disaster. And in Prague I had involved Karel Markus, who had fearlessly interceded simply out of friendship for me, because Noel was my brother. Had he suffered the same fate as I, his family happiness destroyed, his life devastated? And Leon Gecow and Anka, here in Warsaw. It all seemed so horribly clear—provided that what I had read in that trial transcript was true.

During the following days the drama in the curtained room upstairs sharpened by the hour. I was told: "It has taken three weeks to establish the true face of your brother. How much longer will we have to wait for you to cease playing the role of the innocent among bandits? Ninety-nine percent of our work together is done. The facts are clear. All that remains is to substantiate under whose directives you worked in Krakow in 1939 and later in England, in America, on your two trips to the people's democracies, and to corroborate yourself who were your collaborators and what their specific tasks were, and when what you insist on calling a passive role shifted into active partnership."

Night after night we sparred. There were ever more frequent eruptions. I would be summarily sent back downstairs to think, ten minutes later to be hauled out of bed again for another stretch. I was castigated for my incredibly stupid behavior, equivalent to suicide. Falsehood, I was told, had short legs, and truth would prevail in spite of my shortsightedness. I retorted that I doubted that, judging from what was going on in this very room. Again the old problem, in sharper form than ever: in this age of subversion and cold war, how to prove that I am not a camel?

The matter of my brother's activities, far from making the task easier, had only complicated it. I felt increasingly that it would be impossible to clear myself as long as I was isolated here without access to any evidence. Perhaps after years, if they checked every detail of my testimony and were able to obtain relevant facts, they might finally clear me. But what reason was there to assume they would want to? There would be no trial; that was clear by now. They had no evidence that could bear the light even of a communist courtroom.

My fears seemed borne out not only by the frigid atmosphere that now pervaded our sessions, but also by an ominous incident that happened toward the end of that week. As I entered the room one afternoon, I found two strangers staring at me in addition to my usual interrogator. One was a big hulk of a man who overflowed his chair; the other was gray haired, emaciated, and somewhat ascetic looking. Sitting to one side, they held a typewritten page in front of them. My interrogator was obviously nervous as, in a carefully prepared series of questions, he took me over the familiar ground of my work in Krakow in 1939.

The two strangers stared steadily at me the whole time, poker-faced, without a word or reaction. Once or twice they passed a scribbled note to the interrogator, who would nod in agreement. And then at the height of the questioning, in the middle of my predictable response, suddenly the knock came on the door and I was on my way downstairs.

If the end of this phase was approaching, clearly nothing good lay ahead. I needed to formulate some statement, something in my defense that I would insist on having included in the hundreds of pages of questions and answers, a clear, concise statement of who I really was. Perhaps someone in the future would come across it and reevaluate my situation in the light of it. If I were still alive, it might lead to my case being reopened; if I were dead, at least Kate and the boys might learn what had happened to me, and be reassured that I was exactly the person they had known and believed in. All the following morning, therefore, I busied myself formulating a final message for inclusion in my records.

As soon as I was upstairs that afternoon I made my request. "I have a feeling after yesterday's meeting that things look pretty bad for me and that our sessions up here are almost over."

My interrogator made no reply but, taking some paper out of the drawer, beckoned me to draw my chair to the side of the desk and write what I had to say in ink.

"Testament of Hermann Haviland Field," I wrote. I then stated that I had never been aware of the possibility of my brother being an American intelligence agent until the moment I was given the record of the Rajk trial to examine, that his whole life seemed to stand at variance to this allegation, and that I had always believed him to be exactly the person he purported to be. If my brother and his wife had indeed been involved in subverting communist regimes, I wrote, I condemned that activity as contrary to my clearly expressed opinions about proper international behavior. I pointed out that I had assisted my sister-in-law and had enlisted the help of my friend Dr. Markus completely innocently, intending no harm whatsoever to present-day Czechoslovakia, and that Drs. Leon and Anka Gecow had never to my knowledge intended any disloyalty and I had never been involved in any anticommunist activity with them. Then I detailed the objectives of my professional work and the ideals that guided me in my life, in particular with regard to my family. I ended by stating that when eventually this awful mistake was discovered and my innocence established, even if I was no longer alive, my wife and two sons should be apprised of the contents of this last statement, since they had the right to know what their husband and father was truly like. I signed and dated it: December 16, 1949.

As I returned relieved to my seat in the corner, my interrogator took the sheet and read what I had written. He looked up with a sarcastic smile. "Why did you write this?" He sounded amazed. "You thought you could influence me by doing propaganda? Yes, I will put it among your records, but I can assure you the trick didn't work."

That evening, shortly after I had gotten into bed, a strange series of events commenced—events that were to mark a profound change in my circumstances. Their first manifestation was weird indeed. As I lay on my back listening for the cycle of activity that would herald another upstairs session, the bolts of my door suddenly rattled. I jumped out of bed and stood at the wall waiting for the sound of my clothes being dropped on the floor, but instead I heard footsteps approaching. I turned. Shoo and the Mean One stood facing me. Shoo pointed to my head and asked something unintelligible. I shrugged. He told me to bend my head. Had he noticed that my hair had been falling out at a prodigious rate these past weeks? But why would he care even if I lost it all? He looked at me with his wandering eye, full of perplexity. He scratched his shock of hair demonstratively. "Yes . . . yes? *Pan Amerikanski* scratched?"

I nodded. I had been scratching myself, a sort of nervous habit in extremes of worry.

"And? And?" He made a kind of crawling, biting pantomime with his hands, then searched my face for recognition.

"Oh that?" I said, thinking they were asking whether I wanted a haircut. I shook my head and laughed. "*Nie, nie.* Out of the question. Too little."

They both regarded my levity with disapproval, then consulted in a whisper. Shoo, looking sheepish, pointed to my prison shirt: "Give it." I took it off. He pointed to my armpits. Again the nibbling, scratching pantomime.

Again I couldn't help laughing: "Heavens, no, *niema,* nothing, really." I raised my arms as he tried to focus his wandering eye. All right.

Again a conference. He pointed to my long johns. I untied the ribbon. Surely that must be where it itched? A still more detailed inspection. I couldn't keep from laughing. He straightened up and looked offended. "To the wall, to the wall!" All at once his face looked like that of an animal in a frenzy. The two men stalked out carrying my two sole garments with them. I kept on standing stark naked facing the wall.

The door opened again. I was presented with a new ironed undershirt and long johns. I was also given a new sheet and pillowcase and told to pull off the old ones. I remade my bed and slipped back into it feeling horribly clean. So, like everything else here, my scratching my head in desperation had lead straight to a theory: lice!

It seemed very late when I heard the click of the switch above me and the sounds of someone sitting down at the desk. As usual there was a pause of about fifteen minutes while he went over his material, then the familiar sequence: the telephone, the bolts on my door, the suit being tossed onto my cell floor. A few moments later I was herded as usual upstairs.

The door opened. I was surprised. Before me stood an immaculately groomed officer in shining boots and full complement of insignia and ribbons. Except for his bushy mustache, fixedly staring eyes, and ruddy complexion, I hardly recognized my interrogator. He beckoned me to be seated. The encounter had something martial, clipped, and formal about it. I looked at his epaulettes. So this usually quite unmilitary man with his handwoven woolen neckties and tweedy suits was actually a colonel. Why had he chosen this night to reveal himself and create this imposing air? Maybe to leave a final impression? To let me know that my fate had been settled at the highest level?

He broke the silence: "There are one or two minor questions left over still, which I will deal with tonight."

This time there was no sparring, no disagreement. We seemed to be quietly wrapping up the stormy battle of wits that had gone on night after night for over a month until every possible angle of inquiry was exhausted. At one point I thought I heard a car outside. For me? But then as I dictated slowly in German and watched his pen moving across the sheet, the motor picked up and receded, finally disappearing into silence. Soon I had forgotten all about it.

It was a short session, hardly more than an hour. As the Mean One hustled me along the corridor to the stairs, almost treading on my heels, he seemed unusually excited. The red bulb was glowing above the door that separated this end of the building from the central section with the entrance hall: Prisoner passing through to his cell; all others keep out of sight. I almost tumbled down the stairs as the guard kept prodding me—"*Predzej, Predzej!*"

Shoo was already waiting at my door. He pulled the bolts back in succession and inserted the key; the huge door swung open. I stepped toward the threshold and then stopped abruptly. My eyes focused on the far wall. I was looking at the back of a man in prison long johns and shirt, barefoot, black haired, with his hands above his head, immobile as if he were some dummy.

I fell back, looked at Shoo. He must have opened the wrong door. But he was waving his arms excitedly: "Shoo . . . shoo!" I still hesitated. Two cots were crowded in here. There must be a mistake. I glanced at the number above the door. No, no mistake. My cell. Again I glanced toward the motionless figure with upstretched arms.

"Shoo! Shoo!" I was precipitated across the threshold by a strong shove from behind. "Shoo! To the wall and hands up." I worked my way between the cots and, without glancing to the right, squeezed in beside the rigid apparition facing the window grille.

# 11

## Stanislaw

The door banged shut behind us. It was absolutely silent. Out of the corner of my eye I was aware of two raised hands slowly, tentatively coming down—rather like a snail or turtle emerging from its shell, ready at any moment to reverse direction. I had never seen a human being stand like that with hands over his head, and I hesitated to look. It seemed indiscreet, almost indecent, to witness. His hands finally reached his sides, and I turned my head and looked across at him. Uncertainly his head began to turn, again as if in slow motion. Finally, as if two cameras had revolved to focus on each other, we were both staring into each other's face.

I had never seen a face like that. I felt instinctively I should look away, that what I did was forbidden and wrong. I knew too that I would be haunted by that face for the rest of my life. In some ways it was youngish, with rather fine, sharp features framed by coal black hair. But the skin had the opaque pallor of death. It seemed too tight, too set, to be capable of any change of expression, completely masking the person behind it. The eyes were what got me, though. They seemed shrunken, too small for the face, as if fallen back in their sockets. Eyes are usually an entry into the human personality. These into which I was staring revealed absolutely nothing except fear, like those of a trapped wild animal. The human being, the self, had retreated deeply out of sight. We searched each other's faces for several seconds without the slightest acknowledgment of what we were doing.

My glance fell on his white prison shirt and underpants, on his bare feet. I realized I had on my suit and shoes. I took them off and put them in a heap at the door. Hardly had my suit reached the floor, than the door began to open. Immediately the figure at the opposite wall returned to stiff immobility, hands stretched above its head. I returned to my place beside it, my hands firmly at my sides. Behind me I could hear Shoo's shoes on the wooden plank floor. He shouted at me, his propeller arms swinging: "*Schneller . . . Predzej! Verstehen?*"

sprinkling his Polish now with German. Illogically, every time I turned my head and shrugged, he lit into the immobile figure beside me with a new stream of abuse. My neighbor continued to hold his fixed position without flinching. Shoo stamped out of the cell puffing like a bull. The door closed once more.

I crawled under the blanket on my cot, keeping just a small peephole in the shadows as a means of quiet observation. Again in slow motion the hands came down, the face first looking carefully in my direction. Gradually his body shifted away from the wall and he took the two steps over to his cot. He sat down on the edge, keeping his eyes continuously on me. He raised the blanket and slowly crawled in, now staring straight before him.

I hadn't had a moment to reflect until then, so absorbed was I with the events themselves. Now as I peeked across to this stranger lying just an arm's length from me, I began to feel fear. Stories came to me of informers put into the cells with prisoners in solitary. Hadn't that been a constant pattern through the ages of man's inhumanity to man? I could see no other reason for the sudden change, especially now that my interrogation had ended in deadlock. Wasn't it obvious that this apparition of a man was here to gain my confidence? Or perhaps this stranger would confess in interrogation that my face was familiar and then throw in a few superficial facts about my life garnered in casual conversation, and that would be enough to put me on trial. Thus it was that in spite of my quarter year of isolation, I was in no sense happy at the sudden company in my cell. Out of the shadow of my blanket I stared steadily and was amazed at the way my neighbor lay completely immobile on his back, eyes open, exactly as he had stood against the wall.

Again the bolts in the door slid back one after the other. My neighbor sprang up as if an electric impulse had gone through him, and was standing with raised arms facing the window grille before I was halfway off my cot. Again Shoo's heavy boots. This time his wrath was entirely directed against my neighbor, though for the life of me I couldn't see what misdemeanor he could have been guilty of in the short movement of going to bed. At the end Shoo also turned to me, repeating: "*Schneller, schneller! Wand!*" Then he tramped out. As soon as the door closed I turned and slipped back under the covers, and once more took up my watch.

To my surprise my cellmate remained standing at the wall. Gradually he turned and looked at the door. Then his eyes shifted toward me. I sensed a new wariness in them. What had I done? He seemed uncertain what to do next. He looked at his cot, then back at the door, then again at me. He took a few steps forward, then stopped. Then a few more in the direction of the door, as if he were probing something. He turned around and slowly headed back toward the window. Gradually his movements took the form of a hesitant back-and-forth pacing along the narrow space between our cots. Why wasn't he going to bed?

I closed my eyes, pretending to sleep, but could not ignore the rustle as he passed my head. Then he was standing still. I opened my eyes. He had stopped in front of his cot, his back toward me. Then he turned and, very slowly, began to sit down right on the edge of it, keeping his weight partly on his feet as if afraid the cot would collapse under him. A sitting position achieved, he again looked at the door. He was exactly opposite me. I could see his hands resting on either side of him on the mattress. After a while he wriggled backward farther onto the cot and again waited. After another pause, and still in a sitting position, he raised the cover, then swung around and put his legs on the cot too. It seemed as if with each new move he expected a bolt of lightning to strike him. Finally he lay down very slowly, and at once closed his eyes. I kept on staring at him. He was obviously no more asleep than before. What could have brought an adult human being to such a pass?

The next day cell No. 4 witnessed the spectacle of two men silently skirting each other like two suspicious cats, giving each other as wide a berth as the six by twelve feet of their world allowed. It quickly became apparent to me that my neighbor regarded me with at least as much suspicion as I did him. That first morning if anyone had asked us what we wanted most, it would have been to be taken out of the other's presence as quickly as possible.

This ignoring of each other was patently complicated in circumstances such as ours. We both had to use the same pail, and one of us had to carry it to the washroom in the morning and again in the evening. I decided to take it that first morning without question, and my neighbor made the gesture of taking it in the evening. Weren't these two decisions acts of coexistence, even though not a word passed between us? Then, too, there was the matter of pacing in our cell. There was only room for one at a time, the other having to sit at the end of his cot meanwhile. Quite automatically, and again without a word spoken, we conceded each other alternating rights. At lunchtime there was the inevitable dissimilarity of the food. My neighbor looked at my meager raw carrots and eggs in surprise, and I was a little envious of his piled-up bowls of normal food. We both shook our heads and smiled for the first time. And again that night a smile passed as we both pulled our covers over us. We still hadn't uttered a word over the whole first twenty-four hours together, but we had advanced distinctly, each careful not to exceed the other's rate of thawing, nor to suggest a greater interest than the other. Despite no word having been spoken, the assumption on both sides appeared to be the worst: German. Hadn't Shoo thrown in a *Schneller* for the first time instead of his usual *Predzej?*

The second morning there were occasional smiles on each change of the cell-pacing shift. Then that afternoon a momentous thing happened as, near the window, my neighbor suddenly tugged on my arm and whispered in German: "What nationality?"

I was completely unprepared for this and at once felt an instinctive dread. The confirmation I needed: Yes, a German . . . A Gestapo war criminal? What is he after?

I replied, "I don't know."

My answer heightened the worried expectancy in his eyes and at once increased the atmosphere of tension in our cell. He paced back and forth more nervously and, when he thought I wasn't watching, darted worried glances at me as if preparing for the worst. Meanwhile I felt very embarrassed. What incredible behavior in response to the first attempt at conversation! All the rest of the day we kept strictly to ourselves.

Both of us, though, seemed to realize that keeping our distance was a losing battle. For one thing, the cramped space made it impossible to ignore each other. On top of that, we had both evidently seen long stretches of solitude and felt an overwhelming need for human contact. So we kept on observing each other surreptitiously at every opportunity. After my remark he, too, had probably thought the worst—that I was some German Gestapo man being held for war crimes. Who else would refuse to reveal his nationality? Now it was for me to take the initiative. At lunch the next day I pointed to my bowls, laughed, and said in German: "Diet." He asked why. I explained I had a stomach ailment. That was all.

In the evening we said *"Gute Nacht."* Without any further embarrassing questions, German had become our medium. My cellmate warned me the next day that probably we weren't allowed to talk and it could mean trouble. I asked the guard. With a shrug he said, "All right," and then added, "but only in a whisper."

Our first scraps of conversation revolved around food and routines. The questions were innocent on the surface, but full of leads—"What sort of food do you normally eat for breakfast, for dinner?" or "Is it easy to buy everything where you live? Do you have rationing still?" or "Much war damage in your town?"—and then gradually more direct, the usual questions about wives, about children, about work. My cellmate said he was in an industry connected with wine production. I pictured a German wine merchant in my mind. I said I was in engineering. Both were half-truths calculated to mislead, but as the days passed more and more of our real selves began to leak out, in spite of our deep distrust of each other and of human beings in general. Identity was another matter though. We both studiously avoided one particular question: "What is your name?"

I fairly soon came to the relieved conclusion that my companion was Polish, not German, but it was not until just before Christmas that I put his mind at ease with the revelation that my home was four thousand miles away across the ocean rather than over the border in some German town. I was clearly ignorant of details of life in Germany, so he had begun to think I was Dutch or Danish until he spotted still greater holes in my knowledge. Only with Switzerland was I on surer ground, and so until I voluntarily confessed I let him think I was Swiss.

Gradually the wine merchant revealed himself as a man of considerable culture, contrary to the initial image he had evoked. As successive bits of our everyday life were disgorged, we discovered in fact that we had many interests in common. Thus with each passing day the stretches of silence in our cell decreased and the sound of whispering grew (though we still did not know what our full voices sounded like). And with every day our activity increased. Hours of wakefulness shrank as we blotted up ever more of the void in conversation. Still, we touched only generally on our lives and studiously skirted the circumstances that had so suddenly disrupted them.

For my cellmate the fact that he found himself by some strange chance in continual residence with an American represented an opportunity to get a close-up view of a part of the world he had never seen and of a culture with which he had no firsthand acquaintance. Again and again the silence of our cell was broken by the phrase "And in America, tell me . . ." With keen insight he probed systematically into myriad aspects of American life, checking and cross-checking everything I reported. In time it was as if I were his eyes and ears while he sought to capture the presence of my country as if he had once actually lived there. For my part, I found my cellmate an inexhaustible source on Poland's history and culture and customs. He had a knack for vivid description and detailed recollection that at times enabled him to make me forget our drab environment and sit spellbound, visualizing the life of an unknown Polish village in peacetime or of Warsaw in the grip of German occupation and war.

It had been December 16 when I first saw this apparition with hands above head at the far end of the cell. A few days later I was called upstairs, this time to a room at the other end of the corridor. An officer in full uniform remained standing near the door. Seated were Cigarette and the doctor with the big bald head and black horn-rimmed glasses. The doctor questioned me about my ailment and the diet and examined me on a bed. I said I felt better, and he asked me whether I had company or was alone, his tone suggesting that this change was something I should appreciate. I now got the feeling, too, that Cigarette, whatever his other functions, was pretty closely connected with my case; this was the fourth time he had been a more or less silent observer since that first encounter at the airport. When I described him later to my cellmate, he said, careful to reveal no emotion, that he was familiar with this man too.

One thing, however, became untenable with the addition of a second inmate into cell No. 4. Two men continuously in a space of only some 550 cubic feet with a tightly closed double window, and a closed door except when food or clothes were being passed through or we were taken to the washroom, are bound to find themselves struggling from a lack of breathable air. It could be argued that such deprivation was one of many forms of psychological pressure employed while I was under interrogation. Certainly lack of air has a marked effect on one's morale. But neither of us seemed to be under interrogation at that point, so no such pressure was needed. Probably it was for security, out of fear that an open window even at night might enable us to identify telltale sounds and so discover where we were. Or were they concerned that we might catch cold? Or perhaps it was a simple matter of bureaucracy.

Worse was the heat and its effect on odors from the pail, and also the fact that my neighbor was entitled to a daily quota of ten cigarettes. As a result, by the afternoon a thick pall of smoke hung over the cell. He wasn't being thoughtless; I knew that the smoking was for him a last scrap of humanity to cling to. The only concession we were able to win during these first weeks together was that the door be left wide open in the morning and evening when each of us was led separately down the corridor to the washroom.

During these weeks, observation of the inside world of the basement corridor and the world outside our window became less important as we focused on each other. Nonetheless, it did not escape me that on two further occasions there was the sound of a truck engine outside, followed by the cycle of door openings indicating that two more cells were occupied. Thus as the end of the year approached, four cells of a possible eight had inhabitants. Again and again I wondered about a prison system in which a full complement of guards and doormen, plus water, heat, and light, were used for just eight cells. It also became evident that, unlike us, the other inmates spent much time being interrogated upstairs, and I could often hear the excited high voice of the youth who had cried so copiously my first morning here.

December 24 came. Initially both of us retreated deep into ourselves, unable to block out memories of other, happier Christmas Eves. And then in spite of all resolves to remain hard, the floodgates opened and our families entered our minds, thoughts long kept at bay for sheer survival. Even the pacing stopped as the afternoon wore on. Each of us sat gloomily on his cot, he at the foot of his near the door, I up near the window. Soon the silence became unbearable.

"Tell me about Christmas Eve in America." He moved up to the top end of his cot opposite me.

"All right," and I started with my last Christmas in freedom: carol singing at the university and the surprises we'd prepared for the boys—big stockings filled to overflowing and hung at the foot of their beds, the fire engine Alan found on awakening on Christmas morning and the bicycle standing in the middle of Hughie's room. I shifted back to other Christmases, to New England and the low ceilings of our old prerevolutionary farmhouse, the big logs burning in the old fireplace giving the only light while the snow swirled about in the night outside. Or Cambridge, still farther back, carol singing from door to door and Beacon Hill with its bell ringers and open houses. And then the Christmases of early childhood: Zurich and the snow-covered mountains; our surprise for my father as all four of us children played old German Christmas songs to him, my sisters Elsie and Letty at the piano, Noel on the cello, and I on the violin; Mother's pride as she held Father's hand. How clear memory is at moments like this; how much a part of our common European heritage! I could see my cell-mate following the images that overflowed out of my past, and for the first time I felt something breaking through his masked eyes, something intensely human and full of compassion.

I stopped. "Now it's your turn. Tell me about Polish Christmas, the way you visualize it should be."

He began with the Christmas Eve supper, what it consisted of, how it was prepared; the hay that is spread under the tablecloth to symbolize the Manger; the many little rituals associated with the holiday that have fallen into disuse in Protestant countries. He moved on to the Christmas tree with all its decorations and the family, three generations strong, assembled around it, and later still the midnight mass in Warsaw's cathedral. He shifted to the village setting, the peasant hut, the farmyard, and finally the village church at midnight.

The key turned and the bolts rattled one by one. We both went to the wall. When the door closed, we turned. There on the floor stood Christmas Eve supper: a mug each and some bread. Holidays were not for such as us. Except for our own memories, nothing in our prison environment, not even in the smallest particle of food, suggested that this day was different from any other. We both stooped silently and carried our mugs back to our cots.

"Wait a minute." I reached under the sheet and felt for the slit in the mattress. I pulled out some straw and a few threshed ears of wheat. I shook a little of the straw onto the blanket beside him and laid a few wheat ears amongst it.

"Let me have your handkerchief." This I spread on top of the straw and set his mug on it. Then I fixed a similar table in Polish fashion for my mug too. We looked at each other's mugs in silence. My cellmate reached out his hand: "Happy Christmas 1949. You have filled it with the joy of life just now, even as we are..."

He looked at me without flinching: "I am Stanislaw."

For the first time I felt aware of the deep fund of courage in those sunken, searching eyes. I would not let him down.

"I am Hermann. Happy Christmas."

There was a moment of silence. "I hope yours next year will have real hay, and no American to share it." I tried to laugh.

He replied: "One thing... and that is that I know both you and I, wherever we are, will treasure the Christmases ahead more than ever before in our lives, and will never forget this moment now."

We both looked down, then turned to our mug and portion of bread. In thousands of towns and villages dotted thousands of miles over the surface of the earth the candles were being lit, and we too, despite our cellar isolation, had managed to push away the bleakness and feel that we were participants in this pious moment.

# 12

## Cell University

Christmas was a turning point. We had passed from an uneasy coexistence with no escape to active cooperation to maintain our sanity. We still were cautious—that had become second nature after our months of imprisonment. Our own lives were still a carefully maintained taboo.

In circumstances such as ours the need to bridge time is so overwhelming, so big, that even the strongest will begins to crumble. That is why the informer system in prisons has always been so effective. Sooner or later you are bound to confide, to talk about things that are swirling round and round in your head. Sooner or later the unknown stranger who has become your companion in misery—or an ear on the other side of the door—will bit by bit become partner to your thoughts.

Stanislaw and I were acutely aware of the ever-present risk of desultory conversation slipping into telltale reminiscences. Already it was evident, however, that, coming as we did from very diverse backgrounds, we had areas of knowledge new to each other yet not directly related to our lives and the circumstances that had brought us separately into this cellar.

The most difficult period to cope with each day was the endless stretch in the morning between breakfast at seven and lunch at one. Once afternoon came and the shadows of the bars on our window "sun clock" grew longer, time weighed less heavily. With barely five hours to supper, things would then proceed quickly to the day's final stop, bed and release in sleep. So we decided to fill each morning with a pair of lectures, each about an hour's duration, with two additional hours for follow-up questions and discussion. Four whole hours for focused attention. In addition we needed to prepare, which we did silently the preceding afternoon—another hole filled up. The subject would not be announced in advance; instead it would be a surprise to look forward to.

And so started our cell university, which at once became the center of our experience. In spite of the obscured glass and triple-bolted door, through it we managed to open new windows on our life. It not only saved our sanity but managed to enrich us with whole new facets of knowledge. No external inputs were needed, no books, no visuals; the total absence of normal life's distractions produced an intense perceptiveness in both the teller and the listener.

On that morning of December 26, however, the first two lectures were hardly indicative of what the future held. In their way, they had the same tentativeness as that initial question: "What is your nationality?" and the shrugged response: "I don't know." They came from as far out on the impersonal periphery as possible, like the first neutral utterances on a psychoanalyst's couch. His was "Fox Raising," while I came up with "Industrialized Building Methods." Both subjects were handled with expert competence, and neither contained the slightest fragment of the narrator's soul. In the days thereafter we passed from vegetable oil production and the principles of engineering statics, to rotation farming, illumination, climate control, the external environment in building, the history of French painting, and Chinese ceramics. Soon I got started on a cycle on the history of architecture, followed by a sequence by him on Slavic culture and customs, and then on to courses on U.S. and Polish history.

Step by step, as subject followed subject and the weeks began to fill in, we began inevitably to shift away from the periphery. The soul was getting its foothold as we were forced to dig ever deeper, revealing ever more of ourselves and our attitudes toward life. So, too, each became more intensely absorbed in the presenting of his bit, while the other listened increasingly spellbound to the whispered substitute for reality. The mornings began to go by almost unnoticed. Sometimes it was only the rattling of the bolts and the bowls of food slithering in on the floor that pulled us back abruptly to where we were.

In this way we crossed the midcentury divide and left 1949 behind us. Had there been special New Year's Eve celebrations out there to mark the turn? In spite of my resolve to ban destructive yearning, my thoughts had drifted to Kate and the boys, to open house in Cleveland the year before and, as midnight approached, my going upstairs to awaken Hughie as I had promised; the sound of pandemonium coming through the radio from Times Square and the clock beginning to strike, Hughie sitting, still only half awake, among our guests, firmly gripping his calendar and his alarm clock, his eyes riveted on the overlapping hands.

"We must both see the new year in," came a low whisper from the pillow an arm's length away, as if in response to my thoughts.

"But how can you tell? Unless you stay awake until the guards change, you can't be sure you didn't miss it." The oblivion of sleep was too precious. To wait hour after hour would only call up endless reflections that were taboo. "No I'm going to skip it this year," I said firmly. Putting my head under the pillow, I drew the blanket over it so as to escape all sound and the bright light of the cell.

Once during the night I awoke for a moment. My pillow had rolled off onto the floor. I looked across to the other cot. Stanislaw's eyes opened at my movement. I whispered: "Well, has it happened?"

In answer he reached over and shook my hand: "Happy New Year. I heard some factory whistle. We've started 1950."

That morning as I stepped into the washroom with my pail and Fatty held out my toothbrush and towel to me, I sensed a little smile. Instinctively I responded and reached out my hand to shake his. "Happy New Year 1950," I said. But nothing happened. In the last moment, blushing, he drew back his hand and became flustered, and then sputtered crossly at me: "*Was machst du? Schneller. Schneller!*" I had almost sucked him into giving recognition to something that didn't exist down here.

One afternoon as I was sitting on the end of my cot and Stanislaw occupied the aisle, I began to laugh. "Hey, look here," and I pointed to the corner of my pillow. Perched there was a longish brown beetle with two comically large antennae that he was swinging back and forth as he kept on changing his position, poised for a momentous takeoff. And sure enough, a moment later he opened his wings and with a low buzz rose and promptly collided with the wall, crash landing on his back on the floor. I went over and held my finger out to him. Close up, he looked very humorous. His head was the miniature image of an old mare with a long, toothless, drooping mouth that was in continual motion as if he were talking to himself. And in place of ears were those two feelers, much too big for his head, always sweeping ahead like the fingers of nighttime searchlights in the sky. There seemed a droll self-pity in his whole bearing that recalled Eeyore, the donkey friend of Winnie-the-Pooh and Christopher Robin.

"No wonder," Stanislaw chuckled. "What a place to pick for your home. Mustn't be a spark of genius in that little head. Can you imagine, voluntarily?" We both laughed until tears began to run down our faces, looking at the comical creature that somehow had attached itself to us as the third inmate of cell No. 4.

"And what the devil is he doing around in January, of all times?" Stanislaw ventured. "Can't even tell the difference between a radiator and a hot day in August."

Even if he was just a beetle—and the concept of dumbness and species were henceforth interchangeably linked in our minds—he had joined us and so we set out to concede him a place in our company. In the evening we put him in the shadow of the baseboard under my cot, where he was persuaded that it was night even though there was no change in our twenty-four-hour light cycle. When we began to move around in the morning, he would emerge, working his way up the diagonal struts of my cot and eventually appearing on the blanket. In fact, he always kept going toward the highest point, and that was me as I perched on the cot, deeply engaged in our morning program. His journey invariably ended in elaborate preflight gyrations, followed by takeoff and a short arc through the air before the inevitable crash. For food he gradually adapted himself to slivers of raw carrot, his great difficulty in chewing the food being recompensed by the vitamins in the juice, so that he managed to hold his own. Soon we had him spend his nights on the wire mesh grille, where he would not accidentally get stepped on.

Meanwhile, the lack of fresh air was becoming increasingly unbearable. We both knew that in the end our health was bound to break because of it. And so we kept on agitating for the window to be opened, at the same time dragging out our visits to the washroom so the door would remain open for every moment possible. Once Stanislaw was called upstairs, and apparently his appeal then—or perhaps just his appearance—led to the first improvement in this respect. That night someone suddenly opened the window wide as we lay in bed, the freezing January air pouring in over us. I inhaled it ecstatically. Never in my life had I perceived the richness of air—simple air—as I did now. While I lay buried under the blanket with only my nose sticking out, I imagined I was lying on a balcony in a mountain sanitarium in Switzerland, recalling a far-off childhood memory. There was the feel of snow in the air, of wide-open country. Although it was pitch black outside the window, I felt the proximity of the winter night. And now a routine developed in which, we soon noticed, the window was opened by the guard on his way to supper and closed on his return a half hour later. While by the next afternoon the atmosphere was once again oppressive, it was still a huge improvement.

Indirectly, however, this change led to a little tragedy in our cell. That first evening as the window closed, Stanislaw suddenly noticed our friend the beetle lying on the floor on his back with outstretched legs. We had forgotten all about him, and the freezing air had been washing over him through the mesh. I got up and with my toes shoved the beetle toward the radiator pipe, turning him over on his side. It seemed to me he moved a little.

The next morning he was still lying there, but when I picked him up I found him alive, very slowly articulating his legs. As the day advanced he recovered some more, but all the spunk was gone out of him. For the next few days I tended him carefully, but while he began again to crawl about, he was through with the climbing and flying, and his antennae drooped, their ends dragging. He became sicker; a gradual paralysis seemed to be spreading. On top of that he lost whatever reason he might originally have possessed, making laborious expeditions straight across the floor in spite of danger to life and limb. And so, during one such irrational wander, the final chapter was written in the perversity that made him choose cell No. 4 in midwinter as his home: he was accidentally crushed by a shoe.

As January advanced toward February a tentative optimism began to take hold of me. It was clear that my interrogation was over, and with its end had come the end of my solitary life in a vacuum. The tremendous release from tension represented by the presence of another human being whom I had come to regard as a friend and who helped transform hours of nothingness and self-pity into intensive intellectual activity produced a sense of returning normalcy after the storm. I began to fantasize that I might soon be able to pick up my work in Cleveland. I reanalyzed my building project and spotted weaknesses that I would have to correct. I reflected about architectural education and the reorganization of the architectural school at the university under my deanship. I even dared to think again about Kate and the boys.

In our cellar interchanges this optimism meant that I more frequently touched on aspects of life at home. We had passed through a further series of lectures, Stanislaw on French literature, with which he was very familiar, I on the English and American counterparts. It was becoming evident that we were running low on subject areas in which our knowledge could sustain an hour's presentation and the challenge of another hour's discussion. Inevitably we drifted ever closer to the untapped resource of our own life experience. Soon, and quite naturally, I began to describe Valley Farm, going back to its beginning in prerevolutionary days. I told about Squire James Parker, who moved into a settler's cottage there and cleared the forest, becoming a prosperous farmer with a two-story house. I filled in the gaps, my imagination guided by recall of the daily diary he had kept all his life, as had his son. These documents not only gave an intimate picture of life on an eighteenth- and nineteenth-century New England farm, but they also provided valuable commentary on the times in general and the prevailing sense of community. I recounted how the property had entered my life eighteen years before when, on a youthful impulse, I decided to preserve the historic, derelict artifact together with its two hundred acres of forest and abandoned fields.

Stanislaw listened spellbound. Often, hours later, he would ply me with further questions, an indication of how much his mind had become absorbed in the picture I painted of those generations in a far-off land he had seen only through my eyes and my fantasy. Henceforth the Parkers of Valley Farm, whom I had never known, whose derelict farm I had bought only some eighteen years before, seemed to pervade our cell.

One morning Stanislaw said, "What a wonderful subject for an epic novel, a New England saga, these Parkers and this farm of yours in the Shirley lowlands. What fun it would be to write with you about your Puritan Anglo-Saxon New Englanders."

I laughed. "Poor Squire James, let's not cause him such disquiet in his grave."

By now, from bits and pieces of conversation, I had come to the conclusion that Stanislaw's profession until the war had been that of a journalist and editor of some sort. In fact, we both had begun to get a fairly clear image of each other, and at times I was bemused by whatever fate had locked two such disparate souls up together. Predictably, we consistently started from opposite premises growing out of our different cultural backgrounds. To him I represented the unthinkable: a socialist of sorts and apologist for his country's traditional enemy to the East. To me he emerged as a war lover, a representative of a stagnant landowning class with right-wing racist overtones, whose attitudes in the thirties had helped prevent a united front against the threat of German fascism and war. In our intimate isolation, however, we found ourselves taking a new, unhurried look at former assumptions, in a kind of continuous Socratic dialogue that in the months ahead brought us into a new commonality of thought that neither would have believed possible before.

The backdrop to our daily routine was a constant alertness to the world of sounds around us. Just as with a person who has lost his sight, our hearing achieved a level of acuity impossible in normal life. We even seemed to be aware of the impending arrival of a van long before the motor was actually audible, mainly from a change in the usual sound patterns around us—faster steps, a sort of anticipation in the air. We knew at once whether the van was bringing a person or taking one. If it arrived empty, we automatically were swept into suspense: Would it be for either of us? The cellar had gradually filled up, until all eight cells were occupied. In two at least we knew there were pairs of prisoners from the door opening and closing routines. Nighttime traffic up and down the stairs remained considerable, but here there were never any real rabbit hunts, nothing more potent than the Mean One's *Predzej* and an occasional prisoner who for some reason chose to run to and from the washroom.

Fairly soon we came to recognize the characteristic walk of each prisoner who went by, aware also to which cell he belonged. One man had a wooden leg, which we heard tapping by. We also established that his wooden leg was taken away each night with his clothes. One prisoner never took a shower in the washroom on Saturdays like the rest of us, instead receiving the large enamel washbasin in his cell, nor did he get his weekly shave. Clearly it was the youth with the high voice, still with us.

We also learned to identify the coughs we heard, which eventually led to the most dumbfounding discovery of all. One evening I was sure I heard a woman's cough, in cell No. 3 next to us, the very one occupied by the "youth." Suddenly it dawned on me: the person who had shared the loneliness of this cellar with me those first days was a woman. But was that possible? A woman in the middle of a male prison with only male guards, without a moment of privacy thanks to the Judas eye in the door? When I thought about how intolerably oppressive and humiliating I had found every hour in this cellar, I wondered what must it be like for a woman. How well I now understood the haunted crying that day in December.

Now that I had a Polish cellmate who understood the language, the guards tended to ignore me altogether. If anything needed saying, they turned to him to pass it on to me. Shoo had his own swaying, bearlike way of lumbering into the cell and barking to Stanislaw, "Tell your American son of a bitch . . ." Basically I had no objection. In fact, my pretense of not comprehending was often a convenience.

Shoo and the Mean One found us rather amusing. They would sometimes saunter in and ask my neighbor some silly question, such as "How does your American son of a bitch like our country air at night?" When Stanislaw clicked his heels and turned to answer formally, "Very much," the guard would respond: "I wasn't asking you. What about him?"

Stanislaw would translate the question for me making every effort not to smile. By the time I answered I was grinning, and finally all four of us were. But then Shoo, with his typical unpredictability, would suddenly pull himself up and wave his arms and splutter: "Funny, eh? What's funny? Discipline! To the wall. Shoo . . . shoo!" Then they would stomp out. I couldn't help but peek over my shoulder and see that both were as delighted as two kids after a successful prank.

Another guard joined the complement down below. After a few days we named him the Dumb One. He invariably wore a padded Russian jacket, a cap tipped low over his head to hide a strongly receding forehead, and big rubber boots that reached above his knees. He was much too obliging and apathetic to feel anything as enterprising as hostility. Instead he had a habit of seeing significance in a prisoner's smallest behaviors as he peeked through successive cell doors, on more than one occasion sounding alarms merely because he had seen a prisoner look attentively at something or hover too long over the pail.

There were now six guards instead of three, one pair always on duty together for a six-hour stretch with every third day off. On their silent, slippered circuits up and down the carpeted corridor their duties, aside from observing the prisoners, were to give us our meals, which were brought over from another building; distribute and collect our suits; supervise our trips morning and evening to the washroom; handle the complicated up-and-down movement for nighttime interrogation; and keep the cellar clean. Even so, they had long stretches of time on their hands. Games and reading were apparently forbidden, though they were carried on surreptitiously, especially games of chess.

Our cell was in a strategic position for listening, exactly opposite the guard space near the midpoint of the building and close to the bottom of the stairs. And so we continually picked up bits of information from the whispered chatter of the guards, as when they answered the internal phone connecting them to the doorman's room upstairs. Usually the guard said simply, "*Slucham. Dobra*," but there was always the chance of a revealing slip. We often knew which cell was being singled out, since prisoners were identified by cell number and, for pairs, an *a* or *b* suffix. I was 4a, for example. In this way we were able to establish who was in solitary and who had a partner. Polish word endings in which gender is specified constituted another breach of security. Thus on one occasion the guard, in repeating the designated number, confirmed beyond any doubt that our troubled companion next door in No. 3 was indeed female.

Like us prisoners, the guards were supposed to talk only in whispers. But they were only human, and often, in the case of an excited recounting, Stanislaw could make out the whispered sputtering, which he then passed on to me in German. A favorite subject, of course, was women. As everywhere, a few of the guards regarded themselves as authorities and delighted in outlining the juicy details of their conquests, but there were also a couple of greenhorns with their tales of miscalculation. Almost every night a particular guard was on duty, he read out lengthy love epistles he had received and, with the help of his colleague, laboriously fashioned a response.

Our warders had their political courses and Marxist tracts to study, but it seemed they spent as little time or thought on these as they could get away with. In spite of indoctrination, most of them seemed fairly indifferent to us prisoners, doing as their masters bade but showing little overt curiosity or hostility, even though we must have been impressed upon them as the most arch of archcriminals.

And like most people, they could not resist a good joke when the opportunity arose. Some prisoners, like Stanislaw, were given the right to smoke—the point being that an addiction could also be manipulated when convenient. Every morning a pack of ten cigarettes and a matchbox with ten matches were deposited on the end of his cot. In the evening he had to return the box with the ten used matches together with his clothes. Being basically a nonsmoker, I had never asked for any; I also felt that given the condition of my health it would be detrimental, but even more that it might create a carrot-and-stick dependency.

That there were other prisoners with smoking privileges was likely, but we had not been able to establish this definitely—at least not until the day a jokester among the guards had it in for Fatty. We also got a check on the accuracy of the calendar we maintained in the grille of our window, establishing the exact date.

That morning, on returning from the washroom, Stanislaw was told by Shoo that in future no matches would be given with the cigarette pack; henceforth, whenever he wanted a smoke he should knock and a guard would come and give him a light. Some prisoner, we deduced, must have misused the privilege and tried to set himself on fire. Stanislaw was very upset. The last thing he wanted was repeated contacts with the guards and the humiliation of standing at the wall, hands raised, ten extra times a day. Nor could he accept the alternative of chain-smoking his hoard all in one go.

He got a light for his first one when the breakfast dishes were collected. Then at ten o'clock the guard changed and he listened carefully to ascertain who had come on. Fatty was in charge, as his puffing and breathless whispering made clear. Almost upon arrival he was summoned down to the far end to give a light. Hardly had he come puffing back than he was off again with his bunch of keys, hurrying to open another door. As the morning advanced he had not a moment's peace.

Stanislaw erupted: "That beats everything in stupidity! They'll drive not only the prisoners crazy, but also the guards. Just think about it: say only half the prisoners here have cigarettes, that would be six. But that makes sixty extra door openings a day. I ask you!"

I knew he had passed up two cigarette breaks already and I was aware what that meant to a habitual smoker. I tried to commiserate, though I could not resist being amused by Fatty's plight out in the corridor. "Why don't you knock too, since the others do?"

He looked at me gratefully. "Do you think it's all right, just this once?"

I was dying to see Fatty's face. "I'll knock for you." My colleague looked worried but made no move to stop me. Soon the key turned and the bolts slid noisily back. We stood facing the wall, immobile.

"Hallo . . . hallo . . . here," came a panting resigned voice from the door. We turned and Stanislaw went to where Fatty stood, flushed and miserable, holding a burning match and trying to maintain a semblance of orderly appearance. It went out. He struck another. It wouldn't light. The side of the box was all chewed up. He tried again; this time the match broke. Finally he had it. Stanislaw lit the cigarette, clicked his heels in military fashion, and returned to the wall. As he hastened out Fatty was shaking his head; already somewhere else there was the sound of knocking. As soon as the door closed I sat down and burst out laughing. After a pause, the hilarity spread to Stanislaw. Apparently each new knocking incited the urge to smoke on the part of some other invisible inmate, and the situation had become chronic. With his Germanic sense of order and thoroughness, Fatty must have been utterly miserable.

After Fatty went off duty at four we heard ongoing hilarity outside in the guardroom. The next morning the matchbox lay as usual beside the pack as if the previous day had not happened. And one look at Fatty's sheepish face told the whole story. Wasn't it about the end of March? Of course: yesterday had been April first!

I looked at Fatty as I passed into the cell after washing up. "Bad day yesterday," I ventured.

He blushed, then waved his hand good-naturedly. "Come on, come on, quicker," he said and closed the door.

At about that time, each day some workmen came down to cut wood and hammer somewhere at the other end of our basement. We established that they were working inside cells starting at the most distant one, with inmates being shifted overnight to the sixth cell of the other end as they moved, not to be returned until the next morning. We also noticed some narrow pipes lying along the corridor, which I identified as electric conduits. Already the banging had reached cell No. 3. The next day would be our turn. From the sound I ascertained that they were cutting a chase and knocking out an area somewhere high in the brick partition near the ceiling. At once I was intensely curious. What was going on? Heating pipes weren't involved, and anyway they would be much bigger. The only other possibility was lights, but our light seemed perfectly in order.

Sure enough, the next morning it was our turn. Without explanation, as always, we were told to carry our cots, one after the other, to the sixth cell, and then our bucket. The following morning, again just as anticipated, we were told to move everything back. Of course, we at once set to examining our cell to find any telltale changes, but everything looked exactly the same as before. No stray bits of masonry or dust on the floor, the wall the same as ever. On closer inspection, though, we saw that things weren't quite the same. I walked back and forth, pretending to lose interest, sure that an unseen eye was watching to note the extent of our curiosity. What I established was that a rectangular hole had been cut out immediately below the splayed wooden lamp box just beneath the ceiling. Furthermore, a horizontal and then vertical chase had been cut from this point around the box to the ceiling, all painstakingly patched up, replastered, and whitewashed so as to be unnoticeable—except to the trained eye.

If it had not been for the sight of the conduits in the corridor a few days earlier, I too might have missed the change. I analyzed the probable light circuitry and became convinced it had not been involved. What other electrical system could it be? Suddenly it came to me. If I could lift the innocent-looking bottom board of the lamp recess, I knew I would find myself looking straight at a brand-new microphone. Preposterous? In fact, that board showed signs of having been tampered with.

Trying not to reveal my excitement, I managed to convey my theory to Stanislaw. He reflected a moment, then gave a qualified nod. In the following days I kept my ears open for every sound, and sure enough there was electrical work going on on the floor above. Finally, a week or so later when I happened to be called upstairs, I was led to a room at the washroom end of the building. Someone had been forgetful. On the floor against the window stood a table amplifier unit—simply a speaker and a series of knobs, out of the back of which dangled color-coded wires. I got only a flashing view before the guard hastily covered it, but it was enough to see that the contraption was neither a radio nor a gramophone. By the time I headed back to my cell, the item had been removed, and someone had probably been given a good scolding.

I smiled at the delusion of secrecy in a world of human error and frailty. And a second thought brought a still bigger smile: as long as our knowledge was unknown to our adversaries, we could play the game back when the moment was right. Henceforth we dubbed this new presence in our cell "Ivan." Needless to say, we felt considerable awe toward it, but also the possibility of a future ally.

On one occasion I received a dressing down for my habit of not holding my arms outstretched above my head when facing the wall. When Shoo stormed into our cell and raged about my lack of discipline, I pretended I didn't understand and didn't see what was wrong. The situation became tense. As a compromise I raised my closed hands slowly to shoulder height. By now, though, Shoo, with a second guard standing fiercely at his side, was out for blood. Without turning his head Stanislaw whispered to me: "For heaven's sake, Hermann, stop this." I gave in and for the first time four hands reached toward the ceiling in cell No. 4. For months thereafter I smarted daily at this humiliation, but Stanislaw was right. The issue was not important enough to sacrifice other gains we had made that spring.

And gains there had been. With the end of winter weather a new system was introduced with our window. Instead of being opened wide for a mere fifteen minutes each night, it was opened only slightly but remained open until the changing of the guards at 4 A.M., shortly before getting-up time. This meant we had fresh air pouring in on us the whole night. A slight oversight in this routine gave us our first restricted glimpse of the world outside. I woke up one morning toward the end of April to find that the darkness outside was vanishing and that the window had not been closed; indeed, the wings had separated slightly, with about a half-inch opening between them. I slipped off my cot and in a few seconds sized up what was to be seen through the crack and in the triangle along the top. I spotted some big trees a little ways off, and a hedge and bushes close up. The ground was only some three feet above our floor. The branches in bud, the quiet of early dawn, the greenness of the grass, the awakening twitter of birds nearby—a world unseen and untouched for almost nine months: it was hauntingly beautiful.

I wanted Stanislaw to share the moment and tugged at his sleeve. I indicated the window and hurried back under the covers. In turn he took a quick look, then whispered: "How far do you think the wall is?"

I was surprised. I hadn't noticed a wall. Another quick look. Sure enough, there it was, a hundred feet or so away, made of reddish building blocks and running roughly parallel with our building from east to west, with jagged bits of glass sticking out all along its top. It was hard to assess its height, as it seemed to lie on slightly lower land. And behind it, treetops. How strange—my focus had been entirely on the wonder of the everyday world, and as if the barrier that was to keep us from it didn't exist I had looked right past it. So we were in a kind of field with trees and a prison wall beyond, and more trees on the other side.

As the nights shortened, the slightly open window brought us in contact with the sounds of the world outside, especially those of dusk and early dawn, strangely reminiscent of the ones I had listened to six months before in the solitude of that other cellar. And even during the day, when the closed window was supposed to create an impervious barrier, the sound of an outboard motor often came through to us. Then one day, quite close by, we heard two shrill blasts of a steamboat whistle. We turned to each other and grinned. I whispered, "If he does that again, we'll have a steamboat captain in the cell beside us soon. For giving vital information to the enemy."

In fact, just those two short blasts nullified all the involved efforts to disorient us. At once in every cell there must have arisen the picture of the Vistula slowly weaving its way through the flat countryside beneath the Warsaw escarpment. So we were close to the marshy east bank. Hadn't the frogs been telling us so every evening, together with the sudden quacking of ducks? Once that far, the other clues such as trains, trucks, and horse hoofs, the regular transit of an airplane over us, and even the outboard motor fell into their places. Unmistakably, we were not only beside the Vistula but on a bend south of the city. On one side close by was the river, on the other—a little farther off—the main Warsaw-Lublin road and the east-bank suburban railway line. Actually, there was another subversive whistle that came to us when the wind blew from the east in the early-morning hours. It was the high, thin peep of an ancient steam engine that hauled a little narrow-gauge train with farm produce into the city. This was an old landmark of the capital, beloved for its service in the first months after the liberation of Warsaw in 1945 when it had been the only means of communication between the ruined city and surviving suburbs in the forest belt to the southeast.

An improvement of a different kind—it seemed positively regal at the time—came one morning in the form of two square white sheets of paper each, about the size of a small handkerchief. We were instructed to stick them until used in the window grille and warned that we would be held accountable if they did not end up in our buckets. After eight months, and for Stanislaw much longer, without the benefit of toilet paper, we felt buoyed for days by this sudden solicitude. It led to hours of discussion as to motives and portents for the future, and each day the receipt of two further pieces stirred renewed satisfaction. Once or twice the guards did attempt a halfhearted inspection during emptying of the pails, but being human and lazy they very soon forsook this duty.

Finally one day came a big improvement when Shoo walked into our cell and, grinning, asked whether it wasn't a little crowded. As seriously as possible, we agreed: "Yes, maybe a little."

"All right then, *predzej*"—he pointed to my cot—"carry it, one at each end. Shoo, shoo!" and he began to wave his hands. The Dumb One was outside, and he looked commiseratingly at my cot. People always looked at it that way, even Stanislaw. Whenever I said I was going to bed, he would correct me: "You mean your nest?"

The whole trouble came from the way I made my bed. In Poland, apparently, the custom is to throw the covers loosely over one, then roll them tightly around the body in a kind of papoose, part of the sleeper rather than of the bed. In contrast, I tucked in everything tightly around the sides and bottom of the bulging straw sack and wriggled my way in from the top. I had to admit to feeling rather hemmed in whenever I wanted to move and looking with envy at my companion stretched out unimpeded on his expanse of white sheet. So much for the security of habit. "Not a nest at all," I would respond irritably.

Our new home proved to be cell No. 2, which was a full three feet wider than No. 4. After some 160 days in the confines of a six-by-twelve-foot space, this was a momentous change. At last we both could walk—simultaneously—between door and window. Like two animals transferred to a new cage in a zoo, we at once began investigating every inch of the space, particularly the flooring for stains and wear patterns, trying to discern where the previous inhabitant had sat, at which end of the cot he had eaten his food, how he had paced. Stanislaw surveyed the cracks in the boards and produced a longish strand of hair. A woman prisoner maybe? We went over to the pail area: pretty badly stained. A man, we both agreed.

There was a whole new world of sounds at the end of the corridor to check out. Previously our interest had been in the guard's space opposite and the wall on the other side of which people went in and out of the building. Now we focused on the washroom, just one door down. We could observe the precise routines every morning from the moment a prisoner left his cell until he was returned. And what individuality was revealed in each phase of the washroom operation! First the way the pail was emptied and refilled with clean water. Some emptied and flushed at once; others first scrubbed the pail with the long-handled brush and only flushed at the end. Others even dared exploit the occasion by using the WCs directly while they were there.

Even the pail scrubbing revealed much of the scrubber's personality. Some went directly to the washbasin and let a quiet dribble of rinsing water into the pail, than headed to the WC stall, set the pail down, and gave just one perfunctory swish of the brush to satisfy the guard observing from the door, emptied the pail and, back at the washbasin, filled it half full. These were deadbeats for sure, ones who no longer cared. Another would scrub every inch of the pail systematically, then empty it, fill it, empty it again, and only then do the final filling. This was obviously a ponderous individual who had maintained a sense of propriety despite this animal existence. Then there were the artists, whose brush strokes had a cavalier boldness about them; or the defiant ones; or the ones who used pistonlike motions, as against the swirlers. Gradually we got to know each and from where they came, going at once on the alert if any individual were missing.

Then there was the second phase of the washing operation. There were the ones who brushed their teeth first and then washed, and those who did it the other way around; the slow systematic ones and those who considered the act a token exercise or who simply did not have enough teeth to bother about. And finally the washing itself—what a revelation! Some ducked their heads in the water and spluttered and bubbled or blew like whales. It was amazing how much satisfaction could be derived from this noisemaking enterprise, a clear assertion of an inalienable right even in these wretched circumstances. Of course, there were also those it was more trying to listen to, who started their routine with demonstrative coughing and spitting and nose blowing. In the washing, too, a few seemed hardly to come in contact with the water in their desire to return to their cells in a hurry, while others again seemed to be testing the patience of the guards by taking twice as long as necessary.

Interestingly, some were prodded constantly quite irrespective of time, hardly ever escaping a *Shoo* or a *Predzej* even before the pail was emptied. In contrast, one man in particular brazenly settled down in a toilet stall and stayed put as if he were reading the morning newspaper. So there was a whole hierar-

chy in which the guards merely reflected the policy from above, even in these
petty details.

Once more we were able to confirm beyond doubt which cells were solitary
and which contained a pair. If there was only one man, the door of his cell was
left open while he was in the washroom. If one of a pair, it was locked behind
him.

Once a week we had a special intelligence-gathering opportunity: the Saturday shave and shower. In addition to the normal pail-emptying operation,
each prisoner was shaved in turn, sitting on a chair. Then he proceeded to the
showering area, carefully supervised by the guard who controlled the valves and
determined how long a person could take. Invariably there were scraps of conversation—"Not sharp enough," or "Too cold," or "Fine, just right"—and depending on the guard's mood or the inmate's status, a joke or banter about the
grotesque misfit in size of the fresh issue of underclothes or a particularly unfortunate chop by the guard's safety razor.

My insistence on topping off every hot shower with a shot of cold water
provided the guards never-ending amusement. The practice was in the same
category as my bed making. Often the second guard on duty would stick his
head into the washroom so as not to miss the show. I remember Shoo's shaking
his head as he turned to the other guard: "That American son of a bitch . . . *cholera . . . cholera.*"

There was good reason for the guards' disbelief. In the other building,
hadn't I on several occasions heard buckets of water slosh in on someone in the
dark cell opposite me as part of some infernal wearing-down process? Certainly
from the gasps that followed, it had been clear that that water was anything but
warm. While there seemed to be no dark cell here and little sign of overt physical mistreatment, a few nights after we had shifted into our new quarters we listened as a newcomer arrived, someone who evidently was not to get the idea
that life was all roses down here. With the Mean One at his heels, he was hustled
into the empty cell opposite us and a few moments later into the washroom, the
door closing behind him. Unmistakably the new guest was being yelled at to
undress and then told to stand under the shower. Every time he wanted to get
out from under he was met with another round of curses that forced him back.
The fact that no fire had been made for the boiler tank, coupled with the man's
evident lack of interest in getting clean and the Mean One's delight in the game,
made it amply clear why the sight of a prisoner enjoying the icy artesian well
water was almost a threat to the established order of things. That was one thing
that couldn't be used against me.

Another Saturday-morning investigative angle was provided by the periodic haircut. Our game was to try to guess from the pile accumulated on the

floor whose bits belonged to whom. There was some snow white hair, a lot of black hair, and various shades of brown. The haircut ahead of me, the second member of No. 1, went very quickly and the last hairs I located were white. Surely an older man, almost bald, which tallied with the slow deliberation of his movements and his somewhat uneven walk.

Our main interest, however, focused on No. 3, the first prisoner to arrive after me that first night last November. Again we heard the cough, and once the voice itself in the washroom. Although we were now sure it was a woman, that was only the beginning of a chain of observations that baffled us for some days before we came upon its solution. Like all those in solitary, her door was left open when she went to the washroom. But she went through an incredibly long procedure with her pail and seemed to do the whole operation twice over, flushing the WC twice too. The only answer seemed to be that she had two pails in her cell instead of one. But the same happened when she washed and did her teeth. Sometimes she seemed to be washing and doing her teeth all at the same time.

Then Saturday came. We listened carefully. As we had already ascertained, she neither showered nor had a shave like the rest, but merely did the pail routine and returned. After breakfast, however, the big enameled washbasin, together with two pails, was passed in to her. A while later the guards not only fetched these but repeated the operation all over again. It was Polish grammar that finally resolved the riddle. The guard had spoken sharply at the washroom door: "You are not allowed to do that." He used not only the feminine ending, but also the plural one. How stupid we had been! Obviously: two women on the other side of our wall.

Soon we discovered another fact about them. One had some digestive affliction and almost half the time, shortly after the midday food, had vomiting spells. In the weeks that followed we began to consider it a victorious day ourselves when we failed to discern the retching next door. The suffering it testified to in a way became ours as well, and we felt miserable each time at our inability to help.

Time moved fast that spring. Perhaps it was the distance already traveled. The main thing was to remain patient; surely one day all this would end as suddenly as it had started. Yet there were moments almost daily when this façade of confidence threatened to crumble, when the diligently suppressed reality of a world I no longer shared began to push through; still, what I felt was more a rebelliousness against my circumstances than the hopeless despair that had gripped me during the first months.

It was the emerging inner world of fantasy, however, that was primarily responsible for the way the days rolled by. When we started our mini-lyceum the day after Christmas, our combined store of knowledge seemed to promise more than enough material on which to draw, and neither of us could have imagined that we would gradually draw it down. By the end of January, though, each of us had already done thirty lectures. By March we stood at over sixty apiece, with yet a little more having been squeezed out of some subject. What about the inevitable morning when there would be nothing left to whisper and the cell would revert to silence? We had expended our resources lavishly at first: the whole art of antiquity in one session, the entire history of Poland in two. Now, even with strict rationing, we were beginning to scrape the bottom of the barrel: American sports, love in Poland, my first five women, his first ten. Inevitably as our supply dwindled, the component of sheer fantasy became ever more brazen, especially when it came to women. Also, we shifted imperceptibly closer to our own lives in spite of our initial resolve not to. At the rate we were going, there seemed no way to stop this drift, even despite our awareness of "Ivan's" ear in our midst.

Meanwhile, I continually marveled at my cellmate's capacity for sheer fantasy. Often when we were not talking I could sense him becoming deeply engrossed, far off somewhere, almost as if he were unaware of his surroundings. He had already been through a year of this cellar existence before we met. During periods of unbearable suffering, his method of survival had been to isolate himself through a kind of imaginary present. He had a passion for fine food, and so he spent hours conceiving the detailed preparation of festive dinners, the act of sitting down and eating and conversing with his friends, even savoring the actual taste of the imagined dishes. Gradually he advanced to imagining whole plots of action, with himself as observer. As the months had gone by, his consciousness came in the grip of an elaborate epic of Poland during war and occupation. It had gone on day after day without plan, unanticipated events shaping the course of his characters' lives, which he shared; a free replay of the turbulent events in which he had been an active player but with no separation of reality and fiction. When the door had opened and food bowls were set on the floor, he had been surprised and resented the intrusion, swallowing the food down quickly before returning to his private reality. He confessed that when he had been put in here in December with me, he had at first longed for the solitude that allowed the floodgates of his fantasy to open. Had that gone on much longer, I wondered whether he would have dropped into that fantasy existence permanently.

As we struggled to find adequate material for our morning sessions, I suggested he recount his epic to me just as he had lived it, fashioning each day into a chapter. He shook his head at first, glancing up to "Ivan's" ear in our light fixture. Besides, he said, his German wasn't up to it. But I knew time was on my side. And sure enough, early in March he started up, and proceeded to hold me in thrall every morning to a degree I had never experienced from any book. Through his telling, I was able to identify with a world of suffering utterly at variance with my own past. The background was the human and physical devastation that swept Poland during the war years, first in Warsaw under siege, then in Wilno under German and then Russian occupation: Stanislaw in hiding in Poland's forests, later in Warsaw closely following the human horror of its ghetto, a close participant in the hell of the city during the 1944 uprising, in Wroclaw (Breslau) at the end of the war. We fell to calling it "Three W" for its three successive main settings—Wilno, Warsaw, and Wroclaw. There were four or five central characters, the events experienced through their eyes. It was clear that what I was sharing was autobiographical in the deepest sense and that Stanislaw's presence inhabited every scene. Bit by bit it shifted the façade he had tried to hide behind in our first days together. In the evenings as I lay on my back, I relived each scene all over again as if I, too, had been a part of it.

There was something infectious about this world of fantasy. While I had no epic to bring to life, I found myself delving deeper into experiences in my own life, which revealed themselves in a new light. I latched on to them and began to narrate them with a vividness that surprised me. Somehow I had tapped a new level in my memory of which I had barely been aware.

As Stanislaw's epic drew to a close, I was worrying about what might take its place. If we worked out a story together, perhaps he could live it out in fantasy? He suggested I come up with something and then he would decide. I knew it would have to be in settings familiar to him. That excluded America, but what could I supply with my own limited knowledge of his world? Then one night I recalled an account I had read in the papers at home about the difficult task of trying to find missing children taken by the Germans during the occupation from parents either dead or in concentration camps. It could be developed into a story seen entirely through the eyes of such a child.

The story as it evolved in my mind during long wakeful hours was that of a Polish boy, separated from his parents at four or five in the early years of the war when they are seized at night and taken off to a concentration camp. The Nazis give the boy for adoption to a German family in Breslau. He spends his early childhood there as one Willi Neubauer, member of the Hitler youth organization. The war sweeps west in 1945. Breslau is surrounded and besieged by the Russians and crumbles into ruins. Willi's adopted father is killed in an air raid. The town finally capitulates. Willi suffers all the agony of being a German, first under Russian occupation and then as the town is taken over by Poland. As part of the German exodus, he and his adoptive mother join the stream of those expelled. When the war is over, chance brings Willi's real parents on his track, though they of course are looking for Jan, their long lost child. Willi, unaware of his Polish origins, is forcibly repatriated through an American search team, thus losing the last remaining bond in his life, the person who had become his mother. The boy's real parents settle in Wroclaw, until recently the German Breslau, with their newfound child, unaware that he had lived there as a German. Jan (Willi) therefore stands in the middle of two conflicts: that between his dual parents and that represented by the German Breslau of his past and the Polish Wroclaw of his present. The story ends when the German mother and Polish father stand face to face at the deathbed of the sick boy, who proved unable to cope with the aftermath of war.

I knew by now that Stanislaw had settled in Wroclaw at war's end and knew the environment intimately. I, too, had visited the ruined city two years before. And so it was that this story in the weeks that followed came alive in whispered fantasy. We lived Willi. Each evening on our backs we mapped out the next day's chapter. We tried to help him, to understand him and his parents on both sides, who were equally unhappy. We tried to see everything through his eyes, as he would have experienced it. With a haunting tenderness and insight, Stanislaw described the boy's attempts at normal childhood joys and his final agony. And when Willi died, as we both knew he would, a gloom settled over our cell that took days to dispel. For Stanislaw, Willi was his son, for me mine, and for both of us the story raised remembrances of childhood and a bitter perception of our own present suffering. His passing out of our cell existence after those weeks devoted entirely to him left a gaping void for both of us.

"How about a story about life in a Polish village? No hero or central character, just its inhabitants moving in and out of the picture in the timeless continuity over which the world in conflict passes as a mere blip." My proposal had a selfish reason, tailored as it was to what I sensed was the setting closest to my cellmate's heart and one he knew intimately. He would move us bodily into it, and through his eyes it would become a permanent part of my reality too.

And so in the weeks that followed I lived in "Wola," sharing its ups and downs over the previous fifty years. I got to know most of its houses and their inhabitants, from the poorest cowherd's hut to the down-at-the-heels erstwhile Manor House.

We both fell more and more to discussing people and their diverse ways. Often I chose persons I had known and, as my morning contribution, tried to present them in detail. Then of an afternoon we would pace side by side and move our focus from the specific to the general, using cases we knew as our starting point. We asked ourselves the age-old question: What were the levers of human behavior? What lay behind man's endless record of destructiveness, not only toward himself but toward the environment that supported him? How did this jibe with his capacity to feel beauty and delight in creation?

The range of our experiences continents apart had been as diverse as were the traditions of our cultures. He was Catholic, conservative, anticommunist, steeped in Latin culture, with a quick Slavic temperament. He lived by the strong prop of faith, with an underlying dose of mysticism that to my mind bordered on superstition. He countered the disasters that had dogged much of his life, as they had that of his country, with an intense capacity for full enjoyment, the attraction of the existential moment.

And here was I, raised in a Quaker environment of service, of will over pleasure, of reason over faith, of a belief in progress and the essential goodness of man in a world envisioned without violence and with equal opportunity; matured in an atmosphere of stability and middle-class security with only a secondhand knowledge of the real struggle for existence; introverted, trained to the holding in check of emotions boiling under the surface.

We were an intriguing novelty to each other. In normal life our paths would never have crossed, and if they had we would at once have taken a dim view of each other. Here, though, our differences provided a continual source of exploration, with accompanying surprises and even disbelief. They also contributed to a learning process, a hitherto inconceivable widening of horizons that led to our jointly questioning an increasing number of aspects of human behavior and the preconceptions that we both had brought into this cellar.

We outlined another story. I suggested we take a dead-end street in a prewar development venture on the outskirts of Warsaw and show the interaction of the lives of the people who moved in and became neighbors. Ever more strands would connect this motley group under the impact of time and events. Again the war would be the catalyst, and we would show how the same events affected each household in turn quite differently. We would call it "Duck Lane: The Story of a Street." No heroes here.

We started on it, knowing it would carry us well into June. Hidden away in this cellar I got to know the inhabitants of this lane in a way I could never have done traveling around on my own. Through my cellmate's eyes and fantasy I began to develop an understanding of his country and, through understanding, to feel close to it in spite of being a victim of it. It was somewhat the same with him with regard to my America. In this isolated cellar an image was taking shape of that land on which he had never set foot.

At the end of each day we felt strongly that we had lived, and as we lay on our cots we would map out the next morning's work. For there was always another morning. Living in the present of our creation, for the moment we felt happy there. What was in store for Jadwiga now that she had moved into Duck Lane? Almost all the inhabitants were now established there. I looked over to the other cot. Stanislaw was smiling; he whispered: "Just wait and see, I've got a wonderful solution for tomorrow. It will tie all the inhabitants together with one strong thread. Just wait and see . . .".

Something made him stop. We both were listening. Our window was closed, but we could hear the sound of an approaching motor. It maneuvered outside and came to a stop. A moment of silence. Had it brought someone? No. The door opened. It was quiet outside. Someone had turned the corridor switch on. A bunch of keys were rattling. Someone would be leaving. Maybe the man with the wooden leg, or one of the women in No. 3? I jumped out of bed—the key was turning in our door. We stood facing the wall with hands above our heads as we heard the dull thud of a suit landing on the floor. Whose suit? His! I stood numbly as I watched him move toward the door. Yes, his suit. Without a word he was already slipping into it, his face pale, not once looking over to where I still stood. His skin looked suddenly stretched again, his eyes small and deep in their sockets, unseeing, almost as if these months together had never existed.

The door opened. Shoo snapped his fingers. The door closed. I remained standing. I heard some bolts out in the corridor: the cellar door to the entry hall. Then the key of the outer door. The car door banged briefly, the motor started up. Quickly the sound receded. Silence.

I stared at the cot next to me, the blanket thrown back. I crept slowly under my cover. It was all gone. All, as sudden as death. The only trace of these five months: an empty cot against the wall.

# 13

## The Oppression of Time

S ummer 1950, the rounding of my first year in nowhere. When I awoke, full of the plans for another day, I found myself staring at the empty cot, exactly as it had been when Stanislaw jumped out and hurried to the wall. For a long time the evening before I had lain awake, listening for the sound of a returning motor, thinking perhaps he had been taken away for a nighttime confrontation of some kind in town.

Now with the morning it was clear that something more was going on. Witness at a trial? In that case he might be back at the end of the day, or it might even be two days. I carefully made up his cot, exactly as I had so often seen him do it.

The day passed. A second. Still no sign of him. While I kept myself busy preparing some new afternoon lectures and thinking through the next chapter for Duck Lane, the thought kept shooting through my mind: What if he doesn't come back? I looked over to his made-up cot for reassurance. It hadn't been removed to make more room for me. When Saturday came I took off his sheet and pillow case and handed them in with mine. I only got back one of each. And later that day my fears were realized: two guards came in and, without a word, carried out the last evidence of our joint existence. The cot was gone.

I felt I had been maimed, the victim of some brutal surgery. How unconscionably cruel it all seemed.

And then I began to analyze the event and thereby to accept its reality. If Stanislaw had left for good, it meant he had not gone merely for a confrontation or to serve as witness at a trial. There was only one answer: he had gone to his freedom. He had been released. Although he had studiously kept the nature of his troubles to himself, I had over the months pieced together enough to realize that he was no more guilty than I.

So with every day I became more convinced that he was free at last, reunited with his wife and son, whom he had not seen since the fatal day in 1948 when he was suddenly picked up at his office in Wroclaw and disappeared. Now he was experiencing the lushness of June, all the things we had imagined together, and I felt tremendously happy. I sat all day in fantasy, visualizing the progress of his rediscovery of the fullness of life. With his family he would ride the streetcar down the Marszalkowska at rush hour to get the feel of people and to look at the faces all around. They would stroll in the Lajenki Park, Andrzej, whom he had known only as an infant, between them holding their hands.

There was a second reason for my sudden buoyant mood. If he had indeed been freed, it must mean that my freedom could not be far off. After all, they knew that through him there could always be the risk of a leak as to my whereabouts, and in the end that could find its way to Kate or the American authorities. So freedom of either of us was, I believed, coupled with that of the other.

The carefully maintained ban of the past months on drifting to thoughts about Kate broke down and I gave way to a string of fantasies. As quickly as my health would permit, we would go to Valley Farm with the boys, and there among the trees and the wide-open fields of New England we would heal the wounds and replan our future. That my work in Cleveland and my deanship had gone to someone else by now was certain. I would have to start my career all over again. But what did that matter beside the mere fact of once more being part of life?

Although I suddenly had nothing to do all day long, the time went by quickly at first in the constant visualization of my new life ahead and in going over the past months with Stanislaw. I practiced French grammar, which he had helped me to brush up on. And I began to relive the books we had narrated— his wartime epic "Three W," our joint "Willi," and our "Enchanted Village," rationed to a few chapters each day.

At the same time, I discovered a new activity in my cell. It started when one morning I found a handsome spider sitting in the middle of a beautifully constructed web fastened between the bars and the window frame. Apparently she had wandered in during the early dawn before the window was fully closed. Although the web's location made little sense with the window shut, a number of flies had made their way into my cell, and these I caught in turn and released into the window space. Each eventually had the misfortune of becoming tangled in the web and promptly being rolled and packaged and stored with consummate skill by the spider. It was the height of the fly season, and ever more found their way into the cell. The spider became a nervous wreck with the sudden surfeit of nourishment. As our partnership developed I came to call her Lorraine for the double barred cross on her triangular back.

At first Lorraine carefully repaired her overworked web every morning or, if it was too battered, demolished it and started all over again with painstaking craftsmanship. I watched, fascinated. When it was all done, she would test the web for any defects by sitting at its center and jouncing it, changing her position to put her feet on new diagonals; she would then run a communication line up to her lair in a crack between the window head and the wall. Hidden away there, she kept the end of one foot resting on the line, the other end of which was fastened to the exact center of the web. When a fly hit any point on the circular network, the impact was transmitted by the affected diagonals to the center and from there by the communication line to the end of Lorraine's leg. Like a stone she would drop instantly to the center, jounce the web once, twice, quickly judging which diagonal had natural vibrations and which swung slower because of the weight of the fly. Almost faster than I could follow, she would be on her prey, grab it, and start spinning it like a ball of wool, tying down its wings and legs in a bundle of threads. The fly safely packaged, Lorraine would then cut herself loose from the web. Hanging the fly like a market bag on one rear leg, she would hoist herself on the cable to her lair and there hook her still-live burden on a projecting piece of concrete for further processing when the spirit moved her.

Soon Lorraine caught on that, even when her web was not in tiptop shape, flies somehow still turned up. So why go to all the trouble of making new ones? As the pile of fly heads and wings and legs mounted on the window sill, she neglected her housekeeping more and more. Finally I was forced to hand up the half-stunned flies on the end of a straw in order to keep her supplied and reduce the fly population in my cell. In fact, she became so demoralized that she only half sucked out her prey; then, instead of cutting loose every bit of finished meal and cleaning the web, she left them dangling where they were. The result was that even when she had a reasonably good web, her whole vibration system was so jammed that she often made false runs to half-eaten corpses while the live fly got away on the opposite side.

As the weeks wore on it became ever harder to keep up my front of optimism. I demanded to speak to an officer. I was told my request would be passed on. Another week went by. I asked again. And a third time. Finally Shoo came with the devastating answer: "The officer will see you in six weeks." Six weeks of this uncertainty, in this vacuum, and even then no assurance of any end in sight!

I could not concentrate on anything. The spiral thinking of those early months soon held me in its grip once more, lashing me hour after empty hour, day after day. I tried to break it. I worked out a backward calendar: 37 days, 36, 35—a kind of military attrition campaign—34 days, 33, and at the other end zero day, zero hour, when at last I would go upstairs. And so I paced day after day toward zero day and zero hour, the one hope that held me and kept me going like a squirrel in a wheel.

July came. Zero day was approaching. On the morning of zero day I said to Shoo, "Please, it is six weeks and the officer will now see me."

Shoo's eyes wandered. "I will report your request."

Then it became zero day plus two. I asked Shoo once more. This time he flared up, swinging his arms: "I told the officer. You will not see him today, nor tomorrow, nor next week, nor next month, nor next year. You won't see him ever. Understand? Never. Never!"

So all this counting down had been a mirage. I felt sick, had dizzy spells. I lost all desire for food. At about this time the doctor made one of his periodic rounds, and each prisoner was taken upstairs in turn to be examined. When he asked me how I was, I answered with a stream of invective. I said I couldn't stand it any longer and would do something drastic if they didn't at least put an end to this do-nothing existence in a vacuum with no idea what was to become of me.

I was returned downstairs without comment. Back in my cell I kept rushing back and forth, trying to stamp out reality through exhaustion. August 8 was around the corner—Kate's birthday. I would celebrate it by smashing everything I could lay my hands on; I would rip the lamp box out of its recess and stamp on the "Ivan." I would throw the pail with its contents into the corridor. Let them retaliate. I would hit back twice as hard. I had nothing to lose.

The morning of the eighth came. Breakfast arrived. The door opened again; the empty mug was collected. As I stood trembling facing the wall, I thought I heard a thud of something being deposited on the floor. As soon as the door slammed shut I turned and looked. There on the threshold, looking as if it had been left behind by mistake, lay a book. I rushed over and picked it up—the first book I had held in my hands in a year. I turned it over. I smelled it. I leafed its pages. It was in German, a used book, and its name was *Witterzonen der Weltpolitik*. It had a lot of maps and photographs and seemed to be a political, economic, and geographical analysis of the most critical flash points just before the outbreak of World War II: the Mediterranean basin, Egypt, South Africa, Persia, Afghanistan, the route to India, India itself, Russia, China, Japan, South America. But the strange thing was that this was no communist treatise, but a Nazi geopolitical study by one Haushofer in the spirit of the prewar anticommunist pact. I was angry at first, but then I reasoned that perhaps it was the only German book they had found around.

I settled down at the top end of my cot, pulled my feet up, and put the book on my knees. What an incredible experience: sitting and reading real words and looking at real pictures! By lunchtime I had devoured the first fifty pages. Behind the obvious ideological bias there was a great deal of serious historical, social, and economic data presented as a geopolitical foundation, an approach quite new to me. I decided to spend the afternoon analyzing what I had read in the morning and use it as a springboard for new conclusions. My original plan for the day had become quite forgotten. If the book had arrived only a few hours later, events would have taken a quite different and unpredictable course.

In point of fact, this book was no more than a shot in the arm, a temporary escape from the problems that would bear right down upon me again. During the first few days of reading I felt completely absorbed. When I had finished, I started the book a second time, but already I was finding it hard to concentrate. At last I handed it back. Presumably there would be another. A day or two passed and once more I was pacing frantically around my cell, ever nearer the brink of a new upsurge of rebellion. Then one day I again heard something being laid on the floor. When I went over and looked I could hardly believe my eyes: there lay the very volume from my suitcase of 1949, Norman Mailer's *The Naked and the Dead*. I hugged the book and ran my eyes over the English words, the English sentences. I had not heard or seen my own language for a year, and it had already begun to seem like a mere memory, a secret language inside me alone. I read the blurb on the back about Mailer. How typically American and familiar it sounded! I studied the jacket design and then the inside flaps. Finally I began to read.

By now, though, I knew it would take more than Norman Mailer to hold back the impending storm. For a long time August 22, the first anniversary of my incarceration, had been a deadline of hopelessness, and it was rapidly approaching. And Kate, she too would have to conclude that it was all over. After a year's searching and waiting, what could she still expect? My disappearance would have melted under a thousand subsequent events. What my captors had been counting on would have happened: I would have been forgotten. Life would go on without me as if I had died.

August 22 came. I felt so tense that I could not keep down my breakfast. After lunch the same thing happened. I hardly touched my supper nor my breakfast the next morning. Shoo wandered in looking worried and asked if I needed a doctor. I answered, "No, it's not lack of a doctor. It's all this." I swept my hands around the room. His wandering eye almost popped out with puzzlement. "Want no doctor? Maybe here, doctor for here?" and he patted his forehead. Then, not waiting for an answer, he ambled out, shaking his head without his usual *Cholera*.

I felt listless, indifferent about everything. About the third day after Shoo's visit, the key suddenly turned in my door in the middle of the morning. As I faced the wall I heard two people entering the cell. My hands still over my head, I turned and found Cigarette standing before me, a raincoat thrown over his shoulder, and behind him the officer I had seen with the doctor, presumably the man in charge of this building.

Cigarette asked in German why I didn't eat properly. I said I was too tense to, that I had trouble keeping my food down. I said it couldn't go on this way with no one willing to speak with me. He said he would arrange something in the next day or so, then turned and left the cell. So at last they were prepared to have me go up and see an officer in spite of Shoo's "never." What had brought about this change? The only explanation could be concern about my condition, especially about my having almost stopped eating.

The more I reflected on this, the more intrigued I became by the sudden intercession. One thing was sure beyond a doubt: while there might be no intention to free me, they also didn't want to get rid of me physically. They were concerned that I remain alive: that was worth knowing. It could be turned to my account.

All the next day I waited to be called upstairs. Very carefully I formulated what I would say. I would review the events of the last year and say there had been time enough for them to investigate all angles fully. I would therefore demand that I either be put on trial at once or freed. I would go into the matter of basic human rights. As a foreign national I was entitled to full process of law in my defense.

I decided on a deliberate policy of turned back most of my food, pending fulfillment of Cigarette's promise. That afternoon I heard a lot of hammering and sawing outside, and in the late afternoon the silhouettes of some workmen were visible, erecting something that at once cut down on the daylight. Soon the workmen departed, but the obstruction outside remained. I was furious. So they're cutting out the bit of sunlight that in its glow on the painted glass gave these cells a little cheer. The evening came. I went to bed extremely depressed.

An hour or so later I became aware of a sudden surge of activity in the corridor. My door flew open, and something big was maneuvered in. I couldn't help but turn and look. Two guards were carrying an army cot with its straw sack, which they set down along the wall opposite mine. On it lay a blanket, clean sheet, and pillow case.

I was startled, then alarmed. I was to have new company. That was hardly a good portent. You don't go to the trouble of putting together two inmates if you're about to release one of them: that the routine of this basement had already taught me. I lay awake, listening to every sound. How strange—an hour from now, or ten minutes, an unknown man will be lying there in that cot across from me. It was an awful thought. I felt too tired, too weak, to face all the readjustments and difficulties it meant.

As I lay there someone outside reached to my window and opened it. This time, though, it wasn't just pulled ajar an inch or two, but both wings were swung out at right angles to the wall as the warm August night poured over me. I raised myself on my arm and peered into the darkness. The light from my cell lit up a lush mass of stalks and leaves all along the bottom of the window to a board wall opposite, part of a three-sided areaway that was the depth of the open window wings and reached about a foot above them. I could see a large piece of sky full of stars above. So that explained the shadowy object that had been put across my window that afternoon. Well, it was worth it, if it meant having the window fully open all night.

I heard a distant motor. A horn blew. A metal gate clanked. The motor rapidly approached. This was the first time I had heard the arrival of a van through the open window. It maneuvered to a stop close by. Someone was being helped out, was shuffling along the pavement, evidently blindfolded. The outer door of the building creaked open. Now the shuffling was on the cellar steps, in the corridor. Instinctively I settled deeper into my cot and pulled up the blanket, leaving a peephole so I could watch the entry of the stranger.

The bolts fell back. He was coming across the floor already, tall and gaunt, his eyes small and sunken and barricaded against the outside world. His skin was taut and deathly white. Suddenly he faltered and stared at me. Why was he staring that way? My God, why? An uncertain smile now played around his mouth. And suddenly I knew. I tried to smile back, but it wouldn't happen. I felt a convulsion surge through me as I turned to the wall and lay doubled up in tears, crying I did not know whether out of joy to see him or out of sorrow for all the new suffering that had made his face so unrecognizable.

# 14

## As the Second Year Began

Stanislaw deposited his clothes at the door and crept under the blanket. Suddenly we were both laughing out of control, the tears running down our faces.

He became serious. "You gave me quite a fright," he whispered. "I didn't recognize you at first there under the covers. It never entered my head you might still be here. I was sure you were mending fences at your Valley Farm since June at least. What are you doing here still?"

The door opened and Shoo picked up the suit. Probably having watched our funny behavior through the Judas eye, he came lumbering toward us with a broad grin: "How about it—all right? Tell your American son of a bitch we knew you'd like it best here with us." He stared at us with something bordering on bearish paternalism, then abruptly turned and left.

"And how about you? Where have you been?" I looked worriedly at Stanislaw's haggard face.

"Where you were before, and where I had been: over next door. Ever since the night I left you."

"Over next door? You mean in the old cellar? Is it that close?"

"I'm sure of it. It's all one prison compound; I checked all the sounds. I'll tell you about it tomorrow." He paused. "But what happened to you? You look deathly pale and sick."

When we woke in the morning it was already light. Real daylight poured in through our wide-open window over the top of the boards. I raised myself and looked at the little two-by-three-foot enclosure of weeds. It was intoxicating—a mass of long stalks of grass, some dandelions, a number of wild scrawny bushes with little blossoms: a whole lost world in miniature. Had the window been forgotten, or was it to stay open all day?

We got up. People went by outside; we could sometimes see the tops of their heads over the boards. We exchanged further scraps of information as we went about making our beds. When breakfast came, I felt hungry for the first time in weeks. How could it be otherwise with this sudden reunion and with the daylight and hot, scented air of August sweeping over us?

But had I not already decided on a policy? In spite of this happy turn of events, didn't the thing I had asked for all summer still elude me? I was not going to be cheated out of my session with an officer upstairs. I had to know. My failure to eat properly during the past week had clearly become a matter of concern. If I stood my ground, it was the one lever that might get me what I wanted. Sure enough, the next morning my tactics bore fruit. I was taken upstairs and, to my surprise, found myself face to face once more with Cigarette, who was standing bronzed, resplendent in a summer suit, beside the muslin-curtained window. Seated at the table was the pumpkin-headed doctor.

So my chance had come at last. I started carefully to present my plight. Halfway through, Cigarette interrupted me: there wasn't time for me to go on and on this way. Specifically, what were my complaints?

I felt totally confused. These contacts with other people had become so rare and special and filled with importance that they caused a mental paralysis to come over me, making it impossible to deal with anything that had not been carefully rehearsed. Rather like a clumsy schoolkid, I would forget what I wanted to say. I asked for information about Kate and the children. Denied. I asked for accurate information on Noel's supposed crimes. Denied. I asked for a yes or no answer on whether I was to be tried. Denied. I pointed to the tops of the trees outside and said it was a whole year since I had been outside; did he understand what that meant?

He shrugged. "We have time, Mr. Field. No end of time. We can wait until you're ready to speak the truth. It's entirely up to you when and if you ever see trees again." The same formula as a year ago, exactly the same, and meanwhile not a single advance on any point. Well, one small concession as I got up to return downstairs: Cigarette said that the officer who had conducted my interrogation was away but would be back in a few weeks and would see me then.

Back in the cell, Stanislaw tried to comfort me. "What did you expect? It's a lot that you'll be seeing your officer again. It means he has completed his investigation."

He went on to tell me that for his part, for the first time in one and a half years he felt real hope. That night in May when he had been plucked out of the cell so suddenly, he had been driven to Warsaw. There he had been confronted with another prisoner who under pressure had concocted a story of joint terrorist acts against the wartime communist underground. As rescripted by the present regime, then, Stanislaw's role during the war years in the Polish non-communist underground—the Home Army, or AK as it was known—now took the form of a secret collaboration with Hitler's Gestapo to destroy the Armea Ludova, the communist partisans operating largely out of the forests against Germany's communication lines to the Russian front.

Until that confrontation, Stanislaw had been unable to stand up for himself. Face to face that night with his denouncer, though, he had fought back and proved beyond doubt that the deeds described had never happened. The interrogators had fulminated and become rough, but finally gave up. That very night he had been taken back to that awful cellar, where he had spent the past three months in a damp cell. Yet despite the bleak conditions, the violence and the rabbit hunts had subsided. Now with his return here, he was sure a final decision wouldn't be far off.

That first morning we decided to switch to the familiar *du* to celebrate our reunion. We also revealed our last names, a strictly kept secret until then. So my cellmate was Stanislaw Mierzenski, not just Stanislaw. He was the first person in over a year who had a real identity.

Once more we plunged into feverish intellectual activity, bursting with the backlog of these months of solitary nothingness. "You know, I worked out all the rest of 'Duck Lane' over there," Stanislaw reported. "I think it's very good now." And so each morning he narrated another bit to me and together we refined it. For my part, I went over everything I had garnered from the German book, embroidering into it all my associated thoughts in a sort of series of area studies. He was thrilled to see my copy of *The Naked and the Dead,* which I started to translate chapter by chapter.

In turn it led to a whole slew of new questions about American life, sparked by the embattled soldiers' flashbacks to their diverse hometown backgrounds. At the same time, we began recasting "Duck Lane" à la Mailer, interlacing the main story with a succession of biographical flashbacks.

Now that we were again in possession of our identities, we began to reveal more about ourselves. I learned that Stanislaw was descended from small landed gentry in the Poznan area of western Poland. In infancy he had had an Irish nursemaid. His childhood, in a manner characteristic of old Polish families, featured an immersion in French culture, which led to a lifelong interest in French literature. His university studies, however, had been in agronomy so that he might carry on the family tradition and manage their estate as a model experimental farm. At twenty-eight, however, he had tired of that work and decided to become a journalist, starting more or less penniless at the bottom, to find himself a decade later economic editor of *Sczas,* Poland's prewar equivalent of the London *Times.* Thirty-five at the outbreak of the war, he was six years my senior.

At once I suggested that he conduct a course on the principles of modern agronomy. He was willing, and in the weeks that followed I learned about soils, plant growth, fertilizers, the principles of crop rotation, and diversified inter-locking methods of farming. I had to submit to examinations on each phase in turn.

I felt a whole new world opening before me. At night I began to imagine all sorts of schemes for my derelict ex-farm. As if reading my mind, Stanislaw an-nounced one morning that the real test would be to prove myself in a pilot proj-ect. Valley Farm would do for this. The first step was to provide him with a mental map of our two hundred acres, and gradually he referred to this or that field with such accuracy it was as if he had actually felt the soil trickle through his fingers. He was a taskmaster, driving me hard as I sought to bring life into our neglected New England soil on the principles of European agronomy. He brought to my protective attitude to the natural environment a sense of pro-ductive activism designed not to deplete it, but to use it on a sustainable basis.

Meanwhile I watched with redoubled interest the odd collection of plants that had taken root in the rectangular patch of sandy soil outside our window. If only we could reach out and nurture it. I hit upon the idea of collecting the dust that had accumulated in the cracks of our floorboards, mixing this with pow-dered lime scraped from our walls, adding some mouse droppings as fertilizer, and stuffing little wet packages of this mix into the crevices at the bottom of our window grille. It was the tomato season, and we had a surfeit of seeds in our food; I also added grains of rye from my mattress. Using an empty eggshell as container, I watered the bottom of the frame each morning. To our infinite de-light, soon little shoots raised their heads, then slender stems began to make their way slowly up the grille. We had indeed created our own little garden of green tracery, an assertive link to that other world of memory.

We felt buoyed by the creative vitality that had transformed our cell. Even though we could see nothing of the outside world except our tiny weed patch and a section of fall sky with its scudding clouds, sounds flowed in day and night without restraint. Children's voices were carried to us on the wind as they played; on hot days we could hear bathers yelling somewhere. In the evenings we occasionally caught the sound of an accordion, an excursion boat, a radio or gramophone screeching noisy dance music from some loudspeaker, a dredger rattling in the river. And as the fall advanced, the whine of threshing machines was superseded by the putt-putt of a diesel tractor. We experienced a happiness of sorts—a strictly existential happiness that could hold only so long as our wills blotted out everything beyond the present.

Our interest in the goings-on within the cellar receded. We hardly listened to the various sounds through the door, lost track of who was going upstairs. The window, however, continued to bring us new bits of information. Sometimes we caught scraps of conversation that drifted down from an open window above us. We confirmed that the focus of interrogations seemed to be not at all on the present but on the war years, dealing especially with the Polish Home Army and its underground struggle. I gradually got a picture of these cellars filling up with Poles who suddenly found themselves the victims of some fantastic twist of their wartime struggle against the Nazis, making it exactly the opposite of what it had been. An eerie atmosphere seemed to hang over it all, with people being hounded on the basis of present political dictates for things that had happened in completely unrelated circumstances.

One day at the beginning of October I was taken upstairs and found my former interrogating officer, the stocky colonel with the bristly mustache, sitting behind the desk. Beside him lay a thick loose-leaf folder. He seemed ill at ease and at once said he had several questions to ask me, as if trying to head off an initiative on my part. He asked me to describe every contact I had had with visiting Russian architects in the closing days of the war, when I served on an American-Soviet architects committee sponsored by the New York chapter of the American Institute of Architects. Again I told him what I could remember about the committee, which had mounted a major professional effort to help develop emergency shelter for Russia's war-ravaged population. With that over, I brought up my concerns. He had obviously been delaying this moment but had to give in.

I mentioned the two statements regarding my Krakow work and my wartime effort from England to help people lost during the evacuation, both of which had been twisted into a link-up with the British and American intelligence services. I told him they were worthless idiocies that I would repudiate if they were ever raised in a trial. He was quite evidently embarrassed and dismissed the matter by saying he agreed those two statements had little meaning. I then demanded that I should either be tried or freed within a stated period, should be given concrete evidence of my brother's guilt, and should be given information about the whereabouts and circumstances of my wife and children. He wrote each point down and said he would pass on my requests. There was no show of hostility. How unlike Cigarette and everyone else I had encountered over the months! I added that I would like more books and a newspaper. He evaded the issue by saying he didn't know whether the prisoner with me had a right to these. All in all it was evident that the colonel did not relish this encounter at all and felt quite defensive.

Back below, Stanislaw counseled me to go slow and not do anything precipitous. Our routine had progressed to a new stage. With his account of "Duck Lane" and my translation of *The Naked and the Dead* behind us, we needed something to fill the gap. That was why I had asked for books. "Well, if they weren't giving us any," said Stanislaw, "we'll write our own." And why not? Earlier he had suggested that I too tell him a story from fantasy just as he had done so magically for me in the spring and now again. I had protested. Fantasy like his was a rare gift, I said; I had never heard anything like it. He countered that he hadn't been that way before, that prison had brought it out in him and, indeed, had saved him during his months of solitary.

I responded that it was hopeless to get a visually oriented mind like mine to paint through words. He retorted, "You're just lazy, that's all."

He suggested we do a joint book, each reciting on alternate days, chapter by chapter. That should make it easier for me. "I'll start off. We won't work out a general plan like with the others. It will be more fun for each of us if we have no idea where the other will take the story. I'll narrate chapter one tomorrow, and after you've heard it, you can take the characters wherever you wish without knowing what I intended doing, and then in turn I'll have to follow along where you left it hanging."

The first characters in the book were two Poles who had already appeared in "Duck Lane." They were in a truck on their way to Paris from a displaced persons' camp in Germany in 1945. The second major players, not surprisingly, were two Americans, a sergeant and a captain, attached to U.S. Army headquarters in Paris. The focal setting was the Hôtel des Saints Pères off the Boulevard St. Germain, with which I had many associations from childhood family stays. Chapter after chapter unfolded in a broad pattern of Parisian intrigue and night life (this being Stanislaw's lively contribution) with biographical flashbacks like Mailer's to Warsaw, New England, South Carolina, and Dublin. Each day thus brought with it an expectancy, suspense over what new turn of events would arise.

After some twenty-eight breathtaking chapters it came to an end, and both of us felt we had gotten a mighty good show for the money. With its heavy undertone of international intrigue and Parisian night life it seemed the perfect serial for a Paris boulevard paper.

Stanislaw was triumphant. "There you are—not able to fantasize!"

Well, maybe, but I was a nervous wreck after all the nights of toil, chasing an imagination that always seemed just out of reach, while across the way Stanislaw snored along night after night in utter contentment. After only one day's pause we were off again on our second joint adventure. He agreed to set this one in Cambridge, Massachusetts, a truly noble gesture considering he had never been nearer to the place than Berlin. This story was to take a different direction, a psychological study of the love of a mother and daughter for the same man. That was the only guide we set out with, and with our Quaker/Catholic, English/Latin-Slavic, and deep temperamental divergences, a very complicated and fertile portrayal of character and behavior was assured. And in fact, with every chapter we became more deeply involved. Often as I labored hour after hour I felt happy and forgot all time, forgot everything but the tragedy moving steadily toward its as yet unknown climax. When it finally finished and the curtain fell, we both were silent. For hours afterward we still seemed to be far off in that house on Shady Hill Square in Cambridge.

In normal life I would jump off a building before submitting to such an ordeal. A prison cellar was another thing, though; even a piece of wood would begin to imagine things down here. I could now concede the abysmal mental laziness to which the hyperactivity of normal life subjected one. I could see the overwhelming need here to counter the vacuum, to probe on an ever wider scale—a probing that had so amazed me when I had first met Stanislaw. Step by step the necessity to blot out the prison reality had injected this capacity into me too.

We started on a third joint novel, "Dr. Gilbert Little, M.D." The setting was New York and a small Pennsylvania mining town, again a concession by Stanislaw giving me the edge of familiarity. By the time we had finished we found Christmas at our elbow—Christmas 1950, our second one together. How upset we would have been a year before if we had been able to foresee that we would be laying straw on each other's cots a second time. And yet how grateful we were, when it came to it, that we still shared the same cell.

By now the dimension of time had changed. I began to accept that the clock could never be set back, that life could not simply go on where it had been surgically cut. Whatever it held, the future would be unlikely to be a continuation of the past. I began to challenge a lot of concepts I had held over the years, issues I had never faced squarely in my personal life and in my attitudes toward the basic forces shaping our world. I began a slow reappraisal of the political and social confrontation between my society and that of the communists, in which I had become enmeshed. Would I make the same judgments today as I had in 1934, in 1939 and 1945, even in 1949? I doubted it. As if from the distance of another planet from which there was no return, I could look at my former world more dispassionately.

Meanwhile, about the middle of November a change occurred that seemed significant indeed. All that fall the cellar had been in full operation, the prisoners varying in number from eight to twelve with a slight but steady turnover. One Sunday morning our window was suddenly closed, and soon we heard the familiar sound of a motor outside maneuvering into position, once, twice, and then again at intervals of twenty minutes or so, while cell doors opened and closed and feet shuffled past on the corridor. We tried to carry on with our narrations but couldn't concentrate. The unusual activity and excitement of the guards, two of whom were riding back and forth in the van as if it were a holiday outing, told us that something big was going on. Now it was the turn of the man in the cell next to us. We became tense with expectation. So the cellar was being emptied, cell by cell. This was no release of individual prisoners in preparation for a trial, but a wholesale evacuation of everyone from one prison to another.

The van arrived once more. I adjusted my jacket: our turn for sure. Instead, the key was inserted in No. l. We looked at each other and grinned. Alone, just us two? We waited in silence, feeling a growing exhilaration. Something special had happened to us—we were being left behind. That must mean some other course had been decided on for us. Obviously one doesn't operate a whole prison just for two inmates. Our staying on here could only be temporary.

Only gradually did we realize that all our guards had gone with the other prisoners. With each change of watch new faces turned up. So Shoo and the Mean One were in the past. This, too, we regarded as a good augury. There was a casual black-haired fellow and, in contrast, "Blondie," a light-haired peasant type who looked at us with undisguised curiosity. Then there was a rather well mannered city youth who couldn't help fall into the behavior of a very obliging waiter whenever he opened the door. He became the "Reticent One." Only the "Correct One" of the old team had stayed behind, evidently to break in this new batch of greenhorns. The guards accepted us without the slightest show of hostility or fear. They were, after all, mere youths, bubbling over with the fullness of life outside, to whom the hours down here were just a routine to be dealt with.

Two days later we were shifted, to our disappointment, back to the narrow confines of our old cramped No. 4. Why, with all the empty spaciousness around us? The only explanation we could find was that now we were exactly opposite the guard's space and thus easy to observe.

And so, in spite of our poorer living quarters, the oppression of prison weighed lighter on us as 1951 arrived. There was something special in our isolation that had a regal touch. Three guards downstairs, three doormen upstairs, all of them just to service us two. A three-to-one ratio fit for a resort hotel. And on top of that, the operation of a whole building—heating, hot water and showers on Saturdays, food brought in from an outside kitchen—all of it just for us. There was something humorously topsy-turvy in all this, reflected in a sleepy routine developing around us. How could any sort of punitive discipline be maintained in such circumstances?

When the building was quiet and no officers were around, a tendency developed either for the doorman to come downstairs to spend time with his colleague or for the guard to disappear upstairs—on tiptoe so we wouldn't notice we were utterly alone down below. Whenever our door had to be opened for meals or for going to the washroom, the rule was that a pair of guards should supervise the function. This, too, was often conveniently forgotten. Usually the guards were much more interested in each other than in us. Especially Blondie and the Reticent One had a way of wrestling and rolling along the length of the corridor like two bear cubs, leaving us alone in the washroom—where we were now allowed to go together, apparently considered less dangerous than before.

Our basement environment was reflected in changes in our behavior too. Since we were alone, we began to shift bit by bit from whispering to conversation in a subdued voice, for which no one took us to task. We not only dispensed with the hands over head business, but even dared face the door when it opened. And in the washroom we could take our time—each day we stretched it a little further until we could think of nothing more to do. Even the resounding call "*Appell*," the signal for bed and quiet, now was just a tap on our door to suggest the hour had arrived.

Nonetheless, I felt I was continuing to drift into a limbo that was closing in around me. Permanent live storage. If that was so, was there anything left now but to fight to the finish, one way or the other? After Christmas I once more started handing back a little food at each meal. Then I asked to speak to my interrogating officer again. Two days later I repeated my request. I cut back further on the food. I asked a third time. By now I was returning most of my food untouched. On the evening of the sixth day the house officer appeared in resplendent uniform and explained that the colonel I had asked for would see me tomorrow. His eyes said the rest: Would you please now be sensible?

During the night I rehearsed my exact procedure upstairs. I carefully formulated each demand, which I would insist on putting in writing. First there would be a short preamble stating my case and the authorities' failure to grant me the most elementary human rights. In consequence I now would demand either immediate unconditional release or one of three measures to safeguard my rights meanwhile:

(a) consular access to me by someone from the U.S. embassy as an inalienable right of a foreign national;

(b) the opportunity to present my case to a representative of the U.N. Commission on Human Rights so that my circumstances could be brought before that body;

(c) access to a representative of UNESCO to transmit my case to the director thereof, since I had been engaged as an architect in UNESCO's mission of furthering international cultural relations and had fallen a victim of these endeavors.

When I arrived upstairs the colonel looked worried and nervous. I realized that this week of malnutrition had taken its toll on me; I felt exhausted from the mere trip upstairs. I began at once by stating that I had certain requests which I wanted to put in writing. He got out some paper and told me to dictate them to him.

He looked very perturbed. He said that these were complicated matters and would take some time to resolve. Meanwhile, I should try to eat normally and he would see that we got some books to read. I retorted that until one of the three alternatives had been fulfilled I wouldn't be able to regain sufficient appetite to eat normally. He left the room, the doorman taking his place. As he went out he said something about telephoning. And sure enough, some two minutes later he returned and started pacing back and forth in front of me, shooting fierce glances my way.

"The fact of your demanding the American embassy is the best evidence of your hostile attitude. The U.S. embassy is the center of fascist intrigue against the new Poland, and you expect us to give consideration to you while at the same time you play along with them against us? Mr. Field, you are unmasking yourself."

I retorted that it was up to them; I had given them two other alternatives. Furthermore, if they freed me, as far as I was concerned we would be quits. I would make no public issue of what they had done to me. The U.S. embassy simply represented my country; its only role was to protect my civil rights, which the Polish authorities had violated. Once more the officer warned me to be reasonable if I wished to clear the matter up. He rang the bell, and I returned below, disappointed by my failure to get any concrete commitment.

And yet, I hadn't retreated one inch from my position, and now my demands and a way to resolve them were in the files in black and white. They could always be pointed to again. Round two, I finally decided, belonged to me, a feeling that was reinforced when, that evening, the door opened and the house officer entered ceremoniously with the startled guard beside him, both staggering under an armful of books. I could hardly keep from smiling as the two stood there with their goodwill offering, looking hopefully to my face for signs of surprised enthusiasm.

Actually, I was almost beside myself with excitement as I struggled to hold back my tears. I could almost have thrown my arms around the jolly little officer, who, bursting with pride, reached for one volume after another and handed them to me. Except for those two volumes last summer, these were the first printed words I had seen since 1949.

I glanced over to Stanislaw who, spellbound, simply watched as the books passed from hand to hand. I fingered each, looked at the titles. They were all in German, a weird collection on diverse subjects published in East Germany and Russia. I selected one of them, handed the rest back, and thanked them without any visible enthusiasm. The officer and guard left looking rather crest-fallen.

I continued to leave my food untouched except for a token nibble. Obviously they had reckoned that, bowled over by the books, I would stop being so stubborn. They had miscalculated. Now something would have to happen. It did, two days later, when, feeling distinctly weak, I was once more taken upstairs and ushered into the big corner office with the Persian rug and the desk across the far corner. This time I was to be questioned by none other than Cigarette.

"Why aren't you eating?"

"Because of loss of appetite." I reminded him that I had made specific requests for safeguarding of my human rights and I was awaiting action by the authorities.

Cigarette looked at me sarcastically, then said with studied deliberation: "The answer is this. If you insist on continuing with your demands for contact with the American embassy, we can assure you, you will never see the world outside there again," as he nodded toward the window. "If, on the other hand, you give up this silliness I can offer you certain assurances. It lies with you."

I tried to explain that I had waited for a year and a half. I had no choice but to insist on my rights.

He smiled with mock pity. "You forget that you are completely in our power. You will only have yourself to blame, and you will no longer have the companionship of another prisoner. All right then." He pushed the bell for the guard to take me back downstairs.

I felt a dull sense of finality. Wasn't I precipitating myself into oblivion? Yes, I was completely in their power. Was I prepared to risk life itself? That I could be faced with such a decision hadn't dawned on me. There was a knock on the door. "*Proche.*" The guard appeared.

I faltered and gave up. "Just a moment. Yes, I will accept, if you could make my life more tolerable meanwhile and I can look forward to concrete prospects of a resolution."

Cigarette beckoned the guard to leave again. "All right then. The state of your investigation looks favorable."

"But can you suggest when I can expect an end to my imprisonment?"

"We cannot give you any exact limit, but I can say that the balance of time you will still be held by us will be no more than half the time you have already spent here. What else?" He showed marked impatience.

"And what about my wife and children? If I can't have direct communication with them, could I at least be informed as to their circumstances, how and where they are, what they have done to adjust to my disappearance? You can easily establish that from my wife's sister, who lives in East Berlin. And your own files must have information too."

"Yes, I will find out what I can, but it will take some weeks."

"And meanwhile I would like some paper and pencil," and I explained about the narrations Stanislaw and I had worked on, and that we wanted very much to write a joint novel to fill the time. I also again asked for some sort of newspaper and for a chess set to give some variety to our daily life. Finally I reminded him that I hadn't once set foot out of doors.

Yes, he thought that most of these requests could be granted in time.

I returned downstairs, feeling the strain of this encounter more than normally, owing to my weakened condition. Stanislaw comforted me: "What else could you have done in the face of such a threat? And you have won very substantial gains."

And so I had. Already we had the books, and by evening a green school copybook and pencil lay beside our cups on the floor. Immediately we plunged into a fever of activity. All the next day there was hardly a silent moment as we worked out our writing plans and began to sketch out the story we would record. It had been made clear to me that only I had won the right to paper and pencil, so any idea of alternate spells of narrating as we had been doing these past months was out. Instead, we would start by taking the best of our stories so far and recast it. In bed at night, we would go over the bit ahead together. Next morning Stanislaw would flesh it out aloud in his limited German while I took it down and adapted it freely in English. We were sucked into a wave of creative energy, convinced that something unusual and of lasting value would come out of our joint effort.

So it was that on the second day after my visit upstairs, the big moment came when I sat down and opened the copybook at page one and wrote: "DUCK LANE—THE STORY OF A STREET," and under that "PROLOGUE." And off we went, in the first of some 115 copybooks that were to become the main insurance of our sanity in the long ordeal ahead, a total of some sixteen thousand painstakingly pencil-written pages.

I sat perched on the end of my cot as close to the light bulb as possible. With winter weather outside, we had our window only slightly ajar with insufficient daylight coming through the painted glass. Except for short intervals I sat there all day, giving the strip of floor over to Stanislaw. Our routine consisted of writing from breakfast to the changing of the guards at four, whereupon I switched to reading aloud to Stanislaw from our new supply of German books. His eyes had deteriorated so much during his imprisonment that he could not see anything detailed, nor decipher print at all.

Our days became still more packed with the receipt of a Polish newspaper. When the first one lay on the floor beside our lunch bowls, we both dashed for it in a frenzy of excitement. At last, the world outside! What would we find? Poor Stanislaw went almost crazy. He could make out the headlines, but that was all, whereas I could read the rest but with limited comprehension. He grabbed me and pushed me down on the cot and said, "Read it aloud, quickly, here, here!" It was a dispatch from Seoul, Korea. The headline was something about a number of defensive positions that had changed hands, about captured U.S. troops and equipment. What did it mean? My recitation was painfully slow. I had never tried to read Polish out loud; it was hard enough to make sense of the words without being snagged on pronunciation.

Stanislaw looked pleadingly at me as he tried to decipher the queer sounds I slowly produced. After half an hour, with my eyes aching, we had finished the first column. Already we had discovered that there was some big war going on in Korea. But what could it mean? When and how had it started? We had never read such tirades. Not only Korea, but China seemed involved, and in addition to Americans the list of captured prisoners included Britons and Turks. What in heaven's name was going on?

As we proceeded, we became more and more amazed at the paper's hysterical tone. Perhaps a third world war was raging without our knowing about it? And yet we could find no reports of any fighting in Europe.

The impact of this first bit of news of the world outside, in a carefully censored communist newspaper in a language I only vaguely understood, was truly terrifying. Not only was I faced with madness in here, it seemed, but now the world outside on which I counted had erupted in madness as well. The more I thought about it and pieced things together in the succeeding days, the deeper despair I felt. Every day the shadow of chaos and a new rain of bombs seemed closer. To be caught in a prison cellar like in a rat trap only made our perspective more haunting.

The paper, the *Curier Codzeny,* was the organ of the communist-dominated Democratic Party and angled mainly toward the intellectual, professional stratum. It was less blatantly ideological than the Party press and devoted considerable space to literature, science, and art, which gave us a lot of pleasure. But we also felt exasperation. Quite aside from the skimpy and distorted reports on international events, the paper had a way of suddenly not appearing for days on end without explanation. All we could figure was that things had happened that we weren't supposed to know about—a sort of censorship within censorship. From this we developed a kind of tension barometer, based mainly on what news we did not get. If the paper stopped for five or six days or even two weeks steady, chances were there was a political trial in progress. If it was for shorter stretches, it was probably just some international flare-up that they wanted to keep from us.

The chess set came too, finally. It had to be returned each night together with the book we were reading and the notebook and pencil, neatly stacked on top of our clothes. And once outside it was promptly seized upon by the guards, who began playing round after round through the night at their table in the space across from us, often joined by their bored colleague from upstairs.

The whole building, not just the cellar, seemed to have drifted into still water. No longer were we summoned for interrogation. The desks had been moved out upstairs and the rooms converted into dormitories for guards and officers. Now it was all laughter and gossip—even the splash in the early predawn hours from a bladder being relieved via the shortcut of the open window above us—instead of tense exchanges between inmates and their captors. Most of the time we were the only ones in the cellar. Only we two, it seemed, had ended up as permanent fixtures.

But then one day, toward the end of March 1951, I was called out of our cellar somnolence. As I entered the room upstairs I found a fantastic character staring at me from behind the desk. His face was emaciated looking with sunken cheeks and small, close-set eyes, one of which seemed unable to keep up with the other and watered as he looked at me. He was a little fellow with distinctly Jewish features, and at once the idea came to me that this grotesque wreck could only be the survivor of a Nazi concentration camp. In spite of feeling a kind of pity and shyness about staring at him, I also felt ill at ease. There was something sick and unpleasant in that face which I couldn't define. That first encounter provided only a general exchange of remarks in German, which he spoke with an unmistakable Yiddish accent. Thereafter came a scattering of the same old questions I had imagined had been dealt with for good.

These sessions went on almost daily for exactly one month, often extending into night. There was something utterly incongruous about them; surely they couldn't have provided anything of substance. Were they intended simply to dampen further assertiveness on my part? If so, they had exactly the opposite effect. The interrogator's behavior became ever more insolent. Soon he merely snapped his fingers for me to leave when the guard came to take me back below. I retaliated by refusing to give any greeting when I entered the room. As I got to know him better, I was horrified to think what would happen to a prisoner if this creature had full freedom to do as he wished. In addition to calling me up during the afternoon, he began to haul me out of bed and keep me two or three hours upstairs doing nothing. He would sit behind his desk, either doodling or surreptitiously reading a book or newspaper in the drawer to one side of him, making no attempt to question me.

In addition to dropping the Mr., he began using the German familial pronoun *du* to indicate just how insignificant I was. In response I called him *du* too, pretending I mistook it for a sign of friendship that should be reciprocated. He in turn launched into a lot of swearing in Polish, which gave him no end of satisfaction, though its effect was wasted on me.

When he insisted on seeing an American agent in every person I had known and a conspiracy in every smallest action of my life, I retaliated by mentioning various communist luminaries who, I suggested, surely should have been locked up as well. How about Gerhart Eisler, whom the Poles had helped escape from the United States on the *Batory?* Certainly, I ventured, everything pointed to his flight having been merely a bluff in his undercover work for U.S. Intelligence. And had they checked on Beria? And Stalin? In fact, I suggested, what they were doing with me had all the earmarks of an American agent's hand, right here in the Polish MBP.

This was too much for him, and he made a rush at me. I was sure I was about to lose a few teeth, but he pulled back at the last moment and merely cursed me with every word at his disposal and said what I had already surmised: "If it depended on me, I would know how to deal with a fellow with your kind of snout. The time will come when you'll regret every word."

On another occasion when he launched into my guilt and how I would feel mighty small after I'd been tried, I said there was something extraordinarily metaphysical in all this, quite at variance with good Marxist teaching, something very traditional. And I began to tell him about the Massachusetts Bay Colony in the seventeenth century, about a certain town of Salem where a number of women, based on confessions made after being tortured, had been found guilty of consorting with the devil and burned at the stake.

"Just think, three hundred years ago. You see, you're not as original in your security set-up here as you think," I concluded. "In fact, you communists should establish a chair in witchcraft at Warsaw University for the training of new security cadres."

That night he called me up to sit in the corner and, instead of his usual passivity, got out some paper and began to write first a title and then a lengthy statement. Occasionally he glanced at me, hatred in his eyes. I realized I had gone too far. No wonder: my nerves were giving out in this continuous struggle. In spite of myself, the threats that were showered on me each day so haunted me that I couldn't get to sleep at all afterward. His utter lack of interrogatory skill, it seemed to me, often revealed more truth than he perhaps realized. Thus to my ears, his taunts about my never getting out of this cellar again and my having been forgotten long ago by the world outside had more than a grain of truth. And especially his comment that no one knew anyway what had happened to me and where I was.

Another few weeks of this and I would have drawn more out of him than he out of me. Filled with envy and hate he blundered along, closing every possible avenue of contact and critical appraisal of me, his victim. I couldn't help but sense at times that his fanatical outbursts were the result in part of his equating my non-Jewishness with the Nazis and the Holocaust. More than any of the other interrogators I had had, he made me realize that with such creatures any method of interrogation other than terror was impossible. And terror in turn produces ninety-nine false leads, which have to be unscrambled for every true result. But did they really care?

When I reported these latest interchanges to Stanislaw, he grew pale. He had warned me each day: fighting back was one thing, but it was dangerous in the extreme to provoke as I had been doing. Especially that reference to Stalin as an American agent! "How could you?"

Yes, how could I? Was I losing my senses?

# 15

## Unequal Battle

My interrogation ceased as suddenly as it had begun, exactly four weeks after that first afternoon. So it was back to our old routine—and yet it wasn't the same. As long as the fantastic sessions upstairs had gone on, I had hardened myself to parry the humiliations and threats that descended upon me day by day. Only now did I realize how profoundly I had been shaken and frightened.

Stanislaw was strong on faith, I on will. How I now envied him his faith, which had carried him unquestioning through successive crises of his life. In desperate moments I pleaded with him to try to teach me faith. He tried. I tried. It didn't stick. I remained the disbeliever. For his part, he envied me my will-power. A hunger strike was inconceivable to him; it wouldn't last a day. He watched me with dismay as, against all reason, I undertook battle after unequal battle. He had the hard task of sitting by, a mute spectator, suffering for me when I suffered, rejoicing whenever I made a gain, and sharing the price of my defeat. His quiet, ever-tolerant presence and gestures of support enabled me to hold through many of the hardest moments.

More convinced than ever that what I now faced was permanent oblivion, a kind of live storage without end, I decided I had nothing to lose by fighting right to the limits of life itself rather than sitting waiting passively for eventual death. I was sure I had the will to carry it through. It fitted my instinctive response of passive resistance. My main weapon would be an indirect one, and the struggle itself would become a preoccupation, an aid to maintaining sanity.

Gradually a strategy took form. Since my area of maneuver was limited indeed, it seemed important to use these resources in small amounts, always keeping some in reserve. The ultimate weapon would be a final life-and-death hunger strike. That could only be used once so was reserved for the moment when all other means had failed. Under no circumstances could I allow myself to be driven into a corner as had happened in January. I would start by returning only a little food, gradually stepping it up week by week claiming loss of appetite due to nervous tension and hopelessness.

I was strengthened in my determination when one evening Stanislaw returned from an interrogation session with the whole side of his face swollen up. He had obviously been struck on his cheek, just below the left eye. He tried to smile and to calm me: "It's nothing really. Bumped into the door on my way upstairs. Pretend not to notice it, it's better that way." I was incensed and urged him to fight back and refuse his food, but he said that in his case the risks were too great, and anyway he would never have the strength to follow through. So in a way I now had the added incentive of acting as his surrogate.

A week or so after I began to cut down on my eating, I was called upstairs. The doctor and house officer were there. The doctor asked why I didn't eat. I answered evasively that I was too tense and felt disgust for food. He reminded me of the writing material and books I had been given. I replied that there was more to life than that, and that last month's interrogations had caused me to expect the worst.

I cut my food back still further. I became thin and weak. One evening in the washroom as I stooped to pick up the half-full pail I suddenly felt dizzy and then everything blotted out. I came to, being lugged on my back by two guards along the corridor to our cell. At first I had no idea where I was and felt a wonderful sense of relief. The whole load of these years had simply slipped away; it seemed as if I were suspended in nothingness, beyond life. I felt myself being laid down on something soft. There was some whispering. I felt a hand on my forehead and I opened my eyes. I was looking straight into Stanislaw's worried face.

"Hermann, what happened? Are you hurt?"

I tried to say something but couldn't. Disappointment swept over me: I was still in prison. Nothing had changed. At the same time, there was something incredibly sweet in those eyes appealing for me to say that it was all right, expressing simple human affection, a thing that seemed a memory from a distant past.

To my surprise I also saw the worried face of the guard who had slept on the table those first nights long ago in Warsaw. So he was still around. He was talking in a friendly manner with Stanislaw. Clearly he had some new responsibility here; he was no longer just a guard. As we learned in the months ahead, he was in charge of minor housekeeping responsibilities—the kitchen, the issue of laundry, maintenance and repairs—and was also a sort of intermediary between the higher-ups and us. At every crisis henceforth he was to appear in the role of peacemaker, well-meaning friend, or provider of special surprises. He did this so effectively that we began to dub him "Angel." He always had an air of conspiracy about him when he turned up with some tidbit or did some little favor, as if it were quite irregular and done strictly out of warmheartedness.

Actually, we soon decided, Angel was merely the authorities' alter ego, part of an incredibly intricate carrot-and-stick system, turned on and off with a suddenness and inconsistency calculated to drive one crazy.

The guards, too, displayed a whole gamut of attitudes, ranging from blatant humiliation to hotel-like courtesy. These shifts tended to come in cycles, often of long duration, though they could also happen in swift alternation. In January, for instance, Cigarette had threatened me with annihilation one moment and then, when the threat had sunk in, had talked about how good things stood for me and how I could expect to be free within a limited time. Guards would even be shifted in or out according to where we were on the road between stick and carrot. Some guards were picked especially for their bark, others were casual and friendly and wouldn't hurt a mouse. Then there was the intermediate efficient but correct type. Sometimes both carrot and stick were used simultaneously, a sort of double warning of what could be gained and what could be lost, unless . . .

One thing was certain: Angel's appearance always signified an unofficial carrot—to be noticed but involving no true commitment, just between the three of us. And Angel had a flare for the role. It fitted perfectly with his peasant cunning, and combined well with his desire to please and genuine warmheartedness. He was a man delightfully devoid of scruples, with an uncanny knack for turning every situation to his own advantage, for satisfying the wolf without sacrificing the lamb. As time went on, we felt increasingly entranced by him, though without ever losing sight of the game he was playing on behalf of others. Especially irresistible was the fact that a good part of the time he fooled himself too and was tickled pink by our expressions of appreciation. And so we took advantage of his pleasure, making it a point to flatter him, giving him credit, for example, for improvements that were a matter of policy and with which he had no connection whatsoever. Yes, Angel became one of the bright spots in our long stretch in the cellar.

My collapse led to another session upstairs. In addition to the doctor behind the desk, Cigarette was leaning against the window sill, a raincoat thrown like a cape over his shoulders, silently and casually observing the spectacle. Again I was asked how I felt, as if it were the most natural of matters. No reference was made to the incident in the washroom. Then the inevitable question: why didn't I eat? Once more I explained. The doctor said he would prescribe some food I would find easy to eat. Again I mentioned that I had been given no news of my family and that my recent interrogation had involved a complete disregard of the most elementary civility—that I had been told I would never get out of here.

While the doctor examined me Cigarette spoke in Polish to him; the doctor then said, "I am told you have only yourself to thank by your uncooperative behavior."

I turned my head to look at Cigarette. "That's a lie. That's a dirty lie."

Cigarette's flabby face hardened as he rushed at me. "Shut up at once, or else. Do you hear?"

I shouldn't have lost control that way. In contrast to my strategy of passive resistance, this sort of behavior could quickly lead to defeat. I went downstairs trembling, at the same time sure retaliation would follow almost at once. What would it be?

Hardly had I crept into my cot, the door closing behind me, than the telephone rang and there was a muffled conversation outside. Instructions were being given. The door opened. Two guards walked in solemnly. They pointed at me and, without giving me clothes or shoes, told me to leave the cell with one guard in front and the other behind me.

In a second round, Stanislaw joined me. Instead of undergoing punishment we both found ourselves in the fifth cell, more spacious by a third than our previous quarters. Another one of those queer surprises. We had been sweating, awaiting the worst, and when it was all over we found ourselves better off than before.

The real surprise came the next morning with the arrival of breakfast. There on the threshold was Stanislaw's mug as usual, with two slices of black bread with lard and sausage. But beside it stood a mug with a spoon in it and a saucer with four elegantly wrapped Wedel filled chocolates. I looked in the mug: whole strawberries with thick sour cream. And in the door stood Angel beaming. I didn't try to analyze the meaning of this sudden bounty. Lunch consisted of cucumbers in sour cream and some more chocolates. For supper, fruit and milk and two cookies.

For a day or two I gave in to the new indulgence. Then I decided to call a halt. I would return to my old course, starting very gradually to cut down on this food too, to just below the level to maintain weight.

June went by, July came. The stalemate continued. I was in a condition of permanent malnutrition but kept it from reaching a critical point. The high-vitamin diet provided by the raw fruit and vegetables had considerable value. Meanwhile, Stanislaw and I kept up our writing. We had finished "Duck Lane" in April, twenty copybooks full. We had started on an entirely new tack, noting down in written form our endless discussions on every aspect of human behavior. We titled the manuscript "Thoughts on Life from Prison." It reflected the encyclopedic soul-searching we both had engaged in, by ourselves and in an ongoing dialogue. This accounted for another six copybooks.

Toward the end of August we tackled a fourth book, in many ways a direct vehicle for our own suffering. We named it "Angry Harvest." It focused on ruthlessness and self-delusion as lived out by the main characters, the farmer Leon, a sort of Everyman, and the Jewish escapee Rosa, whom he sheltered; on the ensuing abuse of power; but also on the continued ability to perceive beauty. Our story of this fragile balance juxtaposed the outside, everyday world of Leon against Rosa's cellar existence of fear and isolation—the split personality of our own circumstances. It took up another ten copybooks. By the end of it we felt drained.

Meanwhile, the stalemate with my interrogators upstairs seemed to be getting me nowhere. I felt I would have to take the initiative and break it somehow. The authorities' nervousness about my state was apparent too, in many little signs. For example, in the spring several other prisoners had been housed in our cellar for short periods of time, and we again heard the daily routine being carried out in the neighboring cells. Inevitably the day always came when we heard one or the other depart, in spite of such precautions as closing our window and keeping the pump motor running at full roar. To our surprise, however, after their departure the same cell doors continued to open and close as usual—until one day there was a new guard, and he didn't bother with any door except ours (though the next time he was not so forgetful). Finally we were forced to admit the distressing truth: our neighbors in the other three cells were ghosts, figments of the imagination like so much else here. All the time we were still the only prisoners in this cellar, though evidently our captors had surmised—and correctly—that the knowledge that we were not alone would decrease our sense of permanent live burial.

On the night of August 1 we had a new surprise, a woman in the second cell, and apparently fresh from the world outside judging by her impatient banging on the door as soon as it got light in the morning. After breakfast she was taken upstairs, but she didn't return. And yet we hadn't heard the truck come to fetch her. Then the next day our window was closed in the middle of the afternoon. We listened carefully and periodically could hear women's voices outside. Within a few days we understood. The woman was now in one of the rooms upstairs. Each day she was allowed to walk for half an hour with a woman who came especially for this purpose, and probably also guarded her in her room. A woman in itself was a matter of persistent interest in circumstances such as ours, but the most significant discovery was that a prisoner could be held upstairs, and could, if she were a woman and important enough, gain the right to walk outside, a thing I had come to assume impossible. Who, we wondered, might she be?

One summer night as we were lying on our backs on our cots, Stanislaw, seeing that I was wide awake, suddenly said, "Hermann, there's something you should know in case we get separated. I thought about it last year, but when we were together again I didn't feel able to . . ." He hesitated, as if searching for the right words. "It was bound to reopen a wound, and things were hard enough as it was. But you see, it's part of something much bigger and too few people know about it . . . It mustn't be lost. The evil that one man can do when there are no moral constraints. It concerns one Lolo Skozowski . . ."

He stopped and his train of thought seemed to shift. "Remember the picture I gradually pieced together when I slipped into the Warsaw Ghetto and observed how it was inside? Each day worse than the day before right up to the ghetto uprising and the leveling that followed? At first it seemed simply the result of more and more half-destroyed people being herded through the gates, with no way left to keep alive and to remain human . . ."

"Stan, you don't know how often I have lived your images in moments of despair. But tell me, how can you face life after that, face even yourself, after what you actually saw? And what happened in the ghetto in 1943 was still only a prelude to Treblinka and Auschwitz . . ."

Stanislaw continued as if he hadn't heard me: "You see, one of my assignments for the AK was to learn exactly what was going on in the hell behind those walls. Not that there was much we could actually do by then." Again he stopped.

"Something struck me gradually, however. There seemed something predetermined about each day. The operation had the earmarks of a calculated strategy to suck until the last drop. The submerged money flow by which Jews with some small hidden savings tried to buy a few weeks of time was squeezed out of the ghetto by every device. The screw turned unrelentingly, a little tighter each day. Given their unfamiliarity with circumstances in the ghetto, no German could have developed such an unfailing touch."

"So you became convinced it was a local?"

"Yes, an inside Polish job by someone who had an uncanny familiarity with the Jewish community. Can you imagine? Masterminding it right in Gestapo headquarters here."

I recalled the anti-Jewish sentiment I had encountered in my work back in 1939 and shivered.

"By then it was all almost over with the ghetto, and we still hadn't established the identity of the man in charge, though we were getting near."

"So the uprising hadn't happened yet? When was that?"

"In the summer of 1943. After that, with the ghetto gone, the German terror shifted increasingly to Warsaw as a whole. So the ghetto atrocities slipped into the background at first. But then something new drew our attention: the Germans announced a grandiose scheme for resettlement of the many Jews who had eluded the ghetto, living hunted existences, concealed at great risk by friends or by persons providing shelter for extortionary money. The new goal was to smoke out these survivors too, to get those who had escaped the ghetto dragnets and who could be counted on to have hidden assets for the German war machine."

"Posters appeared everywhere advertising a 'generous offer' of the Gestapo in Warsaw: The Hotel Polski downtown would be set up as a free zone. Any Jew in hiding would be guaranteed safe access to the hotel, where he or she could register and, for a sizable fee, receive a false name, a passport with his or her picture inserted in it, and, most important, a prewar emigration visa to Bolivia. The whole transaction would take less than a month, during which time the 'guests' would live under Gestapo protection at the hotel, charges being commensurate with the special circumstances. At the action's closing date, a special Red Cross train would be waiting for them in Warsaw's station to take them through the war zones on their first lap to freedom via an undesignated French embarkation port."

Stanislaw was silent for a moment, then continued: "And can you imagine, it worked. They did emerge—emerged in every condition and mood: hope mixed with disbelief; fear mixed with dread; despair mixed with fatalism. Questioning, when deep inside they must have known the answer. Unable to ignore one last hope. I looked at their faces.

"By now I was sure the same mastermind had been at work. But this time we would find him somewhere in the orbit of that lobby and run him down. We were sure we had him at last. His name was Skozowski . . . and . . . and he was a half Jew originally from Lodz . . ."

Stanislaw went on to describe the day of departure. The festive train was serviced by women in Red Cross uniforms, and a week or so after its departure scenic cards postmarked in Switzerland arrived telling of the happy progress of the journey—which, as the underground shortly learned, had gone no farther than the railway spur into Auschwitz.

"And what about Skozowski?" I asked.

"We shadowed him continuously in a kind of cat-and-mouse game. We could not afford the shooting at sight practiced by our adversaries." He went on to describe how the Polish underground had developed its own judicial system by now. The case was brought to the underground court. It sentenced one Lolo Skozowski of the Gestapo, of half-Jewish origin, from the industrial city of Lodz, to be executed forthwith by an underground execution squad.

"And did they get him?"

"Yes, but unfortunately, in my role as a counterintelligence officer of the underground, it fell to me to head the team. Skozowski had his own Gestapo bodyguard. He clearly was aware by then that we were on his tracks. It happened one night finally, as he emerged from a night spot frequented by the Germans. We were lying in wait for him. We got him before he had a chance."

Stanislaw stopped and reflected: "And that's all of it. That's what you must remember and tell others, Hermann, in case I can't." He hesitated. I could sense that it wasn't really all. He turned toward the wall. "Maybe some other time. Not now."

A few nights later, he said softly: "Are you awake, Hermann? Then I will tell you. No, it wasn't all. Do you recall about the trucking service my wife, Janina, organized after I dared return home from Vilna in 1943? Like everyone, we were trying to eke out a temporary living somehow. But like most things then, it had a dual existence. Hauling was much in demand, with all the destruction and moving going on. But so was the underground's secret distribution of leaflets. Actually, that was the main reason for it all." He described how things were concealed in the special underbody of the vehicle. And inevitably, his house was often a transit point. A network of individuals was involved, but security was such that each person was his own private cell. If anyone were caught, it was essential that Gestapo torture could not lead to anyone else. He had not even been allowed to let on to Janina how her creaky trucking service was being used.

Following the shooting of Skozowski, the Gestapo immediately organized a massive manhunt for Stanislaw. He was under AK orders to disappear completely, shifting every night from one safe house to another. But what about Janina? Neither he nor anyone else was allowed to approach their house, and not knowing of either the manhunt for her husband or the vulnerability of her trucking enterprise, she saw no reason to leave. She was used to his often being away over night. As the days went by, the Gestapo kept the house under close surveillance, sure that Stanislaw would weaken and try to rescue her. Meanwhile, all his efforts at indirect contact proved futile. After a week his worst fear was realized: the Gestapo, tired of the game, dragged Janina out of the house and shot her right there in the street.

"Hermann, it was I who was responsible for her death. If only she had known . . . ," and his voice trailed off. We lay there silent, miserable. Sometime during the predawn hours we must have fallen asleep. Stanislaw never mentioned the subject again.

As the end of my second year approached I felt increasingly driven to make one supreme effort to force the issue of my freedom. I knew that while my life had in effect stopped two years ago, everywhere else life was going on relentlessly. Both time and my captors were conspiring that I should at last be forgotten. I proceeded to plan a careful strategy of stepped-up demands in which the hunger strike would be to the death, the final release if all else failed.

My first step was to write an appeal to President Bierut asking for my release as a matter of simple justice and requesting financial indemnity commensurate with the damage to my career and to my health. For my part, I would agree to regard the matter as closed and would seek to avoid the incident being blown up and used against Poland. This last point was what I placed my main hope on. I handed the document to the guards. Both Stanislaw and I were inclined to believe that in spite of the intense secrecy surrounding us, the MBP would feel bound to pass it up to Bierut. Whatever happened in the future, it would at least establish his co-responsibility.

All the time I was aware of the widening circle of persons here who shared the secret of my presence. In spite of all security, news does have a way of oozing out. Some thirty guards had had a look over the past two years at the mysterious American in their midst; it was bound to get whispered around until another thirty knew of my existence. And over ten officers had had dealings with me. Probably close to a hundred people in the security system knew by now. Wasn't there a good chance that through some indiscretion, or even a defection or the presence of an anticommunist "mole" in the security organization itself, the news would finally reach the American authorities? Even if it didn't, the Poles must be aware of that risk, and this could in itself become a deterrent against any trigger-happy solution.

When after a week there was no response I began to pull my nonexistent belt still tighter. My worsening malnutrition was becoming more evident. I was called upstairs. This time, in addition to the doctor and Cigarette, the house officer, looking very troubled, was present. There was the usual opening inquiry about the state of my health. I responded with specific new physical complaints. One look at me was doubtless sufficient to see how I was faring. Cigarette interposed in Polish via the doctor: My request had been delivered to the president and I would receive an answer in due course. I felt tremendously encouraged. He asked what other complaints I had. I said I had waited over six months for the news promised by him about Kate and the boys. Well, he could give me an answer: My wife and children were in good health. I asked "But where?" In Cigarette's characteristically enigmatic manner, he responded: "Where they should be."

I was almost beside myself. "But where, where do you mean? They were on a visit to England when I disappeared in 1949. What has happened to them since? Are they still in England or did they return to America?"

Again the enigmatic answer that could mean everything or nothing: "They're home and well cared for."

Well, I supposed that meant Cleveland, but did it? I felt almost crazy with the need to know. Cigarette wouldn't budge.

I blurted out, "But how can they have been supporting themselves all this time?"

The response was altogether unlikely: "Your former boss is helping them."

The university? Impossible. They must have suffered enough loss through all this without taking on an uncalled-for obligation toward Kate. Clearly this could not be.

To my surprise, Cigarette went on to say that if it would help me, he would authorize a drafting table and instruments to be set up in another cell to enable me to do some architectural designing. This proposal threw me completely off balance. To be able to do this had been a persistent dream my whole two years in prison; without any doubt it would make my existence here much more tolerable. But at this point a mere improvement was hardly what I was looking for. I had gone too far for that. I was embarked now on the ultimate fight for freedom. The whole implication of this offer was merely a stabilization of the status quo.

On several occasions the previous year I had mentioned drawing, so it was difficult to refuse the offer. I hedged by saying that designing in a vacuum on some pretense building was pointless. I had always visualized working on an actual project. So, I suggested, perhaps I could focus on something real connected with Warsaw. I was very familiar with Warsaw's reconstruction problems and was sure that even in my isolation I could produce something better than what was being done.

Cigarette was amenable: Yes, I could do an office building.

During the next days I was in sharp conflict. I could settle for improvements that would make life here more bearable. If instead I continued to fight on the larger issue, which in any case was unlikely to be achieved, I would forfeit these and might lose everything gained so far, for both of us. It was another riposte in the war of nerves, just as the strawberries and chocolates had been. If I turned the offer down, the stick would descend on me once again. Finally I worked out a compromise. I made a list of alternative suggestions. In place of the haphazard stream of books in German, I requested books in Polish on specific subjects such as biology, history, and biography, which Stanislaw would translate for me. Also some French books and a French grammar and dictionary, to enable me to read aloud in that language. Stanislaw's eyesight had improved, mainly through overcoming an acute vitamin deficiency, and with the help of my glasses—which had recently been made available to me for daytime use—he even could read the newspapers. I also asked for a table, for pictures of Kate and the boys from my suitcase, and finally for leave to take a daily walk outside.

Meanwhile, I ate more of the chocolates and cookies, and even occasional tidbits of cold fried pike or white rolls with ham and butter, to show I appreciated their measures to ease my tension. This fitted another important consideration: much too weak anyway to embark on a full-scale hunger strike in the near future, I had to gain time. So I set myself six weeks for a limited recovery without reverting to anything like normal eating.

September arrived, and still no answer. Once again I asked for paper. This time I wrote a letter to the security minister, Radkiewicz, in which I stated that nothing had come of my appeal to President Bierut and that therefore I was forced to place two alternatives squarely before the minister himself. Either within a month he would give me a clear indication that the process of my freeing was being initiated as expeditiously as possible or I would be left with no choice but to insist on my right, as an American national in Poland, to demand that the U.S. ambassador in Warsaw be sent the enclosed letter telling him of my plight and asking him to request contact with me and to notify Kate of my whereabouts. I ended that if by a month from now neither of the alternatives had occurred, the full responsibility for any consequences lay with Poland.

As the weeks went by, I concentrated spiritually and bodily on preparing for my hunger strike. Slowly I built up my strength, in part concealed from the authorities. I knew my actions bordered on irrationality, yet passivity had become intolerable. As I saw it, the key was being stronger than my captors would anticipate, if only to the extent of a twenty-four-hour edge. This would enable me to test them to the limit, with still a slim chance of pulling out alive if I had miscalculated.

I tried to recall all the examples of passive resistance in my Quaker heritage and the images of Gandhi's hunger strikes. I tried to formulate from these a set of rules that could not be broken, a kind of willed serenity. The idea was to make myself impervious to the world around me, to create an impenetrable psychic cocoon as my armor. In the weeks before I knew I would finally have to act, therefore, I withdrew ever more into myself, to a world of reflection that could not be assailed. I cut movement to a minimum and, while handing back what seemed a considerable amount of food, made a secret store of high-calorie "cake" compacted from my suppers, which I kept hidden away between the mattress and the cot. This I intended to consume secretly during the first three days to give me a head start. As the second week of October approached its end, I felt ready down to the smallest detail. My deadline had passed and nothing had happened. I set zero hour for exactly one week later at getting-up time.

In the predawn hours of that day I ate a number of the cake balls. Whatever I had in me, I knew, would be a clear gain. At breakfast the food for both of us was put in as usual. Mine remained untouched at the door.

The day wore on, and I refused each meal. We were conscious of almost continuous surveillance. The next morning was Saturday. I ignored the guard's request that I go and take my shower and his offer of fresh shirt and pants. Stanislaw went off alone. While he was away, the house officer suddenly walked in and started haranguing me angrily in Polish. I just shrugged my shoulders. After Stanislaw returned the officer was back once more, this time with two guards. Again I was exhorted to get up. I refused. My strategy was simple: stay flat on my back no matter what and don't get excited.

The house officer gave instructions. If I wouldn't get up of my own accord, they would carry me out of the cell. A new guard whom we called Lord and the other guard took me, one at each end, and carried me next door onto a cot already made up. Stanislaw followed with his cot. Clearly the intent was to inspect our cell, and specifically my cot. So my hidden rations were lost to me—a bad beginning.

Sunday came. Monday. Each day the food was taken away without my having touched it, though I did dutifully drink a cup of sugarless tea three times a day. In between I lay passively on my back, my eyes closed most of the time, my mind reliving meaningful moments of my life. Stanislaw read to me from beyond my cocoon for a bit each morning and afternoon. On Wednesday they gave up on the food and just provided the tea. By the sixth day I was quite weak.

That afternoon there was considerable activity upstairs, which I suspected had something to do with me. Sure enough, it wasn't long before our door opened and the house officer plus three guards appeared. I was told to get up, dress, and come upstairs. I asked why and was told the doctor was upstairs. I said I had nothing to see the doctor about and would not go anywhere until my demands had been met. The house officer decided to have me carried upstairs. Okay, let them try. I had practiced just for this moment: I closed my eyes, went limp, and shut myself to the outside world. As a result, even the three guards got nowhere, struggling with my drooping body. For a moment there was consternation. Then someone hit on the idea of rolling me into a blanket and carrying it in hammock fashion with me inside. And this was the precarious way I was transferred step by step upstairs, like a sack of potatoes. To withdraw further into myself, I decided to keep my eyes firmly closed until I was back in my cell and not to let anything provoke me into opening them. I recalled a crisis with another prisoner that spring who had apparently also engaged in a hunger strike. He, too, was carried upstairs, and each time an awful commotion broke out above me. One day he was carried quietly out of the building. My hunch had been that he was no longer alive. Was his defeat in part because he had allowed his waning energies to be dissipated in struggle? I had to avoid this at all costs.

I was carried into a room and laid down on something—an army cot. I could hear feet on the carpet, whispering. There must be a number of people. Suddenly a voice said in good German: "Why aren't you eating?" It was the doctor.

"I do not intend to eat until I have spoken with the American ambassador as I demanded."

After a pause he replied, "Your behavior won't help you. It is my task to see that you eat. If you do not do so voluntarily, we will feed you forcibly. Well, then?"

I replied I had already given my answer and had nothing to add.

More whispering. A chair was pulled near me. Several hands took hold of me and plunked me down on the chair. "Open your mouth." I ignored the instruction. The hands on my arms tightened as someone tried to insert a kind of metal separator between my teeth. I yanked myself away from the hands. There was a momentary free-for-all as my arms were grabbed and pinned behind me. I was so angry that in spite of my weakness I tore myself free once more. It was a strange feeling fighting blind, not once seeing who my assailants were. It also helped. It gave me strength and made it impossible to intimidate me.

The struggle let up as I was held pinned down on the floor. Someone went out and returned. Again I found myself in the grip of strong hands, which wrenched my arms into some sleeves. Before I knew it I was securely tied into a straitjacket, my arms across my stomach. Once more I was lifted onto the chair. I tried to relax and go limp but was jerked painfully back into place. My mouth was pried open, my head held immobile, and next a rubber tube began descending my throat into my stomach. As I choked and retched, a liquid went down but almost instantly was vomited up again. This was repeated several times until I almost lost consciousness.

Well, this was the beginning of a new routine, and as such it had the potential for adaptation. It consisted of some twenty-three hours in which I lay immobile on my back, followed each afternoon with an upheaval upstairs. Each time the feeding session began with the unseen voice of the doctor: "Will you now eat voluntarily?" Unalterably the reply was, "When the American Ambassador has been notified."

Without another word, the next stages followed with me resisting as best I could: ensconced as I was in the straitjacket, my teeth had to substitute for my hands, doubtlessly leaving painful scars on several arms and hands. I learned to enhance my tendency to choke, and parried their greater facility in inserting the rubber tube by intensified vomiting of most everything that went down. Each day most of the contents of the mug that was poured in through a funnel, held aloft like an enema, was splattered on the suits and furnishings in a large circle about me. While the doctor managed always to get a small portion into me, largely through experimenting with different sizes of tubes, it was hardly sufficient to keep me alive.

By the following Thursday evening, exhaustion and depression resulting from weakness had plunged me into feverish desperation. To go on seemed beyond my strength, and yet to stop brought me again face to face with hopelessness. It was a critical moment. The struggle upstairs that afternoon had been especially hard. I had been punched several times in the stomach—to no purpose, as it merely resulted in increased vomiting and retching. After the tube had been pulled out and the doctor had left the room, I noticed through my half-closed eyes that only the young officer and Lord remained. The officer was wiping up the floor around me by pushing a mass of rags with his foot; then he picked them up, wiped my neck and shirt, and plunked the whole filthy mess squarely on my face. I lay motionless, almost unable to breath, but determined not to shake it off myself. Let the doctor and the others witness this too. As the doctor's steps approached along the corridor, the mess was quickly removed by unseen hands.

Friday night after I had been "processed" and brought down below again, Stanislaw was called upstairs. There Cigarette warned him in no way to assist me. He was told my release was out of the question, given present international tensions, and it was firmly impressed upon him that he should dissuade me from this suicidal course if he wanted to see me stay alive. This Stanislaw proceeded to try to do with eloquence, even though it was clear to both of us that he was merely a mouthpiece for those upstairs.

Poor, loyal Stanislaw: How much he must have wanted to be able to convince me. While the presence of "Ivan" was doubtlessly a considerable asset to the authorities, since often enough we slipped up and forgot him, knowing the microphone was there also enabled us to turn the tables. Now, I said things intended specifically for the ears upstairs. I complained of much greater physical weakening than in fact existed, but also spoke with a tone that implied much higher morale than I actually possessed.

Saturday morning was bath day again. This time it was decided to forcibly wash me. A good case could be made for doing so on hygienic grounds, what with my soiled clothes and body, but in view of my emaciated condition, my limp noncooperation, and my firmly closed eyes, it was a delicate operation. The house officer supervised every move, greatly concerned lest I be bumped or dropped. I felt like a china doll.

They laid me in a heap on the floorboards under the showers, as I cursed everything and everyone around me without knowing who they were. This led to a burst of hilarity while I was being washed: evidently some poor devil was getting all wet trying to rub me down. All I could feel, though, was the boards pressing painfully against my bones, so whenever the fellow soaped my arm or leg I kept up my invective: "Gangster . . . fascist gangster."

Again a burst of laughter. Why was this so funny? I was furious. Once I slightly opened my eyes because soap had gotten in them and saw, standing naked above me, Stanislaw. The new attack of abuse died on my lips. I was too weak and miserable to laugh, however, and he was much too startled by my emaciation to care.

Lying on my cot afterward and at last opening my eyes, I was amazed: it was the fifth cell once more, bright and roomy, and beside me stood a little square table—no, *the* table, the one that had disappeared from my cell in the cellar next door almost two years ago. It was like meeting an old friend. I let my hand pass over it to prove it was real. And on it lay the current issue of the popular biweekly illustrated magazine on Warsaw's reconstruction, *Stolica,* which I hadn't seen since my abduction. How wonderful—real pictures of buildings and trees and people in the present. I was quite overwhelmed.

Soon breakfast came. Again I stared. For Stanislaw there was a plate of raw herring and sour cream beside his mug of grain coffee. For me there was a bunch of fresh grapes. What utter craziness. I felt like laughing and crying at the same time. Angel came in triumphantly and asked whether I also had a liking for herring and cream. I nodded. He said, "Tomorrow you also," and beckoned me to drink my coffee. It was as if the whole past week's deadly struggle had never existed. Stanislaw's face showed a mixture of worry and delight. He admitted sheepishly that herring was one of his favorite delicacies. Again I was faced with a desperate struggle. I could have embraced Angel for this surprise party, indeed, just for the table alone. Somehow, I thought, everything would turn out all right now. With the table we would make this place really habitable. In the back of my mind, however, I heard ever more imperatively: The carrot, the carrot! I shook my head sadly at Angel: "*Nie, tylko herbata. Dziekuje bardzo*"—No, only tea. Thank you very much. I lay down and closed my eyes. How easy it was to weaken, how overwhelming the prospect of food after two weeks of this. I went through a long tussle and won. I had the will. I would go on, no matter what, to the bitter end.

Sunday came. We still had the table. As on previous days, there was but one goal: to make it through the afternoon forced feeding. Having turned down the carrot, I could expect the real crisis just around the corner. Monday morning it came. I was lugged upstairs in the rug hammock and laid on the cot. It was not the usual room. Someone mumbled something. A woman's voice asked why I kept my eyes closed. It was the interpreter once more, and the second person hovering nearby was probably Cigarette. I answered that I didn't wish to see those who were mishandling me. Then the same rigmarole as to why I wasn't eating and my usual answer. This time they presented me with an ultimatum: I would stop my hunger strike at once, or else I would be put into permanent solitary confinement with no reading or any other privileges and with no prospect of ever reopening the question of my future. I answered that without at least some definite time limit for termination of my imprisonment I could not consider stopping. It would be better to die of starvation.

Cigarette responded with a flat refusal to give any time limit: "Perhaps two years, perhaps five, perhaps longer. We are not prepared to state." Then, with a changed, taunting tone: "That's up to Mr. Truman. You'll be returning to America someday, a different revolutionary America, one that won't have any use for a Truman."

"What's that got to do with me?" I responded.

"A lot."

"I will continue until this injustice against me has stopped."

"You have until tonight to think it over."

Once more I was hauled downstairs head first inside the blanket and deposited on a cot. I opened my eyes. Everything familiar had vanished except for this solitary bed standing alone in the middle of the floor exactly opposite the Judas eye. Stanislaw, the table, his cot, the books—all were gone. And the window was tightly closed. The old feeling of solitude and isolation, which I had almost forgotten in this year of companionship, swept over me like a death sentence. At last I was fighting stripped of everything beyond whatever strength survived within me.

By Tuesday night I was perceptibly weaker. Wednesday I felt almost unreal, listless and indifferent. I no longer even tried to fight back when the tube was inserted in my mouth. At one point as I vomited I opened my eyes for a moment. Cigarette was standing at the end of the cot, staring at me with fascination. Noticing that I had seen him, he grinned sarcastically: "Feeling good, aren't you. Like this way of eating?"

I didn't answer. There was silence in the room. I opened my eyes again. He was standing over me, waiting. "Well, there'll be an end to this soon. This is your last chance. You haven't got much longer." Another pause. I continued looking at him. "Have you got any last statement you want to give us for your wife and children?"

I answered, looking him straight in the face. "No, that isn't necessary. I have already written a statement. It's in your files. That will do."

When I heard Stanislaw's supper being shoved in next door, I waited eagerly for my usual cup of unsweetened tea. In the absence of food, this bit of liquid three times a day was the one thing that kept me from dehydration. This time, however, they passed up my cell. Later they came and fetched my bucket to empty and then returned it half filled with water. As the evening hours advanced, I found my throat and mouth becoming completely parched and sticky. Most of the night I struggled with thirst until it became unendurable. Toward dawn when I heard the guard go past to the washroom, I crawled out of my cot and, too weak to walk, crept on all fours toward the pail. With a mixture of revulsion and a frenzy of urgency, I dipped my hands into the pail and raised the foul water to my mouth. Wishing to drink as little as possible for fear of infecting myself, I tried to create the illusion of drinking a lot by rinsing my mouth and throat again and again, letting only a part slip down my throat. When I heard the guard flush the toilet at the other end of the corridor, I crept back to the cot. My efforts had strengthened me a little and I fell into a fitful and delirious sleep for some hours. At breakfast time I was again ignored. The door didn't open once that day.

Twice more during the morning and afternoon I crawled over to the bucket. I seemed to be living in a continuously shifting twilight—part reality, part dream, part nightmare, part ecstasy. In moments of lucidity I was haunted by a new interpretation of Cigarette's final remarks the evening before. I had assumed it was a warning that they wouldn't give in and continuation on my part would end in death. Now, with all liquids suddenly being cut, I realized it was they who were precipitating my going under, making certain that I would die. So I had miscalculated. In short, the door had closed last night, not to be opened again while I was alive. After going through the motions of trying to prevent my death, they had reached the point where it fitted them better to get rid of me once and for all. And since this hunger strike was on my initiative, it relieved them of any responsibility. In lucid moments, I came back to a single driving question: Shouldn't I at least maintain life? Losing it was irrevocable. It was the one card I still had. And what about Kate and the boys? If things ended this way they would never be able to find out what had happened.

But I felt too unreal, too listless, to act. It was obviously too late. The last thread had been cut.

After dark there again was the usual flurry upstairs, and a moment later three guards came to roll me into the blanket and lug me up to the corner room. Had I been wrong after all? I heard the doctor's voice: "I'm going to give you an injection now." I opened my eyes. The doctor was holding a huge syringe, the kind I had seen veterinarians use to inoculate cattle. Or . . . another image began to impose itself: those syringes Stanislaw had described being used by Gestapo doctors at Auschwitz on Jews for quick extermination. I tried to recall. Yes, phenol, that was it. And within seconds their victims' hearts stopped beating.

The doctor rubbed a place on the side of my thigh and drove the point in under the skin. I stared in horror as he slowly pressed the clear liquid out. No attempt at forced feeding, no explanation, the row of silent guards encircling me, watching intently, as if expecting something. A diffusing numbness was spreading from my thigh. Suddenly fear broke the dam and rushed into my consciousness. I felt I was suffocating.

"Stop, stop!" Hands held me still firmer. I thrashed my head about violently. "Water, water. Quickly."

A glass of water was held to my mouth. I drank it down, spilling a lot of it in my excitement. They brought another glassful. The numbness had stopped spreading. Was I dying in fact?

"Why the syringe?" I gasped.

The doctor answered, "Extreme dehydration because you have had no liquids the past twenty-four hours."

So this wasn't phenol. No extermination after all. I was still alive, still free to choose.

"But that wasn't my fault. I was willing to drink tea as usual. The guards wouldn't give me any."

The doctor smiled. "Perhaps they were so instructed, it not being the authorities' intention that you should."

He asked me now whether I would be willing to eat. I shook my head. Once more the tube, the retching, the vomiting. It was the last straw. As I was being carried out, I rebelled and thrashed, yelling through the sharp pain that spread over my thigh and leg. "Gestapo! Gestapo!" Muffled, half smothered inside the blanket, I continued yelling. Everyone should hear. On my cot in the cell, I yelled on almost mechanically. It was an agony to lie on my thigh. I stumbled onto the floor and started to tear up my sheets, then pulled the straw from the mattress and scattered it around wildly.

"Gestapo! Gestapo!"

The door opened. The guard we called Dog stood above me and said I would be gagged and bound if I didn't shut up at once. I had spent my last remaining energy. Suddenly I was perspiring all over. I dropped onto the bare cot and sobbed. "Kate, Hughie, Alan—help me. Stand by me now. It won't last much longer." Some time later, I don't know how long, I fell into a dreamless sleep.

That night a mug of tea was placed beside my cot. At breakfast and lunchtime again. However, the struggle of the previous day had sapped what little strength I still had. As the day advanced, I felt increasingly sure that I was rapidly approaching a condition from which there would be no return. So if I still wished to live, I would have to retreat in some form from my ultimate demands.

By the late afternoon I had decided to capitulate, but to do so in such a way as to salvage as much as I could of my previously won gains. As a signal of change, I kept my eyes open while they transported me upstairs. I said I would eat voluntarily if the authorities would, pending settlement of my case, make life here more bearable and meet my needs halfway.

Back downstairs again a huge sense of relief and peacefulness swept over me, almost a gratitude for being alive. I realized instinctively that I was lucky to have pulled out of this in the nick of time, and tried not to concede that actually this unequal struggle had ended in my defeat. The mere fact of having this ghastly seventeen-day nightmare behind me was such a boost that I felt almost happy. And in between spells of sleeping, I was already planning all the things Stanislaw and I would do together in the months ahead.

# 16

## Peepa

There followed one of the most peaceful periods in our cellar. I felt lucky to be alive. The return to normal cell life seemed like paradise.

It had not been an unconditional surrender—more an uneasy armistice. We had won the table and *Stolica*. Shortly thereafter, wonder of wonders, Angel traipsed in bearing a huge red volume, the official *Six-Year Reconstruction Plan for Warsaw,* profusely illustrated with large plates in color, charts and illustrations of historic buildings, and sketches of proposals.

The guards showed a heightened respect for me. They had followed my unequal battle with a kind of sporting spirit, and I felt that in their hearts they had been rooting for me. Lord, especially, went out of his way to smile at me every time he opened the door, and surreptitiously began to bring chess problems from the newspaper for us to solve for him at our table. Only Bear, a heavyset newcomer in April, with rather cool pale eyes and black hair and darkish skin, was a bit standoffish. No wonder: he still carried the marks on his hands of the struggles upstairs.

A week or so after I ended my strike, when I was able to move around again a little, we were transferred to the first cell at the southeast corner, opposite the washroom. And a royal change it was. Not only was the space double cell No. 4 in size, about twelve feet square, but it had a window on each outside wall, so on sunny days we could manage without electric light until dusk. It being November now, we had the east one closed entirely, but the crack and triangle in our south window often enabled us to get a fleeting glimpse of the heads of passersby if they went by close enough.

So it came that for the first time we caught sight of a prisoner aside from ourselves. We had been alone in the cellar all summer and fall, but we knew that the mysterious woman who had arrived around August 1 was kept upstairs in one of the interrogation rooms, and almost every day she was taken for a half hour's walk in front of the building. She was always accompanied by someone, either the interpreter woman or the officer of our building. Whoever walked on the inside passed close by the boards and we could get a momentary glimpse of at least part of the face. The prisoner was short, dark haired, middle aged, with a set face and plodding walk. Her steps were almost like a man's, and she seemed to shuffle slightly, so we dubbed her "the Duck."

In the spring of 1952 our south window was opened fully, and two new elements, unnoticed by the authorities, were added to our observation arsenal. First of all, the whole propped-up frame had shifted away from the wall about one and a half inches as a result of a gust of wind, providing a peephole above each window wing, one toward the building entrance, the other toward the corner.

With a lot of practicing I succeeded in catching the split-second image of people as they entered or left the building. In the long run I identified all the people living upstairs and tracked numerous officers and outsiders. One of the discoveries made through these peepholes was that the truck that had become so familiar over the years, secretly conveying its human freight to and from our cellar, had opaque glass windows on its sides with big red crosses painted on them. Were most of the movements of the secret police concealed that way? I recalled having seen a considerable number of such ambulances in the streets in 1949.

As the sun beat down on the boards in front of our south window, they dried out and shrank after a long rainless spell, leaving quarter- to half-inch horizontal cracks in between—our second observational advantage. Although the boards were some three feet away from the window grille, by focusing on the space just beyond the slit we were able to piece together bit by bit the view outside: tree trunks, the green of foliage, waving grass, spots of color indicating flowers, the far-off pattern of bricks. By shifting position up or down slightly, we could trace each distant item in its entirety: a wall topped with broken glass and illuminated at night by floodlights; the tops of big free-standing trees, which, accented by the mooing of cows, suggested open farming country beyond. In time we pieced together the view to the west too, where beyond another wall the land fell off flat and treeless—apparently swamps gradually giving way to a big band of water that stretched almost to the horizon. Obviously the Vistula.

Adding all this to the cues from our sound world, we now were able to envision our surroundings much more accurately. Our building was in a walled, roughly triangular enclosure, of which two sides, topped by jagged glass, formed the exterior perimeter of the compound. The third, slightly curving wall separated us from other parts of the prison. We were in a peripheral segment away from the main operation.

Cell No. 1 was also ideal for observing the bathroom opposite. At first we were the only prisoners in the cellar, except on Saturdays when the Duck was brought down in the charge of a woman guard, and occasionally we caught scraps of conversation between them. Then suddenly in the beginning of December there was a new influx of prisoners, with almost all the cells filled. So we undertook a new sound exploration. These newcomers were treated better than the ones here in 1950, though there were still wide variations. They had evidently all come from the same place, together with their own guards.

A month later, however, most of them departed. Then at some point we heard a new woman's voice. She was apparently in the sixth cell at the other end. In contrast to the Duck's rather uncultured voice, hers was youthful, cultivated, and cheerful. The guards treated her with respect too, and bantered with her at every opportunity—of which there were quite a few. For some reason, after all the other prisoners had departed, she was allowed to sweep and wash the corridor and washroom floors. It was a limited form of freedom without going so far as to let her walk out of doors. It was also done very discreetly so we wouldn't notice.

But of course we did. In spite of repeated warnings, she had no intention of whispering, always answering back and laughing out in her ringing, captivating voice. Soon we established that she was interested in us too, by the shameless way she spent more time cleaning and scrubbing the floor in the vicinity of our cell door than anywhere else. So we made a special point of giving her leads, without it being obvious to anyone listening upstairs through "Ivan." I would launch, for example, into long descriptions to Stanislaw of life in New York, Cleveland, and New England, to make clear to her that while we spoke in German, I came from America.

What if the whole thing was a provocation? We knew we were taking a risk but couldn't resist. We were enchanted by her constant good humor and femininity, and after each of her corridor sallies we settled into individual fantasies. Stanislaw confessed ruefully, "Hermann, sure, it's fun to indulge in passionate fantasies, but realistically, to share a cell with a woman in such unrelenting proximity, that would soon become torture for both."

Then one day I concluded that it was actually two women up at the other end of the cellar. Frequently after lunch a woman came to the washroom especially to empty and rinse a pail. Quickly we realized the meaning. She tended to vomit her food, just as the resident of the third cell had in the summer of 1950. Was this perhaps the same person, the "man with the high voice"?

April brought another discovery. Through the cracks of our window enclosure I noticed something light in color shifting along from left to right, and then several minutes later back again in the opposite direction. Intense concentration established that it was two people walking in the field a little way down the slope. In fact, they wore dresses in gay colors, and a bit later I found the heads that belonged to them, and soon I got a concept of the two entire persons. They were our two women from the sixth cell, real visual entities at last, even though I could never see more than a narrow horizontal slice of them at one time. One was fairly tall, blonde, with a lively face. I was in rapture; what I saw fitted perfectly to the laughing voice in the corridor. Beside her was a somewhat shorter, black-haired woman, more heavyset, with an ashen face. I couldn't size up her age: something about her suggested that she too couldn't be much beyond her twenties, and yet her manner and appearance were those of an old, worn person, tired of life and terribly sick.

From this beginning developed a daily watching of the "girls," as we came to call them. The guards didn't interfere with them but simply sat on the front step during their half hour outside. As the weather became warm, the girls often spent part of their time just lying in the grass or sitting sunning themselves on a bench in the field. It is difficult for someone in normal life to comprehend the sweet nostalgia that this daily vision provided, especially with the spring and summer air wafting into our cell in a lush setting of green grass and trees and colorful flowers. The girls became symbols of the life that was gone. Just as I delighted in the youthful charm of the one, which somehow prison hadn't broken, I was haunted by the tragic sight of the other. Like Stanislaw, she must have gone through a horrible testing. Indeed, there was something quite pitiful in these two women, one already maimed and aged beyond repair, the other facing an unknown future, who were keeping up a pretense of making themselves beautiful, to be admired, wooed, with no one in fact to admire and woo them. How we wished we could have let them know that their efforts hadn't gone quite unnoticed.

One morning I was awakened by repeated thuds on our floor. A frog had come in through our window! I caught him and took him back to my cot, wondering how I could keep him as a guest. Then an idea came to me. When we went to the washroom, I took him along, unnoticed by the guard, and put him into one of the two washbasins. When we returned to our cell, I left him behind. Would the guard make an inspection before he went and fetched the girls? We heard the girls coming down the corridor. The washroom door closed behind them. The guard went discreetly back along the corridor. Suddenly there was a loud yell from the washroom, followed by exclamations and laughter. The joke had worked.

As the months went by in this forgotten world of ours, I felt an increasing need at least to establish our identity with the girls. They might be released, and if so there was perhaps a thousandth of a chance of my whereabouts becoming known. The washroom was one point of possible contact. The safest communication vehicle would be the scrubbing brush for the pail. We placed the brush in special ways when we were through, knowing that, barring an unforeseen inspection, it would not be touched by the guards before the girls had their turn. But would the girls be alert enough to notice a tiny note stuck among the bristles? It was doubtful. We decided to try to get some signals started around the brush to keep their attention on it. After using it, we soaped it up thoroughly to make foam when they used it, since normally they didn't use any soap on their pail. They didn't react or reciprocate. We balanced the brush on its handle for several days. No response.

Then suddenly another route opened up. There was a new young guard, substituting for one who was sick. In his extreme timidity toward supervising females in the washroom, he simply opened the cell door and fled back to the guard's space, leaving the girls to go down the corridor unaccompanied. First we noticed that the washroom door did not close behind them as usual. That meant they could hear us talk if they listened carefully. But would they? And the guard might decide to follow them after all. Any open remark would be dangerous. So we reverted simply to the method of the winter and talked fairly loudly and distinctly about the United States. "The last time I was on my farm in Massachusetts . . ." "You'd like Cleveland. It's a nice place to live in and we have a first-rate baseball team there . . ." We stopped and listened. It was completely still in the washroom. Then suddenly the WC chain was pulled. Some water splashed in the washbasin. I felt triumphant.

The girls had heard, of that there was no doubt. But had anyone else? We soon got evidence that the authorities were aware of our efforts to make contact or at least suspected we might try. Maybe the girls, too, were chatting too freely in the "privacy" of their cell, unaware of the listening device in the wall. Anyway, some weeks later a big ventilator fan in a sheet metal mounting was installed in the wire frame of the corridor window just outside our cell. It seemed almost prehistoric, and still more so when it was turned on during washroom use, making as much of a din as the pump motor in the room beside the guards. We were amused to find it turned on even on a cool morning with the corridor window tightly closed. Clearly, the sole purpose of the fan was to create an acoustical barrier when doors were likely to be open.

Meanwhile, we had occasion to observe our first-class passenger upstairs, the Duck, more closely. Her solitary confinement, already in its ninth month, had begun to tell on her. Through the cracks in the boards we could see her walking alone now. She waddled along through the grass on an uncertain hectic course day after day, staring straight ahead, her face completely lacking any expression. Sometimes she came straight toward our cell window as if drawn by a magnet, then swerved off to the left.

By the end of April she seemed on the verge of breakdown. Her wandering began to be more like sleepwalking. One evening there was some commotion upstairs. A suicide attempt? She didn't go out the next day. Instead there was a lot of sawing and hammering in the windows of the room above the washroom. It seemed they were installing wire grilles there. Then suddenly a day or two later, there she was walking again, but in a new place to the east, out of our sight, and talking with some other woman. So the Duck had been given a companion. We dubbed them the Ducks henceforth, and their passage each day past our window to the front door became an important diversion. With four women and two men as the sole occupants of this bizarre prison, it all seemed stranger than ever. What was the purpose of this building? Why did we six share it? What was the common denominator?

Our building seemed to be the starting point for breaking in new guards. We could always recognize the greenhorns. Not only did they not know the first thing about our routines, but the other guards were usually too lazy to tell them, so it was left to us to put them on the right track and give them tips on how a guard should behave—of course, from our point of view. Most newcomers were lads in their late teens, awkward and ill at ease. They either tried to avoid looking us in the eye or, having got over their bashfulness, did the opposite and followed our every movement as if we were extremely rare circus animals.

Initially they tended to be shabbily dressed. But life was well rewarded in an organization such as this. First came new jackets, sporty and carefully tailored. Then contrasting pants, immaculately pressed. Then came hairdos as the unruly shock was transformed into a series of shiny waves. And finally the ultimate touch: perfume. Everything began to smell of it, from newspapers and books to spoons and dishes.

Meanwhile, their whole bearing underwent a transformation. Of what interest were a couple of misfit prisoners? Now they had just one focus: the hunting expeditions for women in the city every free night, exploits recounted afterward with pride. And if they weren't chalking up their conquests in touching detail the next day, or sleeping off the aftereffects, they had their sunbathing to attend to out front, assiduously putting on that tan to swagger with. We gave them all names, usually based on first impressions: Clown, the Peasant, the Mild One, the Timid One, the Sad One (later we were forced to rename him Violet—the most extreme perfume addict of the lot).

In fact, it was this parade of guards that reminded us most of the passage of time. Youths whom we had first seen just out of school turned up again months or years later, transformed into men, often wearing wedding rings. Some of those in uniform sported sergeants' insignia. Others had ceased to be guards and had become officers. This was the case of "Friend," who had become a second lieutenant and in December 1951 had taken over as commandant of our building. And in the meantime, our previous house officer had advanced from lieutenant to captain. Time was passing for everyone except us; all were engaged in climbing the ladder of life, while with us everything remained stationary.

Perhaps because of a heightened nervousness brought on by this more relaxed atmosphere, a new safety measure was introduced specifically for our cell. There was already no end of barriers between us and the prison compound outside: a locked outer entry door, a locked inner entry door upstairs, a new locked wire frame door at the base of our interior stairs, and finally the lock and three huge horizontal bolts on our cell door itself. Now suddenly it was weighted down by one more encumbrance—a padlock.

What additional security could this provide? Then it dawned on us: it was not directed against us at all but at the guards, to prevent any unauthorized contact between them and us, such as their coming in to watch us play chess. Now it was rather like being in a bank vault where it takes two different people to open the safe deposit box. The guard had the regular key, but an officer was required for the padlock. This meant the house officer on duty or his designee had to drop whatever else he was doing eight times each day at least to come down below, undo the padlock, and wait until the door could be closed again. Inevitably, the very cumbersomeness bred its own simplification, and the house officer increasingly was replaced by his designee. And who was that? Usually the guard on duty upstairs!

And then one night it happened, human nature being what it is. When I returned from upstairs after a long session with my unpleasant interrogator, whom I had dubbed Horsetooth, the Reticent One was on duty down below alone. The upstairs guard had gone off to sleep, and the Reticent One found himself responsible for bringing me down as well as doubling as doorman for the building. And no one had thought about the padlock! As I stood in front of my cell, this fact suddenly dawned on both of us, an unprecedented problem especially for a not-too-bright guard. He looked at me as if for advice on what to do. To make things worse, Horsetooth was ringing upstairs to be let out of the building. The Reticent One positively wilted as he heard Horsetooth stamping impatiently. He was pulled two ways, and it was clear he was much more worried about a dressing-down from Horsetooth than about getting me safely under lock and key. In despair he shrugged and was about to start upstairs, leaving me to my own devices. If that were discovered, he would be lucky if he were merely fired.

I shook my head and went over to the door of the adjacent empty cell. No padlock there. I pointed to his keys. There was no time to lose; Horsetooth was already peering down the staircase as the door closed behind me and the key turned. Now at least no one had been caught giving me the freedom of the cellar. And in time, reason prevailed—or laziness—and the padlock unobtrusively vanished as suddenly as it had appeared.

As I recovered from my hunger strike we put into operation a stepped-up work program from breakfast to suppertime. Having gained considerable experience since we had embarked on "Duck Lane" the preceding January, we felt an urge to rework and deepen it rather than embark on a new venture. So we asked to be given back the copybooks already written, together with new ones for revisions and expansions. We waited nervously for the response. We had a strong suspicion that each 120-page book—of which there were already fifty or more—had made its way into some furnace, which would make our writing as illusory as the distance traveled by a squirrel in a wheel. To our gratification we were handed volume no. 1 of "Duck Lane" and told that further volumes would be produced as required. So we spent each morning rereading, editing, revising, and adding to our original version, the manuscript increasing to almost double its original size by the time we finished in June of 1952, equal to a two-thousand-page book. It had become a broadly painted epic of the interaction of very diverse human beings in the crisis of war and terror. Whereas in the original version we had relied mostly on events, we now focused primarily on the inner development of the characters, especially through expansion of the biographical flashbacks.

The newspaper usually came a day late, though often not at all or else severely mutilated by excisions. Every second week *Stolica* made it to our cell. It enabled me to follow not only the city's rebuilding, a problem I had been intensely interested in ever since the war, but also the discussions on work elsewhere, especially the shifting design concepts of recent years. Immediately after the war, Poland's approach to town planning and architecture had been very promising, as I had had good opportunity to observe on my architects' study tour in 1947. The ideas then being applied stood out in sharp contrast to the formalistic eclecticism common since the early thirties in Russia. But just at the time of my ill-fated visit in August 1949, a special architectural congress was held at which the recent approach was castigated and Polish architecture and town planning was forced into the Soviet mold. It was part of the whole fantastic swing of which I, too, was a victim.

Now, almost three years later, I was able to get a first view of the extent of the disaster. What had emerged was an architecture of power, not one for living. Behind façades unrelated to the function of the structure, behind monumental colonnaded streets, hid an incredible neglect of standards in housing and school design and basic infrastructure. Above all, architectural and planning criticism and commentary were now smothered in political double-talk. The horrible climax came with the announcement of a Soviet "gift" of a thirty-six-story "Palace of Culture and Science" to be designed and built entirely by the Russians on the most conspicuous site in Warsaw. Completely ignored in all this was the fact that the whole future development of central Warsaw would now be thrown out of kilter. Its bombastic placement and concept spelled final destruction for any logical solution to Warsaw's reconstruction.

I recalled an earlier attempt by czarist Russia to put its oppressive stamp on the city. It was in the time of Czar Alexander, who ordered the erection of the costliest, biggest church in Russia in the main square of conquered Warsaw, with a gold leaf dome of huge proportions to be visible from every point in the city. Its lavish mosaics and gold ornamentation were to reveal Russia's might to endless generations. But the Poles were strangely unappreciative, and one of the first things they did after gaining their independence in 1919 was to pull down this costly treasure stone by stone, converting the site into their Square of Victory. As I looked at the pictures of the model of the new import, of the ground being broken and foundations being laid, of the steel frame beginning to rise, I wondered whether the scenario would repeat itself and some future generation would at great cost knock down this huge, misconceived structure imposed in the best czarist tradition. Watching the work advance in issue after issue, I kept on trying to visualize its nonexistence. As I lay on my cot at night, gradually in my mind the outlines of a counterproject took form. If they failed to give me the promised office building to design, I had a ready alternative.

The pace of our afternoons intensified. First, we read the newspaper and *Stolica*. Then our studies. After months of receiving an indiscriminate flow of German-language books, mostly translations from the Russian, we had recently mapped out specific areas of study and asked for books on these subjects, carefully following the book reviews in the paper for anything new. Now most of our books were in Polish, greatly increasing the range available. Stanislaw translated them into German, gradually being able to do it at normal reading speed. Initially our first priority was biology, especially zoology. For me it was a harking back to my father's field and the interest kindled during my summers as a teen in Woods Hole, Massachusetts, close to the activities at the Marine Biological Laboratory, including Thomas Hunt Morgan's epochal genetic research with the drosophila fruit fly. What irony—one of the first items that came our way was Lysenko's *Agrobiology,* written by the man who all but demolished Russia's outstanding tradition in genetics, replacing it with a pseudoscientific communist dictum that all evolutionary change was environmentally triggered and lacking in inherited mutations. His attack focused especially on Morgan's genetic causative thesis as reactionary capitalist deviation, replacing it with his

own concept of acquired characteristics—or as he called it, "Jarowisation"—
and sending most of Soviet Russia's leading geneticists, including Michurin, off
to Stalin's labor camps. Lysenko was never more than an experimental agron-
omist in the manner of Luther Burbank until Stalin elevated him to lead the
fight to excise the concept of genetically induced change as a driving evolutionary force. Through this book I had the opportunity to take a second look at
Morgan's work.

There followed an excellent Polish college-level textbook on zoology in
which we reveled, and from which I made extensive notes together with mi-
nutely detailed pencil illustrations. The idea was to retain what we had studied
as a kind of reference archive to draw upon and add to. We asked for and received a Polish translation of *The Origin of Species,* and followed this with Dar-
win's *Journey of the Beagle,* which was sheer delight. There followed an account
of a zoological expedition to New Guinea and a recent translation of Mali-
nowski's historic work on the sexual life of the Trobriand Islanders, on which
Margaret Mead's later studies were based. Then our focus shifted to astronomy,
followed by the most recent thinking on Wegener's theories of plate tectonics as
the force responsible for the shifting land and water configurations of our
planet.

And so it went: the origins of humans, the origins of the cell, the role of living substance, the anatomy and physiology of mammals and humankind, general botany. How our world was expanding right in these cellar confines! We
were picking up where we had left off in college decades earlier. How sad that at
the moment in our lives when we have the best chance to draw fully from the
accumulated knowledge of our civilization we are still too young to grasp more
than the surface of it, and later when we are more perceptive, the pressures of
everyday life make such an opportunity difficult if not impossible to grasp.
Now, being no longer part of that world—and possibly never to experience it
again—we responded with an absorption difficult to imagine in that other state
of normalcy. Time had lost all measure, and for each printed page we created
ten times that amount in further speculation over every smallest item.

To our formal studies we also added language lessons, Stanislaw in English,
I in French and half-heartedly in Polish. Stan had a considerable familiarity
with French literature, while for me it was an exciting area of discovery. We
started with Rabelais's *Gargantua and Pantagruel,* then jumped all the way to
Zola's *La Bête humaine* with its unforgettable images of the early days of French
railroading, followed by a biography of George Sand by the French Canadian
André Fornet, which in addition to lively descriptions of her many amorous
affairs with the literati and artists of her day provided a broad panorama of the
intellectual ferment of the time. The tragicomic sequences of her misalliance

with Chopin and their flight across Majorca together with his grand piano in tow brought new humanity to his music; they also stood out in marked contrast to the account of Sand's peaceful merging into the musical household of Franz Liszt and the Countess Agoult.

When all other work was done, we usually finished each day with a round of chess, a game in which, under Stanislaw's tutelage, I gradually came to hold my own.

In spite of our isolation from the world outside, our contacts with nature grew in a peculiarly cellar-defined way. Our most constant and faithful companions now as before were the mice who came every evening to clamber around on the wire mesh, nibbling at the morsels I stuck in here and there. Even Stanislaw warmed up to them after a while and admitted to enjoying watching them play in the window—from a distance.

One night I had heard a thud and later a rustling under the floorboards, and toward morning I spotted a mouse running along our radiator pipe, a captive like ourselves. I took pity on it and provided an escape route via my bed covers and the table against the window. The mouse took the hint and vanished. A while later we both noticed a mouse again up in the window opening. It constantly stuck its nose in and looked down at the floor. We stopped our writing and watched. It became more and more agitated, until finally, hanging by its rear feet from the frame, it let go, hit the radiator, and fell down behind it onto the floor, then disappeared beneath it.

I put a scrap of paper on the floor beside the radiator with bits of bread on it. I also spilled some water nearby when I returned from the washroom in the evening. In the morning all the bread was gone. Also all the paper. I repeated the exercise. Once more everything disappeared, and we could hear the rustle of paper being dragged along under the floorboards. I tore some toilet paper into ribbons. All morning the mouse was busy stashing it away somewhere, obviously using it for a nest. And so it became part of our existence, though we couldn't help wondering why, in all these years, only this mouse had favored us this way.

The answer was not long in coming. We were sitting studying at the table when Stanislaw jumped up as if responding to an electric shock and started shaking his left trouser leg. "For heaven's sake, what's the matter?"

He was still busy with his trouser leg. "I swear, something was climbing up my leg." He looked crossly at me. "I bet it's your sacred mouse." Then decisively: "You'll have to get rid of it."

We settled down to our work again. Once more Stanislaw jumped up and batted his leg. "No, this is too much."

We returned to our studies, but I was puzzled and kept my eyes on the floor along the radiator as Stanislaw read. And soon, in the half dark of the shadow, I was sure I saw a small form dart out and disappear again. And then another, and a third. I tapped Stanislaw's hand. "Shh. Turn slowly and look at the floor behind you." And we both watched as four or five tiny mice scampered in and out from the shelter of the pipe. I was delighted. Now I understood the return of the mouse, her jumping in that night, her swiping all the paper. She must have instinctively sought this escape from the freeze outside, to have her brood. How wonderful! These young ones, born here, would be much tamer. Stanislaw didn't at all look happy at the prospect and nervously tapped his slippers.

And so a new era began in our cell life. I lay awake hour after hour on my cot watching the antics of this mouse family. It was a unique observation post. Usually the activities of free mice happen far from the human eye in the darkness of the night. These, however, lived in the same restricted space as we did, without any awareness of being deprived of their freedom.

Two interesting limitations in the perceptive faculties of mice soon became apparent to me. Neither the little ones nor the mother could perceive me as a whole when I was sitting at the table or lying under the covers. They were dealing with a head, or with hands, or with toes, feet, and legs in dark warm tunnels under my covers—all separate entities that had no connection with each other. The other, related limitation of mouse perception, one that makes the species so pitifully helpless in the face of predators, is that it does not seem to be able to recognize as alive anything which is completely stationary. A spider, a beetle, even another mouse that shows no sign of movement is passed by unnoticed, becoming just another part of the inanimate background and so no longer under observation. No wonder mousing is so easy for a patient cat or owl.

Stanislaw witnessed the development of my bedside zoo with mixed feelings. He had always had an abhorrence of mice, which he gradually overcame to the extent that they stayed on the other side of our window grille. This invasion was quite another matter, however. At night he pulled his cot to the other wall, as far away as possible from me and the table. From the late afternoon on he sat down uneasily in fear of inviting excursions up his legs.

Inevitably the moment came when the young mice wanted to explore farther afield. The end of the mouse latency period? They climbed up the dictionaries and tried to follow their mother's example of jumping up to the bottom of the grille. When one finally succeeded, it quickly got a taste of real life, for it happened to encounter an outside mouse eating in the window frame who at once treated it as an intruder. There followed a wild squealing and tumbling, until finally, battered and terrified, our mouse jumped for its life and landed on the nearest object below. Sometimes all seven mice disappeared through the window opening. If anything went wrong out there in the dark, they would make a dash for it through the screen. A week after the first sally, only five young mice were left. Some days later, only four. One day the mother herself vanished for good.

Finally only one young female was left. She would sally forth through the screen into the window opening and walk right under the nose of a waiting date. If he failed to show any interest, she would clamber onto the bar above him and nonchalantly wander past again. If he responded to the extent of clambering up to her, she would move to the bar below. After a few such gambits, her admirer would lose his cool and start to chase her in earnest. At the wire mesh she'd let him close in on her, only in the last moment she'd fly through the grille without watching where she might land—the table, my head, or the floor. And sticking through the grille meanwhile was the surprised face of her frustrated suitor, too afraid to cross the barrier. But she couldn't stand the end of the game. Hardly had he finished looking for her from on high than she would scramble back over my cot—and me—to the other end of the grille.

Once more the chase was on, and in close encounters she didn't hesitate to peep as if it were a case of bloody murder. And so we came to call her "Peepa." Soon she was managing to entice him in a little farther each time—onto the dictionary, the table top. Finally in the heat of the chase he forgot himself entirely and followed her down my pillow, over my shoulder, along the length of the cot, and then on a wild chase around and around our floor. Peepa's favorite trick was to stop suddenly and sit completely still on the sideline. The other mouse would go shooting right past her in his blind haste, proving in part the species' limited eyesight. Technically, she never surrendered.

We tried to discourage Peepa from being too adventurous out of fear of losing her to some unknown predator. She had become such a known personality, we were by now attached to her. Her attitude was special, since she had grown up with the best of two worlds. She could always enjoy her sallies outside, with full freedom for lone adventures, yet she knew that she had a completely secure home, heated in cold weather, cool when it was hot outside, safe from foe and unwanted friend alike, a place, too, where she could call the shots in the ever-repeating mating game.

Peepa also provided a key nutrient for the window garden that we so carefully nurtured. From our earliest attempts at growing individual rye kernels in the interstices at the bottom of the grille we had shifted to the much more ambitious project of using the two-inch-wide depression on the other side of the grille made by the slanting window sill. Here we gradually built up a layer of gravel, lime, and dust from the floor and our mattresses. The missing element was fertilizer, and this is where our mice helped us out. Seeds were gleaned from the occasional tomatoes in our salads, and from our straw sacks came rye and other seeds such as vetches and lupines. We even managed to hatch three apple seeds during the winter in damp paper laid under the radiator. The result was a miniature garden that we nurtured with infinite patience and that gave us no end of joy. We even had the satisfaction of seeing the vetch climb right up to the top of the window and develop several blossoms.

November, December, and then January 1952 had gone by quietly, almost happily. Partly it was the pace of slow recovery from the events of the fall. In January I asked to be able to start work on a design project and made a detailed list of both instruments and information I would need. Toward the end of February a good drafting table with adjustable slope was set up in our cell. I reported what else was needed, trying to make it especially clear that I could not do anything without instruments and basic documentation.

Meanwhile spring had come, and still there was no sign we would be out walking anytime soon. Although we were aware that the other four occupants of our building had this privilege, we could not point to this fact, as it would have revealed how much we had observed. Finally I wrote to the authorities asking for some indication of what was to become of me. I also requested information on what had become of my brother.

The year following my interrogation I had tended to accept that my troubles had their origins in Noel's purported intelligence activities against the communist regimes as revealed in the transcripts of the Rajk trial, incredible though that seemed. Now, with greater distance and time to reflect on every detail I knew of his life, I was rebelling. That just couldn't be Noel. Why was I never presented with further evidence beyond what little was explained to me that one night? Where was he being held? Probably in Budapest. But if he was guilty, what about his trial there? How much of what was cut out of the newspapers might allude to this very issue? Often we sensed that the focus had shifted from Hungary to Czechoslovakia and even to Poland itself. Even if Noel's relief work during the war on behalf of Hungarians had in fact been an OSS operation against a future communist regime, how could I ever prove that my work in Krakow and my postwar visits weren't of the same stripe? But in my case, I suspected that my captors were in a quandary, stuck in midstream, able neither to move forward to the kill nor to back down and give up. And couldn't the same have happened with Noel?

These reflections hardly served to stabilize my state of mind. I felt a gnawing disloyalty toward my brother for ever having given credence to his possible duplicity. At the same time, I lost the last shred of justification I could concede to the communists for what they had done to me. Under the circumstances, how could the impasse ever be broken? An embarrassing leftover, I had been shifted onto the sidelines outside of time, at best a mere reference file. There could never be a release, never a return to life.

Would the situation ever change except through my eventual nonexistence? I was dominated by the need for movement toward some point, just something, anything. So as the spring advanced, time and again I sent written requests for the right to walk, for information on my future, for a statement about my brother and a true indication as to Kate's and the children's circumstances. I no longer included the question of my release. It had become too unreal.

All my petitions were ignored. My restiveness increased. On the fourth attempt to write and protest, the paper was taken from me and I was forbidden to make any further such requests. Once again I started to return part of my food untouched. Walking outside was at last mentioned concretely. We also noticed that, under Cigarette's supervision, the exterior wall of the prison compound was heightened several courses. We were sure it was related to us. Then suddenly we were told that walking was out.

I was beginning to drift back into a closed world of impulses, closed even to Stanislaw's pleading. I got up late and slipped into my cot early. I refused to be shaved, and then even to leave my cell at all, even for the daily washing.

At first it seemed my behavior was being ignored. One day, however, all the old copybooks of "Duck Lane" were removed to the guard's space, so we couldn't continue our revisions. With no more writing, our demand for books increased, but instead there were ever more delays so that finally we were left with almost nothing to do. This brought me to the edge of violence beyond my control. Twice the doctor saw me upstairs, but on each occasion my excited pleas to clarify my situation fell on deaf ears.

June of 1952 passed. July came. The summer would soon be over, and still we were locked without time in this cell, one more year in our lives gone by with nothing but four whitewashed walls to show for it. I ate less and less, and to offset this loss instinctively limited all bodily movement to a minimum. I lay on my cot most of the day, sat up for a few hours, and walked back and forth slowly for two short stretches each day to keep from getting too weak.

At the end of June the authorities reversed their tack. The carrot once more. The copybooks turned up again, along with some French reading material and a slew of new Polish books. Also some odd blueprints of some German Reichswehr automobile processing buildings in occupied western Poland and some plans dating from the twenties for German small-town post office prototypes, a mishmash that neither the guards nor anyone else could explain. So that was the answer to my request to do a Warsaw office building. I wanted to throw it all back in their faces. The forces driving me could no longer be stopped.

# 17

## London 1951

GRASS WIDOW

When it comes to filling out forms you are either single, married, divorced, legally separated, or widowed. You cannot put "grass widow," yet that is what I was, a married woman whose husband was away. Had Hermann been a prisoner of war, I would have received a stipend from the government. Although his salary had stopped after two months, fortunately he had inherited a little money from his mother; still, I could not use this until a trusteeship had been set up on behalf of Hermann as an "absentee." This was something new in the annals of Massachusetts, where the money was, and meant much poring over legal books, not to mention lawyers' bills. But in the end it made it possible for me to support myself and the children.

If I had tried to live on so little in the United States, I should have had to find a full-time job and had very little time to badger people over Hermann's case. Moreover, the prospect of being alone with the children under these conditions appalled me. Fortunately, my parents were able to let us stay on with them in London, where we shared housekeeping expenses.

Back in Cleveland was our house, heavily mortgaged. I decided to sell it, but since it was in Hermann's name this was not so simple. It meant setting up another trusteeship, this time in Ohio. Dr. Herbert Hunsaker, dean of Cleveland College and Hermann's and my employer, was a wonderful friend and arranged it all.

Everyone seemed to think I should take a job, and certainly my present full-time preoccupation with Hermann's case was producing very little result. The atmosphere of tension must have been very hard on my parents and the boys. Perhaps another interest would make me more balanced and effective.

Sir Henry Bunbury had been director of the Czech Refugee Trust Fund and my boss way back during the first year of the war when I was in charge of housing the refugees. When I left to get married in 1940 Sir Henry wrote my favorite recommendation: "Works well under pressure and always rises to a crisis." Well, now I had my crisis. When he heard of Hermann's disappearance he got in touch with me. He was still an active member of Political and Economic Planning, or PEP, an independent research organization in London, and through him I was given a part-time research job in January 1951.

Developments in Czechoslovakia kept me in a state of constant expectancy. The steady disappearance from public view of Czechs who had been refugees in England during the war made me wonder whether their names had been extracted from Hermann through interrogation. What a wonderful case could be built up if the Russians wanted it! And once Hermann was called a spy, how could they ever let him out alive?

There was much speculation in the West as to why the communists were getting rid of their own men. The prominent were constantly being demoted, and it was reported that many thousand inconspicuous people had also been arrested.

Kopriva, since February 1950 minister of public security, was one of the three Czech delegates to the Cominform—the Communist International, with representatives from the USSR and all the Eastern European countries where the communists had seized power. The whole quarrel with Tito showed clearly that Russia controlled the Cominform, so it was significant that a Czech delegate to that body should be the one to accuse Czech nationals of "Titoite plots and underground activity," in a manner reminiscent of the Rajk trial. Clearly Moscow did not wish this work to be in the hands of the "Londoner" Vaclav Nosek.

In February 1951, Clementis and his colleagues were again attacked, and Vaclav Kopecky, the minister of information who was chairing the investigating commission, said, "Let us remember how the whole international net of Anglo-American espionage was unveiled in connection with the well-known Field, with whom again Vilem Novy was in contact."

This was reported from Prague by the AP correspondent William N. Oatis on February 27. He added that Novy had been missing for about a year and was believed to be in prison. That same month, Clementis was arrested and accused of treason, followed by his wife, Ludmila, some two weeks later. The AP office in Geneva reported this news, adding that reliable sources said that the number of arrests of Clementis's supposed collaborators had already soared into the hundreds.

In April a dispatch was published by the AP from Geneva stating that Noel had been seen in Prague on February 27 at Kolodeji Castle, where he was taken to confront Clementis. He was also supposedly seen by Vilem Novy, who was heard to tell a policeman, "I stood there opposite Field and they (the MVD agents) tried to mislead us. One of them blustered like a madman and knocked me down. Field appeared hardened to it." According to this story, Noel was recognized in the corridor by a former acquaintance to whom he said, "I have the honor to be the guest of Mr. Beria in Lubianka."

"That fellow is worth his weight in gold and is well taken care of by Beria," Pavlo Yudin, editor of the weekly Cominform newspaper, was quoted as saying in an unguarded moment in Budapest.

Elsie wrote to the Associated Press for confirmation of this report. They replied that according to information smuggled out of Prague, Noel was brought there in a special plane on February 22 for questioning in connection with the Clementis affair. He and Clementis apparently were brought together on February 27. One day earlier he was questioned together with Vilem Novy, who was also under arrest. The man believed to be Noel was not seen after that day, and the next day a party of five persons, including two Russian colonels, was brought to the airport under extreme security measures. "Our informant," noted the AP correspondent, "says that even high officials of the Czech Interior Department have not seen the statements taken from Mr. Field and Dr. Clementis on February 27, since the case is completely in the hands of the Russians."

I suggested to the State Department that if Noel had been taken to Prague, Hermann probably had too, and asked them to check the validity of the report, but there was no further confirmation.

A few days after this report, on April 23, William Oatis, the AP correspondent in Prague, was arrested. I did not believe he was responsible for these dispatches, though he had filed several stories on the Clementis mystery. His arrest also served to rid Prague of the remaining Western newsmen.

That same day, Rudolf Slansky, secretary-general of the Czechoslovak Communist Party, published a report on a supposed plot by Clementis, Husak, Novomesky, Sling, and Svermova, people he described as "traitors, cosmopolites ready to sell the interests of their country." Again the world expected a trial and speculated whether the Fields would be produced at it, but none came.

The arrest of William Oatis came just after the release of Robert Vogeler, the American businessman who had been sentenced and imprisoned in Hungary since 1949. Taken into custody just two months after Hermann, he was now once again a free man. I felt an acute sense of failure that I had not managed to achieve the same result for my husband as Lucile Vogeler had for hers.

Mrs. Lucile Vogeler was Belgian born, gutsy, and glamorous. She took every opportunity to goad the State Department on her husband's behalf, and seemed to have a knack for publicity. When she flew to London in March 1950 to see

Dean Acheson, then secretary of state, even though I did not know her, I phoned her. She asked me what the State Department was doing for me, and when I replied that they were doing all they could, she said she thought that was debatable and explained why she believed in publicity. She kindly said she would do what she could for me, although she had been warned to keep her case separate from mine.

The Americans had actually granted some concessions to the Hungarians to get Vogeler's release. It was felt, however, that this did not set a good precedent, and so the British refused to follow it in the case of Edgar Sanders, Vogeler's British colleague, who therefore remained imprisoned in Hungary for another two years.

The trial and conviction of William Oatis was very upsetting, though it had no apparent connection with our family's case. Soon came another mystery: the disappearance of Donald Maclean and Guy Burgess. When this story broke in the papers at the end of May 1951, and was followed ten days after their disappearance by the arrival of two telegrams purporting to be sent by the missing men, I was at once struck by the similarity to Noel's case. Then also, when inquiries began to be made, another telegram was dispatched. In both cases the wires seemed not to have been sent by the men themselves. In Maclean's case there were errors such as only a foreigner to England would make. Since I knew Noel had not disappeared voluntarily, I thought perhaps Maclean and Burgess had not done so either. I rang the American embassy and pointed out the similarities.

The April arrest of William Oatis could not be ignored, and on June 2 the State Department issued a ban on U.S. citizens traveling to Czechoslovakia. Officials cited incidents in the past three years, including the arrest of Oatis and that of John Hvasta of New Jersey in 1948, who was still being held; they also stated that in May 1949 Noel Field had "disappeared en route to Czechoslovakia, and a few months later, in August 1949, his wife, Herta, disappeared under similar circumstances."

We were not too happy about the "en route" but were told that was just a mistake in the way it was expressed to the press.

My job at PEP was interesting, but I was not able to function properly, being too preoccupied with Hermann's case. Elsie, a devoted sister if ever there was one, was also spending an enormous amount of time and energy on it, having given up her medical practice to do so. It was all too much for me to cope with, and in June 1951 I gave up my job.

## THE PAPER BATTLE GOES ON

In January of that year the State Department had addressed a new note to Poland, which was handed personally by Ambassador Flack to the Polish Foreign Office. In it the department recounted that there was no evidence that Hermann had returned to Czechoslovakia after August 15, 1949, and that Poland had not even stated whether Hermann had actually departed from Poland after his known visit. In these circumstances, the department charged, the burden of proof in explaining what had happened to him must remain with the government of Poland. Therefore, the U.S. government held Poland responsible for his whereabouts, safety, and welfare.

The Polish Foreign Office refused to accept the note on account of certain references that it considered objectionable, but people in charge read it and so at least knew the American view. Ambassador Flack followed this up with a meeting with the secretary-general of the Foreign Office, at which the latter stated flatly "that the Polish investigation was completed and that it revealed no information concerning the whereabouts of Hermann Field." However, they did not put it in writing.

As to Noel, Walter Winchell, the American news commentator, in a broadcast in December 1950 said that he was in a Russian prison. Asked by the State Department where he got this information, Winchell said that "it came from the chief of the East German Communists, bragging in his cups." Such rumors were no substitute for news.

Meanwhile, Kopecky's statement of February provided an excuse to ask the State Department to approach Czechoslovakia again. The department therefore sent a note referring to this statement and adding that since Noel and Herta were last seen in Czechoslovakia, the U.S. government, pending the receipt of new information, must hold the Czech government responsible for their whereabouts, safety, and welfare.

## CAUGHT BETWEEN A STAR AND ITS SATELLITES

A fundamental complication lay behind the diplomatic impasse: the relations between the USSR and its satellites. Hermann and his brother had disappeared in either Poland or Czechoslovakia. Neither had gone to Russia, yet there was ample evidence that interest in the two brothers was not confined to the countries in which they had disappeared. It was even possible at the time to believe that the Polish and Czech Foreign Offices were telling the truth when they said they knew nothing about it.

The State Department soon became convinced that the security police of the Soviet Union had an interest in the case. The disappearances, some officials suggested, might actually have been kidnappings carried out by Russian agents operating in the satellites, with the Czechs and Poles being ignorant of the whole proceedings while the Fields ended up incarcerated in the USSR. Alternatively, they might have been arrested by the satellite countries' security police under instructions from their Soviet "advisers." In this case, they were probably still in the country concerned, their presence known to at least a few police officials. Whichever of these two procedures had been followed, it seemed to me that Hermann and Noel could be released only with the approval of the Soviet Union, and I believe the State Department thought the same.

What was Russia's interest in holding these people? Every indicator pointed to a prophylactic policy designed to forestall defection of further satellite states from the Warsaw Pact bloc, as had occurred with Yugoslavia. Stalin had come to distrust the old-time communist leaders, especially those who had taken refuge in the West during the war. Their ideas might have become tainted with affection for the Western countries, or they might think they should choose their own paths to socialism and not unquestioningly accept the guidance of Big Brother—particularly since this often included trade agreements more favorable to the Soviet Union than to the satellite itself.

The appearance of Noel on their side of the Iron Curtain must have been a godsend to the Russians. His relief work had put him in touch with thousands of wartime refugees, among them communists who had become just those men Russia was now interested in. And having picked up Noel, any members of his family were of interest too, especially those who had also done relief work.

The logical thing might therefore have been to approach the USSR itself. This the State Department refused to do, on the grounds that since the Fields had not traveled to Russia there was no evidence of Russian responsibility.

So there was the impasse. Russia could operate in peace while her satellites took the kicks, albeit merely paper ones.

The State Department's notes to the Poles may have contributed to their feeling it was worth keeping Hermann alive, but notes alone were not enough to make them admit anything. And we never succeeded in playing off the Czechs against the Poles.

Why could we not act more decisively? The Fields themselves must accept some responsibility for the State Department's reluctance. Hermann had not called at the U.S. embassy in Warsaw, and was therefore not officially known to be in Poland. Herta, who was meeting him in Prague, waited four days before telling me he had not arrived. However, I did then tell the embassy in London promptly, and the State Department was able to confirm that Hermann's name was listed on the plane to Prague.

When, already in the fall of 1949, Elsie and I had asked what we could do to make the Poles answer, we were told there was virtually nothing. I suggested cutting off Polish imports into the United States, and was told that trade was negligible so they would not care; as for private loans, they could not be stopped, and if private travel were halted the Poles would be delighted.

The question of sanctions kept coming up, and at some point I was told: We would be willing to try a sanction if we thought it had any chance of success, but we feel it would not because the Fields are too important to the Russians, and we don't want to be stuck with the sanction.

So it really came down to conflicting interests between us as a family and our country. Cutting off trade or travel was believed to be against the interests of the United States. And once the battle on getting sanctions was lost, our harassing of the State Department seemed to result only in further polite diplomatic exchanges. This, combined with occasional press stories, sufficed to "keep the case alive." And this Elsie and I proposed to do indefinitely.

## IS THERE REALLY NO LAW TO HELP?

It seemed incredible that in the twentieth century there should be no law that could secure the release of a man held without trial in a foreign country. I searched my mind for possibilities. The Court of International Justice in the Hague sounded just right, but it dealt only with complaints of one government against another, not with individuals. I knew our government would not bring a complaint against Czechoslovakia, which had at least answered its inquiry, nor against Poland, which was "investigating."

Then there was the Red Cross. Surely they should be able to help, regardless of the international situation. But they said they could not. The International Red Cross no longer had missions in Poland or Czechoslovakia, and the national Red Cross societies were under state control.

There was still the United Nations. I approached Trygve Lie, then secretary-general, but he said there was nothing he could do. I also tried to get our country to raise Hermann's case in the United Nations Assembly of 1950. For this Elsie and I got the support of his employers in Cleveland, John Millis, president of Western Reserve University, and Herbert Hunsaker, dean of Cleveland College. They were joined by Edmund Purves, executive director of the American Institute of Architects, and George Zook, president of the American Council on Education. In November the four of them went to Washington to appeal for further action and were seen by Undersecretary of State James E. Webb. His reply to Dr. Millis gave a reasoned analysis of why the United States did not believe this matter could be raised at the UN. He said that the General Assembly had not in the past been receptive to considering individual cases of improper treatment by one country of citizens of another, and it was therefore doubtful that they could get the support of other delegations. If a complaint of the improper treatment of Hermann were nevertheless to be made, it would be essential to have incontrovertible evidence. But, he said, "it appears that the evidence available is less than satisfactory, in that it does not even disclose whether the Polish or Czechoslovak government was responsible for his disappearance."

Whether enough support could have been obtained from other delegations we do not know, because it was never tried. I thought Poland and Czechoslovakia should have been jointly called upon to explain how a man could disappear while traveling between the airports of Warsaw and Prague. But the answer was always the same: insufficient evidence.

In November 1951, when the UN Assembly took place in Paris, I wanted to go there and try again. It would be the first time I'd been out of England since 1949, and I was scared. I thought perhaps the communists would have me disappear, in order to silence further inquiries about the Fields. So my father persuaded an old family friend to go with me.

I managed to get an interview with Eleanor Roosevelt and Dr. Tobias, both in the American delegation, and Benjamin V. Cohen. I had met Mrs. Roosevelt before, back in the 1940s, when Hermann and I had gone to Hyde Park to see her, pleading for refugees. Now I had to plead for him. She told me they had no instruction to bring up our case, or indeed any other specific case. They did, however, have a resolution concerning freedom in communist countries for all normal activities, including those of newspaper correspondents. This, as I guessed at the time, resulted in an appeal for William Oatis, the AP correspondent tried and imprisoned in Prague.

I complained that I was asking much less than their resolution did, merely that no country should hold a foreigner over two years without a public trial. Mrs. Roosevelt sighed and suggested I go to the State Department. I said I had been doing little else for the past two years.

So I went to the State Department's liaison man at the UN, and he said frankly that there was inadequate information to raise our case in public debate.

With the thought of trying to interest other UN delegations in our case, especially those not involved in the Cold War, I also spoke to Sir Benegal Rau of India, who listened sympathetically and promised to do what he could. I later heard that he got the same reply from the Poles as they had given to the Americans.

Then I spoke to a group of newsmen at the UN. The next Sunday, November 25, the *New York Times* reported that I had asked Mrs. Roosevelt and Mr. Cohen to bring my case before the UN Social, Humanitarian, and Cultural Committee but that these two delegates saw no way of doing so.

When I got home, I wrote to the State Department that I could not agree with the position that nothing could be done and that, although we could not be sure whether Hermann had been taken at the Warsaw or Prague airport, the department had adequate evidence that it had occurred on a particular plane journey and that his disappearance was the work of communist authorities, whether Polish, Czech, or Russian. "The public silence of the Department," I wrote, "is leading other people and countries to think that we have less evidence than we in fact have."

There was a reason for this last sentence. While in Paris I had spoken to Sir Gladwyn Jebb of the British delegation to the United Nations. His first question was, How did I know Hermann had not disappeared voluntarily like Donald Maclean and Guy Burgess? I told him I was quite certain that Hermann's disappearance was involuntary, and after that I was promised British support should the United States raise the case.

# 18

## London 1952-1953

I had given up my part-time job in the spring of 1951 because I could not concentrate on it. Yet having freed myself and spent most of my time on Hermann's case, I seemed to have achieved nothing. It was like boxing with a mountain of cotton. It was nightmarish.

Friendship and kindness I received from many sides, and sympathy for Hermann. People realized our plight was primarily the result of a fantastic world situation in which peace was not peace but a sort of veiled international civil war. A man was destroyed not because he had done wrong, but because the world had changed and his actions in an earlier period were being judged by present-day values.

Many times I looked at Hermann's last casual postcards to the children, sent from Prague in August 1949, with pictures of Hradcany castle and cherry blossoms and the ironic message "Did you sing Happy Birthday to Mummy on her birthday?" and his last note from Warsaw: "See you Thursday evening, dear." But always I felt sick and put them away again.

I thought of the hundreds of women whose husbands were missing in the last world war or in Korea. Even the widows were saved this gnawing worry, year after year. Their husbands were dead. There was nothing to be done about it but remake life without them. But how many years can you go on hoping without losing your sanity?

Meanwhile I had my responsibilities as a mother. The boys settled into their London life and school, becoming increasingly like little English boys. But they certainly had not forgotten Hermann. One day I saw written on the telephone pad, in Hugh's childish handwriting: "My father is a good man. He helped the refugees."

Their position would have been a lot worse if it had not been for my parents, who became very fond of them. In the attic my father had a workshop with carpentry tools and a lathe, and there, after school, the boys would sometimes disappear with him. Alan called it "the happy little workshop." The boys also had a hobby of "bus spotting," which involved our going to the London bus terminals on Saturday afternoons, where they checked off bus numbers in little green books, while I read a book on my own. For my part, my best distraction was singing madrigals with friends and neighbors, which gave me a little social life. When Christmas came around we would collect our children and go caroling in the neighborhood.

Most people seemed to agree that we would do good by "keeping the case alive." This meant urging the State Department—either directly or through influential people—to take it up diplomatically whenever an opportunity arose. It also meant getting press coverage. In England this was not easy, the argument being that it was not a British case. Often I was interviewed at length, or gave out a press statement, and nothing happened. But when I hit on anything that was considered newsworthy, the writeups were always sympathetic. In America the position was somewhat different. Publicity was easier to get, but it never failed to put the main emphasis on Noel's colorful past. Neither Elsie nor I was in a position to be authoritative about what Noel had or had not done, so we took the position that we were unconvinced of all allegations until he had a chance to answer them himself.

In December 1951 I received a letter from a Czech who claimed to know that "Field" was in Pankrac Prison, in Prague. We followed this up, but it could not be substantiated. In fact, I think such rumors were common in Prague, since prominent Czechs kept disappearing. Karel Kreibich, a "London" Czech, was recalled from Moscow, where he was ambassador, and on January 23, 1952, the radio reported that Ladislav Kopriva had been relieved of his position as minister of public security. This was remarkable, not only because he had held the position for less than two years, but also because he was the person who, in March 1950, had officially denounced Vilem Novy on grounds of his connection with one of the Fields.

Things were moving fast in Czechoslovakia now. Soon Clementis's arrest was officially announced, and then that of Rudolf Slansky, secretary-general of the Communist Party and deputy prime minister. Slansky had already denounced Otto Sling and Clementis as traitors. Now it seemed he was in the same boat. Otto Sling was chief secretary of the Communist Party regional committee in Brno, a member of parliament, and another "Londoner." His English wife was now stranded without him in Czechoslovakia. Bedrich Geminder, another delegate to the Cominform, soon disappeared as well. One could only guess how many lesser lights were being caught up in this latest turning of the tables. Surely there must be a big show trial in Czechoslovakia before long. Would they hark back to the Fields and produce them?

We could only speculate. In December 1951 the North American News Agency (NANA) had published a report that Noel was in the Lubianka Prison in Moscow, but this proved to have no more grounding than the report that he was in Prague. One could only say it was an improvement on the report the same news agency had published a year earlier, saying that he was being "feted" in the Soviet Union. This Elsie managed to discredit, but there was always the danger of this type of rumor cropping up, with the natural corollary that the State Department should waste no more of its time on Noel's case.

In February 1952 King George VI died. Dean Acheson, secretary of state, came to England to represent President Truman at the funeral. I thought I might manage to see him and so went downtown and stood in the vast crowd that watched the procession. It was a very London scene: a gray day, thousands of quiet people, and the uncannily slow, halting march of the procession as the catafalque disappeared into Paddington Station.

I walked back across the park to Princes Gate and left a personal note for Mr. Acheson, begging for an interview. Once again I was refused, and, while at the embassy speaking to Acheson's assistant on the phone, for the first time there I lost control and broke down. In a few moments the assistant came out to see how I was, and someone produced a cool wet towel.

They could not have been kinder, but I still did not see Acheson. Instead I talked to the assistant, complaining that there had been no diplomatic action in a long time. I left a letter to Acheson asking if Hermann's case could be taken up in Moscow, in the hope that he would either be released or the "pressure of inquiry might induce them to put him on trial in a satellite state, which the family considered would be preferable to oblivion." I also said it was clear that the Czechs and Poles were not free to admit anything, and that if the case were raised in the UN it would be "relevant to the question of passport protection and admission of satellite states to UN membership." I added that I would like to offer all Hermann's savings, about $50,000, in exchange for his freedom. I begged the State Department to continue to petition on his behalf lest the communists conclude that he was expendable.

Throughout 1952 Elsie and I nagged the State Department about raising the case in Moscow. In the summer of 1950 the Russians had been asked whether they had any information, and they had replied that they did not. Since then, however, much circumstantial evidence had appeared suggesting that the Russian security police were involved. We both made efforts to see Ambassador George Kennan before he took up his duties in Moscow. Neither of us succeeded.

Erica Wallach's mother, Therese Glaser, was also having no success in tracing her daughter. One very cold wet day in November 1952 we went together to hear Dr. Dibelius, bishop of Berlin, preach a sermon. Afterward Mrs. Glaser managed to corner him. He was going to Moscow, and she asked him to take an appeal she had written to Stalin. But next day the bishop received a telegram from the metropolitan of Moscow saying that the Patriarch had been taken ill and could not receive him; the trip was off.

My failure to get any action by the UN was underlined when in fact the American delegation did take up the case of William Oatis and the rights of foreign correspondents in Czechoslovakia. But there was no mention of any Fields having disappeared there. Instead, Delegate Tobias's closing remark (as quoted in the *New York Times*) was: "May I ask my colleague from Czechoslovakia what has happened to Mr. Clementis?" And Clementis was not even an American citizen!

In April 1952 the Russians held their World Economic Conference in Moscow, to which a few Americans and Britons were invited. Elsie and I each got in touch with two of these people, asking them to make inquiries. I also wrote a letter to the *Manchester Guardian* reminding those scheduled to attend that Hermann was still missing and that we needed better safeguards for travelers if business trips to Russia were to be resumed. I hoped the Russians would see this letter, and the telegrams we also sent to Moscow, and so be reminded of the case. Shortly afterward I sent an appeal to Stalin himself, asking simply for his help, which I made public. I received no responses. Such moves were made after discussion with officials at the embassy, who sometimes saw no point in them but considered them harmless.

I made no second attempts at the Czech or Polish embassies in London. I had never received a reply to my inquiry at the Polish embassy, and both the Czech ambassador I had seen in 1950 and their ambassador in Washington had by now been recalled to Prague.

The summer of 1952 passed without our being able to make any progress on the diplomatic front, so again we asked the State Department to put the Field case on the agenda for the next assembly of the United Nations.

THE BIG SHOW AT LAST

At last, in the fall of 1952, we were provided with a "newspeg." On November 20 I picked up the phone and a newsman told me that Rudolf Slansky was to be brought to trial for treason. He dictated the names of all the defendants, and here they all came at last, the men who had disappeared: Slansky, Geminder, Frejka, Frank, Clementis, London, Loebl, Margolius, Sling, Simone, and Fischl.

All men who had been in the West during the war. Also Reicin, Svab, and even Hajdu, who, as former deputy minister of Foreign Affairs, had said the Fields were not in Czechoslovakia.

This is the big show, I thought. This is what they have been waiting all this time to do: clean out the leaders of the Czechoslovak Communist Party. But the big question for us was, would they produce the Fields as witnesses? The idea of our family being brought in to testify to a lot of lies was frightening. Yet I felt it was our best hope. Then at least the Czechs could not deny knowing where they were. But if they were used for this purpose, they would also have to be sentenced as spies.

For confirmation that the Fields would be named I did not have long to wait. The complete indictment was published the same day, and in it both Hermann and Noel were referred to as spies. The proceedings were broadcast by Prague Radio and monitored by the BBC.

The indictment ran generally along the lines of that against Rajk and others in Hungary back in 1949. It was clear that the mysterious "Titoist conspirators" in Czechoslovakia, of whom only Pavlik was named in the Rajk trial, had now been identified. It had taken a long time to discover that all these Czechs were also traitors. Slansky must have believed the charges raised in the Rajk trial. How incredulous he would have been if someone had told him that in three years he would be the Rajk of Czechoslovakia! It had been slow business collecting all the defendants and systematically removing the leadership from the various segments of the Czechoslovak Communist Party, so that no effective revolt would be possible.

Now at last came the miserable defendants who had been waiting for years in prison cells. From the Foreign Trade Ministry came Evzen Loebl, who had spent the war years in England, had negotiated trade agreements for the communists after the war, and had disappeared from his office in the fall of 1949. He had been followed into obscurity by Rudolf Margolius, from the same ministry.

Then there was the Foreign Affairs group: Vladimir Clementis, who had flown home into the trap and spent a year working in a bank before finally being imprisoned, and his subordinates Artur London and Vavro Hajdu.

But the housecleaning extended to other ministries too, less connected with the outside world. Finance contributed Otto Fischl, a former deputy minister. National Defense contributed its former deputy minister General Bedrich Reicin. Perhaps costlier would be the loss of Ludvik Frejka, former head of the Economics Department of the president's office. Frejka, a "Londoner," was a prominent economist, and one of the men responsible for guiding Czechoslovakia's conversion from democratic capitalism to a communist planned economy.

The most striking thing about this trial was the inclusion of so many different groups of defendants. Slansky had still been secretary of the Czech Communist Party when Loebl and Novy were denounced, and no doubt would have witnessed their trial with equanimity. But now Slansky himself, former vice premier, was to take the dock with Loebl. And with him stood Bedrich Geminder, the so-called eminence grise, formerly in charge of the International Department of the Communist Party Secretariat and one of the three Czech delegates to the Cominform. No doubt he had played his part in excommunicating Tito. Then there was Josef Frank, Slansky's deputy, and Otto Sling, secretary of the Brno region and incidentally also responsible for party cadres. These were all top brass, men who had devoted their lives to the communist cause.

And there was Andre Simone, a former member of the editorial staff of *Rude Pravo* and a "Westerner." In the trial they said his real name was Otto Katz, "an international spy, a Zionist and Trotskyite."

The final touch was the presence in the dock of Karel Svab, former deputy minister of National Security, the man responsible for investigating those arrested earlier. Probably he himself had arrested several of his co-defendants. Now he was accused of not having done the job properly. My interpretation was different: he knew too much.

The indictment stated that the accused, who were either Trotskyite, Titoite, Zionist, or bourgeois nationalist, or a combination of these, had created an antistate conspiratorial center. They had done this in the service of the Western espionage agencies, their purpose being to liquidate the People's Democracy in Czechoslovakia, restore capitalism, and drag their country away from friendship with the Soviet Union and into the imperialist camp once again—in which, it was charged, Czechoslovakia would lose her national sovereignty and independence. To this end the accused had undermined the regime, frustrated the building of socialism, damaged the national economy, carried out espionage, and weakened the unity of the Czechoslovak people and the republic's capacity for defense.

With all this going on, one wondered how Czechoslovakia had managed to survive. But then, the trials were for domestic consumption. With the welter of circumstantial detail, and the main thesis repeated time and again in the confessions of the accused themselves, the ordinary man in the street might think there really was something to it. How could he be expected to know what his leaders had done in London, way back during the war?

The trial had an anti-Semitic side. All the defendants except Clementis, Frank, and Swab were of Jewish extraction, at least in part. This was brought out, and on it was based the accusation of Zionism, which tied in to the USSR's opposition to Israel's foreign policy. It was suggested that these men were not patriotic Czechs, despite their many years of devotion to the communist cause.

In the Slansky trial the Fields were made to play a large part. Just as in the Rajk case the relief work of the Unitarian Service Committee, during and after the war, was misrepresented as a cover for Noel's recruiting of agents on behalf of Allen Dulles and the Office of Strategic Services, so now this theme was repeated. In addition, Hermann was given a parallel role, supposedly under the cover of the British Committee for Refugees from Czechoslovakia.

The indictment continued, charging that the U.S. imperialists wanted to secure a base for a third world war, to which end the American, British, and French espionage services had, even before Munich, spread their network in Czechoslovakia. "From the end of 1938, in London and afterwards in Krakow, under the pretext of helping Czechoslovak and other refugees, the so-called British Committee, later known as the Trust Fund, was an important Anglo-U.S. espionage agency. . . . This activity was directed by Hermann Field and later by his brother Noel Field, the closest collaborators of Allen Dulles."

The accusation was patently absurd, since Hermann had never had anything to do with Allen Dulles or the OSS, nor did Noel have any connection with the British refugee committee.

I knew a good deal about this organization because I had been employed by it from its inception in 1938 until I resigned in 1940. It was set up soon after the signing of the Munich Agreement, in which the Sudeten areas of Czechoslovakia were ceded to Germany. I dealt with finding accommodations in England. Partly these were delegated by us to local voluntary committees, and partly we ran our own hostels. By the time I left the organization I was head of the department overseeing the housing of some three thousand people.

When all Czechoslovakia was occupied, in March 1939, the voluntary contributions of the British public were augmented by a British-Czech loan that had been earmarked for refugees, and owing to this government money the committee was turned into the more formal Czech Refugee Trust Fund.

After World War II and the communist takeover in February 1948, another sad cycle of emigration began as those Czechs who had gone home to build democracy and could not accept life under the communists decided to flee again. The Czech Trust Fund still existed and gave these people—who in the Slansky trial were called the "treacherous émigrés of the post-February period"—some help in finding homes or employment. Thus the fund itself was targeted by the allegations as well.

When Hitler overran Czechoslovakia, of course, we had no thought of getting the refugees into England in order to make British or American agents out of them, for use after a war that had not yet started, and to overthrow a com-

munist regime that no one anticipated and that would not even exist for another ten years. I doubt even British Intelligence indulged in that much clairvoyance. But now, in the Slansky trial, we saw these theories all carefully worked
out: how all our lifesaving work had had ulterior motives, and how Hermann
Field, instead of being a relief worker doing an emergency job for a few months,
was really an agent of the American "spymaster" Allen Dulles, working in tandem with his famous "spy" brother Noel. A number of prominent English people were also mentioned.

The indictment of the Slansky trial, which was broadcast as proceedings got
under way, gave an excellent resume of the evidence to be given by the defendants against themselves. No doubt the sentences were equally predetermined:
death by hanging for all except Loebl, Hajdu, and London. Thus eleven top-
ranking Czech communists would be eliminated, justifying a shake-up
throughout the Czechoslovak Communist Party and government.

While noncommunists in the West recognized this show trial as a frame-up,
resembling similar trials held in the Soviet Union in earlier years, for the families of those men in Czechoslovakia it must have presented a terrible dilemma.
The wives were loyal communists, true believers, and over the radio came the
voices of their husbands declaring that they had committed treason. Were they
to believe them? Did they feel they had been betrayed by their spouses, or were
they under pressure of self-preservation to join in the denunciation?

But the dilemma extended even to the children. The East German news
agency ADN reported that the son of one of the defendants had written to the
State Court demanding the death sentence for his father, whom he described as
"a creature which no longer deserves to be called a man . . . who was my greatest
and most bitter enemy," and requesting that the letter be shown to his father.
Whether this was a genuine sentiment or the result of being taunted as the son
of a traitor, it was equally shocking.

I at least was free, and could answer back for Hermann. After reading the
indictment I issued a press statement on November 21:

> Apropos of the references to the Field brothers in the trial of Slansky and others in
> Prague, I want to say that my husband Hermann Field has never been involved in any
> kind of spying. The Czech government has not brought any charge against the Field
> family in over three years. Noel Field was arrested in Prague May 12, 1949, and Her-
> mann while traveling from Warsaw to Prague by Czech National Airlines on August
> 22, 1949. It is a fantastic denial of human rights that American citizens should be held
> in this way and their names wrongly used to condemn local nationals.

I showed my statement to the first secretary at the embassy before issuing it.
He said he wanted to consider the matter, that it might be wiser to say nothing.

If the communists were using the Fields to convict local nationals, he suggested, they might let them out without trial after it was all over, if it could be done without losing face.

But I felt my answer had to come at once, so went ahead. It did not make much of a splash in the papers, for only the communists took Czech espionage charges seriously.

I suppose few people in the world shed a tear for the victims of the Slansky trial. Not the "good" communists, to whom they were traitors, and certainly not most people in the noncommunist world. But I could not help being impressed by the personal tragedies involved in this macabre spectacle. Otto Sling, who had an English wife and some children, I could remember long ago as a refugee and as a stout man. In prison no doubt he lost plenty of weight, so that his suit would have become loose fitting. An eyewitness reported that when sentenced to death, he let his pants fall to the ground. I thought of this as one last attempt to tell the world what a farce the whole thing was.

It was a shock to see Hermann described as a spy and his relief work so misrepresented. For the eight days of the trial I watched anxiously to see whether he would be produced but was not really surprised when he was not, nor his brother Noel. There was no need, for who among the communists could challenge the flat statement that an American was a spy?

Other "spies" were mentioned, people who had worked with the same refugee committee or had recently been in Czechoslovakia, like Godfrey Lias, newspaper correspondent for the *News Chronicle,* or Konni Zilliacus, British member of Parliament and a longtime member of the Labour Party, currently an Independent. Zilliacus was, I think, the only one who bothered to respond to the accusations, which he did by radio. I asked the State Department to deny that Hermann had ever been an agent of the OSS, but they never got around to it. By that time, I did not think it mattered much.

Vilem Novy, imprisoned since 1949 but never, so far as I knew, brought to trial, was used as a prosecution witness. This was but one step away from Hermann. Karel Markus, who had also disappeared in 1949, was only referred to. The nearest thing to an admission that the Fields were in fact being held came from another prosecution witness, Oswald Zavodsky, formerly of the Security Police, who said: "When Noel Field was interrogated his espionage contact with (Artur) London was definitely established." And Karel Svab in his confession referred to "those named as agents by Field and Pavlik."

On the basis of these indications from the Slansky trial that the communists themselves knew our people were under arrest, Elsie and I pressed the State Department to take the case up again with the Czech government. I went to the embassy again on November 24, when the trial was still going on, for I felt that to be taken seriously by the Czechs, action must be prompt. I pointed out Svab's reference to "those named as agents by Field and Pavlik," which must mean that the prosecution knew the whereabouts of at least one of the Fields. I also wired Secretary of State Acheson and some Congress people for support, while Elsie paid another visit to the State Department.

As usual, official wheels turned slowly, and I became increasingly impatient. I asked for an interview with Minister Holmes at the American embassy and went there ready to make a fuss. He took the wind out of my sails by saying that Washington was in fact sending a note to Prague. He did not want me to go public with this information, saying that if it became known before the note was actually delivered, it would jeopardize the chances of success.

The department's unwillingness to publish its demarches was always hard for me to fathom. Later on, after this particular note was delivered, I again raised the question of publication, but the department still did not want to do it. Perhaps they expected a rebuff from the Czechs and would not have wanted to follow up the note with stronger action, believing that nothing short of extreme steps would have resulted in the Fields being produced at this juncture. The first secretary's view that eventually Hermann and Noel might be released without trial, provided it could be done without losing face, was in fact prophetic.

The State Department seldom gave its notes publicity. This was a major difficulty in my relations with the press. Since I was dependent on the department's maintaining interest in the case, I did not want to go against their wishes; but I also wanted to keep the press interested, which was hard when I could give them nothing new.

The American note sent at the beginning of December 1952 referred to the remarks of Svab and Zavodsky and said that the conclusion was "inescapable" that the Fields had been questioned while in Czech custody. In view of these disclosures, the U.S. government requested information as to the reasons for the detention of these American citizens.

There was no immediate response, and the department still did not want to publish the note for fear of jeopardizing any chances of success. The press, however, was now showing some interest, and eventually was given the gist of the note.

Elsie and I continued to press Washington to follow up the note, but nothing happened. It was an awkward interim period. The November elections were over and General Dwight D. Eisenhower was the new president. The new secretary of state would take over in January 1953. Perhaps we would have more success then.

Ambassador Wadsworth in Prague received an oral reply from Foreign

Minister Siroky at the end of January 1953. Siroky said he had no knowledge of any change since April 1951, which was when the Czechs denied having information about the disappearance of the Fields. Siroky said that their reply at that time had been based on concrete, established fact, namely that neither brother had ever been in the power of the Czechoslovak authorities. An official note would be forthcoming, but, Siroky warned, "it can contain nothing new."

This statement by the foreign minister was extraordinary. It amounted to an admission that a large number of the leaders of the Czechoslovak Communist Party had been convicted of treason and hanged on evidence that had not been obtained by the Czechs themselves. Although the Fields were not the only "spies" named in the Slansky trial, the assumption that they were spies was in many cases crucial to the prosecution. Was it not important that the Czechs themselves cross-examine such key witnesses? This all confirmed the analysis we had built up over the years, that Russia was pulling the strings in these purges.

It so happened that the Czechs had complained to the United Nations of U.S. "interference in the internal affairs" of other countries, the response to a recent act of Congress that earmarked money for the support of political opposition to communist regimes. I pointed out to the State Department that the Czech denial of knowledge about our family would provide the perfect answer by showing that Russia itself was interfering in Czech affairs. But when the time came, the United States still refused to raise our case in the UN.

Unlike the Rajk trial, the Slansky trial was not immediately published in book form in English. Elsie and I, anxious that no shred of evidence should escape us, therefore compared various translations of the proceedings. In particular we wanted to find the most authoritative wordings in the various references to the Fields' being held prisoner.

I took a Czech translator and laboriously went through the daily proceedings of the trial as published in *Rude Pravo*. The significant fact emerged that all references to the Fields' being held, including what they had "said," had been edited out. But nothing could alter the fact that they had been mentioned in the original Czech broadcasts of the trial.

Robert Vogeler, the American businessman, had been arrested after Hermann and had now been free for two years. William Oatis had taken his place, and now his two years were nearly up. President Gottwald of Czechoslovakia had died, and Zapotocky stepped into his shoes. In sending him formal congratulations, President Eisenhower reminded the Czechs that they could have better trade relations with the United States if they released Oatis, and shortly thereafter, out he came. The Czechs said this was in response to Mrs. Oatis's appeal to Gottwald the previous year, but I found this unconvincing. Why had it taken so long?

The American note on the Fields arising out of the Slansky trial still received no formal answer, so I wrote to President Eisenhower and to the chairmen of the Senate Foreign Relations Committee and the House Foreign Affairs Committee urging them to see that the State Department did not relax its restrictions on Czechoslovakia just because Oatis had been freed: "I do not see why Czechoslovakia should receive trade or other benefits from the United States while the Czech government shows such disregard for America's diplomatic representations on behalf of her citizens still in communist prisons." The Czechs should at least answer the department's note, we argued.

Trade restrictions were lifted, however. They had been imposed, the State Department said, in accord with the resolution passed by Congress that "all commercial relations with Czechoslovakia should be terminated immediately, and should be resumed only if and when the Government of Czechoslovakia restores to William N. Oatis his freedom."

This emphasized once again the importance of imposing a sanction in such a case. But we had been handicapped by our inability to state beyond doubt which country in fact held our people, and perhaps also because we had less influential support in the United States. One university was not a match for the business world represented by IT&T, nor the international fraternity of newspaper correspondents.

That spring of 1953 I had seen Assistant Secretary of State Merchant in London. The department promised to consider our case again, and Ambassador Wadsworth in Prague had another interview with Foreign Minister Siroky on June 22. On this occasion Siroky was reported to have been more friendly.

Meanwhile, Stalin had died, and in July Charles E. Bohlen, our new ambassador to Moscow, was in the United States and both Elsie and I tried unsuccessfully to see him. Through the State Department we asked if the case could be raised in Moscow, but Mr. Bohlen thought the time was not right.

That same month of July 1953 came the dismissal of Lavrenti Beria as head of the MVD, the Soviet Security Police, which seemed to me to open up new possibilities. If Beria were now in disgrace, this might foreshadow a reversal of previous policies. Perhaps the Russians, if approached now, would review their know-nothing attitude of 1950.

Elsie had retained the services of Martin, Ansberry, and Henderson, a law firm in Washington, and in light of recent events instructed them to suggest that the case now be taken up with the Russians. But in August the State Department replied that it had consulted our embassies in Moscow and Prague and "after careful consideration concluded that a further approach to the Soviet Government would not serve a useful purpose at this time."

I was getting pretty desperate by now. The approaches to Czechoslovakia following the Slansky trial had borne no fruit. Our criterion for action thus became not whether it was likely to produce results, but whether it could do any harm. So when Ambassadors Bohlen and Wadsworth were called to Vienna in September 1953 to consult with the State Department, I once again appealed to them to approach Russia. I knew their opinion was that Russia would still deny responsibility, so I put forward another option: since the Russians would surely not suggest that the Czechs did not at least know the whereabouts of Hermann and Noel, since they had been so vital to the Slansky trial, maybe the Russians would use their good offices to induce the Czechs to produce them.

Perhaps as a result of this appeal, Ambassador Wadsworth again approached the Czechs, and Ambassador Bohlen reported that he had sent a personal communication to the Soviet deputy foreign minister asking "whether the Soviet Government can supply us with any information whatsoever regarding your husband, his brother and sister-in-law."

Ambassador Bohlen's opinion was that Beria's arrest did not make an encouraging reply any more likely than in 1950, and he was right. In January 1954 he wrote me that Mr. Gromyko had replied, stating that "the appropriate Soviet authorities possess no information regarding the whereabouts of the persons mentioned." It really did seem remarkable that they had not bothered to find out, in view of the Fields' notoriety as "American spies"!

As to the Czechs, in November 1953 they said they "could add nothing to what had already been communicated to the Embassy." And so they got away with their Slansky trial references, and our year of effort to pin them down was in vain.

The State Department had always said they could do more "if only" they had more evidence. There was always the chance that Hermann had been seen by somebody who would later be free to tell us about it, and we were told that U.S. posts throughout Europe were alerted to this possibility. We also checked up on individual cases ourselves. Elsie paid calls on Robert Vogeler and William Oatis, and I saw John Hvasta of New Jersey after his hazardous escape from a Czech prison in March 1954. We wrote to a few others as well, but none could help.

We had approached the Red Cross early on, with no result. Now, in January 1954, I went back to the British Red Cross requesting that they ask the German Red Cross to look out for any information that might be brought by prisoners of war returning from Russia, and to raise the matter with representatives of the Soviet, Polish, and Czech Red Cross societies. Through the League of Red Cross Societies in Geneva I also dispatched a "Missing Persons" memorandum to their branches in Poland and Czechoslovakia. I received no replies.

Nevertheless, when the League of Red Cross Societies met in Oslo that May, it was stated that the earlier written inquiry to the Polish Red Cross had been received and inquiries had been made, but "the persons interrogated in Poland were not able to furnish the Polish Red Cross Society with any information in the case." They had apparently been afraid or unable to report this to Geneva.

However, I was told that at the Oslo meeting the Polish representative accepted my handwritten personal note to Hermann, which he said he would take to Warsaw. It never reached Hermann. I sent another note through the Russian Red Cross, but that did not reach him either. In fact, we tested the Red Cross's assertion that they were helpless against the security police and found it to be true.

LIFE MUST GO ON

Ever since my abortive attempt at doing a part-time job in early 1951, I had stayed home. But the result of two more years' work on Hermann's case had been very meager. At best we had kept the case, somewhat intermittently, alive. By August 1953 Hermann had been missing four years. He might have been disposed of, or simply died, in any hour of those fourteen hundred and sixty days. How often I wondered whether this had happened, and how impossible it seemed that I should ever know!

I read a number of books by people who had been prisoners of the communists. There was Stypulkowski, the Polish leader who had been invited to Moscow and subsequently found himself held captive in Lubianka Prison, and Alexander Weissberg, the German communist who was sent to Siberia. From such books I deduced that if Hermann had in fact been kidnapped by the Russians, his chances of getting out were not good. His case was so different from the cases of Vogeler and Oatis who, although they went through the ordeal of a trial, could not be made simply to disappear.

When I had last seen Hermann I was thirty-six and still felt young. After a year or two my more pessimistic friends were saying, "Its very sad, but anyway you have the children." Or even, "There's nothing more you can do. You'd better look around for a new husband." Even the children sometimes had the same idea. They kept going over the same old questions:

"Why doesn't Hermann come home?"

"Because he can't. He will as soon as he can."

"How do you know he's alive?"

"I don't. But I think so."

"But he may be dead." And then the startling addition: "Well, if Hermann can't come and be our daddy, why don't you get another one? I'd rather have a new daddy than not have one at all."

And then from Hugh, who loved numbers: "Do you think there's a ninety percent chance that he'll come back, or only a fifty-one percent one?"

I wondered how much harm this eternal uncertainty was doing them. If I spoke with great confidence and always assured them that he would come home in the end, their expectation of a happy ending would be greater. But also perhaps the eventual disappointment.

In fact, of course, my own optimism decreased with the years. I knew Hermann's return was possible but not highly probable. Yet because it was possible, I was prepared to continue on that assumption indefinitely. That meant that I would not accept the suggestion made by a lawyer that in a short while I could have Hermann declared legally dead. Although doing so would have enabled me to collect on his life insurance policies, inherit his property, and, if opportunity arose, marry again, it would also have made it harder for me to continue pressing the State Department, though I know Elsie would have gone on doing this for ever. Suppose I did find a "new daddy" for the boys and one day Hermann reappeared, what a mess I would have been in then! Obviously it was out of the question. Our assumption had to be that he was alive and would eventually return.

Most likely, though, I would spend the rest of my life as a "grass widow." I had had nine years of happily married life and had two sons. Many people had less. But one thing was clear, I could not be a good mother if I spent the rest of my life thinking only about Hermann's problem. I must stop my mind always going on the same tracks, in small circles that by now felt like rabbit burrows through my brain.

I decided to see about getting a job again. I could not return to my lecturing position in Cleveland, but my old university, Cambridge, helped me get a part-time teaching job at a teachers' training college. My pupils were girls aged eighteen to twenty and I taught them English.

It was exciting being a professional woman again. At forty-one I was no longer very ambitious, but I felt I had at least been given a chance to make something of my life after all.

This job meant I had to be away one night a week, and my mother willingly took charge of the boys in my absence. When I was working it was impossible to think of Hermann, and instead of developing unmanageable anxiety as had been the case two years earlier, I found myself able to do my job and maintain some efforts for Hermann as well. Underneath, the main factor in my being able to function was, I think, that I had finally come to believe what I was told: that if Hermann were to come out, it would be because of factors far beyond my control.

# 19

## Breaking Point

"I want to live, Hermann. It's all I have . . . I know it will come out all right in the end. Every night I test the future." He was pleading with me.

"Stan . . . There's no end in sight. None. Not one shred of rational evidence. Instead of reasoning, you envelop yourself in a cocoon of faith or something that you can't explain to me. But it's not reason . . . Stan, I want so much to believe you, but it's no use. It's too late." As much as I wanted to cling to life, in this form it had lost its hold.

He persisted. "You'll sink us both in the end, don't you see? To what purpose? Theirs! You think I'm playing games. Maybe I am . . . for survival's sake. Listen, please. Isn't that what both of us want, above anything else?"

Over the months Stanislaw had increasingly admitted to a conviction that all of life was predetermined and our actions could only make minor ripples within this framework. So he set about trying to peer into that future. I had surreptitiously observed him in recent weeks. He had a way of making little dice out of bread and continually manipulating them at night like prayer beads. At first I thought it was simply to calm himself by keeping his fingers occupied. Watching him more closely, though, I discovered that the way the dice fell gave him the answers he was looking for. The whole thing struck me as childish, but who was I to challenge his approach to survival? He was doing a lot better than I was. And in spite of myself, I always asked him each morning whether he had found out anything significant about our future. How could I afford not to? I, too, had to grasp at every straw to boost my own morale.

Stanislaw was, I was sure, in part conditioned from early youth, having had to deal with survival unemotionally, often without knowing whether the next day would put an end to it. This living in the present was especially characteristic of the whole generation of Poles who had fought through the years of German occupation, drawing as fully from life as they could within the moment. I had been startled in his wartime accounts by the freewheeling license right in the shadow of the constant German terror in the streets of Warsaw. Actually, such uncertainty was nothing new to Poland. The successive invasions that throughout history had swept across the country's indefensible plains no doubt contributed to the heady mix in Polish culture of a romantic affirmation of living and an obstinate perseverance in adversity.

Over our years together I had gone a long way in learning to suppress perception beyond our cellar existence. But unlike Stanislaw, I was always on the verge of rebellion. In contrast to him, the basically sheltered and privileged environment in which I had grown up left me with a sense of disbelief, of unreality that I could not conquer.

Even though Stanislaw's responses reflected a mystical bent drawn from Buddhism and Confucianism in addition to Christianity, the Catholicism with which he had been raised was dominated ultimately by unquestioning faith rather than reason. While I felt a growing respect for the great teachers of these faiths because of their keen insights into human nature, I was unable to share their mystical experience. The nearest I came to it was with the Swiss theologian and humanist Albert Schweitzer and his *Reverence for Life*. He was a bridge of sorts, but still a long way from what I needed. This was a great disappointment to Stanislaw. He was convinced that lack of faith lay at the heart of my inability to cope. Maybe he was right, and I cursed the limitations of my own mind.

One more factor played a role in my despair. It had started in August 1951, when an unmistakable tension had developed around us. Security suddenly increased, and radios blared in the distance full of patriotic music and tirades about the aggressors and a confrontation in Berlin. Our newspaper appeared in censored tatters or not at all. Dislocation in our diets suggested food shortages, and our guards often appeared in uniform. Was the Cold War about to become hot? What if there was bombing? What chance would we have of coming out of the rubble alive? The image of the carpet bombing of Dresden with its nearby Buchenwald concentration camp haunted me. Hiroshima.

Stanislaw, clearly exhilarated, experienced no inner turmoil at these developments, having grown up in an unquestioning military tradition. In one of our early discussions he conceded that he had been excited by the prospect of imminent war in 1939. Some change—any change—was better than the doldrums of the thirties, though of course it had all turned out quite differently in the end. Now, he argued, in spite of the risks of sudden annihilation, wasn't war our one real chance of freedom?

For me it wasn't that simple. I could not see riding on the hope for more violence, more destruction, a final degradation of remaining human values. Would it be worth surviving in such circumstances? Then again, war and a change of regime—weren't these in fact the only things that would ever unlock these doors? In any event, as the summer of 1952 approached a showdown seemed to be brewing, though the impending U.S. elections might effect a delay. And now with summer drawing to a close, war and peace still seemed to hang in the balance. My sense of hopelessness and abandonment only increased.

"Hermann, this won't go on for ever. We may still have a chance, and for that it is infinitely worth holding on. We can still build some joy to hang on to down here. We've done it together in the past. Hermann, don't let go now, I beg you. Please!"

I heard Stanislaw, but I no longer listened. His pleadings hardly penetrated through to me. Nor did the conciliatory moves on the part of our captors which implied leniency if I abandoned my campaign of indiscipline. It was the carrot cycle again. This time it was clear that if I did not behave appropriately, the stick would certainly follow.

And so it did. The storm I had feared and yet precipitated by my own actions was not long in coming. Through the cracks and the window boards we identified Cigarette walking past with our house officer. The bar gate in the corridor clattered. It could only be for the girls or us. The steps came straight to our cell. For some seconds we were aware of an eye observing us through the door. Into the cell walked Friend in full uniform. He came to my cot and in a demanding voice asked why I remained lying down. Without waiting for an answer, he ordered me to get up, put my suit on, and follow him. "Cell inspection," he stated laconically.

I hesitated. I heard Stanislaw's whisper: "For heaven's sake, obey." I got up slowly and dressed. I was aware of the eye watching me steadily; it was Cigarette's. As I approached the door it swung open, Cigarette remaining hidden behind it. So no chance to confront him. I was directed down the corridor and into cell No. 3, the door promptly closing behind me. This cell was only six feet wide and dusty, its window closed, with just a cot with a dilapidated straw sack and the usual slop pail.

Alone—not a book or anything human. All the suppressed rage of these three years broke through the dike I had so assiduously constructed. I looked around for some point of application. I threw myself down on the mattress and started pulling out the straw and scattering it all over the floor. I tore the material to shreds. I tipped over the cot, determined to pull it apart too. As my first fury spent itself I noticed some undamaged ears of rye on the floor. How beautiful they were in this chaos. I picked them up and laid them tenderly to one side. How incongruous life could be.

The door opened gingerly. Blankets and bedding landed on the floor as if nothing had happened. So the "inspection" had merely been a ruse to transfer me without a scene. My fury returned. I would retaliate. Aside from Stanislaw in No. 1 there were the girls in the fourth cell on the other side of the guards' area; I would let them know who I was, and let the guards know too. If my captors refused access to me, I would at least make my presence known to all who could hear. The moment my door was opened at lunchtime, I turned toward it and at the top of my lungs yelled: "*Jestem nie wini amerikanski architekt Hermann Field.*" And a second time. The guards, bending down to place the two bowls and wooden ladle on the floor, afraid to hurry lest anything spilled, were taken by surprise. Friend came rushing to the door, gesticulating wildly and "shushing" as loudly as he could to drown me out.

The door slammed shut. I picked up the basin of soup and hurled it at the metal cladding; then the second one, aiming the pork, potatoes, and cabbage straight at the Judas eye and the invisible person behind it. The door, the frame, the floor, and the pile of blankets on it were now streaked and splotched in one glorious mess. I smiled to myself with satisfaction as I kicked over the slop pail in the nearby corner. Retreating to the dry scattered remnants of the straw sack, I dropped to the floor in exhaustion. I had wanted to rip out the electric light unit in the wall and get my hands on "Ivan" and break his neck, but by now I was too weak.

The door opened, ostensibly for collecting the bowls. I turned where I lay on the floor and with my remaining strength once more yelled out in Polish: "I am an innocent American architect, Hermann Field." The door slammed shut right away. A moment later two guards marched in, one carrying a white towel, the other the familiar straitjacket from the forcible feedings. They advanced warily. I shouted, "MBP guilty! MBP gangsters guilty! Bierut gangsters guilty!" and tried to ward them off with my hands, until they had both arms firmly twisted behind my back. Then I tried to get them with my feet, but it was futile. Not only was I quickly immobilized, but the towel was also tied firmly across my mouth, and I lost consciousness.

I came to as cold water was being splashed on my face. Both guards seemed relieved when I opened my eyes and looked up at them. Under Friend's supervision, they lifted me onto the bare cot. Then one went out to get a broom and without comment swept up as best he could the mess on the floor. The door closed. I lay alone, immobilized, deprived of speech, with nothing in the cell except the cot under me.

The afternoon passed; evening came. Suspended in time, I fantasized innumerable new ways to make trouble. My window had been partly opened at the time of my fainting and not been closed again. At the usual hour in the afternoon the Ducks would be walking past the board enclosure. If only I could wiggle myself out of the gag and straitjacket, I could choose the moment of the

Ducks' passing to yell my name and nationality to the world outside. The girls down here no doubt knew by now; this way the Ducks would too. There would be four witnesses in addition to Stanislaw, and if any of them were released at some point, the secret would get out sooner or later.

That evening I heard the steps of officers outside. They came downstairs. Friend entered my cell and started speaking to me in Polish. I understood enough to realize that he wanted me to promise I would make no more disturbances. I shrugged as if I didn't understand. He went out, and after a whispered consultation the door was closed, bolted, and padlocked. I had had no liquids or food since my very meager breakfast.

As the night progressed I became lost in cycle after cycle of thought, each gloomier than the one before. In the past I had managed to break these cycles finally, but this time the exhaustion and physical pain from my bonds helped convince me I had reached an absolute dead end. Was it cowardly now to say I had suffered enough and wanted simply to put an end to it all? Surely neither Kate nor the boys could expect me to hold out longer. Stanislaw had always said it was my duty to them to hang on to life, not to hasten the end through any weakening on my part. But now there was no Stanislaw either. He, too, was gone. This separation had all the marks of permanence. Now that I was alone, I had a right to do what had been inconceivable as long as our lives and our fates interconnected: just to end it and get peace at last.

I felt better. I had decided. I looked at the knots that bound me. Although every last thing had been taken from my cell, even the pail, one new item had been introduced, exactly the one I needed. The straitjacket had two long, cord-like ties rather like those on a pinafore. A lasso. If I ran and fell on the radiator pipe, it would pull tight so suddenly that even if it didn't break my neck, it would throttle me before anyone could intervene from outside. By the time the guard had given the alarm and someone was sent in search of the padlock key, I could reckon on at least five or six minutes—more than enough time. As the hours passed I kept jiggling the knots. Already I could shift my arms a little inside the sleeves and, through the material, manipulate the rope. A blanket had been thrown over me, so neither the knots nor the movements of my hands were visible from the door.

After several hours of work I was rewarded: the knots came undone. I decided to unravel myself under the covers. Now every moment of unnoticed advance preparation would be vital; I would even prepare the noose and test my plan so as to be able to carry everything out in lightning sequence. It wasn't easy, though, to get the ties unwound without shifting slightly.

I heard Violet's muffled voice on the phone, almost inaudible. I hadn't a second to lose. I tried to finish the noose under the covers, but it wouldn't tighten. I threw the blanket off and began to extricate myself. I jumped off the cot and, hurrying to the radiator, knotted the binding around it. Again I struggled with the noose. I heard steps on the corridor stairs. The noose . . . quickly, the noose. The gag was still in the way, and I pushed it down. The cellar gate was being opened. If it was for me, I was too late. Discovery of my intentions would spoil everything.

I let go of the radiator, took the jacket, and lay down on my back on the cot, then repositioned the gag and pulled the blanket over me. I held my breath.

Steps approached outside my cell; the padlock key was hastily inserted. In a flash the door stood wide open. Friend quickly came to the cot, Angel at his heels. Both were flushed and out of breath. Friend pulled back the blanket. I had lost.

Friend held the jacket up and excitedly demanded an explanation. I remained silent. Once more Friend had Violet and Angel truss me into the straitjacket. Too weak to fight back, I began a verbal lashing. But they didn't know a word of German, and my attempts at Polish were almost unintelligible. All I could do finally was to call names. They told me to shut up. I lashed back: "MBP bandits! Bierut bandits! Red gangsters!"

Friend had reached the end of his patience and drew back his fist. By now Angel was worked up too. He put his grubby hand across my mouth while Violet readied the gag. As they tried to silence me, Angel muttered, "*Cholera, cholera . . . z curwi syn.*"

"*Niet, niet. You* the son of a bitch! You *MBP z curwi syn!* You *z communist curwi syn!* I innocent American!" I kept shaking off the gag as soon as it was in place. They gave up and left me, this time tied securely in the jacket but with nothing over my mouth. And so they beat a retreat, shaking their fists at me as I showered them with abuse.

But what to do now? I had just escaped making a fatal mistake—for indeed, life was the only card I still held. How right Stanislaw had been. Somehow, without realizing what had happened, I had completely lost my bearings. My basically pacifist heritage seemed to have failed me and I had swung into an unfamiliar world of extreme aggression, driving those holding me to violent countermeasures. If I had been injured in these scuffles, if guards had exceeded their instructions and lost their tempers, how easy it would have been to get rid of me altogether.

And yet, how did I know that I was rational now? Each successive act had seemed completely logical at the time. My first concern now was to deal with myself. And so, in utter defeat, I began to probe anew into myself. I decided that henceforth every tactical decision should be subjected to a twenty-four-hour waiting period before I could act on it. As to my present circumstances, the only thing was to accept them and try to regain what I had lost. But would the authorities respond? If not, I feared I would be unable to go on.

Late the next morning I was released from the straitjacket and so could move around once more. I decided to accept the meal routine. Saturday came and when Violet asked if I would take a shower and let myself be shaved, I said yes. He behaved as if nothing had happened and even gave me some shears to trim back the beard that now enveloped my face. Then, after several bad attempts with the safety razor, he handed it to me too. It was the first time this had happened. I felt reassured.

After breakfast I asked to speak to the officer on duty, a fairly young man who had appeared at the time the padlock had been added and whom we therefore dubbed "Padlock." During the conflict of the past days he had shouted at me in German, though previously he had appeared to know no more of that language than the rest. Now he listened politely and noted down my requests. I stated that I regretted the incidents that had arisen out of their ignoring of my needs. I said I would try to adjust my behavior even so, provided that the authorities met me halfway. If they would just reunite me with Stanislaw and reestablish our setup in the first cell, and give me the use of the drafting materials, even without any specific project to design, I would cease to ask about walking and news of my family and clarification about my own future. In addition, I would need to be put back on my diet.

I was weak and found it difficult to walk more than a few minutes at a time. I had to leave part of my food untouched, as it worsened my digestive troubles. I asked for the doctor but received no reply. Meanwhile, to keep my mental balance, I started fantasizing a city planning project and found I could retain the visual images without the need for pencil and paper. I decided to take as my subject the redesign of the destroyed center of Warsaw, by creating a really contemporary capital center with an intermodal transportation center, government offices, cultural buildings, parks, and an orderly traffic solution, all of it tied in with the surviving fragments of old infrastructure with which I was familiar. This project would demonstrate the weaknesses of the "cultural palace" being erected by the Russians at this very moment on the same site.

A week went by and still I had gotten no attention. My digestion had almost ceased to function under the dual impact of ordinary prison food and my return to solitary confinement. Then one afternoon my door opened and in it stood both officers, Friend and Padlock, who beckoned me gruffly to come along. I resisted the impulse to refuse.

We passed the familiar doors upstairs, at each of which in turn I expected to stop. Instead we went through the double swinging doors that separated the central building from this wing. Angel appeared with a heavy raincoat with attached hood. I put it on. The entry door had been opened, and I got my first glimpse of the entry stairs and the semicircular turretlike front wall. At the bottom of the stairs a guard had unlocked the outside door. So I was to leave the building. But why?

Before I had a chance to think, some hands reached from behind and placed the black eye pads on my face. Then other hands pulled the heavy rubber hood of the raincoat over my head. The final touch came as something metal clicked shut around my wrist. I was handcuffed, the first time in all these years.

Outside now, the hands on my arms guided me left. I was walking on the concrete pavement and soon would be abreast of the window of cell No. 1, our cell, Stanislaw's. Would he be watching through the cracks? I was walking outside at last, but in what outlandish circumstances! The concrete path ended. Gravel—a road or driveway. Then grass, slightly uphill. Steps up, a door creaking open. Cold air as from inside an old farmhouse, at once familiar, reminiscent.

We stopped inside. The handcuffs were removed, my eye pads undone. I was staring down a narrow carpeted corridor with doors on either side. But of course, I knew this corridor! I had been here before. Padlock beckoned to me severely. We went down the creaky stairs, those of the rabbit hunts of 1949. It was like a dream, like walking the corridor of a medieval convict ship—dark, dank, narrow, echoing, with only a faint light filtering through the tiny, obscured window in the makeshift WC at its end. So I was being punished by a return to this gruesome subterranean existence, with all its awful sounds.

On and on we went, past the door of No. 4, past the central guard space, down three steps to the lower second half, still farther underground. No. 11 was opened as we approached, dark and clammy; the sill of the small barred and obscured window stood above eye level and there was a naked light bulb in a wire cage on the ceiling. Unlike my cell of 1949, this one had a new plank floor on top of the brick.

At first I thought I was alone in this silent cellar. It had the feel of having been closed up right until this moment. There was an unpleasant odor of dogs, which certainly hadn't existed in 1949. Within a few minutes the cell next to mine toward the center received a prisoner too, then a third, fourth, and fifth cell. I soon established from his steps and the way he washed his pail that the prisoner next door was none other than Stanislaw. So I had pitched him into this tomb as well.

The guards were uncommunicative. Everything was strictly routinized, from getting up long before breakfast in the early dawn until evening *appell* shortly after seven. But the most marked change was that, in addition to being held in solitary without anything to occupy me, I was not even allowed to leave my cell to empty and clean my pail or wash. I was the only one in the cellar treated in this way.

The weeks went by, one after another, with no change and no improvement and a stony ignoring of all my requests to speak with someone in authority or the doctor, or at least to be given a French or German book to read. Nonetheless, I stuck to my resolve never to lose my self-control again. As my strength returned I began to do calisthenic exercises once more, refined to counter the disuse of certain muscles and to accommodate the cramped environment of my cell. Occupying half an hour or so before each meal, they provided a focus for the remaining daytime hours.

On the mental side, I organized my thinking into a carefully rationed program. Mornings and evenings I assigned to architectural design. Step by step I discovered that not only were pencil and paper not a necessity, in fact they tended to freeze concepts and imaginative play prematurely. While the morning period focused on the Warsaw reconstruction project, the evenings were devoted to Valley Farm. First I remodeled the eighteenth-century house room by room, to create a livable year-round home. Then I designed two alternate studio-garage annexes, as entirely modern structures but using local materials and bringing them into close harmony with the old homestead.

The afternoons were reserved for an uncompromising self-analysis of a sort possible only after long years of isolation from daily life. I started by seeking out my earliest childhood memories and each day tackled a further five-year stretch, amazed at how much that had long been forgotten began to show up. Then I tried to explore who I really was, what my driving forces were. It turned out to be a painful operation, but my desire to break through disingenuousness and self-deception and establish basic psychological patterns was uncompromising, even if it meant going back a second or third time to peel off another layer. To control myself, I had to know myself. In a way it continued the investigation into the fatal instability of human nature on which Stanislaw and I had earlier embarked.

As I paced back and forth, my eyes searched for faces out of the past in the stains in the floorboards or the irregular shadows on the plaster. Who would emerge this time?

There, unmistakably, was that familiar profile: my mother, with her distinguished bearing maintained through a life of daunting change. She had always found her own way of coping, in defiance of the static Victorian world of manners into which she had been born in suburban London in 1874. It was on a family excursion to Switzerland's Grindelwald that, in 1901 in the shadow of the Jungfrau, she encountered an eligible young American, my father, and was thrown from her sheltered circumstances into a demanding international life in

Zurich. In that last gasp of illusory civility before the events of 1914 descended on Europe, our villa overlooking the lake was filled with grace and ease as she not only raised four young children but also provided an understanding environment for her husband's dual involvement in his zoological institute and his growing commitment to averting the catastrophe of war. When it came nonetheless, the family evacuated to the safer environment of Italian Switzerland, husband and father only rarely able to be with them. After the war there were a scant few years in the old Zurich—and then, in 1921 with my father's fatal heart attack at age fifty-three, it was all over.

At age forty-seven, her life changed forever, my mother had picked up her four children and headed to far-off America to have them grow up in their father's culture, in the Cambridge of his Harvard days. In a sense, it seemed that not until her tragic loss did she become a person in her own right. While lacking the intellectual pretensions of her new Cambridge friends, she clung to my father's Quaker tradition of social concern and plunged into the issues of her contemporary surroundings.

Untrained in analytical thinking, she tended to respond straight from the heart, with a slightly romantic touch that risked overstatement and disappointment. She worked on behalf of the underprivileged and abused in Cambridge and Boston, then became a partisan for labor in the Lawrence, Massachusetts, textile strikes of the late twenties, putting our house at risk as surety to get arrested pickets out on bail. She became an early activist for Negro rights and, with Beacon Hill friends, joined the protest against the execution of Sacco and Vanzetti. She identified with the struggle for women's equality, felt strongly about full access to birth control information, and scandalized her contemporaries by her support of Judge Ben Lindsey's concept of companionate marriage. The generation growing up was what mattered, she said, and she identified deeply and often uncritically with young people, sometimes to the shock of those her own age. She was sought out by young men and women who sensed she would understand their problems without any moral strictures. And they were right. But looking back now, I felt a pang of conscience. Wasn't her activism inspired in part by a deep inner need to share in her children's aspirations? After all, she considered us the ones who would carry on our father's fight for a better world. To what extent had we misguided her? How fortunate that through her death in 1947 she had been spared our family's disintegration.

And Letty—I easily found her profile, with her characteristic pigtails there in the corner near the door. Age seventeen—that was twenty-one years ago. No later image, no mature face that could have been. Usually I killed the emerging outline in the plaster at once: it was too painful. But now it had to be, had to be part of this process of knowing myself. Four years my junior, she enjoyed a progressive education at Cambridge's Shady Hill School, complete with its rigors, mittens in unheated classrooms and all, while I was given the boy's treatment of the Cambridge public schools, an inequality I deeply resented.

Nonetheless, it was with Letty and her friends that I sought intellectual solace. They read books aloud, read and wrote poetry, and smoked, sometimes in mysterious isolation at dusk on the top platform of Mount Auburn Cemetery's tower or just sitting around on the floor playing Bach and Beethoven on the Victrola. At first, the only male in their circle, I felt an interloper, in no way up to their level of perceptiveness, but persistence paid off and more and more I became tolerated. And it was out of that intense sisterhood that I later drew my first wife, Jean.

But back to Letty—as she entered Cambridge High and Latin School, and I Harvard, an unspoken sympathy drew us ever closer together, which in no way diminished as I began to woo Jean. Then toward the end of her senior year she became critically ill and died suddenly from a botched operation. I felt devastated, as never before in my life or since. I have never fully come to grips with this loss of my seventeen-year-old sister and confidante, with all her eagerness for life and knowledge wiped out. Even now in the cellar stillness I could see the Mt. Auburn crematorium and hear the strains of Bach's Air on the G String, played tearfully beside the casket by her former cello teacher, Jacobus Langendoon of the Boston Symphony. For the rest of the afternoon I relived my sister's short life as I paced back and forth, and tried to construct her in full maturity. Where would events have taken her? How would she have responded to the rise of fascism and the inhumanity in which it had buried us all? Even with the rigorous honesty I demanded of myself, the power of her loss remained unabated.

Weeks of self-examination went by. I knew I was approaching a new vacuum in spite of the daily rationing. Maybe I could do the same thing with others, all the people who had happened to cross my life. What an untapped resource! After three years of cellar existence, seven months of them in solitary with nothing to do, I kept on coming to the point where it seemed I had run through every usable bit of material, only to find that the bone had only been half picked.

Now I rationed my excursions into memory from one to four for each afternoon. I tried to piece together how specific individuals from my past seemed to deal with life, who they really were, what motivated them. Having reconstructed my acquaintances' past lives, I then used what I knew to imagine what lay ahead. A lot was bound to happen to them in their careers, their personal lives, as I took them from a known past to an uncertain future and finally to death.

As this phase wound down, I took the main characters in our books and re-analyzed them similarly to see if they still rang true. I especially became absorbed in Rosa and her cellar existence in "Angry Harvest." No wonder: she had increasingly come to share in our own travails, battling through the timeless days and nights for her sanity and survival, searching human behavior for the meaning behind the ruthlessness of which she was a victim. The perpetual "why." She came to fear the loss of her self, her sense of "I," more than death itself—and in the end she lost. Her cellar was mine. If Stanislaw and I ever found each other again, I would want to return to our manuscript. I had so much to add to our portrait of Rosa, to do her justice, to do us justice.

Time again caught up with me. I hit upon a new game, pretending I was back in Cleveland, dean of the School of Architecture of Western Reserve. I re-examined my plans for reorganizing the school's curriculum, set up courses, then took each course in turn and outlined its contents. The irony was that when the problem had stood squarely before me I had given it but superficial attention, whereas now I had spent weeks on something that was never going to happen, right down to the staffing, allocation of rooms, and scheduling of class periods.

I tried in turn to preoccupy myself with more abstract thoughts—the problem of good and evil, of happiness, of ruthlessness in man and in nature generally. Yet I felt distrustful of my judgments. After all, I was filled with anger and bitterness against my persecutors. The evil to which I had fallen victim was a direct challenge to beliefs I had grown up with, including the hope for a more equitable alternative to weaknesses in my own society. How different Stalin's empire had in fact turned out from what we had once envisioned!

And now? I felt no regret about my past attitudes, merely a sense of sorrow and loss. But was it fair to dismiss the Soviet system in its entirety, any more than it was to dismiss my own capitalist world simply on the basis of transgressions during my lifetime? Wasn't the final score to be found far in the future, reckoned on each society's ultimate adaptability over time? After all, it was my own that had tolerated within it the cancer of fascism, leading to the horror of the extermination camps.

Hadn't our own American constitutional process checked the extremes of the misuse of power and provided a limited system of individual protection? The communists, in spite of the promise of their resource and social planning, their original vision of an equitable future for all, had under Stalin sunk into an opposite and unprecedented disregard of human rights. The actuality had turned out badly flawed.

Yet in face of my personal agony and close view of these terrible faults of communist rule, could I allow myself to become an uncritical capitalist yes-man and a fanatical fighter against communism? As I looked at the true villain, which was the human frailty in each one of us, obviously that was not the rational response. And so I tried to isolate my antipathy toward the communists, as derived from personal experience, from the larger instabilities in the interface between man as an individual and man as a social animal. Wasn't my misfortune just one more expression of these?

In my architectural musings, the more I became absorbed in details of design, the more I yearned to test them out in some form. But my hope of getting drawing materials had well-nigh vanished. Was there no other way? I recalled how in 1949 I had written my name on the ill-fated tombstone design with bits of straw. Perhaps this was my clue. I pulled some straw out of my mattress sack and began experimenting. Within a day or two I had worked out a system. I split the straw into thin slivers of varying lengths and thickness to represent lines. If I laid them on the plank frame of the unused cot in my cell, I could give expression to simple plans.

With practice the "drawings" became ever more precise and telling. Each morning I sat down and prepared the day's store of lines, using a system of modular lengths laid out in bundles on my blanket. First I worked up floor plans of residential buildings I had visualized for the farm. I improved the method by contrasting textures and colors for outside and inside by laying down toilet paper to highlight the floor plans themselves. Then I tried elevations, though somewhat less successfully. After thorough study, I erased each "drawing" and created another in its place.

By now I knew my medium well enough to attempt a much bigger project: the site plan for central Warsaw. I reserved the entire floor between the two cots in the middle of the cell for the plan, a space of about thirty by seventy-two inches. Low-rise buildings were laid out on white toilet paper, high-rises were grayed with a layer of dust. Streets, parking, changes of level and terracing, and other outdoor features were shown by straw lines. Plantings and trees were simulated by fluff and dust collected each morning from the floor and the floor joints. Bits of plaster crushed into white powder made for fountains, play areas, and paths. For the green areas I collected dust by the handful from the bottom of my straw sack. Special monumental features were accented three-dimensionally with vague sculptured masses made of compressed bread. As my work chair I used the slop pail, laying folded blankets on its wood cover and shifting it around the floor to where I was working. At night I lay in bed planning. My dread was that the wind, which often blew in through my window when the door was opened, would scattered the bits of paper and straw. And then there was Saturday, when the guard came in and shaved me unceremoniously as I stood trying to prevent him from walking too far into the cell.

Gradually all the remaining free space of my floor filled in with high-rises and vistas, until the only non-built-up areas were the bare bed frame opposite, my own cot, and a small strip at the door for my food bowls. As I retreated to the island of my bed I recalled Robert Louis Stevenson's poem of the bed that had become a ship, and all of the child's room, features of a vast seascape. Those moments of childhood came back to me too when I was served breakfast in bed on a Sunday inside the habitation I had created out of propped-up sheets and blankets. Now as I looked out over the reconstructed city I saw it peopled and lived in—in snowstorms, on moonlit nights, during hot August afternoons. I marveled at its new beauty, watched its traffic circulate unhampered. In the Warsaw of 1965, life would be restful, creative, free, as an urban environment for happiness at last replaced the hideous wasteland handed down with less and less of humanity by successive generations. Each day I made improvements on the previous night's visual analysis.

Unfortunately, my preoccupation had not failed to be noticed first by the guards and then by the officers. Just as in 1949, the light was on continuously at first, the cellar twilight being considered insufficient for prisoner monitoring. Suddenly, though, apparent economy dictated turning off the lights after breakfast until sunset. As my designing came to a virtual standstill, my tension began to grow once more with the prospect, despite all my efforts, of a steady worsening of my circumstances.

Originally I had supposed that my punitive mistreatment would last a month or so, to teach me a lesson. The month passed. Now September was drawing to a close. The cellar draft and damp cold intensified. While I suffered no overt indignities, all indications were that I had sunk to the bottom of the bottom, with no one caring the least about me anymore. Hermetically sealed off; not a soul willing to talk to me, not even to pay minimal attention to the serious health problems that beset me. As the second month passed without change, I began to fear that this state was permanent. After all, hadn't Cigarette earlier threatened that if I insisted on my demands, I would never see normal life again, would settle into a permanent cellar oblivion?

October. The leaves began to fall. The nights became intolerably cold. I knew that I would not be able to survive for long in such conditions. And so, with the dread that I was at last exhausting all remaining avenues of memory and fantasy, I once more questioned the rationality of trying to survive. It would only end in a loss of sanity. I remembered that in those first weeks in 1949 that prospect had been my biggest fear. Now mere survival carried a new dimension of horror. Either they would have to agree to restore my former circumstances and those of Stanislaw, or I would choose to put an end to my life, calculatedly, as a necessity. I was strong enough to accept that now, and I had the hardness to follow through.

That hardness expressed itself in a half-conscious recall of two poems that ran again and again through my mind, out of the deep past and partly submerged. One, in the imagery of Victorian England, was by William Ernest Henley, with the opening lines:

> Out of the night that covers me,
> Black as the pit from pole to pole,
> I thank whatever gods may be
> for my unconquerable soul.

And the other, the determined plea for human decency in the idiom of the Germany just before Hitler and the Holocaust, was Bert Brecht's *Wiegenlieder*, in which the unemployed worker's wife confides in her infant son lying beside her at night. What came to mind especially were the final stanzas:

> Deine Mutter, mein Sohn, hat dich nicht betrogen,
> Daß du etwas ganz Besonders seist,
> Aber sie hat dich auch nicht mit Kummer aufgezogen,
> Daß du einst im Stacheldraht hängst und nach Wasser schreist.
> Mein Sohn, darum halte dich an deinesgleichen,
> Damit ihre Macht wie ein Staub zerstiebt.
> Du, mein Sohn, und ich und alle unsresgleichen
> Müssen zusammenstehn und müssen erreichen,
> Daß auf dieser Welt nicht mehr zweierlei Menschen gibt.

I turned once again to my only remaining recourse: a hunger strike. This time, though, I would fight it on the limited objective of a return to the life of cell No. 1. It would not be a test of strength; it would simply end in one of two stated alternatives—one of which was death.

I was determined not to repeat the same mistakes. I would be calm, cooperative, agree to wash, commit no breach of discipline. I would even stay dressed and sit on my cot to demonstrate my effort to conform to rules. The main thing was to avoid any provocation, any conflict, anything that could exhaust me and break my morale. I would not struggle against the artificial feeding, if it came to that. I didn't have to fear a deadlock. This round, time would be on my side. The consumption of the doctor's time and that of others, the disturbance of routine, would push them toward putting an end to it, one way or the other.

Monitoring every moment of this struggle would in itself be an improvement over the timeless nothingness that otherwise faced me. Thus the situation the authorities had created made a hunger strike more tolerable than a normal day in my cell. This is where they had miscalculated. Before, I had had a lot to lose; nothing could induce me to stick with what I had now.

The first few days of my strike went by quietly. I had collected some bread during the previous week to occupy myself during the day modeling a little dancing figure, an activity that required almost no expenditure of energy. Along with my food, my tea also disappeared, an old trick that I had rather expected. In theory at least, I was once again without liquids, though actually each morning the washbasin was set as usual on my floor by the door. The angle was too steep for them to watch me closely, and so in the process of doing my teeth and washing I managed to scoop some water surreptitiously into my mouth. I suspected that the authorities were aware of this possibility but chose to ignore it despite the attendant health hazard.

On the fourth day I was shifted to the cell No. 5, opposite Stanislaw. I accepted the move passively, whatever its motivation. The cell was the same size as my previous one, with two bed frames and a plank floor. But the floor was dirty and the cell carried a strong odor of dogs, plus the door was all scratched up. Apparently it had served recently as a kennel!

A casualty in all this was my little female figurine, which brought me a touch of gaiety and beauty. It had vanished without explanation. I was doubly sorry, since I had intended it as a little victory gift for Stanislaw in case I won. On the sixth day I was moved back to my own cell. I was already very weak but managed to walk unaided. That afternoon Horsetooth and two guards came to my cell. Without comment a towel was tied around my mouth and I was led upstairs, walking voluntarily but with support. In an interrogation room with padded door and Judas eye I was set down in front of the doctor.

For three months every request to see him had been turned down. And now here he was. I made it clear that this time I would starve myself to death if my original conditions weren't restored, and if the circumstances for drawing and the right to walk were not granted at last. I made no mention of anything beyond that. The doctor warned me that starving myself would have no positive effect. I retorted that I had tried everything else and this was all I had left. The expected rejoinder: if I refused I would be forcibly fed, and where would that get me? I shrugged. That was up to them. I was told to move to the couch. Would I resist? No, I said, but they would get nowhere in the long run. I had nothing to lose anymore and all the time in the world. I smiled wryly. I had turned their own favorite phrase against them.

In the early afternoon for three successive days I was subjected to the rubber tube again. On the fifth day Horsetooth and Padlock visited my cell in the morning and reported that as long as I continued my hunger strike it was impossible for the authorities to make any improvements. I pointed out that I would accept no deal that didn't include my former colleague and that the first step would be to put us together again and reestablish us in cell No. 1 in the other building.

Horsetooth laughed. My colleague? I wasn't doing myself any good concerning myself with him. I showed strange taste, wanting a former Gestapo agent and fascist criminal as my companion. I retorted that I was sure I knew Mr. Mierzenski much better than the honorable officer in front of me and that I regarded it the greatest privilege in life to have shared the last two years with this prisoner. In an outburst Horsetooth said that he knew very well how to deal with the likes of me, and that if he had his way I'd be eating out of his hand and thanking him for it. I assured him that I knew he wasn't exaggerating. Inadvertently, of course, he had revealed that no physical violence was being planned against me from above. I had weathered the encounter calmly and felt strengthened in my resolve.

I found myself increasingly in a sort of euphoria where what happened to me bore little relation to reality. I was simply floating along toward some undefined end. Let them go on with their game. Somehow the physical discomforts had faded into the background; in a perverse way, I was even rather enjoying all the attention, after so many months of being ignored. Again I reminded myself: I had the time, and the patience. In the end it was they who couldn't afford it. The doctor's practice must be tied in knots, having to drive out here every day, all in all two hours at least from Warsaw, including Saturdays and Sundays. It was fun gumming up a bureaucracy!

And so the twenty-seventh day of my strike arrived. I had become so used to the routine, lying now day after day on my cot anticipating the trip upstairs, curious about what turn it might take next. It was almost as if it weren't about me at all, that I was only an observer.

With satisfaction I noted that I had wasted away in spite of all the feeding. I was amazed especially at the sight of my hips. My thighs and buttocks seemed almost to have disappeared, and my hip bones protruded like those of an emaciated horse. With all the stores of fat in my body used up, it seemed as if the muscles themselves were being consumed: on my upper arms, my chest, and my thighs. I reminded myself more and more of that mixture of bones and dried skin I had seen on mummies. The authorities seemed to recognize the deterioration, instructing that I be carried upstairs rather than having me climb up myself.

That afternoon after the usual forced feeding the door opened and Cigarette stood before me—he who pulled all the wires and regulated every detail of my life from the safe anonymity on the other side of the Judas eye. I felt myself hardening. He was the living embodiment of all my suffering. But this time he couldn't intimidate me. I was far beyond that.

His cigarette was hanging as usual from the corner of his mouth, and he exuded his usual air of truculent indifference. But at once I sensed something conciliatory in his manner, and sure enough, he announced that he was prepared to end my solitary confinement, but that it might take a week or more to find a suitable new man to put with me.

"And why not my former cell mate?"

"He is no longer available. Gone."

I answered as calmly as I could. "I'm afraid it's the only basis that could give me the stability to survive here."

Without another word, I was carried downstairs once more.

What now? Actually, could anything touch me anymore? In my weakened state the easy way now was just to continue on to final release. Let them keep sweating over me. It was okay by me. The intolerable vacuum in time had been replaced by directed activity under my control. I was boss, wasn't I? It was a heady feeling, headier the weaker I became. Hunger had become an accepted state and the need for food preoccupied me less and less. All the usual things that held me to life had become tenuous, far off, theoretical, tired. I was no longer filed away timelessly in live storage. My solitary confinement had ceased to be solitary. I was coming more and more to perceive victory as outwitting them by dying in spite of all their feeding. That would be my final triumph.

Toward the end of the afternoon my door opened again. Padlock and Horsetooth entered, looking solemn, as if they were engaged in an important mission. They told me to put my suit on and come upstairs. They helped me into my clothes, assisted me along the corridor, and then carried me like a child up the stairs with care. For once there was nothing threatening in their manner, but the journey was still painful. With the lack of normal body padding, all points of pressure pushed against my bones. Sitting on the stool, supporting myself on the edge of the desk, had become almost unbearable.

The two men settled down opposite me. Horsetooth began: he had been authorized to say that this evening I would be reunited with my friend. The offer was presented with great solemnity, as if it were a great concession.

I hadn't been prepared for this at all—the nearness of suddenly being with Stanislaw again, who at this very moment was there underneath me, unaware of the upcoming big event. Right now—now—I could release him from his suffering, the suffering I had imposed on him. I struggled to hold back tears. But I mustn't cry. Remember the twenty-four-hour waiting period. No, I wouldn't be a pushover now. I slipped back into the wary watchfulness I had developed during these weeks. I held all the cards. I couldn't lose, provided I stuck to my guns and didn't surrender my hard-fought campaign.

"What about books to study?"

"Yes, you'll get these too," came the grudging reply.

"And the drafting table and drawing materials?"

Yes, they would give me all the paper and pencils I needed.

"Will that include the instruments?" I insisted on an itemized list.

Horsetooth was getting impatient, cursing under his breath: "*Z curwi syn.*" I couldn't help feeling satisfaction. Obviously, successful negotiation and termination of the strike was his job and Padlock's. A return empty-handed would result in a sharp reprimand. Yet everything in him strained for a clash, for a violent subjugation of his special enemy. Padlock interceded just in time. Nonetheless, Horsetooth managed to blurt out that I shouldn't overstretch the bow, that this was my last chance.

I said I had nothing more to say and wished to be taken back to my cell. Padlock again intervened, and they held a mumbled conversation. Padlock got out a piece of paper. They laid it before me with pencil:

"Please, then, write down your points."

I hesitated. If I agreed to do so, I would have lost ground for continuing my hunger strike. It would be taken as evidence that I wasn't really serious about a settlement. Was I? In my weakened state, I wasn't entirely sure.

I stared at the pencil, picked it up, then watched the words appear laboriously as if someone else were writing them down.

Reunion with my colleague
Study books
Copybooks for writing
Newspapers
Drawing materials, including instruments
Drafting table
Diet as instructed by the doctor
Return to cell No. 1 in other building, or its equivalent
Regular outdoor walking . . .

I stopped. The two men consulted. Finally the reply: In principle they could go along with me, but at this point they were authorized to agree only to certain demands. For the rest it would take time to make the necessary dispositions. For example, it was not feasible to shift us back to the other building at the moment, but they would give us the biggest cell here meanwhile. And they would give serious consideration to the walking.

I felt drained, only half aware. I kept on having a vague vision of Stanislaw waiting down below for my answer. In turning away, wouldn't I be betraying him yet again? How could I? How? But I needed time to find my mind. My twenty-four hours. I was sure he would understand that reasoning.

"I will give you an answer tomorrow."

They replied that everything was set to make the shift at once, and my friend and I could have supper tonight together still, that he was expecting it and would be disappointed by the delay.

Finally I nodded. I just couldn't say it out loud.

The two men looked exceedingly relieved, although they tried not to show it. As I was helped along the corridor, a junior officer looked out of the adjoining room and gave me a quick, friendly smile, as if to say, "You did it, chum." In fact, one of the things I had sensed in almost all my encounters with the guards, with Angel and most of the officers except Horsetooth, had been a quiet respect, almost amounting to gentleness. In spite of all their indoctrination, simple human decency had shone through. I felt deeply grateful.

Back in my cell I was at once beset with doubts. For a dubious return to a living dead end, I had traded a release once and for all from this exhausting business of living. But had that really been my goal? It was all becoming so jumbled. I needed more time to clear my faltering mind. This wasn't something to rush into. I dragged myself to the door and knocked.

The guard said, "An officer will come soon."

I waited, impatient to break the news that I couldn't give a firm answer until the next day. The door opened. Padlock appeared.

"Come. Follow me."

I wanted to speak. "Later," he said.

He helped me out into the corridor and ushered me into the dingy cell opposite. Without bedding. Just as I was.

"Just a moment," Padlock said and left before I could say anything.

I heard a cell door open somewhere beyond the guard's space on the other corridor wing. There was a lot of coming and going between there and my old cell. I could hear the rustle of straw sacks being carried, a pail. The door of No. 11 closed, and mine was opened again.

"Please, please . . . follow me." I heard it as if I were sleepwalking.

Once again I faltered along the corridor. The guard rushed to support my arm, afraid I was about to fall. The door of cell No. 4 stood open. I entered. How strange—here once more after all these years. Here in No. 4, where I had arrived one night in early September 1949. Two guards helped me to the straw sack. I sat down, drained physically and emotionally. All the images of those awful months rushed back at me. How far away that was, and how much I had changed in the intervening years, though I had never in the meantime been more than a stone's throw away from this very spot. As I looked about me I spotted, as from a previous life, the familiar stains on the walls that had become personalities to me. Yes, there, close to my straw sack, was Kate's face. I trembled.

The door opened. A guard brought in a second straw sack, asking which frame I wanted. I pointed to where I was sitting, the same spot where I had lain those many nights in terror at the sounds on the other side of the corridor.

The door opened again. I could hear the swish of clothes outside, fast steps. A tall, gaunt man with glazed, fixed eyes passed into the cell. I raised my head with effort and stared into the face turned toward me. In its searching expression I sensed shock, mute horror. I knew it was at the sight of me, sitting there swaying, a mere skeleton, unable to utter even a word of greeting. He turned away and busied himself with his bed. My head sank down to my chest. Tears coursed slowly down my face. There was a stretch of silence. Then I knew he was standing beside me. Slowly I raised my head and looked into his strained, pale features.

"Forgive me, Stanislaw. Forgive me. I have fought for both of us this time . . . that we can continue together . . . and help each other . . . whatever comes. And never again . . . will I take any action that is not ours together."

# 20

## Twenty Months of Twilight

Aand so began the most clearly defined period of these years. Its main characteristic was a final adjustment to the existence imposed upon me, a hardened acceptance that all I had was the present and that even in it strength could be found not only to endure but to find a smidgen of joy, if not happiness. There was a prerequisite, of course: no recall of Kate and the boys—not even for a searing moment. And no questions about a future.

It was a sort of maturing beyond bitterness, beyond the storm of futile struggle and equally futile hate. The storm was followed by a deeper acceptance of myself. I was an infinitely small fragment of the world I lived in, of no more account than a black in South Africa or a coolie in China or a scrounger at an American city dump. My misadventure was well within the mainstream of human relationships past and present, no worse than thousands—no—than millions of human tragedies and degradations occurring unnoticed, unchallenged, across the face of the earth, man's home.

Outside of life and yet still alive, I found myself looking at it as if from another planet. I was suspended in space, an observer after death and no longer bound by any relation to the subjects of my observation. My life hopes lay shattered, my career in ruins; family love was merely a distant memory. I had no stake in all that, any more than someone who had once lived and died. But unlike the dead, I still had the privilege of surveying what life had all been about, and I did so with intense curiosity.

Stanislaw and I found a new unity of purpose. In spite of the promises, there was no return to anything like the level of living in the days of cell No. 1. We continued to be subject to the deplorable conditions of this cellar. Even on the brightest day at noon we would have been in constant twilight except for the hundred-watt light bulb in the middle of the ceiling kept on twenty-four hours a day, with natural day and night only distinguishable in the triangular patch of sky above our window boards.

All through the winter months of 1952–1953 we had trouble also with air, worsened by Stanislaw's need for his ten cigarettes a day. Although he always stood below the slightly open window, a haze of smoke pervaded our cell from morning to night. I knew how much Stanislaw depended on this little luxury and so already in 1950 I had decided to live with it. There was also the dampness to contend with, which the fitful heat in the pipes was unable to dispel and which beset us with a vengeance when warm weather came that spring and summer.

All we had in the way of furnishings, besides our cots, was the high drafting table. With no chair or stool, the only way we could work at it was to pile both mattress sacks on one of the bed frames, and on top of them two wobbly bundles of blankets, sheets, and pillows, then perch up in the air, our feet dangling a foot from the floor. We must have looked a comical sight indeed with our improvised eye shields, teetering on our individual mounds behind the big work surface, like two old scribes in the *Pickwick Papers*.

Everything had its place: the stack of copybooks, the current books for study, our dictionaries and newspapers; improvised drinking straws to counter the dirty mugs; Stanislaw's salvaged cigarette pack wrappings for making notes and spent matches for some still undetermined future use. Also pencils, the day's ball of fresh-bread eraser, and my glasses. Or rather, our glasses: we shared them, Stanislaw wearing them when it was his turn to read aloud. With every item in place along the far edge of the drafting table, the remaining space was clear to use as a joint work area. At mealtimes we laid two sheets of newspaper down as a table cloth on which we set our bowls and mugs. In the evening, our day's work behind us, we lifted the table to one side against the wall and made up our beds for the night.

So there was a daytime setup and a nighttime one. Things continued this way, a well-worn routine, throughout 1953 and well into 1954. We improvised a kind of lamp shade with twigs and toilet paper to direct the light toward our work area in daytime and subdue it at night.

In the first weeks together again our first job was to feed the results of our separate mental preoccupations during the preceding months into our earlier "Thoughts on Life," to represent our present selves. Four months later they had been entirely rewritten. The thing we looked forward to each day was the books Stanislaw translated to me from Polish, with a sprinkling in German and French that I in turn read to him. As in the days of Cell No. 1, we followed a sequence of subjects: Egypt, ancient Greece, and Rome were followed by prehistoric man, whereupon we jumped to migrations of early European peoples, a global economic geography, and the history of China and of India, then to art—first a general survey, then German Gothic art, and finally the Renaissance, a subject in which we reveled.

As a separate category we decided to explore biography to get feedback on some of our theories about human behavior. To our good fortune we were able to start way back with a battered volume of Plutarch's *Lives of the Great*. Then in succession there followed *The Diary of Samuel Pepys* of seventeenth-century England (in a new Polish translation, retranslated into German by Stanislaw); the autobiography of that Florentine Renaissance man and scalawag genius, the painter, sculptor, silversmith, and man of the world Benvenuto Cellini; and those classic Chinese Canterbury Tales, *All Men Are Brothers,* in a translation by Pearl Buck, in turn rendered into Polish and now by Stanislaw into German. Then an interlude with *The Pickwick Papers,* followed by Romain Rolland's monumental trilogy *Jean Christophe*, inspired by Beethoven's life. Then a shift to Albert Schweitzer, the Swiss-Alsatian humanitarian-theologian-physician, Bach scholar, and seeker of the human Christ. His *Reverence for Life* came closest to the concept we were struggling to define for ourselves, his search for meaning an exquisite match between active compassion and the wide sweep of his wisdom, between the life of service he chose to follow in the African jungle community of Lambarene and his preoccupation with Bach and his music. And then Thomas Mann's *Magic Mountain*, so close to us in its isolated world of the tubercular sanatorium and the reflectiveness of people like us placed outside of life but still alive. And on and on it went, this heady exploration, month upon month.

Our reading, whether in books or newspapers, also provided us with opportunities to observe the political, economic, and cultural goings-on inside the communist world. As with that extra sense developed during our prison experience, so we had learned to read between the lines and catch the slightest nuances, often by way of observed deletions. We kept close tabs on every shift in Poland's economic situation. We observed the incredibly bad state of the arts, subjected to extraneous ideological dictums. Most of the current theoretical production was unreadable and grotesque.

And behind it all, we watched the systematic Russification of Poland's own traditional culture. In every field of endeavor, Polish scientists were ignored, prewar books of outstanding merit replaced by a flood of inferior Russian translations—this coming on top of the almost complete obliteration of Poland's libraries by the Germans during the war. Whether a student was studying a science or was working in history or the arts, he was forced to turn to Russian sources, with no effort made to fit them to the Polish need. Thus a zoology or botany textbook would focus entirely on various regions of the Soviet Union.

The most visible imposition of this kind was of course the new "Palace of Culture" in Warsaw, against which I had been fighting my own little war. Day in and day out, Poles, from architects to bricklayers to the general public, were told to go there to learn how to do things. What humiliation these Poles must have felt, given their own high tradition of culture and crafts. It must have been especially galling to a people with the pride and sensibilities of centuries of struggle against alien rule from both east and the west. The communists, in their doctrinaire isolation, were bound to alienate every sector of the population in turn by these methods, even when they desisted from using outright repression.

Our wide-ranging reading and study in turn fed into our writing. Once more we went back to "Angry Harvest." We pored over our old copybooks, then decided to start all over again, with little reference to our first version. It had become in a way a surrogate for the diary we could not write, a symbolic account of the dichotomy between an outside world and the cellar twilight of the hunted. And so during the next eight months, as the seasons changed from winter to the spring of 1953, to summer, and back to winter again, so did the seasons in "Angry Harvest," on Leon Wolny's little farm with its closed shutters out in the Polish countryside.

To our writing we devoted our mornings. After lunch, before we took up our serious reading, we focused on the newspaper *Kurjer Codcziennie*—provided it came. Just as likely it would be missing or lacking part or all of its front two pages. Sometimes there were days on end when all we got was a token in the form of the paper's back page, which consisted merely of announcements, local city items, sports, an amusement guide, radio programs, and a serial novel— everything except news. Even so, little escaped us. Sooner or later we figured out why this or that piece of the paper would be absent on any particular day. Our years of experience had made us experts in the art of learning from omission. Although I never knew the details of the successive Czech purges, I had an inkling that big trials had occurred there. I even discovered that Otto Sling and Vladimir Clementis, the latter minister of foreign affairs at the time of my abduction and both former Krakow and London refugees, were being held up for some reason as archtraitors. I recalled my interrogations of 1949. Could this news have anything to do with my misfortune?

In March 1953 the papers stopped completely for some days. We appealed to Angel to allow the back page at least, so that we might continue reading the serial novel. Of course, that did not really interest us; what we were after was the radio and entertainment news on the reverse side, a great source for clues. Several times when there had been local political trials, their broadcasts were listed in the radio timetable. Our pleas for the serial novel resulted in a return of the back page, though the ban on the rest of the paper continued into a second and third week.

Soon we had our first clue: there had been an important death. Theaters were closed in mourning. It could only be a top leader such as Bierut; but then we discovered he was to broadcast a speech. The only alternative was a leading Russian. Finally the momentous discovery: in the radio column the Katowice broadcasting station suddenly was missing. Instead we saw a new station in "Stalinogrod," but with the same program sequence—everything as usual except the name of the new city, which had sprung up overnight. We were excited but not yet sure, despite such strong evidence. We directed our antennae with redoubled concentration. All that April items were clipped out even when we got the whole four pages—evidently a continuing commentary on a momentous event. It wasn't until the May 2 paper that we clinched our suspicions beyond any doubt. It was the usual picture of the annual May Day parade in Red Square with, underneath, the caption: "Malenkow and other Soviet leaders at the Lenin-Stalin Mausoleum." While there were the usual gaps in the text on the page, no one had looked carefully at the caption or the picture. Even we at first missed the newly chiseled additional name on the face of the tomb.

We were in high humor that day. Not just because of our good sleuthing, but because we knew Stalin's death was bound to mean the end of something—an era at least. There would be a period of uncertainty and instability in Russia, to be sure, but it might in time reflect favorably on our circumstances. The Stalin era had held us in its grip; its passing, we thought, could only bring a change for the better. The best evidence was the way our captors did everything to hide the news from us. Now that we knew, it was galling to continue to be deprived of much of our paper, week after week, because of inevitable references somewhere to Stalin's death. We considered reporting to Angel that we knew and so there was no need to continue this nonsense. But that would reveal our alertness, which could mean that further papers would be judged too dangerous or would be subjected to increased censorship. Or it could raise suspicions of a security leak within our cellar and lead to a whole new interrogation. So we decided to live with it and shrug off the big gashes in the paper that each time told of the "great secret" of Stalin's death.

Our silence soon paid off. In June we noticed a continually rising international tension and a new hysterical tone in the papers. Was war just around the corner? What would it mean to us? With Stalin gone, we had hoped that change would gradually come without the danger of world destruction.

Suddenly no papers. At the same time, a radio in a nearby building was kept on continuously, and at news periods turned up so loud that we began to catch fragments, especially in the comparative stillness of the late evening and early morning—words like "international provocation," "American aggression," "frontier violations," and also something about an enemy of the socialist fatherland. Stanislaw became markedly elated; I felt depressed. Maybe a third world war had really broken out, stretching from Korea to Germany, and we were trapped in the middle. We overheard scraps from a guards' meeting in one of the rooms upstairs, all about curtains, methods of quickly blacking out the cellar cells, assurances that all preparations had been made. We both paced back and forth like caged lions, feeling a mixture of fear and hope and horror. What had happened to all our expectation following Stalin's death?

The summer days wore on. The radio hysteria began to subside, as did the interest upstairs in the broadcasts. There was no blackout. Finally we got our paper again, and we were even allowed to know part of the news—the claim of an attempted provocation to start a new war, a coup that had failed. In fragmented bits the uprising in East Germany of June 22 began to emerge. But in the course of this discovery came something else that we certainly were not supposed to know. It was a speech by one of the East German leaders, thanking the Russians for their decisive help in Berlin and for their timely exposure of the archvillain Beria—Lavrenti Beria, head of the NKVD.

We almost collapsed on our cots, and that night neither of us slept. This was a completely unexpected turn. By the next morning we had decided it was much more significant for us than all the blood and thunder in the divided Germany or even Stalin's death. That Beria's repressive machine had had a hand in my misfortune I was sure. Not only were Beria's men the unseen eyes and ears over the face of Russia, but their henchmen peopled the security machine of each of the communist countries in a network that had seemed unbreakable. Right here, among the MBP officers I knew and did not know, how many were Beria men? Blackie of 1949? Cigarette? Both of them, for sure.

What now? Some hard thinking was no doubt going on. In Russia, purge and policy change were inseparable twins. In this monolithic setup, the purging of Beria in Moscow was bound to cause waves, extending as far as right here.

Our hope was given impetus in December when out of various fragments we gathered that Beria had been executed and that a further shake-up of Russia's NKVD was in progress. To counter our excitement and impatience, we concentrated more than ever on our work, setting ourselves one additional task each. For me it was to pick up, at last, a smattering of Polish. Under Stanislaw's tutelage I began to see the unique reflection in it of Poland's cultural linkage of east and west. It was a Slavic tongue, yet much of its roots, its declensions and endings, were Latin in origin. The result was a richness and precision, of nuances in meaning, that seemed to be missing in my own English.

Meanwhile Stanislaw, who had an excellent ear for languages—he claimed any language was easy after Polish—tackled English with a vengeance. As a small child he had had an Irish nursemaid. Already in 1951 and 1952 he had been working on his English almost daily. So it was no surprise when he announced a

Christmas present to me in 1953 in form of a New Year's resolution to converse only in English henceforth in day-to-day conversation, restricting German to our writing and study periods. With three non-Polish alternatives at our disposal, we now made eavesdropping much more difficult.

The craziness of everything around us had its amusing side. That spring, the shower installation opposite us was expanded to include a washbasin and WC, the proud work of Angel. The WC was on the hot-water pipe, and sometimes, especially on Saturdays, we would watch the almost boiling water go down into the bowl and wonder if it would crack. Each time we sat down we couldn't help thinking of the preheated luxury provided for our bottoms. What class! Naturally, the rubber ball in the tank quickly deteriorated, but the unit had been installed so close to the ceiling that the situation couldn't be corrected without disconnecting and removing the tank itself. And so the toilet sometimes went on a flushing binge at the oddest hours, steaming up the whole corridor before a guard woke up and dealt with the situation.

Because we were on the northeast side of the building overshadowed by a projecting corner, not even in summer did the slightest ray of sunlight come down to us. In July one day, someone started driving holes in the outside wall beside our window. It turned out to be the first step toward bringing more daylight and fresh air into the cells. The three-sided wooden enclosures were removed and replaced with bracketed metal frames with cloudy glass panes along the front, the open wings of the windows obscuring the side view. Some three to four feet long, one and a half feet high, they were tipped at an angle toward the sky, thus allowing almost all the outside light to get down to us. The change had one unintended advantage, as we discovered in time. If our left window wing was closed and the other remained at right angles, we could use the latter as a mirror to see along the length of the outside wall, gaining a wealth of additional information about our surroundings.

The new glass screens had some other unanticipated consequences. Hens often came to dig for worms in the damp corner beyond our window. On one occasion, a hen collided with the glass pane and shattered it, giving us our first real view of our surroundings. It was an almost terrifying experience yet wonderful as well. In the interval before the accident was discovered, we confirmed the circular roadway leading to an invisible gate; grass and fruit trees; and beyond them a brick wall that ran roughly parallel to our building. But the most interesting thing was the building behind the wall. We had been aware of some tall radio masts, swaying aerials. We had heard a radio blaring there, windows being closed and opened. Now we could examine the building itself. It was new, long, and much larger than ours—clearly the administrative center of the complex. The many aerials also suggested that it played a major communications role.

Our guards had become such an integral part of our lives that we regarded them not with fear, but with a mixture of amusement and sympathy. Sometimes they seemed like mere children. They had no comprehension of doing anything bad or inhuman; quite the contrary, they were told they were serving their country. One day a decrepit little old character appeared, completing our current set of guards. A single look at him and I felt almost ashamed at the misery and hardship that this human wreck displayed. He hobbled along as if the slightest gust of wind would knock him over. He was so timid about putting our bowl of soup on the floor that part of it always splashed out. With his utter lack of self-confidence, he managed to turn even the simplest operation into a tangle. At each encounter with him, we were constantly on the alert to spare him from embarrassment. We called him "Gnome." The other guards dubbed him "Little Grandfather." It seemed as if he had been rescued just in the nick of time. As the months went by, he began to fill out. At the same time, he seemed to live in a state of constant disbelief at how well life was treating him. His confidence improved as his self-respect grew. His faded castoffs were replaced by a uniform. The final touch was a brand-new pair of leather jackboots. We loved watching his belated claiming of a corner on life. He was the gentlest of the gentle, unable to hurt because he obviously had seen the reality of pain too deeply himself. He and Angel, being the two older ones about, hit it off very well, and Gnome became Angel's devoted Good Man Friday. Often the two would chat for hours in the guards' space.

Gnome's greatest pleasure came, however, from another prisoner in our cellar who for some reason was allowed out of his cell each morning to sweep the rooms upstairs, carry coal, even to shovel the snow on the path outside. Once I got a glance of him through our peephole: an old white-haired man, frightened of his own shadow. Had that fear been acquired in this building? In any case, he was a favorite of the guards on duty, someone to talk to and keep them company on any bit of make-do work. He and the Gnome were naturals for each other. They set about exchanging accounts of their lives, fragments of which we could often overhear. Gnome had spent most of the war years in Nazi concentration camps. Our white-haired colleague plied him with every sort of question. Gnome's biggest fear now was war, which would be bound to destroy the little island of peace he had found here. Both in their own way, guard and prisoner in the silence of this cellar, were absorbed by the same question: Was there any hope for their final years?

The other guards had their misadventures, as on the day Violet had the trust prisoner help clean some of the empty cells. While the old fellow was up at the other end of the corridor we heard the door next to ours slam shut in a gust of wind. We were reading and didn't pay much attention. But then we became aware of a gentle tugging at that door. What could it mean? Was a new neighbor trying to attract our attention unnoticed by others? We listened. He certainly appeared to be signaling. Should we tap back through the wall? Stanislaw said no, it might be a trap. The tapping became louder, more impatient, and finally turned into banging. He was obviously excited about something. Then a muffled voice began calling: "Hello, hello, hello, hello," accompanied by still harder banging. Suddenly we recognized the voice: not a prisoner at all, but Violet. He sounded utterly desperate, banging and yelling with a vengeance, as if in panic: "Hello . . . Hello!"

That gust of wind must have accidentally locked Violet in. There was no handle on the inside, of course, but why didn't the old man come and let him out? Perhaps, taking advantage of the situation, he had decided to try and make a break for it. Evidently the same thought was driving Violet almost crazy. Maybe we were trying to escape too! Although he obviously had wanted to get out without anyone noticing, the only course for him now was to rouse a guard upstairs. No longer worrying about the ridiculousness of getting locked up with the prisoner outside, Violet began to roar like a lion, banging the door with his boots and fists.

No response. Then the intercom rang. That made Violet go almost wild, and he yelled a whole chain of abuses. In the pause that followed we could hear steps on the stairs. Someone knocked on the corridor bar gate with a key. The lock was never opened unless one saw the guard safe and sound in the corridor, lest a trap be in the making.

"Let me out, you son of a bitch idiot! Let me out!"

The other guard was unperturbed. "What's all the noise? Why can't you come here yourself?"

"I'm locked in, you idiot!"

"Who locked you in?" The guard sensed a conspiracy.

"Nobody! *Cholera,* you blockhead, let me out!"

But the other guard was on his mettle. "*Who locked you in?* Tell me!"

Violet began kicking the door in a frenzy. "The wind! The wind, you stupid son of a bitch imbecile."

The suspicion persisted. "Tell your prisoner to open." But strangely enough, the prisoner had evaporated. There was no sign of anyone in the corridor.

After a moment of reflection the guard said, "Wait," and he ran upstairs. He wasn't going to take any chances. Soon he returned with a second guard. Cautiously they opened the bar gate, came over to the cell next to us, and pressed down the handle as Violet burst forth in a mixture of fury and relief.

"Where is he?" The three headed down the corridor; a door opened. A fourth excited voice joined in. As they came back to our end, we got the gist of what had happened. The same gust that had slammed the door next to us shut had also locked the old fellow in the cell he was cleaning. It had been a wonderful show!

In the spring of 1954 the so-called Bicycle Peace Marathon across Poland, Czechoslovakia, and East Germany took place. Polish youth followed this event with the enthusiasm of baseball fans following the World Series back home. Our guards, including Angel, were swept along in the fever, and were quite convinced that Stanislaw and I felt the same enthusiasm. So at evening bucket time, while I was in the washroom, Angel and the guard on duty would stand in the door of our cell and give Stanislaw a blow-by-blow account of the day's fortunes. When I returned with my pail Angel would grin at me and say, "Wait till he tells you. Krusniak outdid himself today!" On several occasions the news came down earlier via the intercom and Violet would tap softly on our door and whisper the results in great excitement. Our guards and we had become an established institution over the years. They knew us and we knew them, and there was no overt hostility on either side. In some ways, the bond between us seemed stronger than between them and their superiors.

My recovery from my hunger strike of November 1952 was slowed down by continued digestive problems. It wasn't until January 1954, after repeated requests, that I once more found myself upstairs face to face with the doctor. This time, to my surprise, Cigarette was not present. Over the years he had made it amply clear that he was in charge of everything here, right down to the smallest detail—including us. And every week we were aware of his footsteps outside, followed by the cell-by-cell check through the Judas eye. He had not been around during the previous weeks, though, and now I decided he must be sick. In any case, it seemed to me that the doctor was not sorry at his absence. He gave me a thorough examination, prescribed some medicines and food changes, and assured me that things would improve. He even listened without interruption to my usual complaints about unfulfilled promises.

By January 1954 we had exhausted ourselves with the final scenes of "Angry Harvest" and sorely needed a pause. So I pushed harder for the alternative of designing, with Stanislaw to provide some of the facts I needed about Warsaw. The authorities tried to evade the issue by supplying us with more books than we asked for. Then a fine roll of tracing paper appeared, with a T square, triangle, and scale, but still no drafting instruments—probably because they could be misused for violence against myself or others.

With the start of 1954 and the absence of Cigarette, Angel came down below more often, often chatting with Stanislaw during my evening trip with the pail and giving him an extra cigarette. Being in charge of the kitchen, he occasionally added a little surprise to our meals, such as new potatoes in scrapple with a mug of sour milk for supper, or a fresh pork cutlet. On Poland's meatless Tuesdays, instead of tough liver or lungs, we found chicken or goose or carp in our bowls.

May went by. With the arrival of warm weather outside, the cold dampness in our cell became an urgent matter. Stanislaw's health was deteriorating markedly from bronchial problems. His heart showed signs of impending trouble, and it seemed only a step to a fatal lung involvement. I could see his strength ebbing day by day. Something had to be done. Though of course the ultimate goal was to be shifted out of this cellar once and for all, we knew that was unlikely. Instead we used the usual indirect tactic: to ask for the apparently lesser thing—which happened, however, to be more difficult for them—in order to achieve what we were actually after. We demanded that they move us to the sunny side of the cellar, to cell No. 11, which I had occupied before our reunion. The catch was, that cell now held an obstreperous woman prisoner. We knew they wouldn't want to tangle with her by putting her into worse accommodation, nor would they want us to be anywhere near her for security reasons.

Whether it was the result of our strategy or some other factor, the next morning Angel whispered secretively: "Everything will be fine. You'll be out of here by tonight."

# 21

## Final Summer

And so it came that one June evening in 1954, Stanislaw and I suddenly found ourselves in the outdoor vastness of trees and bushes and grass and an endless stretch of sky still holding the suspense of a disappearing dusk. A breeze full of scent and the remembrance of a hot summer day blew into our faces and enveloped us.

When the door had opened, we had been instructed to load all our things on top of our stacked straw sacks and carry the whole affair between us like a stretcher. Already in the corridor we had given up. It was too much for us, especially for Stanislaw. So we were told to shed the mattresses and proceed with our individual loads. For the first time in five years we were making a shift without fear and uncertainty over where we might be headed. Extraordinarily, we had been told in advance that we were returning to cell No. 1 in the other building. There were no handcuffs, no covered eyes. We simply walked up visible steps from the cellar and moved through a visible garden among visible trees quietly rustling in the twilight breeze. Just like ordinary human beings.

At first it seemed like something so forbidden that I didn't dare look anywhere but at Stanislaw's back. Then I raised my eyes cautiously, expecting to be reprimanded. I noticed the objects on either side, still radiating the warmth of the sun that had only moments ago disappeared beyond the horizon. I said to myself: Notice everything, every detail. I tried, but I was too disorganized by the emotions surging through me. As we turned across the gravel drive I glanced back toward the outline of the unknown building that had swallowed me five years before, whose cellar I knew better than anything else in my life. Did it look at all as I had imagined from those hundreds of bits of evidence and deduction? I stared incredulously. Yes, it was all there—one story, overgrown with vines, low, the exact size I'd envisioned, with steps and terrace and balustrades.

And yet it was unrecognizable, utterly surprising. How impossible it is to create a real image of something never seen! It's just like trying to draw a picture of a person on the basis only of a lifetime of correspondence. How different all the bits I had seen and heard from the cellar looked as part of an unknown whole. There were the cellar-window glass shields; there the beam of light from a solitary cell. There was the window of cell No. 11, where I had spent three of the hardest months of my life. There the coal hole under the entrance terrace; there the almost unnoticeable small opening next to it through which I had so often gotten tiny glimpses of the outside world while washing. We turned the corner I knew so well from sound alone. There past the sheet-metal gate it lay, the big mass of the second building, not a light showing anywhere. Dead and deserted. Once more I was dumbfounded at how different it all looked from my firm fantasy, though all the details matched. The door stood open in the round turretlike entryway. Inside, I followed the stairs down into the cool basement with all its familiar smells.

Cell No. 1. Stanislaw was already standing in the middle of the floor staring at me as I entered. He had a deathly white pallor. Perspiration had broken out over his face, although it wasn't warm down here at all. His eyes looked feverish and shiny. He was panting, and as I observed him closer he seemed to be swaying.

"Stanislaw, quickly, sit down. What has happened? Sit down! You've over-exerted yourself."

I recalled intermittent heart pains he had experienced during the past year. They had taken his breath and almost choked him. I was frightened. Padlock, too, had noticed. "You can sit down here while we wait for the rest of the things," he said. Stanislaw sat down unsteadily. "I'm all right, I'm all right." He looked around as if searching for something.

I turned to Padlock. "You see, it was high time to get us out of there."

Actually, it turned out that Stanislaw's faltering was more an emotional than a direct physical reaction. True, in his condition this burdened walk had exerted him unduly. The real cause of his weakness, however, had been the impact of the summer evening, the sudden air and space, the first contact in five and a half years with the world outside. It had pierced the armor of strength he had built up, suddenly disarming him with a flow of feelings that could not be controlled, taking his breath away.

How relative everything is. After almost two years in the ghastly cellar next door, this seemed like paradise, and I couldn't imagine ever wanting anything better or different. Now both the south and east windows were open in their wooden enclosures and the summer air poured through the cell. I pushed the head end of my cot right under the window, letting the stream sweep over my face as I later lay in sleep.

In the morning we sat beside the east window as a narrow band of sun beat through onto us. In the afternoon we shifted to the other window. The various harvests came. Scythes cut through the grass. Once more we set up our garden window screen in the strip of dirt that had survived since our departure in August 1952. Once more rye stalks began to weave their way up through the wire mesh, creating a delicate green tracery. Once more various other plants from windblown seeds activated by our daily watering emerged and were nurtured with constant care. And as before, various representatives of the animal kingdom appeared on the scene.

A big green grasshopper strayed into our washroom, and we transferred it to our cell. In daytime it moved in slow, deliberate strides along the edges of our cots or the window grille, its favorite spot. At nights we locked it into our chess box, since the lure of the out-of-doors seemed strong at dusk and we didn't want to lose our new companion. One of its favorite treats was sugar from the bottom of our tea mugs, which we fed to it on the ends of straws as a kind of bribe not to desert us.

Seeing that our grasshopper became increasingly restive toward the evenings, Stanislaw began the laborious task of building a cricket cage in the Chinese manner. He went at it with the persistence of a goldsmith, using spent matchsticks for bars secured by bands of kneaded bread. He even constructed a sliding door for it. As if sensing its coming imprisonment, the grasshopper took off just before the work of art had been completed, settling down, to our chagrin, only a few feet from our window and taunting us with its sawlike rasping call. Henceforth, however, the little cage became the first bit of handicraft to decorate our cell.

Shortly thereafter our biggest animal venture began, and threatened to disorganize our life completely. It all started when a solitary wasp flew in one day at lunchtime and helped itself to some sugar in the bottom of my mug. The next day at the same time it was back, but in the company of a second wasp. The following day three of them arrived, and then things began to grow exponentially.

I was fascinated, whereas Stanislaw tended to fluster and dodge if any came too near to him. In my childhood I had become very fond of wasps. In the summers in Zurich when we ate lunch out in the garden under a big tree there was always a lot of wasp activity and a lot of rescuing to be done as they landed in the apple juice. I got to know individual ones and gave them names, and my favorite ones were rewarded with the privilege of picking morsels from between my lips. I had always maintained that wasps were much less aggressive than bees and only stung as an instinctive response if they felt threatened individually or collectively. Stanislaw generously agreed to give my theory a test—though actually, the risks were all on my side. I had an allergic response to wasp stings, with serious asthmatic consequences. If I was subjected to multiple stings down here, no one would understand what had happened and no treatment would be possible. So convinced was I, however, that I would not be attacked, I was willing to take the chance.

For better observation and mass feeding, I filled my mouth with sweet tea, which I then dripped through a straw onto the flat horizontal window bar. In effect it provided a continuous drinking trough the length of the window. Each day, as the wasp population grew, I had to increase the amount. Often it took no more than ten minutes for the entire puddle to be sucked up. I also kept the tops of eggshells as supplementary teacups for the wasps, which hung tightly packed over their rims. As we got to know them, they caught onto our habits too. They knew exactly when we ate each meal, arriving in a body before the first whiff of food. Not only that, but they had their chosen routes. Some made a round trip in and out through the same window; others came in by one, flew diagonally across the cell, and went out through the other. We experimented with all sorts of changes in routine, location, and method of feeding, and were amazed at the speed with which the wasps caught on. At lunch we provided a choice in diet by introducing little scraps of meat. We found that they specialized, certain ones persistently going for the meat while the rest shunned it entirely. Our observations also confirmed that unless attacked in their own territory, they did everything possible to avoid battle. Indeed, they stung only as a reflex to pain or to a perceived threat of death. Thus, as I became more and more reassured, I also became bolder in letting them eat out of my hand or from my lips. If it became too much, I was not afraid of driving them off.

The danger came not from dealings, but from wasps accidentally wandering into our clothes and getting squeezed or from one of us laying an arm or hand on an unnoticed stray. Quite unfairly, this usually happened to Stanislaw, who during several weeks ended up with three or four stings. He was philosophical about it, though, and never once cursed the wasp or me for his misadventure.

Meanwhile, the good news had spread to most of the wasps in the vicinity. One morning I counted over three hundred at one time in our window opening. All morning long we lived in a continuous drone, as if we were in the control tower of a busy airport. Our guards began to look in amazement and fear every time they opened the door. I couldn't resist a fantasy of the wasps, as our legions, mounting a counterattack that would allow us at last to burst through our barriers. I would dip my hands and head in the tea and, covered in wasps, approach the guard as he opened the door. I would then charge the guard, who would fall back in panic as the wasps spread to him. We would seize his keys and lock him into the cell while we made off.

Most efforts at close contact with other species are filled with unexpected turns. And so it was with us and the wasps. Gradually we were faced with a monster of our own creation, one that in any situation but ours we could have run away from. The wasp population got completely out of control in spite of our best efforts. When we tried to cut back the food in stages, they simply took possession of our cell until we appeased them in desperation. They also retaliated by arriving ever earlier. Originally they first showed up around 10:30. But then they discovered we also had tea at 8. So, just to make sure, they began to turn up at dawn. As they came out of the semidarkness, they were dazzled by our hundred-watt light bulb; charging into it, they got singed, became frenzied trying to get out of the wire enclosure, and then flopped around the room, many mortally injured—the very situation that could lead to indiscriminate stinging. Here we were in a sudden inferno of wasps that were charging, falling and crashing in pain, crawling around stunned, and dying all over the floor, the covers under which we took shelter, and even our heads. When the morning melée subsided and we finally got up, the floor was strewn with corpses—the first day, twenty or so; the next, over fifty; then close to a hundred. We were not only frightened, but we felt awful at the havoc our innocent contacts had caused. The whole affair had turned into a macabre mass slaughter about which we were helpless to do a thing.

The only solution, clearly, was to turn off the light that attracted them in. This we knew the authorities would never consider. Meanwhile, we hardly dared touch anything or sit or lie down for fear of getting stung by a wasp in agony. Finally we decided to stop all feeding and systematically drive out every wasp as soon as it appeared. It took the best part of a week before the crisis was under control and our cell returned to normal.

Our treatment here by our captors was of a level we had never enjoyed before. What had happened? In all sorts of little ways, a change of attitude was evident. Everyone went out of his way to be friendly to us. In addition to Angel's habit of asking us periodically whether we felt all right, rather as if we were patients in a hospital, he was always thinking up little surprises in the way of food. In response to our interest in greens and fruit, a big bowl of lettuce was added to our regular food, later supplemented by cucumbers, radishes, and tomatoes. Holidays were recognized with something special for lunch.

Our life was eased considerably by something more elusive, an apparent change in policy that was never stated outright. We were now human beings like everyone else, with normal human needs, no longer presumed criminals who deserved what we were getting. The strict isolation and all the security rigmarole remained a given, but beyond that we were becoming two individuals who merited consideration and politeness. Even the padlock system had begun to break down. Often now the officer would just send the doorman down with the key, to be picked up again sometime later during the day. We knew right away from the relaxed manner of the guards on duty if no officer came down, or if it was just Angel. When the guards were alone, they would find excuses to putter around the washroom for a chance to chat with us and joke, often with considerable hilarity on both sides.

Typical of the new informality was Clown's proud announcement that he had just married, and his delight when we congratulated him. Or the occasion of the July solar eclipse when, with no officer in sight, Violet posted himself outside our window boards with his piece of smoked glass and gave a blow by blow description of what he saw, rather like a radio commentator at a baseball game.

The new atmosphere was reflected also in reduced attentiveness by the guards to some of the strictest precautions. This led to my being able to salvage a used razor blade unnoticed from a coal bin in the washroom, thrown there absentmindedly by a guard after I had shaved myself one Saturday. Long experience had taught me never to miss a chance that would not come again; I couldn't afford not to have that blade in my possession. First I hid it in the sole of my slipper, and later in a more secure spot in the crotch of the diagonal legs of my cot.

In July we came upon a bit of news that electrified us. Stanislaw had settled down after lunch at the table to read the newspaper out loud while I paced back and forth. He was scanning the headlines as he smoked. Suddenly he put out his cigarette. In an artificially calm voice, he said: "Let's get going. There's a lot today, so don't interrupt."

Stanislaw began quite casually to read some reports on the summer harvesting, followed by a few foreign items, among them (as if of no special relevance to us) a short account from Moscow about a trial of one Rumin, former head of the interrogation department of the NKVD. It in turn referred to an earlier false sentencing of a group of Soviet doctors on the basis of false confessions, extracted by third-degree interrogation, to attempted murder of certain high Soviet leaders. Now Rumin was being tried for using "impermissible criminal methods" against innocent persons, false detention, and other undefined methods impermissible in the Soviet fatherland.

I stopped dead and stared at Stanislaw.

He waved for me to continue walking and made no comment. He went on to other news bits, about exploration in a cave, about the eclipse. Then he read one or two longer items, including the full, momentous account from Moscow. Rumin, it seemed, was being tried publicly, with a lot of fanfare, for doing what had been going on inside Russia unchecked for decades, and which in turn had been imposed on the new communist regimes after the war.

And those practices pointed directly to these very cellars. From one day to the next, what had been denied all these years with a holy vehemence as "anti-

Soviet slanders" had received implied admission. For some reason, the curtain
of silence and denial that had enabled the elimination of millions of defenseless
people had been slightly lifted. This could not be accidental.

Hitherto, anything relating even faintly to trials in the communist countries
had been carefully kept from us by means of the censor's scissors. This was such
a blatant slip-up that we couldn't help wondering. Could it have been a calculated way of making us aware of what was going on while avoiding any official
statement that could cause trouble—a part of that convoluted method of indi-
rection with which we had become so familiar? The forgetfulness of a guard, or
the appearance of three books on the floor when we had only asked for
one—how often the smallest thing that at the time seemed patently haphazard
had in fact carried important signals.

Stanislaw whispered, "Just imagine, Hermann. Even the lowliest guard of
the MBP hierarchy must have read about this trial asking whether it might apply to him, too, in the end. Each participant in the vast apparatus must have
started reviewing his own role and wondering whether his hands were clean."

And down here? Those dealing with us on a day-to-day basis must have
wondered about us, especially about our having been stuck here without any
progress toward a trial all these five years. Here we were, housed all by ourselves
in this cavernous basement, with dozens of people looking after us. At first we
had been archvillains, involved in some conspiracy that threatened the very basis of their communist world. More and more, however, this angle had become
difficult to maintain. By now we were just special, period. It was only a short
step further to suspect that somehow we were simply an accident, a mistake for
which no one had found a resolution. An embarrassment.

This suspicion was not necessarily favorable. With every passing year that
we had been held incommunicado and untried, hadn't it become more compromising, and therefore more impossible, for the Polish authorities to release
us? In the end, wouldn't our permanent elimination seem less costly than a
public admission of the crime?

But against that, we hoped, stood the firm warning of the Nuremberg trials.
Who in the face of such censure would want to take responsibility for doing us
in? And then there had been Stalin's death and, on top of that, the elimination
of Beria. Yet now with this development, hadn't a face-saving device appeared
that would allow our freedom without disastrous propaganda fallout? Perhaps
in half a year? Or maybe we would have to wait a year still; a decent interval was
surely necessary.

We began to speculate who might become the scapegoat. Almost certainly
someone who had had contact with our cases. Cigarette? He seemed a natural,
and we had not seen him since the first of the year. More and more we began to

wonder. We observed the papers with redoubled care to see if any of the top Polish leaders had disappeared from the news. For a while Hilary Minc, head of the powerful planning commission, wasn't mentioned, but then he appeared again. On another occasion President Bierut himself seemed to evaporate, only to turn up on an important occasion in China.

As the summer advanced our spirits were higher than at any point during the preceding five years. For the first time we openly expressed the thought that a year hence we might well be free men once more—provided, of course, that our health held out and no international crisis erupted. There was a new sense of purpose to our lives, a sense of preparing ourselves and of making the fullest use of the remaining time. I even dared to open a tiny corner of my consciousness to thoughts about Kate and the boys, and I discovered the same thing going on in Stanislaw. Cautiously, then, both Kate and Stan's wife, Alina, were admitted into our cellar world. How our release and reunion with our families would come we still could not imagine, but we were sure it was at last conceivable.

After a bad beginning when I bit him severely during a forced feeding in 1951, Bear became the strongest evidence of the changing relationship between us and our guards. By far the most vivacious of the bunch, he was a happy-go-lucky type, a cheerful opportunist who enjoyed life and was the faithful servant of his masters. With his flashing black eyes and superb self-confidence, he would have made an ideal pirate in a Douglas Fairbanks film. Whereas he had initially shown considerable sulky distrust toward me, he had in contrast tried to demonstrate to Stanislaw that he had no such reservations about him. Now, though, he clearly looked forward to contacts with both of us, as during our morning washing, a leisurely half hour outside our cell, and especially the extended Saturday routines, which became occasions for much kidding and laughter. Once, after the Rumin trial, we managed to bring our remarks guardedly around to our five years in prison without any proven guilt or trial. Instead of shutting us up with the usual formula—"You know very well why you are here"—he retorted that all things were bound to end, they wouldn't just keep us in here forever. And then he abruptly switched the subject as he heard steps passing outside the window.

With this first glimmer of a possible return to normal life, I yearned more than ever to put down on paper the three-dimensional concepts that had been coursing through my mind and seen passing expression in the straw constructions on my cell floor. It was the same creative surge that had produced the stacks of copybooks, filled with our thoughts and our novels. For all his eagerness to complete our second expanded version of "Duck Lane," Stanislaw showed a generous understanding of my need. By now he knew that in me the visual medium would always assert itself over the written one. While time taken for my drawing would create a gap for him, he was sure he could fill it in with some activity of his own. He also enjoyed being a kind of Warsaw database for me. So he joined me in working out a strategy that would at last bring about access to drawing instruments.

The first step was to halt our writing temporarily, declaring that we had finished our revisions. Clearly the vacuum would have to be filled: we couldn't just read books all day. Angel said he understood, and agreed that something would have to be done. The implication was that we were relying on the friendly help of the authorities to solve the problem, putting the initiative in their hands to keep everything on an even keel. Already embarrassed at their failure to come through with the walking, they would want to show goodwill with an alternative that would satisfy us. That was the nub of our strategy. But then when two weeks went by, a third, a month, it became apparent that another option would have to be laid before them.

We thus gambled our final card, with Stanislaw all the while praying that they would not call our bluff. If I suggested an additional possibility as a forthcoming way out of our boredom, one that on the surface seemed quite reasonable and harmless but that would in fact be unacceptable for reasons they couldn't explain to us, they would be shamed into acceding to one of our earlier demands as the lesser evil. The bombshell I dropped, therefore, was a quiet request to be allowed to play the violin. I did it in a manner of naive assumption that this way of occupying myself could have no objection from their side. A violin, after all, could be used neither for committing suicide nor for attack on others, presumably the main concern about the drafting instruments.

While I had no expectation that I would in fact be allowed to fiddle, I proceeded as if I assumed that the matter was unproblematic. Not that I wouldn't have been delighted to play: a major deprivation of these years had been the lack of music. In one form or another it had always been a part of my life, passively or actively.

There had been my violin in my youth, pushed aside under the pressures of later years. I had treasured memories of the duets I did with my mother at the piano, the identical Steinway at which in early childhood I had watched her play four handed with my father on Sunday afternoons in the music room overlooking the Swiss mountains.

I made a careful list, which I handed to Angel: the violin, the bow, the chin rest and resin, and then the music, mostly eighteenth century—Haydn, Handel, Mozart, Bach. Also Beethoven and César Franck. I identified the exact composition and even in some cases the German edition with which I was familiar. It all looked overwhelmingly serious. Stanislaw added to this impression by explaining how I had played all my life, a gross exaggeration.

Poor Stanislaw. "But what if the violin in fact turns up, and not the drafting instruments or the walking?"

I understood his panic: what could be more awful than being locked up with a badly played violin, especially when you have no bent for music yourself?

When Angel found himself staring at the list I handed him, it was all too incomprehensible for him to have any opinion. He seemed relieved, however, at the mere implication of some solution. So after a moment he nodded and beamed all over. Bear, listening in the doorway, was amused beyond words. This new gambit completely fitted his image of me as a crazy American. In the evening as he opened our door, he shook his head bemusedly and laughed. He said it was the best idea ever to improve life down here for such as him, and he began to snap his fingers in syncopated rhythm, saying I was to play all the latest hits.

We were sure that my violin playing request had spread throughout the enclave by evening, and that most of the guards knew about it. Certainly ours did. The next morning Padlock turned up at breakfast time in great consternation, my list in his hands. He appealed to me: Whoever had heard of prisoners being allowed to fiddle in their cells? Nowhere in the world! He agreed that some sort of occupation was needed. "But here in your cell? How could you play? It would be heard all over the area!" Bear, at the door, grinned at the notion.

I replied with studied naiveté: "But what would that matter?"

Padlock did not know how to reply. I pointed out that I was suggesting it only because I couldn't follow my professional bent due to lack of drafting instruments, and walking had been ruled out. He threw up his hands in despair, looked from one to the other of us, then finally burst into laughter himself as he turned to the door.

We paced back and forth, Stanislaw distinctly miserable at the thought the fiddle might win. Meanwhile, I imagined Padlock presenting the matter to his superiors, trying hard not to look silly. That had no doubt happened to Angel when he had gone to Padlock, and Padlock had entered our cell convinced there was something horribly garbled here. But he had found himself unable to challenge my case and so had beaten a retreat. By tomorrow morning it would no doubt be Cigarette's turn to test my sanity.

But there was no Cigarette and no next morning to wait for. Some ten minutes later we heard steps passing briskly outside—Padlock and a second officer. They entered upstairs. We were sure they were heading our way.

The door opened and Padlock and Friend marched in, smiling solemnly. Then they ceremoniously handed over a set of drafting instruments. I bowed and took the black case and opened it. We all stared at the neatly arranged pieces in their velvet slots. I had been right. The violin, according to the logic we had become so familiar with, had given birth to the drafting set. Bear, peering in the door, was shaking his head in mock disapproval. And Stan? He looked as if he had just escaped being put in one of the punitive cells!

At once I set about organizing my work. I had everything I needed: an excellent drafting table; T square, triangles, and scale; a big roll of the finest-quality tracing paper; and now a beautiful new German drafting set that must have cost a mint. There was one final touch of craziness: while I had been granted a whole arsenal of spikes—the shaft of the drop-center compass could be unscrewed into a slender four-inch-long spear, more than enough to reach the heart—I was refused thumb tacks as being too dangerous. (Perhaps they were afraid I would swallow them.) Provided instead was medical adhesive tape.

Several mornings later Bear, acting quite secretive and nervous, had a private chat with Stanislaw in the corner of the washroom. I was filled with curiosity and couldn't wait until we got back to our cell. Stanislaw said he had a very important question to relay to me: Did I know anything about canaries? Why yes, canaries had been constant companions from early childhood in Zurich through high school in Cambridge.

"Good, very good . . . Do you think you could design a canary cage? A beautiful one?" He glanced sheepishly to where the empty grasshopper cage hung on our grille.

It turned out that Bear and a colleague had bought a pair of canaries for breeding. In their spare time they wanted to build a cage in the prison workshop here, but they didn't know the first thing about how to make one. Bear had seen his opportunity: Here was an architect *and* was a set of drafting instruments. Would I take on the task?

I was both startled and amused. After five years of inactivity, this was to be my first concrete project? Here was a client right on my doorstep—and he wanted a canary cage! Well, why not? It would present all sorts of intriguing problems. A bit strange, though: I, who knew all about being confined against my will, turning my creative efforts to confining others.

I shrugged and said yes.

Bear was delighted. "The most beautiful cage you can imagine!" He spread his hands to express the grandeur he envisioned.

I made a number of sketches and let him see them. With his approval I started on a cage with a barrel-vaulted top, made of wire rods and all worked out for mass production in a factory. In addition to plans, elevations, and an explanatory isometric showing the finished assembled cage, complete with perch locations, swing, glass ground-floor protective surrounds, a bath, and a nest housing, I made an identification list with a picture to scale of each piece of wire, metal, glass, and wood, and beside it its dimensions and the number of pieces, with symbols keyed to the plans and elevations. The texts were lettered in Polish with Stanislaw's help.

For a week, every morning found me working feverishly as the project took shape. Finally it was done, and the next Saturday at bath time I handed the roll of drawings over to Bear, making sure he understood every detail. He was immensely impressed that every wire had been accounted for down to the last millimeter and that the drawings were so explicit and easy to follow. I assured him that they could indeed start him on the road to becoming a canary cage millionaire if he went into mass production. To be sure, I doubt whether any canary cage was ever honored with such careful documentation on paper.

No one upstairs showed any interest in what I was drawing. All they cared about was that they had got me off the violin jag. Bear never referred to the project except when he was quite sure he couldn't be overheard, on which occasions he reported on how handsomely the cage was taking shape. The scars on his arm and hand had been forgiven.

Stanislaw was quick to devise a way of dealing with his free mornings. Although he had always claimed clumsiness with his hands, the episode with the grasshopper cage had shown that this was not so. Now he hit on the idea of fashioning a rectangular basketlike receptacle for our window grille to hold odds and ends. First he constructed panels of matches in crisscross pattern in superimposed stories, with a kind of "plywood" bottom made of sandwiches of compressed kneaded bread between matchbox wood. Then he made long strings out of bread of various shades from light brown to black, using graphite and cigarette ashes as toners. These strings he wove into beautiful patterns as borders to cover the joints and finish off the top and bottom. He advanced to making flat braided ribbons of various widths and designs, and circular twisted-strand cords. With each passing day his technique improved, as did his inventiveness. Finally, after some two weeks, the effort was rewarded with a piece almost as strong and hard as genuine basketwork.

As I began at last on the preliminary studies for the development of central Warsaw, Stanislaw started the ambitious construction of an oval food basket for our table. It was to have flared sides and an intricate pattern of overlapping matchsticks on a plane both slanting and curved. I marveled at his patience and perseverance.

The center of Warsaw: each day it became more real to me. In the year and a half since my straw sketches on the cell floor I had studied Warsaw's urban problems through every scrap of revealing information from papers, from the big *Six-Year Plan* volume that again shared our cell, from the biweekly illustrated magazine *Stolica,* and above all from Stanislaw's unbounded knowledge of sites both aboveground and beneath the city's ruins. I made my own scaled street grid, complete with detailed infrastructure data, as the base for the emerging designs. My concept was for a raised central terrace mall extending over an area roughly one thousand by five thousand feet, bounded on two sides by the Marszalkowska, Warsaw's main north-south thoroughfare, and the Jerosolimska, its main east-west corridor. Out of this platform would rise a widely spaced grouping of some sixteen state and local administrative buildings varying in height from five to thirty-six floors.

This complex would directly link at its southern end with the traditional axis of royal historic Warsaw, so-called Saxon Park. The northern part would lie directly above the shambles of Warsaw's main railroad infrastructure, already under reconstruction. In addition to lively retail nodes, there would be a hotel complex and a multimodal transportation center bringing together national, commuter rail and urban subway and surface services, including an in-town airline terminal and ample under-terrace parking. With this layered scheme I would be able to counter the unrelieved flatness of the largely destroyed central city and at the same time provide expansion space for many decades to come in a carefully planned sequencing of growth. A wide variety of restaurants and night spots would be featured, in accord with Warsaw's lively past. The under-terrace edges would have the potential for shopping arcades, while the terrace itself would allow for continuous pedestrian movement paralleling the Marszalkowska, with access to the park and recreation area. Automotive traffic would in turn move unimpeded at the street level below, a separation completely neglected in the ongoing reconstruction of Warsaw.

I approached the project at two scales simultaneously. One was the overall three-dimensional and organic pattern of urban design; the other focused on the detailed design of individual buildings, an open-ended process that could be stretched into years of activity. I made a month-by-month schedule to take me into the summer of 1955. Yes, I would need that long, provided there was no slippage or interruption.

And so with a heat stoked by five years of idleness in my chosen field, I got under way at last. I started by analyzing the restrictions created by existing underground trackage and imposing new patterns for these; I would then move on to the rail platforms, tunnels, and vertical communications (escalators, elevators, stairs), finally ending up eleven stories above ground in a starlit glass night spot atop the hotel complex. To my surprise, I found I had become awkward at expressing myself visually; my sketches seemed clumsily diagrammatic. The material I had gotten my hands on in recent months was of little help, and anyway, what I did observe second hand from newspapers and *Stolica* was so alien it seemed to have no relevance except as a warning of what not to do.

It was especially galling that this awkwardness of expression occurred just when I was driven with a new sense of direction and creative responsibility. Henceforth, I knew, I would insist on the holistic imperatives in design, the inseparable link between the individual artifact and its larger physical, social, and economic environment. Design that violated the integrity of its environment could not be considered good design, no matter how creatively brilliant it was. What I had earlier sensed, and what had driven me out of the architect's essentially exploitive role in the private sector into public-sector planning and design, now provided me with much clearer directives for the future. I was at a new beginning.

While I limited the actual drawing to the morning hours in order to continue our joint work programs the rest of the day, my mind kept on returning to design details, even as I lay on my cot at night or in the predawn hours. I could hardly wait for breakfast to be over to get back to the drawing board and set a whole new sequence of ideas down on paper. Having no place to store the many sheets of tracing paper, I began to hang them up, one beside the other, in a band that gradually extended around our cell. In time a second band took form above it, and a third below. Aside from enabling me continually to evaluate and tie together what I had already done, they gave our cell a homey character, animated by the imagined metropolis outside, one that Stanislaw related to as much as I. He would often stop in front of one of the sheets, and hours later a question on some detail showed that he too had become involved, as he evaluated the design from the "grass-roots" level of a lifelong inhabitant of the city who had experienced its former double life of splendor and squalor and, more recently, its convulsive destruction. So I pretended that he was my client, representing the Warsaw public and administration all in one.

Meanwhile, the summer had passed. We both had found a new contentment in our timeless existence. The approach of my sixth winter and his seventh underground held no fear or desperation for us. By this time next year might not we both be free men, even though our cases had nothing to do with each other?

Surely that was one of the conundrums the authorities were now dealing with: having put us together in 1949, with no contact with other prisoners since, security would never allow one of us to be freed without the other. No matter how unrelated the constructs that had brought the two of us here originally, now we were one single problem. We called our condition "double solitary." Stanislaw's release would be the more pressing in view of the many Poles cluttering up various facilities, all of them in one way or another connected with this ruthless attempt to rewrite Poland's history of the war in favor of the communists.

To admit that they held *me* would be much more difficult. All the evidence pointed to their having carefully obliterated all traces of having picked me up in the first place. However, with Stanislaw out, the secret of my disappearance would become quickly known. So simultaneous release would almost be essential. I didn't envy Poland's government the fix they had brought upon themselves. Our assumptions aside, though, we took some elementary precautions, including making a solemn pact that whichever of us got out first would do whatever he could to spring the other one too.

In my intense preoccupation with my project, I paid only cursory attention to a number of small incidents that, had I been more aware, would have provided me with tantalizing clues about the future. The first came with a visit by Padlock one morning, who asked Stanislaw out of the blue whether he had taken advantage of the amnesty of 1946, which granted immunity from prosecution for wartime actions. This was a great surprise to him, since he had been carrying his amnesty document at the time of his arrest. The fact that he had indeed signed it had hindered the authorities in their interrogation of him; because of it, they hadn't dared to try him publicly on the trumped-up charge of covert subversion in the months surrounding the war's end. Stanislaw mused that it was as if an entirely new person had reopened his case, someone unfamiliar with the details. Still more significant, the raising of the amnesty issue put the emphasis on Stanislaw's innocence. The incident confirmed our hunch that he might be the first one heading for release, perhaps as early as next spring. I stepped up the tempo of my work. Could I squeeze my program down from twelve to nine months?

Some days later—it was late September already—Stanislaw was called upstairs. Again no Cigarette. Instead a newcomer, who asked a number of apparently unrelated questions that were already on the record. Then quite casually, in a sudden change of subject, he said: "And tell me, what is the state of your colleague's health?" and after a pause, offhandedly: "Are you aware of his ever having been beaten or otherwise mishandled?"

Down below afterward, we decided this was just another of the familiar games of misdirection. It hadn't been about Stanislaw at all. The concern had been solely with me, and obviously Stanislaw was the most reliable source. This was an exciting turn indeed.

The next evening there was another surprise. Shortly after we had bedded down for the night and were lying watching the antics of our three current mouse companions as they dashed along the pipes and up and down and across our cots, we heard activity out in the corridor. Someone had come down. As the door swung open we both posed the same question: Which one? Most likely Stanislaw again. I hadn't been taken upstairs since my visit with the doctor half a year ago in the other building. Stanislaw started to get up, but Angel grinned and, shaking his head, pointed at me.

Upstairs I immediately spotted the big shiny head of the doctor behind the desk, and beside him the same officer who had been present in January. I felt let down: Why the doctor? I hadn't asked for him, though in fact I did have a few specific complaints. He smiled and asked me how I felt. He looked me over from head to foot, carefully checked my lungs, heart, and blood pressure, tapped my knees, felt for lymph nodes, ran his finger down my back, examined my mouth and throat, and inspected my rectal complaint. To my inquiry as to my general health, he gave a detailed evaluation.

I had been especially concerned about my heart after all the abuse of the hunger strikes and asked him about it in such a way that might elicit some information about my future.

"For example, will I still be able to go skiing?" A rather ludicrous question in view of my circumstances.

Both men laughed, and the doctor replied, "Certainly you'll be able to, why not? Within the normal scope of activity for a man of forty-four, of course, and with a transition period—not the day after you get out of here." Again he smiled, and as I prepared to go downstairs he added: "In that respect, I think we can do things to speed up your recovery."

When I reentered the cell Stanislaw looked at me expectantly. I told him what had happened. "Why did he want to look you over so carefully?" he asked. "There is something more behind this, for sure. Remember what happened yesterday."

I had had so many disappointments that I held my hopes in check. Nonetheless, as I lay and thought over every detail I had to admit there was something different about all this, though I could not put my finger on just what. Not so much in what was said as in an indefinable feeling, which only an "old bear" prisoner's heightened senses could detect.

The next the morning, in the assured privacy of the washroom, Stanislaw whispered: "Is it 82 Corringham Road? Kate's address in London?"

When I said yes, he asked me to repeat the Polish address I had for him. We had gone through this exercise before, but this time it seemed like the sealing of a sacred promise: neither of us could accept freedom while the other suffered on in this cellar oblivion. Only one fulfillment was possible: the reunion of both our families. We shook hands and looked in each other's eyes, then returned in silence to our cell and to our respective preoccupations.

Soon I was engrossed in a series of perspective studies for the vast interior concourse of my central transportation terminal. Lunch came as usual, after which Stanislaw read aloud from the day's paper. Then in the afternoon we shifted to our current joint studies. We were in the middle of a history of art from the early Christian period to the present, a translation of a monumental work by the French art historian Pierre Labadou. Now we were into English

Gothic architecture, one of my favorite periods, and every now and then I interrupted Stanislaw and expanded on various points from buildings that I knew.

Stanislaw continued to read as I paced back and forth, listening attentively, while my eyes scanned the drawings on the walls. I loved the peacefulness of this hour, the sound of Stanislaw's voice, the wide horizons of our joint explorations, the English cathedrals. It was our earned period of relaxation each day, which in turn provided for hours of discussion later as we lay on our cots.

We gradually became aware of activity outside. Once or twice Stanislaw stopped a moment to listen, then continued. Those definitely were Friend's steps on the sidewalk. And upstairs Bear was calling to another guard outside to get his jacket on and be ready. How often we had heard the bustle of the changing guards, the laughter and chatter, the good-byes, the hurry-ups—fragments of normal life drifting down to us.

My attention was caught by the clicking of the bar gate at the other end of the corridor. It must be Friend. But what brought him down here at this hour? Steps approached. Stanislaw stopped reading. We both looked toward the door as it opened. Must be something special. A new book? Or was one of us going upstairs?

Friend looked flushed and excited. He pointed to me and asked me to precede him upstairs. The room into which I was ushered was empty: no one behind the desk, no doctor, no officer. Friend hurried in breathless behind me and stopped beside the desk.

He knew no German, just a few isolated words, so started off in Polish. I got the gist of it. "You will travel now." He waved his hand toward the window. "Better food. Good diet. Fresh air. Walking. Understand?" I was perplexed. He tried again with some German words thrown in: "Yes, everything. Very good, very good. Walking." Again he pointed to the window. "Just a moment," and he disappeared through the door, leaving me alone in the room. Such a thing had never happened before.

I felt a momentary rush of excitement, but then the "old bear" syndrome kicked in: Hold yourself, Hermann. Hold on. Unknown change would require all my strength and alertness. Feeling seeped away as I waited, tense and watchful. Rapidly a number of scenarios we had discussed passed through my mind. The one that most haunted me was some sort of localized release, perhaps at the price of never being able to return to the West, a renunciation of any reunion with Kate and the boys. A mockery of freedom with an unacceptable price tag? The image grew. Once more the carrot and the stick? What if I backed away, what then? Stanislaw had warned me: Don't close the door if you reach that stage. They would have no face-saving way out after such a maneuver.

Friend reappeared, still breathless. To my surprise I was on my way back downstairs. "In few minute we go auto," Friend said in his broken German as the cell door closed behind me.

Something was wrong here. There was the book lying open on the table, my glasses on it; but Stanislaw was gone, gone without a word of good-bye. Was this a new form of solitary to force some confession out of me? Why else separate us?

There was no time to be lost. My mind focused on the razor blade hidden in the legs of my army cot. It was essential I have it along. If everything went against me, I'd still have one way out. I bent, pried it out, and slipped it into my glasses case, then shoved the glasses in on top and put the case in the outside pocket of my suit jacket.

Already the door was opening again. Friend beckoned to me. I looked around, saw my drawings on the wall, Stanislaw's baskets. I indicated I wanted to take the drawings down. He nodded reassuringly. They would follow me later, he said.

"And where is my colleague?"

Friend waved. "Already gone in auto."

Did that mean ahead of me to the same place? How much I wished they had left us in peace this afternoon. All the carefully, painfully erected structure of our prison life seemed on the verge of collapse.

I followed Friend's bidding and left the cell behind me. Accompanied by him and Violet, I found myself turning off the corridor upstairs, descending through the circular entry, and walking along outside the building in exactly the opposite direction from the one taken that evening last June. Vaguely, as if in a dream, the golden colors of the fall came through to me. Now we were passing through the wall beside the kitchen lean-to, and there ahead of us on the gravel driveway beside the other building stood the Red Cross van, its doors open. At once I was struck by the incongruous sight of a big, worn, upholstered armchair dominating the interior. With some effort I was made to understand that this royal seat was meant for me. I clambered in and dropped down on it, facing the open back doors.

Behind me, Friend placed himself on a small folding seat, and on short benches on either side sat two of our guards. Friend asked me if I was comfortable, and I nodded and laughed. There was something so sublimely ridiculous in the question. Friend, too, and then the guards seemed caught up in the humor as I crossed my legs and settled back into the depths of the chair in mock grandeur, my knees sticking through the frayed edges of what had once been pants.

The door closed and we were off. The lower half of the glass panes on each side were obscured, only the upper part being clear. From my deep seat, then, I could only see things on a level higher than myself: the roof of the building whose damp cellar had housed me for so long, the tops of passing trees, the prison wall, the top of the gate swinging shut behind us.

Through the oval window of the door I could see the dusty road rushing away behind us. A little farther back the outline of a heavy open army truck appeared and disappeared in successive clouds of dust. Clinging to the wood slats behind the driver's cab stood Bear in a big cape, talking animatedly with a guard I had never seen. The roofs of farm cottages flew by as we picked up speed, now on a good macadam surface. From the train and road sounds Stanislaw and I had roughly located ourselves on the marshy east bank of the Vistula, some five miles south of the Poniatowski Bridge leading into the heart of Warsaw, on the outskirts of a suburb called Wawer. If this analysis were correct, I was now on the Warsaw-Lublin highway, heading north toward the city.

Gradually a high embankment appeared on the river side of the road, with people strolling along the top. People, real people in the course of a normal day, probably on their way home from work. For the first time in over five years! I was panting as I saw ever more silhouettes of strollers flitting by at a strange angle above me against the sunset sky. It was as if I were sitting stationary, watching a revolving stage.

Soon the embankment vanished. Blocks of scarred, neglected tenements flitted by. Lights had begun to go on in the windows here and there. A kitchen, a living room, another kitchen, someone lazily leaning on a sill. We swung to the right and stopped. A traffic light. We got going again, swinging left onto a smooth roadbed.

Suddenly I was looking straight into a crowded streetcar that we were slowly overtaking. There was something utterly unreal in the many different faces, the gestures, the various attitudes of talking or staring out of the window. So much color. So much youth. Women—women trimly made up in nicely fitting clothes. Everyone going somewhere in an accepted routine, completely unaware that in this van right beside them I was almost going crazy.

I caught sight of landmarks familiar from *Stolica*, the papers, and the planning book: the National Museum, the Communist Party headquarters—one of the better of the new buildings—and then, as we turned left onto Nowy Swiat, a glimpse of the modern department store a little way up the Jerosolimska. I already knew where we were heading: up Alea Stalina right to the headquarters of the MBP, where I had disappeared five years ago.

A new thought came: This was no ordinary transfer. Release? Perhaps, and indeed, why not? Wasn't everything pointing that way? Just as anticipated, we swung in through the iron gate and into a courtyard. In the windowed walls I at once recognized that far-off past, the view through the muslin curtains. It was dusk by now and twilight already enveloped the courtyard.

The van door opened. I half expected to see Cigarette. Instead I found an official who beckoned me, but instead of leading me to the courtyard entrance he pointed to a black passenger car drawn up right beside us, its rear side door conveniently open to receive me. Before I had time to think I found myself sitting between two impassive men in overcoats and hats; in the front seat another dreary-looking hatted individual sat beside a youthful driver.

We were already creeping along in the half dark behind a similar silent car with colorless men in coats and hats. My case had evidently been settled. Instinctively I felt my side pocket. The glasses case was there.

My dread increased. We were recrossing the very bridge that only fifteen minutes earlier had brought me into the city from the east bank. With every passing minute the traffic was becoming thinner. I tried to distinguish road signs that every so often popped up in the headlights, but they were usually gone before I could make them out. East: Russia . . . Siberia. Another half hour and we would be at the frontier.

Suddenly the car in front slowed down and we came up close behind it. A red light signal popped out on its right-hand side. The car turned and we followed. I missed the sign, but at once I was alert to the change of direction. We were no longer going east but south, on another broad, tree-lined highway.

We crossed a major road junction and this time I caught sight of the word "Lublin." One thing was now absolutely certain: our destination wasn't the Russian border. Perhaps I was just being transferred to another prison. Probably in the car ahead between two similar men was Stanislaw. At the end of this trip we would find ourselves in the same room once more. But where, and why?

We slowed down. The car ahead of us turned right off the highway, and we followed. I again missed the sign. The aroma of pines began to envelop us. We were bumping along a country lane as the forest loomed up on either side. So we were not heading toward Lublin either. My fear returned. A lonely forest at night. Hadn't we set "Duck Lane's" tragic scene of the secret execution and burial of a Jewish family by the Gestapo in a pine forest in this very region? Other cases from the war flashed through my mind. Vilna . . . Katyn. We slowed down, and I tensed instinctively. Were we coming to a halt in this no-man's-land? We swung to the left, and as we did I spotted a sign: Otwock.

So we were in the Otwock pine belt, some fifteen miles southeast of Warsaw. What had Stanislaw said about Otwock, aside from the fact that it lay on the Lublin main line and was also the end stop of the electrified suburban nar-

row-gauge railway? I recalled that it was also a sort of health resort for the Warsaw area, its pines and sandy soil considered beneficial for respiratory ailments.

After another turn I suddenly saw some lights among the trees. I couldn't
believe my eyes. Some distance beyond a high wire fence I saw the outlines of
what looked like a small flat-roofed stucco villa. Its broad windows on both
floors were illuminated, as was a two-story stairwell window over a cantilevered
entrance canopy. Only now did I notice some soldiers with rifles by the road as
we waited in front of a wire-mesh gate, which a man in civilian clothes hurried
out from the villa to open. We drove in and followed a neglected loop driveway
right up to the main door of the house; the second car remained outside the
fence.

I stared at the trim white structure, a pleasant example of the so-called international style. It looked almost corny in its romantic fairy-tale setting, lit up
by the reflection of our headlights on the white sand. The car door opened, a reassuring voice beckoned me to get out, and I sleepwalked along a path, in
through a door, up a carpeted staircase, and into a brilliantly lit, modern living
room warmed by a big glazed-tile oven. A little man with a diminutive mustache and wearing a cap was at my heels. He made a sweeping gesture and
beamed. "*Schön, nicht?* For you. All for you." He spoke in halting German,
pointing through an inside glass door to an adjacent room with a dresser, circular table, modern chairs, bedside lamp, and carefully made up metal bed that
looked as if it had come from a hospital.

"Your bed . . . But you are hungry? Supper, yes? And what?"

I stared at him as if he were crazy. Asking me what I wished! I shrugged
helplessly. I felt weak and asked if I could sit down. He laughed at the question
and quickly pushed an armchair up to me.

"We have eggs and ham and cheese and sausage and milk and tea and rolls
and butter . . . Well, how about it?"

I felt paralyzed.

"Well, leave it to me . . . Meanwhile, my comrade here will keep you company."

The man who had opened the gate held out his hand to shake mine. Was I
allowed to? He was a rather heavyset, somewhat intellectual-looking man with
observant eyes and a big shock of dark hair. He offered me a cigarette and
pointed to the book he had been reading. In good German but with an accent,
he asked if I knew it. It was a new novel by Ilya Ehrenburg. I shook my head but
added that I was familiar with *The Storm*. He continued on the matter of books,
and soon we were talking about Thomas Mann. He asked me about American
literature, and I told him about *The Naked and the Dead,* the last American

book I was aware of. He wanted to know if I had ever done any writing, and I told him about the 112 copybooks filled over the past four years. This immersion into something specific helped me. It was the first time anyone aside from Stanislaw had spoken seriously with me as an equal. It was intoxicating.

A third man appeared, carrying a tray with a plate of four sizzling fried eggs, ham, rolls, butter, and cheese. Behind him hovered the little man with the mustache—he reminded me of the perfect Swiss hotelier—clasping his hands, apologizing for the makeshift meal. Tomorrow morning, he promised, he would make a list based on my preferences and go to the market himself. I shifted to the table. The sight of this profusion of food on real white plates with real cutlery, served on a table complete with white tablecloth, made me feel like a child. Wherever I was and whatever this meant, I would enjoy the make-believe for all it was worth. What harm was there in playing Alice in Wonderland for a spell?

I recalled a picture book I had read to Hugh and Alan once about a boy who, after being tucked in by his mother and going to sleep, had somehow gotten onto his rocking horse and ridden it up and up to a fairy castle, where a princess had beckoned him from a window and invited him to a tea of wonderful things. I felt very much like that little boy now.

After supper the heavyset man asked if I liked playing chess. I agreed to two rounds. It was a first shot at reality. I was promptly defeated both times. I decided to go to bed, not being used to late hours. I was shown into a fancy tiled bathroom. Before crawling under the covers I went to the window and pulled the curtain a little to one side, peering out into the night. It was clear; the moon, almost full, shone through the pine trees onto the sandy soil, which was covered with patches of needles and tufts of grass. A little ways off I could make out the fence and a human form, a sentry, pacing slowly along it.

I lay down, trying to recall the date on our paper that morning. September 29. Every now and then someone would tiptoe into the living room to peek through the open door toward my bed. Although the light from the corridor created a half dark in which I was still clearly visible, I nonetheless felt alone, private—in a real bed, with my light turned off and no Judas eye secretly surveying me.

A new phase of my life had begun, that was clear. Already our cell with my frieze of drawings, the big drafting table and the decorative basketwork, Stanislaw reading about English Gothic cathedrals—my life only some three hours ago—seemed utterly remote. Curiously, though, I felt a new anxiety—the anxiety of facing a world I no longer knew. How would I cope with the myriad problems that would rise before me?

# 22

## Forest Paradise

What a strange feeling, waking up in a real bed! It all seemed incomprehensible—the warmth and hominess of beautiful things about me, the Persian rug on the floor, the heat emanating from the large tiled stove built into the wall between the rooms, the freshly painted white walls, the trim modern furniture, the muslin curtains through which low orange sun rays were already bursting into the room. All of it alien, recalling only long-lost perceptions.

I raised myself on my elbows and peered through the window. A sparse pattern of gnarled pine trees gradually disappearing into a heavy morning mist. Complete forest stillness, and through it all the sun, still below the treetops, glistening on the needles. A gentle breeze, full of the forest fragrance, came in through the slightly open window. The thin tufts of grass in the sand suggested a dune landscape by the sea. Not a sign of a garden or planting anywhere. Some hundred feet from the house was the high wire fence with a wide treeless gash between it and a second similar fence, beyond which the forest continued again uninterrupted.

A horse-drawn rubber-tired peasant cart was jouncing leisurely along the right-of-way, and, almost unnoticeable at first, two gray figures in heavy coats were slowly pacing along the outside of the fence. In addition, between me and the world outside a strong folding window grille locked firmly in place by a padlock. Brand new, it looked as if it had been screwed in place only yesterday, just for my benefit. No jumping out! A glance among the trees nearby further revealed a man in a raincoat standing doing nothing, though on seeing me he smiled cordially. And discreetly tucked away in the third room up here were two more men, who soon picked up their briefcases and left as new men arrived. Low-key but with all the same earmarks as in the cellar. Two barriers outside, me isolated on the upper floor, five men obviously all involved in guarding me—and how many more who were invisible? But I hardly noticed in this wonderful fantasy that had suddenly sprung up around me; most wonderful of all, human beings were smiling at me, and came in just to say good morning, to ask how I had slept, keenly concerned about every detail of my comfort. How about a hot bath? My preferences for breakfast? The morning newspaper? Endless amusement with my attempts at Polish and theirs at German.

The little fellow with the mustache appeared with a notebook and pencil and sat down at my table. The others referred to him as "Commandant," and I could see that he was in charge out here. He apologized that things were still so disorganized. Apparently the whole operation had started only with my arrival. There would be a cook to prepare a special diet for me. Meanwhile, would I give him a list of things I especially fancied? Fruit, chocolates, real coffee, cream, fresh fish—it all went down on the list. He stopped and expressed horror at my battered clothes. And indeed, they did look incongruous in this setting: the remnants of my 1948 suit, the kneeless frayed pants held up by a string around my waist and with a zipper that no longer worked; the collarless shirt; the sockless slippers through which my toes protruded. He nodded: new slippers, a suit, shirt, underwear, necktie, overcoat. He would drive right into town and go shopping.

I had a sinking feeling: my residence here, apparently, was not to be a passing matter, but a new phase of prison life. So I asked about my drawings, my drafting tools. He said they would be sent over, as would my suitcase, which I hadn't seen since 1949. I inquired about walking outside and received assurance that as soon as he had time he would go with me. As a transition I was allowed out on a sun balcony reached from the study, under the watchful eyes of two guards who leaned on the rail chatting. At last, the outdoors I had so long dreamed about! Somehow, though, I couldn't relax. Whatever space I was in, even this one, started me on my back-and-forth bear-in-a-cage walk. For only then could I think.

I quickly sized up my immediate surroundings. The upstairs apartment was my own private territory, three rooms, two of which formed my immediate quarters, the third being the study in the corner with its little outdoor terrace. At the head of the stairs off the landing was a roomy kitchen, unused but fully equipped with china, and at the opposite end of the short corridor, a WC and a tiled bathroom with a big vertical window looking out into the forest, equipped with the same security screen as the front two rooms. The ground floor, which I had no occasion to see, was ruled by the Commandant and his household crew. This was where all the meals were prepared, and it fell to a young, attractively dressed maid to serve my food and tidy up my rooms—the first woman in my immediate proximity in all these years. The Commandant had introduced her, a twinkle in his eye, as being there to meet *all* my needs. I fantasized about the ambiguity of the remark but was in no mood to test it.

Looking from the terrace, I could make out a concrete walk from the front door off into the forest. In among the trees another villa was barely discernible, and apparently the path led to it. It was also the route the guards used when they went off duty. Probably the villa contained another prisoner just like me. Stanislaw?

While I gave free rein to the intoxicating, deliciously lightheaded feeling of being a human being again, I tried to fix my mind at intervals on the meaning of all this. Why was I suddenly in this forest paradise? Why this profuse consideration, just like that bestowed on the little boy in the dream? Three theories took shape in my mind: First, perhaps I was being "tamed" for eventual release. Stanislaw had often described the typical routine in letting out innocent prisoners who had never made it to a trial. If they were released straight from a detention cell, their behavior would be unpredictable. Fragile from years of tension and hopelessness, they were likely to emerge full of rage and resentment and could easily break down. They would shock others by their physical and psychic condition, provoke unwanted gossip and rumors, and serve as concrete evidence of what was whispered about but never publicly admitted: the regime of terror behind the scenes. So there would be a careful program of improvements, similar to the treatment people to be used as prosecution witnesses received to make them more cooperative. It could take various forms, depending on the importance attached to the individual. It might merely be better food, access to reading materials, daily exercise, preliminary contacts with family, a more humane relationship with guards, relaxed discipline; or it could take the form of a complete change of environment, being put together with other prisoners about to be released. Something quite as fantastic as my changed circumstances had, however, never entered our heads.

Against this theory stood the evidence that my new accommodations were not intended to serve just for a week or two. My request to be able to continue my design project was in part a method of testing this question. For a short stay it wouldn't pay to disassemble and transport the table over here. The reply was that it would be sent over by and by, perhaps in a week's time. And later it could be arranged too that I got German-language newspapers and periodicals. This led me to the conclusion that if a release was in the cards at all, it would not be in the near future.

A third scenario loomed, worse even than continuation of my basement life: What if all this was merely a super carrot in preparation for final demands to be placed before me? Might they try to strike a bargain I would no longer have the strength to resist? For all I knew I was already in the first stage of a renunciation of my past identity in exchange for some new existence, submerged and isolated, permanently cut off from my family and from all further chance of outside help.

As the days went by, therefore, I waited with a sort of fatalism for the moment of truth. On the third day the Commandant came along with a suit of medium fit and taste, a coat of similar character, pajamas, socks, a shirt, underwear—in short, all the accoutrements to make me semipresentable, even though nothing quite fit. My delight focused on old friends of the past, salvaged from somewhere: my moccasins, polished up and the strings replaced with real shoelaces. As I tried on the assorted garments and relished the familiar feel of the shoes on my feet, the Commandant remarked proudly that now he could take me for a walk.

That first walk, several laps along the little concrete path in the midst of the trees, I will never forget. I felt drunk and unsteady on my feet, and after five minutes had to give up, out of breath, and lie down upstairs. Whenever I shifted my gaze from the ground in front of me to look at my surroundings I would lose my balance and bump into the Commandant. Only gradually did an explanation dawn on me: for five years I had paced back and forth with my eyes focused on the floor; there had been no distant view, and my visual world had required no adjustment beyond the confines of our cell. As a result, I now felt able to cope with balance only if my eyes were fixed on the path. Added to this was a weakness I hadn't realized until that moment. The stroll, together with the trip down and up the stairs, exhausted me, and in the days that followed I often didn't feel up to a walk, despite my yearning to be outside.

One morning several days after my arrival a young man was ushered into my room by the Commandant, a Captain Wrobelski. Somewhere in his early thirties and in civilian clothes, he had a serious but basically friendly air and spoke fluent German. Thus began a fascinating and illuminating relationship.

Already on his second visit I discovered my new companion, whom I came to call Mietek, to be a broadly cultured individual with an amazing musical memory. At once I grabbed on to this trait in my hunger for an important component of my former life. Throughout my imprisonment there were times when I had become absorbed in recalling every bit of music I knew—in song, on the violin, at concerts, on records, in choral works I had participated in. The result was quite a repertoire of fragments that I hummed or simply "listened" to without sound, especially whole sections of Bach's B Minor Mass and St. Matthew Passion and of the Brahms Requiem. And of course the "Ode to Joy" of Beethoven's Ninth Symphony. This musical recall had been one of my most prized treasures. Now with Mietek at my side the repertoire expanded as he whistled and hummed familiar themes all the way from Palestrina through the baroque period and the Beethoven symphonies to Mietek's Polish favorites, Chopin and Szymanowski.

From music we drifted to literature. I told him about Stanislaw's and my explorations. Once again I was astounded. Such a memory! As we wandered among the trees or sat out on the balcony or lounged on the couch in the living room, he regaled me with classical German poetry, especially Goethe and his favorite, Heine; and German translations of Pushkin and Lermontov; and in another vein, Bert Brecht. He produced several volumes of Goethe for when I was alone. We entered into lively discussions on literary themes, on art in general, and finally on architecture. In this manner, almost imperceptibly, we moved toward the political area.

Before I knew it, I was launched on a critique of present-day Polish architecture. I went after my favorite target, the Soviet Palace of Culture, and my manifesto against it. He listened a bit tensely but without comment. I broadened my critique to recent communist literature in both Russia and Poland. Up to this turn in our discussions the one big reality before us, my five-year incarceration, had been treated as a nonevent.

Then one morning it happened: he asked me point blank what I felt about what had happened to me. In the same manner as we had talked about music, and as if we were talking about something removed from us, I tried without emotion to describe an injustice on which I could speak with authority—not as a personal issue but as part of an intellectual exploration, the uncovering of a cancer at the heart of the communist system of belief. Thus the question came to be: Was what had happened symptomatic of a basically flawed system or simply a sickness that had developed in spite of it and could be overcome?

Had Mietek lured me into a trap? Wouldn't it be his duty to reply charging me with guilt? Could he allow me to get away with such a clear indictment, an implied admission on his part? For a moment his mouth tightened, but to my amazement he made no attempt to deny the colossal wrong done me. In fact, his answer virtually confirmed it.

"At this point," he said, searching carefully for the words, "it is inevitable that you translate everything into personal terms. How could it be otherwise? We can't expect you to form a fair and objective judgment. Maybe that will come. Probably never. But we must separate social goals from the turmoil to which they have been subjected, in which forces were unleashed out of the dark unconscious of man. We must not lose sight of our original goals, whatever happens."

He reflected for a moment, then continued: "We never had a chance. Don't forget, ever since the days of Lenin we have been under siege, trying to avert what finally happened out of that world crusade against us. Has there ever been anything more inhuman than the murder of tens of millions of our people in the Second World War and the devastation of the whole basis of life here? The social fabric, and with it our original goals, were bound to warp, to be smothered in abuse. Fear breeds violence, and violence the abuse of power, and both together breed blindness."

When he paused again, I wanted to retort, What about *Stalin's* millions? But he went on: "In your world, social equity has never been more than a by-product, not the main concern; just a talking point to cover a continued misuse of power for selfish greed. Your immense resources largely covered your deception at home, but not in the exploitation and poverty and violence you maintained in the far-off security of your Latin America, your tradition of misuse of Africans. All I am saying is, there's a balance sheet of good and bad on both sides that we could argue about forever. But the starting point with us communists was concern for man, while your society's has always been personal greed. You can't deny that."

I struggled to maintain the pretense of an intellectual exercise. "But perhaps that's the only way, Mietek, given the limitations of human personality. What happened with your dream seems to prove the point. Marx's construct for a decent society is impressive and seems to have some logical underpinnings, but it ignored the actuality of human selfishness and ruthlessness. As for man's propensity for the misuse of power, just look at yourselves." I blurted this out, unable to hold myself in check any longer.

Mietek tensed perceptibly but, ignoring my comment, continued: "Perhaps it's asking a lot, but if we're to get out of this jungle before it swallows us all up, the individual simply has to take second place. The way you're going, you'll never get out; instead you'll drown in goods of little use and a license to do anything for your own individual ends no matter what the social costs."

I broke in. "And you, you with your vaunted ends that justify any means, look where that has gotten you." I wanted to get beyond Marx. Hadn't Lenin's tactics to gain power in 1918 in fact opened the floodgates to all the excesses of the Stalin period? The basic institutional question; but I shied off. Neither of us had mentioned Stalin. I would let him do so first, and in any case I wanted to avoid shifting from a quiet discursive tone to a distinctly adversarial one. Again and again I felt like bursting out and telling him how transparent I found his efforts to lecture me about his communist paradise. His apparent belief that I might be able to erase the profound schooling of the past five years by a superficial dialogue seemed quite fantastic. I put it down to his youthfulness. And in a sense, I didn't blame him. After all, this was his job: he was a crucial element in the taming process. He knew very well that we would never see eye to eye. He was, however, helping me at least toward a frame of mind in which I could approach problems without rancor or bitterness, whatever happened next.

One day as we shared lunch, Mietek announced mysteriously that I would have a rather important visitor that afternoon, a woman official who had been reviewing my whole case. I was very excited. I would be moving closer to one of my hypothetical scenarios. Which one would it be?

That morning all my architectural drawings and instruments arrived at last, and I was busy assembling the drafting table with one of the guards when the Commandant announced a Mrs. Markowska. She turned out to be a fairly short, dark-haired woman, probably in her early fifties, dressed with typical Polish verve although her clothes were simple. With an alpine hat on her head with a bright feather stuck in it and a loose scarf of native design draped loosely around her neck, her appearance was one of outdoor stylishness. She addressed me in fluent German. As she settled down at the table, she drew a tin of Nescafé out of her bag and some fancy cigarettes. She turned to the Commandant still hovering at the door and asked whether we might have some coffee and pastries while we talked. Her manner was friendly and sympathetic.

She said she had come out to let me know that my whole case was under review by a Communist Party commission of which she was a member and that except for the matter of day-to-day care I was no longer subject to the Security Ministry but a responsibility of her commission directly. Chances were good, she said, that the whole matter would be cleared up in due course, though for the moment she could not go into details with me.

She promptly shifted to my present setup, thus indicating that the subject was closed, and inquired into my needs, state of health, and so forth. I wanted to get some idea where we were heading. "Cleared up," what did that mean? Freedom and reunion with Kate and the boys, or that other route: a new existence in the East somewhere after renouncing any return to the West? The latter seemed more likely. I recalled Stanislaw's warning and remained silent.

Mrs. Markowska reiterated that things hadn't reached the stage where she could discuss my case with me. She hoped however to be able to do so soon. Almost mechanically, I asked her whether she knew anything about Kate and the boys. Yes, she knew that they were well and were living with her parents in London. She added that in fact she had seen a recent picture of them and would try to find it. I was so overcome by this first bit of direct news that I wasn't even startled by the mention of the picture, which could only have been in a newspaper. She reached into her case and pulled out two worn flat cards and laid them face down on the table. She lightly touched the top of my hand as she got up to leave: "For you to look at when you are alone."

As the door closed I stared at the table. I was eager, yet afraid. I recognized the cards. They had been in my suitcase way back when. Two enlargements. Beside the Hudson at the bottom of the Palisades in New York in 1942 on that Sunday when we first knew that Kate had conceived and our Hugh was on his way. I knew I would be looking straight into Kate's radiant face, an image I had carried in my mind for what seemed an eternity. The dam that I had built in my mind would break. But now that had been given official sanction: Kate would again be admitted into my life. Was that clear yet? No matter—I turned the top one over: it was the self-timer one of us together against a large boulder, happy in our innocence. And the other, the close-up of Kate's face that day. I stared and stared in disbelief.

I had to do something to respond to all the feelings welling up inside me. This was it at last. I wanted to shout to Kate across all the hundreds of miles that separated us still. I rushed around the room. Kate, Kate, do you know too? What were you doing just now when I looked at you? My desertion of you is over! You can be with me again in my mind. We are together now. I felt for my glasses case in my pocket and pulled it out. I hurried to the WC and extracted the razor blade from its hiding place. You're not needed any longer. I snapped it into pieces and flushed it down the toilet, shuddering as I watched it disappear. To think that I might have been compelled to use it.

Two days went by and, as promised, Mrs. Markowska once more settled down at my table. This time, she said, she could be more definite. That there had been some irregularities was clear. She would make no attempt to defend the actions of the Security Ministry.

Her admission electrified me. I turned on her and blurted, "Do you know the enormity of what has been done to me and to my family? Tell me, how can such a thing happen in a civilized country? Tell me. Tell me!" I was almost beyond myself, in a confusion of outrage and excitement.

She listened quietly to my outburst, as if expecting it, and waited for me to calm down. Then without protesting she said simply: "We know only too well, and all I can say to comfort you is that we feel deep shame and are determined to see that all this becomes but a bad closed chapter of the past. But you must be patient." She looked intently into my face. "Listen to me. Listen. I have just one request: Are you willing to give us a chance? We will undertake to do everything humanly possible to rectify the injury done to you provided you will show confidence in our sincerity." She paused. "For example, what would you regard as a reasonable approach?"

Suddenly I recalled my letter of 1951 to President Bierut in which I had made a compromise proposal that I thought could enable them to release me. Didn't all of those points still hold today, at least for starters? I asked her whether she was aware of that document. Yes, but she couldn't recall the details. Why?

"The test you mentioned: it's right there. I meant what I wrote then. It is still valid as far as I am concerned. How about you?" I had played a card she had not anticipated.

She reflected a moment, then said that she would look it over and discuss it with her colleagues. More, at this point, she could not say.

The next day we were at it again. She greeted me cordially as she pulled a package out of her case. I found myself staring at my own faded writing on yellowed paper, as if it were an archeological find. Yes, my writing. It all came back to me in a flood. If I could have imagined then that I would someday be looking at it again . . .

"My comrades on the commission and I have looked at this material as you requested, and we feel it to be a valid basis on which to proceed. You see, we are on the road to meeting your test." She flattened the paper out in front of us. "Let's look at each of your points."

When we had finished she looked at me. "We see nothing there that is not negotiable. It's more a matter of applying it to where we are now." She folded the package and put it back in her briefcase. "I see you're very tired. Let's let it rest for the moment. We'll continue tomorrow." She got up. "We'll do some hard thinking, and so will you, and then we'll go on from there." And she abruptly changed the subject.

My mind, too, had shifted to something else—to Kate, the only person I could trust. I pressed for contact with her. This was the real test. Mrs. Markowska declared that unfortunately that was not possible now, but the time would come. So, release was not imminent? She explained that what had happened to me was tied in with many other complications, some beyond Poland's borders. It would take time to unravel. Direct contact with the West would be impossible for the moment. Did I know anyone else I would trust, someone here in the East?

It came to me in a flash: Why of course, Kate's sister lived in East Berlin, married to a German communist who had been rescued from one of Hitler's concentration camps in 1936 and had found a new home in England right through the war. In 1949 he had held a high position in the East German Ministry of Education. I was sure Priscilla, though she might still be a communist, would put Kate's interest ahead of any other loyalties. Until I could be directly in touch with Kate, might not she serve as Kate's surrogate? Surely her involvement would lessen the chance of a new enforced disappearance.

"Yes, there's my wife's sister in East Berlin," and I explained what I knew about her and her husband's whereabouts as of 1949.

Mrs. Markowska took down the information in her notebook. "We'll see what we can do."

The next afternoon to my surprise Mrs. Markowska was accompanied by a shortish, gray-haired man, "Comrade Dluski of the Central Committee. He is leaving tonight for Berlin to find your sister-in-law and bring her back here to stay with you. You see, my comrades and I are doing all we can to help you."

My spirits were high. I understood full well the significance of Mr. Dluski's appearance out here. It was as if they were telling me, Look who is dealing with your case, right at the top. We are sending this busy official to make sure we don't let you down. Now it was up to me. "Where we are now," Mrs. Markowska had said. She was inviting me to start by writing my own ticket. It was part of the test, wasn't it? So, throwing caution to the wind (Stanislaw not being around to warn me otherwise), I began to enumerate specifics:

1. My release must be unconditional. (Although the word "release" had never once been uttered up to now, wasn't that what we were talking about? In any event, she didn't flinch at my use of the word.)

2. The Polish government must issue a statement admitting their mistake and my innocence, and in such a way as to come to the attention of the press in both the West and East.

3. Stanislaw must be released simultaneously.

4. A financial indemnity was to be paid to me—I suggested $60,000 as a minimum, based on lost salary during the five-year period.

5. All medical costs to restore my health must be borne by the Polish government.

6. All my notebooks would be returned to me.

7. I wanted incontrovertible evidence about my brother's whereabouts.

8. And finally, those persons guilty of special misdemeanors against me had to be punished. I was especially thinking of Cigarette, Horsetooth, and one of the guards. That was the least I could do for my unknown fellow sufferers.

There followed a long silence, which she finally broke with the almost off-hand question, "If we were to meet these conditions to your satisfaction, would you be prepared to state publicly that you regarded the matter closed for good?" I thought for a moment, then responded in the affirmative, afraid somehow the whole thing would disappear like a mirage.

Although it was still up in the air, I could see by her manner that I had won. I tried hard to hide my excitement. Instead we said good-bye with great formality, two unequal negotiators on opposite sides of the bargaining table.

Our fifth session followed two days later. Mrs. Markowska's demeanor reassured me at once. Clearly, things were on track. She asked for clarification of a number of details, then requested that I elaborate on my eighth point, which was giving them some trouble. Who specifically did I wish to have brought to justice for acts against me? Would I be prepared to write down a bill of particulars that could be used in a trial?

I felt trapped. Of course Cigarette should be dealt with as he deserved, as should Horsetooth. Maybe even the doctor, for his role in my hunger strikes. But what assurance did I have that Security had no power over me anymore, or that there might not be a sudden reversal? Anyway, the last thing I wanted was to get tangled up in an internal trial. Then again, what about my responsibility toward the others, and especially toward Stanislaw? I said I would think the matter over.

That night I sat long hours writing out a tentative deposition covering Cigarette, Horsetooth, the doctor, and the guard. I had not decided yet how to use it, but I knew that these things must never happen again; I had a moral obligation not to remain a silent accessory. When Mrs. Markowska turned up as usual, I decided to let her read it without yet committing myself to handing it over.

She finished reading and looked up questioningly; I was utterly unprepared for her response. "I'm afraid there is no way we can meet your demand for punishment as regards the main object of your complaint. Colonel Swiatlo, the one you call Cigarette"—and she showed me a picture of the familiar truculent face for identification—"he is no longer under our jurisdiction. You'll have to go to your friends in Washington for help on that. He was their agent all along, and when we finally got on his track he quickly skipped to his masters. Last December, on a supposed mission for us in Berlin, he disappeared and turned up at your consulate there. He's become a hero in your country. He even claims he saved your life." She went on to emphasize that it had been he who had controlled every aspect of my existence; indeed, she said, he had initiated the whole idea of my abduction, and on several occasions had been kept from eliminating me only because of intervention from higher up.

I felt devastated: Cigarette turned hero in Washington, the one human being I could never forgive. It must be some new move to confuse me, especially that bit about his having been a U.S. agent all along. She had overplayed her hand with that remark. I felt bitter and betrayed. I had to be alone. "I would like you to go now," I said.

She got up. "I understand. I understand what you must be feeling, and I see you don't believe me. If you could read it in the *New York Times*, would that help?" I nodded, and she left without my acknowledging her departure.

This turn pushed me into a turmoil of conflicting emotions. So the world—and Kate—knew at last. The thing I had fought for all these years. They could never take that away now—never. But who had told them?

Thus far my distrust had focused entirely on my captors. Now, it seemed, the man I had most despised was an honored guest in my America. I was told that I was bound to be sucked into a huge propaganda splurge of press and radio and congressional committees in tandem with him—I, who would gladly tear him apart if ever we found ourselves in the same room as equals. And I had long ago resolved that the least I could do if I were ever released was to avoid my individual misfortune being blown up on the international scene. The facts should become known, but not as part of a Cold War extravaganza. Now this possibility had been closed. I felt a new sense of persecution. Everyone, even my friends at home, seemed intent on doing me in. Where could I turn? Only to myself or Kate or Stanislaw. The possibility that Cigarette's defection might be related to the new eagerness to resolve my case only faintly entered my awareness.

Next day we were at it again, though I kept my distance in conversation. Mrs. Markowska pulled a battered newspaper clipping out of her pocket and placed it before me. It was from the *New York Times,* as she had promised. The date was September 29, two weeks ago; the front page, and there on the right-hand side a large picture of Cigarette broadcasting over Voice of America, and the caption: "Polish Defector Bares Data on the Missing Field Family." So it was true. Hadn't I been moved out here on the thirtieth? Yet if Kate knew I was alive and where I had been held, why couldn't I at least write a letter to her? And why was I still here?

To my surprise Mrs. Markowska reflected a moment before answering: "There is no official channel. We have not recognized Swiatlo's accusations. There would be no way of reaching your wife without it becoming known—though come to think of it, our London embassy might be the messenger if our Foreign Ministry is willing to take the risk. From our side, we are concerned about the pressures on your wife at present. She might get pushed into making statements that could set back the whole process. But a word of encouragement from you might help. You write something now while I wait. I can't promise she'll get it, but let's try. The decision will of course be up to the ambassador himself."

I couldn't believe it. "You write something now." So casual! My first words to Kate in five years. I retreated to the other room and sat down on the edge of my bed with the pad of paper. I wanted to spill everything out to her in these few moments, tell her that at last it was over, that now all that was left was for us to believe in our future. But did I in fact have any basis for saying that? This gesture might be a trap to keep us both off balance. Hadn't Mrs. Markowska conceded that they had not yet even admitted that they had me?

Going against my original urge, therefore, I referred to my situation with great caution, saying merely that my captors had assured me we would be re-united and that we should be patient and have confidence in them. And then, with heavy heart, I ended on a note of uncertainty. Past experience had left me with little trust—which, for the moment, was all we had to go on. So I urged her to remain calm and take no action. If nothing happened soon and she didn't hear from me, she should feel free to use her own judgment on how to proceed. I for my part promised I would do everything I could to see that we stayed in communication.

Mrs. Markowska looked over what I had written and frowned. "It will be up to the ambassador," she repeated.

I asked, "What about my sister-in-law, perhaps she could be the messenger?"

Mrs. Markowska indicated that they had failed to find her, since she apparently no longer lived in Berlin. They had a lead to Dresden, but in any event I couldn't expect a result right away. Meanwhile, however, she had learned of an English woman who had expressed interest in being of help. She was active in the World Peace Council, which was just now meeting in East Berlin. Her name was Monica Felton. They might be able to persuade her to return to London via Warsaw.

I had mixed feelings about Monica Felton. I had known her as a city planner attached to the Ministry of Town and Country Planning in 1949; she was in charge of planning the town of Peterlee, an entirely new community in England's coal mining area. I associated her with the radical left in postwar Britain, as seemed to be confirmed by the occasional appearance of her name in our Polish newspaper from speeches and interviews that had a distinctly anti-American tone, especially in connection with some visit she had made to Korea. I hesitated, but then my need to communicate with Kate, by whatever means, won the upper hand. It was clear that at this point only someone acceptable to the communists would be trusted to be discreet. I gave in.

Thus began an unfortunate episode of my own creation when, two evenings later, Monica's crippled figure, bent by childhood spinal degeneration, stood in tears before me. Stopping here between planes on her way to London, she would, she said, be glad to act as a personal messenger to Kate. If I would write a quick letter, she would take responsibility for it and no one would be aware of the contact. By tomorrow, then, Kate would know of my love and my faith that things would turn out all right. She had a right to that, while for me it would be a lifeline that none could retract. I went to the other room and wrote. Then, as suddenly as she had appeared, this apparition from the past was whisked away into the forest darkness.

I admitted to Mrs. Markowska that my distrust was directed not just at the Polish authorities, but at everyone. I had learned to rely solely on myself, and now contact with other people had become difficult and alien to me. But . . . could I see Stanislaw?

No, that would be difficult; he was still a prisoner, not under her commission.

What could they tell me about Colonel Gecow and his wife—my friends Lolek and Anka, who had vanished just ahead of me in 1949? She looked troubled. She would find out about them. Then she switched subjects.

The next day I confronted Mrs. Markowska at once: "Have you any news now about Colonel Gecow and his wife?"

She hesitated. "Anna Gecow is well and working in the pediatric clinic. We could arrange to have you meet. Leon Gecow—" She paused; I knew what was coming. "He apparently died in prison of pneumonia. I am sorry . . ."

Already from my interrogations long ago I felt things had gone very badly for him. How much had our friendship contributed to his suffering and death?

"Yes, I would like to see Dr. Anna Gecow." It would be arranged for us to meet in Warsaw.

This led one evening to one of the weirdest moments of those weird days of transition to a world with which I had lost touch. The car stopped at the elaborate entrance of a small Warsaw palace on a dead-end street off Nowy Swiat. I was ushered into a hall of the kind I associated with conferences of heads of state, but it was just me alone among the mirrored panels and plush furnishings. I felt increasingly uneasy. There must be some mistake. I was to meet Anka; I thought this would be in some discreet basement coffeehouse where we could talk in privacy.

And then I saw a figure rushing in, all out of breath.

"Hermann! Hermann!"

We were hugging each other, speechless, crying and laughing at the same time as the sound echoed from the marble walls. Only then did we look at each other through our tears, and we each knew at once what the other had been through.

We drifted over to one of the side galleries and plunked down on a sofa. Someone came in and discreetly put wine glasses and a bottle on the table beside us, along with chocolates and other goodies. Anka's eyes still had the fiery intensity I had always associated with her. Looking at her black hair and dusky skin and high cheekbones, I recalled her remark that one of the things that had saved her in eastern Poland in the early days with the Nazis was that she would be mistaken for a Ukrainian.

Nineteen forty-nine: yes, she said, she was arrested just before my visit to Warsaw. She had been released a year ago after a peremptory trial and allowed to return discreetly to her old work as a pediatrician. She worked and lived at the clinic; there was nothing else left to her life. And then she told me about Lolek. The story about pneumonia was untrue. He had succumbed to desperation and gone on a hunger strike to the finish, his health already thoroughly undermined by abusive treatment during interrogations. The authorities had recently wanted to rebury him in the military cemetery as a form of posthumous rehabilitation, but she had fought against it. It would be a final humiliation. Instead she had insisted on an ordinary grave in the civilian cemetery, beside other members of his family.

And what now? She said she had only one responsibility in life still, which was to see that this sort of deviation in human rights never happened again in Poland. She was sure that that would have been Lolek's position also. Both their lives had been shaped in the fight against fascism and the struggle for a more just social order. Things had gone terribly wrong, but at least Stalin was no more. A return to the old prewar Poland was out of the question. This was a last opportunity to move ahead. Although chances were that too much belief had been warped or destroyed, she would nevertheless be relentless in her pursuit of a better world.

We briefed each other on the past five years. She had shared cells with a number of other women, she said. Her worst interlude had come when she was alone with a woman who had gone mad and every night threatened to strangle her in her sleep. She was sure it had been an intentional form of intimidation. But there had been lighter moments as well. She remembered fondly one young woman with a lot of spirit by the name of Alina. As she described her I couldn't help interrupting: "What was her last name?"

"Mierzenska. Her husband had been seized a year earlier in Wroclaw, a former army officer. His name was Stanislaw. She was released about the same time as I."

I couldn't believe my ears. Alina! Through Stanislaw I had a close image of her, of the strange circumstances that had brought them together during the Warsaw uprising when Stanislaw had interrogated her as a supposed German spy who was brought in to be shot summarily. He had quickly decided it was a case of mistaken identity in the chaos of the stricken city. In fact, it turned out that she was a Grabowska, a direct descendant of Poland's last king, August Poniatowski, whose offspring were not granted royal status. And in a manner characteristic of those tumultuous days, a few weeks later Stanislaw and Alina had become husband and wife.

Anka and I talked deep into the night there alone among the columns and marble and mirrors, both of us pouring out for the first time long-suppressed recollections as well as questions about the past and the future. I was more passive, feeling deeply skeptical about any belief or ideology, especially of the communist stripe, and so mainly listened. Afterward, as I sat alone in the back of the car being whisked through the chill country air back to my forest sanctuary, I reflected how, in the midst of human tragedy, I had nevertheless stumbled on a surprising and intimate piece of the past.

The next morning Mietek surprised me. "I know you still find it difficult to be with people. Soon you will have to overcome this. We had an idea. There's a couple from America here in Warsaw, a Polish nuclear scientist and his wife, an anthropologist from New York. They would love to have you spend an evening with them. Being among your own people, would that help?"

I thought about it. It was a strange idea, and why the sudden solicitude?

"What is their name?"

He pulled a slip of paper from his pocket: Dr. Leopold Infeld and his wife, Dr. Margaret Schlauch. I knew both their names and had even read an article once by Schlauch. The idea attracted me. Why not? With them I might perhaps feel less withdrawn.

And so the next evening found me sitting in what might easily have been a New York apartment, in a room lined with books, decorative tribal sculptures, and pictures, some of them with familiar American subjects. The dining table came straight out of memory, with its place mats, Russell Wright china, silverware, and wine glasses. At first I felt awkward and looked for guidance before making any move. Things were so much easier with just an enamel bowl, wooden ladle, and mug. But the Infelds had an informal cordiality about them, and soon we were talking about common memories of New York during wartime and their reasons for deciding to make Warsaw their home. It was as if I had just dropped in for a visit. No mention of how I came to be here. No surprise. No questions.

It wasn't until Infeld and I had settled down for coffee in his study that he said straight out: "Tell me about your sojourn here." A sad smile passed over his face at the clear understatement. "And you can be completely open with me in the privacy of this room. I know it will not be a pretty story."

I had planned to say as little as possible. After all, I was still a prisoner, and I had indicated to Mrs. Markowska that if they followed through in meeting my demands I would regard the matter as closed. But this was not a potential Cold War adversary; indeed, he was obviously one of their own. If such as the Infelds were prevented from knowing the stark reality, what assurance was there that all this wouldn't happen again? In fact, didn't I have an obligation to speak out?

That, then, is what I did. Step by step I told my story, becoming more and more intense as I poured out a flood of accusations.

Visibly shaken, Infeld only occasionally interrupted me to ask a question. When I finally ended my account, he said almost in a whisper: "Of course we knew in a general way what was going on, but it is impossible in the present Cold War hysteria to sort fact from fiction. Ours is a new, terribly vulnerable society that would even in normal times be beset by inexperience, especially in security matters. So we have tried to live with it. I am extremely grateful to you, Hermann, for having the courage to confront me with the shameful reality. That it is a malignancy deep in our social order, of that there is no question. Is it too late to get it out and salvage at least some of what we promised? If not, it will be up to us here in Poland. The first step is to know the facts."

As the couple bade me good night, Infeld said that he frequently went out to work at the scientists' club, a former country estate called Nieborow. He would love to invite me as his guest. It was in a beautiful rural setting, the former Radziwill residence in its wooded park, an ideal spot for strolling and talking. I liked the idea. I was under the spell of having come out of my protective shell for the second time.

The feeling was a heady and scary one, and I pulled back into myself as I sat shivering in the back of the open car rushing through the October night back to my safe haven. Safe from the assault of a new reality that allowed no space to think things through, in which I had to be on my guard in every human contact. I was glad to be alone again, settled back into the timelessness that was my security.

But that was not to last. As the days passed I sensed an escalating tempo that put such feelings of separation out of my mind. Mrs. Markowska appeared one day with a heavy woolen dressing gown to help with the increasingly cold mornings here. She apologized that it was several sizes too big: it belonged to her son, who had agreed to part with it. I felt rather honored. She had earlier let on that he was Warsaw's leading music critic. Later, that tidbit would help me identify who she really was.

Mietek hinted that things were about to happen, and sure enough one morning Mrs. Markowska, arriving earlier than usual, announced: "Tomorrow you will be a free man." Just like that.

Why now? I had been out here almost a month, no more. How could I possibly be expected to handle such a shift without warning? Now it was I who protested: "But there is so much we haven't agreed upon yet. You have answered only a few of my eight points. Anyway, I refuse to budge from here until you have also freed Mierzenski. And what about my brother? I still have no news about him. You said he had been in Hungary but you didn't know whether he was still alive. That's nonsense! Your security services talk to each other, don't they? I won't believe anything until I can actually talk to him on the phone."

To my surprise, she responded that a phone would be set up that very day in the study for my own private use.

There was no time to lose, she said; they planned to announce that I had been released early the next morning on the first news broadcast. I reminded her that I wanted to be in on whatever statement they made. She pulled out a sheet of typed paper, which I went over: "Hermann Field, an American citizen, has today been released from prison in Poland, where he has been wrongfully held since 1949. He has been cleared of all charges, and full compensation for wrongful imprisonment has been granted to him. Measures are being taken against those guilty of crimes against him."

It wasn't exactly how I would have put it, but it would do. In any case, it left no doubt at all as to my innocence and their guilt: that was what counted.

On the compensation, she agreed it should relate to my lost earnings. We could settle on the exact amount after my release. I had already received the copybooks the previous day. The American embassy would be notified as to my whereabouts, and they could come out and visit me. After that, it was entirely up to me. As simple as that. Beforehand, though, they would like me to give an interview to the AP correspondent, a Polish citizen, for the benefit of the Polish press. He would be free to use the telephone, which would be functioning by then. How about ten in the morning?

I didn't like the idea at all. Although she explained that no foreign correspondents were here at present, I though it would seem mighty strange that after the long silence, I, an American, would give my first reactions to the Polish press, which in essence represented my former captors—and while still in captivity, at that. She retorted that at first there would be a lot of mystification and speculation, which could do considerable harm and which an interview could forestall. I finally gave in. I would just say as little as possible.

And what about tomorrow? How could I just walk out into a world I no longer knew? There was still so much to be settled here. Once in the West again, I would have lost all my leverage with regard to my promise to Stanislaw. But what would be Kate's reaction, what of the public at large, if I deliberately delayed my departure?

I began to dread my first contact with my compatriots at the embassy. What would they think of my not returning with them? And then there was the question of Cigarette. The embassy would have to guarantee that I would never be face to face with him in the same room.

To top things off, I had begun to get an inkling of events at home that I didn't like at all. The Poles had recently installed a short-wave radio, which I listened to, even occasionally hearing my name mentioned in all the cacophony. Selected copies of *Life* magazine and some newspaper clippings made their way to me, as did Alistair Cooke's book *A Generation on Trial*, an analysis of the climate surrounding the Hiss trial. It all made me feel sick. People were being persecuted and hunted not just here, but at home as well. I read about congressional hearings by Senator McCarthy. Would I simply be trading one madness to another? A few of the clippings even hinted at a subpoena when I got back. For what?

I decided to buy time. I would not be rushed off my feet, not by anyone. I was in no position to face a press barrage without knowing what everyone else knew. I would not simply drive off tomorrow in the embassy car to some unknown destination. Instead I would use my old tactics of a twenty-four-hour waiting period between deciding on an action and carrying it out. If only Kate could come out here and be at my side so we could act in unison. At this point I had a right to lean on her.

The evening came. I was transferred to the study and asked to stay there for the night. Workmen, they explained, would be around making preparations, and they wanted no possible leaks through them before the formal announcement. A lot of banging and drilling ensued. I gathered they were taking out all the window bars, which weren't exactly compatible with my being "free."

That couldn't, however, account for all the activity. I recalled the chases cut into the cell walls in 1949. "Ivan"? I had imagined the wiring for that function had already been in place when I was moved out here, but maybe not.

It appeared, then, that in my first contact with my countrymen a third, unseen party would be listening in. How could we talk freely?

# 23

## London 1954

Once in a while the really unlikely chance happens. At the end of February 1954, Bob Wallach, husband of the missing Erica, was told by the State Department that two returned German prisoners said they had seen his wife in Vorkuta, a Soviet work camp near the Arctic Circle.

Then on March 13, 1954, Bob received a Red Cross card from Erica herself. Without doubt it was from Russia, and it had a return half on which Bob could reply to her. After three and a half years of silence, suddenly there came this voice from the Soviet Arctic, telling her family that she had had a wonderful Christmas present: permission to write to them! She wanted to know about her children: How were they? Where were they?

She was well but would like them to send her some things: woolens, hobnailed boots, a toothbrush, and some food. But they should not worry about her. She hoped that she would be let out soon and would spend the next Christmas with Bob and the children.

After this, anything seemed possible. Perhaps now a card would come from Hermann from the Arctic. But we did not forget the difference: Erica had disappeared in Berlin, when Soviet authorities were still in occupation of their zone there. It was technically more justifiable for them to have taken Erica to Russia than any of the Fields. But as to getting Erica out, there was a serious difficulty: she was not an American citizen, but a German made "stateless" by Hitler.

In 1954, Elsie brought her family to Europe for the summer. They started by spending some time in England, and this gave us a grand opportunity to go over everything together. They arrived in June and then went on to Switzerland, where I planned to join her the next month with the boys. It would be a big adventure, but I slightly dreaded it. I had not been abroad since my visit to Paris in

November 1951 and still had some fears. There was, after all, the business of Donald Maclean's wife, Melinda, who had disappeared from Switzerland with her children the previous summer.

Perhaps the State Department also was hesitant, or was it really just a backed-up schedule that made them take six weeks to validate my passport for Switzerland? (Unlike most people's, my passport when renewed had been made valid only for Britain.) But when I was on the point of canceling my hotel booking, the permission finally came.

The boys and I left London airport in pouring rain, but over France the sky cleared and we could peer down at the fields below. The adventure had begun! I felt quite elated for once. Then the landing at Basel and a train journey to Sarnen, where Elsie met us. Finally the cable car in which we dangled over the pine forests and passed up and up beside the great rocks, made pink by the sunset. At last, Melchsee Frutt, nearly three thousand feet up from the valley—and just thirteen hours after we had left Corringham Road.

The air was so wonderful, so stimulating, that for the first few nights I woke refreshed at about four in the morning and could not get back to sleep. Farmyard sounds and smells drifted up through my window and evoked happy memories of earlier vacations I had spent, climbing with my parents or skiing.

Elsie also knew these places well, having lived in Switzerland as a child. Her husband, Joe, and the three children were with her. We went for walks and scrambles among the rocks, and gradually my boys thought less about London bus numbers and more about mountain sights and sounds. I, too, began to feel revived, and when we returned to England a month later was able to face life more cheerfully. I would never have done it without Elsie.

In London again, I got back to work. By an amazing chance, a German woman prisoner, Mrs. Gerland, who had been released from the USSR and to whom I had written, had in fact heard talk of the Fields. She wrote me that she knew the name Herta Field from a German journalist with whom she had been in Vorkuta. She thought the journalist (who was still a prisoner) had been with Herta for some months in 1950–1951 in a Moscow prison, and that later Herta had been transported to Karaganda.

This was only secondhand information, but the story was very plausible, and it strengthened our growing belief that all the Fields had probably been taken to Russia.

We managed to find out the location of the major Soviet labor camps, and were proposing to send Red Cross cards to Hermann, Noel, and Herta in the hope that they would be delivered, and that our family would be allowed to respond. It was a long shot, but seemed worth trying. I visualized Hermann working, possibly in Karaganda, a coal mining area in Siberia where, according to another returned prisoner, the miners were prisoners from many countries. Americans might be among them.

The Cold War seemed to be thawing a little, and there was an increase in unofficial contacts across the Iron Curtain. A delegation of British members of Parliament was planning to go to Moscow at the end of September. This seemed an opportunity I should not miss.

I finally managed to get an interview with Christopher Mayhew, a Labour member of Parliament, who had been on the British delegation to the UN in earlier years. He promised to see what he could find out.

### THINGS BREAK AT LAST

It was September 28, 1954. I was out for the evening with some old college friends; we were going to see *Hedda Gabler*. We'd had supper and were about to head to the theater when I decided to call home, just to check in.

My mother answered the phone. Excitedly, she said that the press had been on to her with an amazing story. A man in Washington called Josef Swiatlo was claiming that he had arrested Hermann in Poland.

Poland! I had long thought of that as an innocent country in all this. But the report was so convincing. Could this be the information we'd been searching for, at last?

I called the embassy, but it was nearly eight o'clock and no one could help me. I dashed to the theater and told my friends what had happened. I was so excited I was shaking, and could hardly talk coherently. But to protect myself against disappointment I said, "Of course, I may find it's just another rumor." All the same, I could not have sat through a play and went home at once.

At home, the phone rang. The press wanted my comment. I wished I had some guidance from the embassy, but Swiatlo's story of how he had arrested Hermann at the airport and of his subsequent imprisonment in Poland was so convincing I thought it must be true. In any case, I must not say anything to throw doubt on it. I said it was the first news I had had of Hermann in five years and I was terribly excited. Then I went to bed, longing for the morning to bring more news.

I rang the embassy as soon as it opened. How reliable was Swiatlo's information? What confirmation did they have that Hermann was still alive, since Swiatlo had left Poland ten months ago? What did they want me to do? Should I make any appeals?

It seemed the London embassy had not been warned that Swiatlo was going to be produced, like a rabbit from a conjurer's hat, and they were as much at a loss as I was. But they cabled Washington for me.

Elsie was still in Geneva. How I wished she were in London with me! Instead we spent a small fortune telephoning each other, discussing what to do, transmitting hopes and fears. For now started one of the toughest periods of all. We were immensely more hopeful, yet there was the awful possibility that it might all once more come to nothing. The tension was terrific.

On September 29 I was able to see from the papers that Swiatlo's statement had been accompanied by notes from the State Department to Poland on behalf of Hermann, and to Hungary on behalf of Noel and Herta, and that for once these were published in full in the *New York Times*.

The note delivered to the Polish Ministry of Foreign Affairs by the American embassy in Warsaw, on September 28, 1954, referred to the fact that inquiries regarding Hermann had never received a satisfactory reply; the State Department now wished to inform the Polish government that the former deputy chief of Department Ten of the Polish Ministry of Public Security, Josef Swiatlo, had revealed considerable information. The note then quoted in detail Swiatlo's account of Hermann's arrival in Poland and his subsequent arrest and detention.

While in Prague, the note went on, Hermann had called Helena Syrkus and Mela Granowska in Warsaw and asked them for help in getting a visa. These calls had been reported to the Ministry of Public Security, whose head, General Stanislaw Radkiewicz, knew the Hungarians were preparing the Rajk trial in which Noel would be implicated; it was therefore decided, with President Bierut's approval, that Hermann should be permitted to come to Poland so that he might be exploited in this connection. Granowska got Hermann a visa, he arrived in Warsaw and was escorted by her to visit Helena Syrkus and Colonel Leon Gecow.

Preparations were made to arrest Hermann when he went to Warsaw airport to fly back to Prague. Swiatlo was told that President Bierut himself issued the instructions, and the border control organization at Warsaw airport was informed of the plan. Hermann, escorted to the airport by Helena Syrkus and Mela Granowska, had passed through customs and entered the waiting room. He was then called into the border control office and arrested. They waited until this moment so that, having passed through customs, he would be officially listed as a passenger on the Czechoslovak Airlines plane bound for Prague.

> The arrest was made by Swiatlo, who invited Hermann Field to accompany him to a waiting car held in readiness by an assistant and a chauffeur. Hermann Field went with Swiatlo to the automobile and, together with the assistant and chauffeur, they drove to a place of detention at Miedzeszyn maintained by Department Ten of the Ministry of Public Security.
>
> It is known that Lieutenant Colonel Piasecki of that Department conducted a

thorough interrogation of Hermann Field. Officials of the Ministry of Public Security recognized that no evidence was uncovered that he was a spy or had conducted espionage on behalf of the American Government and concluded that he should be considered innocent and be protected. It is further known that Hermann Field continues to be in prison at Miedzeszyn, Poland.

In view of the foregoing information the United States Government requests immediate consular access to this American citizen and the conclusion of arrangements for his repatriation at the earliest possible date.

The note to Hungary detailed how Swiatlo had revealed that he and General Roman Romkowski had gone to Budapest and learned how the Hungarian authorities had brought Noel and Herta Field under custody to Budapest when they disappeared in the summer of 1949. Swiatlo had interrogated them separately at the AVH (State Security Authority) Building in Budapest, where they were imprisoned. Noel had stated to Swiatlo that he had not engaged in espionage but was gathering information for a book about the so-called People's Democracies. "In view of this information," the note concluded, "the United States Government requests immediate consular access to these American citizens and the conclusion of arrangements for their repatriation at the earliest possible date."

At the same time, the press was given a biographical sketch of Josef Swiatlo. In September 1948, it seemed, he had been transferred to the Ministry of Public Security, or MBP, in Warsaw and assigned to a special bureau then being set up to prepare cases against Wladyslaw Gomulka, former secretary-general of the Polish Communist Party, and General Marian Spychalski, former chief of staff of the Polish Army, both of whom had subsequently been arrested on political charges and had been held in prison ever since without public trial. This special bureau, reconstituted as "Department Ten" of the MBP in 1951, was charged with the protection of the Polish Communist Party and regime against internal political subversion.

Swiatlo had been deputy director of Department Ten at the time of his defection. He had arrived in East Berlin on a special mission on December 3, 1953, and on December 5 he crossed into the western part of the city and asked for the protection of American authorities there.

It was quite clear that the State Department believed Swiatlo's story. What a miracle that the very man who had actually arrested Hermann should come over to the West! Now my course seemed clear: I must do nothing that might spoil the department's strategy, and I must show that I, too, believed Swiatlo's story. So when the press photographers came to the house, as they inevitably did, the children and I posed full of "smiles of hopefulness," as they said, at the first real news in five years.

Swiatlo gave a second interview the very next day. Elsie phoned in great distress saying that he believed that Noel and Herta were dead, and that Hermann had been "facing death" ten months ago, when Swiatlo left Poland.

Although it was late at night, I phoned the *New York Times*. There was only a man on night duty, and he did not want to read me the story. "It's not pleasant reading," he said.

"I don't mind," I insisted. "I never imagined he was having a picnic. I must know what has been said." So I steeled myself for the worst while he read me the news report:

> After Mr. Field's two hunger strikes, Mr. Swiatlo said, he tried to dissuade his prisoner from making further attempts at suicide . . . but a few months later, when a request for information about his wife and children had been refused him, Mr. Field was interrupted in his attempted hanging. . . . It was before March 1951 when he (Swiatlo) went to Budapest in quest of the deposition about Hermann Field from his brother and sister-in-law.
>
> As recently as early last year however, according to the Polish defector, the Polish President, Boleslaw Bierut, observed to an assistant that "Field lives too long." Such an opinion, as expressed by Bierut, said Mr. Swiatlo, "is the equivalent of a death sentence."

I thanked him and hung up. Poor Hermann! It had been much as I imagined. I knew how he must have despaired, feeling desperate at the prospect of endless years in jail, at his ignorance of what had happened to the rest of us. Imagining, perhaps, that the boys and I had been taken too, or perhaps pushed overboard from the *Batory*.

I went to bed feeling less hopeful. What proof had we that Hermann was still alive? Had he perhaps survived so long only to succumb, not knowing that Swiatlo's information was to become available to the world? This raised the question that came at once to everyone's mind: Why did ten months elapse following Swiatlo's defection before the State Department revealed and used the precious information he brought with him? Ten months, in which Hermann could have died a hundred times, with not a single note sent to Poland? Instead Czechoslovakia had been approached three times, as recently as August! Not only that, but Elsie and I, having not even an inkling of Swiatlo's existence, had in our ignorance and desperation been pressing the State Department and Red Cross. Our Red Cross postcards sent to Russia might confirm that we had no solid evidence where our relatives were. I immediately phoned Elsie in Geneva and asked her to stop the Red Cross from sending them.

Christopher Mayhew, of the British parliamentary delegation just going to Moscow, called me to ask what they should do now. I said that I thought it would still be helpful to ask the Russians to use their good offices with the Poles. He would consult our Moscow embassy before taking any action.

Meanwhile I saw the American consul general in London, and I wrote to Ambassador Flack in Warsaw begging him to do everything in his power to get access to Hermann, enclosing a loving note to be given to Hermann if he succeeded.

I also sent a telegram to Hermann addressed to "Miedzeszyn near Warsaw." Although the post office clerk could find no such place in the international postal guide, he thought it was worth a try. Hermann did not receive it. And through the International Red Cross I sent him a postcard. The special Red Cross receipt card that came back was postmarked "Oct 14, Miedzeszyn poczta Jozefow k/Otwocka." Hermann never received it either.

Thinking that Poland might like a face-saving device that would enable them to say they had released Hermann on humanitarian grounds rather than in response to State Department pressure, I wrote an appeal to the Polish president, Bierut. I went with it to the Polish embassy in London and asked to see the ambassador. They told me he was away in Poland. I then asked for the chargé d'affaires, but he would not see me. Finally I was told to send my request in writing. This I did on October 6, asking that my letter be forwarded to Poland. Two days later I received a reply saying that this had been done. I then sent a note for Hermann, which the embassy said they also forwarded to Poland. He never got it. Whether the Council of Ministers, which had replaced the office of president, ever got my appeal I did not know.

Meanwhile, the days were passing. I was not too concerned whether my notes got through to Hermann; if he were still alive, I reasoned, the Poles would now be doing everything they could to keep him so. Swiatlo's statement had made his position infinitely safer, provided it had not come too late.

What did worry me was that the State Department's note had still received no reply, nor had any action been taken to back up our demands. So on October 8 I sent a request to the department to take "steps to back up its Note and give the Polish Government an incentive to respond favorably." I also appealed to President Eisenhower and the American Institute of Architects for support.

The original statement by Swiatlo in the *New York Times* had hinted at the extent of Hermann's suffering, but also of his strength. How I admired his spirit, which had kept him making demands, even to the extent of going on a hunger strike when that seemed his only weapon.

At times we were hopeful, at others depressed. To try to get to the bottom of all this uncertainty, Elsie arranged for her lawyer in Washington, Mr. Martin, to interview Swiatlo at the State Department on October 11. The Pole was glad to cooperate and gave a detailed account of how he had arrested Hermann, and the conditions under which he was being held up to the time of Swiatlo's defection in December 1953.

Swiatlo confirmed that when Hermann had asked for a Polish visa it was decided, "in cooperation with the main Soviet adviser, who is in the Security Ministry in Warsaw," to let him enter the country and then arrest him. "There was no special direction of spying he was accused of, rather politically spying in connection with his brother."

Swiatlo asserted that neither Noel, Herta, nor Hermann had ever confessed to being a spy, and that he, Swiatlo, believed Hermann to be innocent. Asked why the Polish government never admitted holding him, Swiatlo said: "They would have to have a trial with Hermann to say why they keep him . . . but he does not admit to what they accuse him."

Swiatlo said he had not been present at Hermann's interrogations but talked to him because he was responsible for his living conditions. Hermann wanted to know why his brother was arrested and why he himself was arrested, and he wanted to have some contact with his family and children.

Swiatlo said he had tried to tell him that he should be patient, that eventually the case would somehow be clarified. "Besides the difficult conditions which every prisoner has in prison in Poland, he had an especially difficult condition in the prison. First of all, for a very long time . . . he was alone in his cell in prison. And through this whole time he was not allowed to walk in the prison yard. . . . He started not to take food. . . . He wanted to have somebody else in his cell to whom he would be able to talk at least. In . . . the plan of the Polish government, Field would never see freedom, so they thought it advisable to send to his cell . . . a man who would also never be released, and such a man was sent to him . . . Mierzenski . . .

"Field again started his hunger strike. . . . He tried to hang himself. There was a decision of the Communist Party that he should not be given food. If he goes on a hunger strike he should go, and in this way, rather, should this case be closed or finished. It was not the order not to feed him, that was not the order, but it was rather the intention to allow him not to take food. I sent a physician who was the physician of the Security Office. . . . Beside this, I talked to him and told him that he has always time to finish his life if he has decided to do it, so he shouldn't hurry it, because that would be the last step which he would not be able to take back." So they did forced feeding.

Swiatlo said Hermann had written a letter to the American embassy in Warsaw asking that they should take care of him because he was an American citizen. Naturally this letter was not sent but was put in the files of the case. When he last saw Hermann both his health and spirits were poor.

Swiatlo also told how he and his superior, General Romkowski, vice minister of Polish Security, went to Hungary in August 1949 to interview Noel and Herta regarding people they knew in Poland. After the war they had both worked in Poland on behalf of the American Unitarian Service Committee and had set up a hospital at Piekary, in the industrial area of Polish Silesia.

"Well," said Swiatlo, "the Hungarian authorities showed us quite long confessions that they were admitting to the spying, but in the conversations which we had with Noel he did not admit it at all. . . . The best proof would be if he admitted really to what he was accused of, he would be one of the accused in the trial of Rajk, and he was not."

Swiatlo confirmed that both Noel and Herta had been arrested from their hotels in Prague and taken to Hungary. The Czechs complained about being held responsible for this: "The Czechoslovak attitude was negative as long as Slansky was alive." (Archival information has since made clear that the arrests were made by Czech secret police at the request of the Hungarians and Russians.)

When Swiatlo saw Noel and Herta in Budapest their appearance was "very, very poor. It would look like the Hungarians were working them very hard and wanted to get from them some confessions."

In March 1951 Swiatlo was in Hungary again because the Polish government wanted to "organize a group of the interrogator officers which worked on this case of Field, Noel and Hermann. . . . The Polish government rather wanted that the Hungarians should take Field (Hermann) to Hungary." But the Hungarians told Swiatlo that it was not possible to interrogate Noel or Herta anymore; from this he had concluded that they were no longer alive. Mr. Martin then asked if they might instead have been taken to Moscow, to which he replied: "Everything is possible in this world."

He also knew about Erica Wallach. "As I understand this case she was taken by the Soviets somewhere in Berlin." He thought he had heard this from his boss, General Romkowski.

And what did Mr. Swiatlo think was the real opinion of the high Polish officials regarding Hermann?

"Well, when you are used to being not honest, it is very difficult to become honest, so it is difficult to say. . . . They would say he is an American spy, but very hard and doesn't want to admit . . . and a hard one to break."

And what is the Colonel's own opinion?

"I am very eager to say my own opinion. I had very wide access to all these materials, the same in Poland, Hungary and Czechoslovakia. For me it is quite clear that they are not spies. . . . It was my conclusion when I was in Poland. That probably was not the basic reason I am here today, but anyhow it was one of the reasons I am here today."

When asked what he thought the Polish government intended to do with prisoners such as Hermann, Swiatlo said that they did not want to release them because they would say the government were liars. In any event, he pointed out, the decision to release them would have to be with the consent of the Soviet authorities, and in fact the State Department should have sent its notes to Moscow, not Warsaw.

On reading the transcript of the interview it seemed to me that Swiatlo had no hesitation in answering the questions put to him. I had no way of knowing what was in the occasional pieces "off the record" but surmised they might be harrowing descriptions considered too distressing for the family to read. He did say that, despite their poor physical condition, all the Fields were in full possession of their mental faculties when he saw them. In reporting that Hermann had tried to commit suicide, he did not subscribe to the idea that such an action was a sign of insanity; under certain conditions, in fact, he would consider it quite reasonable, and it was certainly not uncommon.

Swiatlo's detailed account of his own actions in the case, including his arrest of Hermann on the orders of the Soviet adviser in Poland, his interviews with Noel and Herta, and his knowledge of the Czech government's displeasure at their having been kidnapped in Czechoslovakia, confirmed my belief that the colonel was only a cog in a much larger wheel, with its hub in Moscow. The interview threw no light, however, on the puzzling question of why it took so long for Swiatlo to be produced. The State Department would say only that considerable time was required to verify the accuracy of his statements, and that then the department had to wait for the right moment, politically, for his revelations to achieve the desired result: the release of our family.

Elsie paid a short visit to London, then again returned to her family, still in Geneva. I felt so sad seeing her go up into the plane. How much longer would we have to fight this battle?

Returning from the airport, I noticed a newspaper headline: "Hungarian Justice Miscarries: A Startling Admission." The report, from Budapest and dated October 14, quoted a high-ranking Hungarian communist as saying that the leaders of the former State Security Office had arrested many people using criminally improper methods, but that all cases of such prisoners had been examined after the Peter case, and those whose innocence was proved had been released.

This was most interesting. General Gabor Peter had been head of the State Security Office when Noel disappeared and when the former foreign minister, Laszlo Rajk, was executed in 1949. His own turn had come in 1953, when he disappeared, and in 1954 he had been sentenced to life imprisonment for "antistate crimes." Now the Hungarians were backtracking one step further: they were admitting that many people had been falsely accused. Could it be that they would now release Noel, saying it had all been a mistake? It was not impossible.

And if the Hungarians took this line, why not the Poles too? They could simply release Hermann, without a trial. It was something that, as the years went by, had seemed too good to hope for. Now it seemed a real possibility.

Then came another clue. The British parliamentary delegation had returned from Moscow and Mr. Mayhew wrote to me on October 18:

> I promised . . . to send you a written account of my brief talk with Molotov, which took place at the reception at the British Embassy in Moscow.
>
> I said I was acquainted with a charming young Englishwoman, Mrs. Field, who was the mother of two young boys. In the confused and difficult international situation in 1949 her husband, Hermann Field, had disappeared on a plane between Warsaw and Prague. The British Parliamentary Delegation hope very much that Mr. Molotov might make some inquiries. Such inquiries might lead to the conclusion that this was not a matter for the Soviet Union but for the Polish Government. But in a very human case of this kind, the Delegation hoped that Mr. Molotov might be able to find a way round.
>
> Molotov replied—"But you believe in the principle of non-interference? How can I interfere in a matter concerning Poland?"
>
> The firmness with which Molotov stated it was a matter concerning Poland suggested to me that he was familiar with the case. I replied that I was sure that if Mr. Molotov had heard your case from you, as I had, his experience would enable him to find a way round.
>
> He replied—"But how would you feel if other countries interfered in your affairs in such a way?"
>
> I said that on a human problem of this kind I would not hesitate to talk to any of Britain's allies. At this point, however, Molotov firmly changed the subject.
>
> Later I said to Gromyko, who had been listening, that it was a pity Mr. Molotov seemed unable to help in the question. It was a small thing, which could make a great impression on the British Parliamentary Delegation.
>
> After a pause Mr. Gromyko said in a kindly enough tone—"But you see he could not make any other answer."
>
> It is of course true that even if Mr. Molotov had intended to take the matter up with the Poles, he would be careful not to give any indication that he was doing so. Nevertheless, I am afraid his attitude and answers give no grounds for encouragement.

This was interesting. Molotov did not mind saying that it was Poland's affair, which in turn suggested that Poland might finally admit culpability.

## SOME PERSONAL DIPLOMACY

Throughout these new developments I had continued with my teaching job, knowing that I would go crazy being at home all the time. Indeed, if nothing came of all this, how could I afford to give it up? I was forty-two now, and it would be hard to get another job. But in fact working proved impossible and I had to resign, my boss saying kindly that if I needed to I could come back for the next term, in January.

I had no great hopes of getting anywhere through the Polish embassy. They sent me a letter asking the name and surname of my husband, which was strange, since I had previously used personalized notepaper bearing that information. Then they wrote again, asking me for a copy of their letter to me, as they could not trace the file. When I went there to deliver the copy, the embassy appeared practically deserted and I was only able to see a receptionist. Then, coming home one evening, I found two letters from them. The first informed me that I should disregard their last letter and that mine to Hermann had been forwarded to Poland. The second said that the ambassador was now back and he could see me next morning, Saturday October 23.

The next morning I drove down with my father, calling at the American embassy on the way for any suggestions.

This time my reception at the Polish embassy was quite different. While my father waited downstairs, I was taken up to and received by the ambassador. We sat in armchairs before a blazing open fire while he doodled with a pencil on a packet of Wawel cigarettes, decorated with a picture of the great castle on the hill above Krakow, which I had visited before the war.

He said that I would be expecting him to say something, and that I should feel rather hopeful: "You can believe that this question will be settled before too long in a way that will be satisfactory to you."

This already sounded wonderful, and I could feel my heart pounding. I waited for more.

"I have seen your letter to the Polish president. There is now a Council of State instead of a president, but it does not matter. Your letter will be carefully considered. I would like to help you, but you must be careful not to do anything that would make things more difficult."

I wondered what he meant. He explained that these were very delicate matters, and more complicated than I might imagine. They would be more easily settled quietly and without a lot of noise. There were people who would like to exploit me for their own purposes, but they were not in a position to help me. Newspapermen were only interested in getting a story to earn some money. I did not want to be a "film star," with pictures of myself and the children in the papers. Rather, I should be quiet.

I responded that I had been quiet for five years. I did not invite the newsmen, but they were interested in the case.

He continued. I should not think about the past; we were concerned with the future and with how to settle this business as soon as possible. It was a human question. He was sure I loved my husband, and that Hermann loved me and our little boys, and that all I wanted was to get my husband back. But Josef Swiatlo was a provocateur. Now he was saying my husband was procommunist. Had I seen what Swiatlo said?

"Yes, I've seen the press reports of it." I was not going to say anything to throw doubt on Swiatlo.

He went on slowly, while I sat on the edge of my chair straining to catch every word despite his accent.

"Your husband is alive." I felt my heart rise. "And in rather good health. He is not living in bad conditions at all. It is not a prison, rather a villa."

"Have you seen him?"

"No, but I was told about him when I was in Poland on holiday just now."

"It would make the waiting much easier if I could write to him, and he to me. I sent a note for him through this embassy, but I have had no reply."

He said I could write again and bring the letter to him.

"And will you let me know if you have further news?" I asked.

"Certainly. But it is a very delicate situation. I want you to trust me, and I will do my best for you. You should deal only with me, and this conversation, it is just between the two of us, you understand?"

Yes, I understood. But, I thought, it's a bit late now for me to start trusting the Polish ambassador and no one else. The Poles had not done anything to help me so far.

"Of course, you are free to do as you like, but I advise you just to trust me. Other people cannot help you. It is not a question of who was to blame. Five years is quite a long time, and now we want to settle this the best way we can both for you and for me."

He went on a bit more about Swiatlo being a provocateur and how I might spoil it all by behaving badly and indulging in publicity.

"And how long will I have to wait?"

"That I can't say at the moment. But speaking responsibly as an ambassador, I will say that you can feel confident it will be settled in the way you wish."

I thanked him several times for his kindness in seeing me. "You have given me great hope, and I will try to be patient."

He escorted me down the imposing stairway of this once luxurious mansion. My father was waiting, and I introduced them. Then we left.

At once I told my father the news: Hermann was alive and well, and it looked as if the Poles would release him. We went around the corner to a little café and drank coffee while I reported the conversation in detail. Could the ambassador have spoken that way if there were still any doubt of the outcome?

I felt in a quandary, however. Was it true that I might spoil it all by not taking the ambassador's advice to trust him exclusively? How could he expect me to keep this great news a secret? Did he really want me to stop speaking to the American embassy, just at the moment when the American government was seriously looking into the matter?

"How far can I trust the Poles?" I asked my father.

"As far as you can kick them," he replied.

There was one lesson which I thought I had well and truly learned: that without the backing of my government I was nothing. Only his American citizenship would save Hermann. Herta had put his case into the hands not of the U.S. government but of Helena Syrkus, who she was sure was the best person to handle it. And what had Helena done? Simply assisted the Poles in giving outsiders the impression that Hermann was not arrested there. Herta had further advised me to take no official steps, but simply to take my children home on the *Batory* and wait for Hermann to follow by plane "when it was cleared up." I never regretted having disregarded every bit of her advice.

Many times I had appealed to the Poles. I had phoned and written to the Syrkuses, with no reply. I had tried unsuccessfully to get an interview with the Polish ambassador in 1949, and when I finally saw some minor secretary, he was unable to tell me anything. I had appealed to Radkiewicz, minister of public security, and received no reply. Nor had Elsie ever received any help from the Polish embassy in Washington. The Poles had maintained their procrastinating silence or know-nothing replies for five years, until finally it happened: they were faced with the truth, embodied in an American note.

Now they suddenly discovered that they *did* have Hermann, but it was all a mistake. And they asked me to trust them and nobody else.

As far as I was concerned, it was too late. Of one thing I was certain: neither my position nor Hermann's would be strengthened if they thought they could play me off against the State Department. But this did not stop me from worrying that I might lose some valuable news of Hermann by my insistence on sticking to my own government and by my inability to avoid the press.

The American embassy, meanwhile, considered my having been called in by the Polish ambassador a very hopeful sign.

# 24

## London: Battle for a Soul

It was Saturday, and it seemed nothing more would happen over the weekend, so my parents went away and left me in London with the children. In my sleep I heard the telephone ringing. I stumbled to the next room and answered it.

"Mrs. Field? This is Reuters News Agency. We have some good news for you. Warsaw radio has just announced that your husband has been released from prison and cleared of all charges made against him."

"Is it true? Can I really believe it?"

"Oh yes, it's official all right."

I just started to cry. He was safe! At last this was the end; nothing else mattered.

"Mrs. Field? Mrs. Field? Have you a statement to make?"

"I can't . . ."

"Can I just say you are overwhelmed?"

"Yes."

I hung up. Slumped down by the bed, I sobbed out my relief—the end of the strain, the uncertainty, the hopes raised only to be dashed again. I thanked God for the mercifulness of the world to us. That Hermann, who could have died a thousand times, had yet lived; that I, who had expected to spend the rest of my life a widow, was to have my husband back, and our boys their father. Did I believe it was because we had always wanted it so much? No, I knew there were women who loved their husbands as much as I loved mine but who had lost them. No, I believed it was just a great mercy that had been shown me, and I would be thankful forever.

I got up and switched on the light. It was 5:50 A.M. on October 25, 1954.

Hugh had heard the telephone. "What's happened?" he called out.

I went to him. He was standing in the middle of his bedroom. "Hermann's been released from prison."

He started to cry, and we stood with our arms around each other, perfectly understanding.

The phone rang again. This time it was International News Service. I grabbed a pencil and this is what I scribbled down: "Warsaw radio announced that Hermann Field has been released from prison and cleared of all charges made against him. They said that Field was released and received complete satisfaction . . . that this was after exhaustive proof that the charges made against him by Josef Swiatlo were baseless and have been fabricated by American agents and provocateurs . . ."

Well, I was not going to worry about what explanation the Poles gave in order to save face. I wanted confirmation by the BBC, so Hugh and I waited impatiently for the seven o'clock morning news. Sure enough, it came: "Warsaw radio announced the release of Mr. Hermann Field, an American architect, who disappeared while searching for his brother . . ."

There it was! No longer any possible doubt. Hugh was so excited, we had to turn it on again at eight o'clock. "I like to hear it lots of times," he said.

By this time Alan was awake and listened too.

"When will Daddy get here?" they asked.

"I don't know. Of course, Poland's some ways away. But any time now."

I gave them their breakfast, and all the time the phone kept ringing, newspaper reporters and friends who had heard the BBC news.

I got Hugh off to school. (Alan was staying home with an injured hand.) Then I phoned Elsie in Paris, and the American consul general. I told him I wanted Hermann to come to London as soon as possible.

Then my father called. I asked him to come back to London, as I foresaw a deluge of inquiries. While we spoke, the Polish ambassador's secretary appeared at the door. She said the ambassador would like to see me; he was outside in his car and would drive me to the embassy. I told her I could not leave just then, but would come to the embassy on my own a little later

I was not happy about going to the Polish embassy alone, so before going in I stopped at a call box and phoned the American embassy to let them know what I was doing.

I was taken up to the ambassador at once. Had I heard the news? Yes, I had; could I absolutely believe it? Oh yes, it was official. Things had moved more quickly than he had expected, and now I could look forward to having my husband back soon. I think he was sincerely pleased.

That was about all. There was something a little strange about this interview; it seemed so unnecessary. I began to feel apprehensive that something might still go wrong. Later I phoned our consul again. Could the Poles still do anything to wriggle out of it? No, he didn't think so. He felt sure everything would be all right.

I went home. As I neared our house I saw a large number of men hanging around—sure enough, it was the press. I did not want to be photographed posing, after the Polish ambassador's warning about not being a film star, so as a compromise I let them take pictures of me walking up the path with Alan.

Apart from being overjoyed, there was nothing I could tell the press, but that did not stop them. One agency phoned the American embassy in Warsaw, which confirmed that Hermann had been released but said they did not know where he was. Other agencies arranged to meet all planes coming out of Poland to the West. One newspaper offered me a phone call to Hermann at their expense, though because no one knew where he was that was easier said than done, and in any case I did not relish the idea of our first words to each other being recorded in a newsroom. I hung around the house all day hoping for further news.

That evening at around eight o'clock, I had a call from the Polish ambassador's secretary. He had some news for me; would I come to the embassy as soon as possible? My father drove me down, and again waited downstairs.

The ambassador was at his desk and motioned me to sit down. Then he handed me an envelope. I opened it. A long letter in Hermann's handwriting! I felt myself trembling all over, and started to read: "Otwock, Oct. 24, 1954. Dearest, By the time you are handed this the official announcement of my freeing will be in progress . . ."

Here they were, my first words from him in all these years! The proof that he was really alive now, or at least two days ago, and well enough to write a long letter! I read on: "In a world that has long since ceased to exist for me . . . I have taken cognizance of the Polish Government's offer to put at my disposal convalescent facilities . . ."

Taken cognizance! What strange, legal-sounding language. Had he really written this careful, well-organized letter himself? Or had someone been leaning over his shoulder, dictating it? And convalescent facilities offered by the Poles; did this mean he was intending to stay there and convalesce instead of leaving at once? How could he bear it—and how could I stand the suspense? Perhaps the Poles did not want him to come back to the noncommunist world. After all, the communists had not yet admitted holding Noel.

". . . Beyond this I am not willing to take any action affecting our future without discussing it with you. The Polish Government will give you a visa to come to Poland to be with me. Let me know . . ."

So that was it! Instead of Hermann coming out, I was to go there. But was this really Hermann's wish, or someone else's? By looking at his letter I could not tell.

Then at the bottom I read: "P.S. Destroy this letter before leaving the Embassy."

I went on looking at the piece of paper in my hand, pretending still to read. Destroy this letter—but why? Why should I destroy this precious letter, the first word I had received from him in five years, and which I would want to reread over and over again to grasp its meaning. It was in fact the only evidence I had that Hermann really was still alive. Suppose there was still some monkey business and they did not let him out, should I destroy my one bit of evidence? No, I decided. Even though I was disobeying Hermann's first request to me, and even though the ambassador probably knew what that request was, I folded the letter carefully and put it in my pocket.

"Thank you very much. This is the first word I have had from my husband and I'm very grateful for it..."

He rang, and the secretary appeared and took me down in the elevator. I felt almost in a trance. At last I had news from him, and he still wanted me after all these years of silence. But at the same time I felt depressed. It was not going to be so simple after all. He would not be flying out of Poland tomorrow, but instead was waiting there for me. Here was a whole new problem. Hadn't I felt there would be a catch somewhere? Had anyone heard before of an American being released after five years' detention without trial and his captors saying it was all a mistake? No, there was something queer about this case, and I did not know what the game was.

Back home, we all reread Hermann's letter, trying to figure out what was behind it.

I went to bed elated yet worried. How could he imagine that I would want to go to Poland after all that had happened? Actually, the mere idea of setting foot in Poland terrified me. There was still no news of Noel and Herta. I was the one missing link. They had Noel's wife, but they did not have Hermann's. How did I know that Hermann had not been released as bait to catch me? Once I was there, perhaps he would disappear again. No, I thought, I will not fall for it. We have had enough experience in our family of this sort of thing. Hermann, Herta, and Noel and Erica had all followed Noel. I would be a damn fool to do the same thing now, five years later. Once in communist territory, I'd be in their hands—and then what? No, I would have to persuade Hermann to come out, without going to fetch him.

The next day, October 26, the boys and I each got a telegram from Hermann. The one to the boys was so characteristic that I felt he was his old self. They were delighted with it, copied it, and carried it to school in their pockets. An enterprising newsman persuaded us to give it to the press:

HELLO HUGHIE AND ALAN. WHAT DO YOU THINK OF THE IDEA OF HAVING A DADDY
AGAIN? I JUST RECKONED OUT THE LAST TIME WE SAW EACH OTHER WAS ONE THOU-
SAND NINE HUNDRED EIGHTEEN DAYS AGO. I GUESS WE WILL HAVE A LOT TO TELL
EACH OTHER. I TOLD THE DOCTOR TO HURRY ME UP A BIT BECAUSE I WANT TO BE
WITH MY BOYS QUICKLY TOO. MEANWHILE A BIG DADDY HUG TO BOTH OF YOU.
YOUR FATHER

The telegram to me repeated the invitation to go to Poland. At the same
time, the Polish Embassy invited me to go at their expense. I replied that I
wanted my husband to come to London.

At the American embassy I was told that Ambassador Flack had managed to
see Hermann and had given him my note, one I had written several weeks before in preparation for his release. The State Department also published an announcement:

> The Department has been informed that Ambassador Joseph Flack visited Her-
> mann Field yesterday at a sanatorium near Warsaw, to which he had been moved
> from prison in September. Mr. Field said he wished to rest in the sanatorium for
> the immediate future in order to regain his health. He said he has been out of
> touch with the world for five years and therefore he does not feel prepared to meet
> the press or make any public statements for the time being. The Ambassador plans
> to pay a second visit to Mr. Field.

I was asked at our embassy whether I wanted to go to Poland. I said no. I
then asked whether, if I did go, they could ensure that I got out again. They said
that once I was on Polish soil there was nothing they could do to protect me,
and it would be a matter of whether the Poles wanted me to leave. The way of
handling Hermann's release was without precedent and no one knew what the
purpose of it all was.

Deciding the prospects were simply too poor, I walked over to the post office and sent Hermann a long telegram. I told him I had received the Polish
government's invitation to come to Poland, but I did not want to do so. Instead
I was willing to wait until he felt able to make the journey to somewhere where
we could be peacefully alone together, and had asked the American ambassador
to discuss this with him.

The press was intensely interested by now, expecting Hermann to appear
any hour. Our telephone rang so constantly that it became impossible to prepare meals or eat without interruption, but we did not dare disconnect the
phone in case Hermann should try to get through.

On October 27, two days after Hermann's release, I got a call from the
counselor of the American embassy in Warsaw. Ambassador Flack had just
been out to see Hermann, who was about eighteen miles from Warsaw. He had

received my wire, and his condition was quite good. He was being very courageous, but it was hard for him. He was going to telephone me soon, and Mr. Flack wanted to warn me to be as calm as I could. Hermann was prepared to meet me outside of Poland. He could go any time. "You will find he has definite ideas of where he wants to go. I suggest you keep away from the press as much as possible"

I was so excited that I started to cry even while he was speaking. Now everything would be solved quickly! I got myself composed and waited for Hermann's call.

And then it came: his voice all the way from Poland, all the way from 1949! He sounded just the same as ever. It was unmistakably him. My dear, dear Hermann, at last! And he sounded quite calm too, so that between us we carried on quite a rational conversation. But all I remember of it now is the emotion, not the words, like a dream that seems so sensible, yet you cannot remember it when you wake up. What mattered was that I had heard his voice. No longer was there that blanket of silence, no longer did I have to rely on notes from governments or press agency reports. He had proved to me that he was still alive, and that he still cared about me and the boys.

He was disappointed that I had not come to Poland to fetch him, but he thought he could manage to travel the next week.

"I've been thinking where we could go. I'd like you to meet me in Switzerland at Gandria. It's a little village on the lake of Lugano. Mother took me there when I was a child. Maybe Monday or Tuesday. I'll call again tomorrow evening, when the boys are in from school."

Next morning the phone rang again. Warsaw calling. Hermann again? But no, it was for my mother: it was my sister Priscilla. What on earth was she doing in Warsaw?

I listened breathlessly to my mother's end of the conversation. She seemed to be trying to calm her: "Yes, of course I'll meet you at the airport, darling . . . Well no, I can't promise everyone will be there . . . It will be lovely to see you."

My mother had not heard my sister's voice for five years. She turned from the phone looking a bit shaken: "I wish it hadn't happened. Priscilla is in Warsaw. She is seeing Hermann, and soon she is flying here."

"Does she sound all right?"

"I'm not sure. She's too excited. She's talking too much. I couldn't stop her."

So that was it! I was furious. How was it that my sister was suddenly in Warsaw with Hermann? Wasn't this all an effort to confuse Hermann, to get him to swallow the communist line that his troubles were all due to "American provocateurs"? She lived in Dresden in East Germany, not Poland. They had failed to get me to go to Poland, so they were trying other means to see that Hermann did not come out. And of all things, to use my own sister against me!

I could well guess that my sister was not the only person in Warsaw bustling over to Hermann's villa, with bunches of flowers and saying how sorry they were for the awful mistake. But I did not dare ignore the possibility that if I went over there myself to counteract all this, neither of us might get out.

The next day, October 29, I received another summons to the Polish embassy. The ambassador repeated his invitation for me to go to Poland, and said I could bring any other members of my family that I wished, children or grownups. We could make it a short or a long visit, as we wished.

"And why do you want me to go to Poland?" I asked.

"It is your husband's wish. Are you suggesting that we are keeping him against his will?"

"I'm not suggesting anything. But I would like you to tell your government that the best way to clear this up for all concerned would be to encourage my husband to come home quickly."

As I took my leave I remember saying: "My husband is an American, not a Pole. He went as a visitor to your country for one week."

Hermann phoned again that same day. The American ambassador, Joseph Flack, had come to see him, he said, and "I told the ambassador frankly it was all a thing of the past. Over here there are quite a lot of people whose cases are not yet clarified, and until everything is settled I must stay here."

I protested: "This ought to be said by someone else, but your first responsibility is to your wife and children."

What on earth was all this about having to help settle other people's cases? True, nothing had been heard of Noel and Herta yet, but I didn't feel Hermann could do anything for them by staying in Poland.

We spoke again the next morning, and he said a commission had been set up in Poland to investigate why he had been held. He could not leave until they had gotten to the bottom of things and punished those responsible. He must stay another week. "I can't be pushed," he said.

That evening I tried to reassure him: "Don't feel I'm pushing you. Just try to feel close to me." Although I had sold our house in Cleveland, we still had his beloved Valley Farm in Massachusetts. "You've no idea how many friends you have over here. A thing like this shows who are your real friends."

Then he told me that there had been another man with him most of the time. Together they had written books, and he wanted me to go through them with him and prepare them for publication.

"I'm so glad you and Elsie have become close," he said.

"It's because we have gone through so much together, and fought for you so long."

By now Elsie was in London with me, her family still in Switzerland on vacation. Now she spoke with Hermann for the first time, a great excitement for them both. The next day he suggested to her that she and I should go to Poland together, and asked her to help me overcome my fears. The Poles would take care of all expenses.

But Elsie was firm. She told him she would not be beholden to the Poles in that way, and if she came it would be at her own expense. She could not think only of Hermann in this, but also of me and the boys. "Kate has to make up her own mind."

"But I must have her at my side to help. You should both come for a month or so. You know, Elsie, there are other members of the family involved, and other people."

"Of course I know. But I have been with Kate a lot, and I trust her judgment."

Poor Elsie was in a bind. She wanted more than anything to see her brother, but she stuck by me. We racked our brains trying to think of a solution. Not knowing anything of Hermann's state of mind, we feared he might be driven by this conflict into a nervous breakdown.

My daily conversations with Hermann were at the expense of the Polish government. In fact, most days there were two calls, morning and evening, because I told him I could not sleep without knowing he was still safely there.

I found the situation utterly ironic. Here he was in a sort of paradise, in his convalescent villa with every need attended to, after five years in a cellar. He felt so safe he did not want to reenter the world again. I, on the other hand, lived in a state of constant suspense. Whoever had heard of the communists releasing a prisoner and leaving him, convalescent but free, in a lovely villa in a pine woods? Hermann gave me a glowing account of the beauty of his surroundings.

There was as yet no news of Noel or Herta. Could it be that now that Hermann was "free" as far as the Polish government was concerned, he would finally disappear? The American embassy in Warsaw had issued him a new passport, and the Poles had stamped an exit permit on it. Now the Russians could pick him up, and the Poles could simply shrug their shoulders and say, "We don't know where he is. He was free to go wherever he wished." I was worried he could be hustled off in the wrong direction.

Our telephone conversations seemed to get us nowhere. One day I told him they must be terribly expensive and he should show more consideration for the Polish taxpayers. All he had to do was come out.

The nervous strain was beginning to tell on me. I had been chronically nervous for the past five years, but the month of suspense since Swiatlo's statement had made the continued delay especially hard to take. Despite sleeping pills, I often spent the hours before dawn sitting at my desk, composing long letters to Hermann trying to tell him about events that had happened in the outside world since he had disappeared.

On November 2, I sat at the little table by my bedroom window, looking out at the moon in the London sky. It would be looking just the same to Hermann, if he were awake in his villa in the Polish woods. I started to write, explaining why I would not come to Poland. I gave him the facts on how and where Noel, Herta, and Erica had disappeared, and how Erica had been sentenced to death and was now in Vorkuta. I said that if I came to Poland there was no guarantee that I could get out again, and that I was not willing to make Hugh and Alan orphans. "We conceived these children, and you know how much we love them."

I reminded him that he was an American, and that given the great tension between America and the communist world, "no American can vacillate between these two worlds without destroying himself." His choice was to come back to some noncommunist country very soon and rejoin me and the children and all his staunch friends, or stay in Poland without us forever.

I explained that we had lacked proof of where he was arrested, but that the State Department had nevertheless sent many notes to the Poles on his behalf, and I, too, had appealed for their help. They had given none. "Now suddenly the Polish ambassador is all kindness—but they have already shown they do not care about my happiness, by not helping me before . . ."

No doubt he had been told Swiatlo was an American agent, and I understood how he must hate the man, but he should remember he did not know for whom he had been working.

There seemed to be two things keeping him in Poland. One was concern about what would happen to him when he left; and the other was the desire to help those falsely accused like himself. I tried to reassure him on the first point: "I agree that some people have suffered through the irrational feelings aroused by the Cold War, particularly in America. But this does not extend to a degree serious for you . . . I honestly believe, honey, that without the State Department's efforts you would not be out of prison today."

On the matter of helping people, I did not see how he could do so by remaining in Poland, and I told him that Elsie agreed that his presence could have no influence on any decision to clear Noel and Herta.

As to bringing wrongdoers to justice, he should remember he was an American, and it was not his business to interfere in the internal affairs of Poland.

Then I tried to counter the fear he and the Poles seemed to have of the press, and pointed out that although they had their own interests it was sometimes very useful to get facts on public record, such as that he was in Poland now. But of course I would not give his exact location to the press, so he would not be pestered by them.

I ended with an emotional appeal: "If you stay and do this thing, it will break my heart. I have fought for your freedom for five years and only want to save you from making an irrevocable mistake. No one has exerted any pressure on me. I am sitting alone in my bedroom writing this . . . I do beg you to trust my judgment, darling, rather than that of anyone who has been living in Eastern Europe, and arrange to meet me in Switzerland, or Sweden, or any noncommunist country you like. I shall ask the U.S. embassy in Warsaw to let me know that you have read this letter. Your own wife, Katie."

I counted the pages, six sheets written on both sides. Perhaps it would move him.

The sky was getting light. I got back into bed and fell asleep.

The U.S. diplomatic pouch to Poland seemed slow, and most of my letters to Hermann did not arrive until after he had left. But this one reached him.

Every day Elsie and I tried to figure out a way of breaking the impasse. The British had offered a military plane to fly him directly to London, but he turned that down flat. Then there was the idea of meeting in Copenhagen, but that also fell through. It seemed he would not go to any NATO country, given their lack of neutrality in the Cold War. What about Sweden? So we arranged for the Swedish ambassador to Poland to fetch him to the Swedish embassy and give him neutral protection while we worked out how to meet him in Sweden. But this did not work out either.

Finally Elsie went off to Switzerland to see if somehow Hermann could be induced to go there. She discovered that there was about to be an architectural congress in Warsaw, and among the delegates was the Swiss architect Hans Brechbuehler, who had shared a room with Hermann at the congress in 1949. She went to see Hans, who promised to contact Hermann and do his best to persuade him to come out. The Swiss authorities said they would make it easy for Hermann to come to Switzerland, where, they assured her, he would be safe from the Russians, and that they would do their best to protect him from the press.

Meanwhile, Hugh and Alan spoke to Hermann daily, telling him about their school life as if they really knew him well. Though sometimes, when I began to feel we would never get him out, I wanted to say, "If you aren't going to come and be a father to these children of yours, it's not fair getting them attached to you again."

I became worried about the boys' security. The one way of getting me to go to Poland would have been to take my boys there. To reassure me, my father visited the chief of the London police Special Branch for advice; he also kept notes in his diary of where the boys were going to be each day and when they were due to return from school, and he often went to meet them there.

Hermann told me that Ambassador Flack had brought him back numbers of the *New York Times* covering the past five years, and that reading them had been an awful shock. He had known virtually nothing of world events and was horrified by the intensity of the Cold War, and by the political climate generated in the United States by Senator Joseph McCarthy.

Finally, on the morning of November 14, I decided to abandon all diplomacy and, regardless of who was listening in on the line, to tell Hermann the main points of what had happened in the world in the last five years. I started to talk about all the purge trials in which the Fields had been mentioned, about the men hanged in Hungary and Czechoslovakia and imprisoned in Germany.

He tried to stop me, and I said: "You needn't say anything, I'm going to go on." And I proceeded to tell him how Erica Wallach had gone to Berlin, been arrested, condemned to death, and that now we knew she was in a Russian labor camp. I told him that his friend Karel Markus had disappeared in Czechoslovakia, and that I had been told his wife and children had been found dead. And I told him—though really this was for the Poles or Russians, if they were listening—that if anything happened to him and he did not come out there would be no more damned nonsense about American agents, that I knew it would have been Russian agents and I had enough evidence to prove it. Further, if they really wanted the Cold War heated up, they had only to continue this fooling over Hermann and I would see it heated up plenty!

Hermann sounded a little shaken, and I was trembling. Anyway, he knew certain things now. Perhaps my outburst would help him understand why I did not come to fetch him, and why he should not delay any longer. For really, I was becoming desperate. We seemed to have reached an impasse, and I wondered how much longer I could take it. I was living on sedatives and sleeping pills, and even so spent much of each night sitting in my room trying to figure a way out. Since Hermann's release I had lost ten pounds.

I had an image of Hermann hanging on the end of a rope in a deep well, with me forever trying to wind him up to the surface. Only he always got stuck when he neared the top. I could never get him over the hump.

In exasperation, and perhaps just for self-preservation, one day I decided I was beaten. I came into my parents' sitting room. On the mantel shelf was an old snapshot of Hermann and me with the children. I said to my father: "Please put that away, Daddy. I know I've had it."

"I'll put it in my desk," he said, "just for now."

# 25

## Breaking Out

I slept fitfully as the morning hours of October 25 advanced. Shortly before 5 A.M. I turned on the radio to Warsaw. And then it came, the momentous announcement. I recognized my name and some of the key words, including "Joseph Swiatlo," "*amerikanski agent,*" "*provokateur.*" At once I felt uneasy. The statement was much longer than what we had agreed to the previous afternoon, and certainly it was not the same. I waited. Now it came in English:

> Following an inspection ordered by the state authorities in the middle of 1953, certain cases were brought to light of a gross violation of the people's rule of law, and a thorough investigation was ordered in this connection. In the course of this investigation the authorities detected Josef Swiatlo as an agent provocateur of the U.S. Secret Service who, with the aid of forged identity papers and disguising himself and taking advantage of defects in the exercise of control, had managed to infiltrate into the public security organization.
>
> As an agent provocateur, Swiatlo employed various criminal means and false evidence forged by himself to slander and incriminate a number of citizens. Taking advantage of the absence of proper supervision, he selected certain persons and caused them to be arrested on false charges. One of the persons so arrested was an American citizen, Hermann Field, the case against whom was deliberately framed by Swiatlo with particularly provocative perfidy.
>
> Fearing his exposure as the result of the investigation, Swiatlo succeeded in fleeing the country, and today he is openly continuing his provocative work as an exposed agent of subversive U.S. activities, broadcasting lies, calumnies, and fallacies which are as absurd as they are shameless. This provocation is part of the campaign conducted against Poland by Americans who shrink from no method in preparing the way for their aggressive aims. It is notorious that they are making frantic efforts to force through the revival of the Wehrmacht under the cadre of Hitlerites with their criminal Nazi methods.
>
> The investigation has shown that the charges brought by Swiatlo against Hermann Field were groundless. Consequently Hermann Field has been released and has been given full satisfaction.

Other charges leveled against certain Polish citizens have been proved to be false and groundless, and these innocent victims have been released. The investigation is continuing; and measures have been taken against those guilty of lack of vigilance and inadequate supervision.

I felt betrayed. This had no resemblance to what I had agreed to. The first act on regaining my freedom in effect made me an accessory to a campaign by my captors against my own country. What did I know about Swiatlo beyond what he did to me? What did I know about anything at this point? How could I face the embassy people after this anti-American blast?

I hardened: Remember, I told myself, you're in the driver's seat now. First, I would call off the impending press conference scheduled for ten o'clock. I had not wanted it anyway, and now I could not possibly evade the issues that had been raised. I would find myself surrounded by controversy while still on Polish soil; there would be no chance of leaving as a private citizen with the past five years a closed chapter. Second, I would refuse to cooperate in any planned procedures this day. Let the Poles sweat out the mess in front of the whole world.

Mrs. Markowska was alerted to my decision, and she rushed out to Otwock, arriving only half an hour before the interview was to start. She said my action was irresponsible. I retorted that they had put me in an impossible position, one that violated all her promises about my release. Under the circumstances, until all the issues between us were cleared up, I wouldn't be willing to see anyone, including representatives from my own embassy.

It was a standoff. The day advanced, Mrs. Markowska gravitating constantly between me and the telephone line to Warsaw, the tension mounting all the while. She complained that I was creating an international incident, that the U.S. embassy was demanding immediate access to me on the basis of the news release, that the Foreign Office was now involved and could not hold off giving my address here any longer.

There was something comical, but also miserable, about the way this entrance back into life had backfired. After the weeks of preparation, the Poles were visibly put out. They had obviously wanted this to be their day as the initiators of my freeing, a day of celebration on their turf before it was placed irreversibly into American hands. First thing that morning before my rising, they had decked out my front rooms with a profusion of flowers. On the table were bottles of champagne, Wedel chocolates, fruit, and delicious pastries. The commandant had greeted me with great pride as if it were my birthday.

And now? Now we were all upset. It was late afternoon and nothing had been resolved. Was everyone set on pulling me apart when what I needed was to be put together? Suddenly the commandant rushed into my room in consternation: "They're here, the Americans."

Already I could hear the scraping of shoes on the threshold downstairs. I could hardly contain my excitement. The unbelievable moment had come. My countrymen!

Three hearty figures, all out of breath, appeared in the doorway of my room, loaded down with gifts. I wanted to rush to them. Then we would just turn around, go downstairs, and climb into their limousine. I would be surrounded by my own people, not the silent figures with the drooping hats. We would race right through the gate, not even bothering to open it. Who cared? This time it would not be fantasy. The bad dream would be behind me for good. Freedom!

But of course I knew it wouldn't be that simple. I steeled myself and retreated back into my "old bear" shell.

They glanced around the room in surprise. The Poles had apparently tried to steal the show. The tallest of the three spoke up: "Welcome, Mr. Field. May I introduce our ambassador, Joseph Flack. I am Oechsner, counselor at the embassy. And this is our colleague John Dennis, second secretary." His eyes fastened on the festive setting of the room. "We are happy also to share this first moment of freedom with you. A lot of us have worked hard to get it for you."

Mr. Flack approached me and warmly shook my hand. He was a fairly short, older man with white hair and a warm, sympathetic manner. "I have greetings for you from Kate and your sister which were sent some weeks ago but could not be delivered till now. I talked with her today on the phone. Needless to say, she is very eager to see you and is waiting to hear from us here. We'll do everything we can to expedite your being reunited quickly." I put the letters he handed me in my pocket. I would have to be alone for that first moment with Kate.

What familiar faces they had, as if I were suddenly back home. And the sound of English in other than my own voice or its copy in Stan—it was delicious to hear. We settled down around the gift-laden table. Now old friends had been added—a tube of Ipana toothpaste, a Gillette shaving set and brush, a package of Lucky Strikes, some good old American beer, some copies of the New York Times and Life. For a moment the honest simplicity of these tokens of my own lost world broke through to me. We all laughed spontaneously.

My guests inquired about my health, about my circumstances here, and were intrigued by my project drawings pinned up on the cupboards and walls of the room. To all appearances, it was as if I had spent these years as a luxury-class prisoner out here—which was exactly the impression my captors had intended. I touched cautiously on the past saying that until a few weeks ago I had been in the very different environment of a secret interrogation center in Miedzeszyn. They smiled. They were quite familiar with the spot. It was within sight of the Foreign Journalists Club on the east bank of the Vistula. I couldn't help thinking that that was probably one of the reasons I wasn't allowed to walk outside.

I felt increasingly uneasy. I suspected that our conversation was being monitored downstairs. I presumed my guests must have had similar suspicions. How could either side speak frankly under the circumstances? I also supposed that anything I said was subject to leaking by either side to their own advantage against the other. With all the apparent fanfare about my release and its anti-American tone, there would be a lively search for stories. Clearly I was just a chip in a vast poker game. Meanwhile, much was at stake here that had not yet been resolved.

The ambassador was saying that he and his wife would be glad to have me as their guest until my departure from Poland was arranged. Part of me wanted to throw all resolves to the wind and say, "Of course, I'd love to." But how could I? My hands were tied. How could I explain that I had no choice but to stay put for the time being? In the face of unseen ears, I didn't feel free to talk about my ongoing negotiations. I thanked Mr. Flack but indicated that I needed a short breather to adjust to the momentous events that had come upon me so suddenly, that I didn't want to put my health at risk in my weakened condition, that this isolated forest refuge, despite its association with my captivity, provided the quiet I needed to find myself.

Mr. Oechsner shook his head in disbelief, but Ambassador Flack was reassuring, saying that no one wanted to rush me. I should obviously do as I felt best. Was there a telephone available to me? Yes? In that case, if I liked the idea, he would try to get Kate through to me tomorrow evening. They would come out again in the afternoon and then we would see. And I should feel free to call him anytime.

I felt very grateful to the ambassador for easing the tension. I liked him at once (he had commented as an aside that he and I had somewhat similar Quaker backgrounds, which perhaps warmed me to him further). Had I any other immediate needs? I indicated my sketchy knowledge of the outside world, and especially of my own country today. Oechsner agreed to bring out a stack of *Time* magazines and a sampling of *New York Times*es, an implied recognition that my departure might still be some days off. In spite of their going without their prize exhibit and their evident puzzlement at my unanticipated reluctance to leave, I felt this first encounter with my countrymen had ended on a friendly, if uneasy, note.

I was alone at last. I pulled the letter from my pocket. October 4: Kate's words just weeks ago. I was reading her own words. We had made it, after all these years of silence. I grabbed a pencil and wrote:

FREE AT LAST. YEARNING TO SEE YOU AND BE REUNITED. DOING WELL BUT NOT YET
IN CONDITION TO TRAVEL. THEREFORE SUGGEST YOU COME FOR SHORT VISIT HERE
IF THE BOYS CAN SPARE YOU FOR A WEEK. POLISH AUTHORITIES HAVE OFFERED TO
PAY YOUR TRAVEL COSTS HERE AND BACK. SUGGEST YOU GO TO THEIR EMBASSY IN
LONDON FOR VISA AND TICKET. SUGGEST YOU LET AMERICAN EMBASSY LONDON
KNOW WHAT PLANE YOU ARE COMING ON. YOU WILL BE MET AT AIRPORT HERE . . .
LOTS OF LOVE AND CHEER.

And then one to the boys.

When I had finished, I gave the telegrams to the commandant, who promised to have them taken right in to the central telegraph office. He seemed
genuinely moved by the day's events.

Suddenly it flashed through me: we weren't really together yet, were we? I
had turned down the opportunity to see Kate and the boys, when right now I
could be speeding toward them. Had I trapped us in my own twenty-four-hour
rule? But a sacred commitment cut across everything: my pledge to Stanislaw
and his to me.

As I looked back at this first day of "freedom," I felt I had been standing on a
perpetual-motion seesaw that had been trying to throw me off balance. What
would day two bring?

It started with an early-morning stagger-walk with Mietek (I still found it
difficult not to weave), who hinted at important corrective measures being
considered in the Polish security system. He vaguely referred to forces beyond
the Polish border. There would be some housecleaning. But it would be difficult to set things right, with the West waiting to jump at any admission of
weakness.

After breakfast Mrs. Markowska showed up, businesslike as usual but having regained her cordial manner. She pointedly ignored the events of the previous day. "We don't have much time now, and there is still a lot to resolve. The
American press and even your Kate are implying that we are stalling on your
release. First, the matter of indemnity . . ."

She reached into her handbag and pulled out what looked like a large
checkbook. "Here is a check made out to you by the Polish National Bank in the
sum of $50,000. It's the closest to your request we are prepared to go. We are
not a wealthy country. You will be able to cash it anywhere in the West . . . All
we ask is that you do not use the notoriety of your release against us, and that
you agree that we have made all amends possible and that you have no further
demands on us."

She continued: "There is the matter of your health. If we are to cover measures to make good any damage to your health, we must first establish your condition. We are proposing to have you undergo a thorough examination at our best Warsaw clinic, the one all our top party and government officials use. This can be arranged in a few days, but will require a number of sessions before we can make any commitments. At least a week or ten days. Maybe you would like to have Kate be with you during this time, and then join you for a month of convalescence up at Zagopane? All as our guests. That might be all you need." And she laughed at the thought in spite of herself.

I agreed to the sessions at the hospital and dental clinics at the earliest possible dates. There was no way around that if I wanted them to take responsibility for any remedial costs. For all I knew they might be considerable, and these five years must have drained resources at home. All the more reason to have Kate here. I would talk to her about it.

Mrs. Markowska went on to my request for punishment of those I had pinpointed earlier. Aside from Swiatlo, about whom I would have to deal with the Americans, the others were already in custody. It would be useful if I could testify in person. I refused. It would be inappropriate for me, an American citizen, to be involved in an internal criminal process, especially after the twist of their Swiatlo announcement.

My writings with Stanislaw? I was worried they had ended in an incinerator. No, they had been found intact. She added, somewhat amazed: "I'm told there are well over a hundred copybooks." She laughed. "You'll have to wait till there's a truck available!"

I realized she had been holding back on the most difficult question: Stanislaw's release. She regretted that they would not be able to follow my wishes at this time. I was shocked. When? No later than mid-June of next year. His case was tied in with that of a number of high-level Polish political figures still under review. Surely I understood that security and fairness made it impossible to release him ahead of the others.

That was unacceptable, I retorted. Every additional day he spent in that cellar while I was free was simply intolerable. I would stay right where I was until this matter had been resolved. The moment I uttered the words I suspected that this was hardly a threat at this point. They were in no hurry. The embarrassment of not being able to pry me loose would all be with the Americans. For the moment, however, I had no choice. The Poles would grow weary after a while. Anyway, a vague promise of some future date was no good. I didn't trust them for a moment. Only right here and now could I force the issue. The agony of decision making that lay ahead on this issue was as yet only faintly discernible to me.

And so the seesaw continued. That afternoon, in a rapid change of scene, my countrymen appeared once more at my door. Oechsner, true to his word, carried a heavy bundle of publications under his arm. He extricated a *New York Times* from the rest. "Here it is, all about you. The colonel's statement and our two long requests to the Polish and Hungarian governments. Now you'll understand better why you are a free man today, with your wife impatient to receive you in London."

I expressed my thanks. What a lark, being wooed from all sides!

"You'll need a new valid passport. The Poles will require it for their exit visa. We brought along a Polaroid."

We went out on the little corner terrace for better light. I was shocked by the result. I looked unfamiliar, not like myself at all. Flabby and beaten. My eyes were hooded, looking inward; no evidence of seeing.

"I don't want Kate to see this before we meet."

"Don't worry. It will only find its way into the passport we are issuing for your return home."

As we sat around the table I came clean on the three sticking points with the Poles: release of my cell mate, information as to the fate of my brother, and the matter of my health. Mr. Oechsner expressed great surprise that I had taken it on myself to negotiate while still technically in the hands of my captors. Who had ever heard of such a thing? That's what the embassy was here for, after all. And I was hurting someone else grievously—Kate, who despaired with every further hour of uncertainty.

I had steeled myself for this. "It would speed everything up if I had Kate here at my side to help me back into life, after which we could leave together."

Oechsner looked still more dismayed. "But obviously she is afraid to do that. Surely you can understand. The last place in the world she wants to find herself is Warsaw. In any case, you'll have a chance to talk with her yourself in a few hours. She'll be calling you this evening around eight o'clock."

The phone rang exactly at eight. "Mr. Field, this is the embassy. We have Mrs. Field on the line in London. Hold for a moment while we transfer her."

And then suddenly, from far off: "Manchie? Manchie, dear, it's your Kate . . ." In spite of all resolve, I dissolved in tears and, at first, couldn't say a word.

"Manchie." It had always been her most private name for me, a humorous misconstrual of a Swiss term from my childhood, *Maenneli*—little man. "Manchie, can you hear me?" At once I visualized her sitting at the phone by the hall window at Corringham Road in London, near the old grandfather clock. I don't know what my words were when they finally came. Questions about her, about the boys, about Elsie . . .

Then her inevitable question: "When will you be arriving? I'm afraid for you. Until you've left Polish soil, nothing is sure. We couldn't face anything going wrong now. Remember, we three have waited for you these five years. Waiting, just waiting." She became silent. I knew she was struggling on the other end.

I tried to be factual. There were things to clear up still. She would have to be patient. And I didn't feel secure enough to travel by myself into an unfamiliar world. Couldn't she come to be at my side? Being around people was still very difficult for me, I explained. We could have a few quiet days to get reacquainted in my little forest hideout here. I described the beauty of the pines in the misty mornings and in the full moon at night.

I sensed that Kate was trying hard to remain calm. "Manchie dear, you seem to have forgotten what happened to you. Surely you don't now want to put me at similar risk. Think of Hughie and Alan; your sons, Hermann . . ." Our conversation petered out. I assured her we would stay in touch by phone through the embassy, and we would talk together tomorrow at the same time. As I hung up I felt drained of all emotion. I dropped on my bed and fell into the protective arms of a deep sleep.

The next morning—it was the twenty-eighth—Mietek asked me how my conversation with Kate had gone. Then he added that routing our calls through the embassy seemed cumbersome and quite unnecessary. He was authorized to say that henceforth I could communicate with Kate any time and as often and as long as I wished by just picking up the phone. "Simply ask for the international operator."

Meanwhile I spent every spare moment with the big pile of magazines and newspapers left by Mr. Oechsner, trying to catch up with events and attitudes and becoming ever more disturbed as the hours rolled by. What I had dismissed in the Polish papers over the past year as typical communist harangue about events at home turned out to have a reflection in the pages of *Time* and the pictures in *Life*. The United States seemed to be in the grip of a paranoia that spewed nastiness into every aspect of American life. Where was the intellectual integrity I had dreamed about? The traditional warmth in plain human contact I had so longed for? The effort to understand different points of view? The pluralism that was so lacking here?

What sort of security were we hoping for when in the process we lost the security of our own humanity? Stalin's world had done just that, betrayed the hopes for a new social contract by violating elementary human rights, by its slave labor camps, by its rigged trials, by Katyn Forest and the mass killings of dissidents. But that did not give us at home the right to impose on others our own skewed values as the only alternative. How did it look to the Russians to be under constant threat of an atomic bomb from the only source that had seen fit to use it? True, after World War II there was reason enough to believe that Stalin's ruthless determination to protect Russia by a ring of buffer states might have ended in a takeover of all of Europe. Kennan's policy of containment to counter that possibility had seemed a reasonable precaution at the time, a standoff while the dust of postwar instability settled. But by now all this appeared to have degenerated into an insensate anticommunism reminiscent of that which had driven Hitler's Germany.

I felt depressed. Would I once again find myself the odd man out? Clearly the expectation at home was that after my brush with the shocking aberrations of this society I would be a fanatical anticommunist myself. But surely there must be a middle ground, a place somewhere for men of reason. Or had we all passed the point of no return?

In the afternoon my visitors from the embassy again paid a call. I expressed gratitude for our government's response to Swiatlo's revelations and said I wouldn't dispute his general chronology. I went on to report on my reading of the newspapers they had brought. It didn't look that pretty at home, did it, I ventured. I wanted some assurance that I would not be sucked into congressional hearings as a circus partner with Swiatlo. They should understand my feelings about this particular individual. While I would be happy to provide a full report in a serious setting, I would have to refuse point blank to take part in any public extravaganza.

I was reminded that the embassy represented the executive branch and had no control over how Congress conducted its business. They could give me no guarantees. That, I said, wasn't good enough. After what I had been through these five years, I felt I had a right to be left in peace so I could reconstruct my life. I was not prepared to run from one abuse into another one.

An uneasy silence settled over the room, which I broke by asking whether they had any information about Noel beyond Swiatlo's September statement.

No, the Hungarians had not responded the way the Poles had, despite efforts by the embassy in Budapest. Of course, it was possible he was no longer alive. In any case, there would be considerable public interest in him—into which I might be drawn as well.

They gave me the latest papers, which expressed mystification as to why I was still stuck in Poland. Such speculation would only make things more difficult if it continued. The embassy would like to be able to announce a definite day for my reentry into free society. I responded that I still had to have my physical checkup at the Warsaw clinic. Beyond that, though, I felt too insecure to travel by myself yet. Oechsner said they could assure complete protection and privacy: they would fly me out on a U.S. military plane to Frankfurt, where Kate would meet me.

Time was on my side. But what *was* time, anyway? Until very recently, it had almost ceased to exist. Now, everyone was piling in with a stopwatch to throw me off balance.

The question of what had happened to Noel preoccupied my thoughts that evening. The next morning I put the issue squarely to Mrs. Markowska. She was prepared to say one thing: they were both alive. I felt relieved, but in that case felt it was up to the Poles to arrange for me to talk directly to Noel by phone. That was the only way I would believe them. It was absurd to claim that the Polish security machine couldn't get the cooperation of their Hungarian counterparts.

I felt exhausted. It was difficult being all alone in a world that had become so unfamiliar and to be unable to feel trust in anyone. Now in a way I was embattled on both sides: the Poles kept stalling on critical issues, while my countrymen seemed to want to pitch me forthwith into the turmoil that would meet me at home. More than ever I valued the quiet shelter of this island of peace. What was the hurry? I was part of a complex game, and as long as I kept my feelings in check and played it cool, no one could walk over me. Not anymore.

Barely had my colleagues from the embassy left than Mietek rushed in: "You're in luck! They found her at last and have brought her to Warsaw. You see, you can count on us!"

"But who?" I had a sinking premonition even as I asked the question.

"Your sister-in-law!" Mietek noticed my subdued reaction. "Well, how about it?"

What could I say? Everything had changed since I had made my original request. Now all I had to do was pick up the phone every morning and evening and Kate's voice was at the other end. I no longer needed an intermediary. And yet Priscilla had dropped everything and made a tedious, long journey to answer my cry for help. It was not her fault that the whole scene had changed in the interim. At last one of Kate's family would be here in person, the very thing I had been asking of Kate herself without success.

I was too drained of emotion for any show of affection as, later, I stared into the strained, tired face before me. Priscilla's eyes had a strange intensity about them, and a restiveness kept her in constant movement as she responded to my questions about her life the last few years. As the evening advanced into night I repeatedly urged her to get some sleep, but she said she could not.

To my relief I learned that neither she nor her husband had been locked up or physically abused on account of me. Hans had lost his position at the Education Ministry in East Berlin and been transferred to Dresden, to head up a new teacher's training institute. Priscilla had been able to continue her work as an artist, but Hans had been demoted, as had many of their German colleagues. The sudden news of my release, followed by the appearance of an unknown

Polish emissary looking for her, had stood everything on its head, and Priscilla now felt she was being swept along in a kind of euphoria.

Although she hadn't slept for two nights, the light shining from the study where she had bedded down told me that sleep eluded her once again. By the next morning I could see that she was in a state of overstimulation that was feeding on itself, as if she was being driven by a sense of mission to somehow rectify what had happened.

I got in touch with Mrs. Markowska; some sedatives were ordered. Given her state of mind, I dreaded the possibility of an encounter out here between her and the embassy people; I therefore had her driven in to Warsaw for the afternoon. When she returned her condition hadn't improved. I suggested she might want to go on to London, to the quiet of her family. So Priscilla picked up the phone and put in a call to Kate. Her mother answered. At first she urged that her sister come to Poland, but on Kate's refusal she said she would fly to them at the first possible opportunity.

Priscilla took off for London on October 30, her overwrought condition in no way diminished. I could not blame her for her emotional behavior or for the additional load she placed on me. She, like Monica Felton, had turned up here on my own misguided initiative. They had simply been responding to my cries for help.

The world I had reentered was most strange. Day after day assorted Polish players were journeying out to my forest castle, pilgrims of remorse, of self-justification, seeking absolution for having turned on me. I could not reciprocate their tears. Was I expected to feel sympathy toward them for the mistaken views they had had about their world and about me, and the discomfort they were suffering now? Clearly their tears were about themselves rather than about me.

Meanwhile, the paralysis connected with my departure intensified from day to day. Every morning and night Kate and I made another try at undoing the knot, but it only got worse. I felt we were in a fishbowl on the international front-line. How many might be listening in, with their own plans to keep the pot boiling? There were leaks to the press that no one could nail down. I didn't feel I could freely discuss my promise to Stanislaw. And Kate couldn't possibly understand my situation, removed as it was from her reality. In her growing despair that this whole episode might end abruptly in my disappearance for good, she tried to warn me with a detailed account of the disappearances and trials in eastern Europe; I in turn felt only panic at this wide-open discussion, with the one end of the line right here on communist soil.

I told her that I was trying to get acclimatized to being with other people, by making shopping trips to town, visiting the Infelds at their Nieborow retreat, going to concerts, spending occasional evenings with Mietek and his family. To

Kate, each of these ventures represented a new threat, although I assured her I was always accompanied and driven in a chauffeured car.

"But, Manchie, have you forgotten in whose hands you still are?"

In fact, I did feel increasingly insecure, but for another reason: these phone calls, I feared, could become a guide to unauthorized ears for politically motivated terrorism. Wasn't I exposing myself to a hidden risk here? That there were still pockets of underground insurgency against the regime was more than likely. What better way to destroy its international standing than to waylay me, remove me from the scene, and claim the secret police were behind it all? I even sensed a certain uneasiness among my "hosts" out here, with the commandant and Mietek always insisting that I should not cross a busy downtown street alone and should stay close to whoever accompanied me. It didn't escape my notice that the chauffeur had a bulge at belt level under his jacket, which could mean only one thing.

As for the authorities, I felt reasonably sure that they could not back away now from releasing me to the West. That dreaded scenario was gone for good; there was simply too much world focus on the case. That did not prevent them from wanting to do things their own way, of course: departure only when all the excitement had died down; the recurrent invitation for a month in the Tatra mountains with Kate while I convalesced. There had also been an official offer from the Polish Ministry of Reconstruction for a six-month stint as city planner in Lodz to start me back on my career! Or a similar half year of transition in India? By that time Stanislaw, they had assured me, would be free. Then again, I was still met with continuing excuses for failure to effect phone contact with Noel. All these trial balloons had an air of absurdity about them; but how to break the cycle?

Although my rags had long since been replaced by an ill-fitting assortment of garments, clearly something more had to be done about my appearance before I was ready to go forth into that other world. One day without warning, a tailor appeared to measure me for a first-rate suit and winter coat, of materials of my own choosing. The commandant whispered to me that this man was responsible for none other than the president's wardrobe. Was this yet another device to draw out my departure, or was it to make me as presentable as possible? I could play this game too. At the final fitting a week or so later, I pointed out that I expected to be going to the mountains for some skiing, but that would require quite different clothing. Without protest, he measured me for a hand-tailored ski suit. But that wouldn't help, I protested, if I had nothing appropriate for my feet. How about some new shoes? And come to think of it, ski boots were in order too. So a shoemaker shortly joined the work force, with an order to make a set of each.

The competition for my soul extended into exquisite details. There was the amusing occasion when Mr. Dennis of the embassy asked whether I would like to join him at a Rostropovich concert that night in town. Though it was sold out, the embassy was sure they could get an extra ticket for me. But alas, apparently all but one of their three seats had already been spoken for. As if by accident, Mietek mentioned the same concert and said he had cornered two tickets especially for himself and me. Imagine my surprise when, Mietek and I having taken our seats, I found Mr. Dennis, looking quite crestfallen, on my opposite side.

Or there was the incident with the suitcases. Because my worldly goods kept on growing from zero, there would be quite a bit of luggage, whichever route of departure I took. Mr. Oechsner raised the matter and kindly offered a spare suitcase of his own. The next morning, however, without explanation, two beautiful new cowhide suitcases appeared in my room. The commandant merely commented with an offhand grin: "For your journey—Polish style."

And there was my agreement to come for lunch to the embassy, in spite of scowls from the Poles and hints that it might be a one-way street with no return. They drove me there but kept the car stationed outside for my return journey. It was the first time I felt free to talk without the risk of unwanted ears listening in. And yet in spite of all the cordiality and introductions and hamburgers in the cafeteria, I felt out of place, in an environment that had become alien and frightening. It was therefore with a sense of relief that I sped back across the Vistula bridge to my hideout.

# 26

---

# The Mist at Dawn

As days became weeks there still remained three unsolved issues. The first was my fear of traveling alone, combined with my suspicion of every suggested resolution; the second was my need to meet Kate without the fanfare of the press; and the third, and still the most intractable, was getting Stanislaw freed. On the matter of direct contact with Noel I had all but given up.

The first and second impediments quite unexpectedly evaporated owing to a fortunate combination of efforts and circumstances. One morning I got a call from the Swiss legation. A Swiss architect was in Poland as a delegate to an international housing congress in Warsaw and wanted to speak to me. He claimed he knew me and had told the Swiss minister he had joined the congress in part to help me. It turned out to be dear old Hans Brechbuehler from Bern, my roommate at the Bergamo congress just before my disappearance in 1949.

Thus I was promptly invited for lunch at the legation. What fun it was, dropping into Swiss dialect with all its associations! The whole atmosphere was one of family cordiality. Not only did Brechbuehler offer to be at my side throughout the flight out of Poland, but the minister also said he had been in touch with the Swiss police about sheltering me if I chose to go with the architects when they returned to Switzerland in a few days. They understood my need for privacy and would see I got it. I remember that little session at the Swiss legation as some of the happiest moments of those long-drawn-out weeks. At last my dread of journeying in isolation into an uncertain world had been resolved.

And the question of Stanislaw being freed? By now I sensed the Poles themselves were becoming impatient with my delayed departure and the bad press they were getting for it. This may have been a factor in their new proposal: While they could not free him now, they promised that he would be able to celebrate Christmas Eve a free man together with his wife and son. Would I accept that?

That was only some five weeks away. But could I trust them? I replied, "Only if he tells me—here, in person, and in complete privacy—that he trusts that what you promise will be carried out."

They said they could not respond at once; difficult technicalities were involved. I sensed, however, a definite relief on their part. And so I felt the last impediment was dissolving. Now I could confidently assure Kate I would be on next Friday's flight to Zurich via Prague. For sure . . . Friday: only five days hence.

Everything was set at last. The clinical checkups had provided me with a stack of X rays for future reference and a clean bill of health, much to the relief of Mrs. Markowska. The doctors stipulated an extended convalescent stay in the mountains. Since by now it was clear that it would not take place in Poland, Mrs. Markowska handed me a $500 bill, the first I had ever seen, for use in Switzerland.

Everything settled? Not quite. The embassy told me they would be picking me up with the embassy car at 7 A.M. Friday to take me to the airport. When Mrs. Markowska heard this, she vetoed the arrangement at once. "As long as you are on Polish soil, your security is our responsibility. We will deliver you to the plane." She was quite adamant.

"No, I'm not willing to do it that way," I replied. "I was your prisoner. I am now free. You have no rights whatsoever over me anymore. It is for my embassy to claim me."

I took the matter up at once with Ambassador Flack, feeling slightly ridiculous. He took my protest calmly, not wanting to allow for the possibility of a new impediment.

"What if they deliver you to the entrance doors of the airport and we receive you there? You'll be with us at one table while we wait for the plane, they at another. When the flight is announced, they can officially say good-bye in our presence and we will escort you onto the plane." It all sounded childish, but no matter. I went back to Mrs. Markowska with this proposal; she scowled at first and then shrugged and said okay. Everybody's turf was secure, even as everybody's faces were saved.

Monica Felton turned up again in Warsaw, reporting bitterly that Kate, giving no satisfactory reason, had refused to see her. By now I couldn't have cared less and once more regretted that moment weeks ago when, in my isolation, I had accepted her intervention. She hovered on the periphery out here and took it upon herself to advise me at every opportunity of the jungle I was about to walk into.

And then, on Wednesday, the unexpected happened. I first got the news over the radio: Hungary had released Noel and Herta. Had this event been timed to upset my plans once more? Instead of relief and joy, I felt a kind of resentment. Now his freedom, which I had wanted as much as mine, had somehow become disconnected. No—nothing would delay my departure at this late point, not even Noel's being freed, not even his need for me.

And so Thursday and that unforgettable, mad last afternoon and evening in Poland arrived. By then I was in a kind of stupor as events seemed to rush all around me. None of it seemed real. Stanislaw was to arrive in midafternoon from prison for some five hours of "freedom" out here at Otwock with me, then to become a prisoner again for just a few remaining weeks.

Suddenly the thought came: After all these years, what about some presents? Why hadn't I thought of that before! I called the chauffeur, jumped into the car, and instructed him: "The craft shop in Constitution Square, quickly!" And off we went.

It was still early afternoon. I could rely on the chauffeur to get me there and back by four. At the store I felt quite overwhelmed by the profusion of choices. I had not made a purchase on my own in five years. After some deliberation I bought a lovely woven peasant rug from Lowicz in brilliant colors for Kate, then smaller bits and pieces for the boys, for Elsie, and on and on. As we sped back to Otwock I was horrified to see that it was already past five.

Meanwhile, that afternoon, Stanislaw, with neither warning nor explanation, was presented with a full complement of clothes to put on. Outside the cells at Miedzeszyn another chauffeured car was waiting for him, and off they went without explanation in the direction of Warsaw. To be reunited with his family? But if that was so, why didn't they take him directly to Alina? He began to feel dread: might it be some other scenario?

It was only when they headed out onto the Lublin Road to the enclave in the Otwock forest that he was told he was to spend some four hours in freedom "with an acquaintance of yours." Alina after all?

A few minutes later Stanislaw and I found ourselves staring at each other in disbelief, not in our familiar prison tatters, but looking as if we had just come home from work. Stanislaw, out of breath and pallid, glanced around, apparently searching for someone else in my sumptuous quarters. How incongruous my prison drawings all around the walls must have seemed to him. He looked dully at me again. What was the matter?

Suddenly the stack of worn green copybooks caught his eye. He rushed over and began fingering them: "Hermann—I can't believe it! Not destroyed! Our capital . . . you'll see. I always told you so." He had pushed aside whatever disappointment he had so clearly felt in the first moment of our encounter.

There was no time to lose. The sun was already low on the horizon and we had a lot to settle. "Come and let's do together what we never achieved over there. The feel of the pine forest will do you good." I was worried by his pallor. Once out of earshot of the house, I reported on the events of the last few weeks and said that I was to join Kate the very next day. I reminded him of our mutual pledge, and how for weeks I had been holding out for his freedom. The best I had been able to get out of them was "No later than Christmas Eve." And that was the reason for his trip here today. I had to have it directly from him: Would such a delay be acceptable? And how much faith did he have in their promise?

Stanislaw reflected a moment, then responded: "As much as I resent every additional hour down there, I realize that it's a political impossibility to release me much ahead of the many other Poles directly or indirectly involved in my case. You know, you've done unbelievably well. The December date is much sooner than I ever imagined. It will have to happen very quietly; they can't possibly get it all cleared up by then."

"That's just it. What reason do you have to believe them?"

"The announcement of your release and the business about Cigarette have changed everything, not just for you, but by implication for the rest of us as well. Everyone knows now that we are innocent; it's only a matter of time before they have to let us go. And now our meeting here and their promise to you. It wouldn't be worth it to renege. They know you'll be watching wherever you are." He thought a moment. "You and I are only the beginning of change that will go way beyond Poland. You'll see. Remember Stalin's death and Beria's execution and our hunches then. It will come, the end of these years of horror. Maybe in fits and starts and slowly, decades even, but it will happen."

I suddenly remembered and broke in: "And Stan, you won't believe this"—and I told him of Anka's prison encounter and friendship with Alina. I was a bit uncertain whether I should say anything, because he had thought that, despite all the threats during his interrogation, she would not be picked up. His face flushed. "She was so poorly prepared for this kind of testing, but to know she has been out and free for some time . . ." He smiled impishly. "And I want to remind you—I told you I knew something very nice had happened to her at one point, and you were so scornful about my being able to know. You see! Anyway, this is a nice bit to reflect on when I go back tonight for a few more weeks. It will make it a lot easier."

We shook hands. "Christmas Eve, then, with Alina and Kate. Sure. No straw out of any mattress this time."

The evening was closing in on us as we got back to the house. Our stack of copybooks: I should take them all with me for safekeeping. We would make a try with one manuscript first, which I would edit and prepare for submission to a publisher. I would send him a copy and he would then do a Polish version. But which should it be? I had my heart set on "Angry Harvest." I had always felt closest to it, and Rosa had so much of me in her. Stanislaw wondered whether "Duck Lane" might not be more substantial, but then agreed that it was tied in much more specifically with Polish perceptions, whereas "Angry Harvest" was more universal in its message and would be more understandable in the West. We agreed. It would be a difficult undertaking across thousands of miles, but difficulties had never stopped us, had they?

Another handshake, and we sealed our future collaboration.

The phone rang in the study. The commandant reported a call from Zurich. I dashed to the phone: "Yes, it's me, Katie. I'll be there for sure." We quickly went over last-minute details, but the operator cut in: "Pan Field, you have a call from Budapest," and Kate's voice was gone.

Now it was a new voice out of the past: "Hermann, it's Noel, your brother. I was afraid you'd already left. I've been trying for hours."

I broke in: "How is your health, Noel? . . . Not so good? . . . And is Herta with you? . . . I heard the news yesterday. I had been trying to get contact with you for weeks but there always were excuses. Are you really free now? . . . Yes? . . . In a little house your own? Sounds like here . . ." Question tumbled after question, even though it was patently ridiculous to try to cover both our lives in this manner.

And then what I dreaded, came: "Hermann, we owe it to each other to meet before you leave for the West. Can't you postpone for a week and come stay here in the place where we are convalescing?"

Hadn't it been Noel I had been looking for five years ago? And now, when he was found at last alive, I was about to turn my back on him? But I held fast. Kate was expecting me in Zurich in just a few hours. There could be no question; it was all settled.

"I'm sorry, Noel. It's too late."

There was no use discussing it on the phone; I would write to him at length from Switzerland. A sudden thought came: Monica Felton. "There's a woman visiting here, an old planning colleague from England . . ." If he wanted to know more about what had been going on, I was sure she would be glad to return via Budapest and report to him in person on my behalf. We ended the call, sadness and disappointment on his side, sadness and bitter determination on mine. Although I experienced a flash of concern about Monica, I shrugged it off. After all, she was part of their world, not mine. So what did it matter now?

I returned to the living room. Everyone, including Stan, was standing around waiting. Before us a sumptuously festive farewell dinner had been laid out, champagne and all—white tablecloth and real napkins, porcelain plates and real forks, knives, and spoons. Seating ourselves, Stan and I toasted Alina and Kate again and again as the commandant and the house staff joined in.

Then we settled down to our feast, trying to delay the inevitable end of the make-believe.

As our evening wore on in utter unconcern, we occasionally saw a worried face peeking in through the door. Then the commandant started gesticulating that it was time. He whispered in my ear that it was getting to be midnight and Mrs. Markowska and other friends were waiting downstairs to help me pack. Stan and I got up unsteadily and went down and out into the night air, where a car was waiting. His short hours of freedom had come to an end.

"Stan, it sounds crazy, but you must visit us at Valley Farm."

There was a moment of silence. "I will, you'll see." Then, almost as an afterthought: "But only on condition that you and Kate come to celebrate the tenth anniversary of this evening in true Warsaw style somewhere in the Stare Miasto. Don't forget! And we'll get properly drunk. Your Puritan soul will never be the same."

The car door banged. I saw him disappearing among the pine trees, a figure with drooping hat on each side. Stanislaw of cell No. 4, Miedzecyn. Had all that had happened this evening been merely an illusion?

I woke up early on the morning of the nineteenth, despite having gotten only a few hours of sleep. A heavy November mist gently shrouded the irregular outlines of the pines. It was an infinitely precious scene. This little patch of forest stillness represented in miniature the rediscovery of a world that for me had become a mere memory. Its beauty beckoned me: See, it said, there is another side. That it was within a few short miles of the place where man's inhumanity had beat upon me day after day, week after week, year after year, seemed immaterial.

Later, sitting in the back of the open car, I glanced back at the white silhouette of the house as it faded into the mist. It looked sad. Its occupant was gone, its brief moment of being a home over. Ahead of me was another car and behind me a second one, just as on that night of momentous change. But now I was sitting alone in the backseat with my voluminous luggage, while in front the commandant kept up a cheerful chatter, evidently pleased to be my honored escort. The same sequences ensued: the long stretch of open highway, the Poniatowski Bridge, the center of town, past the Lazienki Park, then the road that would end at the airport.

I could see two groups of figures: to the left of the airport entrance, the architects Szymon and Helena Syrkus, Mrs. Markowska, Brechbuehler, and several people I did not know, presumably some of the returning Swiss delegates; and a little off to the right, my countrymen from the embassy. We stopped in front of them. The transfer occurred stiffly, following a strict protocol. I briefly shook hands with each of my caretakers, then moved over to greet Ambassador Flack and Mr. Oechsner. Without looking back, I entered the building with my new hosts, who took me to a table and offered me some coffee. At another table nearby the other group also settled down. For a moment I had the impulse to go over and acknowledge their presence. But no, there were no longer two courts. The official transfer of my body had taken place. Protocol had to be maintained, and anyway, I felt happy where I was. The tensions of earlier visits at Otwock had disappeared, and the embassy people and I engaged in informal chitchat.

Several times there were announcements that the plane from Prague was delayed. I began to feel nervous in spite of myself. This airport had too many memories. Aha, another announcement, in Polish and much longer. I got the gist of it: Our plane had not been able to leave Prague, so the flight was canceled. There was a pause. Then the announcer continued: They had been able to divert a Soviet flight from Moscow to take us on; it should be here in another twenty minutes. I almost froze. At once I recalled Stanislaw's account of the Polish underground delegation in 1945 that took off on a Soviet plane for supposed negotiations and was never heard from again.

Mr. Oechsner said: "Wait. I'll be right back." He wanted to find out details from the airline officials. Soon he returned. He thought it would be okay. The U.S. ambassador in Prague had been instructed to meet the Soviet plane, and Swissair had agreed to hold their flight to Zurich until we arrived for transfer. That had been Oechsner's main concern; he had assured Kate there would be no danger of my getting stuck in Prague. The main thing now was to avoid carefully laid plans unraveling anew. Although I was a bit hesitant, the others managed to reassure me.

And so it was that I got my last glimpse of Warsaw, my enforced and unseen home for the past five years of my life, looking down from a Sovflot plane as it ascended in a big spiral, waiting tensely in spite of myself for the moment it would veer to the southwest onto its scheduled course.

# 27

## Kate

It was the morning of November 18. Fog shrouded the city. My father, who would be coming with me to Zurich, and I were driven to the airport. The plane was due to leave at 9:15. Hermann had particularly asked that I get to Switzerland without the press knowing, so I had intended to fly under an assumed name, but, owing to a misunderstanding, our tickets had been booked in my father's name. When I saw the luggage being labeled with my maiden name, Thornycroft, I wanted to leave the airport and go by steamer and train. But the fog was so thick it was doubtful whether the boats would be crossing the Channel, and if we were delayed we might not reach Zurich before Hermann.

We went to the departure room and waited. The hours passed. Our plane was repeatedly announced as delayed. It seemed to me there were a lot of young men around carrying cameras. I tried to read my paper.

"Excuse me, are you Miss Thornycroft?"

"No," I said, before I could think. After all, I was not.

After a little while the loudspeaker announced: "Will Miss Thornycroft, passenger for Zurich, please call at the reception desk?"

I felt the terror of a hare that has been spotted by hounds. Eyes all around the room seemed to be watching to see which passenger got up. I decided to go on sitting. And then in a little while: "Excuse me, are you Mrs. Field?"

"No." Well, I might as well be consistent and carry this farce through.

We went on sitting. It became midday, and still our plane did not leave. Occasionally others took off into the fog, but not our BEA Viscount. We each ate a sandwich, though I was too nervous to be hungry. Suppose they spotted me and the world press trumpeted the news that I was in Zurich to meet Hermann, would he get stage fright and refuse to come?

The suspense of the last three weeks had been ghastly, but finally he had phoned that he would be flying to Switzerland with Hans Brechbuehler. Elsie's plan had paid off! And the latest news, that Noel and Herta had now been freed by the Hungarians, must have eased his mind as well.

It had been five long years since we had seen each other. Hermann said he had become bald, and I tried to visualize what he would look like. I hoped I had not aged too much, and that he would like my new clothes.

The afternoon wore on. We had been due in Zurich hours ago. Back in Corringham Road, though I did not know it, my mother was grappling alone with a barrage of press inquiries, trying to put them off. The American consulate had sent a message to Zurich that I was surrounded by the press at London airport, and something must be done to avoid my being mobbed when I got to Zurich.

My father and I went on sitting, caught like two mice in a trap. The foggy yellow daylight faded, and it became dark outside. We had sat on the same two chairs all day. At last, at about six o'clock, the loudspeaker announced: "BEA flight to Zurich . . ." I almost wept.

I was wearing my reading glasses, in the faint hope that I would not be recognized; or if I was, Hermann would at least see that I was trying to obey his wishes and travel incognito.

We were ushered out into the night. Many young men with cameras came too. Suddenly flashbulbs started firing. I knew they'd got me.

For the first time in my life I entered a plane not with a silent prayer, but with relief. The mousetrap ordeal was over. We had been in that waiting room for ten hours, and now civilization seemed to reign again. If members of the press had come on board as well, they made no attempt to approach me.

We landed, and as we left the plane my father said, "Remember to smile." An official in British Airways uniform appeared. "Come this way, please, Mrs. Field. Your sister-in-law is here." He siphoned me off from the rest and left me sitting alone in a large glass reception room. In the distance I saw Elsie, surrounded by journalists to whom she seemed to be chatting amiably. Why had she come? I had hoped she would keep well away, in order not to attract the press.

Then another man appeared. "Please come with me. I have a car here. I am from the American consulate." He spoke with a foreign accent. Now I could see how easily it is done! He takes me, and where do I land? In the Soviet zone of Austria perhaps!

The BEA official came over. "How do I know he is from the American consulate?" I asked.

"I swear it," said the BEA man. "I've known him many years."

"Yes, I have been with the American embassy twenty years."

I decided it must be okay, so my father and I drove with him to the hotel outside town where Elsie had booked rooms for us under assumed names. She arrived there a little later, without the press.

Elsie was very excited and told us of her adventures. Apparently she had been at the airport by arrangement with the American consul in order to identify my father and me to the consul's chauffeur, who had whisked us away. Elsie had stayed chatting with the press until told by airport personnel—much to her surprise—to board "her plane for Vienna." She was then led through the plane and out the pilot's cabin to the consul's waiting car. All this had been a device concocted by the Americans and the Swiss to make the press think we were meeting Hermann in Vienna. It had not been her idea, and indeed seemed to me to be going pretty far, and my father thought it quite crazy. But it worked. I believe some unfortunate journalists actually did fly on to Vienna. But I did not much care; I was myself feeling fed up with their attention and concerned only that Hermann might also be taken in by the false leads.

I put a call through to him in Warsaw. To my joy he sounded quite composed; he said he was still intending to fly to Zurich the next morning. I told him that he should ignore any press reports that said we were in Vienna. I would meet him tomorrow at the airport.

Suddenly our call was interrupted: "Budapest, calling Warsaw."

I could guess who it was: Noel. So at the very last minute they were putting Hermann in touch with him! How I hoped he would not try to make Hermann change his plans.

Elsie and I shared a room that night. It was a beautiful room, high up on the Zürichberg, overlooking the city and the lake. It was a double room, and if all went well, the next night I should be sharing it with Hermann.

We both felt the drama of the moment. Tonight everything still hung in the balance. Tomorrow it would have been decided. For me, anyway, the five-year struggle would be over. Won, or possibly, at the eleventh hour, lost?

"You know," said Elsie as we undressed, "you mustn't be too upset if he doesn't come tomorrow. At least we will have done our best, Kate. We couldn't do more."

I knew. I thought he would come; I prayed that by the next night it would all be over. Meanwhile, I was glad to be sharing the room with Elsie, who had been such a staunch sister to her brothers and through this struggle had become a close sister to me. She loved both her brothers, but I knew she felt the tragedy had been greater with Hermann because of its effect on me and Hugh and Alan. For five years she had been fighting our battle too.

Next morning a call came from the American consulate saying that Hermann's plane had left Warsaw, and he was on it. The tension of the morning was terrific for all three of us.

Elsie went off somewhere. My father and I lunched in my room. We were to be picked up by a car from the consulate and driven to the airport. How all this was to be done without the press knowing I neither knew nor cared. Hermann was coming, and that was all that mattered. Everything had been taken out of my hands, and I could only do as I was told. I looked at my father. He was terribly tired and looked ten years older than usual.

At last the phone rang again. The consulate reported that Hermann's plane was just due to land, and the car would fetch me any minute.

How I wished I were already at the airport! Hermann would land and I would not be there. Would he think I had failed him? Elsie was not coming to the airport but would wait at the hotel.

The car came, and my father and I drove off at a good speed. When we reached the airport the plane had already unloaded. We swung in at some back gate, heading to the airport police building. I was to meet Hermann there and come out again quickly to the car.

The car stopped, and I ran into the building. There was a long corridor. "Where is he? Which door?"

A door was opened, and I burst in.

There he was, sitting on a bench. He got up and came over to me. How can I recapture that moment in words? The emotion of it will never leave me, nor the picture of him. Yes, it was my own Hermann. But altered. His face rather pink and white. His head, not completely bald, but bald on top. His hair, graying. He was wearing a light gray gabardine suit that made him look broad shouldered with a large torso, somehow top-heavy, and as he walked rather hesitantly toward me, for an awful moment it flashed through my mind that he had been somehow crippled. This stuffed-out torso, was it covering iron braces, for a broken back or legs?

And his face: it looked frozen. His mouth was contracted as if he were expecting to be hit in the face. His expression was a mask, a protective mask that he wore because he could not afford to have feelings. It was not an expression at all, but an insulation, as from an outside world that dealt him nothing but blows.

I flung my arms around him and kissed him. "I will look after you, darling, always," I told him over and over, at the same time realizing that he was not wearing iron braces, that it was nothing but an overpadded Polish suit, with the breast pockets stuffed full of papers. He held me close, but the frozen expression did not leave his face.

I had no thought of time, but we must have stayed long together, for someone came in and said we should be going.

Outside was my father, and we packed into the consular car again and drove off. Soon another car was following us, and our driver started to take unexpected turns to shake it off. It wasn't easy, and we increased speed. At last I begged them to slow down. "After all this," I protested, "it's not worth getting killed just to escape the press." Finally we did escape, our imaginative Swiss chauffeur driving around the back of the elegant hotel Baur-au-Lac, thus throwing off our pursuers and allowing us to arrive back at our hillside hotel undetected.

I ran upstairs to Elsie. She had been waiting all this time, pacing the room and chain-smoking. She looked terribly tired.

"Elsie, he's here. And he's okay. But don't be shocked. His expression is strange." And looking at her face, tired as it was, I could see how different our life had been from his. Her face was not a mask, but a mobile mirror of her emotions. When they met, it was the same. Elsie was laughing, almost crying. Hermann's face was emotionless.

All afternoon we stayed together in the hotel bedroom—Hermann, Elsie, and I. We just sat, gently letting him take in the world again, letting him look out of the window over the city where he had been born. We just sat quietly, knowing that we had won. The five years' hell was over now, and in time love would thaw out that mask and he would dare to feel again.

# Epilogue

O ur account ends with our reunion in Zurich more than forty-five years
ago. Noel and Herta had been released a few days earlier in Budapest. The
Polish government kept its word to Hermann and released Stanislaw Mierzenski just in time for Christmas 1954.

Noel and Herta, who had each spent over five years in solitary confinement
in a Budapest prison, surprised their family and the world by choosing to stay in
Hungary. The Hungarian government had exonerated Noel of all charges of
spying, and he subsequently made it clear that he regarded the whole episode as
a Stalinist aberration for which the communists had made amends. (Later Noel,
in an article titled "Hitching Our Wagon to a Star," made it clear that his heart
was still and would always be with the communists.) The health of both Noel
and Herta had been seriously undermined, and the Hungarian government
committed itself to providing medical care for the rest of their lives. With his
American money, Noel bought a small house on the hill above Buda, where
they lived until Noel's death in 1970. Herta remained there until her own death
in 1980.

We finally visited them in Budapest together in 1964, when Noel was working for the *New Hungarian Quarterly*, a cultural periodical in English, for which
he ensured the correctness of its language. Hermann last visited them in 1969,
when Noel seemed withdrawn, his faith somewhat shaken by the Soviet sup-
pression of the Czechs during the Prague Spring of 1968. He was still, however,
unwilling to discuss his past actions with his brother and remained a believer in
communism to the end of his life.

In 1993, Hermann gained access to the files of the Hungarian Ministry of
Interior and was able for the first time to learn how his brother had been
treated. Right at the outset, Noel had been subjected to brutal interrogations
and driven into making a false confession. This was used in the Rajk and Slansky trials, despite the fact that he had promptly repudiated it and, indeed, in-

sisted on his innocence through all the subsequent years of his imprisonment. This information confirms the statement by Josef Swiatlo that when he was sent to Budapest to interrogate him, Noel refused to admit to any guilt. This may be why he was never produced in either trial as the key witness.

In October 1955 Erica Wallach was finally released from Vorkuta, the Soviet labor camp in the Arctic, where she had been on a railroad-building gang. It took two years before she was granted a visa to join her husband and children in the United States. She wrote about her experiences in her book *Light at Midnight.*

As for ourselves, we spent our first two months together in the Swiss mountains, then returned to London and invited the press to an overflow session in the living room at Corringham Road. The reunited family stayed on another year in England before a final homecoming in 1956.

Hermann was anxious to make something of the creative writing he had done with Stanislaw, and *Angry Harvest* was published in the United States in 1958 and simultaneously in Poland as *Okiennice* in a version prepared by Stanislaw. It appeared in German as *Bittere Ernte* and in Swedish as *Fruktans Väg,* and an adaptation was shown on NBC's Kraft Television Theater. More recently it was made into a West German film, which was a finalist for an Academy Award. It justified Hermann's and Stanislaw's conviction that their struggle to survive carried within it the reward of creative achievement.

On their last night together in Poland in 1954, Hermann and Stan had searched for some assurance of continuity in their friendship. For Stan it meant seeing the actual Valley Farm of his imagination. For Hermann it was the promise that he would join Stan in a Warsaw coffeehouse to celebrate the tenth anniversary of their release. The first became reality in 1960, when both the Polish government and our own made it possible for Stan to spend a year in Boston to complete, with Hermann, their manuscript of *Duck Lane,* which was published in the United States and Poland in 1961.

When 1964 came along, Hermann was determined to fulfill his part of the friendship pact. Sadly, Stan died of cancer while we were on our way to see him. But we met his widow, Alina, and with her went around Warsaw, even driving out into the country far enough to see in the distance the walled compound where Hermann and Stan were incarcerated for so long. Hermann visited both Stanislaw's and Lolek's graves. They were buried in the same cemetery.

The impact of a five-year disappearance is not confined to the principal actors involved. Our boys, Hugh and Alan, were deprived of their father during some very formative years, and when he returned they had to get to know him again and become readjusted to their native country. We both had wanted another child, and our daughter, Alison, was born in 1957.

The evidence suggests that Hermann and Noel survived only because they were American citizens. But Kate learned early on, in a lesson more recently repeated in the case of the hostages held in Lebanon, that the interests of people taken prisoner in enemy territory are directly opposed to those of their own country. Despite support from Hermann's professional colleagues, no sanctions were taken on his behalf, nor for his communist brother. Nevertheless, the persistent inquiries by the State Department must have given those in charge of the Fields an uncomfortable feeling that it would be unwise to have them disappear for ever.

When the Poles released Hermann in 1954, they said that "the charges made against him by Josef Swiatlo are baseless and have been fabricated by American agents and provocateurs." We dismissed this charge as a face-saving device. The idea, however, was later picked up by a British journalist, Stewart Steven, in his book *Operation Splinter Factor*. He suggested that in fact Swiatlo had been an American agent ever since 1948 and that the CIA had deliberately led the communists to think the Field brothers were expendable in order to facilitate a self-destructive purge of the communist satellite leadership and so discredit communism throughout Europe. Soviet and Hungarian intelligence files do not substantiate Steven's claims. The show trials only made the satellite countries more subservient to the Soviet Union and created an atmosphere of intimidation within them. There can be no doubt that they were a deliberate policy, formulated by Stalin and carried out by Beria and his subordinate, General Byelkin, operating through Soviet "advisers" in each of the satellite countries. This particular stage ended with the death of Stalin and the execution of Soviet secret police chief Lavrenti Beria, events that caused Josef Swiatlo to flee from Poland and reveal to the United States his 1949 arrest of Hermann.

The underlying reasons for the trials rest in the international situation at the end of World War II. The Soviet Union had lost some twenty million people and been physically devastated. The United States, on the other hand, had kept war from its own shores, and American troops remained in Europe. We were implacably opposed to the spread of communism, and the wartime marriage of convenience between the Western capitalist states and the Soviet Union was being replaced by the old geopolitical struggle between the two economic and social systems, now with the added threat of mutual nuclear annihilation.

In order to rebuild Western Europe and prevent its populations' falling prey to the promises of communism, the United States instituted the Marshall Plan of economic aid. For the West's military security, the North Atlantic Treaty Organization was formed, which included American forces. On the other side, the Soviet Union created the Cominform to complete Soviet political dominance over the satellite communist parties, and the Warsaw Pact for military security.

Meanwhile, civil war had been raging in Greece, and the enunciation of the Truman Doctrine, stating that the United States would hold the line against communism in Greece and Turkey, assured the defeat of the Greek communist partisans.

Yugoslavia was unique in having achieved communism through its own partisan efforts against the Nazis and not through Soviet intervention, and it therefore had considerable indigenous strength. Its remarkable wartime leader, Josip Broz, known as Marshal Tito, looked toward a confederation with Bulgaria and Albania. Moscow, however, perceived this plan as a threat. This conflict of interests came to a head in July 1948 when the Cominform passed a resolution against "Tito and his clique." The Yugoslavs lost, and the pro-Tito Albanian minister of the interior, Koci Xoxe, was secretly tried and executed through the intervention of the Russian security police. This was the precursor of the infamous show trials in the other satellite countries.

The trials had little to do with communist ideology, and a lot with geopolitics. They were a prophylactic operation against future defections from the Soviet bloc. Therefore, even loyal followers of the Moscow line such as Laszlo Rajk and Rudolf Slansky had to be sacrificed, their innocence of any past deviation irrelevant. The purpose of the trials was to eliminate strong characters, strike terror into the hearts of all communist functionaries, and so ensure control of the satellite communist parties by Moscow. Indeed, ever since the internal show trials in Moscow in 1937, Stalin's hold on power had derived from his constant cleansing of the party leadership. These new trials merely spread the practice into neighboring countries.

The policy worked, at least for a time. Each show trial led to a spate of arrests and secret trials of hundreds, sometimes thousands, of lesser communists. But the policy did nothing to resolve the internal, particularly the economic, problems in the satellite countries. These resulted in the Hungarian Uprising of 1956 and the Prague Spring in Czechoslovakia in 1968, both of which Moscow suppressed by force. Twenty-one years later, in 1989, the whole system of controlling Eastern Europe from Moscow collapsed. Shortly thereafter the Soviet Union itself imploded.

While the show trials were clearly motivated by the foreign policy interests of the Soviet Union, for presentation to the public where they took place they had to be given another rationale, one that would effectively conceal Moscow's hand in them, be plausible, and direct hostility toward the supposed enemies of the "People's Democracies." For this purpose the enemies chosen were successively "Titoism," "Anglo-American imperialism," "bourgeois nationalism," "Trotskyist deviation," and "Zionism." Links between the selected victims and one or other of these forces had to be found, or manufactured.

It was thus extraordinarily fortunate for Beria, charged with carrying out Stalin's policies, that the American Noel Field, who knew so many returned exiles through having aided refugees from Hitler during World War II, could be induced to come into communist territory.

After the Unitarian Service Committee had terminated Noel's position because of his communist sympathies, and since it was the era of Senator Joseph McCarthy, Noel hesitated to return to the United States. Already in 1948 he had expressed a desire to report on developments in Eastern Europe as an independent journalist, and traveled there extensively. An application the next year for permission to go to Czechoslovakia triggered surveillance of him by the agents of NKVD chief Beria. Noel was granted a visa, and on May 5, 1949, he went to Prague. On May 12 he was abducted, taken unconscious to Budapest, imprisoned, and immediately interrogated by Soviet and Hungarian intelligence. There is ample evidence that this was done at the behest of the Russian general Byelkin and through the Soviet advisers in Hungary.

Noel, and later Hermann, were important because they could provide the names of communists with whom they had been in contact during their respective refugee work, Hermann's before the war in Krakow, Noel's before and during the war in France. At the same time, their captors attempted to extract false confessions from them of being American anti-Soviet agents. They could then have been produced as witnesses in impending trials, thus implicating any defendants they had known, who could therefore be presented as agents of a foreign power. Noel's wartime contact with Allen Dulles, in charge of the American Office of Strategic Services in Geneva, evidently sufficed for this purpose, even though this connection had not continued after the war.

According to the investigations of the Slansky trial undertaken by the Czechoslovak Communist Party at the time of the Prague Spring of 1968, and published in the Piller and Kolder reports, dozens of names of Czechoslovak Party officials were obtained from Noel. The Hungarian interrogation files put the number of Hungarians, Poles, Czechs, and Germans identified by Noel at several hundred. Although he repudiated his forced confession of having been an American agent, his name was freely used in the Rajk and Slansky trials, where he was identified as the American mastermind of subversion.

Because of the simultaneous accusations against Noel in the Alger Hiss trial at home, his wife, Herta, hesitated to report him missing to the State Department and instead persuaded Hermann to go to Czechoslovakia and Poland and quietly ask questions about his brother's disappearance. With the opening of the Russian, Czech, and Hungarian files to researchers, it is clear that Noel was in touch with Soviet intelligence during the 1930s but was distrusted by the Russians thereafter.

Hermann's chance arrival in Eastern Europe was an additional bonus for Beria. But because he had never had any connection with any intelligence service, in the Slansky trial when it came to dealing with the refugees who had fled to England, often only the surname Field was used. The assumption could be that Noel was meant, though he had never had anything to do with the emigration to Britain.

One point should not be lost sight of. Both brothers risked their lives to help refugees from Hitler before and during World War II. A minority of these were communists who returned home to become important in their native countries, only to be liquidated by the Soviets ten years later. The majority survived both Hitler and Stalin and were able to live out their lives in many parts of the world, rather than being buried in Buchenwald or reduced to ashes at Auschwitz.

*Valley Farm, Shirley, Massachusetts, 1999*

# Photographs

Dr. Herbert Haviland Field,
Zurich, 1919.

Nina Field with her children, Noel, Elsie, Hermann, and Letty, Zurich, 1919.

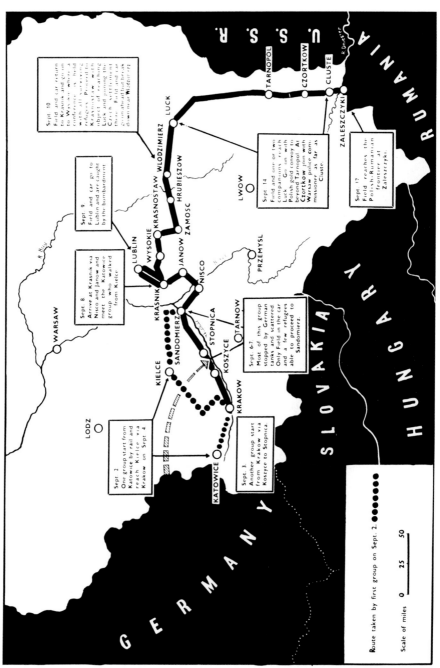

Route of Hermann Field and Krakow and Katowice refugees in September 1939 in effort to escape Germans.

Collective farm in the Volga German district of the USSR, 1934.

Hermann in Krakow, 1939.

Hermann and Kate in Czechoslovakia with mayor of Moravska-Ostrava, former refugee leader in Krakow, 1947.

Hermann in Cleveland, 1948.

Kate in Cleveland, 1948.

Erica Wallach with Noel Field, Geneva, 1940.   Erica Wallach, Warrenton, Va., 1962.

Drs. Leon and Anna Gecow in their
apartment in Warsaw, 1947.

Noel and Herta Field in ruins of Warsaw, 1948.

Early view of residence at Miedzeszyn before its conversion as part of secret interrogation center complex, in cellar of which Hermann was held for several years.

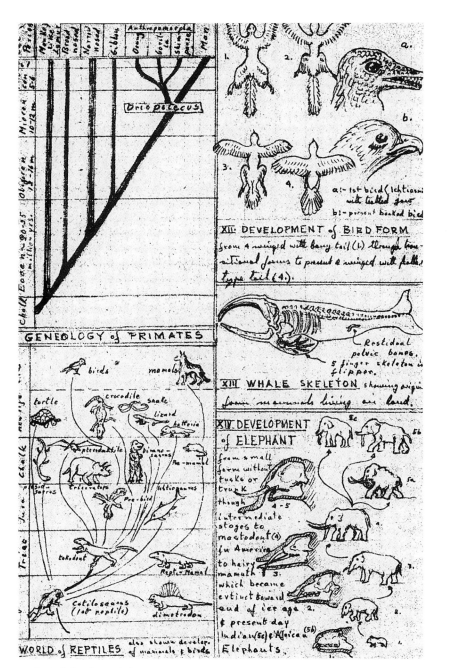

Zoological sketches, Miedzeszyn, 1953.

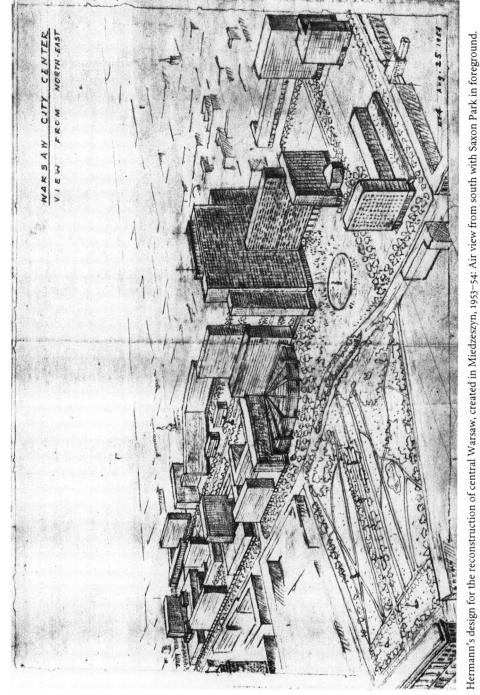

Hermann's design for the reconstruction of central Warsaw, created in Miedzeszyn, 1953–54: Air view from south with Saxon Park in foreground.

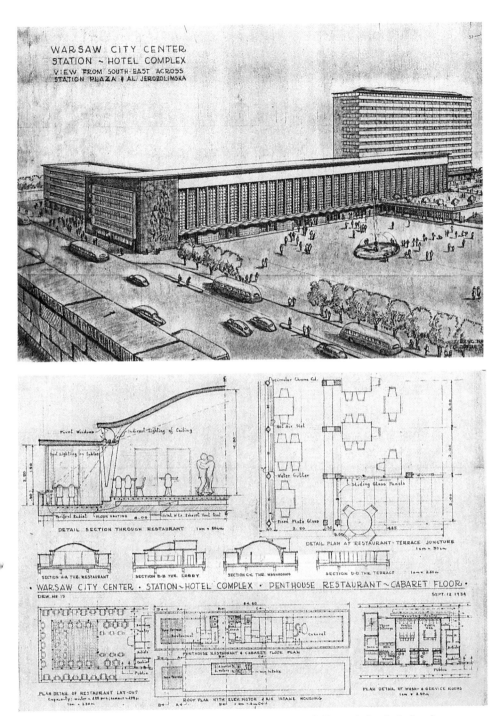

Warsaw project: (*top*) Intermodal Transportation Center and hotel; (*bottom*), details for hotel penthouse restaurant. Miedzeszyn, 1953–54.

Mrs. Hermann H. Field · 82 Corringham Road · London N.W.11.

October 5, 1954.

His Excellency .
    The President of the Polish People's Republic
Warsaw, Poland.

Your Excellency:

I humbly beg your help on behalf of my husband, Hermann Field, now a prisoner at Miedzeszyn, where he has been for over five years.

As President of the Polish People's Republic I appeal to you to consider that he has suffered enough, and to allow him to come home to me and his two little boys.

I love my husband with all my heart, and I do not want my sons to grow up with bitter feelings against your country. We ordinary people long only for peace and goodwill, and I sincerely believe my husband's release would help in this.

I promise you that if my husband is quickly released I can heal his wounds and the past will be forgotten.

I beg your Excellency to listen to this plea from a wife and mother who has suffered so long, and cannot bear much more.

I am your Excellency's humble servant,

Kate Field.
Kate Field.

Appeal letter by Kate to the president of Poland, August 1954.

Kate with her parents and sons,
London, 1955.

Hermann during his release, Otwock, October 1954.

Stanislaw Mierzenski after his release,
Warsaw, December 1954.

Dr. Elsie Field, Geneva, 1954.

Josef Swiatlo at press conference,
Washington, D.C., 1954.

Hermann and Kate's arrival at Victoria Station, London, February 1955.

Television interview outside home of Kate's parents, London, February 1955.

Hermann and Stanislaw at Valley Farm, Shirley, Mass., 1960.

Kate and Hermann, 1992.

Hermann outside
prison wall of
Secret Police inter-
rogation center,
Miedzeszyn, 1993.
(Photo by Werner
Schweizer)

# Afterword

## Norman M. Naimark

I n her 1965 biography of Noel Field, *Red Pawn*, Flora Lewis described the young man Hermann Field as "tall like his older brother but more lithe and not so gangly, more elegant and not so tweedy, more confident and not so intense." From spending time with him in person, she concluded, "Hermann had become an immensely distinguished-looking urbane man who inevitably led women meeting him to grope in their memories for the name of a familiar movie hero face that his suggested."[1]

Hermann Field was eighty-eight when I met him in September 1998 at the convention to the American Association for the Advancement of Slavic Studies (AAASS) in Boca Raton. Still handsome, if rather shorter, slighter, and bent a bit with age, Hermann leaves a lasting impression on anyone who encounters him. His honesty and openness, intelligence and warmth, remind one of the forthright personalities of many Holocaust survivors, who have seen it all and bear witness by refusing to indulge convention or artifice. In brisk language and with an unerring penchant for important detail, Hermann delivered a paper at the convention and answered questions about the making of his autobiography, *Departure Delayed*. A passionate goal of his is to see the book appear in English and to talk about its implications for understanding the history of communism in the Soviet Union and Eastern Europe. (The book has already appeared in both Polish and German.)[2]

Thanks to the interest of Stanford University Press, *Departure Delayed*, now titled *Trapped in the Cold War: The Ordeal of an American Family,* will become a

---

[1]Flora Lewis's descriptions of Hermann can be found in *Red Pawn: The Story of Noel Field* (Garden City, N.Y.: Doubleday, 1965), pp. 7, 78.

[2]Hermann and Kate Field, *Opozniony odlot: Wokowach zimnej wojny* (Warsaw: Panstwowy Instytut Wydawniczy, 1997); in German as *Departure Delayed: Stalins Geisel im Kalten Krieg* (Hamburg: Europäische Verlagsanstalt, 1996).

standard item in the growing literature on the Cold War and "High Stalinism." Hermann's sheer intelligence and human insight will surely establish the book alongside such classics as Artur London's *The Confession* and Arthur Koestler's *Darkness at Noon* as a primer for the psychology of internment and the pathology of prison warders in communist countries. Though never a communist himself, Hermann explores the kinds of psychological pressure and mental torment to which purge victims were subjected. He also embodies the amazing resilience of those who were able to withstand the highly developed NKVD system of extracting confessions. Like the haunting films *The Confession* by Costa-Gavros and *The Interrogation* by Richard Bugajski, Hermann Field's memoir shakes us to the core in its portrayal of the twentieth-century reality of terror. There is no understanding communist systems without coming to grips with the problem of inquisition, confession, and purge that is at the heart of Hermann Field's and and his brother Noel's cases.

Noel Field was born in 1904 and Hermann in 1910. Their father, Herbert Haviland Field, a biologist by profession, directed an international scientific bibliographical institute in Zürich. The brothers grew up in a cultivated home, dominated by their parents' Quaker, pacifist, and progressive values. They were exposed early on to European cultures and languages; they both attended Harvard and excelled at their studies. As a young man, Noel was profoundly influenced by what he saw as the martyrdom of the Italian-American anarchist radicals Sacco and Vanzetti. While Noel began his career in the U.S. State Department in the late twenties and went on to work with the League of Nations on disarmament issues, Hermann pursued his passion for urban planning and architecture. In the 1930s, both were antifascists and both sympathized with Soviet peace initiatives, as did many progressives in the West. Both were deeply moved by the Spanish Civil War and became involved in efforts to aid victims and opponents of fascism, especially those on the Left. As a League of Nations representative in Spain in 1938–1939, Noel helped to repatriate foreign participants in the Republican struggle. He then served as director of the American Unitarian Service Committee relief mission in Marseilles in 1941, working day and night with his wife, Herta, to provide relief for antifascists and leftists, while helping to transport those in danger to safety in Switzerland. Hermann met his second wife, Kate Thornycroft, in England, where she worked for the British Committee for refugees from Czechoslovakia, later the British Czech Refugee Trust Fund. Hermann joined these efforts and became deeply involved in helping refugees from Czechoslovakia, many of whom were antifascists and leftists of Jewish background. First in Prague and then in Poland, Hermann helped them flee the Nazi-run Czech protectorate for Poland and then the West. His tireless relief work in Katowice and Krakow with Czech refugees came to a crashing end in September 1939, with the Nazi occupation of Poland. Yet even during the early days of the German invasion, Hermann stayed with his charges, seeing them to safety despite dangers to his own life.[3]

The similarities in their antifascist biographies played an important role in their parallel arrests, internments, and interrogations from 1949 to 1954—Noel in Hungary and Hermann in Poland. But the subtle, though crucial, differences in their politics and philosophies held profound consequences for the content of their experiences. Noel Field had most certainly become a communist by the end of the 1930s, and even if he did not directly belong to the American Communist Party or any other formal party organization, he provided information to Soviet intelligence operatives and worked for Soviet interests. Fatefully for Noel and those communists he had helped and befriended, he also used all of his European contacts, including an old family friend, Allen Dulles, to aid his work of getting leftists out of occupied France. Noel also contacted Dulles, who was OSS European chief in Switzerland and later director of the CIA, to help German, Hungarian, and other Central European leftists return home after the war. Recently released documents make it clear that Noel and Herta remained communists to the bitter end.[4] Even after their release from prison in 1954 they chose to remain in Hungary, defended the Soviet invasion of the country in 1956, and eventually joined the Hungarian Communist Party.

Hermann was different, as was Kate. They were progressives, pacifists, and, in Hermann's case, a youthful sympathizer of Marxism. But both were far too independent of mind and interested in family and profession to devote their lives to a party. To be sure, after the war Hermann was interested in the architectural and planning issues involved in rebuilding devastated communist Eastern Europe. He also bridled at what he saw as dangerous anticommunism emerging within Western governments and societies after the war. But before being drawn into the tornado of Stalinist arrests and trials, Hermann wanted nothing more than to begin his new job building an architecture program at Western Reserve University and to settle his young family into their new house in Cleveland.

Noel's ongoing commitment to communism derailed Hermann and Kate's

---

[3]In a letter of December 28, 1998, Professor Igor Lukes of Boston University notes that "Karel Markus, Vilem Novy and scores of others quite simply owed their survival to Hermann's refusal to cut and run."

[4]For the most up-to-date research on the Field case, especially on its connections with the Slansky Trial, see Igor Lukes, "The Rudolf Slansky Affair: New Evidence," *The Slavic Review*, 58, no. 1 (spring 1999): 160–88. New material about Noel Field's connection with Soviet intelligence in the 1930s has been analyzed by Allen Weinstein and Alexander Vassiliev in *The Haunted Wood: Soviet Espionage in America—The Stalin Era* (New York: Random House, 1999), pp. 4–11.

plans. Because of growing suspicions about his communist sympathies, the Unitarians dropped Noel from their European operations. Noel was hesitant to return home to the United States, worrying that he might be drawn into the 1948 investigation of alleged communists in the State Department sparked by Whittaker Chambers's testimony to the House Un-American Activities Committee. Noel, after all, had been a friend and colleague of Alger Hiss.

As a result, Noel turned to the East for support. He looked for jobs in journalism and writing, traveling to Czechoslovakia, Poland, and eastern Germany and visiting old communist acquaintances, now often in important positions of power. There is good reason to believe that the case against Noel was cooked up by Hungarian and Soviet intelligence, who then informed the Czechs to set a trap for him in Prague.[5] When Noel was lured back to Prague in May 1949, therefore, he was seized by Czech secret police agents and moved unconscious to Budapest. There he was held in solitary confinement, interrogated, and brutalized until he was exonerated and released in November 1954.

Herta, Noel's wife, went to Prague at the beginning of August 1949 to find her missing husband. She, too, was eventually arrested, moved to Budapest, and subjected to the same bitter fate of isolation cells and incessant interrogation. But before her arrest, she contacted Hermann to ask for his help in locating her husband. No doubt her own communist attachments and alienation from the U.S. government made it hard for her to seek help from the American embassy. In any case, Hermann agreed to search for his brother and flew to Prague. Able to learn nothing about Noel's disappearance from the Czech authorities, Hermann then flew to Warsaw to contact old friends and acquaintences in the Polish government to ask for their help. Facing a mysterious wall of silence in Poland, Hermann went to the Warsaw airport to fly back to Prague to report his findings to Herta. Before boarding his plane, Hermann was seized by Polish secret police on August 22 and placed in solitary confinement. In addition to the disappearance of Noel, Herta, and Hermann, Erica Wallach, a foster daughter of Noel and Herta, was arrested by East German police in Berlin as she sought to locate the Fields, looking to friends in the German Communist Party for help. Erica spent five years in Soviet exile in Vorkuta for her efforts.

There is still considerable uncertainty about the precise reasons the Soviets arrested Noel and Hermann Field. Noel was accused of being the centerpiece of a vast conspiracy of East European communists, whose real sympathies lay with the deviant Yugoslavs and the reactionary West. Certainly, Noel's biography

---

[5]On the abduction of the Fields, see the most comprehensive book on the East European purge trials, George H. Hodos, *Show Trials: Stalinist Purges in Eastern Europe* (New York: Praeger, 1987), p. 27.

contained all the necessary elements to arouse Soviet suspicions. He was of elitist background, pacifist upbringing, and he had worked for the State Department. He was friendly with the likes of Allen Dulles, the American spymaster, and he had close ties with Spanish Civil War veterans and East European communists who had spent the wartime years in exile in the West instead of in Moscow. He had helped leftists of various persuasions and nationalities, including many Jews, to move back to their homes in 1944–1945. The antagonisms of the Cold War hardened after the Czech coup of February 1948 and the beginning of the Berlin Blockade in June of the same year. The anti-cosmopolitan campaign, directed against Jewish leftists in particular, gained ground at the end of 1948 and the beginning of 1949. Stalin's worries about enemies among East European communists grew exponentially as it also became clear in late 1948 that the Yugoslav deviation was turning into heresy and defiance. Discipline in the newly emerging Soviet bloc would have to be insured by the traditional Stalinist means of purges and show trials. Stalin and Beria dispatched NKVD "advisers" to all the capitals of the People's Democracies in order to quicken the hunt for "enemies of the people."[6] Development of the Noel Field case was ideal for this purpose. It served as the central delusional conspiracy behind the Stalinist purges in Eastern Europe, including the Rajk trial in Hungary (September 1949) and the Slansky trial in Czechoslovakia (November 1952).

Once Noel Field had been identified as a potential agent of the imperialists, Titoists, and Trotskyites, it was easy to implicate his wife, Herta, his foster daughter, Erica, and—of course—his brother Hermann. Hermann's work helping Czech antifascists in 1939 and his visits to Poland after the war were transformed in the imagination of his captors into critical pieces of a network of counterrevolutionary activity headed up by Allen Dulles and Noel Field. Hermann's arrest and interrogation was supervised by Josef Swiatlo, a colonel in the Polish security service charged with developing the case against alleged enemies in the Polish United Workers Party, Wladyslaw Gomulka included. Swiatlo personally arrested Hermann at Warsaw's Okecie Airport. During Hermann's more than five years in detention, Swiatlo—"Cigarette" in Hermann's memoir—represented the forces of evil, the man who dictated the terms of Hermann's internment. In a bizarre intersection of Cold War stories, Swiatlo defected to the West in 1954 and revealed, among other secrets of the Soviet bloc, that Hermann and Noel were alive and in detention in Warsaw and Budapest, respectively. The Poles alleged that Swiatlo was already working for the CIA when he arrested Hermann. But it seems more likely, given the brutal convic-

---

[6]Newly released Soviet documents on the East European purge trials have been published in "Delo Slanskogo," *Voprosy istorii*, nos. 3 and 4 (1997).

tion with which Swiatlo performed his job in the period described by Hermann, that the Polish colonel defected to the Americans in Berlin because of worries about his own neck after the arrests of Beria and the Hungarian police official Gabor Peter.

Hermann was finally freed from Polish internment in September 1954 and was reunited with his wife, Kate, and their two boys in Switzerland in November. In coming to terms with what had happened to them as a family, Hermann wrote down detailed recollections of his time in prison. At the same time, Kate recorded her own unsuccessful efforts in Britain and the United States to locate and free her husband, providing background about the "Noel Field Affair," as it soon became known in the West. Kate's narrative was infused with careful analyses of the East European purges, which she followed systematically in the press and in available documents. But both were nervous about publishing their story in the atmosphere of the Cold War. After all, Noel and Herta had chosen to remain in Budapest, "behind the Iron Curtain," and Hermann had close Polish friends from his internment and before whom he wished to protect. Thirty-five years later, with the Cold War waning and a successful career as an architect and planning educator behind him, Hermann, together with Kate, returned to their memoirs and prepared them for publication.

*Trapped in the Cold War* reads with all the immediacy and tension of the time. Although the reader knows the outcome, Hermann and Kate tell their stories as they experienced them—from internment in Hermann's case, from London in Kate's—imparting to the narrative the breathless terror and anxiety inherent in their situations. As an architect, Hermann demonstrates phenomenal control of the details of his surroundings. The cell he inhabits, the windows, chairs, cots, the sounds and the light, are all frighteningly real. His attachments to mice and insects, his need to draw and to learn, and his relationship to his warders—"Angel," "Fatty," "Shoo," "Horsetooth," "Violet," "Blackie," "Padlock," et al.—draw the reader into his daily struggle with confinement and isolation. Hermann's story is highlighted by an unusual and unique event in prison literature of this genre: his deep friendship with Stanislaw Mierzenski, a Pole who was interned with Hermann for wartime Home Army activities. The two wrote novels together (of which *Angry Harvest* and *Duck Lane* were later published).[7] They lectured to each other and taught each other, thus working to stay alive emotionally and intellectually under the harshest of circumstances. Even when Hermann was exonerated by the Poles and released, he refused to

[7]Hermann Field and Stanislaw Mierzenski, *Angry Harvest* (New York: Thomas Y. Crowell, 1958) and *Duck Lane* (New York: Thomas Y. Crowell Co., 1961). The former novel was also published in German, Polish, and Swedish; the latter in Polish.

leave the country until he was assured of Stanislaw's liberation. They had made an emotional pact that would ensure this loyality, and Hermann stubbornly adhered to its terms.

The Cold War remains a central facet of our identity as Americans. Historiographical arguments about its origins and causes remain lively, even after the collapse of the Soviet Union. Fascinating new materials are being released from Russian and East European archives that document the secret background of a terrifying series of crises and confrontations, from the Berlin Blockade and Korean War to the Cuban Missile Crisis and Soviet invasion of Afghanistan, that endangered the fate of civilization. In a revival of sorts of the dramatic McCarthy period, the stories of Alger Hiss, Whittaker Chambers, and the Rosenbergs are being retold and reexamined in light of this new documentation. With the renewed public interest in the era of Stalinism and the Cold War, the appearance of Hermann and Kate Field's memoirs is an important reminder of the human costs of the Soviet-American confrontation. It is impossible to calculate the "losses" of the Cold War the way one can enumerate the losses of the world wars. Whether one argues that "fighting" the Cold War was necessary or not, few could doubt its negative effect on progress, tolerance, and world brotherhood over the past half century. Hermann and Kate Field's memoirs remind us that better ways are possible if only we have the determination to find them.

# Identities of Names in Text

Miedzeszyn   A top secret hideaway where "disappeared" individuals suspected of international conspiracies and intrigue against communist rule were held and interrogated. Originally it consisted of just a single-story building, a converted small landowner's villa near the east bank of the Vistula, south of Warsaw, not far from the foreign journalists' club. A similar building was added in 1949 close by, and later still a third, larger structure, designed as a communication center. Together they formed a walled-in high-security enclave.

"Cigarette"   Col. Josef Swiatlo, deputy head of Department 10 of the Bezbieka at Miedzeszyn, the Ministry of Public Security (MBP), the top secret department dealing with counterintelligence. He was in charge of Hermann until his defection to the West in December 1953. Originally from Krakow, he spent the war years in Russia and trained there under Beria until his return to Poland. After Beria's trial and death sentence in the aftermath of Stalin's death, he had reason to fear the same fate for himself in Poland, having been responsible for many irregularities on his watch.

"Blackie"   Col. Rozanski, head of the 5th (investigative) Department of the MBP. He was especially feared by prisoners for his brutal interrogation methods and was himself sentenced to a prison term on this account in 1955.

1949 interrogation officer   Col. Henryk Piasecki, also a deputy head of Department 10. He claimed in 1955 that following his interrogation of Hermann in 1949 he became convinced of his innocence and was removed from the case.

Mela Granowska   Polish Jewish prewar resident of Krakow who dedicated herself to helping shelter refugees and acted as ombudsman during the September 1939 flight from Krakow. She spent the war years in Russia. In 1949 she held a responsible position in the energy ministry. She arranged lodging for Hermann during his ill-fated visit to Warsaw.

The "Duck"   Zofia Gomulka, wife of Wladyslaw Gomulka. She was secretly arrested together with her husband by Swiatlo in the summer of 1951 and brought to Miedzeszyn, where she was housed upstairs in the second building that at the time held Hermann in its cellar. Her husband was similarly housed "first class" over the cellar of the older building. Until 1948 Wladyslaw Gomulka was deputy prime minister and head of the Communist Party; he was then sidelined until his 1951 arrest.

The intent was to make him the central figure of a Polish conspiracy trial, similar to that of Rajk in Hungary, with supposed connection to Hermann Field and Leon Ge-cow. His interrogators never succeeded in breaking him, however, and the trial never took place. He was released in 1955 and returned to power in 1956.

"Mrs. Markowska"    Luna Brystigier, an old-line Communist, member of the Central Committee, and deputy head of the notorious 5th Department of the MBP. She was a leading figure in Party politics and intrigue. In 1954 she headed the commission to investigate irregularities in the MBP, part of her assignment being to negotiate the freeing of Hermann.

"Horsetooth"    Lt. Col. Fidelis Ventland of the MBP.

The doctor    Dr. Gangel, an internationally known Polish physician attached to the MBP. He was later investigated for his role in the mishandling of prisoners.

Gottwald    Klement Gottwald, president of Czechoslovakia following the communist takeover in 1948. Under Soviet and Hungarian pressure he authorized the seizure of Noel Field in Prague in May 1949. He died in Moscow in March 1953.

Monica Felton    English town planner in charge of development of Peterlee new town. She participated in Hermann's reconstruction tour that visited Poland in 1947 and in the early 1950s became active in the communist-dominated World Peace Council.

# Notes

CHAPTER 4

All correspondence detailed in the text is in the possession of Kate Field.

CHAPTER 8

The indictment of Laszlo Rajk was reported in the *Times* of London, September 10, 1949, and the proceedings were subsequently published in English as *Laszlo Rajk and His Accomplices before the People's Court* (Budapest, 1949), with full public information.

The first formal note regarding Hermann was sent by the U.S. State Department to the Polish Foreign Office on September 13, 1949, with follow-up enquiries by the American embassy in Warsaw on September 14. The Polish acting foreign minister gave an oral reply on September 28 in which he stated that he was "really mystified."

All correspondence between Kate Field and the State Department is in her possession.

CHAPTER 9

Kate Field issued her first press statement on December 29, 1949, including with it a telegram she had addressd to Secretary of State Dean Acheson.

The *New York Herald Tribune* (European edition) published an Associated Press report from Prague, "London Czechs are accused of Wartime Plot," January 6 and 20, 1950.

Telegrams to Vaclav Nosek, Czech minister of the interior, and Stanislaw Radkiewicz, Polish minister of public security, from Kate Field were published in the *News Chronicle* newspaper, London, February 16, 1950.

Ladislav Kopriva's *Report to the Meeting of the Central Committee of the Communist Party of Czechoslovakia, Feb. 25, 1950,* was reported on the BBC and in various newspapers on March 3, 1950. Kate Field's response was reported by *Reuter's News Agency* and printed in the *News Chronicle,* March 3. On April 13 the State Department suggested to the American embassy in Prague that, in view of Kopriva's statement, a further enquiry should be made regarding Hermann.

The following individuals approached the State Department on Hermann's behalf during 1950:

Robert A.Taft, senator from Ohio; Frances Bolton, representative from Ohio; John S. Millis, president of Western Reserve University, Cleveland, Ohio; Herbert C. Hunsaker, dean of Cleveland College, Western Reserve University; George F. Zook, president of the American Council on Education; and Edmund R. Purves, executive director of the American Institute of Architects.

On May 5, 1950, the American Institute of Architects (AIA), Washington D.C., issued a press statement entitled "American Architects not attending Warsaw Congress because of Hermann Field Disappearance." The text of the AIA resolution said in part: "It did not appear seemly for the American Institute of Architects to participate in the next Congress of the U.I.A. [Union Internationale des Architectes] or to receive professional hospitality in such Congress so long as one of its members had disappeared in Poland, the country which is host for the next Congress of the U.I.A., or in any other country associated with Poland."

On June 16, 1950, the United Press reported from Prague that two British diplomats had been expelled.

On September 1, 1950, the East German newspaper *Neues Deutschland* reported expulsions from the East German communist party; that account was translated and published by the *News Chronicle*. On October 26 the *New York Herald Tribune* (Eur. ed.) quoted an AP report from Berlin, "East German Reds Purge Party Again."

On November 7, 1950, the *New York Herald Tribune* (Eur. ed.) reported that Antonin Gregor, on behalf of Czechoslovakia, had signed a trade agreement with Moscow.

On December 4, 1950, the *New York Herald Tribune* (Eur. ed.) printed an AP report from Prague, "Nine Churchmen Convicted of Treason and Spying."

All Kate Field's correspondence with the State Department and others is in her possession.

CHAPTER 17

The arrest of William Oatis was reported from Prague on April 23, 1951, and printed in the London *Times* on April 24. As a consequence of this action, the State Department issued a press release on June 2 banning travel by Americans to Czechoslovakia.

Records of Kate's interviews and correspondence with officials of the American embassy in London and with the State Department are in her possession.

CHAPTER 18

Reports on Dr. Dibelius, Bishop of Berlin, were printed in the *Times* of London, November 21, 1952.

The trial of Rudolf Slansky et al. was broadcast by the BBC Monitoring Service, Summary of World Broadcasts, Nov. 24–27, 1952, and subsequently published in Czech by the Czechoslovak Ministry of Justice as "Trial of the Leadership of the Anti-State Conspiratorial Center Headed by Rudolf Slansky" (Prague, Nov. 1952). Excerpts from the radio broadcasts of the proceedings, including the sentences, were published in English on December 1.

On June 8, 1953, the State Department wrote to Alexander Wiley, chairman of the Senate Committee on Foreign Relations, in connection with the Field case. On July 13

James Henderson, lawyer representing the Field family, wrote to Secretary of State John Foster Dulles, receiving a response on August 25. Kate Field wrote to Charles E. Bohlen, ambassador to the USSR, on September 22, and received a response on January 11, 1954. All correspondence referred to is in her possession.

## CHAPTER 23

On September 28, 1954, State Department press releases nos. 535 and 536 detailed notes sent to Poland regarding Hermann, and to Hungary regarding Noel and Herta, together with biographical material on Josef Swiatlo.

The transcript of the interview of Josef Swiatlo with Mr. Martin, representing the Field family, on Oct. 11 is in the possession of Kate Field, as is other correspondence.

## CHAPTER 24

The release of Hermann in Poland was reported in the press on October 28, 1954.

## CHAPTER 26

The release of Noel and Herta in Hungary was announced in the press on November 17, 1954.

Hermann's arrival in Zurich on November 19 was covered in the *New York Times* on November 20, 1954.

# Annotated Bibliography

Brandt, P., J. Schumacher, G. Schwarzrock, and K. Suhl. *Karrieren eines Aussenseiters.* Berlin: Verlag J. H. W. Dietz Nachfolger, 1983. A biography of Leo Bauer, who, together with Erica Wallach, was tried and sentenced to death for treason in 1950 by a Soviet military court in Berlin. Their sentences were reduced after Stalin's death to twenty-five years in a work camp in Siberia. Bauer was released October 1955.

Checinski, Michael. *Poland: Communism, Nationalism, Anti-Semitism.* New York: Karz-Cohl, 1982. A detailed examination of the Polish security apparatus based on extensive interviews with its victims and those once responsible for their plight. Includes chapter on Department Ten of Polish MBP.

Connolly, Cyril. *The Missing Diplomats.* London: Queen Anne Press, 1952. A contemporary account of the disappearance of the British diplomats Guy Burgess and Donald Maclean in May 1952.

Cooke, Alistair. *A Generation on Trial.* London: Rupert Hart-Davis, 1951. An observer's account of the first and second Hiss trials and of the attitudes that bore upon them.

de Gramont, Sanche. *The Secret War: The Story of International Espionage since World War II.* New York: G. P. Putnam's Sons, 1962. Contains extensive biographical material on Noel Field, as also on Erica Wallach.

Field, Hermann. "From Krakow to Roumania." Chapter in *I Was Lucky to Escape.* London: Lindsay Drummond, 1940. Account of his September 1939 trek with the refugees.

————. "The Polish Tragedy." *The Fortnightly* (London), March 1940. An eyewitness account of the German invasion of Poland, the strategy of encirclement, the total collapse of Polish military and civilian defense, and the Russian countermove from the East.

Field, Hermann, and Kate Field. *Departure Delayed. Stalins Geisel im Kalten Krieg.* Hamburg: Europäische Verlagsanstalt, 1996. The German edition of *Trapped in the Cold War.*

————. *Opozniony Odlot. Wokowach zimnej wojny.* Warsaw: Panstwowy Instytut Wydawniczy, 1997. The Polish edition of *Trapped in the Cold War.*

Field, Hermann, and Stanislaw Mierzenski. *Angry Harvest.* New York: Thomas Y. Crowell, 1958. [Also Apollo paperback and British, Polish, Swedish, and German editions.]

———. *Duck Lane*. New York: Thomas Y. Crowell, 1961. [Also in Polish edition as *Kaczory*. Warsaw, 1961.] A sharply abbreviated version of the original manuscript.

Field, Noel. "Banishing War through Arbitration: A Brief Sketch of the Post-War Arbitration Treaties." Washington, D.C.: National Council for Prevention of War, 1926. A thirty-eight-page brochure, and Noel Field's first writing on this subject shortly before he joined the U.S. State Department.

———. "Hitching Our Wagon to a Star." *Mainstream,* Jan. 1961. A seventeen-page biographical article written in 1960 in Budapest, ten years before his death, in which Noel reaffirmed his political beliefs.

Gecow, Anna. "The War Years and 1949 to 1954." Paris, 1984. Unpublished taped autobiographical conversations with Hermann Field.

Gordon, Stewart. "The Cloak and Dollar War." London: Lawrence & Wishart, 1953. A seventy-two-page brochure in which a British communist defends the show trials and the claim that the Field brothers were U.S. agents.

Grossmann, Kurt R.. *Emigration. Die Geschichte der Hitler-Flüchtlinge, 1933–1945.* Frankfurt: Europäische Verlagsanstalt, 1969. A description of the plight of the anti-Nazi refugees from Germany, Austria, and the Sudetenland and of the efforts to save them.

Hoare, Geoffrey. *The Missing Macleans.* London: Cassell & Co., 1955. The first full-length account of the defection in 1952 of the British diplomat Donald Maclean, followed by the equally mysterious disappearance of his wife, Melinda, with her three children twenty-seven months later.

Hodos, Georg Hermann. *Show Trials: Stalinist Purges in Eastern Europe, 1948–1954.* New York: Praeger, 1987. A history of the show trials and their origins by one of the victims of the Rajk trial, interspersing the events and their interpretation with glimpses of the author's prison existence. Includes biographical data on the Field brothers and Erica Wallach and a description of the preparations for the Gomulka trial in Poland, which never took place.

Hubback, David. *No Ordinary Press Baron: A Life of Walter Layton.* London: Weidenfeld & Nicolson, 1985. A detailed account of Lord Layton's distinguished career in economics, international diplomacy, and journalism, including a chapter on his efforts on behalf of Hermann Field.

Hungarian Government Printing Office. *Laszlo Rajk and His Accomplices before the People's Court.* Budapest, 1949. The official account of the trial of Rajk and those indicted with him.

Jowitt, the Earl. *The Strange Case of Alger Hiss.* London: Hodder & Stoughton, 1952. A contemporary account of that trial.

Kaplan, Karel. *Dans les archives du Comité central.* Paris: Albin Michel, 1978. The author, as a member of the Czech Communist Party's 1962 Kolder Commission to investigate the abuses leading up to the Slansky trial, and in 1968 as secretary of the Piller Commission set up to rehabilitate defendants in that trial, had unique access to the inner workings of the interrogation process. He succeeded in salvaging the interrogatory material when he left the country in 1976.

———. *Politische Persekution in der Tschechoslowakei, 1948–1972.* Cologne, 1983. Further aspects of the trials in Czechoslovakia.

———. *Die politischen Prozesse in der Tschechoslowakei, 1948–1954.* Munich: Oldenburg, 1986. A more general handling of the material presented in Kaplan's *Dans les archives.*

———. "The Prague Political Trials of 1952." *Review of the Society for the History of Czechoslovak Jews* (New York) 2 (1988): 65–121. Another account on the same subject.

———. *Report on the Murder of the General Secretary.* Columbus: Ohio State University Press, 1989. The most authoritative examination of the communist show trial process based on Kaplan's firsthand knowledge of the interrogation and trial documents of the Slansky trial of 1952 in Prague. As a former member of the commissions set up by the communists themselves in the 1960s and 1970s to review all the material, Dr. Kaplan had unique access to files never fully released to the public.

Kapp, Yvonne, and Margaret Mynatt. *British Policy and the Refugees, 1933–1941.* London: Frank Cass, 1997. A critical review by two former administrators in the wartime period of the Czech Refugee Trust Fund.

Kiessling, Wolfgang. *Partner im Narrenparadies. Der Freundeskreis um Noel Field und Paul Merker.* Berlin Dietz Verlag, 1994. An account of the circle of the underground relationships built up around Noel Field's activities on behalf of German communist refugees between 1941 and 1948, which Stalin built into his conspiracy web against them.

Koch, Stephen. *Double Lives: Spies and Writers in the Soviet War of Ideas against the West.* New York: Free Press, 1994. A controversial interpretation of Soviet global penetration and management of the antifascist Left during the 1930s, World War II, and the early years of the Cold War, based on personal interviews and correspondence with survivors of the period and partial access to hitherto inaccessible files.

Koltai, Ferenc. *Laszlo Rajk and His Accomplices before the People's Court.* Budapest: Budapest Printing Press, 1949. The official transcript of the trial.

Lewis, Flora. *Red Pawn: The Story of Noel Field.* Garden City, N.Y.: Doubleday, 1965. The most extensive biographical account to this day.

Loebl, Eugen. *Die Aussage. Hintergrunde eines Schauprozesses.* Stuttgart, 1978. Background of events leading to the Slansky trial of 1952, by one of three survivors among sixteen sentenced.

———. *My Mind on Trial.* New York: Harcourt Brace Jovanovich, 1976. A detailed account covering the events leading up to the trial, his years of interrogation, the trial itself, and his efforts to create a new belief system to replace the Marxist economics that had guided his adult thinking.

———. *Stalinism in Prague: The Loebl Story.* New York: Grove Press, 1969. A blow-by-blow account of Loebl's passage through the Slansky interrogations and trial, including a description of the trial proceedings with the examination of each of the fourteen defendants, the verdicts and sentences, and Loebl's release in 1960 after eleven years of imprisonment and rehabilitation in 1963.

Loebl, Eugen, and D. Pokorny. *Die Revolution rehabilitiert ihre Kinder. Hinter den Kulissen des Slansky Prozesses.* Vienna, Frankfurt, Zurich, 1968. An analysis in German of the Slansky trial.

London, Artur. *The Confession.* New York: Ballantine Books, 1971. Another description by one of the three survivors of the Slansky trial of his experiences as defendant and the circumstances of his release after sixteen years in 1968.

Lukes, Igor. *Czechoslovakia between Stalin and Hitler: The Diplomacy of Edvard Benes in the 1930s.* New York: Oxford University Press, 1996. A scholarly account of the tragic slide of Czechoslovakia into dismemberment.

———. "The Rudolf Slansky Affair: New Evidence." *Slavic Review* 58, no. 1 (spring 1999). Recent research in Prague, bringing to light further material relating to the Field case.

Marat, Stanislaw, and Jacek Snopkiewicz. *Ludzie bezpieki.* Warsaw: Wydawnictwa ALFA, 1990. A detailed account of the operation of the Polish security organization during the period of communist rule, with biographies of all those in leading positions or involved in major prosecutions and trials.

Mosley, Leonard. *Dulles.* New York: Dial Press/James Wade, 1978. A biography of Allen, John Foster, and Eleanor Dulles, stretching across two world wars and the early years of the Cold War, including the OSS period.

Murphy, Kenneth. *Retreat from the Finland Station: Moral Odysseys in the Breakdown of Communism.* New York: Free Press, 1992. An account of the decline of communism from the beginning of the 1917 Revolution to the failed putsch against Gorbachev in 1991, as seen through the lives of leading revolutionaries such as Bukharin, Djilas, Imre Nagy, and Dubcek and writers such as Gide, Koestler, Silone, and Solzhenitsyn.

Pelikan, Jiri. *The Czechoslovak Political Trials, 1950–1954.* Stanford: Stanford University Press, 1971. [The Piller Report.] Analysis of the Czech trials from the records provided by the 1968 Piller investigative commission.

———. *Ein Frühling der nie zu Ende geht.* Frankfurt am Main: S. Fischer Verlag, 1976. Recollections of the Stalin years in Czechoslovakia and the moment of hope in 1968 called the "Prague Spring" before Soviet tanks arrived, putting an end to it.

———. *Pervertierte Justiz. Bericht der Kommission des ZK der KPTsch über die politischen Morde und Verbrechen in der Tschechoslowakei, 1949–1963.* Vienna, Frankfurt, Zurich, 1972. [The Kolder Report.] The author uses his unique access to the interrogatory files at the time of the Kolder Commission in 1962 to throw light on the methods used to obtain the confessions in the Slansky trial.

Rositzke, Harry. *The CIA's Secret Operations.* New York: Reader's Digest Press, 1977. A former Soviet area specialist's coverage of declassified information.

———. *The KGB: The Eyes of Russia.* Garden City, N.Y.: Doubleday, 1981. An account based on twenty-five years of experience in the CIA's Soviet area.

Schmidt, Dana Adams. *Anatomy of a Satellite.* Boston: Little, Brown, 1952. A contemporary account by the *New York Times* correspondent in Prague at the time of the events leading up to the major trials, including that of William Oatis.

Schweizer, Werner. *Noel Field: The Invented Spy.* Documentary film and video, in German; with English voice-over versions. Zurich: Tschoint Venture Film Productions, 1996. A full-length account of Noel Field's personal and political life and his entanglement in the Rajk trial, based on archival material in Hungary's Ministry of Interior, with testimony from surviving participants, including Hermann Field.

Slanska, Josefa. *Report on My Husband.* London: Hutchinson & Co., 1969. The first part of this book comprises official documents relating to the wartime period, Slansky's rise to power, and his interrogation and trial. The second part is his widow's recollections of the earlier wartime years and of her husband's ordeal and her tribulations in the period following his execution.

Slingova, Marian. *The Truth Will Prevail*. London: Merlin Press, 1968. An account by the widow of Otto Sling, a defendant in the Slansky trial who was executed.

Smith, R. Harris. *OSS: The Secret History of America's First Central Intelligence Agency*. Berkeley and Los Angeles: University of California Press, 1972. A comprehensive and detailed account of the OSS in wartime Europe and the immediate postwar period in East Asia, including the Allen Dulles–Noel Field relationship.

Steven, Stewart. *Operation Splinter Factor*. New York: J. B. Lippincott, 1974. Report on a purported covert CIA operation in which Joseph Swiatlo was supposedly recruited as an American agent in 1948 and masterminded seizure of the Fields as part of a CIA effort to precipitate the show trials. Based on undocumented material.

Swiatlo, Joseph. "Behind the Scene of the Bezbieka and the Party." New York, Munich: Radio Free Europe, 1955. Transcripts of the Swiatlo broadcasts during 1954–1955, throwing considerable light on the circumstances of the holding of Hermann Field as presented by Mr. Swiatlo.

"The Swiatlo Story." *News from behind the Iron Curtain* (New York, Free Europe Press) 4, no. 3 (March 1955). A thirty-three-page condensation of Swiatlo's original broadcasts on the inside workings of the Polish communist power structure and its security arm.

Szasz, Bela. *Volunteers for the Gallows: Anatomy of a Show Trial*. London: Chatto & Windus, 1971. An inside view by one of the victims of the purges in Hungary that led to the Rajk trial.

Toranska, Teresa. *They: Stalin's Polish Puppets*. New York: Harper & Row, 1989. [Also in Polish as *ONI*. London: Aneks Publishers, 1985.] Interviews with some of the key Polish figures involved in the Field case such as Jakub Berman.

Vogeler, Robert A. *I Was Stalin's Prisoner*. London: W. H. Allen, 1952. An account of the circumstances leading to the author's arrest and trial in 1949 and of the period of his detention until his release in 1951.

Wallach, Erica. *Light at Midnight*. Garden City, N.Y.: Doubleday. 1961. Wallach's account of her arrest, trial, and detention in various East German and Soviet prisons and labor camps in the period from 1950–1955.

Weber, Hermann, and Dietrich Staritz. *Kommunisten verfolgen Kommunisten*. Berlin: Akademie Verlag, 1993. A collection of contributions by participants of a conference on Stalin's terror and the cleansing of the Party in Russia in the prewar period and in the satellite countries after 1945.

Weinstein, Allen, and Alexander Vassiliev. *The Haunted Wood*. New York: Random House, 1999. An account of Soviet espionage in the United States, based on new Russian archival information.

# Index

Library of Congress Cataloging-in-Publication Data

Field, Hermann H.

   Trapped in the Cold War: the ordeal of an American family / Hermann Field and Kate Field ; afterword by Norman M. Naimark.

     p.  cm.

   Includes bibliographical references and index.

   ISBN 0-8047-3590-5 (alk. paper)

   1. Field, Hermann H., 1910–.  2. Europe, Eastern—Politics and government, 1945–1991. 3. Cold War.  4. Political prisoners—Poland—Biography.  5. Americans—Europe, Eastern—Biography.  I. Field, Kate, 1912–.  II. Title.

DJK50.F54    2000

947'.0009'045—dc21                                    99-042202

This book is printed on acid-free, archival-quality paper.

Original printing 1999

Last figure below indicates year of this printing:

08  07  06  05  04  03  02  01  00  99

Designed and typeset by John Feneron